Theological Bible Commentary

Theological Bible Commentary

EDITED BY
Gail R. O'Day
and
David L. Petersen

WESTMINSTER
JOHN KNOX PRESS
LOUISVILLE · KENTUCKY

Unless otherwise indicated, Scripture quotations are from the New Revised
Standard Version of the Bible, copyright © 1989 by the Division
of Christian Education of the National Council of the Churches
of Christ in the U.S.A., and are used by permission.

Book design by Sharon Adams
Cover design by designpointinc.com

First edition
Published by Westminster John Knox Press
Louisville, Kentucky

This book is printed on acid-free paper that meets the American National
Standards Institute Z39.48 standard. ♾

PRINTED IN THE UNITED STATES OF AMERICA

09 10 11 12 13 14 15 16 17 18 — 10 9 8 7 6 5 4 3 2 1

Library of Congress Cataloging-in-Publication Data

Theological Bible commentary / edited by Gail R. O'Day and David L. Petersen.—
1st ed.
    p. cm.
Includes bibliographical references.
ISBN 978-0-664-22711-1 (alk. paper)
1. Bible—Commentaries.   2. Bible—Theology.   I. O'Day, Gail R., 1954–
II. Petersen, David L.
BS491.3.T44   2009
220.7—dc22

2008030396

Contents

THE OLD TESTAMENT

THE NEW TESTAMENT

Introduction

The world of biblical studies has changed significantly during the last fifty years. Investigations concerning philology, history, the cultural contexts of the Old and New Testaments, and the formation of biblical literature dominated much of the conversation during the first two-thirds of the twentieth century. Those topics continue to be important. However, new ways of studying the Bible, especially literary and social scientific analysis, achieved prominence during the last quarter of that century. During that same period, biblical scholars became acutely aware that "presuppositionless" scholarship was a chimera. As a result, scholars began to recognize the ways in which their beliefs and cultural formation—religious and otherwise—influenced their work. Another important topic emerged at about the same time, an interest in construing the Bible as canon—attending to the text as Scripture for varied religious communities. The coalescence of all these factors has now led to a blossoming of interest in theological readings of biblical texts.

The communities of readers of biblical texts also have changed in the past fifty years. Not only has the community of biblical scholars grown more diverse, than it was say, in the 1950s, but the notion of what it means to be religious, of how one relates to a religious community and to religious authority also have changed dramatically. Nondenominational churches, retreat centers, spirituality and theology reading groups, for example, have generated new readers of the Bible and new forms of reading communities. The increase in denominationally based Bible study programs has created a community of readers whose grounding in the biblical material leads them to engage substantive theological issues in the Bible.

This volume meets a need both in biblical studies and in Christian religious communities for a resource that puts the best of scholarship in conversation with the theological claims of the biblical texts. In conceiving this volume, our goal was to create a resource that modeled diverse ways of thinking theologically about biblical literature. This volume's distinctiveness is in the way it conceives of the practice of biblical theological reflection. Its starting point is the theological richness and diversity of the biblical texts as books of the Bible. To take such an approach to biblical theological work means that theological reflection begins with and receives its fundamental shape from its engagement with fully formed biblical books.

Such a starting point for biblical theological engagement is more unusual than it seems at first glance. In this volume, theological reflection is not centered on favorite or seminal passages, nor on scholarly constructions of the biblical material and its theological trajectories (e.g., the Deuteronomistic History, the Tetrateuch, Q, the historical

Jesus), nor on overarching theological themes—"covenant," "justification by faith," "creation," "incarnation"—whose roots are in the biblical material. This biblical theological commentary is *textual* theological reflection, contingent on the fully formed biblical books. Further, this approach does not privilege one biblical book over another. This volume is not predicated upon the notion of a theological center or fulcrum for either the Old or New Testament. Each biblical book serves as the basis for theological reflection in this commentary.

Yet this emphasis on canonical form does not produce a "canonical" reading in the conventional sense of that term. There is no attempt to create a uniform theological voice out of canonical diversity, nor is the theological perspective of one biblical book measured against or harmonized with the theological perspective of another. Nor do the authors write from the conviction that one theological norm or one way of understanding and doing theology should receive pride of place. Instead, the volume contains a series of individual theological commentaries that together offer a glimpse into the wealth of theological perspectives that the contemporary reader can find in the Bible. What all the essays have in common is a commitment to address fundamental theological issues from the perspective of a careful analysis of biblical literature.

The diversity of theological methods and approaches in this commentary reflects the theological richness and diversity of the biblical books themselves. No single methodological template has been followed by the authors (other than the very general organizational rubrics of "introduction" and "commentary"). For some of the volume's contributors, the exegetical theological engagement leads to reflection on primary theological themes (e.g., the nature of God, what it is to be human, the nature of human community), while for others this engagement leads to theological reflection through the lens of a particular biblical book on a range of topics (war and peace, justice, poverty) that were important topics in biblical times and remain so today. The common thread that runs through the commentary is the recognition that theological reflection on biblical texts is an essential intellectual and theological practice that can and should be undertaken from as many perspectives as possible. Careful literary analysis, acute attention to historical and social issues, concern for gender, ethnicity, and other dimensions of social location, concern for the formation of biblical literature and its traditions: all can yield theological insights. The more questions that are asked of the biblical text, the greater the theological yield, especially since biblical literature itself broaches such a range of topics.

Theological reflection like that practiced and modeled in this commentary can lead to a wide range of activities—preaching, teaching, individual learning. This commentary does not presuppose any single use or any particular reading community, but is conceived as a resource for readers interested in exploring the theological implications of biblical books. Each individual commentary is a freestanding piece, but the full picture of the Bible's theological perspectives emerges when the reader reads across the commentaries just as he or she would read across the canon.

As a whole, the volume invites the reader to engage the biblical books themselves and their exegetical details as the stuff of theological reflection. This volume understands and embodies theological reflection as a move into the specifics and exegetical richness of biblical texts, not a move away from that exegetical richness into abstraction and proposition. This combination of theological reflection and exegetical attentiveness is what holds the two parts of its title, "theological" and "Bible," together. One of biblical scholarship's distinctive contributions to the theological enterprise is its predisposition to notice the particular, to attend to the details, to notice the difference it makes when God speaks as a still small voice, in the whirlwind, or when God's Word becomes flesh, and to enable each of those expressions of God to have its full say.

Gail R. O'Day
David L. Petersen

Contributors

O. Wesley Allen Jr.
Associate Professor of Homiletics
    and Worship
Lexington Theological Seminary
Lexington, Kentucky
Luke

Samuel E. Balentine
Professor of Old Testament
Union Theological Seminary—Presby-
    terian School of Christian Education
Richmond, Virginia
Numbers

Craig Bartholomew
H. Evan Runner Professor of Philosophy
    and Professor of Religion
Redeemer University College
Ancaster, Canada
Ecclesiastes

Nancy R. Bowen
Associate Professor of Old Testament
Earlham School of Religion
Richmond, Indiana
Ruth; Esther

Brad R. Braxton
Senior Minister
The Riverside Church
New York, New York
1 Corinthians; 2 Corinthians

Michael Joseph Brown
Associate Professor of New Testament
    and Christian Origins
Candler School of Theology
Emory University
Atlanta, Georgia
Romans

William P. Brown
Professor of Old Testament
Columbia Theological Seminary
Decatur, Georgia
Psalms

Allen Dwight Callahan
Cambridge, Massachusetts
1 John; 2 John; 3 John

L. Juliana Claassens
Extraordinary Visiting Associate
    Professor
Department of Old and New Testaments
University of Stellenbosch
Stellenbosch, South Africa
Isaiah

Stephen L. Cook
Professor of Old Testament
Virginia Theological Seminary
Alexandria, Virginia
Ezekiel

Katharine J. Dell
Senior Lecturer, Old Testament Studies
Cambridge University
Cambridge, England
Job

Joanna Dewey
Harvey H. Guthrie, Jr., Professor
   Emerita of Biblical Studies
Episcopal Divinity School
Cambridge, Massachusetts
Mark

Frank H. Gorman Jr.
Muncie, Indiana
Leviticus

Patrick Gray
Assistant Professor of Religious
   Studies
Rhodes College
Memphis, Tennessee
Hebrews

Theodore Hiebert
Francis A. McGaw Professor of Old
   Testament
McCormick Theological Seminary
Chicago, Illinois
Genesis

E. Elizabeth Johnson
J. Davison Philips Professor of New
   Testament
Columbia Theological Seminary
Decatur, Georgia
1 Thessalonians; 2 Thessalonians

Luke Timothy Johnson
R. W. Woodruff Professor of New
   Testament and Christian Origins
Candler School of Theology
Emory University
Atlanta, Georgia
James

Melody D. Knowles
Associate Professor of Hebrew
   Scriptures
McCormick Theological Seminary
Chicago, Illinois
1 and 2 Chronicles

Steven J. Kraftchick
Associate Professor in the Practice
   of New Testament Interpretation
Candler School of Theology
Emory University
Atlanta, Georgia
1 Peter; 2 Peter; Jude

Deborah Krause
Professor of New Testament
Eden Theological Seminary
St. Louis, Missouri
1 Timothy; 2 Timothy; Titus

Tod Linafelt
Associate Professor of Biblical Studies
Georgetown University
Washington, DC
The Song of Songs

Elizabeth Struthers Malbon
Professor of Religious Studies
Virginia Polytechnic Institute and State
   University
Blacksburg, Virginia
Mark

Carleen Mandolfo
Associate Professor of Religious Studies
Colby College
Waterville, Maine
Lamentations

Gregory Mobley
Professor of Christian Bible
Andover Newton Theological Seminary
Newton Centre, Massachusetts
Joshua; 1 and 2 Kings

Carol A. Newsom
Charles Howard Candler Professor of
   Old Testament
Candler School of Theology
Emory University
Atlanta, Georgia
Daniel

Julia M. O'Brien
Paul H. and Grace L. Stern Professor of
  Old Testament
Lancaster Theological Seminary
Lancaster, Pennsylvania
*Hosea; Joel; Amos; Obadiah; Jonah; Micah;
  Nahum; Habakkuk; Zephaniah; Haggai;
  Zechariah; Malachi*

Gail R. O'Day
A. H. Shatford Professor of Preaching
  and New Testament
Candler School of Theology
Emory University
Atlanta, Georgia
Introduction; Revelation

Dennis T. Olson
Charles T. Haley Professor of Old Testa-
  ment Theology
Princeton Theological Seminary
Princeton, New Jersey
Exodus

David L. Petersen
Franklin N. Parker Professor
  of Old Testament
Candler School of Theology
Emory University
Atlanta, Georgia
Introduction

Sandra Hack Polaski
Richmond, Virginia
Galatians

David Rensberger
Atlanta, Georgia
John

Stanley P. Saunders
Associate Professor of New Testament
Columbia Theological Seminary
Decatur, Georgia
Matthew

Carolyn J. Sharp
Associate Professor of Hebrew
  Scriptures
Yale Divinity School
New Haven, Connecticut
Jeremiah

Matthew L. Skinner
Associate Professor of New Testament
Luther Seminary
St. Paul, Minnesota
Acts

Daniel L. Smith-Christopher
Professor of Theological Studies
  (Old Testament)
Loyola Marymount University
Los Angeles, California
Ezra and Nehemiah

Ken Stone
Professor of Bible, Culture, and
  Hermeneutics
Chicago Theological Seminary
Chicago, Illinois
Judges

Brent A. Strawn
Associate Professor of Old Testament
Candler School of Theology
Emory University
Atlanta, Georgia
Deuteronomy

Patricia K. Tull
A. B. Rhodes Professor of Old Testament
Louisville Presbyterian Theological
  Seminary
Louisville, Kentucky
1 and 2 Samuel

James Buchanan Wallace
Assistant Professor of Religion
Christian Brothers University
Memphis, Tennessee
Philemon

Sze-kar Wan
Professor of New Testament
Perkins School of Theology
Southern Methodist University
Dallas, Texas
Ephesians; Philippians; Colossians

Harold C. Washington
Professor of Hebrew Bible
Saint Paul School of Theology
Kansas City, Missouri
Proverbs

Abbreviations

AB	Anchor Bible
ANET	*Ancient Near Eastern Texts Relating to the Old Testament*, ed. J. B. Pritchard, 3rd ed. Princeton: Princeton University Press, 1969
ANTC	Abingdon New Testament Commentaries
AOTC	Abingdon Old Testament Commentaries
FCB	Feminist Companion to the Bible
ITC	International Theological Commentary
JSOTSup	Journal for the Study of the Old Testament Supplements
KJV	King James (Authorized) Version
LXX	Septuagint
MT	Masoretic Text
NASB	New American Standard Bible
NIB	*New Interpreter's Bible*, ed. Leander E. Keck. 12 vols. plus index. Nashville: Abingdon, 1994–2004
NICOT	New International Commentary on the Old Testament
NIV	New International Version
NJB	New Jewish Bible
NJPS	New Jewish Publication Society Version
NRSV	New Revised Standard Version
OBT	Overtures to Biblical Theology
OTL	Old Testament Library
SBLDS	Society of Biblical Literature Dissertation Series
SBLSymS	Society of Biblical Literature Symposium Series
WBC	Word Biblical Commentary

The Old Testament

Genesis

Theodore Hiebert

INTRODUCTION

No biblical book is more important for theology and ethics than the book of Genesis. It contains the foundational narratives, images, and concepts in Western religions about the nature of God, of human identity, of religious life and community, and of the world as a whole. Its ideas play a central role in some of the most controversial debates in modern culture: about the origins of the universe and of human life, about human responsibility for the environment, about the proper relation between the sexes and sexual identity itself, about ethnicity and race, and about land and politics in the Middle East. It is thus a book whose theological and ethical perspectives are of interest not just for personal edification and reflection but because they continue to influence the shape of society today.

A significant reason for the lasting power of Genesis's ideas is that Genesis is about origins. Origin stories are always more about the present than they are about the past. Origins determine essence and define character. The way in which something is made establishes its nature for all time. When a culture tells stories of its beginnings, it is telling stories about itself, about who it is and what it was meant to be. So the readers of Genesis, just as its storytellers, have always seen themselves in its stories and characters, and

their understandings of these stories have played a major part in their own definitions of God, themselves, and the world. But Genesis is not only about origins; it is itself the starting point of Western religious thought. Standing as it does at the beginning of our religious history, its ways of thinking have ever since determined the modes of thought, set the rules of engagement, and drawn the parameters for religious reflection and experience. It is now nearly impossible to think theologically or to act ethically without being influenced, consciously or unconsciously, by the ideas of Genesis. This makes it immensely important to continually examine and reexamine the theological and ethical perspectives of the book itself.

Until the modern era of biblical studies, interpreters read Genesis as a flat story, with a single author and point of view; and when they encountered inconsistencies they did their best to explain them as apparent discrepancies, which could with care be harmonized into one seamless narrative and theological perspective. Some modern scholars still prefer to deal with the final form of Genesis as a single literary whole, but most now regard the book as a compilation of different Israelite traditions with different origins, settings, and perspectives. The consequence of reading Genesis as a compilation of traditions means that Genesis does not present us with a single theological or ethical perspective; rather, it contains multiple perspectives from Israelite life and experience. This fact itself is a theological issue, since it raises the question whether theological and ethical reflection is best served by a single honored point of view or by multiple voices with different perspectives that have gained respect.

The theological and ethical studies that follow take as their starting point the broadly held view in contemporary biblical studies that the book of Genesis is a compilation of various Israelite traditions. While there is continuous debate about how to identify and divide these traditions, the classic position is that they may be identified with one or another of three great schools or authors. The oldest, the Yahwist (J), preserves Israel's earliest accounts of itself and presents these accounts from the perspective of Israel as an agrarian society during the Davidic monarchy. The Elohist (E) preserves alternative ancient traditions that appear to reflect the interests of the northern rather than the southern kingdom. The Priestly Writer (P) is the latest, working after the monarchy during the Babylonian exile or the postexilic period to record his traditions—though they may in themselves be more ancient—and to combine them with J and E to produce the book of Genesis we have today. P presents his traditions of Israel's beginnings from the perspective of Israel in exile as a religious community centered in ritual and worship. Thus in this commentary I describe the theologies of Genesis rather than the theology of Genesis, but I do so in such a way that those who prefer to read Genesis as a single narrative may still profit from these observations.

Until the modern era of biblical studies, interpreters also read Genesis as if it were written in and to their own worlds. They effectively collapsed the eras of the writer and the reader and therefore deemphasized the differences between the social and cultural realities of the biblical world and of their own. One of the most important contributions of the modern historical approach to biblical studies has been to clarify the concrete details of life—social, cultural, political, religious—in antiquity and to show how different ancient society was from society today. The profound insights into divine and human reality in Genesis still communicate to the modern reader across such a cultural divide, but at the same time these insights are cloaked in the cultural realities of the world from which they come. To understand the theological and ethical perspectives of Genesis, and to reflect upon them with critical respect, their ancient cultural context must always be recognized and given careful thought and assessment.

COMMENTARY

Creation (Gen. 1–3)

The book of Genesis contains two distinct accounts of creation, the story of creation in seven days attributed to the Priestly Writer (1:1–2:4a) and the story of creation in the garden of Eden attributed to the Yahwist (2:4b–3:24). The aim of the Priestly account is to present the universe as a perfectly ordered sacred structure. This account is designed with two literary patterns, one in time and one in space, both of which have religious purposes.

The temporal pattern, which describes creation in seven days, divides time into ordinary time, the period of six working days, and sacred time, the seventh day of rest. It informs the reader that the temporal rhythms of the universe are centered in sacred time, most basically the Sabbath. The spatial pattern superimposed on this temporal pattern divides the six days of creation into two panels of three days each. On the first three days the realms of light and darkness, sky and waters, and land and vegetation are created (1:3–13), and on the second three days these realms are populated with stars and planets, birds and sea creatures, and land animals and humans (1:14–31). All of creation in this pattern flows from the top down, revealing to the reader a universe that is a perfect hierarchy with God at its apex. Sacred time and space were especially important for Israel's priesthood and its supervision of Israel's rituals and worship throughout biblical history, but they were particularly crucial in exile when Israel had to reconstruct an identity apart from its land and political institutions.

The Yahwist's account of creation, while deeply religious in its own way, is not so much interested in the origins of sacred time and space but in the origins of the society, economy, and culture of ancient Israel. Its focal point is not heaven but earth, in particular the domestic world of the Israelite farming family. In this account God begins creation by fashioning the first human from arable soil (2:7), and God assigns humanity to cultivate that soil (2:15), thereby explaining Israel's character as an agrarian society in which nearly every Israelite family practiced subsistence agriculture. God's climactic creative act, after producing plants and animals from the same arable soil, is to form a second human from the first, thereby establishing the sexes, marriage, and the family as the foundational unit in a kinship society and as the primary source of production in an agrarian economy (2:21–24). Such social and economic realities characterized the Yahwist's audience and, indeed, all Israelites throughout biblical history.

The character of God. Priestly and Yahwistic creation traditions present contrasting portraits of God that are normative for these traditions throughout Genesis and that have become crucial aspects of God's nature in later theology. The Priestly Writer emphasizes God's sovereignty: God resides in heaven at the pinnacle of the universe's hierarchy, issues commands to bring the world into being, and creates a world perfectly ordered in time and space. The Yahwist, on the other hand, emphasizes God's human traits: God shapes the first human from the soil (2:7), experiments in order to produce a true partner for the human being (2:18–25), walks in the garden (3:8), converses with people (3:9–13), and—if we take the text at face value—does not know everything (3:9–11). These contrasting images of God have been combined in classic theology in the claim that God is both transcendent, that is, distant and completely other than human, and immanent, that is, accessible and in close relationship with humans and human experience.

While both characteristics of God are usually combined in any particular modern theology, one or the other, depending on the theologian's context, community, and contemporary challenges, is invariably emphasized, as they were by the Priestly Writer and the Yahwist. The Priestly Writer's image of a transcendent God is related to his hierarchical conception of reality and to his self-understanding of his priestly role in that hierarchy, as the mediator of God's presence to Israel through ritual and worship and as the intercessor for Israel to God. The Priestly Writer's sense of God's transcendence could only have been heightened by the tragedy of the exile, in which Israel's religious leaders—including the great prophet of the exile, Second Isaiah—sought hope not in the ordinary securities of life, which had disappeared, but in the power of the sovereign creator of the universe. The Yahwist's more accessible and anthropomorphic conception of God, on the other hand, is related to the more popular expressions of religious life and worship in the familial and kinship social settings that characterize life in the Yahwist's epic traditions. In the Yahwist's narratives, contact with God is not confined to priestly mediation but is more varied and immediate: God appears in various places, to different kinds of people, and in many forms and manifestations.

The origins of the universe, I: Making or ordering? One of the most influential theological claims made about the biblical view of creation is that God created the universe out of nothing (*creatio ex nihilo*). This claim rests on the judgment that Gen. 1:1 starts with a prepositional phrase: "In the beginning God made the heavens and the earth." A clear statement about God creating out of nothing, however, appears for the first time only in the first centuries BCE and CE among both Jewish (2 Macc. 7:28; *2 Enoch* 24:2) and Christian interpreters (Rom. 4:17; Heb. 11:3), years after the composition of the sixth-century Priestly creation story. This belief that God preexisted the universe and all of its matter obviously emphasizes God's transcendence and power, and thus it reflects in some respects P's own sense of God's sovereignty. At the same time, it gives P's own conceptions of God's sovereignty a new and different meaning.

In the ancient Near East and in the Bible, creation was viewed not as making matter but as ordering chaos. According to this viewpoint, the world began when God gained control of primordial chaos—usually represented as untamed water—and imposed upon it the orders of the universe, standing guard to restrain the primordial chaotic forces and ensure the lasting triumph of order (*Enuma Elish*, *ANET*, 60–72; Pss. 74:12–17; 89:6–15). This view of creation appears to be the actual Priestly view, if we read Gen. 1:1, as many scholars now prefer to do, as a subordinate clause introducing the primordial waters of chaos: "When God began to create the heavens and the earth, the earth being a formless void with darkness on the surface of the deep and the wind of God sweeping over the waters, God said, 'Let there be light.'" Many creation accounts in the Bible and ancient Near East begin with just such a subordinate clause (*Enuma Elish*, *ANET*, 60–72; Gen. 2:4b; 5:1). Such a conception sees God's sovereignty not in the absolute origins of matter, a theological issue in which the authors of Genesis do not seem to be interested, but in the establishment and preservation of the orders upon which the universe and human life depend. While not addressing the issue of ultimate origins, the Priestly conception of creation is a dynamic understanding of God's sovereign power in creation, since it focuses not only on the beginning of creation but upon God's continuing work to sustain and preserve it.

The origins of the universe, II: Creation and evolution. The debate between creation and evolution is one of the most divisive cultural controversies in the United States, especially as it bears on the teaching of science in the public school curriculum. The debate began in 1859 with Charles Darwin's classic argument for evolution in *Origin of Species*, reached a high point in 1925 when John Scopes was found guilty of teaching evolution in a Dayton, Tennessee, high school, and shows no signs of abating, due to the continuing efforts of supporters of creationism and its stepchild, intelligent design. A poll in 2005 found that nearly two-thirds of Americans believe that creationism should be taught alongside evolution in public schools, while just over a third favor replacing evolution with creation.

This debate is only the latest stage in a very old dispute, going back to the early church fathers and rabbis, about the proper way to understand the Bible when its picture of the universe differs from science's picture. But it has become particularly intense after the major scientific discoveries that challenged the human-centered character of the biblical universe: Copernicus's thesis that decentered the earth, geologist's findings about the earth's vast age, and Darwin's theory of the evolution of life on earth. In these conflicts, theologians have taken one of two approaches: that the Bible is the enduring standard to which science must conform or that the Bible's picture may be accommodated to new scientific viewpoints.

The basic difficulty of the first approach, represented today by creationists who take the Bible as a scientific standard, is best illustrated by the Copernican revolution in the seventeenth century. Because Copernicus and his disciple Galileo contradicted the plain meaning of Scripture that the earth was the center of the universe and that the sun moved around it, the church condemned their teachings that the earth is a planet revolving around a motionless central sun. This crisis in the authority of Scripture took Christians a long time to resolve. It took two hundred years before the church removed Galileo's books from its list of prohibited books. This was a hard lesson to learn, but the church finally recognized that some aspects of biblical cosmology, in this case the earth as the center of the universe, could no longer be taken as adequate scientific descriptions in light of new discoveries.

If we are to learn from this lesson in the church's history, we must acknowledge that the accounts of creation in Gen. 1–3 are based on an ancient cosmology that is not only earth centered but that contains many other features no longer accepted by contemporary scientists or by the general public. In the Priestly creation story, for example, the earth is fashioned as the center of the universe before the heavenly bodies are formed to move above it (1:9–19). Furthermore, the earth is stationed between two great reservoirs of water, one held back by the dome of the sky and the other resting below in which the earth's pillars are sunk to keep it stable (Gen. 1:6–10; 1 Sam. 2:8). The earth itself appears as a flat plain with boundaries marking its edges (Job 28:24), with either a square shape divided into quadrants with corners (Isa. 11:12) or a circular shape (Job 26:10). In all of these respects, biblical authors—the Priestly Writer, the Yahwist, the psalmists, and others who describe creation—accepted a view of the universe common in the Mediterranean world in the first millennium BCE but superseded by subsequent scientific advances.

Knowing this, we are in a position to better understand the relation between the Bible and modern science. Biblical creation accounts reflect the view of the universe accepted at the time of their composition as the best explanation of natural phenomena. In this regard they share with modern science a key concern: the aim to describe the structure of the universe and account for its origins in terms that made sense of the world as humans observed it (in antiquity without technological assistance, of course). At the same time, biblical accounts differ from contemporary science in two important ways. First, as we have just seen, the view of the universe reflected in biblical creation accounts is an ancient one that has been superseded by later scientific discoveries. Thus, while biblical conceptions include "scientific" observations and conclusions, these are part of the history of science and cannot be used as modern scientific standards. Second, biblical accounts not only describe the origins of natural phenomena, but also explain the origins of cultural (agriculture, family) and religious (Sabbath) realities. Thus biblical accounts do not limit themselves to the explanation of natural phenomena within a closed materialistic system, as do contemporary scientific theories, but they provide a holistic account of beginnings in which natural, cultural, and religious beginnings are integrated into a common story.

Recognizing the difficulties with taking the Bible as the enduring standard to which science must conform, we must consider the merits of the opposite approach, that is, accommodating biblical accounts to new scientific viewpoints. The two most popular attempts of this kind are both attractive on the surface but also problematic upon further analysis. One of these approaches takes the biblical creation accounts to be ultimately compatible with modern science if read properly. For example, if we take the seven days of Gen. 1 as figurative expressions for epochs, we get around the conflict in the length of time of creation; moreover, the general development of the universe and of its life forms—from simple to complex, from the seas to land—looks a lot like the explanations of evolutionary geologists and biologists. The basic problem with this approach, however, is that it misunderstands the true nature of biblical creation accounts and their cosmology. Biblical cosmology is simply an ancient one, completely different in its worldview from modern ones, and any attempt to squeeze it into a contemporary system will fail more often than succeed.

A second attempt at accommodation circumvents the problems of the first by claiming that biblical creation stories are essentially theological (or poetic or mythical) and not really about science at all. The Bible and science do not conflict, because they are different kinds of literature with different purposes. The two literatures are supplementary, not contradictory, and we may draw our theology from the Bible and our view of the universe from science. This approach accurately claims that biblical creation accounts incorporate theological perspectives while scientific explanations do not, and it appears to provide a simple escape from the conflict between biblical and scientific viewpoints. It does so, however, by disregarding the "scientific" aspects of biblical accounts—their attempt to explain the structure and origin of natural phenomena in light of the cosmology of their day—and it thereby undervalues the theological importance of the natural world and its role in biblical thought.

An approach that more accurately reflects the nature of the biblical stories and is more productive for contemporary theological reflections on the Bible and science acknowledges two facts about the biblical view of creation. First, the Bible shares with science the aim of explaining the origins of the observable universe, but its explanations are based on an ancient cosmology no longer accepted in the contemporary world. Second, the Bible is more holistic than modern science, combining its explanations of the origins of natural phenomena with explanations of Israel's own cultural, ritual, and theological realities. Because it contains ancient—not modern—cosmological assumptions and because it combines explanations of cosmic origins with explanations of Israel's own cultural and religious origins, the biblical view of creation is not an appropriate subject for science instruction in public education. At the same time, the biblical view of creation provides a model for the theological reflection of contemporary Jews and Christians, in its aim to integrate cosmology, culture, and theology in a holistic account of beginnings. These stories challenge modern theologians to do for today what biblical theologians did for their age: provide a compelling explanation for the contemporary view of the origin of the universe and its life as the design of a divine being ordering it all toward a greater purpose.

Human identity and culture: Common humanity and ethnic particularity. The Bible's creation stories make a number of important claims about the nature of human life, one of which is the belief that all people share a common humanity. This is not to say that the first chapters of Genesis provide a generalized, universal account of the origin of the world and human history, as is widely claimed. Both P and J write about beginnings in very particular terms, P describing creation as the origin of Israel's unique religious rituals and J describing creation as the origin of Israel's own agrarian economy and kinship society. Thus biblical authors view the human race as a whole through the lens of their own ethnic particularity. At the same time, by tracing their descent not just to the nearer ancestor from whom their own ethnic group descended—that is, to Jacob/Israel—but to the ancestor of all human beings, both writers affirm that they are members of one human family. Through these creation stories, then, biblical writers set their own ethnic identity into the larger context of a common human identity. This belief in a common humanity has provided assurance and power to oppressed minorities throughout history, who have challenged their second-class status with the Priestly view that, as descendants of the first human, all are created in the image of God (1:26–27).

Human identity and nature: Master or member of the universe? The Priestly view of human identity as created in God's image, which has provided such a positive affirmation of our common humanity, has come under fire in recent years from another quarter, those who advocate for the well-being of the community of life as a whole. As the environmental crisis has intensified and historians and ethicists have investigated the values that have led humans to exploit nature, some have traced the roots of these destructive values to the Priestly image of human identity as the master of the universe. By describing only humans as bearing the image of God, P separates human life from all other forms of life and sets it above them. Even worse, P grants humans almost unlimited power when God gives them dominion over all other life (1:26–28). According to some ecologists, this image of humanity has given people the false idea that they are separate from nature and that they have the power to control it and use it as they see fit. It is difficult to say how much this image is to blame for the environmental crisis, because many ideas and events in postbiblical times also influence the way people behave today, and because people of many other religious traditions and cultures have also abused nature and contributed to the crisis. But this image of human identity has played such a large part in Jewish and Christian theology that it bears reexamination in light of the current crisis.

The view of humanity in Gen. 1 fits squarely into the Priestly conception of a hierarchical universe, where humans are just below God and above everything else (cf. Ps. 8:5–6). The dominion God grants them is potent: the Hebrew verbs are elsewhere used for the rule of kings over their subjects and masters over their servants. Yet the context of the creation story as a whole puts clear restraints on human rule. First, humans are granted rule only as God's representatives. This is the ancient meaning of the image of God: it gives humans not a special nature but a special function, the role as the mediator

of God's purposes on earth. For this role as God's agent, trustee, or designated manager, modern theologians have used the term "steward" (though the term itself is not employed in Gen. 1). As a result, the term "stewardship" has become adopted in religious and secular culture alike as the model for caring for the environment. Together with granting humans representative rule, Gen. 1 also affirms the worth and integrity of the world of nature to be ruled, repeating seven times after the creation of each part of nature: "God saw that it was good." The Priestly human is thus very powerful but commissioned to represent God's rule over a world God deemed good.

A point overlooked by ecologists is that J's image of human identity contrasts sharply with P's. In J's story, humans are placed in their environment not to rule but to serve: the Hebrew verb usually translated "till"—when God puts the first human in the garden to till it and keep it (2:15)—basically means "serve." Thus the human is commissioned to respect and assist creation rather than to manage it. Furthermore, J's first human is made not in God's image but from the soil, as are all other forms of life (2:7, 9, 19), and so humanity is not separated from other life but shares its nature. J, therefore, sees humanity more as an integrated member of the world of life than as its master. J's image reflects the contemporary ecological insight that all forms of life are members of a complex ecosystem and dependent upon one another for the health of the whole, and it provides a necessary antidote to the potential hubris of the powerful Priestly human. In the end, these two images reflect the unique ambiguity of human life, and both are necessary to reconstruct a healthier role for humanity in the natural environment, a role that at once respects and serves the whole and exercises responsibly the unique power humanity possesses.

Human identity and morality: Is human nature fallen? Most modern readers believe that the Bible's second creation account, the story of the garden of Eden, is an account of "the fall." According to this interpretation, the first couple's disobedience changed human nature so that it acquired two permanent defects to be transmitted to all future generations: human nature became corrupted, controlled by sin; and it became mortal, subject to death. This interpretation originated among Jewish interpreters before the birth of Christianity (Sir. 25:24; 4 Ezra 3:21–22), though it was later abandoned by Judaism. The convert Paul adopted this reading from his Jewish heritage and used it as a framework for understanding the redemptive work of Christ: just as the first Adam introduced sin and death into the world, so the second Adam, Christ, redeemed humanity from sin and death (Rom. 5:12; 1 Cor. 15:21–22). Though Paul is the only NT author who uses the concept of the fall to interpret Jesus' life and ministry, his view has become the dominant understanding of human nature in Christianity.

The Eden narrative's author, the Yahwist, is intensely interested in human nature, and has set up the story to explain exactly what human nature is. His narrative device to explain human nature comprises the two trees, the tree of life and the tree of the knowledge of good and evil (2:9, 17; 3:22). J's first claim is that humans, unlike God, are mortal. Humans are made mortal by God as part of their nature: the first human is made out of the soil, to which he returns at death (2:7; 3:19). Death is therefore natural and not a fallen state. To keep humans from changing their nature and acquiring immortality, God makes sure they will never eat from the tree of life (immortality) by expelling them from the garden (3:22). God's punishment for the first couple's disobedience is not death, a part of human nature as God created it, but pain in childbearing and in cultivating the soil (3:16–18).

J's second claim about human nature is that humans, like God, possess the knowledge of self-consciousness and moral discernment. Humans are created with naiveté and a lack of self-consciousness (2:25), but they acquire the Godlike knowledge of self-consciousness and moral discernment by eating the fruit of the tree of the knowledge of good and evil (3:5, 10–11, 22). The knowledge acquired is not a corrupted nature subject to sin, but rather a Godlike knowledge that gives humans the consciousness of self and the ability to make moral choices that is so basic to human identity. Indeed, future generations—like Cain, whom God assumes can make a good or a bad choice (4:7)—have the power of discernment and the ability to choose moral or immoral lives (Deut. 4; Ezek. 18). Thus for J, as for other ancient Near Eastern theologians (*ANET*, 75, 90, 101), human nature possesses two fundamental qualities: unlike God, who is immortal, humans are mortal; but like God, who is wise, humans are also wise, having acquired the knowledge to choose between good and evil. This ancient view that wisdom is a quintessential human trait is still preserved in scientific language, in which the designation for the human species of the primate family is *Homo sapiens*, "the one who is wise."

J's creation story and its interpreters have thus bequeathed us two views of human nature with great explanatory power and with serious consequences for understanding both individual and social behavior. According to Christian theologians who inherited Paul's legacy, each human being possesses moral discernment but also a corrupt nature that inevitably leads to disobedience and sin. People are ultimately incapable of choosing a life of goodness and well-being and can only experience such a life through a divine act of redemption. According to J and Jewish theologians who have inherited his legacy, each human being possesses the potential and power to make moral or immoral choices, and each individual thus bears the responsibility to choose wisely. These contrasting views of human nature continue to surface in one way or another not only in theology and ethics but in psychological theories, social philosophies, and public policies. They urge upon us a constant vigilance concerning our assumptions about human nature and their consequences in the way we behave toward individuals and in the way we construct social policies.

Human identity and gender. The garden of Eden has been a key source for the discussion about the proper relationship between men and women in Judaism and Christianity. Interpreters have discovered in this text very different constructions of gender. Historically, the garden narrative has been used to support the subordination of women to men by interpreting the woman as weak and blameworthy, primarily at fault for the couple's sin: she listened to the serpent, ate the forbidden fruit first, and then gave it to her husband (3:4–6; Philo, *Creation* 151–52, 165–66; 1 Tim. 2:13–14). In recent years, feminist interpreters have disputed this interpretation, arguing that the story presents the equality of men and women as an ideal. According to this approach, gender is introduced into the Eden narrative only when the second human being is made from the first, at which time women and men are pictured as partners of one another (2:20–25). The woman and man act together to disobey God, and the woman's later subordination is the consequence of human sin, not God's design for human relationships (3:16).

Both historical and modern interpretations have attributed more to the narrative than it says. On the one hand, J's Eden narrative reflects the norms and practices of a patriarchal society. Biblical society throughout history was patriarchal, patrilocal, and patrilineal: it placed authority with the male head of the household, located the family in the man's house, and figured descent through the male's line. These social structures are reflected—even legitimated—in the garden of Eden, where the male is made first (2:7), makes his wife a member of his household (2:24), represents the couple before God (3:9–11, 22–24), is criticized for listening to his wife (3:17), and is given authority over her (3:16). While the P account, in which the sexes are created together as part of a single human-

ity, appears to reflect more equality (1:27), P tradition in the remainder of Genesis is even more strongly patriarchal than J (5:1–32).

While accepting patriarchy as the norm, J also develops a counternarrative running throughout Genesis that critiques patriarchal structures by developing strong women characters whose actions subvert men's authority, determine the outcome of events, and further the fulfillment of God's promises. Such a counternarrative begins here where the first woman, as Phyllis Trible has shown, is the active theologian—in contrast to the passive male—debating with the serpent and eating the fruit by which humans acquire the Godlike knowledge of moral discernment (3:1–6, 22). The legacy of the Bible as a whole, as of these creation accounts in particular, is an ancient patriarchal worldview constantly challenged by subversive individuals and voices.

The Primeval Age (4:1–8:19)

Traditional interpretation defines the primeval age as the first eleven chapters of Genesis, and it describes this age as an era in which human wickedness, characterized primarily as hubris, escalated. Beginning with the disobedience of the first couple, human transgressions became more and more heinous, growing worse with Cain's murder and the corruption of all humanity before the flood, and culminating in the arrogant attack on God by the builders of the tower of Babel. This catastrophic failure of the human race during the primeval age is regarded as the backdrop of the new age, when God abandons humanity and selects for special attention a particular people, the children of Abraham. While this interpretation of the primeval age has gained almost universal support, the theological analysis that follows will challenge most of its key assumptions and will provide a fresh theological perspective from which to read the beginning of Genesis. The primeval narrative combines P and J traditions that carry forward the unique perspectives we have already observed in the Bible's two creation narratives.

Cain, Abel, and social conflict (4:1–16). The first episode of the primeval age after the world is created is about murder, the ultimate breakdown of human relations and community. It is a J story, with many parallels—disobedience, dialogue with God, exile—to J's Eden narrative, and it shows that J viewed the first age of human history as a flawed age when all relationships were under strain. In this story the relations between people, people and God, and people and nature are all threatened. Many explanations for this conflict and the disintegration of human ties have been proposed, and we can eliminate most of them. The story is neither about universal human discord nor about hubris. Nor is it about the ancient territorial conflict between shepherds (Abel) and farmers (Cain), or about the cultural conflict between the Israelite immigrants (Abel) and the Canaanite farmers (Cain).

The story is about a family, just as the story says, and that family is typical of the society created in J's Eden narrative. This family is a single kinship unit with an agrarian economy, in which, as is typical, older sons work the fields and younger sons tend the sheep (vv. 1–2). The human conflict is, specifically, sibling rivalry. It is sparked when God accepts Abel's sacrifice and not Cain's. The reason for God's selection, in spite of scholarly obsession to find an explanation in the sacrifices or behavior of the brothers, is not stated by the storyteller and is not the point of the story at all (vv. 4–5). The story is about fraternal conflict and how to respond to it when it arises, as it inevitably does. God's primary speech in the story puts before Cain the alternatives: master your anger and resentment and save your relationship to your brother, or submit to your anger and destroy it (vv. 6–7).

Cain's dilemma will dominate each family narrative in Genesis—Isaac versus Ishmael, Jacob versus Esau, Joseph versus his brothers—and the challenge will always be the same: when conflict arises between brothers, will it be negotiated to save life and preserve the family or will it destroy life and social ties? Each of the familial conflicts during the second age of human history, as we shall see, is negotiated to avoid murder and preserve life. The story of Cain and Abel provides the negative image of these stories, and it is therefore a cautionary tale describing the consequences when resentment triumphs over relationship, when one member of the human community denies, as did Cain, that he is his brother's keeper. Thus the story of Cain and Abel deals with the health of human community not as an abstraction; rather, it grapples with this ideal in terms of the most intimate, powerful, and difficult of human relations, the relationship of siblings.

The flood and the destruction of the world (6:5–8:19). While the flood has traditionally been seen as an episode in the middle of the primeval age, it is actually the final, climactic episode. Common sense tells us that the flood's worldwide destruction necessarily ends one phase of life on earth and begins another. Furthermore, other ancient Near Eastern accounts of the flood see it as the dividing line between two eras of human history, the second of which is the age in which their own authors and audiences live. Finally, as we shall see, the biblical stories that follow the flood are not about the end of the previous age but about the re-creation of the world and the beginning of a new era of human history. The J and P flood traditions are not set side by side as were their creation stories, but they are interwoven to produce an apparently coherent narrative. The astute reader, however, will notice inconsistencies in such matters as the name of God, the chronology of events, the cause of the flood, and the descriptions of animals taken into the ark.

Customarily, the major theological concerns about the flood have been about the historicity of the biblical account. The apparent lack of any geological or historical evidence for a global deluge has sent believers and adventurers scurrying to find the ark or to locate geological evidence to prove the historicity of the flood, a quest that seems almost insatiable, given the constant flow of new books and television specials about it. The discovery in the nineteenth century of a Babylonian account of the flood (now known to be part of the Epic of Gilgamesh, *ANET*, 72–99) very much like the biblical story was taken by some to confirm the biblical account, but it raised questions about the historicity of the biblical text. It is unlikely that the historical question will ever be solved to everyone's satisfaction. The biblical flood story certainly contains historical memories of a flood or floods, but the nature, extent, and location of such a flood are no longer possible to determine, nor will they be solved by the ark quest. More importantly, these traditional concerns, though understandable, avoid the key theological ideas in the story itself and distract attention from the real point of the account.

The flood story is about catastrophe, our fear of it, our attempt to make sense of it, and our hope to survive it. The fear of catastrophe—the onslaught of chaos and the disintegration of the orders that make life possible—is a deep and universal human anxiety, to judge from the fact that accounts of worldwide destruction, usually by floodwaters, come from all continents and cultures. The P version of the flood describes the waters of chaos, restrained at creation, breaking through their barriers and engulfing the world (7:11; cf. 1:6–9). Our attempts to make sense of the flood catastrophe, from Sunday school curricula to scholarly commentaries, tend toward the sentimental. We focus attention almost entirely on the tiny ark and its small group of survivors, overlooking the breathtaking devastation of plant, animal, and human life. This is understandable, since survival is the point of the story, but such an interpretive slant fails to deal adequately with the depth of loss and with the tenacity of hope and survival in the face of it.

Both the Yahwist and the Priestly Writer in their own ways explain catastrophe as punishment for sin (J: 6:5–8; P: 6:11–13). Theirs is the standard way to explain misfortune in the Bible and in ancient Near Eastern theology more generally. But a massive catastrophe like the flood, just as any disaster today, raises the problem of innocent suffering—were all the children and animals guilty?—and thereby of God's justice. The book of Job raises just this challenge for Israel's traditional theology of sin and punishment represented in the theology of both flood authors. Can all suffering, in the life of one individual or in great catastrophes, be attributed to sin and guilt, as do the authors of the biblical flood story? Many modern readers will feel more comfortable with Job's attempt to get beyond the sin-punishment equation than with these authors' confidence in it, especially when trying to make sense of modern disasters. Yet modern readers may still appreciate the flood authors' courage to face great tragedy squarely and to affirm that it never entirely overcomes the life and order in God's creation. Indeed, the first covenants in the Bible, which directly follow the flood, are designed to highlight God's guarantee that life and order will always triumph over chaos in the new era of human history.

The Ancestral Age: Israel's Place in the World (8:20–50:26)

The stories that follow the flood in Genesis describe the re-creation of the world after the flood, the spread of humanity throughout that world, and the emergence of the people of Israel among the cultures of that world. The first episodes in this larger narrative—the accounts of Noah's family, of the dispersion of humanity from Babel, and of the elaborate branching out of the family tree of the world's citizenry—are more properly understood as the introduction to this second age of human history than as the conclusion to the primeval age, as they have customarily been understood. From now on, the reader must practice a special kind of double reading. These stories must be read as the storyteller's past, the stories of the ancient families from which humanity, Israel's neighbors, and Israel itself descended. At the same time, these stories must be read as the storyteller's present, where the ancient characters and families represent the peoples and nations, now composed of their descendants, with which the storyteller and his audience are familiar. Each setting, character, and plot is just as much about the present national and political realities of the biblical authors and their audiences as they are about their past.

The first biblical covenant (8:20–9:17). The new era of human history following the flood is inaugurated by God's first formal covenant, which will define the nature of God's relation to the world from this time forward. Both versions of this covenant, J's and P's, emphasize God's relationship to the world as a whole rather than to humanity alone or to selected individuals within it. In this covenant, God promises to preserve creation and its orders so that it is never again threatened by the return of chaos. In J's account God guarantees the productivity of the agricultural economy upon which biblical society depended by promising "seedtime and harvest" in perpetuity (8:20–22). To keep this promise, God adopts an approach to the world and its people different from the approach described in J's primeval traditions, when God punished sin by cursing the ground, making farming painful and precarious (3:17–19; 4:11–14). In the new era God promises to keep creation stable and productive in spite of human sins (5:29; 8:20–22).

The P version of this covenant is the first of three covenants by which P divides the past into periods: (1) the covenant with Noah, his descendants, and all living things, by which God establishes a relationship with the world and all of its life at the beginning of the new age (9:1–17); (2) the covenant with Abraham, by which

God establishes a relationship with a particular family (17:1–27); and (3) the covenant with Israel at Mount Sinai, by which God establishes a relationship with a particular people (Exod. 31:12–18; cf. Gen. 2:1–4). For P the third covenant is the climactic one, since it institutes the rituals, institutions, and practices over which the priesthood presides and which define Israel as a religious community (Exod. 25:1–31:18). Yet this final, highly particular covenant between God and Israel as a worshiping community is situated by the Priestly Writer within the larger context of God's first, foundational covenant with the world as a whole.

In this covenant, God enters into a permanent and indissoluble relationship with all living things, guaranteeing the well-being of all forms of life in the new age (Gen. 9:9, 10, 12, 15). While interpreters have claimed that God began the new age with the abandonment of humanity and the selection of a particular family within it (Gen. 12), Priestly tradition states the opposite: God initiated the new era with a new commitment to humanity as a whole, and not just to humanity but to the entire community of life that people share. This conception of God's relation to the world as a whole is preserved in Judaism in the belief that in the covenant with Noah, God provided humanity with enough commandments, if observed, to ensure the salvation of all. This covenant between God and all living things has also been used by environmental ethicists to provide a theological justification for biodiversity, the protection of every species of life.

The origins of ethnicity and cultural pluralism (9:18–11:32). Following God's covenant with creation and humanity to initiate the new age, the Yahwist and Priestly Writer describe the dispersion and differentiation of the human race, from the family of Noah to the multicultural world within which Israel's ancestors emerge. The value of ethnic identity and cultural diversity has become a primary concern in the modern world, because of the growing cultural diversity of individual societies and of new cultural and religious conflicts worldwide. Members of modern faiths are on a new search for a theological basis for understanding cultural identity and difference, a search in which biblical images and ideas play an important role. Biblical attitudes toward ethnicity and cultural pluralism in these ancestral narratives describing their origins must therefore be understood clearly and their consequences for conflict or cooperation evaluated carefully.

The stories of humanity's and Israel's ancestors in Genesis provide no simple standpoint or doctrinal principle for viewing ethnicity and diversity. They are a valuable resource for contemporary reflection, rather, because they reflect in their own place and time the common human struggle to embrace one's own ethnic particularity and also to live among, respect, and build relationships with those of other ethnicities. Israel's stories of itself, as all cultural narratives, have distinct ethnocentric elements, which take Israel's own culture as the point of orientation and standard by which other cultures are viewed and judged. At the same time, Israel's stories have a pluralistic sensibility, by which other cultures and peoples are acknowledged and valued for their role in the world. In the ancestral narratives we find no easy answers to contemporary conflicts, but by studying them closely we may better understand the origins of our modern attitudes and gain new insights into the nature of the tension between identity and difference and how our biblical tradition has faced them.

The Yahwist's traditions about the dispersion and differentiation of the human race after the flood comprise primarily two narratives: the story of Noah and his sons (9:18–27) and the story of Babel (11:1–9). The account of Noah and his sons clearly emphasizes the ethnocentric dimension of Yahwistic thought by introducing a theme that will dominate all ancestral narratives: God's selection and elevation of Israel and its culture over its

neighbors (e.g., 17:18–21; 27:29). It is not necessary to determine exactly what infraction Ham committed in order to understand the point of the story, which is expressed by Noah's blessings and curses. One line of humanity, the line of Shem from whom Israel's own ancestors will descend, is blessed by God, and another line, the line of Ham from whom the Canaanites (Israel's ancient enemy) will descend, is cursed and made subservient. This story is clearly designed to deal with the intense military and cultural conflicts between Israelites and Canaanites that accompanied the rise of Israel as a distinct people and that were familiar to the Yahwist and his audience. They contain at once a strong censure of the Canaanites and an acknowledgment of their ancient relationship as common members of Noah's family.

There is no justification for interpreting this story, as it has been in American history, as theological justification for the enslavement or segregation of African Americans. Because the inhabitants of North Africa are among the descendants of Ham in the Priestly genealogy (10:6–7), proslavery and prosegregation preachers have taken Noah's curse as a mandate for the enslavement of all members of the black race. Ham is, however, the ancestor not only of North Africans but of the inhabitants of most of the Middle East including Mesopotamia, the Arabian desert, and the Phoenician coast. Moreover, it is not the North Africans but Canaan, the ancestor of Israel's old enemy, whom Noah curses. Finally, the Yahwist does not use race, here or elsewhere in his narratives, as a cultural marker. The later use of this story to oppress African Americans has nothing to do with the Bible and everything to do with the social agenda of its interpreters.

The second Yahwistic story explaining the spread of humanity is the story of the "tower of Babel," so called because its interpreters have taken the tower as the key to the story. They have viewed the tower as an attack on heaven and on God's authority, and have considered it the climactic act of hubris in the primeval age (11:1–9). By turning the people's actions into an attack on God, interpreters have believed God's response to be an act of punishment. They have therefore believed that God's dispersion of peoples and the differentiation of their languages is a divine curse and judgment upon humanity. This traditional reading of the story of Babel paints the Yahwist as stridently ethnocentric with a pessimistic view of cultural pluralism, and it claims that the Bible's foundational account of cultural diversity believes it to be a tragedy for humanity.

This interpretation, however, goes beyond the story itself, which mentions neither pride nor punishment. According to the story's own explicit claims, the people's motive for building Babel was not an attack on God but the universal human impulse to stay together, to preserve a unified culture and identity (v. 4). Furthermore, the story mentions this motive without censure or judgment. In its conclusion, the story presents God's dispersion and differentiation of humanity not as a punishment or a penalty, but as God's intervention to counteract the homogeneity of humanity and to implement an alternative plan for the postflood world (vv. 5–9). That alternative plan is to diversify the human race in order to create a multicultural world. Thus the Yahwist's account of the origin of the world's cultures and the introduction of difference embraces both ethnicity, by describing without judgment the people's quest for identity, and cultural pluralism, by identifying diversity as God's intention for the new era. It is a remarkably optimistic explanation of ethnicity and cultural pluralism for an author who is at times strongly ethnocentric.

Priestly traditions of the spread of humanity after the flood—recorded in the genealogies scholars have called the Table of Nations (10:1–7, 20, 22–23, 31–32; 11:10–27, 31–32)—are, like the Yahwist's, distinctly pluralistic. These genealogical traditions record the branching out of the peoples and cultures descending from Noah's three sons as a natural development of events in the postflood world (10:5, 20, 32). Indeed, P certainly regards such cultural dispersion and differentiation as the fulfillment of God's command to multiply and fill the earth in God's first covenant of the new age (9:1, 7; cf. 1:28). At the same time, P traditions also give special attention to the descendants of Shem, the line from which Israel's ancestors will emerge (10:22–23, 31–32; 11:10–27, 31–32). In these narratives and genealogies, both writers place special emphasis on God's relationship to Israel and its ancestors, but they do so not by claiming God's abandonment of humanity or judgment of it, as traditional interpretation has believed. Rather, both authors present God's relationship to Israel as one dimension of God's relationship to the larger, multicultural world God created after the flood.

The Abraham traditions (12:1–25:18). Among all of Israel's ancestors in the book of Genesis, Abraham holds the most prominent place. For the biblical writers themselves, J and P, as well as the Elohist (E), whose traditions begin with Abraham, Abraham is Israel's archetypal ancestor, the founding father and standard by which all others are measured. For J in particular, Abraham is also the prototype of David, the founder of the kingdom of Israel and the Davidic dynasty, during which time J lived and put his traditions of Israel's beginnings into their final form. For modern readers, Abraham has taken on new importance as the father of the three great monotheistic religions, Judaism, Christianity, and Islam.

Abraham: The father of Judaism, Christianity, and Islam. In an era when conflicts have characterized the contact between Judaism, Christianity, and Islam, Abraham has become a symbol of their inherent relationship and of the possibility of cooperation rather than hostility among them. By claiming common descent from Abraham, all three religions identify themselves as members of one family. Judaism regards Abraham as its biological and spiritual father. Its members claim that they share common descent from Abraham, through Isaac and Jacob, and that they share the special covenant relationship with God established in the covenant with Abraham (Gen. 15, 17). Christians regard Abraham as their spiritual father. The apostle Paul explained God's inclusion of Gentile Christians among the people of God by designating Abraham as the great exemplar of faith, the individual who first demonstrated that the faith (of anyone), apart from the works of the law (of Judaism), made one righteous before God (Gen. 15:6; Rom. 4:3, 9, 22; Gal. 3:6). Islam also regards Abraham as one of its greatest spiritual leaders. Its adherents claim that Muhammad is a descendant of Abraham through Ismail (Ishmael) and that Abraham was a preeminent model of the submission to God fundamental to Islam.

Abraham is thus a powerful symbol of unity in a time of conflict. Yet biblical traditions themselves are complex, combining ethnocentric and pluralistic elements and thereby containing the seeds of both conflict and cooperation. On the one hand, the stories of Abraham reflect the severe ethnocentric notion that only one son may be chosen and only one line of descent favored. For one son, Isaac, to be fully included in the family, the other son, Ishmael, must be excluded (Gen. 16:1–16; 21:8–21; cf. 17:18–21). On the other hand, this exclusivity is tempered throughout these narratives by the motif that Ishmael too has a crucial role in God's purposes. In all traditions, Ishmael is the great patriarch Abraham's son, and, moreover, the firstborn son, the most honored position in the family. In both J and E traditions, God appears directly to Ishmael's mother Hagar to protect her and her son, and in both instances Ishmael is the recipient of the covenant promises of nationhood and uncountable descendants that God first made to Abraham (16:7–12; 21:13–21; cf. 12:1–3; 13:16). In P traditions Ishmael is

Abraham's favored son, is promised descendants and nationhood, is the first to be circumcised with the sign of the covenant, and cooperates with his brother Isaac to bury their father (17:18, 20, 23–27; 25:9). The contemporary reader must recognize the complexity of the biblical legacy of Abraham and consider carefully the ways it can be employed to further conflict or create cooperation among its heirs.

The Abrahamic covenant (Gen. 15, 17). The covenant with Abraham exists in two versions, J in Gen. 15 and P in Gen. 17. Both versions of the covenant focus on God's promise to Abraham that his heirs will be innumerable and that they will inherit the land of Canaan. The religious rituals that accompany these two versions of the covenant, however, differ greatly. In the J account, the covenant is sealed when a flaming torch passes between the halves of the carcasses of slain animals, which symbolize the fate of the covenant party who violates the covenant. This ancient Near Eastern practice may lie behind the J expression "cut" a covenant (15:18; NRSV "made"). In the P account, the covenant is sealed by the circumcision of its male members, and any who are not circumcised are excluded from the covenant community (17:9–14). For P, this covenant introduces a new era of history. Just as God's first covenant with the world, whose sign was the rainbow, guaranteed the stability of creation (9:7–17), so God's second covenant with Abraham, whose sign was circumcision, guaranteed God's care of a particular family.

Biblical theologians have invested much energy in a debate over whether these covenants are conditional, in which the divine-human relationship depends upon a human response, or unconditional, in which God takes sole responsibility for the relationship. In one respect, such a debate turns on the Christian approach to law and grace, by which salvation is viewed as based either on obedience or on God's free gift. The insight that biblical covenants are based primarily on the language and conventions of kinship, which defined and structured Israelite society, makes this a false dichotomy. As Frank Cross has shown, biblical authors view God as the divine father of the family with which he has entered into relationship. God is referred to as father in personal names—Abram means "the father [i.e., God] is exalted"—and is identified as the head of Israel's ancestral families—Jacob calls God "the God of my father, the God of Abraham, the fear [possibly, 'kinsman'] of Isaac" (31:42). The Hebrew term *hesed*, often translated "kindness" or "steadfast love," is a kinship term signifying the loyalty inherent in the intimate bonds of a family or larger kinship group (19:19; 39:21). Thus the covenants between God and the ancestral families are conceived as kinship relationships, and such relationships are always characterized by mutual obligations and privileges. There are no unilateral covenants in a kinship society. God's protection and promises in the Abrahamic covenants are accompanied by Abraham's own trust and obedience (15:5; 26:4–5) and by his faithful attention to covenant obligations (17:23–27).

The role of land in Genesis.   One aspect of the Abrahamic covenant that has presented a particular moral dilemma in contemporary American and Middle Eastern politics is God's promise of the land of Canaan to Abraham and his descendants and the consequent displacement of other peoples (15:18–21; 17:8). Some members of the conservative wings of Judaism and Christianity have brought God's promises to Abraham to bear on the contentious and divisive conflict between Israelis and Palestinians. Specifically, they have argued that God's promises to Abraham are eternal and therefore legitimate Israel's possession of all of the occupied West Bank in which a Palestinian state has been proposed. The actual sites where God promises Abraham and his descendants land— Shechem (12:6–7), Bethel (13:3, 14–17), and Hebron (13:18; 15:17–21)—are cen-

ters of Palestinian culture in the West Bank today.

The biblical authors apparently had their own moral concerns about the possession of land and displacement of peoples, as we can see in J's explanation that these promises would not be fulfilled until the societies of the displaced had become so corrupt as to merit judgment and exile (15:13–16). For the contemporary reader, however, the key to understanding God's promises of land in the Abrahamic covenant is to recognize that both J and P considered them to pertain to, and to be fulfilled in, the political realities of their own times. J, who lived and recorded his ancestral traditions in the early days of the Davidic monarchy, saw the promises of land and descendants to Abraham fulfilled in the Israelite kingdom, with its own territory and robust population. P, who lived and collected Israel's traditions during the Babylonian exile, saw these promises fulfilled when the Persian Empire sponsored the return of the Israelite exiles to their ancestral homeland. To take these promises of land out of the biblical context for which they were intended thus distorts their purpose and makes them susceptible to modern political agendas. A secure Israeli-Palestinian peace can only be accomplished by ensuring justice for both Palestinians and Israelis in light of current realities, not by political agendas based on biblical texts intended for different social and political contexts.

The ambiguity of ancestral behavior.   All of the heroes in the ancestral era, from Noah to Jacob's sons, including the archetypal Abraham, act in ways that seem peculiar and at times even immoral to contemporary readers. Are they to be considered paragons of virtues to be emulated or practitioners of vices to be avoided, or both? And how should such judgments be made? P characterizes Abraham and his heirs in completely favorable terms as upright and righteous figures (17:1–2; 21:4; 28:1–5; 35:9–13). E too presents an exemplary Abraham, explicitly defending Abraham's character in his own version of parallel traditions, when J stories put Abraham in ambiguous positions. For example, E preserves the integrity of Abraham and Sarah in the foreign king's court (20:1–17; cf. 12:10–20; 26:6–16) and provides divine legitimation for Abraham's expulsion of Hagar and Ishmael (21:8–21; cf. 16:1–14). Even J honors Abraham as a praiseworthy figure, emphasizing his trust and obedience (15:6; 26:4). Yet it is primarily in the J narratives that Abraham and his family reflect the kind of behaviors that have led Elie Wiesel to describe Israel's ancestors not as heroes but as antiheroes (personal communication).

One reason for J's occasionally anti-heroic presentation of Israel's ancestors is theological: J wants to emphasize God's actions over human efforts in the well-being and success of the ancestors and their descendants. God rescues Abraham and Sarah from Pharaoh's court (12:10–20); provides a child for Sarah, Abraham's primary wife, even though she was past childbearing age (18:1–15); saves Abraham's nephew Lot from the destruction of Sodom and Gomorrah (19:12–26); and ensures that the second son, Jacob, would acquire the blessings of the firstborn, Esau, in spite of Isaac's wishes (25:21–34). By opening the barren wombs of Israel's matriarchs, God steps in to fulfill the promises of descendants (16:1; 18:10; 25:21; 29:31; 30:22). The manifestly human characterization of the ancestors, then, is a constant reminder that God rather than the ancestors themselves is the ultimate source of their and their descendants' existence and prosperity.

A second reason for the occasionally unusual behavior of the ancestors is J's viewpoint that God regularly acts counter to human conventions and expectations. In a patriarchal society like ancient Israel's, the two most powerful figures are the father, who is head of the household, and the firstborn son, who will inherit the father's role. Latter-born sons and women possess less power and play secondary roles. Yet this pattern is usually reversed in J's stories. Israel's matriarchs normally play a larger role in determining the transfer of power to the new generation than do the patriarchs (21:10–11; 27:5–10). And in each new ancestral generation, the firstborn son fails to inherit customary power in the family (21:12–13; 27:36–37; 49:1–8). According to J, this reversal of social convention is described as God's plan for the ancestral families (18:13–14; 25:21–23).

To counteract social convention, however, matriarchs and second-born sons must employ their power in ways that circumvent socially sanctioned structures of authority, since this very system of social authority contained within it the structural discrimination against women and younger sons. The deceit Rebekah and Jacob used to subvert the sanctioned social authority of Isaac and Esau has troubled readers, yet this was one of the only devices available for subordinate individuals to challenge the structures that excluded them. When J connects these subversive challenges to institutional power with God's plans, he may be reflecting his experience of and support for David's rise to prominence, since David was the youngest son from a family outside the royal court of Saul. Yet J may also champion the larger view that God often intervenes in human history to support those excluded by society's institutional structures.

Some aspects of the behavior of Abraham and of Israel's other ancestors, however, are best explained not as theological lessons but as the consequence of social practices and mores that differ from modern Western practices and mores. A number of these ancient practices—such as polygamy (16:3; 25:1), incest (19:30–38), and owning slaves (12:16; 16:1)—are not only different from modern practices but are against the law in many contemporary societies. Others, not illegal, may simply seem puzzling or strange to some modern readers: arranged marriages and the exchange of goods accompanying them (24:52–61), special diets to increase fertility (30:14–16), peculiar breeding practices (30:31–43). Still other ancient practices and mores, such as patriarchal social structures, are still part of contemporary society but are being strongly challenged in many modern contexts. All of these examples show that the stories of Israel's ancestors in Genesis reflect the ancient customs and practices of the time, and that these stories may not be taken as theological or ethical guides without critical reflection to determine which practices are to be rejected as immoral and inhumane and which are to be accepted as ethically exemplary.

The most problematic episode in all of the ancestral stories is E's account of God's command to Abraham to sacrifice his son and Abraham's willingness to carry it out (Gen. 22). Interpreters have traditionally escaped this ethical predicament by reading the story as a polemic against child sacrifice, since God substitutes an animal for Isaac (22:12–13). But this interpretation undermines the point of the text, that Abraham is honored because he was prepared to sacrifice his son (22:12, 15–18). Child sacrifice was practiced in the ancient Near East and in ancient Israel (Exod. 22:29–30 [22:28–29 Heb.]; Ezek. 20:25–26). Another way to resolve this dilemma, championed by Søren Kierkegaard, is to consider God above all human moral codes and absolutely free to act in divine wisdom. A third approach, which avoids the interpretive and moral pitfalls of these first two approaches, is to recognize the practice of child sacrifice as a sanctioned ancient custom—like slavery—that must be recognized today as absolutely contrary to genuine ritual and morality, as it was already recognized by some authors in the biblical period (Deut. 12:31; Jer. 7:30–32).

The Jacob traditions (25:19–36:43). Jacob
is the most complex of Israel's ancestors. On the one hand, he is the quintessential ancestor of Israel, since it is only his descendants, the children of his twelve sons, who can call themselves Israelites. As the prototype of his people, he is granted the name by which they will be known, Israel (32:28 [29 Heb.]; 35:10). While Abraham and Isaac too are ancestors of Israel, they are also the ancestors of Israel's neighbors, the Ishmaelites (16:11–12), Midianites (25:2), Edomites (25:30), and others (25:1–4). On the other hand, Jacob is synonymous with trickery and deceit, the techniques he uses to acquire power in his family and to acquire possessions in his wives' family. Indeed, his original name, Jacob, means to displace or unseat. His two names, Jacob and Israel, thus symbolize the complexity of Jacob's identity and of his theological and ethical position in the narratives of Genesis.

Jacob's questionable character as Israel's ancestor. Jacob, like his own ancestors Abraham and Isaac, is an exemplary figure. He is the recipient of all of the benefits of the covenant God made with Abraham: innumerable descendants, land, nationhood, and blessings (28:13–15; 35:11–12). He receives God's constant protection, inside and outside the land of Canaan (28:15; 31:3–9). He is buried in the tomb of his fathers Abraham and Isaac in the land God promised him (49:29–50:14), and even the Egyptians grieved his death (50:11). During his lifetime, he founds the Israelite sanctuary at Bethel (28:18–22), serves his father-in-law Laban faithfully (30:26), obeys God's commands (31:3, 13, 17), and mediates the blessings of God to others (30:27–30). He embodies the best ancestral qualities, sharing the benefits and upholding the responsibilities of the covenant relationship between God and Israel's ancestors.

Yet it is Jacob's crafty schemes and cunning maneuvers that the reader remembers best, his "theft" of the birthright in his own family (27:1–45) and his "theft" of the best animals in Laban's flocks (30:25–31:18). The biblical authors, however, appear to view these aspects of Jacob's behavior in much more positive terms than the modern reader. Jacob's acquisition of the birthright and of Laban's prime flock are presented both as God's own designs for Jacob and ultimately as events in which God was implicitly involved (25:22–26; 27:27–29; 31:4–16). This divine support for Jacob may be best understood in light of the larger pattern in Genesis, which we have already noticed in the Abraham traditions, by which God's plans for Israel's ancestors are furthered by women and secondary sons, that is, by those outside the positions of power in society held by fathers and their firstborn sons (see "The ambiguity of ancestral behavior" above). By vesting complete authority in the father and his firstborn heir, Israel's kinship society disenfranchised others, who, like Jacob and Rebekah, used the means available to them to gain access to the powers denied them. By placing God on their side, the authors of Genesis appear to offer an implicit critique of the rigidity of kinship structures and to see God's activity in the quest by the disenfranchised to share in the power and benefits of the family and society.

Wrestling with God. The most fascinating and theologically intriguing story in all of the Jacob narratives is the account of Jacob's wrestling a mysterious assailant at the Jabbok River on his return from exile at his father-in-law Laban's home (Gen 32:22–32 [32:23–33 Heb.]). The story is fascinating theologically because we are not sure if Jacob's opponent is God—the narrator refers to him as a man (v. 24) but Jacob identifies him as God (v. 30)—and because, if the opponent is God, we are not sure what this kind of a wrestling match tells us about God's nature and relationship to people. The story's presentation of Jacob's assailant in such a mysterious way has led to all sorts of interpretations about his identity. Jacob's opponent has been interpreted as a river demon; as a prefiguration of Esau, whom Jacob was about to encounter; and as Jacob's own self.

From the point of view of the Yahwist who narrates this story, Jacob's opponent is certainly God. This mysterious figure is not unlike the Yahwist's other depictions of God, who is humanlike and accessible and is sometimes a liminal figure occupying the threshold between human and divine realms (18:1–15; see "The character of God"). At the same time, this encounter between God and Jacob is unique because it contains the element of struggle, in which God is both an adversary and a benefactor. God attacks Jacob and wounds him, leaving him with a limp (vv. 24–25), but God also blesses Jacob and gives him the name Israel by which his descendants will be known (vv. 28–29).

This two-sided nature of God is not unique but reflects the profound ambiguity of the encounter with the Divine in the Bible (and in other religious traditions as well), which Rudolf Otto has described as a strange harmony of contrasts. On the one hand God is wholly other than human, so awesome and overpowering that it is dangerous even to enter God's presence: Jacob marvels that he has seen God and is still alive (vv. 30). On the other hand God approaches humanity with gracious intent, acting to ensure Jacob's protection and blessing (v. 28–29). The name God gives Jacob, "Israel," which J takes to mean "God (*'el*) struggles (*yisra*)," captures this paradox of religious experience, and it identifies Israel as a people who will forever live in this tension between divine majesty and power and divine graciousness.

Sibling rivalry and international relations. The rivalry between Jacob and Esau that dominates the Jacob traditions is one of the most colorful and ethically complicated relationships in Genesis. Like other stories in Genesis, this story is meant to be read on two levels: the level of the family, in which the rivalry between Jacob and Esau represents the contest for power among brothers in a single household; and the level of the nation, in which the rivalry between Jacob and Esau represents the tensions between the nations of Israel and Edom that constitute their descendants. The way in which this double-leveled rivalry is described in the Jacob traditions reveals the values held by the authors of Genesis about the resolution of conflict both within the family and on the larger international scene.

On the family level, J, who is primarily responsible for these rivalry stories, presents the conflict between the brothers without simplifying it as a contest between a villain and an innocent victim. On the one hand, J recognizes Esau's right to the birthright because he is the firstborn and the favorite of the great patriarch Isaac. On the other hand, J lends support to the excluded second-born son by portraying his theft of his brother's birthright as the plan of God and of the great matriarch Rebekah. More than establishing blame for the rivalry, J is interested in exploring a path toward a resolution that avoids violence (see "Cain, Abel, and social conflict"). In this case, reconciliation is achieved when Esau—the party who possesses good reasons for revenge and who also has the power to carry out an act of vengeance (32:11 [12 Heb.])—takes the initiative to lay aside his grievances, reestablish contact with his "enemy," and bring about a peaceful resolution to the conflict (33:4–10). Reconciliation is achieved when the party with the power to determine the outcome of the conflict uses that power for a peaceful rather than a violent response. Without such a magnanimous act, the cycle of revenge is without end.

On the level of international relations, J explores through this rivalry the complex relations between Israel and its neighboring nations, in this case the nation of Edom (25:30). On the one hand, this story legitimates the hegemony of Israel over Edom, whose ancestor was thoughtless enough to sell his birthright (25:29–35) and whose descendants were made subservient to the descendants of Jacob in Isaac's blessing (27:29). But on the other hand, this story advocates great respect for Edom. The nation of Edom is not viewed as foreign or alien but as a brother, sharing much of Israel's own identity and deserving the honor and privileges of a member of one's own family. When conflict does arise between

these nations, it is resolved not by violent means but by reconciliation and the exchange of gifts. Perhaps most striking of all, it is Israel's neighbor Edom that is the more powerful party in this story and that initiates the act of reconciliation by which the two parties may live in peace. Thus J grants international magnanimity not just to Israel, which we might expect, but to Israel's neighbors as well.

The Joseph traditions (Gen. 37–50). While composed of elements of the three great Genesis traditions—J, E, and P—the stories about Joseph give a stronger impression of a unified account than the collections of narratives about Abraham and Jacob. At the family level, these stories contain the same dynamics of sibling conflict and resolution we have seen in the other families in Genesis. But at the national level, these stories narrow the reader's attention from the relations between Israel and its neighbors to the relations between the main subgroups that make up Israel itself. Each of the sons of Jacob is the ancestor of one of the twelve tribes of Israel, so that the description of the relationships between the sons of Jacob in these stories also becomes an account of the nature of the community that makes up the kingdom of Israel at the time these stories were told.

The dreamer and his brothers. The story of Joseph and his brothers at the conclusion of Genesis is one of the most memorable human dramas in the Bible. It has been relived by millions of modern viewers at shows of Timothy Rice's and Andrew Lloyd Webber's *Joseph and the Amazing Technicolor Dreamcoat*. Like the stories that precede it in Genesis, this story deals with social conflict and its resolution in a kinship-based society. Here too the narrators avoid presenting conflict and assessing blame in simplistic terms. The narrative recognizes the primary claim of Joseph's older brothers to prestige and power in the family (37:10), and it pictures Joseph himself as a cheeky kid who rubs his family the wrong way

(37:1–11). At the same time, Joseph is described as the favorite of the patriarch Israel, and his claims to greatness are presented as God's own plans for him and his family (37:4–9; 39:5, 41:37, 50:20).

In this narrative as in the preceding ones, biblical authors are more interested in the resolution of the conflict than in its origins. And the drama of this resolution may be the most poignant one in the Bible: Joseph, recognizing his brothers, who do not at first recognize him, weeps with them because of the pain of the family's past and the joy of its future (45:1–15). Within this emotional narrative are embedded the key values held by its authors about community, its sustenance, and its health. At the key points in the conflict, its resolution by violence is narrowly averted when those with the power to change the course of the conflict and who have good reason to seek vengeance choose reconciliation over violence. At the moment when Joseph's life is threatened by his brothers, both Reuben— the privileged firstborn, whose action is described in E traditions (37:19–22, 24)— and Judah—the fourth-born who receives the family's primary blessing and whose action is described in J traditions (37:18, 23, 25–27)—intervene to save Joseph's life. At the narrative's climax, when Joseph has both the power and the motive to avenge his brothers' betrayal, he decides not to retaliate but to reestablish the relationship that his brothers had severed. Throughout the book of Genesis, these stories of conflict and reconciliation hold up the values of courage and compassion over those of accusation and retaliation.

The role of David in Genesis and in the Bible. The figure of David as the quintessential leader of the people of God and as the mediator of God's designs in the world towers over both Old and New Testaments. He and his family are adopted into a special relationship with God to establish and rule the kingdom of Israel as a nation among nations (2 Sam. 7:1–17; Ps. 89). Thus David fulfills the great covenant promises to Abraham, Isaac, and Jacob that their descendants will become a populous nation in the land of Canaan. It is to David's family that in a later period many Jews looked for a messiah to restore the fortunes of Israel. And it is from David's family that Jesus of Nazareth, proclaimed as the Messiah by the first Christians, was born (Matt. 1:1; Luke 3:31).

Though he is never mentioned in Genesis, David exerts a profound influence on the traditions of Joseph. At their larger national level, the stories of Joseph provide a kind of internal communal map of the people of Israel at the time of the monarchy when these traditions of Israel's ancestors were first solidified. In the J traditions in particular, David's tribe, the tribe of Judah, is singled out through the stories of its ancestor Judah for special respect, privilege, and power. Judah is instrumental in saving Joseph from death (37:25–27), a fact with wide national significance when it is recalled that Joseph is the ancestor of the northern tribes, Ephraim and Manasseh, which David unites with the south to create the united monarchy (Gen. 48; 2 Sam. 5:1–5). Judah's role as the one to unite all of the brothers/tribes of Israel is seen also in his leadership in the protection of Benjamin and in the brothers' reconciliation with Joseph (Gen. 42:1–45:2). Finally, Judah's receipt of the family patrimony and hegemony over his brothers in Jacob's final blessing reflects the prominence of the tribe of Judah upon the rise of David to power over all of Israel's descendants (49:8–12). Jacob's great blessing of Judah, from whose lineage Jesus of Nazareth would also come, is interpreted later by early Christians as prefiguring Christ.

Tamar and the restoration of the marginalized (Gen. 38). To modern sensibilities, the story of Tamar is one of the strangest and most ethically troubling in the Bible. It involves Tamar, the ancestor of David (vv. 27–30; Ruth 4:18–21), in sexual intercourse with her brother-in-law (v. 8), in coitus interruptus (onanism, v. 9), in prostitution (vv. 15–16), and in sexual intercourse with her father-in-law (vv.

24–26). Part of the explanation for this kind of behavior may be found in J's antiheroic presentation of Israel's ancestors (see "The ambiguity of ancestral behavior"). Another part of the explanation may be found in ancient social customs unknown in modern Western societies. One of these customs is levirate marriage, in which a widowed woman sleeps with her deceased husband's brother to produce an heir who will be considered the heir of her husband to carry on his name and patrimony (Deut. 25:5–10). While this custom violates modern sexual norms, it was an ancient Israelite practice that promoted stability within kinship structures and protected the widow by producing sons to provide her with economic support.

The key to addressing the ethical difficulties of the story, however, lies in the imbalance of power in a patriarchal society. At her marriage, Tamar moved away from the authority of her father and came under the authority of her husband, Judah's son Er. At Er's death, she came under the authority of the patriarch of her husband's household, her father-in-law, Judah. But Judah abdicated his responsibility to her when he failed to produce an heir for her and her deceased husband by neglecting levirate marriage laws (vv. 11, 14). Failed by Judah in whose household she now belonged, she no longer possessed standing in the household of her marriage or of her birth. Because of the failure of the men who had power over her, she as a woman lost her place in society.

Dislocated and unjustly disgraced by the irresponsibility of patriarchal power, Tamar initiates a plan to rectify her undeserved predicament. She poses as a prostitute to produce a male heir from her husband's family, luring Judah into the sexual liaison that he should have provided her through levirate marriage. When she averts death for sexual activity outside marriage by producing Judah's signet, cord, and staff, her subversive plan is vindicated by Judah's own words: "She is more in the right than I" (vv. 24–26). J's primary ethical concern in this story is the abuse of patriarchal power, and the ethical value he honors is the right of those robbed of their standing to act to recover their rightful identity and status in their society. The story is not a modern feminist argument for fundamental changes in Israel's patriarchal society, but it does call attention to the abuses of patriarchy and it does place righteousness solidly on the side of those who challenge their unjust marginalization (see "Human identity and gender").

Egypt in Genesis and in the Bible. The Joseph traditions and the book of Genesis as a whole end not in the land of Canaan, which is promised to the ancestors and their descendants and which is the focal point of the ancestral stories, but in the land of Egypt. When a severe famine grips their homeland, Jacob and his family are forced to emigrate from Canaan and relocate to Egypt, where they reside when Genesis concludes. Because of the enslavement of Jacob's descendants in Egypt in the book of Exodus that follows, the pharaoh, his armies, and the Egyptian people have come to symbolize evil and oppression in biblical traditions (Exod. 15; Isa. 19; Ezek. 29–32). This negative image of Egypt has been emphasized in the modern period by liberation theologians, such as Gustavo Gutiérrez and James Cone, who have taken the exodus as the archetypal liberation of the oppressed and Egypt as the archetypal oppressor.

The view of Egypt in Genesis and in the Bible is complex and includes, especially in the Joseph traditions, a profound element of respect and high regard. There are, of course, details critical of Egypt in these stories, such as Potiphar's wife's false accusation of Joseph (chap. 39) and the claim that all of Egypt's sages could not interpret dreams as Joseph could (41:8–13). Yet the image of Egypt in the Joseph traditions is overwhelmingly positive. Above all, Egypt is recognized as the savior of Israel whose very existence was threatened by famine (45:5–8; 50:20–21). God reveals the future to

Pharaoh so arrangements can be made to survive the famine (41:25); the pharaoh elevates and honors Joseph as his top administrator (41:40); Joseph marries the Egyptian priestess Asenath, whose sons Manasseh and Ephraim are the ancestors of the most powerful and populous tribes of northern Israel (41:45–52); Jacob's family flourishes in Egypt (47:27); and the Egyptians mourn Jacob at this death (50:7–11). These elements of the Joseph traditions present Egypt not as a furnace of oppression but as the safe haven in which Israel's life was preserved and nourished.

Such positive aspects of Egypt in biblical traditions have been particularly important in Afrocentric biblical interpretation. Afrocentric interpreters emphasize Egypt's identity as an African country and, as such, its and Africa's role as one of the fountainheads of human civilization. Thus Egypt is not only the land of enslavement but also the culture that sustained and nurtured the descendants of Israel. It was in Egypt that Israel became a populous and strong people, that Moses was educated in the court of Pharaoh, and that the powerful northern tribes of Manasseh and Ephraim were born of an Israelite-Egyptian marriage. Afrocentric interpretation thus calls attention to the ways in which African peoples and cultures have influenced and contributed to biblical history and religion.

This more rounded view of the role of Egypt in biblical experience and religion has important consequences also for the contemporary period in which strong tensions exist between the Islamic East and the Christian West, tensions that have been described as a clash of civilizations. In such a charged environment, biblical interpretation that emphasizes Egypt as the symbol of oppression and evil simply exacerbates the stereotypes of the Middle East cultivated by extremist parties, by some media, and by much government rhetoric. Recovering an image of Egypt in the Bible that incorporates the positive dimensions of its portrayal by the authors of the Joseph traditions provides us with a more accurate understanding of the book of Genesis and with a more realistic standpoint from which to repair relationships and build bridges between East and West.

Bibliography

Cross, Frank Moore. *From Epic to Canon: History and Literature in Ancient Israel.* Baltimore: John Hopkins, 1998.

Kierkegaard, Søren. *Fear and Trembling: And the Sickness unto Death.* New York: Doubleday Anchor, 1954.

Otto, Rudolf. *The Idea of the Holy.* New York: Oxford University Press, 1958.

Trible, Phyllis. *God and the Rhetoric of Sexuality.* Philadelphia: Fortress, 1978.

Exodus

Dennis T. Olson

INTRODUCTION

The book of Exodus contains one of the OT's most influential master narratives: God's *liberation* of enslaved Israel from Egyptian tyranny (Exod. 1–18), God's *formation* of Israel into a servant people of God dedicated to obedience around the laws and covenant of Mount Sinai (Exod. 19–24), and God's *restoration* of a broken covenant relationship in light of Israel's disobedience in the golden calf/tabernacle cycle (Exod. 25–40). The interplay among these themes of liberation, formation, and restoration create compelling dialectical tensions: human freedom versus human obligation, divine judgment versus divine mercy, God's sovereignty versus God's suffering and compassion, God's nearness and God's otherness. These and many other theological polarities and tensions within the book of Exodus make it a rich, complex, realistic, and mature resource for biblical-theological reflection.

This richness of Exodus derives in part from the variety of literary genres that have been woven together: narratives of various types, poetry, commandments, laws, and ritual instructions. The poem of Exod. 15, the Ten Commandments in Exod. 20, and the Old Testament's earliest collection of laws in the so-called Covenant Code in Exod. 21–23 are probably among the earliest traditions in Exodus. These earlier traditions have been taken up by various writers and editors and joined with later narratives, laws, and other material over hundreds of years of development.

The theological complexity of Exodus also stems in part from its interweaving of at least two major theological strands within ancient Israel: (a) the distinctive and more easily identifiable Priestly tradition that dominates Exod. 19–40 (with interests in the cult, ritual, tabernacle, and temple traditions), and (b) a variety of non-Priestly traditions that dominate Exod. 1–18. Certain key points of great drama and importance in the plot line of Exodus have acted like magnets, attracting a number of different traditions in a dense cluster of edited material. These densely edited clusters include Exod. 14–15 (Israel's rescue through the Red Sea), Exod. 19 (the beginning of the covenant at Mount Sinai), and Exod. 32–34 (the golden calf and God's restoring of the broken covenant relationship). These three nodal points help guide us to the three high points in the Exodus narrative along with their corresponding themes: liberation (Red Sea), formation (covenant at Mount Sinai), and restoration (golden calf).

The book of Exodus likely reached its final form sometime in the sixth or fifth century BCE, after the Babylonian exile of Judah in 587 BCE and the return of the exiles back to Judah in the Persian period of Israel's history. With its themes of liberation, formation, and restoration, Exodus helped to address the theological crisis of the exile and the need for God's people to regain their sense of identity, purpose, and relationship to God as they reconstituted themselves as a sociopolitical and religious community. The final form of Exodus provided a powerful resource of traditions that had been used, shaped, tested, and formed over generations and in various contexts and circumstances. Exodus has continued to be a vital theological resource for countless generations of people of Jewish and Christian faith.

COMMENTARY

Liberation: God's Rescue of Israel from Egyptian Slavery (Exod. 1–18)

A new pharaoh, a new oppression (1:1–22). The dramatic Exodus story of liberation begins with a rather mundane census list of the Israelite clan of Jacob, which numbers seventy people (1:5). The family of Jacob rapidly multiplies in dramatic fashion (1:7). By the time they leave Egypt, their number will grow to six hundred thousand men of military age besides women, children, and the elderly (12:37). This assumes a growth in population over 430 years (see 12:40) from seventy to an amazingly large population of nearly two million Israelites. Although historically improbable, the narrative presents the rapid growth of the Israelite people as a way to affirm God's faithfulness in making a sizable down payment toward fulfilling the earlier promise to Abraham and Sarah that their descendants would become a great and numerous nation (Gen. 12:21; 13:16; 15:5–6). However, this good news of Israel's prolific growth is endangered by a new pharaoh who does not know Joseph and his family. The new pharaoh radically alters Israel's situation in Egypt—from that of welcomed guests to oppressed slaves—and thereby returns them to Joseph's earlier status as slave before his rise to power in Egypt (Exod. 1:8; see Gen. 37:25–38; 41:37–45).

The first individuals to join God's struggle for justice and life against Pharaoh are women: the Hebrew midwives Shiprah and Puah. Pharaoh commands them to kill all the Hebrew male babies but to let the female babies live. Ironically, Pharaoh sees no threat from Israelite females, yet they are the very ones who begin his undoing. The midwives engage in the Bible's first acts of civil disobedience for the sake of justice. They save the lives of both boys and girls and in the process protect the birth of a special child named Moses, the one who would overthrow Pharaoh and lead Israel to freedom. As so often in the Bible, God uses what is low and despised in the eyes of the world to shame and overthrow the arrogant and the strong (1 Sam. 2:1–10; Jer. 9:23; Luke 1:46–55; 1 Cor. 1:26–29).

Three short narratives of attempted deliverance (2:1–25). Exodus 2 places three brief stories of attempted rescue side by side, stories that share some basic features: (1) the rescue of the baby Moses by Pharaoh's daughter (2:1–10), (2) Moses' slaying of the Egyptian foreman and the Israelites' rejection of Moses' authority (2:11–15), and (3) Moses' rescue of the seven women of Midian from menacing shepherds at a well in the wilderness (2:15–22). All three narratives involve an attempted act of deliverance with Moses as either the object or subject of the deliverance. In the end, Moses becomes an "alien" (Heb. *ger*) in a foreign land and thus names his son "Gershom" (2:22). The Egyptian pharaoh seeks to kill Moses (2:15). The Hebrew slaves disown him (2:14). And the wilderness dwellers called Midianites refer to Moses as "an Egyptian" (2:19). On his way to becoming the leader of Israel, Moses experiences the same alienation and loss of status as Israel experienced in its slavery. Nonetheless, in Exod. 3 and his encounter with God, the "alien" Moses finally finds his true home.

The burning bush and the call of Moses (3:1–4:31). At the base of Mount Horeb (also known as Sinai—19:11), Moses encounters an unquenchable burning bush while herding sheep in the wilderness. The fiery bush is an icon of the Divine. The burning bush expresses both God's merciful accommodation, coming down from the mountain of God to meet Moses, and God's awesome holiness, the unquenchable fire being both dangerous and attractive at the same time. God instructs Moses to remove the sandals from his feet, a gesture that not only honors the holiness of this ground but also testifies that Moses has at last found his home (3:5). Removing sandals in the ancient world was done as both an act of reverence at holy places and an act of familiarity and hospitality at one's home. Moses hides his face because he is "afraid to look at God" (3:6). Later in Exodus, Moses will receive a unique opportunity to see a glimpse of God's back (33:17–23).

God calls Moses to go back to Pharaoh and lead the Israelites out of their slavery in Egypt and travel to the promised land of Canaan (3:7–10). As in some other biblical narratives (e.g., Jer. 1:1–10), Moses resists the call and raises a number of objections to which God responds. Moses complains of his own lack of qualifications (Exod. 3:11), the Israelites' anticipated reluctance to believe or follow Moses (4:1), Moses' lack of eloquence (4:10), and Moses' desire that God send someone else (4:13). The most theologically significant objection is Moses' complaint that the people will ask Moses about the name of this God and Moses will not know how to answer them (3:13). God responds by revealing to Moses God's special name, "I AM WHO I AM" (3:14 NRSV). A better translation of the name from the Hebrew might be "I Will Be Who I Will Be" (my trans.). This divine name is built on the Hebrew verb "to be" and is related to the Hebrew divine name used frequently throughout the Old Testament, "Yahweh" or YHWH (the transliterated Hebrew consonants without the vowels, translated as "the LORD" in most English versions). In the Jewish tradition, this special name of God is considered so holy that it is not to be pronounced (hence the absence of vowels). In Exod. 3 this special divine name both reveals and conceals something about who God is. The fuller meaning of God's mysterious name and character will unfold at certain crucial junctures throughout Exodus (20:2–6; 29:45–46; 33:19; 34:6–7). The divine name is important since it gives Moses and the Israelites unique access to God and God's power through prayer and worship.

A brief and enigmatic encounter between God and Moses erupts in the narrative in 4:24–26. After just having called Moses to become the leader of Israel's liberation, God attempts to kill Moses! Moses' wife Zipporah intervenes by circumcising her son, touching the foreskin to Moses' "feet" (a probable euphemism for genitals), and then declaring, "A bridegroom of blood by circumcision." In response to Zipporah's actions, God relents and lets Moses alone. Modern readers have difficulty understanding this story. It is apparently related to traditions about Israel as a firstborn son (4:22), Moses' firstborn son, circumcision, and a ritual associated with marriage. In the larger biblical tradition, however, this divine attack against one who is specially related to or called by God for a special mission is not without precedent (Jacob in Gen. 32:22–32; Balaam in Num. 22:22–35; Joshua in Josh. 5:13–15). In each case, the surprise attack or threat against the one called by God inculcates a fearful reverence, awe, and a deep sense that God and not the human is ultimately in control. God can just as quickly become an enemy as an ally if the community strays from God's chosen path. That will become abundantly clear in the golden calf episode (Exod. 32:1–35). Moreover, Zipporah's rescue of

Moses raises the possibility that God's decision to destroy can be changed, a lesson that will also play a crucial role in the golden calf story (32:14).

The ten plagues and Pharaoh's resistance (5:1–13:16). During Moses and Aaron's first encounter with Pharaoh, they request a three-day journey into the wilderness in order to sacrifice to the Lord. Pharaoh responds that he does not "know" Israel's God and will not let Israel go (5:2). Pharaoh's response sets up an important theological dynamic. Throughout the following chapters, God will be concerned that not only Israel but also Pharaoh and the whole world come to know God as the powerful deliverer of Israel and judge of Egypt (8:22; 9:16, 29; 10:2; 14:4, 18; 32:12). God's name will be known and "resound through all the earth" (9:16).

God sends Moses and Aaron in a series of encounters with Pharaoh that result in ten plagues upon Egypt (7:14–13:22). The plagues are a series of what the OT scholar Terence Fretheim calls "ecological disasters" in which God allows nature to overrun its boundaries to excess in response to Pharaoh's breaking the boundaries of human justice and decency in Egypt's cruel oppression of the Israelites. The Nile River turns to blood, frogs overrun the land, gnats swarm out of control, flies invade, disease attacks cattle, boils come upon cattle and humans, hail falls, locusts swoop in, darkness covers the land, and finally all the firstborn male offspring of Egyptian families and animals die. What humans do in their history can have disastrous consequences and repercussions in the world of nature. A sense of poetic justice emerges from certain parallels between what Egypt did to the Israelite slaves and what the plagues do to the Egyptians. For example, Pharaoh's decree to kill Israelite babies in the Nile River (1:22) finds echoes in the first (7:20–21) and the tenth plagues (12:29).

A complex interaction of human and divine wills appears in the repeated motif of the hardening of Pharaoh's heart throughout the plague cycle. This motif has played a large role in theological debates on the relationship of divine determinism, predestination, and human freedom of the will. The metaphor of Pharaoh's hardened heart appears in three phases in the plague narratives. In the first phase, God predicts ahead of time that God will eventually harden Pharaoh's heart so that he will refuse to let Israel go (4:21; 7:3). In the second phase, when the plagues begin, the subject of Pharaoh's hardening of his heart is either himself (8:15, 32) or is unspecified (7:13, 22; 8:19; 9:7). Thus Pharaoh is initially the one largely responsible for his own recalcitrance. Time and again he stubbornly refuses God's command to set Israel free.

It is not until we reach the third phase (in the sixth of the ten plagues—9:12) that God enters for the first time as the subject who hardens Pharaoh's heart. God determines that Pharaoh's repeated and willful stubbornness had by the sixth plague escalated to a point of no return. Like a rowboat entering the edge of a whirlpool, Pharaoh had been paddling his own boat for too long in the wrong direction. Pharaoh had too often tried and tested the divine forbearance and eventually became caught in the vortex of inevitable divine judgment. Israel's prophets and the Psalms speak in a similar way about Israel's own escalating rebellions leading to inevitable judgment and exile (Jer. 15:1–2; Ps. 81:11–12).

Even as God hardens Pharaoh's heart in the later plagues (beginning in Exod. 9:12), however, the biblical narrator and Pharaoh himself continue to affirm Pharaoh's own moral responsibility and role in bringing the judgment upon himself (9:27, 34a). Thus the plague stories suggest a complex interplay of divine sovereignty and human responsibility, not entirely reducible to either divine determinism or human freedom.

God's slaying of Egypt's firstborn is a troubling event. One should not minimize its horror. Nonetheless, the following comments may help the reader understand the event within its ancient biblical context. First, although God has employed the human assistance of arms, hands, and staffs of Moses and Aaron throughout the other plagues, it is God alone who carries out the slaying of the Egyptian firstborn (11:4; 12:23). The tenth plague is not a model for human imitation or a pretext for humans committing violence in the name of God. Second, the narrative insists that much of the moral responsibility that led to this tragic point lies with Pharaoh and the Egyptians. The previous plagues were warnings and glimpses of the great tragedies that would unfold if Pharaoh continued his resistance. The story reminds us about the particular responsibility of human leaders and politicians who can lead a nation or group down paths that bring tragic consequences. Just as Pharaoh had tried to take away God's firstborn son Israel, the divinely created moral order of the world led to Pharaoh and Egypt losing their firstborn sons (4:22–23). Third, the narrative affirms that all firstborn among the Israelites belong to God (13:2, 13). And if God is the God of all the earth (19:5–6), then God has the right to claim back for Godself any firstborn among any nation as God does with Egypt in the tenth plague. In the Israelite understanding, God's claim on the firstborn served as a sign that the whole people and the whole earth belong to God.

Exodus 12 and 13 weave together a vivid narrative with a set of ritual instructions for the Festival of Passover to be observed by all future generations. These chapters help the reader to see how the narrative of a definitive past event becomes actualized as an ongoing ritual for a community of faith (12:14). The narrative of the tenth plague became both an etiology or explanation for the origins of the annual spring festival of Passover with its roasted lamb, unleavened bread, and other symbolic foods, and a retelling of the exodus story to be remembered and passed on as a defining master narrative from generation to generation. The Passover remains a central festival for the Jewish tradition with its overriding theme of freedom from bondage. The Passover

and the complex network of images and themes attached to it—remembrance and actualization, deliverance from bondage and death, association with the firstborn son, the lamb that was sacrificed, darkness and night, the blood that protects from death, the wine of the Passover meal, the unleavened bread—all provided a rich matrix out of which the Gospels portrayed Jesus' institution of the Lord's Supper as a rite founded on the celebration of the Passover meal with Jesus' disciples "on the night in which he was betrayed" (Mark 14:12–25; Matt. 26:17–29; Luke 22:7–23).

One final story of note in this section is the Israelite "plundering" of the Egyptians (Exod. 12:33–36). God had predicted that the Egyptians would eventually be so desperate to get rid of their Israelite slaves that the Egyptian masters would gladly give them their silver and gold jewelry and fine clothing (3:21–22; cf. 11:2–3). What God has predicted comes true, and 12:36 draws the conclusion: "So they plundered the Egyptians." The conclusion interprets the entire sequence of plagues leading up to the death of the firstborn as a kind of holy war or struggle against Pharaoh. Israel's plundering of the Egyptians signals that God has won the victory over Pharaoh. This plundered silver and gold will be carried into the wilderness, where it will be used to build and furnish the tabernacle, the holy shrine symbolizing God's presence (chaps. 25–31, 35–40). This same plundered gold will, however, play a negative role in the construction of the golden calf, an act of apostasy and idolatry that proves to be a near-fatal misstep by Israel at Mount Sinai (chap. 32). In the history of biblical interpretation, this "plundering" of Egypt offered biblical support to those who sought to justify plundering the riches of ancient Greek philosophy and rhetoric in the construction of Christian theology and doctrine.

The Red Sea and the final defeat of Pharaoh and his army (13:17–15:22). Various tensions and doublets within chaps. 14–15 have led scholars to discern three different versions of the Red Sea event. Two prose traditions about the Red Sea event have been woven together into one composite narrative in chap. 14, and a third retelling of the Red Sea story appears in poetic form in the Song of Moses in chap. 15.

In one of the two prose versions in chap. 14 (the non-Priestly version), Moses reassures the people that God will fight for Israel, and Israel only needs "to keep still" (14:14). God drives the waters of the Red Sea back by a strong east wind, and the divine cloud somehow throws Pharaoh's army with its chariots and horses into a panic so that they rush into the sea and drown. Israel remains "still." There is no mention of the people crossing through the Red Sea. God does all the fighting.

In the second prose version (chap. 14, the Priestly version), God commands Moses to raise his staff over the waters of the Red Sea, whereupon the waters divide. A path of dry ground opens up between two receding walls of water, and Israel passes through on the dry sea bed safely to the other side. The Egyptian army follows the Israelites into the sea but drowns when Moses stretches out his staff once again and the walls of water return. The walls of water being separated and dry land appearing recall the Priestly creation story (Gen. 1) in which God's creation involves separation, boundaries, walls of the firmament holding back the primeval waters of chaos, and dry land appearing (Gen. 1:1–9).

The third version of the same event appears in the poetic Song of Moses, a victory hymn praising God for the defeat of Pharaoh and his army by drowning them in the sea (Exod. 15:1–10). The imagery and language recall ancient myths about a divine battle against an entity named Sea that represents the power of chaos in the cosmos (Pss. 77:16–19; 114:3–6). The song in Exod. 15 elaborates on additional victories of God over enemies on land in which the earth (not the sea) swallowed them (15:11–12).

The song also recounts how God guided Israel to God's "holy abode" (15:13) and the "mountain of your own possession" (15:17). The song reinterprets the one-time victory at the Red Sea against Pharaoh as an ongoing paradigm of God's victory against all Israel's enemies and an assurance of God's protection of Israel on God's holy mountain. The "mountain" may be Mount Sinai, which is the place of God's dwelling in the wilderness (19:1–25; 24:1–14), or Mount Zion in Jerusalem, where God's temple will eventually be built in the land of Canaan (1 Kgs. 8; Ps. 48:1–3).

Finally, a brief account of "the prophet Miriam" singing and dancing with "all the women" in praise of God's victory over Pharaoh forms an epilogue to Moses' song (Exod. 15:20–21). Miriam is the sister of Moses and Aaron (2:4, 7–8; Num. 26:59), and a female prophet like Deborah (Judg. 4:4) and Huldah (2 Kgs. 22:14). Micah 6:4 lists her (along with Moses and Aaron) as one of the three leaders of the Israelites in the wilderness. Miriam's song begins with the same words as Moses' song (Exod. 15:1, 21). This repetition has led some scholars to surmise that the longer version of Moses' song was originally attached to Miriam and only later came to be attributed to Moses.

Initial challenges on the wilderness journey (15:22–18:27). Just as God had earlier responded to Moses' objections to his initial call (3:11–4:17), so God provides water and food in response to the legitimate complaints of Israel as they enter the desert of the Sinai Peninsula. Similar complaints about food and water in Num. 11:1–9, 31–35, and 20:1–13 will provoke God's anger and punishment because the circumstances have changed. At the beginning of the wilderness journey, however, Israel's concerns about basic food and water are deemed legitimate and God responds appropriately.

The first episode at Mara (meaning "bitter," for the bitter water there) interprets the challenges of Israel's desert sojourn as a "test" (15:25) of obedience to

God's commandments and statutes. The wilderness experience of crisis, strained resources, danger, and vulnerability create a crucible for testing faith and obedience. Obedience will bring God's healing (Num. 21:4–9; Deut. 7:15; Ps. 103:3), but disobedience will bring the same plagues upon Israel as fell upon the Egyptians (Exod. 15:26).

Israel's concern moves from water to food in the manna story (chap. 16). The manna story offers a profound reflection on work, greed, materialism, fear, contentment, and trust. The command to rest on the seventh or Sabbath day anticipates one of the Ten Commandments (Exod. 20:8–11). These wilderness images of undrinkable water becoming drinkable (15:25), of manna raining down from heaven (16:4), and of quail coming up and covering the ground (16:13) suggest the reversal of some of the earlier images of the plagues against Egypt. During the plagues, the Nile River had turned to blood and become undrinkable (7:14–24). A devastating hail had rained down from heaven (9:22–26). Swarms of destructive locusts had "come up" and "covered the surface of the whole land" (10:12–18). The similarities but also the differences between these destructive images and the more positive images of sweet water, delicious manna, and succulent quail imply that God is at work to overturn the ecological upheavals of the earlier plagues, restoring nature's ability to provide water, food, and life rather than chaos, death, and destruction.

The challenges and testing in the wilderness continue as Israel complains again about the lack of water (17:1–7) and is attacked by the Amalekites (17:8–16). One notable detail in the Amalekite story is that when Moses stands and raises his arms during the battle, Israel prevails over the Amalekites. But when Moses lowers his arms from weariness, Israel suffers defeat. Aaron and Hur assist Moses in holding up his arms. Their assistance illustrates the lesson Moses will learn from his Midianite father-in-law Jethro in the very next narrative (18:1–27). Effective leaders share authority and distribute responsibility among others in the community. This wisdom comes from Jethro, a Midianite priest and not a worshiper of Israel's God. The narrative affirms the possibility that knowledge and wisdom from a religious or cultural outsider may be helpful and true, as long as it is also tested against what God commands (18:23). In a later narrative, God will command Moses to implement a similar administrative reorganization (Num. 11:16–17, 24–25; Deut. 1:9–18).

Formation: God's Covenant with Israel at Mount Sinai (Exod. 19–24)

Israel's arrival at Mount Sinai (19:1–25). After three months ("on the third new moon"), the Israelites arrive at Mount Sinai. Sinai is also known as Mount Horeb, the same "mountain of God" where Moses first encountered God (3:1). God had promised Moses in that first encounter that God would bring Moses and Israel back to this same mountain of God as a midterm sign of assurance that God was with him and had the power to fulfill God's promises (3:11–12). Such provisional signs of hope and assurance along the way strengthen courage and resolve to continue the wilderness journey all the way to the promised land of Canaan.

Exodus 19 is another complex amalgam of interwoven traditions. So much is invested theologically in this momentous event that many varied traditions have been allowed to come together and contribute to the shape of the present form of Exod. 19. This complexity draws attention to the importance of this text and the event it narrates: God's formation of Israel into a special covenant partner with the God of all the earth (19:5–6). The diverse traditions in Exod. 19 offer an array of elements associated with God's presence. In 19:1–8 God only speaks; no visual images accompany the divine reality. In 19:9, however, God is in a "dense cloud." In 19:16 thunder and lightning appear alongside a thick cloud as God draws near. In 19:18 God's appearance is described using the imagery of an earthquake: fire, smoke, and violent trembling of the mountain. Most of the chapter assumes that God speaks from the top of the mountain (19:3, 20), while 20:22 states that God spoke from heaven. Different traditions specify who can ascend the mountain to meet God. Most of the chapter assumes that only Moses is allowed to climb Mount Sinai; anyone else who even touches the mountain "shall be put to death" (19:12, 20). However, 19:13b suggests that the whole people "may go up on the mountain." And 19:24 implies that Aaron may come up the mountain along with Moses but no one else. One may widen the lens even further to include Exod. 24, which also portrays God on the mountain. There Moses, Aaron, Nadab, Abihu, and seventy elders of Israel "went up" Mount Sinai "and saw the God of Israel" (24:9–10). Remarkably, the imagery of a thunderstorm and violent earthquake is replaced by a tranquil outdoor banquet scene on top of Sinai: "they beheld God, and they ate and drank" (24:11). Clearly, the literature associated with Sinai is made up of diverse traditions concerning the presence of God and those particular Israelites associated with this momentous event.

The Ten Commandments (20:1–22). These ten commands form the central core of Israel's covenantal obligation to God (20:1–11) and to fellow humans (20:12–17). The commandments begin with a declarative preamble that affirms God's already existing relationship with the people of Israel: "I am the LORD your God, who brought you out of the land of Egypt, out of the house of slavery" (20:2). The commandments that follow are not so much the conditions upon which the covenant is established as the guide by which Israel is to live more deeply into the covenant relationship that already exists due to the initiative and mercy of God.

The special status of the Ten Commandments or Decalogue among the many other laws in the Old Testament is evident in numerous ways. The uniquely terse style of the commandments, the repetition of the Decalogue in Exod. 20 and in Deut. 5, the claim that they alone were "written with the finger of God" (Exod. 31:18), God's mediation of the Ten Commandments directly to the Israelites without the help of Moses (20:1), and the placement of the stone tablets with the commandments inside the ark of the tabernacle (25:21) all point to the special nature of the Ten Commandments. Their importance for ethical reflection has continued in the faith traditions of both Judaism and Christianity.

The first commandment, "you shall have no other gods," is first not only in sequence but also importance (20:3). Israel's catastrophic violation of this first commandment in worshiping the golden calf will threaten the very foundation of the covenant God established with Israel (32:7–10). The proscription against idols (20:4–6) is taken by some traditions as a separate commandment (e.g., the Calvinist or Reformed tradition), while others (Jewish, Lutheran, Roman Catholic, Eastern Orthodox) understand it to be a commentary on the first commandment. Earlier, God had revealed to Moses a special divine name: "I AM WHO I AM" or "I Will Be Who I Will Be" (see 3:14). The open-ended character of the name invites readers to follow God's character in Exodus and to perceive the fuller meaning of that name as it is revealed: " I am the LORD your God, who brought you out of the land of Egypt, out of the house of slavery . . . a jealous God, punishing . . . to the third and the fourth generation . . . but showing steadfast love to the thousandth generation of those who love me and keep my commandments" (20:2, 5–6). The commandment against the wrongful use of the divine name (20:7) reflects the conviction in the ancient world that names conveyed the essential character of a person or god and provided access to their attention, their power, and their resources.

The Sabbath commandment (20:8–11) is the longest of the Ten Commandments and integrates obligations to God (the seventh day of rest is holy to God), obligations to other human beings (the mandated rest benefits family members and workers, including alien residents), and obligations to nonhuman creation (even livestock need regular days off). The observance of the Sabbath day of rest is motivated by the human imitation of the image of God resting on the seventh day of creation (Gen. 2:1–3).

The commandment to honor father and mother is probably most concerned about the care of elderly parents (20:12). The prohibition of "murder" is aimed at any killing not sanctioned by the community, including personal acts of revenge (20:13). The command not to steal concerns property (20:15), whereas the command against false witness concerns the preservation of a person's reputation, especially in judicial cases and disputes. The coveting commandment was aimed especially at the rich and powerful. To "covet" an object or person involves both the inner yearning as well as the initial steps leading to stealing something that rightfully belongs to others, especially that which belongs to the poor and less powerful in the community (20:17).

The Book of the Covenant: Additional laws (20:22–23:19). Most scholars consider this group of laws to be one of the oldest legal collections in the Old Testament. These biblical laws have several parallels in subject matter and form (case law) to ancient Babylonian laws. The laws alternate between religious concerns and criminal, social, and economic matters. Placed immediately after the Ten Commandments, these laws illustrate how the commandments might function in daily life. The first set of laws are cultic in nature and expand upon the first commandment's prohibition against worshiping other gods or idols of "silver" and "gold" (20:22–26). This will be the commandment that Israel breaks when it worships the golden calf (32:1–24). The principle of the law of just retribution ("life for life, eye for eye")

seeks to limit the extent of any act of revenge and thereby to protect the community from escalating violence and counterviolence (21:22–25). Israel's own experience of being aliens in the land of Egypt motivated the laws against oppressing a resident alien or other marginalized people in the community. If foreigners within Israel are abused and cry out to God, then God will heed their cry and bring deadly plagues upon the Israelites as God did with the Egyptians when Israel cried out in pain (22:21–24; 23:9; see 3:7; 6:5–6).

Promises and instructions on Israel's future entry into Canaan (23:20–33). God promises to send an angel as a divine representative to protect and fight for the Israelites on their way to the promised land of Canaan (23:20, 23). The angelic warrior had appeared already in 14:19 and will be promised again in 32:34 and 33:2. The angel will reappear in Josh. 5:13–15 and Judg. 2:1–5. God warns Israel that the angel's character is strict and unforgiving: "he will not pardon your transgression" (Exod. 23:21).

A second covenant-making ceremony (24:1–18). Exodus 19 and 24 provide differing accounts about the ratification of the covenant on Mount Sinai. The two chapters form bookends at the beginning and end of the covenant-making process. Diverse and dramatic images appeared in chap. 19: images of clouds, smoke, fire, thunderstorm, and earthquake with diverse accounts of who did or did not ascend the mountain to meet God. Exodus 24 presents a different version of the same event, and depicts a much more quiet, subdued, and peaceful encounter between God and the Israelites. There is also a clear and consistent hierarchy. The people are at the foot of the mountain. The high priest Aaron and his two sons, Nadab and Abihu, along with seventy elders ascend part of the way up the mountain. Their experience of God is visual, not auditory: they "saw the God of Israel" (24:10–11). Moses and his assistant

Joshua ascend to the very top of the mountain to encounter and speak with God more directly (24:1–2, 9–14).

The Israelites have heard and know God's laws, and they have pledged themselves to obedience three times (19:8; 24:3, 8). However, that resolve to obey God's commands will soon crumble in the golden calf episode when they break the covenant and create a nearly fatal crisis in the relationship between God and God's people (32:1–35).

Restoration: The Golden Calf and the Tabernacle (Exod. 25–40)

Detailed instructions for building and furnishing the tabernacle (25:1–31:18). The story of Exodus has moved from God's *liberation* of the Israelites from Egyptian slavery (Exod. 1–18) to the *formation* of the covenant people of Israel at Mount Sinai (Exod. 19–24). The third phase of the Exodus narrative moves into an arduous process of *restoration* of the covenant between God and Israel after Israel dramatically breaks the covenant by worshiping the idolatrous golden calf. The golden calf is a clear violation of the first of the Ten Commandments (20:3), offering an alternative to the tabernacle-building project that dominates the last half of Exodus. The tabernacle is the only proper and divinely ordained vehicle of God's assured presence in the midst of Israel as they travel through the wilderness and into Canaan. The tabernacle is an elaborate portable shrine or sanctuary, God's mobile home after Israel leaves Mount Sinai. The detailed instructions for the construction, arrangement, priestly personnel, and inner furnishings of the tabernacle appear in 25:1–31:18. The construction of the tabernacle will be put on hold and the whole project will be endangered by Israel's rebellion when they make a golden calf (chap. 32). In the end, the tabernacle will be built, a tangible sign of the restoration of the covenant and an assurance that God does indeed contin-

ue to dwell among God's people in spite of their sinful rebellion (35:1–40:38).

God issues instructions to Moses for the construction of the tabernacle in a series of seven speeches (25:1–31:18), which mirror God's seven-day construction project of creation in Gen. 1:1–2:4. Like the creation story (Gen. 2:1–3), the tabernacle directives end with a law about the Sabbath (Exod. 31:12–17). Moreover, just as the spirit of God "swept over the face of the waters" at creation (Gen. 1:2), so the spirit of God comes upon the creators and builders of the tabernacle to guide their creative work (Exod. 31:1–11). The tabernacle is finally dedicated on New Year's Day, a day associated with the first day of creation by ancient Israelites (40:2, 17). Thus Israel's building of the tabernacle became the means by which Israel participated in God's creational building and renewing of the whole creation.

The ark of acacia wood appears as the first item to be made (25:10–16). The ark is the most important item in the tabernacle's inner room, the Holy of Holies. The ark had various roles throughout the Old Testament. It is a sign of God's presence in Israel's battles against enemies (Num. 10:35; 1 Sam. 4:3–5). The ark with the cherubim on its lid functioned as the visible "mercy seat" where God's invisible presence was enthroned and could be encountered (Exod. 25:17–22; 1 Sam 4:4). God would continue to issue commandments to Moses from the mercy seat of the ark (Exod. 25:22; Num. 7:89). The ark was also the box that contained the "covenant" or "testimony," the two stone tablets of the Ten Commandments "written with the finger of God" (Exod. 31:18; Deut. 10:1–5). Together the ark and tabernacle symbolized the worship of God, the obedience of the people, and Israel's mission in the world.

God states clearly the tabernacle's theological meaning and purpose at the conclusion of the instructions for ordaining priests: "I will dwell among the Israelites, and I will be their God. And they shall know that I am the LORD their God, who brought them out of the land of Egypt that I might dwell among them; I am the LORD their God" (Exod. 29:45–46). The open-ended name of God first disclosed in Exod. 3:14 as "I AM WHO I AM" or "I Will Be Who I Will Be" has been developed at various points in the Exodus story. God's name unfolded to include the God who "brought you out of Egypt, out of the house of slavery" (20:2) and even more, a "jealous God, punishing . . . to the third and the fourth generation . . . but showing steadfast love to the thousandth generation" (20:5–6). In the tabernacle instructions, the name is broadened still further to include the ultimate purpose of God's liberation of Israel from Egypt: "that I might dwell among them" (29:46). The near presence of God in the midst of Israel is God's ultimate desire and purpose, and the tabernacle is the vehicle and sign of assurance of that divine presence (25:8). But before the tabernacle can be built, Israel puts its whole existence and life with God in jeopardy by succumbing to the temptation to worship and attach itself to another god and another vehicle of divine presence, the golden calf.

Israel worships the golden calf (32:1–35). The golden calf debacle and its aftermath endangers God's ultimate goal in the Exodus story: that God, enthroned in the tabernacle, would dwell in the midst of a liberated Israel, formed into God's obedient covenant people as a holy nation and a royal priesthood, on the move toward the promised land (19:5–6; 23:20–33; 29:46). The Israelites grow impatient and gather around Aaron, Moses' brother and high priest, who is in charge during Moses' absence, and request that he "make gods" for them (32:1). Aaron instructs the people to give him their gold jewelry, presumably the gold that the Egyptians had given to the Israelites when they departed from Egypt (12:33–36). Aaron takes the gold, and forms it in a mold, and casts an image of a calf (32:4). Aaron will offer an alternate version of events when Moses confronts him later (32:24).

The people worship the image as representing the gods who brought them out of the land of Egypt (32:4), an illegitimate transfer to the golden calf of the name of Israel's God in the preamble to the Ten Commandments (20:2). In contrast to an earlier scene of obedient worship on Mount Sinai when Aaron and the elders "beheld God, and they ate and drank" (24:11), Aaron and the people "eat," "drink," and "revel" as they worship the forbidden golden calf (32:6).

Meanwhile, God informs Moses on top of Mount Sinai of the divine decision to let God's wrath burn against the Israelites for their apostasy and to "consume them" in the wilderness. Israel's sin is so grievous that for the first time in the Pentateuch God threatens to end the relationship with Israel. God offers to destroy the Israelites and start over with Moses alone. God offers to Moses the promise originally given to Abraham back in Gen. 12:2: "I will make of you a great nation" (Exod. 32:10). Moses resists the offer and instead pleads for God to change the divine decision to destroy Israel. Moses reminds God that Israel is God's people (32:11), that destroying Israel would be bad for God's international reputation (32:12), and that God had promised Israel's ancestors that God would bring their descendants to the land of Canaan (32:13). Remarkably, the narrator reports: "And the LORD changed his mind about the disaster that he planned to bring on his people" (32:14). Moses' earlier arguments with God concerning his own call had not changed God's mind (3:11–4:17), but this prayer of intercession and his advocacy on behalf of other people (here Israel) had a special power with God that did indeed change the divine mind. The conversations between God and Moses in Exodus affirm a theology of prayer as genuine engagement between two partners, an engagement that could at times change God's mind.

God's change of mind concerned the planned destruction of Israel. But the consequences of the disobedience linger—the broken covenant symbolized by Moses smashing the stone tablets (32:15–19), the death of many of those most directly involved in the golden calf episode at the hands of the newly ordained Levites (32:25–29), and a plague sent by God (32:35). Israel incurs some of the same judgment of death and plague that came upon Egypt earlier in Exodus during the ten plagues. Moses also confronts his brother Aaron, who was supposed to be in charge during Moses' absence. Moses had defended and advocated for the people of Israel before God. Moses had acted as a true leader who takes responsibility and joins his fate with those he is called to lead. In contrast, Aaron tries to pass the buck and excuse his actions by blaming the people (32:22), lying about his own role in the construction of the calf (see 32:4 and 32:24).

Archaeologists have recovered numerous cultic images of calves and bulls in the iconography and statuary of the ancient Near East and ancient Israel itself. It is likely that the golden calf story has some historical relationship to the story of Jeroboam, the king of northern Israel, who set up two golden calves at sanctuaries at Bethel and Dan in the north as rival worship centers to the Jerusalem temple in the southern kingdom (1 Kgs. 12:25–30; cf. Exod. 32:4, "your gods"). The cultic images were viewed as a symptom of the idolatry and sin of the northern kingdom and its kings and a reason for the eventual conquest and exile of the north by the Assyrian Empire (722 BCE). In Exod. 32 this originally antinorthern tradition has been reshaped as a paradigm of disobedience that applies equally to all Israel, north and south. Judah and Jerusalem were as susceptible to such idolatry and apostasy as the northern kingdom. Indeed, Judah eventually suffered the same fate of conquest and exile at the hands of another empire, the Babylonians, in 587 BCE.

How does a holy God dwell in the midst of a sinful people? (33:1–34:35). Moses continues to argue with God, seeking clarity about how God will be involved in leading the Israelites to Canaan. God had previously offered only an angel to lead Israel (33:2), but God now offers a further concession, "My presence will go" (the Hebrew does not include the NRSV's addition, "with you"; 33:14). God's presence will go, presumably alongside or ahead but not in the midst of Israel. But Moses is not satisfied. Moses seeks to push God further and insists that God must not only go alongside Israel but God must "go with us," that is, "in our midst." Moses insists on nothing less than the tabernacle-with-God-dwelling-in-the-midst-of-Israel plan being reinstated in all its original glory. Moses knows that the only thing that makes Israel distinct from every other nation is that God is "with us/in our midst" (33:16). Otherwise, Israel is like Egypt or any other nation.

Remarkably, God agrees to everything Moses asks because of the unique bond between God and Moses (33:17). God restores the broken covenant, symbolized by the restoration of two new stone tablets to replace the tablets that Moses had broken (34:1, 4, 27–28; 32:15–16, 19). The restoration of the relationship becomes possible not because of any change in the Israelites but because of Moses pushing God to reveal something deeper about the name and character of God. The name of God has unfolded in various stages throughout the book of Exodus, moving from "I AM WHO I AM" (or better, "I Will Be Who I Will Be"—3:14) to "the LORD . . . who brought you out of the land of Egypt . . . a jealous God, punishing . . . but showing steadfast love to . . . those who love me and keep my commandments" (20:2, 5–6) to "the LORD their God, who brought them out of the land of Egypt that I might dwell among them" (29:45–46). Moses insists that this last expansion of the divine name, "that I might dwell among them," not be lost.

As God passes by Moses and Moses sees the back side of God, God proclaims one of the most significant theological descriptions of the character of God in the entire Old Testament: "The LORD, the LORD, a God merciful and gracious, slow to anger . . . forgiving iniquity and transgression and sin, yet by no means clearing the guilty" (34:6–7). This revelation of the divine name is clearly intended to be compared and contrasted with the earlier version in 20:5–6, which described God's character as "jealous . . . punishing" and only secondarily "showing steadfast love." In this climactic revelation, God is not first of all "jealous" or "punishing." God is now revealed before everything else as a God of "steadfast love," a quality that is put front and center. The "steadfast love" section of God's description expands with the presence of numerous additional adjectives: "merciful and gracious, slow to anger, and abounding in steadfast love and faithfulness, keeping steadfast love for the thousandth generation." The condition or qualification that God would show steadfast love only "to those who love me and keep my commandments" back in 20:6 is dropped. Instead, in its place is the assurance that God's character includes "forgiving iniquity and transgression and sin" (34:6–7). God's punishing to the third and fourth generation will remain (34:7). Disobedience will continue to generate consequences, but divine judgment occupies a secondary role in the deep character of God. Thus it is God's own merciful and forgiving character alone that makes possible the opportunity for God to restore the covenant and to dwell in the midst of Israel through the building of the tabernacle.

This unique encounter and revelation of the divine name to Moses creates a divine aura that causes Moses' face to shine (34:29–35). The shining face and the veil that he wears set him apart as a unique human mediator between God and the people. Moses bears in his body something of the holiness and mystery of God's intense interactions with certain called and chosen human beings who stand between God and God's people.

The construction of the tabernacle, the seat of God's dwelling in the midst of Israel

(35:1–40:38). Exodus 35 begins an extensive section dealing in great detail with the actual construction of the tabernacle. The precision and detail lavished upon this building project testify to its central importance as the tangible and mobile sign of God's presence in the midst of Israel as they leave Mount Sinai and travel through the wilderness to Canaan. The detailed instructions and process of construction resemble the detailed account of the building of Solomon's temple (1 Kgs. 6–8) and the detailed description of Ezekiel's vision of a new temple in Jerusalem (Ezek. 40–48).

The instructions for building the tabernacle in Exodus were first given in chaps. 25–31. The golden calf crisis (chap. 32) had endangered the tabernacle project. However, the resolution and restored covenant in chaps. 33–34 enabled the tabernacle construction to move forward. Just as the Sabbath law had concluded the detailed instructions for building the tabernacle at the end of chaps. 25–31 (31:12–17), the Sabbath law introduces the actual work of construction (35:2–3). The people give offerings willingly to support the building project, and all the instructions are carried out in detail (35:20–29). God's spirit guides the workers and inspires them to teach others (35:30–35). All the work is done eagerly "in accordance with all that the LORD has commanded" (36:1).

Two major work projects bracket the book of Exodus. Pharaoh's oppressive empire had enslaved and exploited Israelite workers against their will. In the construction of the tabernacle at the end of Exodus, the people gladly contribute to building the tabernacle. The tabernacle is the sign of God's holy, gracious, merciful, and forgiving presence in their midst, a presence that offers them mercy, blessing, protection, and purpose in their newly restored vocation as God's royal priesthood and holy nation (19:6).

The completion of the tabernacle "on the first day of the first month" (40:2) marks the beginning of the seasons and festivals of the new cultic year and also commemorates, in the Priestly calendar, the first day of creation (Gen. 1:3–5). The Priestly tradition associated with the tabernacle tradition in Exodus viewed God's construction of the universe in the creation story in Gen. 1:1–2:4 as a process of providing order and structure out of chaos that enabled the beginning of time and the flourishing of life. In a similar way, Israel's careful attention to the precise construction of the tabernacle out of the chaos of the wilderness and the golden calf apostasy (Exod. 32) enables the order and structure necessary for the beginning of Israel's worship and cultic life that will be further elaborated in the book of Leviticus. In the final climactic scene at the end of Exodus (40:34–38), God's "glory" and "cloud" cover and fill the tabernacle just as they had covered and settled on Mount Sinai (24:15–18). The journey to the promised land can now continue.

Bibliography

Brueggemann, Walter. "The Book of Exodus." In *NIB* 1:676–981.

Childs, Brevard. *The Book of Exodus*. OTL. Louisville: Westminster John Knox, 1974.

Fretheim, Terence. *Exodus*. Interpretation. Louisville: Westminster John Knox, 1991.

Gowan, Donald. *Theology in Exodus: Biblical Theology in the Form of a Commentary*. Louisville: Westminster John Knox, 1994.

Meyers, Carol. *Exodus*. New Cambridge Bible Commentary. New York: Cambridge University Press, 2005.

Leviticus

Frank H. Gorman Jr.

INTRODUCTION

Literary Context and Content

Leviticus is the literary and theological center of the Pentateuch. Exodus 19:1–2 reports the Israelites' arrival at Mount Sinai, and Num. 10:11–28 reports their departure. Their stay at Mount Sinai is a formative moment in the nation's history. Exodus 40:17–38 reports that the presence of Yahweh filled the tabernacle when Moses completed its construction; Leviticus follows immediately with instructions for the tabernacle cult. Thus the book assumes that the presence of Yahweh dwells in the midst of the community. Leviticus answers the Israelites' question, "How are we to live in the presence of Yahweh?"

A primary literary and theological element of the book emphasizes that Yahweh gives ("and Yahweh said") instructions to Moses for the community (see 4:1; 5:14; 6:1, 8, 19, 24 [5:20; 6:1, 12, 17 Heb.]; 7:22, 38; 8:1; 11:1; 12:1; 13:1; 14:1; 15:1; 16:1; 17:1; 18:1; 19:1; 20:1; 21:1; 22:1, 17, 26; 23:1, 9, 23, 26, 33; 24:1, 13; 25:1; 27:1). The book opens with the statement, "Yahweh called to Moses from the tent of meeting and said to him, 'Speak to the Israelites and say to them . . .'" (1:1–2a, my trans.), and closes with, "These are the commandments that Yahweh commanded Moses for the Israelites on Mount Sinai" (27:34, my trans.; cf. 26:46). Leviticus addresses the whole community and provides ways for the community to shape, to understand, and to enact its existence in the presence of Yahweh.

Leviticus includes the following elements: two series of instructions concerning sacrifices and offerings (chaps. 1–7); the consecration of the priesthood, the founding of the tabernacle cult, and the death of two of Aaron's sons, Nadab and Abihu, when they offer "strange fire" before Yahweh (chaps. 8–10); instructions concerning the purity and impurity of food, of contact with animal carcasses, of giving birth, of scaly skin afflictions, and of genital flows (chaps. 11–15); the ritual for the annual Day of "Atonement" (chap. 16); a section generally referred to as the Holiness Code, which contains a variety of instructions and the call for Israel to be holy (chaps. 17–26); instructions concerning economic issues relating to the sanctuary (chap. 27).

A large block of Priestly material (the Priestly [P] traditions and the Holiness [H] traditions), begins in Exod. 24:15 and extends to Num. 10:28 (with the exception of Exod. 32–34). The whole of Leviticus consists of Priestly materials. The P traditions and the H traditions reflect theological differences on key issues (e.g., the holiness of the people, the holiness of the land). This means that the Priestly

41

materials reflect theological diversity. Whether the Priestly materials are best understood as a "source" or a "redaction," and questions concerning the historical period in which the Priestly materials were written and achieved their present form remain critical issues in the analysis of Leviticus. Readers must recognize that an exilic or postexilic origin for the composition of Leviticus does not eliminate the possibility that the ritual practices prescribed in Leviticus may reflect much earlier origins.

Generally, Leviticus is viewed as a "rule book" or "instructional manual" for the priests and the tabernacle cult. The book does indeed include instructions directed to the priests: Yahweh to Moses to Aaron and the priests (e.g., 6:8, 24 [1, 17 Heb.]; 16:1–2b; 17:1; 21:1, 16; 22:1, 17), Yahweh to Aaron alone (10:8), or Yahweh to Moses and Aaron (11:1; 13:1; 15:1). As noted above, however, the book is addressed to the whole community. From a literary and theological perspective, the priesthood, although institutionally set apart, remains within the wilderness community. Information directed to the priests is significant for the whole community. For example, the question concerning who eats the sacrificial foods is as important for those who bring sacrifices as for the priests. This is true, in part, because sacrifice is both a ritual and an economic practice.

In addition, recent ritual, anthropological, and cultural studies have questioned whether the texts provide enough detailed information to enact the rituals effectively. If true, these texts were not written primarily as instructions for the enactment of rituals. Early Judaism recognized the need to supplement the rituals of Leviticus with details and information not found in the biblical texts themselves (the Mishnah provides excellent examples).

Finally, Israel experienced occasions when no fixed sanctuary existed to which the people could bring their sacrifices. Those people taken to Babylon in the sixth century would certainly have experienced this. In that they were unable to offer legitimate sacrifices, how were they to worship Yahweh? Both Sabbath observance and circumcision became more significant in this period; both could be practiced without a central sanctuary.

Another way in which Israel was able to practice its obedience to Yahweh in this context was through the reading and hearing of "sacred" texts. Reading and hearing were translated into ritualized activity. If the Priestly materials were written during the exile or after, a ritual view of reading and hearing would have informed the writing of Leviticus. The act of reading, understood as ritual enactment, became one source for creative theological constructions.

Such a view neither seeks to undermine the importance of Israel's ritual activity nor to reduce ritual to word (or enactment to theology). Rather, the argument takes seriously that Leviticus addressed the Israelite community at a time when the enactment of rituals at a central sanctuary was not a possibility. Reading and hearing became ways in which the whole community might enact and observe the words of Yahweh. If true, this view opens new possibilities for reading and interpreting Leviticus.

For example, this view suggests that the "reality" of the tabernacle exists in the texts and will be experienced only in and through the reading and/or hearing of the texts. In the same way, the "reality" of Yahweh's presence in the tabernacle must be experienced in and through the reading and/or hearing of the texts. A theological reading of Leviticus must include historical awareness of the reality of Israel's past existence, but it must also include awareness of the reader's context and existence. For the contemporary reader, the tabernacle and the God who dwells within it exist only in the text. The practices are no more available for the contemporary reader than they were for the people of Judah who were taken to Babylon.

The basic approach to the tabernacle has been to view it as a literary reflection of the Jerusalem temple. Thus, if the Jerusalem cult practiced sacrifice, which it undoubtedly did, then the same must be true for the tabernacle cult. Such a view, however, fails to recognize the significant differences between the Jerusalem temple and the tabernacle. The most obvious one is that the tabernacle is portable, whereas the temple is a fixed structure. The tabernacle texts may well be designed to offer alternatives to the ritual sacrifice practiced in the temple. In addition, the portability of the sacred text may well be a reflection of the portability of the tabernacle and the divine glory. Leviticus as a literary construction is both portable and inhabited by Yahweh. Because of this, the text of Leviticus guarantees the possibility that ritual activity may be practiced at any time and in any land.

Imaginative engagement with these texts may well be the best (if not the only) way to experience the glory of Yahweh residing in the tabernacle and the tabernacle cult. Imaginative construal may be the way that the reader or hearer experiences the forgiveness offered by the expiatory sacrifices (e.g., 4:35; 5:10, 16). Imaginative struggle with the texts may itself be part of the ritual activity of reading and hearing. A theological reading of Leviticus that recognizes the importance of reading, hearing, and imagination does not avoid the historical realities of ancient Israel.

Theological Themes

Three theological themes inform the whole of Leviticus. First, Yahweh's words to Israel at Mount Sinai reflect the Priestly theology of creation. In Gen. 1:1–2:4a Yahweh creates the cosmos by speaking; at Mount Sinai Yahweh creates the Israelite community by providing ("speaking") the divine instructions. Both Gen. 1:1–2:4a and Leviticus understand creation as an ongoing process. The order and the well-being of both the creation and the community are dependent not only on the words of Yahweh but also on the actions of the people. Human sin disrupts the life of the community; human obedience through ritual activity repairs the disruption and restores the community. Through the enactment of ritual activity and the prac-

tice of holiness, the Israelites participate in the ongoing well-being of the community.

The ongoing well-being of the community is also significantly related to the ongoing presence of Yahweh in the tabernacle. Human sin and impurity are the primary threats to Yahweh's presence in the tabernacle; if they are left unattended, Yahweh will leave the tabernacle. The divine departure and absence would be the undoing of the Israelite community (see the blessings and curses in Lev. 26). Israel's identity and self-understanding are based, in part, on the ongoing presence of Yahweh in the tabernacle. The divine presence must be understood in terms of divine promise and human enactment.

Second, the Priestly materials consistently emphasize the holiness of Yahweh. The P traditions focus on the holiness of the tabernacle, the priests, and sacred occasions. The H traditions are characterized by the call for the Israelites to be holy as Yahweh is holy (see 19:2; 20:7, 8, 26; 21:15, 23; 22:16, 32; cf. 11:44–45; Num. 15:40) and extend the concern for holiness to the people and the land. The call for the people to be holy is based on and expressed in the self-identification of Yahweh: "I am Yahweh your God" or "I am Yahweh" (see 19:2, 3, 4, 10, 12, 14, 16, 18, 25, 28, 30, 31, 32, 34, 36, 37).

Although the P traditions and the H traditions have different emphases, both include a concern for cultic and social enactments. Both practices are elements of what it means for Israel to be holy. The H traditions, in particular, emphasize the importance of justice and integrity in the life of the community. A theological reading of Leviticus must explore the nature of holiness in terms of enactment. Readers must be clear: enactment is not opposed to critical reflection, because critical reflection creates opportunities and possibilities for critical practice.

Third, a guiding concern of the Priestly traditions has to do with the purpose of the "sin sacrifice." The traditional view speaks of "atonement" or "expiation." Milgrom argues that the "sin" sacrifice is better understood as a "purification" sacrifice designed to purify or purge the tabernacle of impurities (see 10:10; 15:31; 16:16–17). "Sin sacrifice" is especially misleading in relation to impurities associated with giving birth, an unclean skin affliction, or a defiling genital flow. These reflect the purity/impurity system and must not be confused with sin. These impurities require a purification sacrifice, not a sin sacrifice. In that this sacrifice not only purifies sacred space, but also reconsecrates sacred space

(see 8:14–15; 16:18–19), the notion of "restoration" is often operative in relation to this sacrifice. In several instances, complex ritual processes conclude with the statement that the ritual process accomplished "expiation" (14:18–20; 16:24). The best approach is to try and understand the nature of each ritual process and the purpose of specific sacrifices within their specific contexts. The final result of the expiatory sacrifices is "forgiveness" for the person offering the sacrifice.

COMMENTARY

The Sacrifices and Offerings (1:1–7:38)

Leviticus 1:1–6:7 (5:26 Heb.) and 6:8 (6:1 Heb.)–7:38 constitute two distinct series of instructions concerning sacrifices and offerings. Five distinct types are detailed: the whole burnt sacrifice ("the burnt offering," 1:2–17; 6:8–13 [6:1–6 Heb.]), the grain offering (2:1–16; 6:14–23 [6:7–16 Heb.]), the sacrifice of well-being (3:1–17; 7:11–36), the "sin" sacrifice (4:1–5:13; 6:24–30 [6:17–23 Heb.]; traditionally "the sin offering"), and the reparation sacrifice (5:14–6:7 [5:14–26 Heb.]; 7:1–10; traditionally "the guilt offering"). These rituals allow a person to experience and give concrete shape to the experience of joy, celebration, thanksgiving, sin, guilt, and forgiveness in the presence of Yahweh. The texts say very little concerning Yahweh's role or "experience" in the sacrifices. Several texts note that the smoke of the burned animal provides a "soothing aroma for Yahweh," that is, to soothe Yahweh and remove Yahweh's anger (see, e.g., 1:9, 13; 2:2; 3:5; 4:31).

The sin sacrifice (4:1–5:13; 6:24–30 [6:17–23 Heb.]) is at the heart of the Priestly materials. Three types of sin sacrifices may be distinguished: when the blood is brought into the tent (on behalf of the high priest and the community; 4:1–21), when the blood is placed on the outer altar (for a chieftain or an individual; 4:27–35), and a presentation that need

not require blood (the graduated offering; 5:11–13). The first two types are associated with sins of commission, the third with sins of omission. Both are concerned with the restoration of the holy place to its ideal status: clean and holy. The sins of the Israelites, along with nonsinful impurities associated with the body, generate impurity that defiles the tabernacle, Yahweh's dwelling place. The disruption caused by the impurity is twofold: defilement and "deconsecration" of the holy place. The "sin sacrifice" repairs two problems through two distinct acts with the blood. Leviticus 8:14–15 states that Moses placed the blood of the sacrifice on the horns of the altar to cleanse it and poured the remainder out at its base to reconsecrate it (cf. 16:19). The sin sacrifice restores sacred space and produces forgiveness for the offerer.

The sins of commission refer to the inadvertent doing of things that ought not to be done. "Inadvertent" suggests that the offender did the act without being aware that something about the situation made the action sinful. When the offender realizes that the act was wrong and recognizes the guilt associated with it, a sin sacrifice is required to cleanse and reconsecrate holy space as well as to generate forgiveness. The sin of the high priest or the community requires that the blood be taken inside the tent, whereas the sin of a chieftain or a common person requires that the blood be placed on the horns of the outer altar. The severity of the first two is greater than that of the latter two and the impurity associated with it moves further into the tent.

The sins of omission (5:1–13) are cases in which a person fails to do something that should be done. These cases require both confession and the presentation of the sin sacrifice. Specific cases are noted: failure to provide information in the context of a sacred call to testify, contact with an unclean animal carcass, contact with human uncleanness, and the failure to follow through on an oath. These are not inadvertent, because failure to do them requires recognition and awareness that one is not doing them. This need not mean that these are the high-handed sins of Num. 15:30–31. These may be a form of sin that is to be placed between the inadvertent and the high-handed. As such, the graduated sin sacrifices may reflect an understanding of sacrifice that is not precisely the same as that reflected in the other two types of sin sacrifices. These sacrifices, however, conclude in the same way as the others: expiation and forgiveness.

The reparation sacrifice is required when a person violates something sacred, an action understood as a trespass against Yahweh (5:14–6:7 [5:26 Heb.]). Reparation is required when a person swears falsely in matters relating to (1) a deposit or pledge, (2) robbery, (3) fraud, or (4) a lost item that has been found and kept secret. The "false swearing" makes Yahweh a party to the deceit. The disruption caused by such trespass requires both a sacrifice and the payment of a penalty equal to the value of the violated item(s) plus an additional one-fifth of its value. The call for reparation recognizes the close relationship between Yahweh's integrity and the integrity required in social interactions.

Blood, Sacrifice, and Food (Lev. 17)

Leviticus 17 consists of five rulings concerned with issues relating to sacrifice and the consumption of blood. The first two rulings (vv. 1–7, 8–9) require that well-being sacrifices and whole burnt sacrifices be offered at the entrance of the tent of meeting. In effect, this requires that all sacrifices be brought to the entrance. Failure to do so is associated with the bloodguilt of murder. The killing of an animal must take place at the holy place in order to avoid the guilt associated with murder. The third ruling (vv. 10–12) provides the rationale for the requirement: Yahweh has designated the blood to be placed on the altar as the means to accomplish expiation for the people. This may indicate that the blood expiates for the slaughter of the animal. The blood belongs to Yahweh and Yahweh requires that the blood of sacrifices be placed on the altar. The fourth (vv. 13–14) and fifth (vv. 15–16) rulings are concerned with the blood ritual for animals killed in the hunt and purity concerns related to the eating of animals found dead in the wild.

The life of an animal is in its blood (Gen. 9:4). Leviticus 17 associates this view with the prohibition against eating the blood. The explanation for this is not forthcoming. Although the blood of the animal may be required to expiate for the slaughter of the animal, the blood of the well-being sacrifices must not be eaten. The rulings address the relationship of life, food, and sacrifice and reflect a concern for understanding the ways in which the sacrificial act takes shape within the struggle of life and death.

Leviticus and Ritual Enactments

Leviticus 1–7 identifies the basic types of sacrifice and the situations in which they are to be offered. They are associated with the human experiences of thanksgiving, joy, sin, guilt, and forgiveness. Leviticus also prescribes more complex rituals that involve multiple sacrifices. These complex rituals are of three basic types. *Rituals of founding* bring something into being or create something new (see Lev. 8–9 for the founding of the priesthood and the tabernacle cult). *Rituals of maintenance* function to keep in place, preserve, or mark something already in existence (see Lev. 16; 23; Num. 28–29, the yearly calendar of sacred times and practices). *Rituals of restoration* restore a situation or state that has been disrupted (see Lev. 14:1–32, the restoration to the community of a person recovered from an unclean skin affliction). Some rituals may include more than a single purpose. All three types reflect creation theology: the creation of something new, the maintenance of something already in existence, or the restoration of something to its original state.

A ritual of founding (Lev. 8–9). Ritual founding takes place in four distinct but significantly related ways in Lev. 8–9: (1) the tent and its utensils are consecrated (made holy); (2) the institution of the priesthood is inaugurated; (3) Aaron and his sons are ritually located in the Holy Place to serve as priests (the first priests set apart into their institutional role); and (4) the beginning of the priestly ministry of sacrifice. These rituals are one-time enactments that take the reader into generative moments of Israel's origins. When Aaron and his sons offer the sacrifices and offerings for the first time (chap. 9), fire comes from the tent, consumes the sacrifices, and ignites the sacred fire on the outer altar of burnt offerings (see Lev. 6:8–13 [6:1–6 Heb.]). The people see the fire and recognize it as a sign that Yahweh is indeed present with them.

Moses places blood from the ram of ordination on the left ear, left thumb, and left big toe of Aaron and his sons. This use of blood is found elsewhere only in the restoration ritual for a person recovered from an unclean skin affliction (14:10–20). Both of these rituals pass the participants from one status to another and from one location to another. An unclean skin affliction requires the afflicted person to leave the camp, a form of social death that reflects the encroachment of death in the eating away of the skin (see Num. 12:10–13). The restoration of the person from outside the camp to inside the camp reflects a passage from death to life.

The ordination of Aaron and his sons ritually moves them from their ordinary status in the community to their status as priests located in the Holy Place. Although the ritual locates them within the realm of the holy, they are designated as the ones who are to pass back and forth between the holy and the common. As mediators between Yahweh and the people, they stand with one foot in the holy and one foot in the common. Thus they exist within an ambiguous and dangerous state.

Numbers 16:41–50 [17:11–15 Heb.] recognizes the danger associated with their service. As a plague begins to kill Israelites, Aaron takes fire from the altar, burns incense, and makes expiation for the people. The text states, "he stood between the dead and the living until the plague was checked" (Num. 16:48, my trans. [17:13 Heb.]). The priests stand between life and death in order to perform expiation for the people. The people give voice to this fear in 17:12–13, my trans. [17:27–28 Heb.]: "We perish! We are dead! We are, all of us, dead! Anyone who draws near to Yahweh's tabernacle will die. Ah, we will die and perish." The priests are located in a dangerous place that is always and ever a single act away from death. This is their permanent location—between life and death with the necessity of stepping into the world of the common in order to do their work in the realm of the sacred.

In both rituals the placement of the blood on the ear, thumb, and toe functions as part of the ritual passage of persons from one status to another, from one location to another. In both cases the ritual passage is understood in terms of life and death. The movement into a new status and location is understood to a degree as a creative process. Something new is coming into being in and through the ritual. Creation is understood as both restoration and location. In the world of the Israelites, birthing involves new life as well as the encroachment of death (see Lev. 12).

A ritual of restoration (Lev. 14). The ritual for the restoration of a person recovered from an unclean skin affliction, as already noted, moves the person from outside the camp, a place of death, to inside the camp, a place of life (Lev. 14:1–20). An interesting and unusual element of this ritual is the use of the two birds (vv. 4–7). One bird is slaughtered over "living (fresh) water" and its blood caught in an earthen container. The live bird is then dipped into the blood of the slaughtered bird, some of the blood is sprinkled on the recovered person seven times (an act said to cleanse him), and the live bird is set free into the open country. The ritual of restoration cleanses the person from impurity associated with the skin affliction (the sprinkling with the blood) and removes it, or eliminates it, from the community (the freeing of the live bird; cf. the two goats in Lev. 16). The concern of the ritual is not only the impurity of the flaking skin condition, but also the threat posed to the community by the encroachment of death, which was symbolized by the "diseased" skin of the unclean person.

Rituals of maintenance (Lev. 16; 23). Leviticus 16 prescribes a ritual that is to be observed once a year. As part of the yearly cycle of observances, this ritual functions to mark time and to move the community from one status to another within time. This is the only day in which Aaron (the high priest) enters the Most Holy Place, takes the blood of the expiatory sacrifices with him, and sprinkles it on and before the covering of the ark (vv. 11–16). The ritual cleanses the most severe disruptions of purity and reconsecrates the Holy Place. The ritual restores the Holy Place to its normative status and as such functions to maintain the status of the holy space (through re-creation).

A central feature of the ritual is the use of the two goats, one for Yahweh and one for Azazel, between Aaron's first and final ritual washings (vv. 4, 23–24). Having filled the Holy of Holies with smoke (a sign of the presence of Yahweh; see Exod. 19:18; 40:34–38), Aaron takes the blood of a bull (for his household) and a goat (for the community), both "sin sacrifices," into the Most Holy Place. He sprinkles blood on top of and before the cover of the ark (often translated "the mercy seat") and then places blood on the horns of the outer altar and sprinkles the altar seven times with blood: "Thus he shall cleanse the impurities of the Israelites from it [the altar] and reconsecrate it" (Lev. 16:19b, my trans.; cf. 8:14–15).

After exiting the Most Holy Place, Aaron puts his hands on the head of the live goat, confesses the Israelites' iniquities, transgressions, and sins, puts them on the head of the goat, and sends it into the wilderness to Azazel (16:20–22). In this ritual, the wilderness and Azazel, a wilderness demon, are associated with chaos, the resulting status of the Israelite community should Yahweh depart from its midst. The blood rites cleanse and reconsecrate the Holy Place; the live goat sent to Azazel bears the sins of the Israelites to the place of chaos. The sins of the people, the possible cause of defilement and the departure of Yahweh from the tabernacle, are sent to the place of chaos because of their ability, if left ritually unaddressed, to bring about the chaos of the divine absence. Chaos is put in its place and thereby separated from the community.

Between his two ritual washings, Aaron enters into the Holy Place and then into a state of ultimate defilement. He places the sins of the people on the head of the goat. The ambiguous and dangerous status of the high priest is made clear in this ritual. Aaron holds together in his person the holy and the sinful. In breaking down the boundaries between these two absolutely distinct realities, he brings into being the ritual possibility for a new creation, a return to order and well-being. Again, restoration is the means of maintaining the very good order of the camp and Holy Place.

Leviticus 23 provides a list of sacred occasions that the Israelites are to observe (cf. the more complete list in Num. 28–29). The ritualized year gives structure and order to Israel's communal life. Sacred times and observances provide a means for maintaining the cycle of the year by marking critical moments to be observed as reflections of Yahweh's creation of the times and the seasons (Gen. 1:14–15). In observing the prescribed times, Israel marks out the reality of the temporal nature of God's creation. In observing the sacred times, the community participates in the maintenance of the well-being of Yahweh's creation.

The sacred observances provide opportunities for Israel's reflection on its identity, its agricultural life, and its community history. The Year of Jubilee, to be observed in the year following seven times seven years (Lev. 25:8–12), also emphasizes Israel's existence within time and provides an image of the future that includes the restoration of the community to economic well-being (Lev. 25). For those with debts, the debts are to be forgiven. For those who have given the use of their land as a means of paying debts, the land is to be restored. The land belongs to Yahweh, and Yahweh has assigned a piece of the land to every Israelite (vv. 23–24). In the Jubilee, the land must return to the Israelite whose land it is.

Chapter 25 also recognizes the importance of relatives in difficult economic situations. If an Israelite was in debt, a relative, known as the redeemer, could pay the debt and secure release for the person. Redemption is construed as an economic issue. In the Priestly perspective, Yahweh is concerned with debt, land, and related economic matters in relation to the lives of the Israelites.

The Priestly Ministry (Lev. 21–22)

The priestly ministry, however, includes more than just ritual activity in the Holy Place (e.g., manipulation of sacrificial blood, burning the sacrifices on the altar, burning incense inside the tent). The priests are also responsible to watch over and protect the tabernacle cult from intruders. Access to the Holy Place, and therefore to Yahweh, was a critical concern in Israel

(e.g., see the rebellions in Num. 16–18). The Priestly materials indicate pointedly that only Aaron and his descendants are to serve at the altar as priests. Priestly holiness is detailed in Lev. 21–22. No person with a "defect" was allowed to work at the altar (see the list in 21:16–23). Additional constraints were placed on their family relations in matters relating to death and marriage (21:1–15). Their sanctuary duties also included determining payments for vows or penalties for transgressions of Yahweh's holy things (chap. 27; 5:14–6:7 [5:26 Heb.]). This demonstrates the important role they played in economic matters as well as the importance of economic matters in relationship to the tabernacle cult.

A critical aspect of the priestly duties included distinguishing between both the holy and the common and the clean and the unclean. They were also to teach the Israelites Yahweh's instructions (Lev. 10:10–11). For example, the priests were responsible to decide if a skin affliction was unclean or not (Lev. 13). In this way, the priests were involved in the construction and maintenance of order and holiness in the camp and community.

The Purity and Impurity Rulings (Lev. 11–15)

The purity/impurity instructions in Lev. 11–15 follow the death of Nadab and Abihu in the Holy Place (Lev. 10). Impurity is not the same thing as sin, and the purity/impurity instructions are not primarily parts of a moral or ethical system. Leviticus 11 is concerned with the animals that may be ingested and the animal carcasses that make one unclean by contact. The purity/impurity concerns in Lev. 12–14 reflect what may be termed biological or pathological processes of the body. The purity/impurity instructions recognize the body as a significant and essential element of Israel's theology. These instructions provide a means to construct identity through a set of practices associated with the body. The construction of the body and the construction of theology are woven together in these rulings. These instructions indicate, to a degree, the relationship that exists between the body and the divine presence.

Chapter 11 addresses two primary issues: What is considered a clean and edible animal and what is the nature of the impurity generated through contact with an unclean animal corpse? Edible *land* animals must chew the cud and have true hoofs, characteristics of the domestic animals suitable for sacrifice (cattle, sheep, and goats). Fish, the *water animals*, must have fins and scales to be edible. Inedible birds, the flying *air animals*, are identified in a list (probably carrion birds). These three sets of animals reflect the categories of creation identified in Gen. 1:1–2:4a: land, water, and air. Creation theology provides the context for the purity/impurity rulings on edible and inedible foods. Finally, winged swarming things that walk on all fours are forbidden unless they have jointed legs above the feet and leap on the ground, and animals that swarm on the earth are prohibited.

The instructions in Lev. 12–15 share several elements. First, they are directly related to the body. Second, the impurity of a woman when she gives birth, the ritual for the person recovered from an unclean skin disease, and the impurity associated with abnormal flows all share an extended period of time to restore their purity. Restoration from these impurities requires the presentation of a purification sacrifice. Third, these impurities are understood in the context of the struggle of life and death. When a woman gives birth, she not only brings a new life into being (a creative act), but she also experiences, through the loss of blood, the encroachment of death. The background for this view is the Priestly belief that "the life is in the blood" (Gen. 9:3–5; Lev. 17:10–12, 13–14). To give birth is to lose the life that is in the blood. The flaking away of the flesh by a skin impurity is viewed as the encroachment of death made visible as the flesh is eaten away (see Num. 12:10–13). The genital flows, normal and abnormal, are understood in part as the misuse of creative fluids. This concern reflects God's blessing of human beings at creation, "be fruitful, multiply, and fill the earth" (Gen. 1:28), as well as Israel's ongoing struggle to survive as a community.

Family and Society (Lev. 18–20)

Leviticus 18–20 forms a redactional unit. Chapters 18 and 20 address issues relating to sexuality and family. Chapter 20 provides punishments for relationships prohibited in chap. 18. Chapter 19 is a miscellaneous collection of cultic and social rulings that opens with a call for the people to be holy just as Yahweh is holy. These rulings present a significant image of the way Israelite society might appear if lived according to the H traditions.

In order to be holy, Israel must set itself apart from the other nations (18:1–4, 24–30; 20:22–26). The practices of the other nations defiled them to such a degree that the land itself was defiled and spewed them out. Yahweh's instructions provide the means for Israel to be holy, to separate itself from the other nations, and to live on the land. Family relations and sexuality are central to Israel's life on the land constructed in contrast to "the others" who previously lived on the land.

Two basic relational categories inform the rulings in chap. 18: (1) blood relations and (2) relations based on marriage. The chapter identifies appropriate and inappropriate sexual partners on the basis of these two categories. Verses 19–23 list five additional prohibitions: sexual intercourse with a woman during her menstrual flow, sexual relations with a neighbor's wife, presentation of children to Molech, sexual relations with another man as with a woman, sexual relations with an animal (the only one specifically addressed to men and women). These rulings reflect a concern for the birth and survival of legitimate children. If the Priestly writers believed that men and women have a limited number of opportunities to produce children, they would want to protect both fertility practices and the lives of children. Legitimate sexual partners could be only distant members of one's family; legitimate sexual activity must be limited to situations most likely to produce children.

The diverse rulings in chap. 19 include three statements concerning family, two about farming practices, eleven about cultic practices, and thirteen about social concerns. The H traditions understand cultic practice and social justice to be of equal value in terms of the practice of holiness designed to reflect the holiness of Yahweh.

Chapter 26 concludes the Holiness Code and reads like the conclusion to a covenant document. Israelite obedience will lead to prosperity, fertility, productive land, and peace. Obedience will also ensure Yahweh's continued presence in the midst of the people. Israelite disobedience will lead to curse. The litany of punishments intensifies until Israel is consumed by the land of its enemies. Hope remains, however, if the people change their ways and make expiation for their sins. Their return to the land of promise remains a possibility. Israel's life on the land is located within the possibilities of blessing and curse. These possibilities are also the context for the families of Israel.

Conflict, Conversation, and the Divine Will (Lev. 10:16–20; 24:10–23)

Leviticus 10:16–20 reports a dispute between Moses and Aaron concerning the priestly consumption of the expiatory sacrifices. Aaron thought the consumption of the sacrifices would be inappropriate in light of the death of his two sons Nadab and Abihu (10:1–2). Moses is angry, but agrees with Aaron at the end of the story. The story demonstrates that conflict and conversation are able to lead to a consensus concerning the will of Yahweh.

Leviticus 24:10–23 relates the story of a man who committed blasphemy. He used the Name (Yahweh) in a contemptuous way with no regard for its sacred nature. When Moses asks, Yahweh instructs him to have the community take the man outside the camp, lay their hands on his head, and stone him to death. The situation provides an opportunity for Yahweh to provide instructions concerning "murder" in the community: killing another human being (bear the guilt, put to death), killing a beast (restitution), and maiming a fellow Israelite (the law of equity, a fracture for a fracture, an eye for an eye, a tooth for a tooth). These rulings seek balance and restitution for the victim rather than punishment for the "criminal." In this context the rule of equitable response must serve as the background for the death penalty. The reader must also recognize that the principle of equity seeks to limit violence and to create balance between the initial offense and the response to it.

Both examples demonstrate that the Priestly writers recognized that the will of Yahweh might be determined in the midst of conflict and conversation as well as in response to situations that arose and demanded a new ruling. Conflict, conversations, and situations may well give rise to the discovery of the will of Yahweh.

Bibliography

Gorman, Frank H. *Leviticus: Divine Presence and Community.* ITC. Grand Rapids: Eerdmans, 1997.

Houston, W. *Purity and Monotheism: Clean and Unclean Animals in Biblical Law.* JSOTSup 140. Sheffield: JSOT Press, 1993.

Jenson, P. P. *Graded Holiness: A Key to the Priestly Conception of the World.* JSOTSup 106. Sheffield: JSOT Press, 1992.

Levine, Baruch A. *Leviticus.* JPS Torah Commentary. Philadelphia: Jewish Publication Society, 1989.

Milgrom, Jacob. *Leviticus.* 3 vols. AB 3. New York: Doubleday, 1991–2001.

Numbers

Samuel E. Balentine

INTRODUCTION

The English title, which comes from the Latin (Vulgate, *Numeri*) and Greek (Septuagint, *Arithmoi*) translations, provides a first clue for reading the fourth book of the Pentateuch. This title accents the "numbers" of Israelites who made a forty-year journey from Sinai to the border of the promised land. A first census (Num. 1) enumerates the twelve tribes who came out of Egypt, covenanted with God, and are now preparing to embark on the journey toward becoming a "priestly kingdom and a holy nation" (Exod. 19:6). A second census (Num. 26) counts the twelve tribes of a new generation who have reached the plains of Moab. Five additional lists, each also naming twelve tribes, occur at the beginning, middle, and end of the book (Num. 2; 7:12–84; 10:14–18; 13:1–16; 34:16–29). Taken together, these seven numberings of the twelve tribes create a coherent and conventional three-part plotline: (1) twelve tribes set out for the land of promise (1:1–10:10); (2) representatives from the twelve tribes spy out the land and with God's help overcome both internal and external obstacles to reaching it (10:11–21:35); and (3) twelve tribes arrive in the plains of Moab by the Jordan, there to receive their allotted inheritance in the land of Canaan (22:1–36:13). On first reading, then, the "numbers" tell the story.

The Hebrew title of the book, "In the Wilderness," which comes from the first verse in the Masoretic Text (1:1), provides a second clue for reading. The phrase "in the wilderness" occurs at both the beginning (1:1, 19; 3:4, 14; 9:1, 5) and end of the book (26:64, 65; 27:3, 14; 32:13, 15; 33:8, 11, 12, 15, 36) and is thus an apt geographical orientation for the whole of the journey toward the promised land, which according to Num. 33 comprises forty stations "in the wilderness." The largest number of occurrences—fourteen out of thirty-one total—are, however, clustered in the middle of the book, chaps. 10–25 (10:12, 31; 12:16; 14:2, 16, 29, 32, 33, 35; 15:22; 16:13; 21:5, 11, 13), which accent the Israelites' response to various difficulties encountered along the way, especially at Kadesh. While some biblical texts describe this time in the wilderness positively (e.g., Hos. 2:14–15 [16–17 Heb.]; 11:1–4; Jer. 2:1–3), Numbers does not. Immediately following their embarkation, the people complain about the lack of food, water, and basic provisions (Num. 11:4–6; 20:2–13; 21:4–9); Miriam and Aaron revolt against the leadership of Moses (12:1–16); a majority refuse to believe that they can occupy the land (chaps. 13–14), despite assurances from Joshua and Caleb that God "will bring us into the land and give

51

it to us" (14:8); a cadre of Levites, led by Korah, challenge the priestly authority of Moses and Aaron (chaps. 16–17); and in a covenantal breach that parallels the golden calf debacle in Exod. 32, the people prostitute themselves with Moabite women and their gods, which culminates in the death of the first generation who came out of Egypt (Num. 25:1–18). This sordid account in Numbers is paradigmatic of the assessment of Israel's disobedience in the wilderness that dominates in the Old Testament. The psalmist offers a representative view:

> How often they rebelled against him in
>   the wilderness
> and grieved him in the desert!
> They tested God again and again,
>   and provoked the Holy One of Israel.
>   (Ps. 78:40–41; cf. Ps. 106:13–33;
>   Ezek. 20:10–17)

On this second reading, then, "numbers" alone do not tell the whole story this book conveys. Israel's journey "in the wilderness" is fraught with challenges that effectively change the calculus for everyone involved—for a chosen people who must live in a world inhabited by others, for leaders who must mediate God's requirements for holy living to a people who question their authority, and not least for God, who must calibrate expectations for obedience with the inviolable covenantal promise encoded in the words "I am the LORD your God" (Num. 10:10; cf. Exod. 20:2).

The different titles for the book introduce but do not exhaust its challenges, for as many commentators have noted, Numbers is the most complicated composition in the Pentateuch. In terms of *literary sources*, the beginning (chaps. 1–10) and end (chaps. 26–36) of the book can be clearly identified with the Priestly tradition. As such, the frame for Numbers extends the Priestly account of the tabernacle's construction (Exod. 25–31, 35–41) and the ritual instructions for holy conduct inside its sacred precincts (Lev. 1–27), along with additional instructions

stipulating that holiness is also the prerequisite for Israel's journey toward the promised land. The middle of the book (Num. 11–25) is an amalgamation of Priestly and non-Priestly traditions; in some places different traditions report on the same incident, thus thickening its interpretation by adding multiple perspectives. In terms of *literary structure*, the book juxtaposes law (chaps. 5–6, 15, 18–19, 26–27, 28–30, 34–35) and narrative (chaps. 11–14, 16–17, 20–25, 31–33). Read separately, the laws are divine prescriptions that require obedience, irrespective of time or place; the narratives describe everyday life under the changing circumstances of the wilderness journey. Read in concert, the laws are not independent of the narrative; instead, they chart a course, then move with and respond to the changing conditions the narrative presents. The narratives do not merely track the successes or failures of everyday life in the shadow of the law; instead, they provide specific contexts in which the law shines more brightly by adapting to on-the-ground realities. In terms of *historical context*, the Pentateuch locates the events reported in Numbers in the presettlement period. From this perspective, the book looks forward to a journey to Moab yet incomplete and to a promise of land yet unfulfilled. The compositional history of Numbers, however, locates the final form of the book in the sixth century. From this perspective, it looks backward to a journey that seems to have deadended in Babylonian exile and to a promised land once obtained but now seemingly lost forever. The hermeneutical challenge is to search for meaning inside the tension of these two perspectives. On the one hand, we read backward—as a people exiled from our hopes and expectations—in order to remember where the journey should have led us and why it did not. On the other, we read forward—as those whose faith is faint but abiding—in order to remember where the journey still leads and how we might yet realize its promises.

COMMENTARY

The Priestly frame (chaps. 1–10, 26–36) provides the overarching structure for theological reflection of Numbers. This frame accentuates two principal criteria that must be met if the people departing Sinai are to reach their final destination in the land of Canaan. The first, addressed in chaps. 1–10, is the requirement for Israel to be a holy people, not only by faithfully observing the prescribed rituals inside the tabernacle (as spelled out in Leviticus) but also by faithfully living in accord with the claims of these rituals outside the tabernacle, where the obstacles to obedience are far greater. The census in the first chapter foregrounds the challenge: God commands Moses to count "everyone in Israel able to go to *war*" (1:3, repeated thirteen times). Toward this end, Israel is to prepare for the march by organizing itself around the tabernacle, the central symbol of the presence of God, which provides critical orientation for every step and every decision that the journey will require. Immediately encircling the four sides of the tabernacle are the priestly families, custodians and mediators of the holiness of God, and surrounding them, the remaining tribes of Israel, with their respective tents facing toward the tabernacle (Num. 2). Additional instructions adumbrate the favored status and the special responsibilities of the priests, especially their administration of the rituals that prevent and/or eliminate the defilement of the holy (Num. 5–6).

A second principal criterion that frames the Priestly perspective on Israel's journey through the wilderness emerges in Num. 26–36. A second census, which reiterates but does not stress the mobilization for war (26:2), sets the table for additional priestly instructions concerning the cultic calendar and sacrificial responsibilities (chaps. 28–29), the fulfillment of vows by laypersons, especially women (chap. 30), and the rules for participation in holy war, especially the purification of warriors and the proper handling of acquired booty (chaps. 31–32). Numbers 34–36 adds an important new word. The criterion of holiness is prerequisite not only for the journey *toward the land;* it is also an abiding imperative for the way Israel must live *in the land.* The protective role played by the priests encamped around the tabernacle in the camp will extend to the land, where priests have the special charge for administering forty-eight "cities of refuge" (35:6–8). These cities reflect concern about how to deal with persons who are guilty of shedding blood, whether intentionally, as in the case of homicide, or accidentally (35:16–28). In Priestly theology, "blood pollutes the land, and no expiation can be made for the land . . . except by the blood of the one who shed it" (35:33; for the trajectory of this concern, see, e.g., Gen. 4:10–11; 9:6; Lev. 17:10–12). The theological rationale for incorporating this concern into civil law is provided in Num. 35:34: "You shall not defile the land in which you live, in which I also dwell; for I the LORD dwell among the Israelites."

The common theological thread in the two framing criteria identified above is the holiness of God, a central concern in all Priestly texts. The root word for "holy" (*qdsh*) contains the seminal idea of being "separate" or "set apart," a condition that, by extension, creates divisions or boundaries between what is holy and what is not. At a foundational level, God is holy and therefore set apart from all that is common. At secondary levels, God ascribes holiness to places (e.g., the tabernacle), times (e.g., the Sabbath), persons (e.g., the priests), and objects (e.g., the land), all of which are similarly set apart from their respective common environments. Two corollary associations are also important. The holy is at once awesome and dangerous; it both attracts, for one wishes to come as close as possible, and it repels, for one fears coming too close. Because proper maintenance of the boundaries between the holy and the common is so crucial, great care must be taken not to transgress or defile them.

The goal of Priestly religion is to create and maintain *boundaries* that *join* a holy God and a common people in life-giving ways. While the Israelites were encamped at the holy mountain of Sinai, where the "glory of the LORD filled the tabernacle" (Exod. 40:35), this goal must have seemed eminently attainable. Once the command comes to depart Sinai and journey through the wilderness, the challenge becomes significantly greater. God's presence, transferred from the glory inside the tabernacle to the cloud by day and the fire by night outside (Num. 9:15–16; 14:14), is now on the move. As God's location shifts, so too must the boundaries between the God who leads and the people who follow. New geographical locations mean that the boundaries joining *God and Israel* must now be redrawn in order to factor in *other nations*, who have different identities, loyalties, and imperatives. Are these "others" inside or outside the journey that binds God and Israel? New questions about insiders and outsiders create internal tensions for the tribes of Israel, who must now decide who has the authority to answer them. Is leadership to be entrusted to Moses alone or to Moses, Aaron, and perhaps their sister Miriam? The account of the rebellion in Num. 12 indicates that the issue was contested. Does leadership devolve to one special branch of the priestly family, the Levites, to whom the book repeatedly assigns special responsibilities (e.g., 1:47–54; 3:40–51; 8:5–26; 35:1–8), or to all Levitical clans (Gershon, Kohath, Merari)? The report in Num. 16–17 of the rebellion led by Korah, from the Kohath clan, reflects the competition for leadership within the priestly families. Intersecting with all these questions about the boundaries required to protect God's holiness against both external and internal threats is the Priestly concern with defilement. This issue is manifest in various ways in Numbers, for example, physical conditions that render persons ritually unclean (5:1–4; 19:1–10), moral offenses that violate the sacred (5:5–10; 35:9–34), and defilement through improper vows (6:1–21; 30:1–16).

In sum, the Priestly frame for Numbers accents a journey that begins and ends with a unified people ensconced inside boundaries that keep them safely connected to the blessing of a holy God (6:24–26). At the same time, both the frame (chaps. 1–10, 26–36) and the center (chaps. 11–25) of the book invite faith communities to ponder the theological ramifications of living *inside* the imperatives of a holy God and *outside* the summons of the world, that is, whatever or whoever we label as the "other."

Israel and Other Nations

Israel's journey from Sinai to Moab, which necessarily involves engagement with other people, presents a double-edged challenge. On the one hand, Israel must travel through foreign lands while remaining detached from their indigenous cultural and religious values. On the other, it must respect the people it encounters along the way, as well as their prevailing customs, for they are the conduit through which Israel must pass if it is to reach its destination. As the book of Numbers makes clear, navigating this challenge is no easy matter. Two paradigms emerge; both invite serious theological reflection.

First, a people called to conform to the holiness of God may regard the "other" as an enemy who must be defeated in order to remain true to God's hopes and expectations. A number of episodes buttress this understanding, sometimes with unsettling theological reverberations. When Sihon, king of the Amorites, refuses Israel's request for safe passage through his land, he is soundly defeated, and his towns are captured (21:21–32). When the Edomites (20:14–21), the Canaanites living in Arad (21:1–3), and Og, king of Bashan (21:33–35), launch preemptive attacks to thwart Israel's advance, they too are defeated. When the

Midianites seduce Israel into apostasy (25:6–18; cf. 25:1–5, a duplicate account concerning the Moabites), Israel wages holy war against them, which requires killing the kings, all males, all male children, and all nonvirgin women (31:1–17). In a disquieting caveat, Moses instructs the Israelites to keep virgin women "alive for yourselves" (31:18).

These texts depicting the "other" as enemy present serious problems for any interpreter who tries to use them as models for ethical conduct in the modern world. They cannot be simply lifted from their ancient context and used as blueprints for waging war against all those who do not share our values. Nor can they be simply dismissed or disregarded, as if they preserve only time-bound witnesses that no longer hold any importance for contemporary believers. If one is to evaluate these texts properly, their unsettling aspects must be fairly measured against several mitigating factors. Other nations become opponents, and sometimes enemies, when they actively oppose God's plans; they are not targeted for war simply because their values and conventions are different. As Numbers makes painfully clear, especially in its sweeping account of the death of the first generation to come out of Egypt, the chosen people of Israel may also be judged severely when they oppose God's plans. Indeed, Israel may impact negatively the ability of other nations to discern what God is doing in the world, for they may misinterpret Israel's failures as God's powerlessness (14:13–19). The alternation of law and narrative throughout the book provides an additional angle for interpretation, especially in the gruesome account in Num. 31 of the holy war against the Midianites. A principal issue here is the treatment of foreign women. When the Israelites avenge themselves on the Midianites (see the precipitating events in Num. 25), they initially kill all the males but spare all the women (31:9). Moses and Eleazar the priest repudiate them for violating the rules for participating in holy war. The women who

seduced the Israelites to "act treacherously against the LORD in the affair of Peor" (31:16) cannot be brought into the Israelite camp, because their presence would defile the holy. Those women (32,000 according to 31:35) who had not participated in the sexual affairs at Peor, those "who have not known a man by sleeping with him" (31:18), must be spared. The text does not specify what keeping them "alive for yourselves" (31:18) means, but we may reasonably assume from other legislation concerning the treatment of women captured in war (cf. Deut. 21:10–14) that sparing their lives opens the possibility that they may be incorporated into the Israelite community and, upon marriage to an Israelite, be granted full citizenship.

A second paradigm for evaluating Israel's distinctive status among the nations also merits close attention. A people called to image God's holiness may regard the "other" as an ally, not an opponent, as a partner to be welcomed into the journey to the promised land, not a stranger to be feared or excluded. Several texts do little more than hint that Israel must work out its identity in relation to, even if in separation from, the others they encounter along the way. Numbers 9:14, which opens the celebration of the Passover to resident aliens, indicates that outsiders have their place in Israel's ritual observances. Numbers 10:29–32, along with several other pentateuchal accounts (Exod. 2:15–22; 3:1; 4:18; 18:1–27), reports that Moses seeks and receives guidance from his father-in-law, Hobab/Jethro, the Midianite, who is also invited to join Israel on the journey, with the assurance that "whatever good the LORD does for us, the same we will do for you" (Num. 10:32). The most extensive contribution to this paradigm is found in Num. 22–24, the remarkable tale of Balaam, the foreign seer, who is hired by Balak, king of Moab, for the express purpose of cursing the Israelites. Balaam refuses, saying that he cannot do what God has not commanded, and instead of cursing Israel, he blesses them. In so doing, this non-Israelite becomes an agent who sustains the very blessing by which God first summoned Abraham and his descendants toward the land (cf. Gen. 12:3 and Num. 24:9b), the blessing that continues even now to chart Israel's course in the wilderness (Num. 6:24–26).

Priests, Levites, and Other Leaders

The mandate to be holy requires not only that the Israelites carefully navigate the external boundaries between themselves and other nations. It also requires attending to internal boundaries that demarcate the responsibilities of leadership within the community. Numbers 2–3 offers an idealized and hierarchical description of the camp. The tent of meeting in the center of the camp, at which God appears, symbolizes the highest level of holiness. One step removed from the tent are the priests and the Levites. Their positions relative to the tent signal a second and third level of proximity to holiness: on the east, the most prestigious side, are Moses, Aaron, and the sons of Aaron (3:38); on the other three sides of the tent of meeting are the Levitical families, the Kohathites to the south (3:29), the Gershonites to the west (3:23), and the Merarites to the north (3:35). Encamped around the priests and Levites, at one step further removed from the center of holiness, are the twelve tribes in groups of three, each group positioned in descending levels of prestige and importance: to the east, Judah, the most dominant tribe, flanked by Issachar and Zebulun (2:3–9); to the south, Reuben, flanked by Simeon and Gad (2:10–16); to the west, Ephraim, flanked by Manasseh and Benjamin (2:18–24); and to the north, Dan, flanked by Asher and Naphtali (2:25–31). When this carefully organized camp sets out on its journey toward the promised land, the ideal structure is subject to disruption. We should not be surprised that on-the-ground realities create internal disagreement and even rebellion within the community concerning who is best positioned to mediate the imperatives of holiness.

The texts that evidence this dissension are clustered in the middle of the book (Num. 10–25). Two may be singled out as illustrative. Numbers 12 reports rebellion among those closest to the center of holiness, Moses, Aaron, and in this case, Miriam, their sister. The pretext for the revolt is that Moses, who has married a foreigner—a Cushite woman—has gone outside the boundaries of the holy, which his complainants argue annuls his authority as a leader. In response, God declares that Moses has special status (12:6–8), which means that his leadership is authoritative, even when it divides the community of the aspiring faithful against itself.

Numbers 16–17 reports a still more internal dissension within the Levitical families and the tribes. Although the text is a composite, the general outlines are clear. Korah, a Levite from the family of Kohath, Dathan and Abiram from the tribe of Reuben, and 250 unnamed leaders challenge Moses and Aaron's leadership. The challenge comprises two arguments: Moses and Aaron have claimed for themselves leadership roles, yet they have failed, because Israel is now worse off in the wilderness than when in Egypt, where even as slaves they lived in "a land flowing with milk and honey" (16:13–14); and because "all the congregation are holy, every one of them, and the LORD is among them" (16:3), there is no need for a social structure that accords power and responsibility to only a few. The conflict is resolved by God's public affirmation of Moses and the Aaronide priests, now purged of Levitical dissenters. The severity of the punishment on those who have challenged Moses and Aaron—the households of Korah, Dathan, and Abiram are swallowed alive by the ground, the 250 leaders are consumed by fire, and 14,700 die by plague—invites a frightened question from the survivors. "We are lost, all of us are lost! Everyone who approaches the tabernacle of the LORD will die. Are we all to die?" (17:12). The sequel to this episode in chap. 18 provides the answer by reinforcing the division of priestly responsibilities. The Aaronide priests will protect Israel from the wrath of God by performing rituals at the sanctuary and the altar (18:1, 3, 5). The Levites will play a subordinate role by performing duties at the tent of meeting (18:2–4, 21–26).

These texts report dissension within the community but without regularly exploring the dynamics behind the conflicts. Various people complain about being excluded from the decision-making processes, their leaders rebuke and judge them, then reassert their own authority, now reinforced with divine validation. Seldom do the narratives permit us to see behind the curtain, where the tension plays itself out. This is especially true with respect to Aaron and the Levites; although they are often addressed, they rarely speak. The texts offer a much fuller profile of Moses, who provides a model for assessing the psychological (and theological) wear and tear of the conflict.

Moses is clearly an extraordinary leader, whose special status is confirmed when he speaks with God "mouth to mouth" and "beholds the form of the LORD" (12:8; cf. Exod. 33:11, 17–23). For all this, the narrator reminds us that "Moses was very humble, more so than anyone else on the face of the earth" (Num. 12:3). But Moses is also a very human figure, vulnerable to self-doubt (11:14), self-pity (11:11, 15), and intemperate behavior (16:15; 20:10–11). Still more instructive are his candid complaints about God's justice and mercy. When God becomes angry at the people's complaint about lack of meat, Moses is displeased (11:10; literally, "in the eyes of Moses it was evil") and asks God a series of protesting questions: "Why have you treated your servant so badly" (11:11; literally, "Why is there evil to your servant?"); "Why have I not found favor in your sight?"; "Did I conceive all this people? Did I give birth to them, that you should say to me, 'Carry them in your bosom, as a nurse carries a sucking child'?" (11:11–12). Implicit in these questions are accusations that strike at the heart of foundational assumptions about

God's character. Servants of God—like Moses—merit divine *favor*, not divinely nuanced "*evil*." Moses did not give birth to "all this people," God did; Moses is "not able to carry all this people alone, for they are too heavy" (v. 14), a point reasserted multiple times (vv. 11, 12, 13); only God has the capacity to birth and carry a people in accord with divine expectations. When God appears to grow impatient with the people's refusal to "believe in me" and then announces intentions to disinherit them one and all (14:11–12), Moses in turn grows impatient with God and asks if God's intentions are authentically Godlike. Is it worthy of God to "kill this people all at one time" (14:15)? Does not God's own nature require that justice be tempered by mercy and forgiveness? Pressing the point, Moses dares to quote God to God, in the hope of reminding the Almighty of covenantal promises to be "slow to anger, and abounding in steadfast love, forgiving iniquity and transgression" (14:18; cf. Exod. 34:6–7 and its reverberations in Deut. 7:8–10; Jer. 32:18; Pss. 86:5, 15; 103:8; Joel 2:13; Jonah 4:2; Neh. 9:17). Perhaps most remarkable, despite Moses' audacity, God neither silences nor rebukes him. To the contrary, when Moses pleads with God to change divine intentions, God responds positively (Num. 14:19–20). Indeed, when one surveys Moses' multiple intercessory interventions on Israel's behalf (11:2; 12:13; 14:13; 16:22; 21:7), it is evident that God too must make adjustments in the wilderness, where the boundaries between the obedience expected and the divine mercy required are constantly shifting.

Men, Women, and Gender Boundaries

The differences between women and men in a society defined by a patrilineal system, such as ancient Israel, create additional and still more complex boundary issues. Where male lineage is the key to identity, women are ascribed status by virtue of gender; their role in the community derives more from the accident of their birth than from the merit of their deeds. They are, by virtue of their genealogy—as descendants of father Abraham—*inside* the boundaries that define the chosen people of Israel. They are at the same time, however, by virtue of their gender—their birth as females, a fact over which they have no control—*outside* the male-dominated power structures that regulate their lives. This patrilineal system is evident in Numbers, and it represents yet another instance in which interpreters must negotiate the gap between ancient customs and contemporary ethical and moral sensibilities. As Numbers deals with this issue inside its own world, we may discern theological truths that remain important.

Women have a presence in both the laws (5:11–31; 27:1–11; 30:1–16; 36:1–12) and the narratives of Numbers (12:1–16; 25:1–18; 31:1–54). They are therefore both actors in the unfolding drama that is Israel's journey to Canaan, and the objects of the laws that will order and govern their lives inside the land's promised blessing. The following examples must suffice as illustrations that invite theological reflection.

Numbers 5:11–31 is legislation that deals with Israelite women suspected of adultery (the general concerns here are writ large with specific respect to foreign woman in the narrative of Num. 25). The male perspective of the legislation is clear. If a man has legitimate suspicions that his wife has been unfaithful to him, or if he is merely overwhelmed by "a sprit of jealousy" (5:14), he may bring her to the priest for a resolution of the matter. The priest administers a ritual (5:15–31) that involves disheveling the woman's hair, placing special offerings in her hands, requiring her to take an oath, and requiring her to drink a potion, the effects of which will determine her guilt or innocence. If her "womb discharges" and her "uterus drops" (5:22, 27)—a physical sign of a punishment that strikes at her capacity to bear children—then she is guilty and shall henceforth be regarded as "an

execration among her people" (5:27). Her only recourse is to accept the verdict and say, "Amen, Amen" (5:22). If she does not evidence these symptoms, then she is innocent, the proof of which will be her continuing ability to bear children (5:23–26). If she is exonerated, her husband bears no guilt for having falsely accused her (5:31).

This text is problematic for modern interpreters for many reasons. Nonetheless, readers should weigh its importance against two mitigating factors. First, the text defines the issue of concern as "going astray," literally, "breaking faith" (5:12). Though the charge is here laid against a woman, it is in fact not gender-specific—elsewhere it applies to men (e.g., Moses, Deut. 32:51; Uzziah, 2 Chr. 26:16–18; Ahaz, 2 Chr. 28:19, 22–25), the Israelites in general (Josh. 7:1), and individual tribes in particular (Josh. 22:16, 22). In Priestly legislation, "breaking faith" is the equivalent of "sacrilege," that is, the offense is primarily against God—not against another human being—as is made explicit in Num. 5:6: "When a man or a woman wrongs another, breaking faith with the LORD, that person incurs guilt." Second, although this legislation permits an innocent woman to be accused falsely, an indefensible humiliation on any grounds, it also bars her husband, the false accuser, from deciding the outcome of the trial. As the potential offense is against God, any punishment that is warranted must come from God alone, not the husband or the larger community. Thus, for all its cultural and theological limitations, this text ultimately aims at protecting a woman against a husband's jealousy. In a patriarchal society, where males hold the preponderance of power, legislation that draws some such boundaries of protection around women—and others the status quo may systematically deny a voice—should not be dismissed as archaic or theologically insignificant.

Several texts invite consideration of the ways in which women courageously challenge conventional boundaries that would otherwise leave them outside God's blessing. Miriam's challenge to Moses' leadership in Num. 12 is one instance. With Aaron, her priestly brother, she complains that Moses' marriage to a Cushite woman nullifies his role as leader of the community. When judged against postexilic legislation prohibiting Israelite marriage with foreign women (concerns not unrelated to the composition of the final form of Numbers), Miriam is right to object. Yet the text reports that she, but not Aaron, is judged for having raised the issue. Her punishment is both physical affliction—she becomes "leprous as snow" (12:10)—and social ostracism—she is "shut out of the camp for seven days" (12:14). Even so, the text ironically places God on the side of Miriam. When Moses prays for her healing, God answers positively his prayer, to which the narrator adds these words validating her importance for the journey that lies ahead: "the people did not set out on the march *until* Miriam had been brought in again" (12:15; emphasis mine).

A second set of texts reinforces the depiction of women as legitimate challengers to authority. In 27:1–11 five daughters of Zelophehad, from the family of Joseph, challenge Moses by arguing that the legislation (see 26:52–56) permitting only sons to inherit land is inadequate. Their father died in the wilderness, leaving no sons, only five daughters; hence to follow the law would mean that their family will have no place in the land of promise (27:4). When Moses brings the case before God, God concurs with the daughters' challenge and instructs Moses to change the existing case law: "The daughters of Zelophehad are right in what they are saying; you shall indeed let them possess an inheritance.... You shall also say to the Israelites, 'If a man dies, and has no son, then you shall pass his inheritance on to his daughter" (27:7–8). A sequel to this episode occurs in 36:1–12. It both endorses the previous ruling—"the descendants of the tribe of Joseph are

right in what they are saying" (36:5)—and (re)contextualizes it within prevailing conventions. The daughters may inherit the land, but they must marry within their own tribe (Manasseh), lest through intertribal marriage one tribe's gain results in another's loss (36:6–9). Here, as in Num. 12, the role of women in challenging, shaping, and thereby clarifying, even securing, the boundaries between insiders and outsiders invites careful reflection.

Locating God in Numbers

The pressing need for the community that journeys through the wilderness to the promised land is to locate God within shifting contexts that are constantly rescribing the boundaries between what is inside and what is outside the requirements of holiness. Numbers suggests that it is not only Israel who is on the move; God is as well. God's location in Numbers, that is, God's presence in relation to the people, is complex and does not yield to neat categorizations. The following observations must be held in constructive tension.

There is a constancy in God's presence as profiled in Numbers that hovers over Israel's entire journey from Sinai to Moab. God leads and guides Israel through the wilderness, provides for Israel's needs along the way, and sustains the journey through all obstacles with healing, blessing, forgiveness, and restoration, all signs of God's unfailing commitment to keep covenant with the chosen people. At the same time, Numbers portrays God's presence as both intermittent and unpredictable. The cloud by day and pillar of fire by night that serve as visible symbols of God's presence at the tabernacle come and go, sometimes lingering, sometimes moving quickly, as God chooses (9:20–22). When these symbols are visible, God is present and available to talk with his servant Moses; when they move, God is on the move, and the people must follow and wait for the next occasion when God chooses to enter into dialogue with Moses. The nature of divine revelation also varies. With Moses, who alone is permitted to stand inside the tent, God speaks intimately, "mouth to mouth" (7:89; 12:8; cf. Exod. 33:9, 11). All others stand outside the tent; with them God is present by sight, but not by sound. As the cloud and fire that move with the tabernacle both reveal and conceal God's presence, so the ark serves as a tangible symbol of both God's presence and absence. When the ark can be seen, as for example in times of war, then God is present and Israel's victory is secure (Num. 10:35–36); conversely, the absence of the ark signals God's absence and Israel's certain defeat (14:43–44).

The clearest affirmation in Numbers of who God is and how God is present with Israel is found in 23:19:

> God is not a human being, that he
> should lie,
> or a mortal, that he should he should
> change his mind.
> Has he promised, and will he not do it?
> Has he spoken, and will he not
> fulfill it?

While the substance of this text deserves careful attention, what is most striking in the first instance is that it is spoken by Balaam, a foreigner, one who might be regarded as outside the boundaries Israel constructs for itself and its God. On close inspection, there is a curious inversion (or subversion?) of the boundaries between so-called insiders and outsiders. As Israel journeys through the wilderness, conforming as best it can to the demands to be separate to and for God's holy purposes, the boundaries it constructs become increasingly regressive. At its widest point, the line is drawn between Israel and other nations; then it is drawn between the priests/Levites and the other tribes; then between the Aaronides and other Levites; then between males and females. Gradually the circle of insiders believed to have

most favored status with God, those permitted to stand in closest proximity to God's holiness, becomes smaller and smaller. It is therefore instructive to note that God often refuses to stay within the boundaries Israel constructs. God is on the side of Moses, who marries a foreign wife; on the side of Balaam, a foreign seer; on the side of Miriam and the daughters of Zelophehad, all of whom, by God's estimation, if not always by Israel's, have something important to contribute to the journey through the wilderness.

A final observation returns us to the idealized description of the tabernacle at the center of Israel's camp (Num. 2). God's location at the heart of Israel's journey, in essence as the defining center of its identity, is the dominant view in the Priestly tradition and is clearly enormously rich in its theological implications. Nonetheless, Numbers preserves oblique but instructive hints that God moves from the center of the camp (10:21) to its front (10:33), on occasion even moving ahead of Israel by days, months, or longer periods (9:21–22). Both spatially and theologically God blurs the boundaries between what Israel considers central and marginal.

The most suggestive of these texts are 11:26–30 and 12:4, both of which place the tent of meeting *outside* the camp (cf. Exod. 33:7–11). The former text reports that the spirit of God "rested" on Eldad and Medad, who were not at the tent of meeting, which was outside the camp, but who were instead within the camp. Moses is informed that unauthorized persons were "prophesying in the camp" and is asked to stop them. He refuses, saying that he cannot limit where or how God chooses to be present. In his words, "Would that all the LORD's people were prophets, and that the LORD would put his spirit on them" (11:29). The latter text, Num. 12:4, occurs in the context of Miriam and Aaron's complaint against Moses' leadership. God summons Moses, Miriam, and Aaron to the tent outside the camp for a resolution of the matter. As previously noted,

Miriam is punished by being quarantined outside the camp for seven days. Clearly, the punishment has to do with a woman who has transgressed conventional boundaries of what the community deems acceptable behavior. Nonetheless, this text suggests that even outside the camp, Miriam remains within God's presence, for sometimes, from God's perspective, outside is inside. One interpretive strategy for resolving this apparent contradiction is to attribute these conflicting reports of God's location inside and outside the camp to different authors or traditions. Another is to stay inside the tension of where the final form of the book called "Numbers" and "In the Wilderness" locates God in Israel's journey to the promised land. A subtle clue of which option the book tilts toward comes, once again, from Balaam, an outsider who stands, ironically, at the center of God's hopes and expectations for Israel:

How can I [read "we"] curse whom God has not cursed?
How can I [read "we"] denounce those whom the LORD has not denounced?

(Num. 23:8)

Bibliography

Douglas, Mary. *In the Wilderness: The Doctrine of Defilement in the Book of Numbers*. Oxford: Oxford University Press, 2003.

Dozeman, Thomas B. "The Book of Numbers." In *NIB* 2:1–268.

Levine, Baruch A. *Numbers*. 2 vols. AB 4. New York: Doubleday, 1993–2000.

Olson, Dennis T. *Numbers*. Interpretation. Louisville: Westminster John Knox, 1996.

Sakenfeld, Katharine Doob. *Journeying with God: A Commentary on the Book of Numbers*. ITC. Grand Rapids: Eerdmans, 1995.

Deuteronomy

Brent A. Strawn

INTRODUCTION

The English title, Deuteronomy, comes from the Septuagint, which employed *deuteronomion* ("second law") in translating Deut. 17:18. While perhaps infelicitous, "Deuteronomy" is a fortuitous rendition that captures a central aspect of the book: its seconding nature. In Hebrew, Deuteronomy is named after its opening clause—*'elleh haddebarim* (1:1), typically abbreviated to *debarim*, "words." This title is revealing because Deuteronomy contains more reported speech—Moses' farewell address—than any other in the Pentateuch. Finally, a rabbinic designation, *sepher tokahot* ("book of admonitions"), is also appropriate because Deuteronomy is thoroughly sermon-like.

Scholarly consensus has long held that the "book of the law" discovered in Josiah's time (2 Kgs. 22:8) was Deuteronomy, or, more precisely, some form of its core. This theory is supported by two observations: (1) Josiah's reform corresponds with Deuteronomic emphases, especially cult centralization (2 Kgs. 23:1–20; Deut. 12:2–28); and (2) Josiah is the only king said to "incarnate" the Shema (2 Kgs. 23:25; Deut. 6:5). If this consensus is correct, much of Deuteronomy dates to the seventh century. Portions of the book probably predate that period (2 Kgs. 22 reports its discovery, not its composition), but other parts almost cer-

tainly postdate it. Chapters 4 and 28–30 betray awareness of the exile. Indeed, it is widely held that those responsible for the Deuteronomistic History (DtrH) took their orientation from Deuteronomy, prefixing it to their account of early Israel and the monarchy. A first edition of DtrH may have been produced in Josiah's time. But DtrH was subsequently updated in the exilic period, following the cataclysm of 587/586 BCE. It is thus an apologia of judgment and exile—one rooted in Deuteronomy's presentation of covenantal obedience or disobedience and the blessings or curses that result.

Deuteronomy must be read on at least three different levels, corresponding to three different ancient audiences: (1) the *literary level* of Moses in Moab addressing the second generation of Israelites who have left Egypt; (2) a *monarchic audience* that can be associated with Josiah's time; (3) the *exilic audience* reflected in chaps. 4 and 28–30, and by the use of Deuteronomy as preface to DtrH.

Attention to these various contexts thickens theological interpretation because Deuteronomy affects each audience differently. Moses' exhortations to the literary audience prior to land-taking are warning prior to possession. For a monarchic audience that has inhabited the land for generations, Deuteronomy is agenda for the present. It is but a short step from that agenda to explanation after judgment for the exilic audience. Those who have experienced "all these words/things" (4:30; 30:1)—especially the curses (28:45)—can easily deduce that they were caused by disobedience. Yet Deuteronomy also contains instructions for those in exile, offering this belated audience an agenda for the future (4:25–31; 29:1 [28:69 Heb.]–32:47). Like the literary audience, the exilic audience waits outside the land, hoping for another chance to occupy it. Contemporary audiences will resonate in different ways with these three contexts.

Reading Deuteronomy using the three rubrics of rhetoric, revision, and repetition provides insights into key characteristics of the book.

- *Rhetoric.* Deuteronomy is thoroughly rhetorical, not simply in terms of stylistic construction, but because it is *persuasive.* Everywhere Deuteronomy is making a case, convincing the reader to hear and obey. One example is the extensive use of motive clauses in the laws (e.g., "so that you might live long in the land"). Such language makes the commandments eminently reasonable, encouraging adherence to them.
- *Repetition.* Deuteronomy repeats prior pentateuchal material; there is also much internal repetition of important phrases, verbs, and subjects. This macro- and microrepetition combine to help the reader focus on the salient elements to be learned: ultimately, the careful enactment of the commandments.
- *Revision.* In its repetition of canonically prior texts, Deuteronomy revises significant narratives (e.g., Deut. 1:19–45; Num. 13–14) and laws (e.g., Deut. 15:16–18; Exod. 21:2–11). These revisions demonstrate that time and circumstance matter: laws change accordingly, stories are told differently.

Deuteronomy's three Rs intersect: repetition serves the rhetoric of obedience, revision is necessitated by persuasive intent.

The book's rhetoric lives on revision and repetition.

Moses' "last will and testament" is actually a series of addresses demarcated by four important superscriptions (1:1–5; 4:44–49; 29:1 [28:69 Heb.]; 33:1). Each of the resulting units has its own formal and temporal focus: *stories* of the *past* (1:6–4:43), *commandments* for the *present* (5:1–28:68), a *covenant* for the *future* (29:1 [28:69 Heb.]–33:29), and *blessing* and *departure* (33:1–34:12).

Deuteronomy also manifests *a decalogical structure.* Chapters 1–4 provide background for the repetition of the Ten Commandments in 5:6–21. The "great commandment" of 6:5 is a positive articulation of the first commandment, which is followed by a sermon based on that text (chaps. 6–11). The "statutes and ordinances" in chaps. 12–26 then contain case law sequentially keyed to the Ten Commandments.

A *covenantal substructure* comparable to ancient Near Eastern treaties also appears in Deuteronomy. Covenantal elements underscore the real, political, and reciprocal nature of Deuteronomy's content. That the correspondence with ancient examples is inexact, however, complicates questions regarding dating and relationship. So, while the idea of covenant helps readers in thinking about the book as a way of life or polity, it is not a sufficient description of the book's genre.

A better generic clue is found in the term *torah,* which is used throughout the book. Indeed, the phrase "book of the law" occurs prominently (17:18; 28:58, 61; 29:21 [20 Heb.]; 30:10; 31:24, 26) and arguably refers to Deuteronomy in other settings (Josh. 1:8; 8:31, 34; 23:6; 2 Kgs. 14:6; 22:8, 11; Neh. 8:1, 3, 8, 18; 9:3). In Deuteronomy "torah" means more than "law code," though the book includes numerous laws, and "torah" certainly encompasses those. But torah is also something that is expounded (1:5), explained (6:20), and taught (4:1, 5, 10; 6:7). Deuteronomic torah might thus be compared with a catechism.

Deuteronomy is sufficiently complex that it is best to include all of these conceptions—covenant, polity, catechism. However, it is important to include one further category: amended constitution. The Ten Commandments have constitution-like status in Deuteronomy. But the book's revisionist rhetoric amends even that constitutional text along with its constitutional event, the covenant at Sinai. That event/text, whether found in Exodus–Numbers or in Deuteronomy's recollections, is updated and adapted. Deuteronomy itself is constitutional, then, only insofar as it is amendable. It is a constitution with amendments that functions to model and commend further amendment in the future. This last point is somewhat ironic in the light of the "canonical" formulae in 4:2; 12:32 (13:1 Heb; cf. 5:22).

To speak of constitutional revision raises a final generic analogue: the Gettysburg Address, which many people think reinterpreted the U.S. Constitution. In Deuteronomy "Moses," like Lincoln, altered a preexisting constitution from within, changing it, even bringing it to its own condemnation (cf. Deut. 28), by offering something new but not entirely discontinuous in its place. Gettysburg worked: people believe the Constitution means what Lincoln said it meant.

Deuteronomy also worked: the story in 2 Kgs. 22–23 and the theological civil war waged in seventh-century Judah show as much, as does DtrH writ large, along with the influence of Deuteronomy's theology elsewhere in the Old Testament (e.g., in the book of Jeremiah).

Indeed, one might say that wherever one goes in the Old Testament, "Deuteronomy is always somehow there" (McConville, p. 10). Deuteronomy deserves pride of place in any discussion of Scripture's center. It is literature of mature theological reflection, literarily unnecessary for the plot development of the Pentateuch (only Moses' death stands between Num. 36 and Josh. 1), but theologically essential for all that follows. Deuteronomy is thus the end of the beginning: the climactic conclusion to the Pentateuch. It is also the beginning of the end, because even at this early (literary) point, the ground rules are established. All that follows is judged by Deuteronomy's standards. Those standards prove to be more than Israel's monarchs can handle. Deuteronomy thus initiates the slow demise of one stage in Israel's political history. But Deuteronomy knows of life *beyond* judgment and exile—a life guided, in no small way, by this particular book. The end, with Deuteronomy's help, turns out to be just another kind of beginning.

COMMENTARY

Setting the (Rhetorical) Stage: Stories from the Past (1:1–4:43)

The book's first superscription (1:1–5) offers important background data and introduces several Deuteronomic themes. It covers *who, to whom, what, where,* and *when.* Even *how* is discussed—Moses speaks "just as" Yahweh commanded (1:3), initiating Deuteronomy's accent on precise obedience (1:19; 2:37; 5:12; 6:25; 20:17; 34:95). Perhaps the only question that remains unanswered is *why.* But 1:2 offers a hint, noting that the trip from Horeb should take eleven days—1:3 opens *forty years* later! Verse 2 is thus no

innocent aside, but a not-so-subtle hint of Israel's disobedience at Kadesh (1:19–45). This allusion highlights another of Deuteronomy's emphases—the impact (good or otherwise) of previous generations on later ones (4:37; 7:8; 8:18; 9:5; 10:15).

The transition from 1:5, which anticipates an exposition of "this torah," to 1:6, which recounts the departure from Horeb, is somewhat odd. Narration of past events dominates the first three chapters and is interwoven elsewhere (cf. 4:10–20; 5:2–31; 6:16; 8:2–4, 14–16; 9:8–29; 10:1–11; 18:16–20), but the shift in 1:5–6 may be a rhetorical tactic that makes the reader wonder when the substance of torah will be given. This transition, along with the other flashbacks, demonstrates that one expounds torah precisely by retelling the story. This rehearsal of the narrative is consistent with the semantic range of *torah*, on the one hand, and the generic complexity of the Pentateuch (the Torah par excellence), on the other. Both torahs—"this torah" and the Torah—constitute a complex amalgam made up of law and story. Expounding torah means, in no small part, telling it again and again, and then again once more.

For Deuteronomy, the exposition of torah via retelling involves the writing in (inscription) of the present audience into past events. The forty years following Horeb included the death of the first generation and the maturation of the second. The latter group now stands in Moab. But Moses' rhetoric allows no generational divide. He speaks only of "us," of the Lord "our God," and how the Lord "spoke to us" and told "us" what to do. Throughout Deuteronomy Moses repeatedly writes the second generation and their children into the story of the first generation. A classic example occurs in 5:3, which states that God made the Horeb covenant not with "our ancestors . . . but with us, who are all of us here alive today." However, not all of those now in Moab were at Horeb, and most of those at Horeb are now dead (2:14–15). Again, Moses will permit no us versus them, no old versus new. There is only "us": "all of us here alive today." Later he will instruct the second generation to follow his lead and write their own children into the story (6:20–25).

This inscription is two-edged: positive and negative. Later generations are made the beneficiaries of God's delivering acts (6:21–22) and are placed again at Horeb as recipients of the Lord's commandments. In this way, they become part of the exodus generation from a theological perspective. But they are also written into the story of disobedience. If they were in Egypt, then they were also at Kadesh

(1:19–45). If they were at Horeb, then they also worshiped the golden calf (9:8–21). If they are beloved of Yahweh, in no small degree because of the ancestors (7:8; 8:18), then they, like their predecessors, "have been rebellious against the Lord as long as he has known you" (9:24). Deuteronomy's inscription makes readers at once slaves redeemed by the Lord and rebels spurning the Lord's instruction. This biblical book regularly positions readers in and among the poles of Horeb and Kadesh, of covenant and calf. These poles, joined with another locus—exile—function to press incessantly the covenantal decision upon the reader.

The story of Israel's journey through Transjordan (2:1–3:7) makes up a large part of the past Moses narrates; it moves from the theologically evocative to the theologically disconcerting. At first, God commands Israel not to engage the Edomites, Moabites, or Ammonites in battle for two reasons: (1) Edom and Moab are identified as kin (2:4, 8–9, 19), a noteworthy claim since the political relationships between Israel and these groups were often strained; and (2) God claims to have given these peoples their territories in terms altogether similar to God's gift of Cisjordan to Israel (2:5, 9, 19; cf. 2:12b). These groups are also said to have faced prior inhabitants related to the Anakim and Rephaim, whom Israel will later face (2:10–12, 20–23). Most remarkable of all, however, the Lord is explicitly credited with the destruction of those who inhabited these lands before the Ammonites and Edomites entered them (2:21–22; the same may reasonably be inferred for the Moabites and Caphtorim in 2:12, 23).

This is nothing less than a story of multiple conquests. Evidently, God is in the resettlement business—not just for Israel—just as God is in the exodus business—again, not just for Israel (Amos 9:7). While, on the one hand, the God of multiple conquests renders the already difficult conquest narrative still more problematic; on the other hand, this claim democratizes the problem. God, who clearly loves Israel beyond all others (7:7–8), nevertheless acts in analogous and benevolent ways for others, even others who will become Israel's bitter enemies. God gives land to Israel and to other nations and assists them in removing dangerous prior inhabitants.

To be sure, these dangerous inhabitants are demonized. They are called by strange names and presented using mythical categories: they are unnaturally tall, irredeemably wicked (1:28; 2:10–11, 21; 9:4; 20:18; cf. Gen. 6:1–4; Num. 13:33). Such literary (and theological) techniques are undoubtedly attempts to legitimize the *herem* or "ban," which was part of Israel's holy war practice (2:34; 3:5; 7:2; 13:15, 17 [16, 18 Heb.]; 20:17; cf. 7:26). This demonization may be viewed from at least two different perspectives. Like the plural conquest, such characterizations appear even more unpalatable to modern sensibilities: no one could be that wicked, genocide is always condemnable. Yet demonizing the prior inhabitants suggests that they are already larger than life; their presentation may be more theological (and literary) than historical. History and theology are not mutually exclusive in Deuteronomy. It is Og, whose bed can still be seen in Rabbah (3:11), after all, who was the last of the Rephaim (3:11); it is the Canaanites who were the offspring of the Anakim (1:28). Even so, later prohibitions of intermarriage and covenant making with the nations (7:2b–3) are completely nonsensical if the ban had been thoroughgoing. Indeed, 7:22 admits that a quick and complete extermination is impossible. For every audience after the literary one, the injunctions to destroy the ancient inhabitants of the land are of decidedly mixed significance.

Obviously, conquest, settlement, and holy war are complex topics that admit of no easy answers. Insofar as Deuteronomy itself speaks about them in more than one way, the book resists simple-minded approaches or unsophisticated appropriations. Moreover, insofar as the book addresses multiple audiences, the demonized inhabitants are both more and less than real people. A precedent of sorts may thus be found here for an allegorical

interpretation of these nations, if only because Deuteronomy itself interprets them theologically: they threaten Israel's commitment to Yahweh (7:4; 12:30–31). Deuteronomy's worldview is stark. There is the Lord's way and there are all other ways, which are disobedient—"unwilling," as it were—and which challenge Israel's faith. Sihon is the first to represent an unwilling way (2:30), and he is punished. Israel's own earlier unwillingness met with identical results (1:26, 34–35, 45). But since Israel's unwillingness was somehow overcome, so may other unwillingnesses be challenged (cf. 10:10; 29:20 [19 Heb.]). If so, Deuteronomy may undercut somewhat the stringency of the "ban" and offer a way forward.

Moses' death is the only element that advances a plot in Deuteronomy. His death thus looms large and can be felt throughout. In 1:1–4:43, for example, the plan to share judicial authority (1:9–18) offers a subtle hint of Moses' finitude. Despite his incomparability (34:10–12), he was unable to do everything by himself. Another example is present in those passages where Moses "blames" his failure to enter the land on the Lord's anger because of Israel (1:37; 3:26; 4:21). This motif stands at odds with God's own perspective (32:51; cf. Num. 20:1–13). Perhaps Moses' revisionist rhetoric has run amok at this point. Alternatively, one might see in these passages not defensiveness but identification—perhaps even a vicarious, suffering identification—between Moses and the people Moses leads and loves. Nevertheless, Moses cannot give up the hope of crossing the Jordan. When he prays for entrance, his skillful entreaty (3:23–25) is to no avail. God's response is decisive: "Enough from you! Never speak to me of this matter again!" (3:26).

His death outside the land certain, Moses addresses Israel directly in chap. 4, drawing conclusions from the stories just recounted. Stock Deuteronomic language begins in earnest here: Israel is to *hear* and *observe* the *statutes and ordinances* because this leads to *life* and *landholding* (4:1, 4–5).

But, not unlike the movement in 1:5–6, Moses delays offering the statutes and ordinances, retelling instead the encounter at Horeb in the form of a sermon on the prohibition against venerating images (4:9–20; cf. 5:8–10).

Moses exhorts Israel not to forget the covenant (4:23) with a motif drawn from the Horeb theophany (4:11–12): Yahweh "is a devouring fire, a jealous God" (4:24). He then stresses the very real possibility—if not reality—of Israel's failure (4:25–31). This passage, which reveals knowledge of Israel's exilic future, is bleak. It is not only Israel's foes that can suffer the ban; Israel can experience that selfsame fate (4:26; 8:19–20). Such is the end for those who trifle with a devouring fire, a jealous God.

But, as later in Deuteronomy, chap. 4 also knows of something beyond punishment and exile. There is future seeking and finding, returning and listening (4:29–30). And there is future remembrance, for Yahweh is more than just fire and jealousy. Yahweh is merciful—he will not abandon, destroy, or forget (4:31). God is plainly capable of both punishment and restoration, but the divine scales are tipped decisively toward mercy. After all, punishment extends (only) three or four generations, but steadfast love to thousands (5:9–10).

The first unit of Deuteronomy ends with a curious denouement: the establishment of cities of refuge (4:41–43). This may be simply a minor detail in Moses' retelling, but perhaps it is more—a proleptic signal that the Decalogue to follow in chap. 5 must be *interpreted*. "You shall not murder" (5:17), certainly! But is unintentional homicide the same as murder? Clearly not (4:42; 19:1–13), and so 4:41–43 anticipates Deuteronomy's penchant for legal revision, which is showcased most extensively in chaps. 12–26.

Commandments for the Present (4:44–11:32)

Deuteronomy's second superscription (4:44–49) reiterates that Moses is giving

torah (1:5) but adds the "decrees and the statutes and ordinances" (4:45; cf. 4:5). This conglomeration is a commonplace in Deuteronomy's parlance: torah and commandment, statute and ordinance, decree and testimony are all mixed up and mixed together. If it is not entirely clear where one leaves off and another begins, that is how Deuteronomy wants it: *all* of it is important, *all* of it must be heard, *all* of it must be obeyed—in detail and quite precisely. Ultimately, however, this "all" is quite simple. Its simplicity begins, and in a real sense ends, with Horeb—both with what Israel did not see there (4:15–16) and with what they did hear. What they heard was the Decalogue.

The Ten Commandments. Only a few remarks can be made about the Deuteronomic Ten Commandments (5:6–21). The Decalogue makes clear that Yahweh's law giving and Israel's law keeping is predicated on one thing only: the prior, gracious activity of God (5:6). It is no small matter, then, that the Jewish tradition counts 5:6 not as the prologue (as many Christians do) but as the first commandment: Remember what God has done for you. "Bad" memories—such as slavery in Egypt—are not to be repressed; they are transcended through the exodus gospel, never via denial.

The Decalogue's significance is highlighted by its repetition in Exodus and Deuteronomy, and by the fact that it is unmediated—all Israel heard these words . . . and shuddered (cf. 5:5; 18:15–16). The subsequent structure of Deuteronomy also accentuates the Decalogue's centrality. The Ten are the heart of Deuteronomy, the center of its torah. Even so, Deuteronomy's Ten differ from those in Exod. 20. Questions of historical priority need not detain us; it suffices to be amazed that even the Decalogue, which has constitutional status in Deuteronomy, is not above revision. The first major difference is found in the Sabbath commandment, where the prohibition of work is justified not by God's rest (Exod. 20:11) but by Pharaoh's oppression (Deut. 5:15). Israel knows what it is like never to have a break (Exod. 5:5–14). So they are never to live like that again, nor are they to be Pharaoh to others. A second important revision is found in the coveting commandment. In Deuteronomy this is divided into two, placing the neighbor's wife first and using a different verb to describe coveting her (*hmd*) versus the desire (*'wh*) for other things. Some have thought this to be a positive, egalitarian move vis-à-vis Exod. 20:17. That judgment may go too far; Deuteronomy, too, is thoroughly patriarchal. Nevertheless, there is a trajectory begun here that takes steps in a positive direction for women.

The Ten repeat themselves and, in so doing, are simplified. Indeed, that there are only Ten in the first place (Deut. 4:13; 10:4; cf. Exod. 34:28) is already a reduction because, depending on how one counts, there could be more than that. Even the standard Ten fold in on themselves: the first two are of a piece (the "them" in Deut. 5:9 must go back to "other gods" in 5:7); the two coveting versets can be combined (5:21a-b); false witness (5:20) might relate to wrongful use (in court?) of God's name (5:11); the Sabbath rest (5:12–15) can be connected to the honoring of aged parents who are no longer economic producers (5:16). This compounding of the Ten is further underscored in chaps. 12–26, which interprets them. The central law code also folds into itself, anticipating later sections and repeating earlier ones, so that it is not always clear where the exposition of one commandment ends and the next one starts. This mimics the Decalogue's tendency toward simplification so that the reader ends up with just a few commandments, and ultimately just one.

The ultimate commandment is, of course, the first one (5:7) along with its correlate, the prohibition of images (5:8–10). As the Decalogue is the heart of Deuteronomy, this admonition constitutes the heart of the Decalogue. This point is made already in the fourth chapter's sermon and is reiterated later in the

book, most immediately by the sermon that follows in chaps. 6–11.

Preaching the first commandment. The sermon's central point is found in 6:4–9. The precise translation of 6:4—known as the Shema, after the opening imperative in Hebrew—has been debated, though it probably involves a mandate for the exclusive worship of Yahweh (cf. 4:35, 39; 32:39). The meaning of 6:5 is clear, regardless: Israel must love God with everything it is ("heart, soul") and everything it has ("might"). This is simply a repetition of the negatively constructed first commandment in positive terms. But how, exactly, does one love God in this way? Verses 5–9 begin to answer that question, as does the rest of Deuteronomy. "These words" are to be kept in the heart (6:6), incisively taught to children, and discussed constantly at all possible times in all possible locales. Even the Israelite body is marked by these words (6:8), as is Israelite space: they adorn the doorpost (*mezuzah*) of the home and are written on the city gates, the place where the elders gathered and where justice was meted out (6:9). In sum, there is not a body, a place, an area, a time, or a relationship that is not dominated by "these words"—which at one level refers to the entirety of the Book of Words (Deuteronomy) itself.

This, then, is how one loves God: it has much to do with attending to these words, which, in turn, have much to do with remembering God's past beneficence that motivates adherence to the torah. "Loving" God is similar to language found in ancient Near Eastern treaties that spoke of political loyalty in these terms. Still, Deut. 6:5 is filled with rich emotional dimensions. Israel must *love* Yahweh (cf. 10:12; 11:1, 13; 13:3 [4 Heb.]; 30:6). This loving includes obedience, but it also includes the exclusive devotion that characterizes the marital bond. Israel must love God. That means Israel must love no other.

Not surprisingly, then, the rest of the sermon in chaps. 6–11 concerns other possible paramours. The first is not an ancient deity, like Baal or Dagan, but it is just as dangerous: *plenty*. Acquisition of land brings prosperity (6:10–11), which can become a means to forget the Giver. Israel must not forget (6:12). Exclusive devotion to Yahweh (6:13) means forsaking other gods (6:14)—especially the ones covered with silver and gold (7:25)!

The *gods of the nations* constitute other objects of desire. They are so tempting that the only response is a complete dismantling of Canaanite religion (7:4–5). Both the result and reasoning behind these practices must not be overlooked: it is because Israel is a "holy people" and God's "treasured possession" (7:6). Both phrases recall Exod. 19:5–6, which also deems Israel to be "a priestly kingdom." Election with isolation from, even destruction of, adversaries so as ultimately to be of service to all seems illogical, but that is how Deuteronomy imagines Israel's role. Perhaps only those who are holy and undivided in loyalty can intercede on behalf of others.

The high calling of Israel is, ironically, a third major threat. Israel might misunderstand matters and think too highly of itself. In a word, Israel faces the god of *self-exaltation*. Deuteronomy counters this challenge in several ways. First, Israel is reoriented. Its election is rooted in Yahweh alone and God's unfathomable choice of the ancestors (7:7–8). Second, Israel is instructed on the role of its own agency. In three passages Israel is counseled not to "say to yourself" (7:17; 8:17; 9:4)—each of which dismantles specific aspects of an inappropriate self-perception. These too are false gods, but exceedingly subtle ones.

The first mentioned is *the untrusting self*. Small in size, Israel may despair in the face of enemies (7:17; cf. 7:7). If only Israel had *more*—strength, people, weapons of mass destruction—they might stand a better chance. But this is to turn to other gods—the gods of war—and to trust in them, not in Yahweh. Instead, Israel must remember what God has already done and believe God will do

it again (7:18–24a). Not militarism, but God. Not the militarized self, but God. Not the untrusting self, but the story of God's deliverance.

The second passage concerns *the overconfident self*. In contrast to the wilderness, the land is full of plenty, with all the problems that creates (8:7–16; cf. 6:10–11). In light of God's provision in the wilderness (8:3–4) and provision of land (8:7), Israel must not think that it achieved these things on its own (8:17). All gifts, including wealth, are from God (8:18). This wealth (and the getting of wealth) is not an end in itself, but theologically utilitarian, serving only to demonstrate God's faithfulness to the ancestors. Again *God's* agency, not Israel's, is highlighted, reorienting Israel to its past, to its faithful God, and to its faithful forebears.

The last passage covers *the immodest self*. With God fighting for them against the demonized Anakim (9:1–3), Israel might be tempted to overestimate its own righteousness. The importance of the ancestors already refutes such a notion (7:8b; 8:18b; 9:5b), but it is further obviated by highlighting the wickedness of the nations (9:4–5a; cf. 12:31). The inherent wickedness of the nations should not be overstated, however. Discussion of their wickedness is largely a rhetorical move subverting any claim to land-deserving righteousness on Israel's part. The passage clearly stresses the wickedness *of Israel itself*. This is why Moses proceeds to discuss the golden calf debacle (9:8–21), which he has refrained from mentioning until this point precisely because it definitively rebuts the immodest claim to righteousness. As it turns out, the golden calf is just the coup de grâce in a history of disobedience (9:22–24; cf. 1:19–45; 6:10–15). This point, too, ought not be overinterpreted. The presentation is thoroughly rhetorical, the aim to refute the immodest self clear. Most of those hearing Moses' words did not participate in these disobediences. They are simply being inscribed into them—for better, for worse.

The sermon concludes in 10:12–11:31. In light of all that has been said, what must

Israel now do (10:12)? The answer involves key Deuteronomic verbs (fear, walk, love, serve, keep) and their objects (Yahweh, all God's ways, the commandments and decrees); as always, obedience is for Israel's own good (10:12–13). The answer includes two imperatives (10:16): (a) Israel must circumcise its heart—a unique metaphor—indicating that the innermost self is to be marked by *covenant*, not by mistrust, overconfidence, or immodesty (cf. 30:6; Rom. 2:29); and (b) it is to cease being stubborn (cf. Deut. 9:6–7, 13, 24). Israel's history of disobedience (9:22–24) must end. And it will end. It ends "today," in the now of covenant decision. Moses calls Israel to that decision in 11:1, offering them a choice between blessing and curse (11:26–28). This choice and the associated ritual involving Gerizim and Ebal (11:29) prefigure later material (27:4–26; 30:15–20) even as they draw those texts back to the theological center of Deuteronomy: the Decalogue, the Shema, and the sermon on the first commandment.

**Amending the Constitution,
or: Repeating and Revising
the Decalogue (12:1–28:68)**

Although not one of the four editorial superscriptions, 12:1 serves as the heading for the long-promised (4:1, 5, 14; 5:1; 6:1; 7:11; 11:32; cf. 4:45; 5:31) but until now delayed statutes and ordinances. These run through 26:15, at which point Moses again calls Israel to decision, offers blessings and curses, and delineates accompanying rituals (26:16–28:68; cf. 10:12–11:32). The statutes and ordinances are explicitly said to be "for life in the land" (12:1; cf. 4:5, 14; 5:31; 6:1). They are thus revised law necessitated by the new situation of landed-ness (e.g., 12:8–9). Even so, the revised product bears notable and recognizable resemblance to the original. It is unclear whether the authors of Deuteronomy intended to replace all preexisting legal materials, though it is clear canonically that Deuteronomy does *not* replace them but only supplements, repeats, and revises. This is, after all, the "second law."

If there is a tensive relationship between certain laws in Deuteronomy and elsewhere, this need be no more disconcerting than the fact that the amendments to the U.S. Constitution revise it. Such is the nature of amendment! But the original does not disappear. Amendments *depend* on the original constitution for their legitimacy, even as the constitution is now only accessible in its new, amended form. Consequently, the statutes and ordinances: (a) demonstrate the necessity of ongoing revision to biblical material in light of changed times and circumstances; and (b) model the way in which that revision stands in recognizable continuity with what has gone before.

The (ten) statutes and ordinances (12:1–26:15). The statutes and ordinances are related to the Decalogue in both content and order. Although not all scholars agree on this point, it has significant exegetical support, underscores again the centrality of the Decalogue, and offers considerable theological insight. This correspondence means, at the very least, that the statutes and ordinances afford further insight into what the typically terse and open-ended Ten might mean. It also suggests that the central law code, so often underutilized in theological analysis, is fundamentally related to no less important a text than the Decalogue. The statutes and ordinances thus merit close attention and repay theological investigation.

The following chart identifies the correspondences between the Ten Commandments and the statutes and ordinances:

Statutes and Ordinances	*Commandment*
12:2–13:18 [19 Heb.]	The first commandment (no other gods, no images)
14:1–21	On not misusing God's name
14:22–16:17	Keeping the Sabbath
16:18–18:22	Honoring "parents"
19:1–22:8	No killing
22:9–23:18	No adultery
23:19 [20 Heb.]–24:7	No stealing
24:8–25:4	No false witness

25:5–12	Not coveting the wife of the neighbor
25:13–26:15	Not coveting the possessions of the neighbor

Since a full discussion is not possible here, a few examples must suffice to demonstrate the ways in which the statutes and ordinances illuminate and characteristically expand the Ten.

1. The commandment about misusing God's name may concern *public* misuse, which means it would include hypocrisy. This interpretation is supported in 14:1–21, which bases a number of prohibitions on Israel's status as a holy people and treasured possession (14:1–2). Israel's "taking up Yahweh's name" means that all aspects of its life must bear signs of its covenantal relationship, avoiding signs that indicate otherwise.

2. The verses that correspond to the Sabbath commandment concern various aspects of worship (14:22–16:17). A series of sevens in 15:1; 16:7; and 16:9 suggest that the Sabbath should not simply be understood as one day per week (though it is that). Sabbath is also part of a larger structure or way of life: there is a Sabbath-like quality to the year of release, festivals, and offerings. These latter imply, in turn, that the Sabbath was a day for worship (a point unexpressed in the Decalogue) and that there is an intrinsic connection between worship and justice (15:1–18).

3. The section 16:18–18:22 extends the commandment concerning parents by broadening the categories of "mother and father." Judges and officials, kings, Levitical priests, and prophets are also authoritative, parent-like figures. Each group has authority and is worthy of respect. But each also has limitations and restrictions, boundaries beyond which they must not trespass. The honor due these "parents" is thus neither blind nor naive. Judges, for example, must seek justice and that alone (16:20). The king must eschew all accoutrements known from ancient royal ideology (17:14–20). He is not to

hoard possessions nor exalt himself. He is allowed one possession only: a copy of "this torah" (Deuteronomy!) which he is to read continually in order to obey God. This is no ordinary king. This "king" is, in reality, a designated reader—reading torah on behalf of the community.

4. The section 24:8–25:4 is not as clearly delineated as the others, nor as obviously related to the prohibition against false witness. It is like the others, however, in that it broadens the Decalogue's command to apply to a number of subjects. In this case, the emphasis is not on "false witness" but on "your neighbor" (24:10, 13). The statutes and ordinances function to answer the question "and who is my neighbor?" (Luke 10:29). Among the "neighbors" one should consider and help are: the Levitical priests and the diseased; the neighbor who borrows; the poor, whether Israelite or foreigner; families in extreme legal circumstances; aliens, orphans, and widows; judges and litigants; and, last but not least, the hard-working ox (cf. Deut. 22:6–7; 20:19–20; 1 Cor. 9:9; 1 Tim. 5:18). The true neighbor is "the one who shows mercy" (Luke 10:37).

5. The section 26:1–15 mandates a liturgical offering once the people are safely settled. The offering is a thankful response for the gift of land (26:3, 10) and culminates in celebration, which is characteristically extended to the Levites and the aliens (26:11; cf. 12:12, 18–19; 14:27, 29; 16:11, 14). Further, 26:12–13 adds that the tithe is to be given for the Levites and aliens, along with orphans and widows, so that all may eat their fill. To connect 26:1–15 with the tenth commandment is to extend coveting almost beyond recognition. No longer is it only about desiring and taking (Mic. 2:1–2), it is also about hoarding and refusing to give to others— both God and neighbor, especially the less fortunate neighbor. This principle implies that it is possible to covet one's own goods. According to the book of Deuteronomy, all goods belong to Someone Else—Yahweh, who gave the produce that is offered (26:10) and the

bounty that is experienced (26:11; cf. 6:10–12; 8:7–10; 11:9–12, 14–15; also 1:25; 11:17; Lev. 25:23). To covet and hoard is to fundamentally misunderstand the meaning of God's gift.

The statutes and ordinances end with the Israelite in full blossom, neither transgressing nor forgetting any of the Lord's commandments (Deut. 26:13). The Decalogue, even the detailed statutes and ordinances, *can* be kept (cf. 30:11–14). This is a remarkable assertion in light of so much that is said to the contrary in the final chapters of Deuteronomy.

Ratifying the covenant (26:16–28:68). The central core of Deuteronomy concludes with the ratification of the covenant, features of which hark back to 10:12–11:32. Moses stresses that this agreement is marked by mutuality (26:17–19; cf. 27:9–10; 29:13 [12 Heb.]): Israel has agreed to obey God and, consequently, to be Yahweh's treasured possession and holy people; Yahweh has agreed to be Israel's God and to set them high in praise, fame, and honor. Israel must physically manifest this agreement by the public writing of the laws on plastered stones (27:1–8) and by the public litany of curses recited by the Levites and affirmed by the tribes (27:11–26; cf. 11:29–30). These plastered stones are a national mezuzah (6:9), marking Israel's land with "all the words of this law" (27:3, 8). The recitation is a liturgical act of attention to these crucial words. Deuteronomy must be repeatedly written, read, and affirmed.

All seems well, but then comes chap. 28, which is of signal importance in the book. Like other ancient treaties, it contains a list of blessings and curses either of which may result, depending on the behavior of the people. This is nothing new in the parlance of treaties. What is unexpected, however, is the dominance of the curses. Whereas only eleven verses contain blessings (28:3–13), the curses are expansive (28:15–68). The preponderance of curses has led many scholars to relate

Deuteronomy to Neo-Assyrian treaties, which also contain a preponderance of curses. Be that as it may, the ultimate significance of the curses is theological. Two points are worth pondering.

First, the curses undo Israel. All of the prior blessings are systematically and thoroughly refuted. The curses proceed even further, portraying a people who are stricken with disease, who inhabit a deathly land (28:21–24, 28–29, 35–36, 59–61), and who are utterly defeated by their enemies (28:25–26). Israel is finally bereft of its God-given land. In a stunning reversal of 6:10–11 and 8:7–10, others now benefit from Israel's possessions (28:30–33, 38–44). And Israel is alienated from its Lord, serving other gods (28:36). All that is left to Israel is the horror associated with its name (28:37). The curses will be "a sign and a portent forever" (28:46). The horrendous vision of chap. 28 is thus one of cataclysmic destruction and involuntary exile. Israel will go mad in the process (28:28, 34). Among other horrors, it will resort to cannibalism to survive (28:53–57).

Second, at every point in this nightmare, Deuteronomy makes clear that Israel's undoing is Yahweh's doing (28:20–22, 24–25, 27–28, 35–37, 48–49, 59–61, 63–65, 68). Israel has been transformed from a blessed people to insane cannibals in the space of one chapter. This profound shift is due to the contingency inherent in Deuteronomy, the "if" of covenantal obedience. Astonishingly, the chapter even seems to *expect* the curse: the "*if* you will not obey" of 28:15 turns into "*because* you did not obey" in 28:45 and "*because* you did not serve" in 28:47. This inevitability of future failure may simply be the mark of the exilic audience of Deuteronomy. Still, it raises the serious question of whether covenantal retribution is at its end. Tragically, the contingent future now appears altogether certain: it is one of inescapable disobedience and doom. That is where chap. 28 leaves the reader. Yet, while chap. 28 and the Israel it envisions are at an end, Moses and Deuteronomy are not yet finished.

The (Additional) Moab Covenant for the Future (29:1 [28:69 Heb.]–32:52)

The significance of the third superscription is heavily debated. Does Deut. 29:1 conclude 12:1–28:68 (as in the Hebrew versification, which counts it as 28:69)? Or does it introduce the words that follow (as in most English versions)? The weight of the evidence favors the latter option, which means that the words *following* 29:1 (28:69 Heb.) constitute the Moabite covenant. This also means that what has come before has been Deuteronomy's rearticulation of Horeb's covenant for life in the land.

That the Moab covenant exists at all is extraordinary. It demonstrates that a covenant with God, even one akin to Horeb, can be made elsewhere. Covenant making does not happen only on divine mountains (Exod. 3:1); it can also take place down in the valley, on "foreign" soil. Moreover, as foundational as Horeb is, there is yet Moab with which to reckon. Deuteronomy has been revising Horeb from the start, but the Moab covenant is the book's definitive revision.

Still, the Moab covenant is not completely novel. There are elements of continuity (repetition) and discontinuity (revision). In terms of continuity, it is still important to remember the past (29:7–8 [6–7 Heb.]; cf. 2:26–3:22), especially God's delivering acts (29:2–3 [1–2 Heb.]; cf. 29:5 [4 Heb.] with 8:2–5). Obedience is still mandated (29:9a [8a Heb.]; 30:2, 10, 16, 19–20; cf. 4:26; 11:26–28) and the prohibition of idolatry remains a central concern (29:16–20 [15–19 Heb.]; 31:16; cf. 4:16–19; 5:8–9; 7:5). The discontinuous elements, however, are most striking. One is the startling claim that the Israelites have been divinely prevented from understanding matters until "today"—the making of the Moab covenant (29:4, 10 [3, 9 Heb.]). Horeb is like seeing through a glass darkly, Moab face-to-face. Another twist: earlier in Deuteronomy, the present generation was emphasized over both former (5:3) and later generations (11:2). But Moab is not only for those now present, it is also for those *not* present (29:15 [14 Heb.]). Moab is about *now and later*; it extends into the future and unto future generations in a more pronounced way than what has come heretofore.

Future periods and peoples will know of the Moab covenant because they will have this book of torah (Deuteronomy), which explains Israel's calamity (29:21, 27 [20, 26 Heb.]; cf. 30:1). But Moab promises a future of blessing that trumps all exile and curse (cf. 30:3–4 with 28:36–37, 41, 64–68; cf. 30:9 with 28:18, 63). Chapter 28 (and Horeb) may have ended in inevitable failure, a failure still lingering in chap. 29, but Moab knows of a future *beyond* failure that is every bit as inevitable (cf. 4:25–31). That future involves blessing that surpasses the ancestors who are everywhere so important in Deuteronomy (30:5). Then Moab promises the unthinkable: a future that transcends the covenantal contingency that brought Israel to its cataclysmic end (chap. 28). Covenantal contingency is still present in Moab (29:9b [8b Heb.]; 29:20 [29:19 Heb.]-30:5, 15–20; 31:16–21, 29), but there is something beyond it—or, better, *Someone*: Yahweh, who will enable and enact Israel's obedience. This is nowhere clearer than in the contrast between 10:16, which *commands* the Israelites to circumcise their hearts, and 30:6, which *promises* that God will do this very thing for them *and* for their descendants. The astonishing result is automatic enactment of the Shema: loving Yahweh with all the heart and soul.

God's role in helping Israel keep the commandments undergirds 30:11–14. The commandment is "not too hard for you, nor is it too far away" (30:11). It is, rather, "very near to you . . . in your mouth and in your heart for you to observe" (30:14)—evidently because God put it there within reach, because God is the one who came down from heaven and crossed the sea to give it (30:12–13). The commandment is now attainable and observable because God has made it so.

The future Moab envisions is a future without Moses. He must ready Israel for life without him—by writing the torah down, commanding its regular reading, and specifying its privileged place alongside the ark (31:9–13, 26). The reading, hearing, and seeing of this torah will result in proper fear, obedience, and long landedness. This torah—Horeb to Moab—is in place, as a witness (31:26), for the time when Moses is gone.

Israel needs this witness, because when Moses dies, the people will stray (31:16; cf. 31:27–29). The Moab covenant now teeters on the brink because 31:17–21 is just as deadly as chap. 28. There is only one hope: a song that will confront Israel (31:19, 21). What is this song that Moses is told to write and recite (31:19, 22, 30)? Elsewhere, Moses writes the book of torah (31:9, 24), and it is that book that witnesses (31:26). But the song also witnesses (31:19). This overlapping language intimates that the song (32:1–43) *is* torah. At the very least, the song is a poetic version of torah. Poetry must complete the law, torah must include song— perhaps because poetry is eminently memorable: it will not be lost from the children's mouth (31:21). And, for Deuteronomy, remembering means obeying (5:15; 8:2; 9:7; 11:2; 15:15; 16:12; 24:18, 22).

The song is torah because it captures the movement present in Deuteronomy. It begins with God, the perfect Rock (32:4), who is affronted by perverse children (32:5). These well-cared-for children (32:6–15a) became spoiled: they overate and grew fat. Following Mosaic precedent, the song then inscribes the audience into the poem at this precise point: "you grew fat" (32:15b). The children's satiety—*your* satiety—leads to rebellion and pursuing other gods (32:15–18; cf. 31:20; 6:10–15; 8:7–20), which can only lead to God's punishment (32:19–26). The only thing that prevents God from totally annihilating Israel is fear of sending the wrong message to the nation Yahweh uses as the punitive instrument (32:27a).

This is a crucial turning point. God is no longer intent to destroy Israel. The "no people" God used have become overconfident (32:27b; cf. 8:17) and have misun-

derstood the situation. They have succeeded only because God has given Israel up (32:30). But then the song's inscription weighs in. Israel finds itself within the song and interjects: "their rock is not like our Rock" (32:31). At the very moment when they are given up, they claim that Yahweh is still their God—more: their Rock! Israel's unexpected clinging to God leads Yahweh to promise to avenge the people at their lowest point (32:36, 41, 43; cf. Jer. 30:15–16). In reaction to God's about-face, Israel erupts in doxology, praising the Lord who protects them. In a span of forty verses, they have been transformed from "degenerate children" (32:5) and gluttonous idolaters (32:15), to recipients of the Lord's wrath (32:25) and desperate clingers to God (32:31); and, finally, to vindicated victims who praise God for justice and absolution (contrast chap. 28). This song is Deuteronomic torah: it takes Israel from past blessing (the ancestors, Horeb), into disobedience and judgment (Kadesh, calf, exile), and out the other side (Moab) because of the inexplicable mutuality of the covenant that binds Israel to God despite the worst punishment, and that binds God to Israel despite the worst disobedience.

In the end, this torah song is a duet sung with Joshua (32:44). This can only mean that Moses' end is very near. He hears God's command to ascend the mountain and die (32:49–50), but, for once, Moses does *not* obey. He has one final word for his beloved Israel first.

Moses' Deathbed Blessing and Departure (33:1–34:12)

Blessing at last (33:1–29). The final superscription states that Moses' last word to Israel is one of blessing (33:1). This extensive blessing mentions each tribe by name (though Simeon is missing) and provides some counterbalance to the earlier curses. The poem is difficult at several points, but the general sense is clear. The blessings concern life (33:6), God's help against enemies (33:7, 11), safety (33:12), productive land (33:13–16), joy (33:18), enlarged territory (33:20, 23), or general blessedness (33:24–25; cf. 33:22). After blessing the tribes, Moses directs their attention to the *Blesser:* their incomparable God (33:26; cf. 4:34–35, 39; 32:39). Belonging to this incomparable God makes Israel itself incomparable (33:29; cf. 4:6–8, 33; 7:7–8; 9:4–5): incomparably blessed (33:29a), incomparably saved (33:29b), incomparably triumphant (33:29c). Moses' last words are of unbounded praise for the Lord and for the Lord's people. That is how Moses' Deuteronomic sermon finally ends: blessing and praise, God and Israel, together.

The triumph and tragedy of Moses' life (and death) (34:1–12). Chapter 34 finally recounts Moses' long-expected death. He says nothing but follows Yahweh's instructions (34:1; cf. 32:40). With God's help, he is able to see the entirety of the land (34:1–3; cf. 3:27) and then dies "at the LORD's command" (34:5). Deuteronomy notes that Moses could have entered the land: he was old, but his sight was unimpaired, his vigor unabated (34:7; cf. 31:2). He could have entered, but he did not. That means he was *not allowed* to.

Deuteronomy ends, therefore, on a tragically triumphant note. God and Israel are not the only "incomparables" (33:26, 29): Moses, too, is incomparable (34:10). Joshua's wisdom is derivative, coming only through Moses' investiture. Israel listens to Joshua only because of God's command *to Moses* (34:9). The last verses of Deuteronomy go so far as to blur the line between God's deeds in Egypt (34:11) and Moses'. In most instances, "the mighty deeds" and the "terrifying displays of power" that Israel saw are ascribed to *God* (3:24; 4:34; 5:15; 6:21; 7:8, 19; 9:26; 11:2; 26:8). Here, they are credited to *Moses* (34:12) in an unmatched encomium that is one of the most striking examples of divine-human synergy in all of Scripture.

But for all the triumph of Moses' life, his death is tragic. The time for his mourning comes and goes within the span of a single verse (34:8). Despite what happened at Meribath-kadesh (32:51; Num. 20:1–13), Moses comes close to living the perfect human life. But even perfect lives, as Job would insist, are never free of tragedy—perhaps because they are, finally, only human. Moses is incomparable, to be sure, but he is buried in an unknown tomb (34:6). Moses is unrivaled, without doubt, but the time for his mourning is over. New leadership—empowered by Moses—is now in place. A new torah—in continuity with, but appropriately amended and adapted from Horeb—is written, placed beside the ark, ready to be followed, ready to be broken, with words of blessing and curse, explanation and reproof, for all that follows in the land. That so much of the rest of the Old Testament, and so much of the rest of human life, continues to operate by Deuteronomy's standards shows just how effective Moses and his book truly were.

Bibliography

Brueggemann, Walter. *Deuteronomy.* AOTC. Nashville: Abingdon, 2001.

McConville, J. G. *Deuteronomy.* Apollos Old Testament Commentary. Downers Grove, IL: InterVarsity Press, 2002.

Miller, Patrick D. *Deuteronomy.* Interpretation. Louisville: John Knox, 1990.

Olson, Dennis T. *Deuteronomy and the Death of Moses: A Theological Reading.* OBT. Minneapolis: Fortress, 1994.

von Rad, Gerhard. *Deuteronomy.* Translated by Dorothea Barton. OTL. Philadelphia: Westminster, 1966.

Joshua

Gregory Mobley

INTRODUCTION

Holy War in Joshua

The medium is the message for the book of Joshua. Its contents assume the shape of a battle account.

1. Reconnaissance of enemy territory: Israelite spies are sent to Jericho (Josh. 2:1–24).
2. Ritual preparations for warfare: Joshua leads the Israelites in a crossing of the Jordan that recalls the exodus from Egypt, oversees the establishment of the sacred monoliths at Gilgal, and choreographs a series of rites, the circumcision of warriors and the celebration of Passover, to ensure divine support. An anecdote in which a divine messenger appears to Joshua concludes this section and confirms the sacred readiness of the Israelite camp (3:1–5:15).
3. The battle: beginning with their miraculous conquest of Jericho, the Israelite forces under Joshua violently take their promised land from the indigenous peoples of Canaan (6:1–12:24).
4. Distribution of the spoils of warfare: Joshua apportions the conquered territories to the various clans that constitute Israel (13:1–22:34).

Both the contents and shape of Joshua are dominated by warfare. This singular focus presents a theological problem more monumental than the walls of Jericho for interpreters who identify themselves with the biblical tradition and who strive to seek meaning and receive guidance from its witness. Many traditional readings of Joshua assume that the Israelites under Joshua had a divine mandate to conduct genocide, that it was their manifest destiny to conquer, with God on their side, the Judean highlands, Mount Ephraim, the Galilee, the coastal plain of Palestine, and a section of northwest Jordan. "By this you shall know that among you is the living God who without fail will drive out from before you the Canaanites, Hittites, Hivites, Perizzites, Girgashites, Amorites, and Jebusites" (3:10). This verse from early in the book refers to "driving out" these peoples. But the Bible describes that activity more explicitly in its report of what happened when the Israelites came to the Canaanite village of Makkedah: "Joshua took Makkedah on that day, and struck it and its king with the edge of the sword; he utterly destroyed every person in it; he left no one remaining" (10:28). Similar descriptions are given for the Israelite treatment of settlements at Jericho (6:21), Ai (8:24–29), Libnah (10:29–30), Lachish (10:32), Gezer (10:33), Eglon (10:34–35), Hebron (10:36–37), and Debir (10:38–39). The Hebrew word translated above as "utterly destroyed" is a form of *herem*, sometimes translated as "holy war," when it often means something more like "ritual execution" or "martial human sacrifice."

Why did ancient Israelites imagine that God wanted them to erase every vestige of alien peoples and cultures from their midst? The traditional answer is that foreign peoples and cultures were seen as cancerous cells that had to be killed so that the youthful body of Israel and Yahwistic faith could grow up straight and true. It seems inconceivable that the same God whose initial evaluation of creation was "very good," who made a covenant with all life following the flood and pledged never to utterly destroy the world, would have commanded the Israelites to ethnically cleanse the land of milk and honey of peoples also created in the divine image.

This is a theological problem posed by the book of Joshua. In Joshua the sun can be stopped (10:12–14). Whatever theological light Joshua contains threatens to be eclipsed by the holy wars it chronicles.

But these same texts in Joshua that Templar officers used to recite while their medieval knightly peers ate in silence, seeking to inspire their righteous performance in combat against "infidels," have also inspired African American Christians to persevere with dignity in the face of numerous oppressions, giving them a radiant hope that walls of injustice would come tumbling down.

Does it help to know that, despite Joshua's ideology of annihilation, the Bible elsewhere suggests that things did not happen this way? Villages and population groups supposedly erased in Joshua reappear in Judges (cf. Josh. 10:36–37 with Judg. 1:10; Josh. 10:33 with Judg. 1:29). Does it help to know that Joshua is part of a longer literary project, known to scholars as the Deuteronomistic History, spanning Joshua, Judges, Samuel, and Kings? And that this long work was probably composed in the late seventh or sixth century BCE, at a time when religious reformers in Judah feared the imminent demise of their culture?

At such a time, during the reign of Josiah (640–609 BCE) and/or during the early exile, these reformers imagined that only the most radical form of differentiation and separation of Judahite culture from its neighbors would preserve its survival. There is no historical evidence that the Israelites conquered the peoples of Canaan in the Late Bronze Age (ca. 1200–1100 BCE). Skirmishes between Israelites and Canaanites undoubtedly took place, but these were probably more like the border raids and blood feuds depicted in Judges than the wave of conquest described in Joshua.

It is more likely that Joshua reflects the ideology of the era of its composition, the middle of the first millennium BCE, rather than the ideology of its narrative setting, the late second millennium. During Josiah's late-seventh-century reform, for instance, there was a campaign in Judah to eradicate rural shrines and their priesthoods in order to centralize worship in Jerusalem and preserve a faith whose host culture was under tremendous pressure to assimilate and disappear (2 Kgs. 23:1–20). The likelihood that the conquest depicted in Joshua never happened—it probably rewrote ancient history in order to inspire a radical purging of non-Israelite culture from Judah centuries later—blunts the sharp point of the book's martial rhetoric, but it does not obliterate this serrated edge that cuts at the foundations of the ethical ideals formulated in both Judaism and Christianity.

Moreover, the book of Joshua itself is often at odds with this triumphalist martial rhetoric. As noted above, non-Israelite peoples persist even when other texts say they were wiped out. The deepest contradiction appears in the story about Rahab (Josh. 2:1–22; 6:22–25).

The narratives in Joshua do not paint vivid portraits of Israelite heroes. The book does not present such things as Jacob's chicaneries, Moses' self-doubts, Ehud's left-handed dexterity, Gideon's insecure penchant for oracles, Samson's libido-driven wanderlust, Saul's tragic derangement, David's music and murderous ambition, or Elijah and Elisha's cranky intensity. The dominant character is Joshua, who is a speech giver, ritual leader, and colorless commander. Joshua never descends from his pedestal to reveal any humanizing details.

There are beautifully drawn cameos in Joshua's book, but they are of secondary, non-Israelite characters. There is Rahab, the Canaanite prostitute with a heart of gold (Josh. 2; 6). There is a collective character, the villagers of Gibeon (Josh. 9), whose cunning survival skills match those of Israelite patriarchs such as Jacob (Gen. 25:29–34) and matriarchs such as Tamar (Gen. 38:12–30). Rahab and the Gibeonites are the very kind of endearing and crafty underdogs that biblical narratives love. And they are not Israelites.

In a book primarily about chosen people, the most sympathetic and vivid description is devoted to an outsider, Rahab, whose pluck, tenacity, and fidelity to covenant in the face of adversity offers model behavior. A book whose most explicit theological theme is God's covenant with Israel reserves its most colorful storytelling for a narrative where a non-Israelite initiates a covenant with Israel (Josh. 2:12).

In the story about Rahab Providence irrepressibly, mischievously breaks through the surface narrative of the book of Joshua. Her charms and wisdom serve as a muted yet unmistakable counterpoint to the dreary accounts of the mayhem committed by men. Though faint, the countermelody sung by this Canaanite woman is not extinguished by the central movement of the book, the martial music of Joshua's chorus on the march.

The Place of Joshua in the Biblical Canon

The book of Joshua is integrally connected to the books that precede and follow it. Joshua follows Deuteronomy and supplies the next chapter of the story: after the death of Moses at the close of Deuteronomy, his handpicked successor Joshua leads the Israelites into the promised land. Judges, the book that follows Joshua, chronicles the fortunes of the next generation of Israelites, their frontier triumphs and misadventures in the land.

Though modern readers might not share the ancients' enthusiasm for Joshua, it was clearly seen as a high point in the narrative arc of the books Joshua–Judges–Samuel–Kings that follow the Pentateuch (or Torah). God miraculously gives a series of military victories to the Israelites, they come into possession of the land, and they peacefully apportion it among their tribes and clans. Joshua's era is remembered as a golden age when a prophet like Moses led them (Josh. 1:5; 11:15). With the single exception of one miscreant, Achan in Josh. 7, Joshua and his generation are neither grumblers nor idolaters like their ancestors in the wilderness; they are neither blood feuders nor Baal backsliders like their descendants in the era of Judges. Immediately after the notice about Joshua's burial place, the book inscribes a noble epitaph for the era in some of its final lines: "Israel served the LORD all the days of Joshua, and all the days of the elders who outlived Joshua and had known all the work that the LORD did for Israel" (24:31).

Once again, readers face a theological conundrum. The narratives testify that the conquest of Canaan demonstrated that the Lord was faithful and had fulfilled a promise to Abraham (Gen. 13:14–15). The extermination of pagan viruses from the landscape was necessary so that pure faith in the Lord could develop in healthy ways. Biblical authors considered it to be a book with a happy ending (cf. 1 Sam. 12:8; Ps. 105:44–45; Heb. 11:30–31). But the actions described in Joshua are morally reprehensible: genocide, ethnic cleansing, cultural revolutions that seek to eradicate traditional practices, and the seizure of territory from indigenous peoples by colonists who imagine themselves as righteously entitled.

How should one think about this issue? Carefully and with a double consciousness. On the one hand, we must not smooth over the friction between the contents of Joshua and our better nature. On the other hand, the book of Joshua contains many themes of theological interest and unless, like Thomas Jefferson, one wants to take scissors to our Bibles and remove those sections one finds objectionable, the reader is left to struggle with the theologically and ethically uneven amplitude of Scripture. Even more, every honest soul who looks to the Bible as a guide to understanding the personality of the Creator and the purpose of life eventually faces this truth: Ultimate Reality does not conform to our, or any generation's, ideal projections. The book of Joshua is as good a place as any to explore the theologically and ethically uneven amplitude of this Creator, whom Judaism knows as the LORD and Christianity as the triune God.

The Theology of Covenant and the Book of Joshua

The biblical idea of covenant.   The primary theological contribution of the book of Joshua is its emphatic restatement of the idea of covenant, that the relationship between YHWH and Israel reveals the structure of the bond between the Creator and creation. The book of Joshua does not break new ground here; it assumes the backstory of the Torah, the Pentateuch. At its most basic, the biblical view of covenant represents a culturally encoded expression of something universal, namely, moral cause and effect.

The priestly and prophetic inventors of the concept borrowed political ideas from their time and region and translated them into a theological doctrine. The treaties and agreements that ancient potentates entered into with client peoples—and archaeologists have provided us with many examples of such diplomatic covenants from the Bronze and Iron Ages in Syria-Palestine—provide us with the clearest examples of the structures of covenants in ancient Western Asia. A ruler offered protection and benefits to the ruled in exchange for obedience and tribute. The particulars of this exchange were spelled out in documents that enumerated the promises and penalties that bound each party to the other.

David Schloen has demonstrated that these political covenants themselves are a secondary development drawn from the era's dominant patriarchal culture. The relationship of king to subject, or of lord to servant, was an extension of the relationship between fathers and families. The basic cell of the body politic was the unspoken bond between generations in a traditional culture. Fathers had a sacred trust to protect and nurture those in their care (including wives), and the recipients of this care owed fidelity and respect to their patrons. This structure bound fathers to families, husbands to wives, parents to children, older siblings to younger, masters to slaves, landowners to tenants, mentors to apprentices, officers to the rank-and-file, elders to villages, warlords to territories, kings to states, emperors to regions, and, ultimately, deities to worshipers.

Biblical scholars have emphasized the parallels between the formulations in political covenants unearthed by archaeologists and biblical texts that follow the same format. This insight should not obscure a deeper truth: the fabric of all social life in the biblical world was covenantal and based on familial models. Every social encounter, whether between individuals or groups of people, was understood either as hierarchical (parent to child) or peer-based (sibling to sibling). Even acts as common and, at first glance, as politically innocent as greeting rituals expressed the structure of covenants. Dominance and submission were embodied in the choreography of body language (the main biblical verbs for "to worship" in both the Hebrew Bible and Greek New Testament have identical meanings, "to physically bow down before," as the warlord Joshua does before his angelic superior officer in Josh. 5:14).

Biblical covenants involved emotional qualities. The ancient world was acutely oral, intensely social, and overwhelmingly personal. Fathers were not remote

Victorian domestic figureheads, rulers were not distant administrators, the gods were not Unmoved Movers. These conventional hierarchies were embedded in personal relationships. William Moran has demonstrated that ancient covenants often utilized terms for "love." Moran's insight helps readers understand that the biblical call for Israel "to love" the Lord its God was an exhortation to "obey" the terms of the covenant. The concept of the love of God in Deuteronomy, an idea upon which the book of Joshua builds, is neither mystical nor intangible. In other words, to "love" God is to keep God's commandments (Deut. 6:5–6; John 14:15).

Moran's insight also helps readers understand the personal nature of covenants. These terms for love that the Bible and ancient diplomatic texts used to express the bond between superior and inferior parties in a social pact were identical to the terms used to express, in other contexts, friendship, familial bonds, and physical intimacy. Deeper even than the conventions that assigned superior and inferior status to parties was the bond of relationship, of mutuality, and of interdependence. This means that once parties had entered into covenant, the contingencies of a relationship could overrule the constraints of hierarchy. Abraham could reverse the covenantal dynamic and deign to teach the Lord about justice (Gen. 18:16–33). After the golden calf incident, Moses could tell the Lord, who was intent on destruction, "You repent, you turn; do not destroy *your* people" (Exod. 32:11–14, my trans.).

This personal aspect of these covenants cannot be fully measured by either the mathematics of tit for tat or the mercantile exchange of benefits for services. Covenants had something effluent and elusive at their heart, the chemistry of relationship.

And what of the contents of Israel's covenant with the Lord? If one steps back from all the details—from all 613 laws Jewish tradition enumerates in the Mosaic instruction, from all ten of the commandments, from the priestly code

that the Torah contends governs all commerce between Creator and created—one discovers that God created reality to work according to moral cause and effect. The biblical view of covenant enshrines this truth in religious language. The covenant proclaims that God is reliable and that the universe operates according to causality. As Donald Harman Akenson observed, this formulation of causality in religious terms allowed the Israelites to think historically and to plot the fortunes of their culture along the graph of divine justice, that is, to narrate the story that has become our Bible.

The primary fact of covenant is the personal relationship of reciprocity between Creator and creation. In addition to duty and obligation and convention, the biblical idea of covenant expresses, in Hebrew terms, divine *hesed*; in Greek, *agape*; in plain English, love.

Covenant in the book of Joshua. The book of Joshua opens with a divine speech that refers to the covenants God made with Abraham (Josh. 1:6) and Moses (1:7–8) and ends with Joshua's speech about the terms of the covenant (23:1–16), followed by a ceremony in which the community makes its vows to live by this pact (24:1–28). The opening and closing chapters of the book, respectively, frame the covenantal dynamic: the primacy of divine initiative (1:1–9) and the corresponding human response (24:1–28). In between, the literary landscape of Joshua is filled with icons and monuments that are memorials to divine patronage and serve as rallying points for community solidarity: the ark of the covenant, the box that contained Mosaic scrolls (Josh. 3), and the Gilgal monoliths that commemorate the twelve tribes, their deliverance at the Red Sea, and their crossing of the Jordan into the promised land (Josh. 4).

This book claims that Joshua and his generation lived up to their side of the bargain (24:31) and reaped the benefits. But they are not the only covenant partners portrayed in the book. In the narrative that spans Josh. 2–6, Rahab proposes a covenant to the Israelite spies who lodge in her establishment: "Now then, since I have dealt kindly with you, swear to me by the LORD that you in turn will deal kindly with my family" (2:12). The Hebrew verb translated twice above as "deal kindly" is a form of the word *hesed*, "steadfast fidelity." In the story of Israel's conquest of Jericho, Rahab extends *hesed* to the spies, and the Israelites return the favor to her and her family (6:25).

In Josh. 9 the inhabitants of the Canaanite village of Gibeon under false pretenses maneuver the Israelites into a covenant of peace with them; the Gibeonites masquerade as recent immigrants themselves with no territory worth conquering: "We have come from a far country; so now make a treaty [Heb. *berit*, "covenant"] with us" (9:6). The Israelite leaders who received the Gibeonite embassy did not seek divine counsel ("So the leaders partook of their provisions, and did not ask direction from the LORD," 9:14), and fell for it. But a deal is a deal, a covenant is a covenant, and the Israelites live up to this oath they made in vain, letting the Gibeonites live and, later, defending them (Josh. 10). On theological and social levels, then, the book of Joshua emphasizes the centrality of covenant.

Structure

The book of Joshua is made up of four basic parts.

1. The first section, Josh. 1, relays a call to arms up and down the chain-of-command. The Lord commissions Joshua to lead the Israelite tribes into Canaan and to inherit the land promised to their ancestors (1:2–6) . . . with this proviso. Joshua and the people shall succeed only if they obey the Mosaic teaching (1:7–9). Joshua passes the commission on to his officers (1:10–11) and to the militia of the Transjordanian tribes (1:12–15). They in turn vow their allegiance and exhort Joshua to be as good a leader as Moses had been (1:16–18).

2. The next section, Josh. 2–12, mixes battle narratives with descriptions of religious ceremonies. Its largest set pieces are two relatively long accounts about the conquest of Jericho (Josh. 2–6) and of Ai (Josh. 7–8); both include descriptions of rituals. In these eleven chapters one finds the most entertaining and vivid material of the book: the stories about Rahab and the spies, the miraculous tumbling of the walls of Jericho, Joshua's cunning stratagem that defeats the inhabitants of Ai, and the ruse of the Gibeonites that enables them to make peace, at an ironic cost, with the Israelites.

3. Joshua 13–22 represents a topographic tour de force and narrative nadir in its exhausting demarcation of the territorial allotments granted to each of the Israelite tribes.

4. The final section, Josh. 23–24, focuses on exhortation. Joshua waxes Moses-like in a long farewell speech to the people, admonishing them to remain separate from the nations through devotion to the Torah (Josh. 23). Then Joshua leads them in a rite of commitment to this covenant (Josh. 24).

COMMENTARY

Be Not Afraid (1:1–18)

The initial chapter of Joshua contains a divine speech directed to Joshua (1:1–9). It is a "war oracle," the words a religious intermediary gave to combatants on the eve of battle (e.g., Deut. 20:1–4). A person heading into battle typically asked a yes/ no question, "Should we engage the enemy?" "Is it time to mount an assault?" "Is this person guilty of a transgression?" In response, the priest manipulated an oracular device—for example, the sacred dice, the Urim and Thummim—to provide an answer (e.g., Josh. 7:16–19; 1 Sam. 14:36–42).

If the response was positive, then the priest announced the call to arms through a formula drawn from a mixture of these phrases:

Do not be afraid.
Be strong.
Be brave.
Do not be terrified.
Do not panic.
For YHWH accompanies you.

The war oracle provides the matrix for these refrains ("Be not afraid"; "the LORD is with you") that become enduring features of biblical rhetoric.

The phrases soon moved beyond martial contexts. The prophet Second Isaiah employs them to embolden exiles to return to Judah (Isa. 43:1–7). The prophet Haggai uses them to exhort the community to rebuild the temple (Hag. 2:4–5). The angel Gabriel addresses them to a young woman facing an unexpected pregnancy (Luke 1:28–30).

If one imagines that the scroll of Joshua emerged as part of the Deuteronomistic History during the time of Josiah's reform or, alternately, a few decades later during the exile, then these exhortations in Joshua to be strong and trust in God had already exited Israel's military discourse. The exhortations involve the communal resilience and solidarity necessary for the community of Judah to survive Assyrian and Babylonian degradations, and to resist the cultural assimilation that would destroy the Mosaic vision. The Bible itself spiritualizes the war oracle, as subsequent Jews and Christians would, extending the call for courage to every arena of existence.

Still, even in these secondary contexts where the war oracle has been transformed into the oracle of encouragement, the stakes remain grave. Physical as well as moral courage are necessary for the spiritual life. "It is appointed for men once to die" (Heb. 9:27, my trans.), but not twice. The exhortation that dominates the initial section of Joshua, "Be not afraid," invites readers in every age to live fearlessly in the face of illness, catastrophe, and oppression.

The Wars of YHWH (2:1–12:24)

The memorable stories in Joshua all occur in this section, beginning with the long account (Josh. 2–6) of the conquest of Jericho.

The conquest of Jericho (chaps. 2–6): Linen. The Jericho story has a sandwich structure. The initial reconnaissance and final seizure of the town are featured in the first and last chapters of the unit (2:1–24; 6:1–25). In between, a sizable embedded section (Josh. 3–5) locates some of the signature elements of Judahite culture—the practice of circumcision, the celebration of Passover, the founding of a pilgrimage site at Gilgal—in the landscape of Israel's initial generation in Canaan.

Rahab, a Canaanite woman who hides the Israelite spies on the roof of her bordello, is the central character in the Jericho story. The details related to "flax" (2:6) provide a unifying element throughout the adventure. Flax is a wetland, reedy herb that was cultivated both for its oil and for its fibers, which were woven into linen. The sheaves under which the Israelite spies hid (2:6) were flax stalks that had been soaked in order to articulate the fibers that, once dry, could be manufactured into cloth.

The production of linen from flax was a woman's industry in ancient Syria-Palestine, as suggested by the description of the "virtuous woman" in Prov. 31: "She seeks wool and flax, and works with willing hands. . . . She makes linen garments and sells them" (Prov. 31:13, 24).

So, in this story, the reader has a window into the economic life of one such virtuous Iron Age woman. Rahab had her cottage linen industry. Furthermore, it is likely that both the rope with which the Israelite spies escape through her window (Josh. 2:15) and the scarlet cord that marks her house as protected (2:18) were her handiwork. Thus this unlikely outcast hero makes everything happen in the story: she initiates the covenant with the spies (2:12) and she is the mediator of their salvation.

The story features another window (2:15). This is the first, but not the last, biblical story to employ the motif of a male hero escaping through a window; it also occurs in stories about David (1 Sam. 19:12) and Paul (Acts 9:23; 2 Cor. 11:32). This recurring motif functions as a counterpoint in stories about male heroes. Even the heroes depend ultimately on the kindness of others, upon grace, to survive.

The conquest of Ai (chaps. 7–8): Joshua's javelin. The narrative about the conquest of Ai presents another structural sandwich: the battle narrative has two parts (7:2–5; 8:1–29) that surround a middle section describing a ritual (7:6–26). The Israelites' initial assault on Ai is repulsed (6:2–5). A second assault succeeds because of a ruse (8:3–8). In between, the account of Achan's violation of the code of holy war—he had taken forbidden plunder—explains that the initial failure was due to a lack of holiness.

Joshua 8 has many of the necessary parts for a classic biblical adventure story. Joshua turns the first defeat at Ai into a strategic advantage: he leads the main force right up to the city gates, enticing the forces of Ai to leave the city and chase the Israelites back into the hills, just as before. But this time, a smaller elite band of warriors goes into hiding north of the town. Once the Canaanites leave their settlement to chase Joshua and his camp, the special forces enter the defenseless town, and the men of Ai find themselves caught in a vise of Israelites forces.

The story in Josh. 8 includes several vivid details such as the javelin that Joshua raises to signal his army (8:18, 26), and the smoke of the burning city that sends the men of Ai into a panic and, at the same time, informs Joshua that the ambushers are now inside the town (8:20–21). There is, however, minimal personalizing detail about Joshua's javelin that might rival Gideon's trumpet or David's wadi stones as iconic of folk tradition.

The ruse of the Gibeonites (chap. 9): "We are your servants." The Canaanite villagers from Gibeon avoid destruction by impersonating recent immigrants. They don the garb of itinerants and deferentially beg for terms of peace from Joshua. In their pleas, they repeat the phrase, "We are your servants" (9:8, 9, 11). Israel's leaders, flattered and fattened (9:14a) by the Gibeonites, agree to these terms without consulting for divine direction (9:14b). The penalty that the Israelites must pay for their impiety, cupidity, and stupidity is the loss of Gibeon from their estate. In a final twist, however, the Gibeonites receive their just deserts as well. They get precisely what they asked for: perennial survival and perennial servility (9:22–27).

The campaign against the Amorites (chap. 10): Stones. The motif of "big stones" is the structural beam that spans the narrative of Josh. 10 in which the Israelites defeat a coalition of five Amorite militias and execute their warlords. The Lord sends "huge stones," hailstones, that add to the panic of an ancient army in chaotic retreat (10:11). The Amorite leaders seek refuge in a cave that becomes a prison once the Israelites roll "large stones" against its mouth (10:18). After the Amorite kings are removed from the cave and ritually murdered, their corpses are buried under a mound of "large stones" (10:27).

The narratives in Josh. 2–10 demonstrate the bracketing style and moralistic theology common to biblical storytelling, a style rooted in the world of oral communication. A motif mentioned early in the story—the sheaves of flax on Rahab's roof, a javelin, the Gibeonites' deferential snare that eventually entraps them, the boulders of Josh. 10—all undergird the narrative, granting a sense of closure to the audience and a mnemonic aid to the storyteller.

This oral style comes with a world-view. For these storytellers and their audiences, reality did not have loose ends. It was as ordered and just as the verbal and structural symmetries of these stories. Underdogs triumph, fools are punished, and miscreants are discovered. These stories proclaim that there is closure, both narrative and moral. These stories take place in a world enveloped by an invisible moral atmosphere that ensures the operation of ethical cause and effect. Furthermore, the Invisible Hand has a deft touch, imbuing the science of causality with levity and artistry, with poetic justice, as when the Gibeonites hoist themselves on their own rhetorical petard.

Later biblical books such as Ecclesiastes and Job will challenge the idea that human fortunes transparently reveal the workings of divine justice. But the principle, though challenged in some biblical Wisdom literature and compromised daily in human experience, remains in force. Every second, on innumerable levels, the chain of causality binds reality together. Faith in God's justice is tempered by Ecclesiastes' complaint that a mist of vanity obscures human apprehension of the divine will and by Job's testimony, credible still, that life is unfair. But faith in divine justice, the idea at the heart of so many ancient didactic stories, is essential for all who would live with purpose and hasten to love.

Dividing the Spoils (13:1–22:34)

The boundaries of this section of Joshua are clearly marked by the verbal repetition of address to the Transjordanian tribes (cf. 13:1–32 and 22:1–32). Also the resumptive phrase that begins the final section of the book ("Joshua was old and well advanced in years," 23:1) returns readers to the beginning of this section (13:1) before embarking on the tedious and circuitous land survey in chaps. 13–22.

The bald claim of this section is that God has taken territory from indigenous peoples and given it to a favored people, Israel. These chapters provide the details of how this territorial plunder was to be apportioned among the winners. What did this account about the distribution of land mean for ancient Israelites?

According to this story, God had given each Israelite clan and family a stake. God was the owner of this land, of which each family served as tenant. The allotments provided the basis for a family's economic subsistence over generations. Farms that became alienated from clans due to indenturement and debt were to be restored to them in years of Jubilee (Lev. 25:8–17), so that transgenerational poverty did not cripple families. On each of these holdings was a family burial plot or cave. On their family farms, every Israelite was nestled against the bosom of its patriarchal and matriarchal ancestors.

From a historical distance, then, as when Elijah champions the rights of the farmer Naboth against the seizure of his land by a corrupt king (1 Kgs. 21), the boundary lists and territorial arrangements of Josh. 13–22, as some part of a land system, served a crucial social good, offering a measure of order and a basis for fairness in land dealings. It provided the basis for the lawful and peaceful expression of territoriality, that basic human impulse that, unchecked, issues in a rapacious and murderous Darwinian free-for-all. This section of Joshua does not, however, help to resolve a matter that continues to bedevil humanity, namely that all systems of territorial law, however thoughtfully formulated and faithfully practiced, inevitably serve the interests of whoever happens to occupy the land when the system is enacted.

Covenant Renewal (23:1–24:33)

In the final chapters of the book, Joshua reviews the covenant and God's fulfillment of the divine end of the bargain ("not one thing has failed of all the good things that the LORD your God promised concerning you," 23:14), and then asks the Israelites to reaffirm their commitment: "Choose this day whom you will serve." This covenant is conditional ("If you forsake the LORD . . . then he will turn and do you harm," 24:20), yet is it based on the primacy of divine bounty, the gift of "a land on which [they] had not labored, and towns that [they] had not built, . . . the fruit of vineyards and oliveyards that [they] did not plant" (24:13).

The covenant renewal at the close of the book reminds every generation of the freedom to choose, in its day, and by its terms, whether it will keep faith with the biblical God. There is something fragile about this covenant. It is as if the world is suspended by a frayed rope above an abyss. The cords of that rope consist of faiths made good, promises kept, and loyalties repaid. Every promise kept, every covenant honored, and every virtue performed is crucial to the fate of the world.

But what of the ghosts of the Canaanites who worked that land, who built those towns, and who planted those vineyards? They haunt all sacred pageants that reflect these narratives. These ghosts do not ask readers to live without covenants and commitments, without identities and territories. They do, however, ask readers to balance particular covenants, the covenant revealed through Moses for Jews, the covenant with Jesus Christ for Christians, with the covenant God made with all humanity through Noah. The Noahic covenant expresses God's commitment to the preservation of

all life and demands in return that humans check their murderous impulses, prohibiting them from killing any bearer of the divine image (Gen. 9:1–17).

Joshua 24 does not include a description of the sky above Shechem on the day that Joshua presided over the rites that close the book. Can one not imagine Noah's rainbow arcing in hope and judgment over the entire landscape of Joshua?

Bibliography

Akenson, Donald Harman. *Surpassing Wonder: The Invention of the Bible and the Talmuds.* 1998. Repr. Chicago: University of Chicago Press, 2001.

Moran, William. "The Ancient Near Eastern Background of the Love of God in Deuteronomy." Repr. in *Essential Papers on Israel and the Ancient Near East,* edited by Frederick E. Greenspahn, 103–15. New York: New York University Press, 1991.

Nelson, Richard. *Joshua.* OTL. Louisville: Westminster John Knox, 1997.

Schloen, J. David. *The House of the Father as Fact and Symbol: Patrimonialism in Ugarit and the Ancient Near East.* Winona Lake, IN: Eisenbrauns, 2001.

Trible, Phyllis. *Texts of Terror: Literary-Feminist Readings of Biblical Narratives.* Philadelphia: Fortress, 1984.

Judges

Ken Stone

INTRODUCTION

The book of Judges offers a narrative account of Israel's past between the death of Joshua and the birth of Samuel. In its canonical form, the book includes several passages that articulate a clear theological interpretation of this period. According to this orthodox interpretation of the past, the period of Judges was characterized by a cyclical pattern that is set in motion when the Israelites break covenant with their God, YHWH, and worship other deities. Angered by such worship, YHWH hands the Israelites over to non-Israelite oppressors. When the Israelites cry out, YHWH raises up "judges" who deliver the Israelites from their enemies. After the death of a judge, however, the Israelites return to the worship of other gods, thereby continuing the cycle of oppression and deliverance.

While this theological framework is important for understanding the book of Judges, the stories inserted into the framework often reveal a more compli-cated world. Here we find individuals whose actions cannot always be characterized neatly as righteous or wicked, moments at which God's actions or intentions are either unclear or troubling, ambiguous or fluid boundaries between "Israelite" and "non-Israelite," conflicts among the Israelite tribes themselves, and unexpected developments that are often related to matters of gender. If one reads the individual tales of the judges while asking how clearly those stories illustrate the theological framework, one discovers much variation. Thus the theological significance of Judges cannot be derived only from the orthodox interpretive framework. Rather, the complicated structure of Judges encourages readers to acknowledge, and to grapple with the theological implications of, the tension that usually exists in religious traditions between stable orthodox frameworks and the heterogeneous realities of the lives of the people of God.

COMMENTARY

Chapters 1–2

Judges opens "after the death of Joshua" (1:1), and its first chapter focuses on attempts by Israelite tribes to take possession of Canaan. Particular emphasis is placed on Judah, which is identified by YHWH as the tribe that will go up first against the Canaanites (1:2). The initial selection of Judah by YHWH may point toward a theological bias on the writer's part. The tribe of Judah is understood in the Bible to form the core of the southern kingdom of Judah. YHWH's statement that "I have given the land into [Judah's] hand" (1:2) would resonate with an audience sympathetic to traditions about YHWH's covenant with the Davidic dynasty in Judah, or about YHWH's identification of the temple in Judah as the place for proper worship.

Although Jerusalem, eventual site of that temple, is not yet a Judahite city at the beginning of Judges, Judah captures it and destroys its inhabitants (1:8). Judah destroys other Canaanite cities as well, sometimes with the assistance of the tribe of Simeon. However, Judah is not able to destroy "the inhabitants of the plain," who have iron chariots (1:19). Other tribes, too, are unable to drive former inhabitants out of their territories, though some of these inhabitants are subjected to forced labor.

Since God has promised Canaan to the Israelites, the continued existence of these other peoples is a theological problem with which Judges wrestles. At the beginning of chap. 2 (my trans.), a "messenger of YHWH" reminds the Israelites that YHWH forbade them to make covenants with inhabitants of the land and commanded them to tear down altars of those inhabitants. Because Israel has disobeyed these edicts, YHWH allows inhabitants to remain in the land as adversaries for the Israelites. Thus, according to 2:1–5, the continued existence of non-Israelite inhabitants follows from Israelite disobedience.

These themes are given an expanded, and slightly different, theological interpretation in 2:11–23. According to this passage and several similar ones scattered throughout the book, the Israelites during the period of the judges continually anger YHWH by worshiping other deities, such as the god Baal and the goddesses Astarte and Asherah. YHWH, in angry retribution, causes or allows enemies of the Israelites to oppress the Israelites and prevail over them in battle. When moved to pity by the groans of the Israelites (2:18), YHWH raises "judges" who deliver the Israelites. Yet once a judge dies, the Israelites anger YHWH again, even surpassing previous generations in their wickedness. Thus the cycle continues. According to this passage, YHWH allows non-Israelites to remain in the land not only as punishment for disobedience (2:21), but also to "test" Israel's covenant faithfulness (2:22).

When reading these theological interpretations, it is helpful to remember that Judges constitutes one part of a larger theological account of Israel's past, found in the books of Deuteronomy, Joshua, Judges, Samuel, and Kings. This narrative complex (sometimes called the "Deuteronomistic History") interprets the imagined past of the Israelites by evaluating it against covenant stipulations found in Deuteronomy. Failure to live according to these stipulations is blamed for disastrous events, including those that finally bring the independent nations of Israel and Judah to an end. Such devastating events are understood by the Deuteronomistic History as divine retribution. Passages such as Judg. 2:11–23 encourage the reader of that longer story of Israel to interpret the period of Judges in terms of a persistent tendency of the Israelites to order their lives according to practices of their neighbors rather than the demands of God.

Readers have long noted that the opening chapters of Judges contain several interpretive problems. Some of these problems involve contradictions between the books of Joshua and Judges. For example, certain cities that are said by the book of Joshua to have been destroyed completely during the period of Joshua, such as Hebron and Debir, are still in existence and inhabited by non-Israelites at the beginning of Judges. Such differences highlight that the Bible is a collection of numerous traditions, which often stand in tension with one another, and not the single, unified book that it is sometimes made out to be.

From the point of view of theological ethics, more serious problems concern the assumptions about warfare that underlie

Judges. While recounting Judah's military exploits, Judges tells us that Judah and Simeon destroyed a city called Zephath, which "they devoted to destruction" and renamed "Hormah" (1:17). This new name is derived from the same word that, in its verbal form, is translated as "they devoted to destruction." The word refers to the Israelite custom of *herem*, also called the "ban." According to biblical traditions about *herem*, YHWH sometimes demanded the total destruction of an enemy city's inhabitants, including all men, women, children, and animals. This type of slaughter is attributed to Judah in 1:17, and the specification that YHWH was with Judah during this period (1:19) underscores the writer's assumption that such annihilation was divinely approved.

Throughout history, readers of the Bible have been troubled by this tradition of divinely ordered massacre, which appears also in several other biblical books. Scholars have sometimes explained it away by suggesting that it shows how debased the Canaanites were, but there is no historical evidence to support this suggestion. We know from archaeological evidence that the Moabites, who used nearly identical language to speak about the same military custom, practiced it against the Israelites themselves while associating it with their Moabite god rather than YHWH. Thus the practice of *herem* seems not to have been distinctive of Israel, historically. Both the practice of *herem* and the attempt to justify this brutal practice by appealing to divine approval are examples of ways in which biblical literature rests on assumptions that Israel shared with its neighbors. Recognition that many modern people of faith reject such assumptions about violence and the Divine is crucial for any responsible theological use of the Bible.

Troubling assumptions about gender also pervade Judges, which includes more female characters than most biblical books. Yet some of these characters act in unexpected ways. In 1:12 Caleb, acting like a typical patriarch, promises his daughter Achsah to any man who captures the enemy city of Kiriath-sepher. When Caleb's kinsman Othniel captures the city, Caleb gives Achsah to Othniel. Yet Achsah, though treated like property, shows herself to be assertive. Although women rarely own property in the Hebrew Bible, Achsah demands and receives watering springs from her father (1:15) to go with her field (1:14). Thus her story shows that even when constrained by unjust social structures, oppressed persons may act to improve their circumstances.

Chapter 3

At the beginning of chap. 3, nations left in the land to "test" Israel are identified. Intermarriage between Israelites and other nations is noted with disapproval and cited as a cause for the worship of other gods.

Attention then returns to Othniel. Under the influence of the "spirit of the LORD," Othniel "judges" and serves as "deliverer" for the Israelites (3:9–10) when they are punished for apostasy. The role of the "spirit of the LORD" in his actions underscores the charismatic nature of leadership in Judges. However, irony is introduced when the author observes that Othniel, kinsman of Caleb and "son of Kenaz," is apparently a Kenizzite rather than an Israelite (Num. 32:12; Josh. 14:6, 16). Kenizzites are included among the nations whose land YHWH has promised to Abraham (Gen. 15:18–21). Logically, they could have been considered enemies of the Israelites. Yet this Kenizzite functions as deliverer and judge for Israel. Thus the boundaries between Israel and its neighbors are blurred, thereby suggesting that the "nations" are not always viewed as negatively as the beginning of chap. 3 implies.

The stories of deliverers continue in chap. 3 with the tale of Ehud, a Benjaminite who kills the Moabite king Eglon, thereby providing Israel with a period of rest in the cycle of oppression and peace. The humorous story of this assassination (involving body waste and body fat) is probably derived from folk narratives that were given new meaning when inserted into a theological framework.

Another deliverer, Shamgar ben Anat, is noted in a single verse (3:31), though his name recurs once in chap. 5. Linguists point out that his name is Hurrian rather than Semitic. Thus his identity as an Israelite is also in doubt. His appellative, "ben Anat," which literally means "son of Anat," is often understood to mean simply that he was from the town of Anat. However, the appellative may be related instead to the war goddess Anat, associated in ancient Near Eastern texts with warriors, and could indicate that Shamgar was a non-Israelite mercenary. Once again, hints of ethnic and religious heterogeneity are found in the stories of Israel's judges.

Chapters 4–5

Chapter 4 introduces Deborah, a woman prophet and the only female judge mentioned in Judges. Translators call her "wife of Lappidoth" (4:4), but her marital status is actually unclear. The phrase "wife of Lappidoth" is obscure and may be rendered "woman of torches" or "fiery woman." The insistence on giving Deborah a husband could result in part from discomfort among biblical interpreters with a strong, unmarried female character who commands men. The identification of Deborah as both prophet and judge, however, indicates that even in the patriarchal world of ancient Israel, it was possible for some women to take on political and religious leadership roles.

Accompanied by Deborah and led by the Naphtalite Barak, the tribes of Naphtali and Zebulun defeat a powerful Canaanite army with YHWH's help. While most of the Canaanites are killed, the Canaanite commander, Sisera, flees to the tent of Jael, a Kenite woman whose husband's clan is at peace with the Canaanites. Though Jael pretends to offer Sisera hospitality and a hiding place, once Sisera is asleep she kills him by driving a tent peg through his head. The

enemy of the Israelites is slain not by an Israelite but rather by a non-Israelite who, in fulfillment of Deborah's prediction (4:9), is a woman.

These events are referred to again in chap. 5, a lengthy poem often referred to as the "Song of Deborah." The poem, which is difficult for even skilled linguists to translate, is considered by many scholars to be one of the oldest texts in the Bible. Its version of events is somewhat different from that in chap. 4. Here, for example, other northern tribes in addition to Naphtali and Zebulun participate in the battle; and Jael apparently kills Sisera while he is standing up rather than while he is asleep (5:26–27). Moreover, Shamgar ben Anat is represented here as a contemporary of Jael rather than a predecessor (5:6).

The poem is sometimes cited by those who find evidence of a revolutionary theological perspective, favoring the economically or socially marginalized, in the Bible. An obscure passage seems to pit an Israelite peasant class against a caravan trade that would have circulated between urban Canaanite centers (5:6–7). In that context, Deborah, "a mother in Israel" (5:7), is praised for rallying tribes who are victorious over "the kings of Canaan" (5:19). As in chap. 4, YHWH is credited with a spectacular victory that appears to involve miraculous intervention on behalf of the oppressed.

While YHWH is identified explicitly as the God of Israel (5:3), the picture of YHWH that we find in this poem, marching to the accompaniment of thunderstorms while the earth quakes and mountains shake (5:4–5), recalls representations of such storm gods as Baal in nonbiblical Semitic texts. Moreover, the tribes of Reuben, Dan, and Asher are criticized for failing to participate in the battle, as are Gilead (an area east of the Jordan that seems to be understood as a tribe in the book of Judges) and an otherwise unknown group referred to as Meroz. Clearly, there is dissension among the Israelite tribes. Simeon, Levi, and Judah are not even mentioned.

Chapters 6–9

When the Israelites again worship other gods, YHWH causes them to suffer at the hands of the Midianites, who disrupt Israelite food production. In response to the cries of the Israelites, YHWH calls Gideon, a member of the tribe of Manasseh, to deliver Israel from the Midianites. After receiving a miraculous sign, Gideon, at YHWH's command, destroys both an altar to Baal and an *asherah*, a tree or a cultic object made of wood, which may have been associated with the goddess Asherah. These objects apparently belong to Gideon's own father, Joash (6:25). Yet when the townspeople, upon discovering Gideon's deed, threaten to kill Gideon, Joash intervenes on Gideon's behalf, pointing out that Baal himself should "contend" against the person who tore down his altar, if Baal is a real god. This story functions as an explanation for Gideon's other name, Jerubbaal, which means "Let Baal contend" (6:32). While the author of Judges clearly considers the worship of Baal and Asherah to be reprehensible, the story of Gideon also shows that many Israelites considered such worship quite normal.

Gideon, inspired by the "spirit of the LORD" (6:34), gathers an army from several northern tribes. Before leading his troops to do battle with the Midianites, Gideon demands and receives additional miraculous signs involving dew and a fleece of wool (6:36–40). YHWH, however, is concerned that a battle won by too large an army will convince the Israelites that they, rather than YHWH, are responsible for victory. Thus YHWH orders Gideon to follow procedures that reduce the number of soldiers from thirty-two thousand to three hundred. With YHWH's assistance, Gideon and his small force bring about the defeat of the Midianites.

After quarreling with members of the tribe of Ephraim (8:1–3), Gideon kills two Midianite kings. The Israelites then attempt to persuade Gideon to become their king and establish a hereditary dynasty. Gideon rejects the offer, assert-

ing that YHWH alone should rule over Israel (8:23). This assertion reflects a strain of biblical thought, also found in 1 Samuel (e.g., 1 Sam. 8), which, for religious reasons, views kingship negatively. Its association with Gideon might seem to indicate that Gideon was a zealous devotee of YHWH. Yet Gideon also fashions an "ephod" of gold, which apparently becomes an object of worship for the Israelites and the family of Gideon (8:27). Because an ephod is normally an object of clothing, sometimes worn by a priest, scholars suggest that this golden ephod may have been worn by an idol. In any case, the reference to the ephod causes the story of Gideon to end on an ambivalent note. There is peace in the land for forty years under Gideon (8:28), but Gideon and his family are associated with apostasy. The consequences of his leadership are thus not entirely good or entirely bad, but rather ambiguous. As it does in several other cases, the book of Judges here shows divinely chosen leaders to be flawed human beings, capable of doing great things with the help of God's spirit but capable of acting in dubious ways as well.

The negative perspective on Gideon's family is intensified by the story of one of his sons, Abimelech, whose name ironically means "my father is king." Gideon, who has many wives, is said to have seventy sons (8:30; 9:5). However, Abimelech's mother is referred to as Gideon's "concubine" (8:31), a female sexual partner who apparently has a lower status than a wife. This institution of concubinage is accepted in the Hebrew Bible, but Abimelech's status appears to be differentiated from that of Gideon's other sons by the fact that his mother is only a concubine (cf. "slave woman," 9:18).

Abimelech kills all of his brothers except the youngest, Jotham, who hides in order to survive. Abimelech is then declared king at his mother's hometown of Shechem, a city in the territory of Ephraim that served as a site for covenant making in Josh. 24. Jotham uses a parable to warn the leaders of Shechem that their selection of Abimelech as king may have disastrous consequences for them.

After Abimelech has ruled Israel for three years, God sends an "evil spirit" (9:23) to stir up dissension between Abimelech and the rulers of Shechem. This association of God with an "evil spirit" may seem strange to modern readers. It occurs elsewhere in the Bible in the story of Saul (1 Sam. 16:14–15; 18:10) and reflects an unusual willingness, on the part of some biblical writers, to consider God the cause of developments that are acknowledged to be morally ambiguous. The consequences of God's "evil spirit" are negative for individuals affected by it. Here the conflict between Abimelech and Shechem culminates with Abimelech's destruction of Shechem and its temple, and the slaying of Shechem's population. When Abimelech subsequently attacks the city of Thebez, however, he is mortally wounded by a woman in the city's tower who drops a millstone on his head. Wishing to avoid being remembered for having been slain by a woman, Abimelech orders his armorbearer to kill him. Both his death and the massacre of the Shechemites are attributed by the narrator to God, who wishes to punish Abimelech for the slaughter of his brothers, and the people of Shechem for having made Abimelech their king.

Chapters 10–12

Chapter 10 opens with brief reports about Tola, from the tribe of Issachar, who judges Israel for twenty-three years; and about Jair the Gileadite, who judges Israel for twenty-two years. These reports are followed by another account of Israelite apostasy, which causes YHWH to turn Israel over to Ammonite oppressors. Once again, the Israelites cry to YHWH for deliverance. On this occasion, YHWH at first refuses to deliver Israel, replying to their cries scornfully that they should ask for deliverance from the other gods they worship (10:14). Once the Israelites put away their other gods, however, YHWH is no longer able to watch Israel suffer. This account of alternating divine anger

and divine compassion leads to the story of Jephthah the Gileadite.

Because Jephthah, a "mighty warrior" (11:1), is the son of a prostitute, the other "sons of Gilead" (or Gileadites) refuse to allow Jephthah to share in their territorial inheritance. Jephthah therefore becomes the leader of a band of outlaws. After the Ammonites attack Israel, however, the elders of Gilead persuade Jephthah to return and serve as their "head and ruler" (11:11, my trans.) and fight against the Ammonites. When the king of the Ammonites refuses to heed Jephthah's initial attempt to persuade him to refrain from attacking Israel, "the spirit of the LORD" comes upon Jephthah and Jephthah marches out against the Ammonites.

At this point in the story, Jephthah makes a vow to YHWH that will have serious consequences. The vow seems superfluous, since Jephthah already has "the spirit of the LORD" that elsewhere in Judges allows deliverers to accomplish their deeds. According to the vow, if YHWH delivers the Ammonites into Jephthah's hand, Jephthah will offer as a burnt offering "the one coming out of my house to meet me when I return in peace from the Ammonites" (11:31, my trans.). Does Jephthah assume that "the one coming out of my house to meet me" will be an animal or a person? While this question has vexed and divided commentators, the text itself provides no answer. It does tell us, however, that YHWH delivers the Ammonites into Jephthah's hand.

When Jephthah returns home, it is his daughter, his only child, who comes out to meet him. Though Jephthah tears his clothes in distress, both Jephthah and his daughter seem to assume that since the vow to YHWH has been made, it must be carried out. Jephthah's daughter asks only that she be given two months to wander in the hills with her friends and "bewail my virginity" (11:37). At the end of two months, she returns to her father "and he did to her the vow that he vowed" (11:39, my trans.).

The sacrifice of Jephthah's daughter raises difficult theological and ethical questions. The story clearly presupposes that vows made to God have to be taken seriously, even if the consequences are troubling. But what is God's view of the matter? The text does not tell us. It is striking that YHWH, who gives Jephthah the victory he asks for immediately after the vow has been made, does not prevent the human sacrifice. In that respect, one cannot help noting the contrast between this story and the story of Isaac, whose sacrifice at the hand of his father is first commanded by God but then prevented by a "messenger of YHWH" in Gen. 22 (my trans.). Some commentators compare this story as well with the story of Achsah in Judg. 1, for in both stories daughters are given away by fathers in exchange for military victory.

Although the text does not give an evaluation of either Jephthah's vow or the sacrifice of his daughter, it does note that the sacrifice gave rise to a women's ritual in Israel. Each year "the daughters of Israel" spend four days commemorating the daughter of Jephthah (11:39–40). Thus even if the story does not explain the troubling silence of God at certain terrible moments, the actions of Israel's daughters may point toward the most appropriate human response in such moments: memory and lament. That Jephthah makes his vow after YHWH's spirit comes upon him also indicates that divine inspiration is no guarantee against foolish or tragic actions.

After the death of his daughter, Jephthah and the Gileadites become embroiled in a conflict initiated by the tribe of Ephraim. As in the time of Gideon, Ephraim is blamed for the dissension. Here, though, Ephraim pays a heavy price for its petulance. The Gileadites kill forty-two thousand Ephraimites, who are recognized by the fact that they pronounce the Hebrew word *shibboleth* as "sibboleth."

Jephthah leads Israel for six years before he dies. He is followed by three judges who are listed with very little detail: Ibzan of Bethlehem, Elon the Zebulunite, and Abdon son of Hillel, an inhabitant of Ephraim.

Chapters 13–16

Like the story of Ehud, the stories about Samson are probably based in part on older folkloric traditions that, in our Bible, have been incorporated into a theological framework. Even in their current context, the Samson narratives are rather different from other sections of Judges. While Samson, like other deliverers, is associated with "the spirit of the LORD," he never leads an Israelite army. Rather, his exploits against enemies of the Israelites grow out of his personal conflicts, which are often associated with his liaisons with women.

The Samson narratives begin in chap. 13 by noting that YHWH has given the Israelites into the hands of the Philistines. The story focuses initially on Samson's father Manoah, who belongs to the tribe of Dan, and Manoah's wife, who like many women in the Bible is barren. A messenger of YHWH appears to Manoah's wife twice, announcing that she will conceive and that her son should not drink wine, eat anything unclean, or allow a razor to touch his head. The boy will be a "Nazirite" (cf. Num. 6:1–21) and will deliver Israel from the Philistines.

Immediately after noting that the "spirit of the LORD" has moved Samson (13:25), the author of Judges tells us how Samson notices a Philistine woman and asks his parents to get her for him. Samson's parents view this request negatively, and try to persuade Samson to choose an Israelite woman instead. Many commentators also take a dim view of Samson's desire for foreign women, perhaps because the book of Judges has already spoken about intermarriage between Israelites and non-Israelites negatively (3:5–7). Yet the text explicitly attributes Samson's desire for the Philistine woman to YHWH, noting that YHWH is looking for a reason to act against the Philistine oppressors (14:4). Like the Hebrew Bible as a whole, the book of Judges is inconsistent in its attitude toward intermarriage between Israelites and non-Israelites, viewing such marriages negatively in some cases while making allowance for them elsewhere.

When the Philistines threaten to burn her and her father's house, Samson's wife finds out the secret answer to a riddle that Samson has asked the Philistines and gives the answer to them. This discovery leads to a series of skirmishes between Samson and the Philistines, in the course of which Samson's wife and her father are burned alive by the Philistines, a fate that she had earlier tried to avoid. Numerous Philistines also die at the hand of Samson. At one point in the conflict, Samson is turned over to the Philistines by the tribe of Judah, but escapes and kills a thousand more Philistines. When Samson spends the night with another Philistine woman, a prostitute from Gaza, the Philistines attempt to kill him again; but Samson escapes once more and carries away the city gates.

Only in 16:4 does Samson finally meet Delilah, the woman whom readers most often associate with him. Delilah is never called a Philistine. Since the valley of Sorek where she lives is on the border between Israelite and Philistine territories, her ethnic identity remains ambiguous. For eleven hundred pieces of Philistine silver, Delilah finds out the secret of Samson's strength and how he might be subdued. Three times he gives her untrue answers, and each time Delilah carries out exactly the actions Samson describes. Thus by the time Samson tells Delilah truthfully that his strength will abandon him if his head is shaved, there can be little doubt that Delilah will shave his head. Once she does so, Samson's strength leaves him. The Philistines are able to bind Samson, put out his eyes, and force him to grind at a mill in prison.

When he is brought to a Philistine temple to entertain the Philistines, Samson, whose hair has begun to grow back, prays for divine assistance and destroys the temple. Numerous Philistines are killed, as is Samson himself. Yet Samson's prayer indicates that he is seeking personal revenge for having been blinded (16:28) rather than trying to deliver Israel from Philistine domination. Indeed, his story ends without any reference to deliverance or peace in the land, such as we find in the accounts of other judges. Nevertheless, the text specifies that Samson "judged" Israel twenty years (16:31).

Chapters 17–18

The last five chapters of Judges are noticeably different from the others. No judges or deliverers are mentioned here, and the stories focus largely on conflicts internal to Israel. The five chapters are knitted together with the observation that "in those days there was no king in Israel," twice in this form (18:1; 19:1) and twice with the additional comment that "each man did what was right in his own eyes" (17:6; 21:25, my trans.). Thus, in contrast to the stories of Gideon and Abimelech (which presuppose a negative view of kingship), the chaotic events narrated in chaps. 17–21 are recounted in such a way as to imply that kingship might be preferable for Israel. YHWH appears, but only briefly.

Chapter 17 introduces Micah, a man in the hill country of Ephraim who returns eleven hundred pieces of silver to his mother. Although the mother is not named, the amount of silver leads some readers to imagine that she is Delilah. Micah's mother gives two hundred pieces of the silver to make an image, which Micah uses to create a shrine at his home. When a Levite from Bethlehem passes by, Micah persuades him to become a priest at the shrine.

In chap. 18 Micah's Levite is visited by five spies from the tribe of Dan, who are searching for a new home for the Danites. After the Levite assures them of YHWH's approval, the spies locate a remote northern town called Laish and persuade their fellow Danites to move there. When they pass Micah's house again, the Danites steal Micah's image and other religious objects and persuade the Levite to come north with them to serve as priest for the entire tribe of Dan. The Danites then destroy the town of Laish and slaughter its peaceful inhabitants. When the city is rebuilt, the Danites rename it Dan and set up the image stolen from Micah. It is possible that this strange story is meant to disparage the origins of a religious site at Dan, which becomes the object of much criticism later in the Deuteronomistic History. However, the Levite apparently worships YHWH (18:5–6) and is associated with Moses (18:30).

Chapters 19–21

Chapter 19 introduces another Levite in the hill country of Ephraim. This Levite's concubine leaves him for her father's house in Judah. The reason for her departure is unclear. Hebrew manuscripts suggest that she acted like a prostitute, while Greek versions indicate that she was angry with the Levite. Since divorce was normally initiated by men rather than women in ancient Israel, it is possible that the mere fact that this unnamed concubine leaves the Levite caused her to be viewed by men as acting like a prostitute.

The Levite travels to Judah to retrieve his concubine. On the way home the Levite, the concubine, and the Levite's servant stop for the night in Gibeah, a town in the tribal territory of Benjamin that is closely associated with Saul in 1 Samuel. When an old Ephraimite living in Gibeah gives the travelers shelter and food for the night, the men of Gibeah surround the house and threaten to rape the Levite. In a move that parallels Lot's actions in Sodom, the old host offers his own daughter and the Levite's concubine in place of the Levite. Although the Gibeahites reject that offer, the concubine is thrown outside and raped all night. She returns to the house and falls at the door, but we are never told when she dies. When the Levite finds her in the morning, he carries her home, cuts her body into twelve pieces, and sends those pieces throughout Israel to call the tribes together.

The Israelites, hearing what has happened in Gibeah, ask the tribe of Benjamin to turn over the Gibeahites, who will be punished by death. When Benjamin refuses, the other Israelite tribes, with YHWH's approval (20:18, 21, 28) and assistance (20:35), do battle against the Benjaminites and defeat them. Although twenty-five thousand Benjaminite soldiers are killed, six hundred remain alive. The Israelites want the tribe of Benjamin to survive, but swear that none of their own daughters will be given to Benjamin as wives. After consulting YHWH, the Israelites slay all the inhabitants of Jabesh-gilead (which refused to send soldiers to the war against Benjamin) except four hundred virgins, who are given to the Benjaminites as wives. Two hundred more young women are abducted as wives from a religious festival at Shiloh.

The actions recounted in chaps. 19–21 are among the most horrible in the Bible, and they illustrate the chaos into which Israel has fallen without a king (21:25). Clearly, the author of Judges views the events at Gibeah negatively and assumes that Benjamin is wrong to protect the Gibeahites. However, the actions of other characters are disturbing as well. The Levite seems to assume that the crime in Gibeah was committed primarily against him, and only secondarily against his concubine (20:5). The Israelites show little hesitation about kidnapping young women as wives for Benjamin. Indeed, they appear to believe that these kidnappings are approved by God, since the kidnappings follow prayer. Moreover, YHWH, who clearly is present in the story and participates in the battle against Benjamin, says nothing against the kidnappings or the slaughter at Jabesh-gilead.

The book of Judges ends on a troubling note. The ability of God's people to commit horrifying atrocities, even while praying and seeking God's will, is made clear. Yet God's own role in these atrocities also remains more ambiguous than readers of the Bible may expect or desire.

Conclusions

A number of the theological emphases found in Judges are potentially valuable for readers who come to the Bible looking for contemporary relevance. The insistence upon loyalty to YHWH above all other deities may still encourage faithfulness to God over all competing loyalties.

The book's representation of YHWH as a God characterized by both judgment and compassion may remind us of the simultaneous importance of both justice and mercy for biblical theology. Recognition of the contribution of the spirit of God to effective leadership in Judges, and acknowledgment that such leadership is sometimes embodied in the book by the most unlikely candidates, may serve to check the human tendency to choose as leaders only those individuals who are most clearly characterized by prized human qualities. And the book's emphasis upon maintaining a distinctive identity as the people of God may encourage caution about any uncritical adoption of popular ideologies by communities of faith.

Nevertheless, much about Judges is hard to assimilate theologically. Readers are rightly disturbed by certain theological, ethical, and social assumptions that are accepted uncritically by the author, including assumptions about the religious justification of genocide or the treatment of women as property to be given and taken. The book's violence shocks many readers, especially those who, on the basis of other biblical texts, emphasize peace as a religious goal and way of life. The unsettling silence of God at such tragic moments as the sacrifice of Jephthah's daughter, or the rape of the Levite's concubine, leads to difficult questions about the author's notions of God.

At the same time, in some places details of the book seem to undermine some of its own assumptions. For example, the emphasis upon a clearly marked Israelite identity stands in tension with the important roles played in the book by such characters as Othniel the Kennizite and Shamgar ben Anat, both of whom are represented as judges in Israel yet neither of whom is necessarily Israelite; or by Jael the Kenite woman who kills an enemy of the Israelites. The negative perspective on intermarriage between Israelites and non-Israelites is hard to reconcile with the report in chap. 14 that God is responsible for Samson's desire for a Philistine wife.

At no point do all the tribes act in unison, and the various tribal groups that appear in the book do not correspond exactly to lists of Israelite tribes found elsewhere in the Bible. Even the undeniable prevalence of male dominance in the book is partly undermined by the role of Deborah as prophet, judge, and military leader; or by the assertiveness of Achsah when she demands property from her father.

In these respects and more, the book of Judges proves to be a problem for readers who assume that theological interpretation of the Bible requires the extraction of simple truths from a clear and consistent text. Yet the book's resistance to such widespread assumptions might be one of its most important characteristics. When readers compare the internal parts of Judges with one another, and when they compare details of Judges with details of other biblical books, they come to realize more fully that both the book of Judges and the Bible as a whole are actually characterized by heterogeneity and even contradiction. While this feature of Judges and of biblical literature is sometimes seen as a difficulty to be overcome by theological interpretation, recognition of heterogeneity and tension inside the Bible may enable us to accept and live better with the heterogeneity and tension that also, inevitably, characterize our own religious communities.

Bibliography

Boling, Robert. *Judges*. AB 6A. Garden City, NY: Doubleday, 1975.

Brenner, Athalya, ed. *A Feminist Companion to Judges*. FCB 4. Sheffield: Sheffield Academic Press, 1993.

Gunn, David. *Judges*. Blackwell Bible Commentaries. Oxford: Blackwell, 2005.

Schneider, Tammi. *Judges*. Berit Olam. Collegeville, MN: Liturgical Press, 2000.

Yee, Gale A., ed. *Judges and Method: New Approaches in Biblical Studies*. 2nd ed. Minneapolis: Fortress, 2007.

Ruth

Nancy R. Bowen

INTRODUCTION

The book of Ruth is a short story. It is located in the Writings section of the Hebrew Bible. In Judaism it is considered one of the five festival scrolls (or Megilloth) and is the liturgical reading for the harvest festival of Weeks (cf. Exod. 34:22). In the Greek Old Testament, Ruth follows the book of Judges, a location that reflects the setting of the book "in the days when the judges ruled" (Ruth 1:1). The date of composition is debated. The concern for Davidic lineage (4:18–22) argues for a date during the monarchy. However, issues of family, fertility, and foreignness were central concerns of the postexilic period.

COMMENTARY

Two famines, a lack of bread (or food) and a lack of men (husbands and sons), drive the plot of Ruth. The story focuses on the ways in which Ruth and Naomi will obtain the bounty of food and family. The theological issue is God's (non)involvement in both of the crises and their resolution. This issue is complicated in Ruth by the lack of direct speech or action by God. As a result, interpreters offer differing judgments about the presence of the Deity in this story.

Elsewhere in the Bible, famine is a manifestation of divine judgment (see 2 Sam. 21:1; Jer. 11:22; 14:15; 27:8; 44:13; Ezek. 5:11–12; 14:13; Amos 8:11). But whether the famine in Ruth (1:1) is God's judgment is not directly stated. Since the book of Judges recounts Israel's ever increasing sin (Judg. 21:25), the setting "when the judges ruled" implies a connection between the famine and divine displeasure. Conversely, abundance of food can be a sign of divine blessing (see Isa. 30:23–26; 43:18–21; Joel 2:22–26). Naomi decides to return to Bethlehem because "she had heard in the country of Moab that the LORD had considered his people and given them food." That God had stopped the famine remained hearsay.

Naomi invokes divine blessing in her speech to Orpah and Ruth (1:8–9). The expression "deal kindly" occurs also in 2:20 ("kindness") and 3:10 ("loyalty"). The Hebrew word *hesed* is most often translated "steadfast love" (especially of God in the Psalms). It is much more than "niceness." It concerns ultimate commitments (cf. Mic. 6:8). Naomi hopes that God will measure up to Ruth and Orpah's level of commitment, especially Ruth's (1:16–17). Should God do so, then

Orpah and Ruth will "find security" (cf. 3:1). In Naomi's next speech (1:20–21), it is questionable whether Naomi believes God will measure up.

In the bitter description of her own personal experience of God, Naomi names God as "the Almighty" or Shaddai. Elsewhere Shaddai is associated with the promise of numerous offspring (Gen. 17:1–7; 28:3–4; 35:9–12; 48:3–4). In contrast, Naomi laments her loss of offspring, as well as the possibility of future offspring. The term *Shaddai* also occurs when both Abraham and Israel are renamed (Gen. 17:1–7; 35:9–12). In related fashion, Naomi ("pleasant") wants her name changed to Mara ("bitter"). If Shaddai was responsible for her initial fullness, then she can only be bitter that the same Shaddai has decided to deal harshly with her by rendering her empty. Naomi's bitterness may reflect the belief that blessing is a reward for obedience and calamity is a punishment for disobedience. Then, like Job, there seems to be no reason for God to treat her this way. But without a direct speech from God about this matter, the relation between God's action and Naomi's life remains ambiguous.

Naomi's only other reference to God is the invocation of God's blessing upon Boaz when Ruth recounts her day in the fields, "Blessed be he by the LORD . . ." (2:20). It is unclear whether Naomi is referring to God's or Boaz's kindness; the Hebrew syntax is ambiguous. Since Naomi held bitter feelings toward God, she may be expressing gratitude for Boaz's assistance to her (she is living) as an act of family loyalty to her husband (he is dead). If, however, the reference is to God, then Naomi is claiming that God has maintained covenant loyalty, even though her circumstances make it appear otherwise. Overall Naomi's speech reflects an experience of God as capricious—who brings famine and abundance, who brings fertility and barrenness, who is harsh and kind, but with no clear connection between the action

of an individual and how God responds to them.

Boaz frequently speaks of God. The greeting and response between Boaz and his workers exemplify a belief in God's presence and care (2:4). In his first encounter with Ruth, Boaz hopes that God will "reward" Ruth for all she has done on Naomi's behalf, including the sacrifice of leaving her family and home country (2:12). Boaz asks God to repay Ruth for what it has "cost" her to support Naomi. "Full reward" denotes completion and perfection. Boaz asks God not to shortchange Ruth or cheat her out of what should be hers. Boaz believes that God is obligated to reward those who seek refuge under God's wings (Pss. 36:7; 57:1; 61:4; 91:4; cf. Deut. 32:11). Boaz next speaks of God, employing the language of blessing, when he awakes to find Ruth at his feet (Ruth 3:10). Boaz expresses a belief in blessing as a reward for obedience. Overall Boaz's speech reflects an experience of God as one who responds fairly to a believer's obedient actions. Life is blessed by God, who is obligated to reward those who are faithful. The contrast between Naomi's and Boaz's theology might reflect how differences in class and gender shape theological perceptions.

God is mentioned by the townspeople at the end of the transaction between Boaz and another kinsman. They petition God to grant offspring to Ruth, thereby building up Naomi's "house," or family (4:11–12). The people affirm the belief that offspring are a result of divine action. And indeed, this is the case. The only direct action that God takes in the entire book is to cause Ruth to conceive (4:13).

The inclusion of Ruth, a foreigner, into the Israelite community is also a central issue in this book. Ruth is not merely foreign, she is a despised Moabite (cf. Gen. 19:37; Num. 22–24; Deut. 23:3; Isa. 15–16; Jer. 48). Other biblical traditions suggest that foreign wives bring foreign gods, which lead the people astray (e.g., Num. 25; Ezra 9–10). The theological problem of potential apostasy that Ruth posed is resolved by her covenant with Naomi (Ruth 1:16–17). Ruth vows to take Naomi's God as her own and swears by the Lord as a sign of her new allegiance. But beyond this Ruth never speaks of God. But maybe she does not have to. All of Ruth's acts echo divine activity: she provides them with food, she is kind and loyal to Naomi, and in giving birth to Obed she restores Naomi to the fullness she had lost. Ruth *is* God to Naomi and therefore provides Naomi with an alternative theology—God as a loving, abiding presence who goes where she goes and will be with her even till death.

Bibliography

Linafelt, Tod. *Ruth*. Berit Olam. Collegeville, MN: Liturgical Press, 1999.

Pressler, Carolyn. *Joshua, Judges, Ruth*. Westminster Bible Companion. Louisville: Westminster John Knox, 2002.

Sakenfeld, Katharine Doob. *Ruth*. Interpretation. Louisville: Westminster John Knox, 1999.

Webb, Barry G. *Five Festal Garments: Christian Reflections on the Song of Songs, Ruth, Lamentations, Ecclesiastes and Esther*. New Studies in Biblical Theology 10. Leicester: Apollos, 2000.

1 and 2 Samuel

Patricia K. Tull

1 SAMUEL

INTRODUCTION

In the Hebrew manuscript tradition, 1 and 2 Samuel constitute a single book, relating Israel's transition from a tribal society led by various regional "judges" to a dynastic monarchy. It forms part of the narrative extending from Joshua through 2 Kings, which most scholars refer to as the Deuteronomistic History. Although the Jewish canon places 1 Samuel after Judges, Christian tradition interposes Ruth between these two books, since it concerns David's ancestors in the time of judges.

Most scholars think the Deuteronomistic History was essentially completed during the Babylonian exile. Distinctions in writing style and subject matter suggest that it was assembled by redactors from various shorter narratives. Diversity of sources and redactional layering can be seen, for instance, in the introduction of David to Saul for the first time twice (1 Sam. 16:18–21; 17:55–58). Theological and ideological tensions are also evident, particularly around the roles of human leaders in relation to God's rule. However, the nature, extent, dating, historicity, and purposes of 1–2 Samuel's various source narratives have been debated at length without consensus. Many scholars have abandoned trying to reconstruct the history of the book's formation and have trained attention

instead on the literary, psychological, and theological genius of its final form.

Some of the Bible's longest and most ethically complex stories are found here. Trials and temptations besetting leaders emerge as dominant themes, as one ruler after another arises with great promise, struggles to build or maintain his power, encounters obstacles, and finally succumbs to opposing forces within his soul and within the environment. First Samuel begins with the aging priest Eli and his two unworthy sons presiding over the temple at Shiloh, and narrates their replacement by Samuel, who fills the roles of prophet, seer, man of God, priest, and judge. When the people of Israel object to Samuel's installation of his own sons as judges, and request a king instead, God directs Samuel to anoint Saul. But an array of forces, both human and divine, result in Saul's failure. Meanwhile, Samuel has, at God's prompting, anointed a rival leader, the youthful David. Whereas Judges portrayed a leadership vacuum, suspense here revolves around a surplus of intended leaders. The question dangling throughout the second half of 1 Samuel and into 2 Samuel is not who will be king but how David, the shepherd who becomes in quick succession court musician, military hero, royal son-in-law, palace renegade, and finally Philistine agent, will acquire the throne.

Arranged around this plotline are stories drawing attention to a host of vivid characters, from Samuel's mother Hannah to the widowed, dying daughter-in-law of Eli, to an incredible hulk named Goliath, to Saul's offspring Michal and Jonathan, to the ill-fated priest Ahimelech and the Edomite Doeg who murders him, to the surly Nabal and his quick-thinking wife Abigail, to the trusting but misled Philistine Achish, to the frightened but compassionate woman of Endor, to the devoted inhabitants of Jabesh-gilead who rescue Saul's body from Philistine dishonor.

At issue throughout is not only the nature of human existence, but the mysterious and often troubling role of the Divine. God is manifest through direct speech, prophets' messages, the casting of lots, meteorological phenomena, astounding coincidence, and the possessing of characters by prophetic or evil spirits. A God who is clearly independent of human will nevertheless shows surprising receptivity to human actions, continually adapting to make the best of unfolding events, showing favor and disfavor at will for reasons not altogether clarified. Such a characterization of God may reflect lingering ancient understandings of the Divine as powerful, immortal, but not necessarily irreproachable, and can be fitted to later Christian understandings only uneasily. To a

remarkable degree, however, these portraits reflect the universe we inhabit, which does not operate on principles of fairness, though it can be influenced by human initiative.

Various cultic objects unfamiliar to modern people also play roles. The ark of the covenant, the central symbol of God's presence, appears several times, starting in the temple of Shiloh and ending in Jerusalem with David. Stories about it make clear that it is not an object to be manipulated but a site of divine presence whose dangerous power must be respected. The Urim and Thummim, associated with the priestly ephod, are frequently used for inquiring of God by the casting of lots. Although Saul himself is chosen by this process (1 Sam. 10:20–22), he enjoys little benefit from their use (14:37–42; 28:6). David, on the other hand, consults the lots regularly and successfully (23:2–6, 9–12; 30:7–8; 2 Sam. 2:1, 5:19, 23–24).

The Hebrew manuscripts of 1–2 Samuel are among the most poorly preserved in the Bible, with significant textual corruptions and omissions of material that in many cases has been better preserved in the Septuagint Greek (LXX) translation. To reconstruct a more accurate text, English translations have increasingly relied on the Qumran scrolls as well as the LXX and other ancient translations. At times the ambiguities on the manuscript level mirror or augment those of the narratives themselves.

COMMENTARY

1 Samuel 1–4

First Samuel begins with a family traveling to worship year by year and, like many families, annually repeating its own tiresome holiday drama. Two women share one man. One wife has all the children; the other has reassurances of her husband's love that do nothing to address her plight: in a society structured on women's fruitfulness, she is childless. The apportioning of sacrificial offerings reopens this wound

every year. Because of manuscript discrepancies, English translations characterize Elkanah's gift to Hannah variously: as only one portion, though he loves her; as a double portion, *because* he loves her; or as a prime portion. No matter which it is, someone is left unhappy. Elkanah's strained attempts at fairness cannot mask inequities disrupting domestic peace.

Hannah leaves the feast one year to petition God in the temple of Shiloh, where Eli is sitting. Weeping, she vows that if given a son she will give him to God's service. In a brief exchange that raises questions about both his eyesight and his spiritual vision, Eli mistakes her distress for drunkenness, is corrected, and blesses her, and she leaves comforted. God remembers her, and she bears a son, whom she names Samuel. In due time she returns to hand him over to Eli's care.

Hannah's exultant song announces themes prevailing throughout the Old and New Testaments, down to Mary's song in Luke 1. A series of parallel clauses that portray the just God as defeater of the powerful and defender of the powerless is summed up in the statement, "Not by might does one prevail." The final verse leaps ahead, foreshadowing that God "will give strength to his king, and exalt the power of his anointed" (2:10).

Hannah's song celebrates her own reversal of fortune. Yet other reversals quickly appear. Eli's sons, barely mentioned before, receive a scathing review: they are scoundrels abusing priesthood, sacrifices, and worshipers. Descriptions of their sin and their father's feeble reprimands alternate with affectionate portrayals of Samuel. Their fate is sealed when a man of God delivers a retraction of God's promise that Eli's family would serve God forever. Instead, Eli's sons will be killed on a single day, his descendants will perish, and God will "raise up a faithful priest" (2:35).

The familiar story of God's calling the young Samuel by night and being mistaken three times for Eli follows immediately. At Eli's instruction, Samuel responds to God and hears the message, which confirms the prior one: "the iniquity of Eli's house shall not be expiated by sacrifice or offering forever" (3:14). Eli demands to know what the frightened Samuel heard, and responds with resigned acceptance.

Eli is harshly judged for his sons' abuses, and becomes the first of the book's rejected leaders. Blind and undiscerning as he is, in comparison with those who follow, Eli shows himself decent, kind, and God-fearing. As Samuel grows up, God is revealed to him regularly and he is established as a reliable prophet.

First Samuel 4 links Eli's story with that of the ark of the covenant, which resides at Shiloh. During a war with the Philistines, Eli's sons bring the ark to the battlefield hoping its presence will assist their victory. Ironically, it is the Philistines who recognize its power and, despite their fear, defeat the Israelites, kill Eli's sons, and capture it. News of the ark's capture is repeated five more times in seven verses. Upon hearing it Eli dies, and his daughter-in-law dies giving birth, mourning her husband, her father-in-law, and the "glory of God" that she says has departed from Israel. But the ark has a story of its own that will continue in subsequent chapters.

Major themes are previewed in 1 Sam. 1–4. The story of the four-hundred-year dynasty of King David begins with a childless woman's tears, a priest's demise, and a military and spiritual defeat. Yet this is not the end. As Hannah said: "The LORD is a God of knowledge, and by him actions are weighed. The bows of the mighty are broken, but the feeble gird on strength" (2:3–4). At many junctures in the history of faith, as in this story, visions have been scarce and the word of God rare. But the lamp of God, sometimes burning dimly, does not go out (3:1–3). Even in dismal times new leadership arises through whom God speaks and acts.

1 Samuel 5–6

First Samuel 5–6 follows the captured ark to Ashdod, where it is placed in the temple of the Philistine god Dagon. In a sequence filled with farcical repetition, Dagon's statue is found repeatedly prostrating himself in his own temple before the ark of Israel's God. Then the effects on the population are described. Like the Egyptians who, the Philistines remember, were struck with plagues (4:8; 6:6), the Philistines are plagued with tumors in every city to which the ark is moved, until their religious leaders instruct them to return it to the Israelites with a golden guilt offering. The two cows pulling it on a cart walk straight to the Israelite border, where it is joyfully received. Even for the Israelites the ark is not a safe object—some who look inside it die and, duplicating the Philistines' reaction, their neighbors send it to another town.

This fanciful story pokes fun at foreign oppressors and their gods while hardly leaving Israelites unscathed. Though the Philistines do not quite have the traditions straight, they seem more aware than the Israelites of the power of Israel's God in the past and the futility of trying to control divine symbols in the present.

1 Samuel 7–15

Twenty years later, Samuel calls the people to recommit to God. When they gather, the Philistines attack, but at the people's bidding Samuel prays and the enemies are routed. This narrative follows the pattern of threat, prayer, and deliverance frequent in Judges; however, Samuel leads the people to renewal before, not because of, an imminent threat. His leadership is evidently working.

When Samuel grows old he places his two sons in office, but they are no more honest than Eli's. As before, the people point out the problems. This time they also propose change. Rather than these judges, they want a king to "judge" them.

Samuel reacts badly, but the response of God, who speaks regularly and easily to Samuel, is mixed: "Listen to the voice of the people in all that they say to you; for they have not rejected you, but they have rejected me from being king over them" (8:7). Elsewhere in Scripture, human kingship is not viewed as competing directly with divine rule. Deuteronomy 17:14–20 grants the nation divinely chosen kings, but limits royal acquisitiveness and subordinates the king to God. In Judges the son of Gideon who conspires to rule succumbs to his own violence (Judg. 9), yet kinglessness is associated with lawlessness (Judg. 17:6; 21:25). In the Psalms human kingship

represents, rather than replaces, divine reign (see, e.g., Ps. 72). Yet here both Samuel and God fear they are being displaced. Samuel warns the people at length of the demands a king will place on them.

Saul is introduced as a young man seeking his father's donkeys. Going to Samuel for help, he is instead invited to a feast and anointed king. Samuel foretells a series of signs confirming God's participation, but his instructions are ambiguous. On the one hand, he says, "When these signs meet you, do whatever you see fit to do, for God is with you" (10:7). On the other hand, he tells Saul to go to Gilgal and wait seven days, "until I come to you and show you what you shall do" (v. 8). The story skips over the first two signs and details the third.

Samuel then summons the people, scolds them again, and proceeds to choose a king by lot. When Saul is picked, he is discovered hiding. No interpretation is given of this or of previous gestures downplaying his own significance. Together they suggest that kingship is not Saul's aspiration; he seems willing but not eager to cooperate. His tolerance toward "worthless fellows" who question his effectiveness suggests magnanimity. Almost immediately comes an opportunity to show leadership by defending the town of Jabesh-gilead from the Ammonites. This success seals his kingship.

Samuel takes the opportunity to call everyone to Gilgal to "renew the kingship" (11:14). There Saul and the people rejoice, but Samuel delivers a chapter-long speech drawing attention to himself, confirming his fair dealings with all, reviewing their ancestors' sins, and once again scolding. To underscore his point, he calls down rain to ruin their wheat crop, eliciting a frightened confession. Though he then reassures them of God's care and his prayers, he concludes with: "if you still do wickedly, you shall be swept away, both you and your king." No retiring pastor has yet preempted his successor's installation as effectively as Samuel did Saul's.

Regnal words such as appear in 13:1 customarily accompany a king's ascension (see, e.g., 1 Kgs. 14:21). But the MT is corrupt (reading "Saul was a year old when he began to reign and he reigned two years over Israel"), and the verse is missing from the LXX. Though English translations cope variously, this manuscript flaw seems an appropriate opening to three episodes in which Saul's reign is destroyed. In the first, he encounters Samuel's ire; in the second, he blunders into a confrontation with his army; and in the third, he incurs divine rejection. Even though Saul's reign will persist until his death eighteen chapters and some years later, its fruitless end is declared by Samuel in the same chapter in which it formally begins.

Saul's encounter with Samuel at Gilgal is confusing. When he first anointed the young Saul in secret, Samuel described three events that took place immediately, as well as instructions to wait a week for a meeting in Gilgal. Readers may have assumed this episode occurred offstage long ago, especially since much time has passed and they have already met in Gilgal.

Now Saul is no longer young, but has a grown son. An army has been recruited; victories have begun. The Philistines gather to attack at Gilgal, fearful troops begin to desert, and then as if in a nightmarish time warp, Saul is waiting seven days for Samuel, who does not come. In narrow straits between the Philistine threat, waning morale, and Samuel's orders, Saul makes an executive decision to proceed with prewar sacrifices. Immediately Samuel arrives. Neither apologizing for his delay nor acknowledging the crisis, he upbraids Saul, saying his kingdom will not continue and God has sought out someone else. Saul's exact offense is unclear, and commentators struggle to reconstruct it, augmenting the impression that he was given a test with no correct choices.

Although Saul has shown leadership before, from now on his blunders help undermine his reign. Having been snared in unresolved conflict between Samuel and the people, Saul cannot but fulfill Samuel's dire predictions. Yet his sin is not royal greed as Samuel predicted, but misplaced zeal. In the midst of a battle his son Jonathan is winning, Saul displays more piety than military sense, issuing a curse on anyone who tastes food before the battle's end. When Jonathan inadvertently transgresses, and God ignores Saul's inquiries, Saul swears death on whoever violated his oath. Discovering Jonathan's transgression, he prepares to execute him. But the soldiers intervene, saving their hero and undermining their king, whose integrity has become rigidity.

God had not originally welcomed the monarchy, but had accommodated popular wishes. It has been Samuel, not God, who has opposed Saul. God's turning point comes in chap. 15. Following Samuel's instruction, Saul defeats the Amalekites, but contrary to orders, he captures their king alive and retains the best of the animals. Whether or not he intends a sacrificial offering as he says, God interprets the delay in killing all as disobedience. Samuel confronts Saul and they argue. When Samuel declares divine rejection, Saul asks for pardon. Samuel refuses, and their verbal struggle is protracted and painful. Latitude for decisions and grace for mistakes are not given to Saul.

Readers may recognize Samuel as an unyielding leader unable to apprentice another as Eli did. We may see in Saul a trainee willing to please, whose confidence erodes with every scolding, and ask why God allows Samuel's jealousy to undermine Saul's reign. At points in the biblical story God appears singularly wise, patient, and providential. At other points, God seems to learn by trial and error. Samuel claims that God "is not a man, that he should repent" (15:29, my trans.), but both God and the narrator confirm that God had indeed "repented" (vv. 11, 35). Although Saul has not been told when to step down, his dynasty is doomed and his reign blighted. He will seesaw back and forth between rigidity and humility, between savagery and nobility, losing ground not only in God's eyes but in those of his family and readers.

1 Samuel 16–20

At God's initiative, Samuel anoints another monarch. This problematic leadership redundancy is signaled on the literary level by other redundancies that draw curiosity and upset logic. David is introduced to Saul twice; Saul tries to kill David twice through matrimony and twice with a spear. Saul falls into prophetic frenzies twice, prompting the same saying twice. Two of Saul's children love David and rescue him from their father; Jonathan does it twice. David departs from the palace twice, and twice runs to the Philistines, who twice repeat the same saying about him. He twice declines opportunities to kill Saul, and twice upbraids him, eliciting two confessions. Samuel sees Saul for the last time in his life twice—and once more after death. In the end we will hear two conflicting accounts of Saul's own death. Attention alternates between two parallel narratives, the painful story of Saul's downfall and the winsome story of David's rise. Unsurprisingly, tradition has preferred the latter, more sanguine narrative, in which providence prevails for good rather than ill.

The well-known tale of David's anointing follows the biblical pattern of favoring the younger, less obvious candidate. God claims to ignore appearance, yet David's good looks are noted twice (16:12; 17:42). "The spirit of the LORD came mightily upon David from that day forward," and "the spirit of the LORD departed from Saul, and an evil spirit from the LORD tormented him" (16:13–14). Saul's condition ironically leads him to hire David to play music to soothe him. Saul becomes the first of many, including his children, the servants, and all Israel and Judah, identified as loving David.

The challenge by the Philistine warrior Goliath occasions David's second introduction to Saul. Displaying both ambition and zeal, David visits the battlefield and inquires about Goliath until he is brought to Saul and assures him that he can defeat the giant, which he does with a single stone. Thus David appears as a nimble warrior, outwitting stronger opponents—capacities he will soon need in relation to the king himself. Saul's son Jonathan is captivated. In a gesture signaling his future abdication, he gives David his robe, armor, sword, bow, and belt. Almost immediately Saul envies David's growing popularity. Within twelve verses he tries four times to murder him, finally using the love of his daughter Michal as bait, persuading David to bring a hundred Philistine foreskins as a marriage gift, in the vain hope that he will die trying.

Chapters 19–20 relate four rescues. Twice Jonathan attempts to persuade Saul against seeking David's death. In between, first Michal engineers his escape through a window, then David flees to Samuel, and everyone Saul sends after him, finally including Saul himself, falls helplessly into a prophetic frenzy. Finally, David returns to confront Jonathan with his father's deeds, persuading him to test Saul's reaction to David's absence at the new moon festival. Jonathan fashions a baroque system of signals involving archery practice, a servant, and prearranged messages, to let David know whether it is safe to return.

The timing of this exchange is strange, since Saul's murderous intent is now public. As with other episodes that defy logic, the redactor's purpose in this redundancy of escapes is suggestive but not explicit. David's place within Saul's household has been ambiguous, with Saul alternately welcoming him sincerely, welcoming him duplicitously, and driving him away. His leaving has left a marriage dangling. Yet his deepest ties are with the heir to the throne himself, the one who should be his greatest rival.

As arranged, Jonathan offers David's excuses, eliciting his father's attempt to spear him just as he did David, signaling that he too senses the identification between them. The next morning Jonathan carries out his coded message and they meet for a tearful parting.

Saul's deterioration is precipitous. Like Samuel, Saul takes out his rejection on the subsequent leader. In an unusual move, the storyteller flatly reports Saul's thoughts and feelings several times, rendering Saul's feelings obvious to all, while the inner life of others, especially David, remains veiled. Sympathy Saul may have elicited previously is lost, while Jonathan, Michal, and others model a growing sympathy for David, who frequently asks, "What have I done?" (17:29; 20:1, 32; 26:18; 29:8).

Does David deserve the sympathy he elicits? Michal loves David fiercely, but his feelings for her are not reported. Jonathan's generosity is showcased at length. That David reciprocates his love here can only be inferred (cf. 2 Sam. 1:26). As Saul's misdeeds become more pronounced, David displays patient trust that God will confirm his future. Only as the narrative progresses are we made aware of the complications around David's innocence.

1 Samuel 21–26

Attention alternates between David and Saul, who devotes more time to pursuing David than to ruling Israel. Although Saul accuses all of conspiring against him, he receives plenty of help, even from towns indebted to David. But without God's support, Saul's attempts continue to be frustrated.

David tells the priest Ahimelech at Nob that he is on a secret mission for Saul and needs supplies. Ahimelech gives him the holy bread and Goliath's sword. David flees to the Philistine city of Gath, but when he is mistakenly but presciently identified as Israel's king, he feigns insanity and finally flees into the wilderness of southern Judah, where other outlaws join him. Meanwhile, Saul sits under a tamarisk tree holding his spear, a tableau that both recalls his attempted murders and foreshadows his own burial. Accus-

ing his own servants of conspiracy, he elicits from Doeg the Edomite a report against Ahimelech, claiming that the priest inquired of God for David. Saul sends for the priests and confronts Ahimelech, who in his innocence praises David. When Saul orders his men to kill the priests, they refuse, but Doeg slaughters them and their entire town. Ahimelech's son Abiathar alone escapes to David.

Chapter 23 outlines the movements of pursuer and pursued as they receive and act on intelligence messages. Having made himself odious not only to his children and followers but to God, Saul now finds his greatest support among distant cities of Judah, who inform him of David's movements. For his part, David consults God through the ephod brought by Abiathar.

A series of close calls leads to the next episode, in which Saul humiliatingly and providentially tends to personal matters in the very cave where David is hiding (chap. 24). Despite prompting, David refuses to kill Saul, calling him "the LORD's anointed." He will use this description of Saul a total of nine times as events unfold, drawing attention to his own status as the Lord's anointed. After Saul leaves, David calls to him, holding up a scrap of cloak that David has cut off, reenacting Samuel's earlier words: "The LORD has torn the kingdom of Israel from you this very day, and has given it to a neighbor of yours, who is better than you" (15:28). Following David's lengthy profession of innocence, a humbled Saul acknowledges, "you are more righteous than I" and "you shall surely be king" (24:17, 20). A similar scenario will be repeated two chapters later, when David takes the sleeping king's spear and calls to him from a distance, eliciting another confession. David's second speech takes a brisker, more formal tone, while Saul vainly and profusely apologizes.

David's nonaggression toward the Lord's anointed does not, however, translate to an overall pattern. Between these two episodes, David and his men, as self-appointed protectors of a rich man's flocks, attempt to claim a reward—appropriately enough—at fleecing time. When brusquely refused, David prepares to slaughter the household. He is restrained only when quick-thinking servants alert the quick-thinking wife, Abigail, who brings provisions and profuse apologies for her husband, who as she points out is named Nabal, "fool." In this episode Abigail momentarily takes David's own role, prevailing through diplomacy over a stronger aggressor, saving him from unjust violence. She receives his gratitude in return. When she tells her husband of the averted disaster, he is stricken and dies, and she marries David.

David's scrupulous trust in divine vindication shames his pursuer. Yet he summarily takes up the sword to avenge an insult. His genius in relation to powerful foes must be supplemented by a broader ethic in order to succeed once he himself attains power. Though he recognizes wisdom in the restraint Abigail encourages, it remains to be seen whether he will rule by discretion, or be ruled by indiscretion, once his adversaries are overcome.

1 Samuel 27–31

An averted slaughter followed the first of David's demonstrations of nonviolence. Actual slaughter follows the second. Ignoring Saul's promise of amnesty, David again retreats to the king of Gath and is given the city of Ziklag. There he makes his living raiding villages and killing inhabitants, while telling King Achish he is attacking Judah and its allies. This ruse keeps him from harming Israelites. It also reveals his duplicity toward one who trusts him, marks his distance from youthful valor, and brings into question his sincerity at past points. Suspense builds when Achish unwittingly calls David's bluff, recruiting him for the war against Israel.

It is noteworthy that the storyteller withholds judgment both here and elsewhere. Only halfway through 2 Samuel will David's action be explicitly judged.

Evil does not spring from a pure heart overnight, however, and the biblical narrative is too realistic to claim even founding ancestors as altogether godly models. As with sudden discoveries of unsuspected wrongdoing in our world, the question left open is, how far back does the path to David's later sins stretch? At what point does diplomacy cross over into duplicity, when does deceit become self-deceit, self-defense become wanton aggression? These questions are left open to interpretation.

Attention returns to Saul, who now faces the Philistines without any divine response to his many inquiries—not by dreams, lots, or prophets. In an episode fraught with desperation, Saul breaks his own decrees by asking a medium to consult the dead Samuel, who even in life was the last person from whom he could expect a hopeful word. An unsurprisingly irritable apparition tells Saul much more than he needs to know: God "has turned from you and become your enemy . . . has torn the kingdom out of your hand, and given it to your neighbor, David" (28:16–17), and tomorrow he and his sons will die. Whereas before Samuel's threats were harsh but inexact, now Saul's replacement is explicitly named, in case he had any doubt.

Saul is simply undone; courage fails him. He falls full length on the ground, filled with fear, empty of strength, terrified. In a consoling gesture, the medium takes charge and prepares him a meal before his last, predetermined battle.

Back among the Philistines, David and his men prepare to fight. At the last moment the other Philistine rulers challenge Achish's judgment, eliciting from him the affirmation, ironic to readers, that he has found no fault with David. For the fourth time in six chapters David accepts profuse apologies. Swearing by Israel's God that David has been honest, and calling him "as blameless in my sight as an angel of God" (29:9), Achish sends him away. Upon returning to Ziklag David and his soldiers discover that raiding Amalekites have taken their families and belongings. So while Saul and his sons are dying, David is far away pursuing Amalekites and bringing back spoil with which to curry favor with the elders of all the towns David had been claiming to have pillaged.

The scene changes one last time to a critically wounded Saul, begging his armor-bearer to kill him, offering one more opportunity for a loyal soldier to refuse a bad order. In a Shakespearean finale, Saul falls on his own sword and the armor-bearer follows suit. His enemies behead him and fasten his and his sons' bodies to a city wall. In a courageous act of gratitude, creating an inclusio with Saul's first victory, the men of Jabesh-gilead steal the bodies, burn them, and give the bones a dignified burial under a tamarisk tree.

God's opening action in 1 Samuel is a generous response to a barren woman's prayer. But God also plays a darker role. Saul's undoing can be traced, like that of Absalom, who will die "hanging between heaven and earth" (2 Sam. 18:9), not only to his own failures but to the prior actions of others, including God, who placed him in an unprecedented position for which he did not ask and in which he had no latitude to succeed. The result is both a won-derfully wrought heroic tragedy and a theologically intricate image of divine grace through the portrayal of its absence. Like those of Noah and Job, Saul's story, deceptively simple on the surface, opens to reveal complex questions of suffering and evil.

It is striking that the third failed ruler in 1 Samuel (after Eli and Samuel) receives such an intricate tale. The revision of Judah's history in 1 Chronicles allows Saul less than a chapter, dismissing him with ringing judgment, collapsing all ambiguities: "Saul died for his unfaithfulness; he was unfaithful to the LORD in that he did not keep the command of the LORD; moreover, he had consulted a medium, seeking guidance, and did not seek guidance from the LORD. Therefore the LORD put him to death and turned the kingdom over to David son of Jesse" (1 Chr. 10:13–11:1). The preservation of his tale in 1 Samuel does more justice to the realities of Saul's world and our own.

Saul's years of mistakes offer David time to grow into leadership and opportunity to consider how he will do the job better. Second Samuel will show whether the next leader handles success more gracefully than his predecessors have handled failure.

INTRODUCTION TO 2 SAMUEL

The narrative of 2 Samuel begins immediately after the death of King Saul, and tells the story of David's rise to kingship, the consolidation of his power, and the disastrous events growing out of his sexual misconduct and murderous plot. David's reign continues into the first two chapters of 1 Kings, which chronicle his death and the succession of Solomon.

Second Samuel evidently originated from the redacting together of several traditions and stories. Scholars have discerned a continuous narrative encompassing at least 2 Sam. 9–20 and 1 Kgs. 1–2. Although some have seen here an eyewitness report justifying Solomon's reign, others have viewed the story as either crit-ical of David or ambiguous in its sympathies. More recently scholars have seen the entire narrative, beginning with 1 Samuel, as a subtle and well-told novel that by balancing sympathies highlights the ethical and pragmatic dilemmas of leadership, the conflicts between personal and public life, and the inevitable ambiguity of human motives.

The sparely narrated but thickly woven plot of 2 Samuel resounds with ironies, incongruities, intertextual linkages, and psychological acuteness. David and his reign stand at the center. Shifts in his character are revealed as events unfold, and David moves from an unshaken confidence in his partnership with God to a more profound recognition of God's independence from his wishes. Divine plans to mold a nation intersect with David's ambitions, but supersede them as well. In contrast with much of 1 Samuel, the portrayal of God in 2 Samuel remains understated, visible only at certain dramatic junctures, creating an overall sense of a just order working itself out in relation to the kingship despite, and sometimes even through, human evil.

Besides David and God, the one character present throughout is David's general Joab. A ruthless pragmatist loyal to the throne, Joab carries out campaigns, assassinations, and retaliations, some authorized by David and many not. His violence helps bring David's inner conflicts into sharper relief. Many other vivid characters appear, including several members of Saul's family, several children of David, and others arrayed around the king—prophets, military leaders, and friends. The beautiful Bathsheba, doubtless the most famous supporting character, remains a mysterious figure whose feelings and motives have eluded centuries of readerly curiosity.

COMMENTARY

2 Samuel 1–4

Second Samuel opens just after Saul's death and David's return from defeating Amalekite raiders. A messenger arrives from the battlefield, a person whose story resembles but does not square with the version in 1 Sam. 31, in which Saul committed suicide. Playing his cards carefully, the Amalekite messenger appears to mourn, though he brings David the king's crown and armlet. He claims to have killed Saul, but only at his request. Readers know this is a fabrication; David and his companions do not.

David's reaction is passionately upright. He has the hapless Amalekite executed for having destroyed "the LORD's anointed" (1:14), and voices a lament. The lament's threefold refrain, "how the mighty have fallen" (1:19, 25, 27), is appended with more and more dramatic phrases with each repetition— first, an announcement of Israel's "glory" slain on the high places; then a gradual movement from beyond Israel's borders toward the central subjects, Saul and Jonathan, portrayed as mighty warriors, united in life and death, reflecting Jonathan's persistent loyalty despite the many disharmonies between father and son. Reasons for mourning Saul are economic, but grief for Jonathan is personal: "I am distressed for you, my brother Jonathan; greatly beloved were you to me; your love to me was wonderful, passing the love of women" (1:26).

Immediately on the heels of this lament, David inquires of God and moves to Hebron to become Judah's king. He sends a message to Jabesh-gilead, wooing a city loyal to Saul. But David's long-awaited ascension to Israel's throne will not be as easy as he hopes. Opposing forces appear immediately: Abner, commander of Saul's army, makes a fourth son of Saul king, the evidently young Ishbosheth (Ishbaal in the LXX and NRSV). One of the first casualties in the lengthy war that ensues is Joab's brother Asahel, killed by Abner.

Ishbosheth's insecure position crumbles when he accuses Abner of sleeping with Saul's concubine Rizpah. Abner indignantly vows to make David king, and sets out to do so. David tells Abner that he must first bring his wife, Saul's daughter Michal, who was long ago given to another man. That pure politics have overrun familial affection is underscored in the snapshot of her husband Paltiel, weeping behind her until Abner orders him away.

Abner visits David and is happily received. But Joab, claiming that Abner is deceiving David, murders him in retaliation for his brother's death. David immediately and at length distances himself, declaring his own innocence, cursing

Joab, ordering him to mourn, weeping at Abner's grave, voicing a lament, and refusing to eat. "All the people took notice of it, and it pleased them; just as everything the king did pleased all the people. So all the people and all Israel understood that day that the king had no part in the killing of Abner son of Ner" (3:36–37). David's lengthy campaign to hold Joab guilty overpowers even this narrative summary, and he gets in three more exclamations before the scene closes, including the ironic statement, "Today I am powerless, even though anointed king; these men, the sons of Zeruiah, are too violent for me" (v. 39).

The next chapter details the assassination of Ishbosheth while asleep in his bed. The two men who present the rival royal head to David have evidently not been watching him carefully enough. Their only thanks is immediate execution.

None of this bitter history remains in the rewritten version of David's enthronement in Chronicles, in which immediately upon Saul's death all Israel makes David king. Second Samuel's narrative is much grittier. God is not portrayed as participating in the several events that destroy Saul's dynasty, and David likewise proclaims his innocence. Some readers admire David's restraint, viewing the opportune deaths as providential. Other readers, suspicious of David's protestations, view him as grieving for appearance' sake, or even as secretly manipulating events. Whatever the actual causes, David's climb to the throne has become inevitable.

2 Samuel 5–10

Several events now consolidate David's kingship. Twenty chapters and nearly as many years after his secret anointing by Samuel, Israel's elders anoint him king in 2 Sam. 5, which bursts with repetitions of "king over Israel." Immediately he makes the Jebusite city of Jerusalem his capital, with a palace built by King Hiram of Tyre. When the Philistines hear that their erstwhile vassal is now their enemy's king, they come seeking him. In a reversal of the humiliation of 1 Sam. 4:11, the Israelites defeat them and carry away their gods. The trusting Achish, who had sheltered the renegade David, is completely forgotten.

Chapters 6 and 7 finesse a response to earlier concerns that a king would displace God's rule. David seeks to unite church and state: first, to bring to his new city the ancient tribal symbol of divine presence, the ark of God; and second, to house it permanently near his palace. In both cases God will weigh in; this partnership is by no means controlled by the king. When David tries to bring the ark from Abinadab's home where it resided through Saul's reign, it proves no safer for human manipulation than before: Abinadab's son Uzzah attempts to steady it on the cart and is killed. Enraged and afraid, David leaves it in a Gittite's home.

After three months David sets out again to bring the ark to Jerusalem. But this parade likewise ends in an exchange of anger founded on history. Michal's rage, sparked by David's alleged exhibitionism, is best understood in relation to her entire story. Having been traded for Philistine foreskins, abandoned by the husband she loved, and extradited from a kindly marriage, Michal exhibits disdain for the king-turned-buffoon as passionate as her former love for the shepherd-turned-hero. David's stinging retort emphasizes his freedom to debase himself and yet retain honor, since God has elected him to replace her own father.

Michal's subsequent childlessness is one of several dead ends in Saul's genealogy, with more to come. Whether it results from her choice, David's, or God's is left unstated. By contrast, David's descendants immediately receive an eternal promise. Chapter 7 is a theological centerpiece not only of this book but of the Deuteronomistic History overall. David expresses to the prophet Nathan his wish to build a "house" for God. God relays through Nathan that, on the contrary, it is God who will build David a house—that is, a dynasty. Reaching both backward and forward in the story, God says of David's unborn son: "I will not take my steadfast love from him, as I took it from Saul. . . . Your house and your kingdom shall be made sure forever before me" (7:15–16). Eli, Samuel, and Saul all failed to see their sons succeed them. This fourth time around, succession is assured.

Having secured the crown, the city, the ark, and the promise, David defeats surrounding neighbors, showing little mercy. Both Jonathan and Saul had presciently pleaded for amnesty for their family (1 Sam. 20:14–15; 24:21–22). While David has not directed the demise of Saulides, neither has he overseen their preservation. But once his kingdom is fully secure, he remembers Jonathan's kindness and asks: "Is there still anyone left of the house of Saul to whom I may show kindness for Jonathan's sake?" (2 Sam. 9:1). The relationship between this episode and the Gibeonites' request to execute seven of Saul's sons and grandsons in chap. 21 is unclear. On the one hand, his question shows ignorance of Mephibosheth's existence, suggesting that this episode precedes 21:7, in which he spares him. On the other hand, Mephibosheth is already being depicted as the sole survivor, suggesting that this episode follows the others' deaths. Chapter 9's author may have been unaware of the other story, or may have chosen to suppress it. The author of chap. 21, however, carefully avoided contradicting this one.

Mephibosheth had been dropped by a nurse and crippled the day his father died. Now he himself has a son, and lives in the non-Israelite Transjordan. After learning of him from Ziba, servant of Saul's family, David brings Mephibosheth to stay with him and restores his ancestral land, which is to be managed by Ziba. This transaction is couched in royal magnanimity, but it undeniably brings the king benefits: oversight of potential rivals and legitimated use of Saul's land. Its resonance with the end of 2 Kings, where the captive Davidic king sits at the Babylonian royal table, suggests a limbo of neither imprisonment nor freedom.

God's involvement has so far been inconspicuous. Such tacit approval affords David latitude to choose his course without prophetic strictures such as Saul endured from Samuel. The story is not blind to Machiavellian practicalities in violent times. David shows both military ruthlessness and a realistic valuation of alliances. Chapter 10 shows David attempting to extend friendship to the neighboring Ammonites and changing his policy quickly when his envoys are humiliated. The war that ensues becomes the setting of King David's most famous conquest.

2 Samuel 11–14

The next events occur at the pinnacle of David's success, in what should have been his golden years. Chapter 11 is well known but widely misapprehended. Renaissance paintings focus on the woman bathing, smiling seductively, on her own roof or even in an open square. But the storyteller's eyes are on King David, who spies her from his own roof. In no place is Bathsheba blamed by Nathan, God, or the narrator. Modern movies detail a love affair, but the terse narrative could hardly show less romance. David strolls; he sees; he inquires. The woman is wife of one of his renowned fighters, and daughter of another (2 Sam. 23:34, 39). Nevertheless the king sends and takes and lies—doing far worse than Samuel had warned of kings: "He will take your daughters to be perfumers" (1 Sam. 8:13). Her reaction is understated: she goes when taken, she returns, she conceives. Bathsheba's single independent act is to send a two-word message suppressing both panic and recrimination but denying David the privilege of standing aloof: "I'm pregnant" (11:5). What confession would have cost the king we cannot know; his futile cover-up costs many lives, beginning with Bathsheba's husband and other soldiers. Sovereignty has limits: a king can take a body but can control neither biological processes nor human responses.

Bathsheba's visit to the palace lasts four words. Uriah's visit lasts four days, 128 words unfolding excruciating suspense. Despite the king's coercion, Uriah is too loyal to the troops to enjoy his wife and home. His uprightness contrasts sharply with the king's irresponsibility.

Joab cannot follow David's orders to betray Uriah without the help of others. Instead, he deliberately botches the battle, killing many soldiers. Seething anger permeates his overdetermined report. But this is nothing next to the scathing message Nathan brings from God. David had told Joab, literally, "do not let this thing be evil in your eyes" (11:25), but we soon hear, "evil was the thing David did in the LORD's eyes" (11:27). Nathan's main points are not rape or adultery, but murder and wife stealing. He uses a story inviting royal judgment to indict David of thoughtless killing for the sake of appetite. Interpreters have sought in vain to allegorize this parable (Is the poor man Uriah or Bathsheba? Is the lamb Bathsheba or Uriah? And who is the visitor?), but the culprit's identity is clear. Nathan's stinging pronouncement, "you are the man" (12:7), forces David to recognize his deeds. God has given him much, but he cannot take everything he pleases.

Judgment follows in a blunt series of parallel clauses describing God's prior actions for David, David's actions against God, Uriah, and Bathsheba, and God's planned actions against David, including the death of Bathsheba's child, violence in his household, and sexual usurpation.

Children should not have to suffer for their parents' sins, and yet they do. The storyteller leaves the precise link between David's deeds and the ensuing family tragedies unscrutinized but inescapable. Nor does the narrator dwell on the anguish of others harmed by David's sin, whose various griefs peek through the crevices of a narrative that relentlessly spotlights the king.

David's strange behavior surrounding his infant's death is remarked by his servants. The one who fasted and mourned at length for Saul, Jonathan,

and Abner ceases to mourn his own son when it becomes clear God is not listening. Is this admirable assent to divine decree, or resignation, or callousness? Unlike Saul's, David's divine rejection is temporary, ending with the birth of Solomon, whom God favors.

The aftermath nevertheless continues to unfold, as David's children repeat his own behavior against one another, forcing upon him the divided pain of loving both victim and victimizer. His oldest son replicates his sexual machinations, and his daughter forcefully articulates her tragedy. Word choice intensifies the irony: Amnon "loves" Tamar, so he wants to "do something to her." His "wise" friend Jonadab, understanding what "love" means, prescribes tricking David into "sending" for Tamar—as he once sent for Bathsheba. It works perfectly.

Amnon discovers, like his father, that he can seize a woman's body but cannot control the outcome. When no justice is forthcoming from their father, Tamar's brother Absalom persuades David once again to send, snaring Amnon for murder just as Tamar had been snared for rape and Uriah for betrayal and death.

When Absalom flees to his maternal grandfather, David mourns for his son day after day. Which son he grieves is not specified. Finally, according to the NRSV: "the heart of the king went out, yearning for Absalom; for he was now consoled over the death of Amnon" (13:39). This translation hangs on a textual corruption and several ambiguous words. Equally likely is its opposite: "David longed to march out against Absalom, for he was grieved about Amnon, because he was dead." This ambiguity plunges readers into confusion mirroring that of a king missing his moral compass.

Now Joab reenacts a previous event. Like God two chapters before, Joab sends a messenger to lead David into a judgment designed to implicate him. His messenger, a woman described as "wise" like Jonadab, faces a task far more complex than Nathan's, calling the king not to condemn an evildoer, but to arbitrate between competing theories of justice. After three speeches, she teases out a reluctant ruling. Attempting to apply the ruling to the king, she becomes oddly incoherent, saying literally: "Why did you think thus about the people of God? From the king's saying this thing, as being guilty in order for the king not to bring back his outcast one . . ." (14:13). By the time her garbled speech ends four verses later, she has retreated from oracle back to ruse. Recognizing the contrivance, David identifies Joab's involvement. He agrees to return Absalom to Jerusalem, but refuses to see him. Their meeting two years later is brief, formal, and wordless.

Unlike Eli, Samuel, and Saul, David had emerged from troubled years in great triumph, with every resource firmly in hand and great potential to rule well. Yet his own success undoes him. Although biblical prophets preach often against greed, violence, and abuse of power, few stories portray more vividly the devastation wreaked by such wrongs. Few stories show more powerfully the heartbreaking consequences, not the least of which is the squandered opportunity to use power to benefit rather than destroy others. Yet readers through the ages have winked at the king's evil, either finding it titillating or blaming the woman he spied and took. Renouncing violent abuse of power, whether sexual, political, or military, still lies beyond our collective grasp.

God is rarely seen intervening to protect victims from powerful foes, and terrible consequences still play themselves out in history and families. Yet prophets still demand change. The biblical story asserts that the unseen God does watch, and that those who abuse power will not be able to hide their crimes. This is a point of hope for many who pray with Jeremiah, "Why does the way of the guilty prosper?" (Jer. 12:1). Poetic justice still emerges, even if ambiguously and late.

2 Samuel 15–20

Absalom immediately begins plotting insurrection. His story thinly reenacts that of David with Saul. Exiled from the palace, Absalom garners admiration and gathers supporters, steals the people's hearts, and is declared king in Hebron. But unlike his father, Absalom indicates no faith; his one mention of God is a ruse (15:7). What unfolded for David as divine blessing unfolds for Absalom by human wit alone.

Whereas Saul had marched out to attack David, David retreats from Absalom. He has already shown himself more skillful as underdog than as ruler. Now several encounters with supporters, detractors, and profiteers reveal glimmers of the David of old, characterized by strategic wisdom and pious humility. The king who lost his religion while comfortable now regains it in the midst of crisis.

The king first encounters Ittai the Gittite, leader of six hundred Philistine mercenaries, who asserts his loyalty despite David's protests and is permitted to join the retreat. Next he meets the priests bringing the ark from Jerusalem. Unsure of his standing with God, he refuses to take the ark. Instead he commissions them to send him news from Jerusalem. When he hears that his counselor Ahithophel has joined Absalom's insurrection, he garners the strength to pray that God "turn the counsel of Ahithophel into foolishness" (15:31). Almost immediately he recognizes a potential answer in the form of another friend, Hushai the Archite, whom he asks to find Absalom and give him false advice.

Next he meets two fellows who attempt to capitalize on his misfortunes. Mephibosheth's servant Ziba brings supplies and a tale of his master's vain hope of restoration to kingship. As if an exiled king had power, David quickly grants Ziba all of Mephibosheth's property, displaying his mistrust of Jonathan's son. Finally, a relative of Saul named Shemei arrives, cursing with dangerous accuracy: "Out! Out! Murderer! Scoundrel! The LORD has avenged on all of you the blood of the house of Saul, in whose place you have reigned" (16:7–8). David declines Abishai's offer to behead him.

In Jerusalem Hushai greets Absalom with flattering doubletalk. Upon Ahithophel's advice, Absalom pitches a tent on the palace roof—where David's troubles began—"and Absalom went in to his father's concubines in the sight of all Israel" (16:22)—just as Nathan had predicted. Ahithophel tersely offers to go assassinate David alone, ending the battle. But Hushai offers a flowery, flattering counterproposal that Absalom wait for reinforcements and ride out himself for a full-scale war. God's participation is glimpsed: Absalom follows Hushai's advice because God ordained it so. Hushai sends word to David, who crosses the Jordan River immediately and meets more friends bringing provisions.

David's preparations for battle are detailed. With great pathos and ambiguity, he requests that Absalom be gently handled. After the lengthy buildup, the battle itself takes only three verses. The statement that "the forest claimed more victims that day than the sword" (18:8) both hints at divine participation and prepares for what follows: Absalom's head is caught by a tree and he is found "hanging between heaven and earth" (v. 9). The argument that ensues between Joab and the soldier who found him reveals Joab's ruthless reputation and the differing construals the king's order regarding Absalom might inspire. Joab, who has killed so many for the king, does so once again.

Much more narrative space is given to David's reception of the news. Five verses relate Joab's conversation with Ahimaaz, who begs to take the message. A race ensues between him and a Cushite messenger. Ten verses build the suspense and chronicle the king's reaction. Showing no interest in the victory, he asks only about Absalom. Ahimaaz pretends ignorance, but the Cushite replies with a stately circumlocution: may all the king's enemies be like that young man.

The king hears the political only to extract from it the personal: "O my son Absalom, my son, my son Absalom! Would I had died instead of you" (18:33).

Here readers are given one of the very few unobstructed views of David's heart. David's climactic lament strikes hard on common experience.

As the scene enlarges, emphases shift drastically: "The victory that day was turned into mourning for all the troops" (19:2). This moment crystallizes what has been taking shape for many chapters. David's public servants have been used repeatedly to cover his private sins. The entire nation has become embroiled in a family brawl, and twenty thousand are dead. After having failed for many years to react effectively to repeated instances of violence that have ravaged his children, his reaction at this point, pathos-filled as it is, comes far too late in family and political history.

Joab is hardly the type to offer sympathy, but his brutality may still shock, as he reframes the meaning of what has happened. This army saved the king's life and those of his family. To weep for Absalom who hates him is to despise all who love him. If he does not speak kindly to his troops, not one will stand with him again. The king receives the troops, his silence signaling the gap between familial and public roles.

Episodes as David returns to Jerusalem mirror those of his leaving. Shimei meets him crying for mercy. David swears that he will not die (but see 1 Kgs. 2:8, 36–46). Mephibosheth meets him with a story contradicting Ziba's. Rather than investigate, David splits the property between him and his servant. David invites his benefactor Barzillai to live with him in Jerusalem, but the old man declines, sending a younger man in his place.

Rebellion breaks out again, this time sparked by a Benjaminite named Sheba. This episode eerily echoes several previous events, as if all possible story lines have already been told. Without needing to state his reason, David grants Joab's command to Amasa, who had been Absalom's general. Amasa is sent to rally Judah, but when he is delayed, Joab inserts himself into the action, kills Amasa, and takes charge. Sheba is pursued to the city of Abel, and the rebellion halts when Sheba's head tumbles over the wall, the last of several beheaded enemies of David, from Goliath to Saul to Ish-bosheth. A final note declares Joab in command of the army.

This story will continue four chapters later with another tragic split in David's household sparked by his son Adonijah's pretensions to the throne, a split that will divide David's supporters and result in murders authorized by the king extending beyond his death. The one Shimei called a man of blood dies broken and bitter. Unlike most everyone else, he dies in bed.

First Chronicles 20:1–3 preserves only the minutest sliver of the story that has been detailed in ten excruciating chapters in 2 Samuel, overviewing only the capture of Rabbah by Joab and the taking of booty and slaves. Uriah is remembered only in a list of warriors, while Bathsheba is utterly forgotten, and Amnon, Tamar, Absalom, and Adonijah appear only as names. So it is in most families: ancestors die along with their heartbreaking stories, and all that remains are names and dates, if even these. The decision by the author of Chronicles to omit these stories testifies to their disturbing power. But it is for this very reason that such stories should be remembered. As Maya Angelou has said, "History, despite its wrenching pain, cannot be unlived, but if faced with courage, need not be lived again" ("On the Pulse of Morning").

2 Samuel 21–24

The final four chapters fit the book loosely, a miscellany organized into an envelope structure. At the core are two poems in which David describes his life and relationship with God (22:1–51; 23:1–7). Framing them are two lists, orna-mented with anecdotes, of David's war-riors (21:15–22; 23:8–39). Framing these are two stories of divine punishment for royal misdeeds, first by Saul and then by David (21:1–14; 24:1–26).

The first affliction is a three-year famine. Though it occurs during David's

reign, it is attributed to Saul's killing of Gibeonites. When David asks the Gibe-onites what amends can be made, they request seven of Saul's descendants. Two sons and five grandsons are given them for ritual murder. Rizpah, the mother of the two sons, guards the bodies for weeks, until David buries their bones.

The second affliction results from David's taking a census. After David con-fesses it as sin, a prophet offers him a choice of three punishments. He chooses three days of pestilence, which kills sev-enty thousand. The plague ends when he buys a threshing floor in Jerusalem and builds an altar.

Following the first affliction is a brief section describing battles with the Philistines in which four giants from Gath are killed by four of David's men. One note stands in conflict with David's own story: "Elhanan son of Jaare-oregim, the Bethlehemite, killed Goliath the Git-tite" (21:19).

Complementing this section are anec-dotes and lists of David's renowned war-riors—three of the greatest, two others, and thirty more. Remarkable here is the inclusion of Eliam, son of Ahithophel and father of Bathsheba (23:34). Standing out at the end of the list is Uriah the Hittite (v. 39). Standing out for his absence is Joab. These lists suggest that national security depended not on David and Joab alone, but on the collective strength of many skilled soldiers.

Enshrined in the middle are two poems attributed to David, complementing the Song of Hannah in 1 Sam. 2, and sounding similar notes: "You deliver a humble peo-ple, but your eyes are upon the haughty to bring them down" (22:28). Yet in the con-text of David's story their piety raises uncomfortable questions. The first psalm narrates divine rescue from enemies, metaphorized as "mighty waters" in a cos-mic battle. The reason given for God's deliverance is the speaker's blamelessness (vv. 21–25). About midway the oppressed speaker becomes a warrior crushing opponents with God's help: God "trains my hands for war . . . I pursued my enemies and destroyed them . . . I beat them fine . . . foreigners came cringing to me" (vv. 35, 38, 43, 45), showing the ease with which one who begins as a victim dangerously continues to claim victim status long after circumstances are reversed. Its ultimate irony lies toward the end: after descriptions of consuming enemies, striking them down, destroying, crushing, stamping, David says "you delivered me from the violent" (v. 49), showing how the certainty that one is blameless and blessed authorizes the infliction of suffering on others.

Similar irony appears in the companion piece in chap. 23, where David reports God's word to him: "One who rules over people justly, ruling in the fear of God, is like the light of morning, like the sun rising on a cloudless morning, gleaming from the rain on the grassy land" (23:3–4). The next verse is puzzling, as if its unintended honesty were a Freudian slip. According to the NRSV and most other recent translators and interpreters, it reads as a question seeking an affirmative answer: "Is not my house like this with God?" But the Hebrew shows no marker for a question; a literal translation yields something close to the LXX and Vulgate as well as the KJV and other premodern English translations: "For my house is not so with God," a rendering that seems to fit the context of the poem in 2 Samuel better than the thrust of the poem itself, as if the two were at odds with each other.

In the heart of these final chapters lie two poems that would sound more convincing elsewhere—in David's glorified tradition in Chronicles, for instance, which makes of the story of the altar on the threshing floor a jumping-off point for David's planning and sponsorship of the building of Solomon's temple. The ambiguities of these poems can be evaluated in differing ways. They may suggest the impossibility of purity in politics and give David credit for intending to honor God, sinner as he was. Or David's ability

to intone these words may be viewed as a gift of forgiving grace. Or they may reflect a ruler so caught up in his own rhetoric that he cannot see his resemblance to those he denounces.

Many ethical and theological themes in 1–2 Samuel resound in contemporary events: those who lead must serve rather than abuse their followers; power does not reside in armies, wealth, strategy, talent, or prior promise, but is given by God. And justice, even divine justice, appears in no predictable or wooden fashion, but unfolds slowly through the twists and turns of human events. The books of Samuel invite readers to sharpen their moral vision, beckoning no simplistic formulas or easy pronouncements, demanding full recognition of the many-sided nature of human existence before a God whose plans intersect but by no means coincide with their own.

Bibliography

Alter, Robert. *The Art of Biblical Narrative.* New York: Basic Books, 1981.

Birch, Bruce C. "The First and Second Books of Samuel." In *NIB*, 2:947–1383.

Brueggemann, Walter. *First and Second Samuel.* Interpretation. Louisville: John Knox, 1990.

Clines, David J. A., and Tamara C. Eskenazi, eds. *Telling Queen Michal's Story: An Experiment in Comparative Interpretation.* JSOTSup 119. Sheffield: JSOT Press, 1991.

Exum, J. Cheryl. *Tragedy and Biblical Narrative.* Cambridge: Cambridge University Press, 1992.

Green, Barbara. *How Are the Mighty Fallen? A Dialogical Study of King Saul in 1 Samuel.* JSOTSup 365. London: Sheffield Academic Press, 2003.

Gunn, David M. *The Fate of King Saul.* JSOTSup 14. Sheffield: JSOT Press, 1980.

———. *The Story of King David: Genre and Interpretation.* JSOTSup 6. Sheffield: JSOT Press, 1978.

1 and 2 Kings

Gregory Mobley

INTRODUCTION

The scroll of Kings begins with David in decline, shivering next to the maiden Abishag. How the mighty have fallen. That had been David's own line composed for the funerals of his crazed mentor Saul and beloved comrade Jonathan (cf. 2 Sam. 1). This tepid opening establishes a tone of weariness that dominates much of the books of 1 and 2 Kings, a single scroll originally. David, the giant slayer, scourge of the Negev, warlord of the six hundred, prince of Hebron, king of the houses of Ephraim and Judah, founder of Jerusalem, the sweet psalmist of Israel, David the mutilator and musician, David the harem master, husband to at least seven wives and sire of more than twenty children: the great man whose territory eventually extended from "the River" (Euphrates) to "the Great Sea" (the Mediterranean)—and he cannot achieve circulation to his extremities even when cuddled by the most beautiful girl in Judah (1 Kgs. 1:1–4).

The scroll of Kings concludes with details about events four hundred years later. It is the end of everything: the city of David, the capital cities of Samaria and Jerusalem, the network of market towns and provincial capitals, the army of Judah. Above all, the end of Kings describes the destruction of Solomon's temple, the Iron Age embassy where YHWH, Creator of the heavens and the earth, received pilgrims and accepted tribute, the house whose bedrock foundation capped the Well of Souls and whose Edenic chambers and pillared solidity proclaimed through architecture that the Lord was in heaven and all was right with a world that found its center on Mount Zion, in the sacred city of Jerusalem, in the Middle Kingdom of Judah, in the Holy Land of Eretz-Israel.

What remained at the end of the scroll of Kings? The priesthood remained, and at least one of its members in Babylonian exile composed or completed a vast historical chronicle of the dynastic era in Israel (also known as Ephraim) and Judah. The full work was a tetrateuch—Joshua–Judges–Samuel–Kings—and it told the story of the people Israel from its entry into Canaan to its exit to Babylon. (Note: the term "Israel" in the Bible and in this essay can refer to the entire culture, the patriarch Jacob, and the territorial state that from ca. 922 to 722 BCE existed in Galilee, and Jezreel Valley, and the Samarian highlands north of Jerusalem.)

The house of David remained, just barely. According to the final paragraph of the scroll of Kings (2 Kgs. 25:27–30), the Davidide Jehoiachin was released from confinement and allowed to dine in the gilded cage of Evil-merodach's palace in the imperial capital with the other exiled West Asian potentates.

Most of all, a prophetic tradition remained after the fall of Jerusalem to the Babylonian army in 587 BCE. This prophetic tradition began in the ninth and eighth centuries on the highlands of Ephraim, was borne south by northern emigrés to a village called Anathoth after the fall of its host culture in 722 BCE to the Assyrians, and eventually captured the allegiance of some Jerusalem priests by the end of the seventh century BCE, one or some of whom composed the scroll of Kings.

The scroll of Kings marks the end of so much. As literature, Kings marks the end of the Joshua–Judges–Samuel–Kings corpus, the Former Prophets. Canonically, Kings marks the end of the Primary History, Israel's sacred narrative of cosmic, terrestrial, and national life that spans Genesis through Kings. Theologically, Kings marks the end of an era. It represents the final grand statement of Iron Age theology.

The cataclysms of the destruction of the temple and the exile of elite Judahites, along with the demeaning quality of colonial life and the accumulated debris from generations of deferred dreams, would inspire subsequent Judahite writers in the late exilic, Persian, and Hellenistic ages—such as the authors of Isaiah 40–55, Job, Ecclesiastes, and Daniel 7–12—to question implicitly and explicitly the efficacy of moral cause and effect as an explanation for everything, and reflect more deeply upon the meaning of suffering, the origins of evil, and the justice of the divine government. The scroll of Kings never gets to these marginal, less-traversed places in the theological landscape, but its written witness became the platform on which later visionaries would take their stand and catch their breath before formulating their advances.

The Scroll of Kings as a Prophetic Oracle

The scroll of Kings, eventually the books of 1 and 2 Kings, was understood in two different ways by the ancients, as a prophetic oracle and as a historical chronicle. The former is the more ancient and the more Jewish, to count the scroll of Kings among the prophetic literature of the Bible. The latter view, which may have originated among the Jewish community of Alexandria who produced the Septuagint in the second century BCE, would eventually become the dominant view in Christianity, that Kings is among "the historical books," a corpus expanded to include Ezra, Nehemiah, Chronicles, Esther, and Ruth (all found in the final section of the Hebrew canon, "the Writings"), that follow the Pentateuch and precede "the poetical books." We must pause to consider the implications of viewing the scroll of Kings according to the former view, as a prophetic oracle. Although 1 and 2 Kings assume the form of a historical chronicle, they represent the translation and extension of the performance-oriented, primarily oral prophetic tradition into chronologically sequenced prose, a new development in literature.

What is prophecy? Though we are accustomed to imagine prophetic vision as foresighted, as seeing forward, prediction is not the focus of biblical prophecy. Rather, biblical prophecy is about "seeing through." "Then Elisha prayed, 'O LORD, please open his eyes that he may see.' So the LORD opened the eyes of the servant, and he saw; the mountain was full of horses and chariots of fire all around Elisha" (2 Kgs. 6:17). The prophet sees through the veil of appearances to glimpse a different reality. The prophet, as in the above anecdote about Elisha, sees a world that is charged with the grandeur of God, and glimpses the cosmic realities, here celestial horses and bands of angels, that are invisible to the prophet's peers. Prophetic vision penetrates everydayness to go deeper than conventional wisdom in order to reveal the story behind the story. For instance, while everyone else in Amos's mid-eighth-century culture heard the faint but ever increasing noise of the Assyrian war machine under lion-festooned standards gearing up for campaigning in the west, the prophet alone heard the roar of a different beast, the Lion of Judah aroused and on the prowl against God's own people because of the economic and ritual corruptions of Jeroboam II's administration in Samaria. The Assyrian army was merely the Lord's tool of judgment against Ephraimite society.

Occasionally, this type of prophetic vision did uncannily foreshadow the future. But this was not because prophets gazed through crystal balls; rather it was because, under the surface of reality, under the river of time, there is another river whose course, cut into the earth during creation week, is foundational and paradigmatic. Tides—of creation to chaos and from chaos to re-creation, of exile and homecoming, of divine mercy and judgment—undulate below the surface, and it is by these eternal wave functions that the prophets marked time and announced seasons.

We might understand it this way: true prophets—and there were plenty of false ones—were those with a sixth sense, not for hearing voices or seeing visions or sensing intangible perceptions (though that is how the ancients told it), but for registering those tremors of the transcendent reality beneath and behind the surface of the mundane.

For the priestly historians who composed the scroll of Kings, the Mosaic tradition, the Torah, served as the lens for interpreting the deepest, truest story of the dynastic era in Israel and Judah. Though the word *torah* has often been translated as "law," it is better understood as "instruction." That is, the Mosaic torah was considered to be the instruction manual for human life. Those persons who followed the instructions, observing its times and seasons, its patterns and progressions, were in tune with the underlying principles that structured the cosmos, and approached a state of harmony with God and creation, their word for which was *shalom*. Those who lived contrary to these patterns were moving against the grain of creation and courted disaster.

This Mosaic tradition can now be identified with the biblical literature of Genesis, Exodus, Leviticus, Numbers, and Deuteronomy. We cannot be sure how much of this corpus was extant when Kings was composed, and whether it circulated through oral or documentary media. Nevertheless, this tradition, whether authored by Moses (a traditional view) or merely associated with his legend in order to grant it religious legitimacy (a modern view), the core of what came to be known as the Written Torah, offered the perspectives that prophets and prophetic-minded historians so immersed themselves in that they could claim to divine the deeper wellsprings of meaning beneath the showy parade of events, the ebbs and flows in God's management of the world.

The authors, or author, of Kings (note: scholars fiercely debate whether Kings had single or multiple authorship; I will not take a position on this question here) may or may not have been prophets themselves, but they valorized prophets and used the prophetic method to compose their chronicle of the reigns of ruling houses in Shechem, Tirzah, Samaria, and Jerusalem from the eleventh to the sixth century BCE (i.e., ca. 1000–560 BCE). Every dynasty and era was judged according to how it measured up to the standards of the Mosaic teaching, especially as these were formulated in the Deuteronomic tradition.

The Deuteronomistic tradition and the composition of Kings. We employ the term "Deuteronomic tradition" rather than Deuteronomy, the ultimate written expression of these ideas, because the book of Deuteronomy as we know it was undergoing its final composition at the same time as that of the scroll of Kings. Readers curious about the academic debates concerning the growth of the book of Deuteronomy, and the different ways in which that work may have influenced the writing of the tetrateuch of

Joshua–Judges–Samuel–Kings, should consult the commentaries.

For our purposes we will assume that the book we know as Deuteronomy is the final form of a tradition that developed over centuries. This tradition began in the northern culture of Israel, traced its origins to Moses himself, had associations with the Levitical priests of the premonarchical shrine at Shiloh (most notably Eli and Samuel), was championed by the heirs to this priesthood and a series of Ephraimite prophets such as Elijah and Elisha in the ninth century and Hosea in the eighth century, and was carried south to Judah after the collapse of Samaria in 722 where it was preserved and augmented with southern, Judahite religious traditions by northern immigrants in the village of Anathoth, Jeremiah's hometown just north of Jerusalem. In the seventh century (perhaps) this tradition of religious teachings associated with Moses began to be formulated into a written document.

Eventually, by the time this work assumed its current form, during the exilic period, this collection of religious teachings had been shaped into the form of a covenant, the very kind of political treaty that Assyrian and Babylonian tyrants "offered" to their subjects. Deuteronomy in its final covenantally styled form thus represents a sacred declaration of independence from the Mesopotamian superpowers: Israel's constitution was given to Moses on Sinai by YHWH; the only treaty it would recognize was the one granted by the Creator and ratified through the generations by the community.

The key link between this Deuteronomic tradition and the scroll of Kings is this. The dramatic climax of Kings is the reign of the Judahite king Josiah in the final decades of the seventh century. According to 2 Kgs. 22–23, a forgotten scroll was discovered by the priest Hilkiah, who claimed to have found it among the holdings in the archives of the Jerusalem temple. This scroll, which claimed to be the very words of Moses, was authenticated by the prophetess Huldah, and inspired

King Josiah to reform the religious life of Judah. The tenets of Josiah's program—the centralization of worship, the performance of Passover in a certain style, the iconoclastic purging of divine images—are identical to those promulgated in the book we know as Deuteronomy. In addition, the very words used in the description of Josiah's reform—allusions to "covenant," to loving the Lord with "all one's heart and soul"—are reminiscent of the diction of Deuteronomy.

This suggests that during Josiah's reign, the Deuteronomic tradition was "discovered," or began to be formally composed (we must remember that no ancient religious reform based on new ideas would have been respected; it had to be linked to an ancient worthy to have legitimacy in this traditional culture). Alongside this scroll of Deuteronomy, initiated in Josiah's reign and completed by Judahite priests in exile, a companion history was composed. This history, written by priests who were fellow travelers of the Josianic-Deuteronomic reform, picked up Israel's story line after the death of Moses and chronicled the fortunes of Israel from the days of Joshua, through the settlement in Canaan and the frontier days of the judges, to the beginnings of the monarchy under Saul and David, and finished by sketching the four centuries of the dynastic era in Israel and Judah (the subject of the book of Kings) up until the Babylonian exile.

This priestly history eventually spanned four scrolls, comprising the books we know as Joshua, Judges, 1 and 2 Samuel, and 1 and 2 Kings. Since this historical work shares so many parallels with Deuteronomy, it is customary for scholars to refer to the quartet of historical scrolls from Joshua through Kings as "the Deuteronomistic History." Consider, for instance, the way in which so many major speeches from a variety of speakers (e.g., Joshua, Samuel, David, and Josiah) speak in the same accents throughout the History: the voice of Moses from Deuteronomy (cf. Deut. 31 with Josh. 23–24, 1 Sam. 12, 1 Kgs. 2, 1 Kgs. 11, 2 Kgs. 22–23).

Commissioned by Josiah to write a history that culminated in his late-seventh-century reforms, or bitterly inspired by the exile to articulate what went wrong with the dream, or both, priestly historians wrote "the prophetic history of the kingdoms of Israel and Judah," the interpreted history, a national chronicle that judged every era and king according to how it measured up to the standard of Mosaic tradition in its particular Deuteronomic form.

The Compositional Texture of Kings

These historians who produced Kings were conservative in their poesy; their achievement was as much an act of compiling and editing as of writing. These historians drew on two major types of sources: (1) official, archival material from the palace and temple precincts such as court annals from both Israel and Judah (e.g., 1 Kgs 11:41; 14:19, 29), various expressions of administrative trivia (1 Kgs. 4:7–19, 22–28), and the design of the temple (1 Kgs. 6–7); and (2) legends about prophets, many of which have the earmarks of originally oral composition. These historians used the outline of reigns from the court archives in order to sequence their narrative, spliced in their didactic asides, their rantings and Deuteronomic ratings of each reign, and paused every so often to highlight scenes in which prophets bested kings.

The scroll of Kings thus consists of big traditions (edited official records) and little traditions, a corpus of tales about prophets set mainly in rural villages that highlight the moral heroism of legendary prophets such as Elijah and Elisha and many other named and unnamed prophets, and sketch indelible portraits of various common people. This contrast between the clichéd formulaic texture of the accounts about the rote mendacities, petty corruptions, cruel injustices, and bungling statecraft of the big shots, and the vivid, quirky folktales about the little people—lepers, Syrian house slaves, rural juvenile delinquents, family farmers, roving bands of itinerant,

undomesticated seers and the informal network of women who fed and sheltered them—may hold theological significance itself. The meek inherited and kept vital the traditional faith of Israel throughout the monarchical era.

The Meaning of the Title, "Kings"

The ancients were not keen on titles. Titles of works were scribal retrieval devices, not authorial creations that added another layer of meaning to a work. The correct sense of the title of the scroll of Kings is captured in the Greek title of the work in the Septuagint, "Reigns." The Hebrew word for "kings," *melakim*, refers not to the protagonists of the scroll—its heroes are the prophets, not its parade of potentates—but to its subject matter, the chronicle of the era of kingship, when there were functioning royal dynasties in Israel and Judah, from ca. 1000 to 600 BCE.

When and by Whom Was Kings Written?

The scroll of Kings could not have been completed before the mid-sixth century BCE because its final paragraph, a note about the fortunes of the exiled King Jehoiachin, is dated to the thirty-seventh year of his exile in Babylon. Since Jehoiachin was among the first wave of Judahites deported to Babylon in 597 (cf. 2 Kgs. 24:10–12), this takes us down to ca. 560. As noted above, the composition of the scroll could have been initiated several decades before it was completed, during the reign of Josiah, the patron of the Deuteronomistic Historians.

Nowhere does the text of Kings name its author. According to the Talmud, the prophet Jeremiah was its author. Most modern scholars are conditioned to reject the ancient traditions about the authorship of biblical books (e.g., that Moses wrote the Pentateuch, that David wrote the Psalms), and most attribute the composition of Kings to an unknown member(s) of that late-seventh- and sixth-century Judahite priestly subculture that produced the scroll of Deuteronomy, that is, someone within the circle of Deuteronomistic Historians. The biblical scholar Richard Elliott Friedman is a rarity among modern scholars in his commonsensical contention that no major work of literature was ever written by committee. He further observes that the book of Jeremiah is itself full of Deuteronomistic language. We cannot know whether Jeremiah was the Deuteronomistic Historian—again the work contains no ascription of authorship—but if readers desire to imagine an ideal author in order to humanize and emotionally deepen their reading experience, then the talmudic tradition that Jeremiah wrote the scroll of Kings is not a bad choice.

Theological Themes in the Scroll of Kings

Moral cause and effect. The dominant theological principle of the scroll of Kings is that God administers justice on the basis of moral cause and effect, rewarding virtue and punishing vice. Though this doctrine is often termed "Deuteronomistic" because it is formulated so often and so memorably in Deuteronomy (e.g., Deut. 28), it is more properly termed "Iron Age theology," because it can be found outside Deuteronomy, even in the religious literature of Israel's neighboring cultures such as in a ninth-century BCE Moabite text, the Mesha inscription. The book of Kings provides a moral audit of every dynasty and era, and explains how every prosperity was the fruit of righteousness and every disaster grew from idolatry or injustice.

When the Babylonians took scores of Judahites into exile in a series of early-sixth-century deportations and when they destroyed the temple in 587, they also indirectly destroyed the unchallenged efficacy of this Iron Age theology. In subsequent decades and centuries, biblical writers such as the author of Isa. 40–55, the author of Job, Qohelet, and various apocalypticists would reconsider whether moral cause and effect was an adequate explanation for human fortunes. The punishment of the Judahites seemed immeasurably greater than their sins. Second Isaiah suggested that some suffering might be redemptive (Isa. 52:13–53:12). Job subpoenaed God only to have the Almighty explain that the universe is exquisitely complicated and that divine justice transcends the binary moral categories of "innocent" or "guilty." Qohelet shrugged his world-weary shoulders and concluded that a misty, vaporous atmosphere of "vanity" inhibits mortals from seeing the divine patterns. The apocalypticists, such as the author of Dan. 7–12, claimed that the very patterns that were so opaque to the author of Ecclesiastes were, to the contrary, crystal clear. The times and seasons had been "revealed" (the meaning of the Greek term *apokalyptō*) to them. The apocalypticists came up with a conspiracy theory: the reason why the chosen people continue to suffer is because a demonic, universal network is dedicated to destroying them at every turn.

The Iron Age theology of Kings did not die. Moral cause and effect remained—and remains—operative. This theology was like Newtonian physics, a viable and enduring explanation for the basic operating system, but less useful the farther one moved toward the margins where light bends, time curves, the wicked continued to flourish, and the righteous continued to languish. The scroll of Kings formulated its conservative, traditional Iron Age thesis so securely and persuasively that it endured long enough for other progressives to critique and question it, and eloquently enough to explain the quotidian realities, the diurnal cycles of history where the rise and fall of bodies in motion and of souls in moral combat were still recognizably linear, predictable, and orderly. The scroll of Kings is the final grand statement of the Iron Age theology.

The essential beneficence of God. We might express this foundational idea in many ways: that the world has a loving Creator and so life is not designed to break people's hearts; that there is a heavenly host and so the universe is ultimately hospitable toward life; that the first thing to say about God is, as Exod. 34:6 puts it, "the LORD, the LORD, a God merciful and gracious, slow to anger, and abounding in steadfast love and faithfulness."

The book of Kings has its own particular way of describing divine beneficence, by emphasizing the promise God made to David to maintain the Davidic dynasty (e.g., 1 Kgs. 11:26–43; 15:1–4; 2 Kgs. 8:16–19; 22:1–2). This expression of God's unmerited care for the Davidic house, the city of Jerusalem, and the temple on Mount Zion is so parochial that it might not inspire litanies of assent in the modern age; it was probably hard to sell in the Iron Age outside Judah. But this is the narrowly coded way that Kings formulates its hope that, despite human failings and foibles, though the mountains should tremble and kingdoms totter, that no matter how long the night, there will be evening, there will be morning the next day; God will help Jerusalem for the sake of David when the morning dawns (cf. Ps. 46). Also, note that this scandalously partisan expression of the historian's faith in God's ultimate mercy is consistent with the theological style of the Hebrew Bible, which everywhere eschews the abstract for the concrete, and whose God is revealed in the details, not the generalizations.

The essential contrariness of humans. The doctrine of sin is also culturally coded in Kings. The scroll of Kings does not refer to a primeval trespass as the paradigm for human rebellion. For Kings, the sins of the tenth-century Ephraimite king Jeroboam—the erection of rival shrines to the Jerusalem temple—haunt and doom the northern kingdom of Israel (e.g., 1 Kgs. 12:25–33; 2 Kgs. 10:28–31; 17:21–23). The sins of the early-seventh-century Judahite king Manasseh—the importation of foreign elements into Judahite religious practice—ultimately bring about the down-

fall of the southern kingdom of Judah (e.g., 2 Kgs. 21:1–16, 21; 24:2–3).

We must pause here to reflect on the theological complications inherent in this critique of rural shrines and of popular religion. Jeroboam I was the first king of Israel, who led the northern tribes to secede from the rule of Solomon's son Rehoboam in the final decades of the tenth century. Jeroboam decreed that two shrines, at Dan in the far north of his kingdom and at Bethel in the far south, would be the pilgrimage centers for his culture. Must we consider this accommodation for the religious and cultural life of his subjects—the alternative was for his people to make their pilgrimage to Jerusalem, capital of a society with whom he was at war—the mother of all idolatries and the reason why Samaria fell to the Assyrian war machine two centuries later?

And what is idolatry? In the abstract, many might rally round to condemn worship of and allegiance to anything less than Ultimate Reality. But who decides by which sequence of phonemes this Reality is addressed and through which constellation of symbols the sanctuary is adorned? The perspective of the book of Kings is ultraorthodox in its definition of correct religious practice in Iron Age Judah. Moderns might want to think twice before labeling the religious ideas and symbols of others as idolatrous and joining crusades against "pagan" religion. Josiah's purge of Canaanite religion in late-seventh-century Judah climaxed in a ritualized mass murder of country priests (2 Kgs. 23:19–20).

Rightly or wrongly, the priestly historians who composed the scroll of Kings believed that the survival of their seventh- and sixth-century community of Judahites was at stake, that the only way that the community in covenant with YHWH would survive the military adventurism of Mesopotamian tyrants and the degradations of exile was to maintain the strictest forms of religious purity and to protect the mystery of the unimaged I AM against every compromise, hybridization, and synthesis with other religious systems. The ferocity of their particularity protected the core of the faith of ancient Israel and enabled it to survive cultural devastation, exile, and centuries of colonial status. In subsequent centuries Judaism and Christianity would emerge from this matrix with their pluralities of belief and dissent and their diverse latitudes of openness toward other religions.

This is a theologically complicated task: to understand the roots of the antipathy in Kings for rival religions and alien symbols, *and* to resist demonizing the historians who constructed this foundation for our faith, *and* to find ways of cultivating continuities with our spiritual ancestors, *and* to boldly dissent from ancient formulations that could serve as charters for purges, crusades, and pogroms against those who do not worship as we do. Still, this might be the very task we must embrace if we hope, as the composers of the scroll of Kings did, to play our part in bearing our faith safely through a dangerous time.

An Outline of the Scroll of Kings

The scroll of Kings can be divided into five sections:

1. The Template	1 Kgs. 1–11
2. Prophetic Heroism	1 Kgs. 12– 2 Kgs. 13
3. Freefall	2 Kgs. 14–17
4. The Dynamics of Prophecy and Order	2 Kgs. 18–23
5. A Theology of Exile	2 Kgs. 24–25

The first section, 1 Kgs. 1–11, details the transition of the monarchy from David to Solomon. The latter reign, among the dozens depicted in the northern kingdom of Israel and the southern kingdom of Judah throughout 1 and 2 Kings, receives the most detailed attention of them all, most of it admiring. This could be because the seventh- and sixth-century historians who composed Kings remembered this tenth-century Solomonic administration as a golden age for their culture. But we might also imagine that the prominence given in Kings to the Solomonic era was motivated more by prospective hopes for the future than by nostalgic retrospection. For Solomon is hardly portrayed as the ideal king: he "clings" (1 Kgs. 11:2) to his foreign-born wives rather than to the Lord (cf. Deut. 11:22), indulging their non-Israelite religious practices and traditions (1 Kgs. 11:4–8).

Solomon's four-decade reign receives a full quarter of this chronicle that spans four centuries because it serves as the template for the hoped-for renaissance of their society following the exile. According to this template, the remnant of Israel and Judah, northern and southern tribes, would honor a single ritual center, the temple in Jerusalem. That temple would be reconstructed according to the Solomonic blueprint, whose details are lovingly recorded in 1 Kgs. 6–8. All subsequent kings, like Solomon, would be Davidic heirs who exemplified wisdom (Solomon's legendary sagacity is profiled in three full chapters, 1 Kgs. 3–4 and 10) rather than martial heroism. Royal military adventurism held no interest for these historians, who had seen enough of siege, devastation, and campaigning in their lifetimes.

The next section, 1 Kgs. 12–2 Kgs. 13, the heart of the entire work and the longest and most lively section of the scroll, depicts the prophetic heroism that generation by generation kept Mosaic faith alive throughout the monarchical era.

The third section, 2 Kgs. 14–17, leaves the narrative of the prophets to concentrate on the eddying, spiraling decline of the northern kingdom, whose capital Samaria fell to the Assyrian army in 722.

The penultimate section of the scroll in 2 Kgs. 18–23 depicts the false spring of kingship in Judah under Hezekiah (2 Kgs. 18–20) and Josiah (2 Kgs. 22–23). During the reigns of these two admirable monarchs—interrupted by the miserable royal pair of Manasseh and Amon (2 Kgs. 21)—a workable synthesis of royal power and prophetic justice was achieved (from the ancient perspective at least) as Hezekiah relied on the counsel of Isaiah and Josiah on Huldah and the legacy of the Mosaic prophetic tradition contained in the book of the Torah discovered in the temple.

The final section of Kings, 2 Kgs. 24–25, describes the end of a world, the fall of Jerusalem to the Babylonians, as a whimpering, drawn-out tragedy of ineffectual statecraft and as the long overdue collapse of a structure, Israelite and Judean kingship, that had been compromised from its beginning by infidelity to Mosaic instruction.

COMMENTARY

The Template (1 Kgs. 1–11)

The subjects with the most theological significance in the initial section of the scroll, covering the Solomonic era, are wisdom and the temple. I also discuss a third issue, the use of the term "satan" in 1 Kgs. 11, because though marginal in Kings, the idea of "Satan" continues to attract theological interest.

Wisdom. This theme is encapsulated in the story about how Solomon was granted a single wish, whatever he desired, by the great Jinn of jinns in 1 Kgs. 3. "At Gibeon the LORD appeared to Solomon in a dream by night, and God said, 'Ask what I should give you'" (1 Kgs. 3:5). Our storied oriental ruler (Sulayman in Arabic tradition) did not ask for the superpowers and bejeweled trinkets common to such tales, for "long life or riches, or for the life of [his] enemies" (1 Kgs. 3:11), but merely that the Lord grant his servant "an understanding mind to govern your people, able to discern between good and evil" (1 Kgs. 3:9).

The theme is underscored throughout 1 Kgs. 1–11, beginning with David's deathbed counsel to his son (2:6, 9), and continuing after Solomon's above request with the anecdote in 1 Kgs. 3 that classically illustrates Solmonic wisdom—the king's incisive adjudication of the civil case that reunited an infant with its true mother (3:16–28). The next chapter catalogs Solomon's organizational savvy and learned observations about the natural world. The long section related to the temple in chaps. 5–8 honors him as the pious architectural patron of what was for Judahites the singular wonder of the ancient world, their Colossus of Rhodes, their pyramid of Giza. In chap. 9 an account of the accomplishments of Solomon's administration is capped by his great victory, not over a Philistine giant or an Egyptian pharaoh with his chariot corps, but over the Queen of Sheba in a royal battle of wits.

I cannot do justice here to the depths of the ancient Hebrew idea of *hokmah*, "wisdom." Wisdom was a way of life, a philosophy, and at times even a personification for God as the creator of the patterns that beautify and unify the world. I can only say this: the portrayal of Solomon as the paragon of wisdom, especially in light of the contrast the historians made between Solomon's sagacity and the demonstrated physical valor of the earlier leaders in the Deuteronomistic Tetrateuch such as Joshua, Samson, Saul, and David, forges a new platform for heroism (Solomon himself apologizes for his lack of martial experience in 1 Kgs. 3:7). Hidden among these folktales that illustrate and the clichés that testify to Solomonic wisdom is an elusive jewel that will serve as a marker, first of Judahite, then of Jewish, culture: the elevation of the sage rather than the man of war to the highest position in society, and the cultivation of learning in the service of justice rather than the arrogation of power as its most cherished ideal.

Solomon was offered his choice of gifts from God. This section of Kings with its emphasis on wisdom reminds us of another of the many gifts that the Bible has added to the world: by championing sagacity over physicality the biblical writers redefined heroism (cf. Prov. 24:5).

The temple. Four chapters in this initial section of the scroll of Kings are devoted to Solomon's construction of the temple (1 Kgs. 5–8), a testimony to its importance as the supreme sacred space in ancient Judahite culture. I will not detail here its architectural subtleties and ritual details, but I must comment on the theological symbolism of Solomon's temple in Jerusalem. The First Temple represented a creation story written in architecture.

The temple had three sections. Using the terms in the NRSV of 1 Kgs. 6, they were (a) the vestibule, (b) the nave, and (c) the inner sanctuary. The vestibule was the forecourt, an entrance area guarded by two immense pillars, "Boaz" and "Jachin" (1 Kgs. 7:21). These pillars were free-standing: they did not support the roof of the temple; rather they symbolically supported the dome of the sky. Close to them, also outside the structure proper, was a bronze basin filled with water, "the molten sea" (7:23–26). We should recall that in ancient Near Eastern creation traditions, "the sea," Hebrew *yam*, often symbolized the chaos that had to be defeated or controlled in order for there to be an orderly world. So the forecourt of the temple proclaimed in masonry and metallurgy that the Deity worshiped at this site controlled the chaotic waters above the earth by supporting the dome of sky with sacred columns, and contained the chaotic waters below the earth within the boundaries of sacred basins. On Mount Zion, on the banks of the Edenic Gihon (cf. Gen. 2:13, 1 Kgs. 1:33, 38, 45), the chaotic vitality of the primeval waters was channeled, controlled, and transformed into the River of Life.

The nave of the temple was a large, enclosed limestone chamber with cedar panels on the sides and a cypress floor. The cedar panels were decorated with carvings of palm trees, flowers, and cherubim (1 Kgs. 6:29). Architecturally, this assemblage of carved wood and dressed stone represented nothing less than a sacred grove on a divine mountain. The nave of Solomon's temple was symbolically the garden of Eden. Crossing the threshold of the temple, its priests entered sacred time and space, the first morning in Eden's forest, and through appropriate rites and intermediaries regained a lost intimacy between the Creator and the community.

The way in which the nave depicted a sacred Edenic arbor has immense theological significance. Through worship at this house, the community believed that it received a dose of creation, and was renewed daily, every Shabbat, and every holiday. If we extended this ancient view to our world, then we would envision community worship as a return to the garden, a place where the community leaves mundane time and enters the time of "as it was in the beginning, is now, and ever shall be," joining the ancestors and all creation in a renewal of the primeval "very goodness" that God intended for the world. Our culture may have forgotten this, but it unwittingly preserves this truth in language that speaks about the Sabbath as a day for "recreation," that is, re-creation.

The inner sanctuary of the temple, the Holy of Holies, contained two statues. Images of cherubim—the sphinx-like monsters that guarded the borders around sacred places in ancient mythologies—menacingly sat as divine bodyguards in this Iron Age throne room of the King of the universe. The inner wings of these hybrid winged lions rose toward each other. The charged stillness where these cherubim's wings kissed, a void measured in millimeters, served as the focal point for encountering the mysterious, invisible, unimaged Creator of the heavens and the earth.

The design of this ancient shrine broke the patterns of contemporary sacred architecture and opened a threshold to a religious world we still inhabit. For the Jerusalem priests who ventured on behalf of their community into the deepest privacy of the divine apartment in

God's very house saw nothing, and then everything. Here in the inner sanctum of Solomon's temple we approach the architectural expression of the Mosaic revelation that God is one, and that the divine identity transcends every mortal attempt to outline its fearful symmetry in images.

"Satan" in 1 Kings 11. In the final chapter of this initial section of Kings, the Hebrew word *satan* occurs three times, translated in the NRSV as "adversary" (1 Kgs. 11:14, 23, 25). These adversaries are rival warlords, Hadad in Edom and Rezon in Syria, whom the Solomonic government was unable to pacify and who bedeviled the united kingdom on its northeastern and southeastern borders throughout Solomon's reign. These *satan*s represent wholly human opponents. There is not a hint here of the later evolution of the idea of Satan in Jewish and Christian thinking. Through soundings in later biblical and extrabiblical Jewish and Christian literature we can chart the evolution of the term *satan* from its Iron Age meaning of "opponent," to its Persian period usage as the name for a member of the divine court who conducts moral audits of human virtue ("the Satan," i.e., *hassatan*, of Job 1–2 and Zech. 3), and finally to its use in the Hellenistic and Roman periods as the name for the mastermind of the cosmic criminal underworld who leads his network of demons in their gleeful vandalism of all stable structures.

The cosmology of the composers of Kings is uncompromisingly monistic; there is no room for the modified dualism that develops in some apocalyptic pockets of later Second Temple Judaism, and which became the norm in early Christianity. In the latter worldviews, God, the angels, and the saints have been engaged in spy-versus-spy combat with Satan and his demons since the first morning and will remain so until the last day. Readers can decide for themselves about the devil's existence and theological utility, and what they think about the extrabiblical traditions concerning the primeval

fall of Lucifer. Based on the use of the term *satan* to refer to terrestrial political adversaries in 1 Kgs. 11, however, it seems clear that at the time of the writing of Kings the devil had not yet fallen from the pages of the Bible.

Prophetic Heroism (1 Kgs. 12–2 Kgs. 13)

The next major section of the scroll of Kings follows a chronological course to sketch the fortunes of Judahite and Ephraimite societies over the two centuries following Solomon. The narrative moves back and forth between the two rival political states and duly catalogs each reign in formulaic terms (e.g., 1 Kgs. 14:19–15:34). The focus of this section, however, is on, and the most lively narration devoted to, accounts about the prophets who troubled these kings.

We will consider the theological implications of several themes in this section of the scroll of Kings, which highlights prophetic heroism. Readers are familiar with the names of the prophets Elijah and Elisha, but there are many more whose stories are usually ignored in children's Sunday school lessons and adult homilies. In order to impart a sense of the ubiquity of the prophetic presence in 1 and 2 Kings, I list them all below.

The Roster of Prophets in 1–2 Kings
1. Nathan of Jerusalem (1 Kgs. 1)
2. Ahijah the Shilonite (1 Kgs. 11:29–39; 14:1–18)
3. Shemaiah of Jerusalem (1 Kgs. 12:21)
4. "A man of God" from Judah (1 Kgs. 13:1–34)
5. "An aged prophet" from Bethel (1 Kgs. 13:11–33)
6. Jehu ben Hanani (1 Kgs. 16:1–7)
7. Elijah the Tishbite (1 Kgs. 17:1–19:21; 21:1–29; 2 Kgs. 1:1–2:12)
8. Elisha ben Shaphat (1 Kgs. 19:19–21; 2 Kgs. 2:1–9:37; 13:14–21)
9. "A certain prophet" in Israel (1 Kgs. 20:13–43)
10. A company of prophets (1 Kgs. 20:35–43)
11. Micaiah ben Imlah (1 Kgs. 22:13–28)

12. Jonah ben Amittai from Gath-hepher (the subject of the prophetic book of Jonah) (2 Kgs. 14:25)
13. Isaiah of Jerusalem (2 Kgs. 19:20–20:19)
14. An anonymous (generalized) prophetic voice (2 Kgs. 21:11–15)
15. Huldah from Jerusalem (the only female prophet in this corpus) (2 Kgs. 22:14–20)

Tough love: The code of the prophets (1 Kgs. 13). After the account of the division of the Davidic united state in 1 Kgs. 12, where Rehoboam, Solomon's son and heir, succeeds in alienating the northern tribes by conscripting their commoners for royal building projects and Jeroboam I, an Ephraimite leader, initiates their rebellion that ends in secession, we have our first tale about prophets. Because the savagery of the story in 1 Kgs. 13 serves as an ideal prophetic primer, I will give an extended treatment of it.

The first movement of the story, in 13:1–10, is conventional in that it depicts, like so many stories that follow in Kings, an angry prophet condemning a monarch for erecting an illicit shrine. The anonymous prophet, referred to as "a man of God from Judah," travels a few kilometers north, to the pilgrimage shrine in Bethel, confronts there King Jeroboam, and calls for the destruction of this shrine set up as a rival to Solomon's temple. In a preview of a speech that another Judahite prophet would deliver in the same shrine a little more than a century later (Amos 7:10–17), the jeremiad of this man of God from Judah carries the day. The shrine is destroyed and a violent interlude injects the scene with additional energy and urgency: when the king extended his arm to silence the prophet, Jeroboam's arm magically withers before the prophet restores it to its original form. A prophet has injured, healed, and thoroughly bested a king.

Then there is a detail added at the end of this first scene that sets up the drama in the second scene (13:11–32). Grateful or wary, Jeroboam extends hospitality and gifts to the seer, but the man of God refuses them. "If you give me half your kingdom, I will not go in with you; nor will I eat food or drink water in this place. For thus I was commanded by the word of the LORD" (13:8–9). So our man of God refuses any royal succor or blandishments and begins his chaste journey home to Judah, a tightly wound ball of prophetic austerity and obedience.

But in the next scene the virtue of our hero is undone when another prophet, described as "an aged prophet from Bethel," tests the fortitude of the, presumably, younger man. The aged prophet deliberately sets out to intercept the Judahite seer, encounters him, and invites him home for dinner. The Judahite prophet maintains his ascetic devotion—his food is to do the will of the one who sent him— and refuses the Bethelite prophet's hospitality. Then the prophet from Bethel tells the Judahite a lie. A heavenly messenger had given the aged seer a new directive, the man from Judah was supposed to—no, commanded to—dine at the home of the local master (13:18).

So the young prophet walks into the trap and dines in Bethel. Even before the meal is finished, the aged prophet castigates him for disobeying the terms of his original divine command to abstain from any eating or drinking in, presumably ritually contaminated, Bethel. Once sated, saddled on a donkey, and, we must assume, shaken by these shifting winds of divine inspiration, the young prophet is sent home. He loses his life, the punishment for disobeying the full terms of his original orders (13:26), when a lion attacks him on the way back to Judah (13:24).

This conclusion to this first prophetic narrative in Kings is chilling. The virtuous prophet delivers his message unerringly—an oracle about the fate of the shrine of Bethel that was treasured and remembered by fellow prophets for generations (2 Kgs. 23:15–18)—and his reward is to be seduced by a deceptive superior into violating a peripheral aspect of his mission. And he pays for this misdemeanor with his life.

But the story still is not over; it has one more unpredictable twist. The aged prophet retrieves the Judahite seer's body. The corpse had been spared any mutilation by the lion (1 Kgs. 13:28), an amazing providence because in the ancient view the body had to be corporeally intact and integral in order for its host to gain a restful forever in Sheol. The aged prophet then grieves over his "brother" (13:30), inters him in his own family tomb, and commands his own sons someday to bury him right next to his fallen comrade.

Though it has plenty of competition, this account is one of the most bizarre stories in the Bible. What kind of prophet, speaking here of the seer from Bethel, forces his junior to undergo such an ordeal, concocts a lie to tempt him to betray a sacred vow, utters an "I-told-you-so" when the Judahite's death is reported to him, but then honors him with proper burial rites and tender attestations of kinship?

What kind of prophet is this? Keep reading the scroll of Kings. What kind of prophet commands a fellow prophet to strike him and when the latter refuses, summons a lion to devour his lamblike friend? The story about this anonymous prophet is in 20:35–37. And with the outcome of a battle and scores of lives at stake, what kind of prophet toys with a desperate king who needs a divine omen on the verge of battle by giving him a false oracle? Micaiah ben Imlah does, in 22:15. And what kind of prophet projects a lethal force field that fells those royal lackeys, sent by the king to summon him, who do not ask in a nice way, and spares those who say please? That is from a story about Elijah in 2 Kgs. 1:9–15. And what kind of prophet responds to the jeers of a gang of unruly boys by inciting a bear to maul them? That prophet is Elisha in 2 Kgs. 2:23–24.

Another example of the martial intensity of the prophets' subcultural code (*semper fi*) is in the story in 2 Kgs. 2 about how Elijah directed his disciple Elisha to withdraw from following him. Three times Elijah told Elisha to back off, three times Elisha refused to abandon his master on the latter's lonesome journey into the Jordan Valley where he would exit the mortal frame (2:1–2, 4, 6). Elisha passed his three-part ordeal and his tenacity was rewarded by a double dose of Elijah's charismatic power (2:9–14).

These are the tales of the ancient Israelite prophets. These uncompromising, undomesticated mountain men from the highlands of Ephraim and river rats from the jungly wilds along the banks of the Jordan River practiced a code of tough love, of fierce love, where half-right was never good enough. Even if we allow for the exaggerations and over-sized characterizations common to folktales—and many of these accounts have those qualities—the prophets in the books of Kings refuse to conform to our projections of ideal ethical heroes.

The word that best describes the protagonists of the above stories might be *odd*. As it turns out, and as Walter Brueggemann has written, "odd" is not a bad English translation for the Hebrew *qadesh*, "holy." The biblical word *qadesh* carries the sense of "separate," "different," even "odd." These bizarre prophets with their animal-skin mantles were walking-talking incarnations of this holiness and oddity, and thus exemplified the wholly otherness of the God whom they served. Judging by these stories, the prophets held themselves and their societies to the highest standards. These grim tales illustrate that the violation of these standards, even casually, had fatal consequences.

Modern heirs to this prophetic faith must exercise great care in interpreting these stories, adjusting for the fairy-tale qualities of these Iron Age narratives about beasts that serve as agents of moral retribution and the naughty children who get eaten by them. Imagine them as drawn from the same world of raw folktales that we find in the Brothers Grimm. But if we censor or ignore these wild stories, we may lose touch with something vital to both biblical faith and its portrait of God: the awesome turbulence of the created world and its Creator, the fatal consequences of infidelity to covenant, the spiritual tenacity necessary for discipleship, and the edgy difference and oddity of the religious life that asks so much of and offers so much to believers.

The prophetic voice (1 Kgs. 14–16). In this section of Kings that details an era that spanned about a century, from the mid-tenth century to the mid-ninth, the royal house of Judah maintained a precarious stability. Rehoboam's Judah was invaded by Pharaoh Shishak of Egypt, and he and his son Abijam had border skirmishes with Israel. The next Davidide, Asa, formed a political alliance with Syria that forced Israel to concentrate on defending its northern borders and withdraw from the disputed territories in the border region of Benjamin. Then Asa was succeeded by a king who is remembered as virtuous, Jehoshaphat (1 Kgs. 22:41–46; 2 Kgs. 3:14).

In contrast to the century of peaceful succession of Davidic descendants in Judah, the northern kingdom of Israel was plagued with political instability during this period. Jeroboam, the first king of Israel, survived to leave his throne to his son Nadab, but the latter was assassinated by the warlord Baasha. Baasha, founder then of the second dynasty in Israelite history, survived to leave his throne to his son Elah, but Elah was murdered by his cavalry commander Zimri. Elah, according to 1 Kgs. 16:9–10, was "drinking himself drunk" with the royal steward when Zimri overtook him. Zimri, this junior officer who led a coup d'etat, did not live long enough to leave his throne to heirs—indeed, he did not last a week, before the commander of the Israelite army, a man named Omri, attacked him in his palace in Tirzah. Zimri, who never constructed a royal house, set fire to the palace and killed himself in its white heat. We should note this as well: each of these dynastic transfers, when Baasha killed Nadab to end the reign of the house of Jeroboam and when Zimri killed Elah to end the reign of the house of Baasha, was accompanied by the mass murder of every member of the royal families.

There is a theme of theological interest in this section that reads like a gangster epic—call it "Murder, Inc."—as rival warlords and their networks vied for control of the northern region and cleaned house every couple of generations. The historian provides an editorial backbeat to all the bloodletting, namely, that there was always an Ephraimite prophet in the midst of all this murderous chaos. The words of Ahijah of Shiloh (1 Kgs. 11:29–39) shadowed the house of Jeroboam (14:1–18). Jehu ben Hanani (not to be confused with a later Israelite king who was named Jehu) troubled the house of Baasha with his insistent critique of its corruption (16:1–7). It is as if in every dynasty, in every era, there was always a prophetic voice to check the excesses of kings and to insist that power be wedded to justice. This is not a new theme in the Deuteronomistic History: Samuel performed this function in Saul's day (1 Sam. 13). Nathan immortalized it in David's court when the prophet told King David, "You are the man" who killed Uriah the Hittite (2 Sam. 12). Nathan demanded that King David answer for the death of Uriah, and David—and this is equally significant—did not have his general and hit man Joab come back from the front lines to kill Nathan also but instead confessed, "I have sinned against the LORD." For every culture that has been influenced by the ideals of biblical justice, this story remains foundational because this is when that goddess on the statue holding the scales outside the Supreme Court building in Washington, DC, received her blindfold.

The classic prophetic tales (1 Kgs. 17–2 Kgs. 13). In this section of Kings we encounter the most famous prophets in the Ephraimite tradition, Elijah and his disciple Elisha, who along with Micaiah ben Imlah (1 Kgs. 22) took turns troubling the Omride dynasty in Israel, especially during the reign of its most infamous king, Ahab, and his queen, Jezebel.

Here the scroll of Kings, which had been structured up till now by regnal formulas, changes its tempo, and the voice of a didactic royal chronicler gives way to that of a storyteller.

One great story follows another: Elijah's food miracle and resuscitation of a dead boy in the village of Zarephath (1 Kgs. 17:8–24); the contest on Mount Carmel, a kind of priestly Olympics, between Elijah and four hundred priests of Baal (18:17–40); Elijah's Mosaic pilgrimage to Mount Horeb, where he receives his own revelation of the Lord, not in the thundering style familiar from Exodus but in "a still, small voice" (19:4–18); Elijah's championing of Naboth, the family farmer who was murdered and had his estate seized by royal chicanery (chap. 21). There is the tale about Micaiah ben Imlah, the prophet whose integrity and principled contrariness even Ahab grudgingly respects (chap. 22). Elijah ascends to heaven with bands of angels (2 Kgs. 2:11–12), and Elisha parts the Jordan (2 Kgs. 2:13–14). The stories about Elisha keep coming: he performs food miracles (4:1–7, 38–44), helps barren couples conceive (4:11–17), brings the dead back to life (4:18–37), and heals the Syrian general Naaman of leprosy (chap. 5).

Let us pause to analyze one story in more detail, an obscure account in 2 Kgs. 6–7 that captures the mixture of miracles and moralisms that is so characteristic of the prophetic narratives about Elijah and Elisha. Four leprous men outside Samaria, besieged by the Syrian army, finally give up any hope for charity from a royal capital whose lords and ladies inside the city walls have been reduced to cannibalism (6:24–30), and decide to head for the Aramean camp. They intend to throw themselves on the mercy of their enemies and, short of that, prefer a quick death by the sword to the drawn-out agony of starvation. "So [the men with leprosy] arose at twilight to go to the Aramean camp; but when they came to the edge of the Aramean camp, there was no one there at all" (7:5). What happened to the Syrian army? "The LORD had caused the Aramean army to hear the sound of chariots, and of horses, the sound of a great army, so that they said to one another, 'The king of Israel has hired the kings of the Hittites and the kings of Egypt to fight against us.' So they fled away in the twilight" (7:6–7).

This story about the twilight transfer of a well-stocked camp from an evil army to a quartet of misfits whose wheezing, halting, noisy approach is amplified by divine instrumentality into the sound of an approaching cavalry charge, predates folktales like "The Bremen Town Musicians" by millennia. In the Grimms' fairy tale, four discarded domestic animals long past any usefulness to their human masters band together for survival and come across a robbers' camp. The donkey's braying, the hound's barking, the cat's mewing, and the rooster's crowing so frighten the cutthroats that they flee their cabin, leaving their food and drink to the four disabled "musicians." The Bible employs this variant of an ancient and widespread folktale to its own purposes. The four lepers serve as the agents who bring about the fulfillment of an oracle uttered by Elisha, who had predicted this reversal of fortunes the day before to a king. The miraculous audition heard by the Arameans is described in the terms of the celestial army referred to in other Elijah/Elisha tales (2:11–12; 6:17).

The details in this single story—about these human outcasts who put an army to flight, about a prophet who knows better than a king, and about the helpless people whose God rescues them from the rapacious assaults of enemy forces—captures the winning, underdog mentality of so many of these narratives in the central section of the scroll of Kings. The tone of this story and of the other Elijah and Elisha tales breaks from the ennui of the sections of Kings that catalog one inept reign after another. In the little traditions, in the folktales from the scroll of Kings, common people and roving bands of their prophetic champions move among farming villages and rural holy sites (Mount Carmel, Mount Horeb, the Gilgal monuments from Joshua's day), sustaining the Mosaic faith and supporting one another in spite of evil governments. They constitute the faithful remnant that the writing prophets always promised would make it through any disaster (Isa. 10:20–21; Jer. 23:3; Amos 5:15; Mic. 2:12), the righteous who survive because of their faithfulness (Hab. 2:4).

The prophetic underground (1 Kgs. 17; 2 Kgs. 2, 4, 6, 8). This section of Kings begins in 1 Kgs. 17, where Elijah, without any birth or call narrative, appears as abruptly as he will later disappear (1 Kgs. 17:1; 2 Kgs. 2:12). The mysterious entrances and exits of prophets to and from center stage and the scenes that depict single prophets standing up to monarchs and their courts, military units of fifty men, and priestly battalions of four hundred inspire images of lone voices crying in the wilderness. But that was not the case. The Ephraimite prophets belonged to a social network.

In three stories, villagers in Zarephath (1 Kgs. 17:8–24), Sidon (2 Kgs. 2:19–22), and Shunem (2 Kgs. 4:8–37) provide safe houses and support for prophets. There are references throughout this section of Kings to prophetic bands, the disciples, peers, and comrades among whose ranks prophets were taught, tested, and tied together in a fraternity of dissent. Elisha's gang even builds a prophetic clubhouse on the banks of the Jordan (2 Kgs. 6:1–7). The lore about the prophetic subculture included the traditional trope of "the foolish disciple," as Elisha's servant Gehazi functions as a comic Sancho to his Don Quixote–like master, prefiguring the comic (and tragic) bumblings of a later Galilean prophet's disciples.

The prophets were not solo performers but rather the leaders of an entire underground band of fellow travelers that included wealthy matrons (2 Kgs. 4:8), spouses (4:1), sympathetic villages (2:19), servant girls (5:2), and their own cantankerous core group of seers. Prophets in any age are produced by and depend on the base communities who train and sustain them.

The still small voice (1 Kgs. 19). One of the better-known prophetic tales is that of Elijah's encounter with God on Mount Horeb (also known as Mount Sinai) in 1 Kgs. 19. On the lam from the royal couple of Ahab and Jezebel because he and his associates had slaughtered the entire Samarian priesthood (1 Kgs. 18:40), Elijah sought refuge at the very shrine where his hero Moses had once glimpsed the flanks of the divine physiognomy (Exod. 33:12–34:10). But it would not be the fire this time, unlike in the Sinai/Horeb material from the Pentateuch (see Exod. 3, 19–34). In 1 Kgs. 19 the Lord does not appear in the old style with all the conventional special effects of Semitic storm deities who rode clouds, snorted zephyrs, and spoke thunder.

The Lord passes by Elijah not in the wind or earthquake or fire (1 Kgs. 19:11–12) but in "a still small voice" (19:12 KJV). The Hebrew phrase may also be translated as "the sound of a thin whisper." We might imagine it as the faint rush we hear when we place a conch shell to our ear.

If we consider biblical religion historically, as developing through time, then this account marks a cosmic turning point. This is a place where Israelite religion broke away from and differentiated itself from its regional climate. Prophetic ethical monotheism here parted company with the alpine theatrics of Baal Hadad, the Canaanite storm deity who was the Lord's chief rival for the affections of Israel during Elijah's day. This story reveals a new facet of the diamond-like complexity of the biblical God: wholly real, as indispensable as air, yet as elusive and imperceptible and modest as the faintest wind that barely stirs the leaves on a tree.

Rightfully, we might consider this quiet, even mystical, approach of the Creator a theological advance on those many biblical and extrabiblical images of an intimidating deity who revels in tree-splitting, earthshaking displays. At the same time, if we get too comfortable with this single divine manifestation and its breezy resonance with other attractive theophanies—the wind that creatively hovers over the face of the abyss on creation morning (Gen. 1:2) or the dove that alights on Jesus' shoulder following his baptism (Matt. 4:16)—then we falsify the biblical record. The God of the Bible remains a moving target, impossible to pin down, fiercely free to return in the whirlwind of Job and marching out to war trailed by celestial hosts in the apocalyptic scenarios of Daniel and Revelation.

Prophetic justice (1 Kgs. 21). Elijah's intervention on behalf of a rural family destroyed by the rapacious, quasi-legal machinations of a royal family illustrates the prophetic standard of justice. The account in 1 Kgs. 21 assumes that readers know about the Israelite attitude toward landownership. The family farms passed down from generation to generation were considered sacred trusts granted by a divine landlord who, in actions associated with the great ancestor Joshua, had equitably parceled them among the tribes, clans, and families (Josh. 13–21). Furthermore, there were traditions formulated in priestly teaching and imparted Mosaic authority (e.g., Lev. 25:13) that held that mortgaged land debts were to be forgiven every fifty years, the Year of Jubilee, so that chronic poverty did not take root among lineages disadvantaged by whatever economic inequities had inevitably accumulated over time. These priestly traditions ensured that families, at least every fifty years, could return to self-sufficiency on their own land, to the farms that linked them to their God and to the commonwealth of the twelve tribes of Israel from Joshua's day and to their ancestors who slept restfully beneath them in family tombs.

But Naboth's ancestral family farm happened to abut a royal vacation home in the fertile Jezreel Valley. When King Ahab offered to buy it from him, or trade for it, Naboth took his stand with Moses, Joshua, and the Levitical priests of old. His words, "The LORD forbid that I should give you my ancestral inheritance" (1 Kgs. 21:3), meant that for Naboth, he would be damned if he lost that land, estranged from every covenant that was holy to him.

Jezebel, Ahab's queen, is portrayed as the driving force behind the royal scam to have Naboth executed on trumped-up charges of treason and his land confiscated (21:13–14). That a Phoenician woman is depicted here as the epitome of evil while her Israelite husband is merely ineffectual and passive (21:5) is suspiciously patriarchal and parochial. According to the folksy ethnocentrism of Kings, yet another good Israelite boy has been ruined by a foreign wife, as Samson and Solomon had.

Jezebel's (and Ahab's) plot bears the malevolent imprimatur of due process. Evidently Ahab could not risk the naked seizure of Naboth's estate, so Jezebel's administrative worldliness (she grew up in a royal palace in Sidon) comes in handy. She dispatches the text of Naboth's alleged blasphemy in official documents ("[He] cursed God and the king," 1 Kgs. 21:13), and she sees to it that the local worthless "sons of Beliyyᶜal" (the Hebrew phrase) produced to testify to the charade met the Mosaic standard that there be two witnesses in such cases (Deut. 19:15). Following a rigged trial, Naboth is stoned by a mob for his alleged blasphemy, his corpse left in a field as carrion. The loss of his life, the economic ruin of his family, the transgenerational crippling of his clan— add to these injuries the haunting degradation of the postmortem assaults visited upon a discarded corpse that prevented Naboth from resting peacefully in the patriarchal bosom of his ancestors.

But "then the word of the LORD came to Elijah the Tishbite" (1 Kgs. 21:17). The crime may have had the cover of law but it was noted by a more supreme court. Elijah issues his prophetic indictment of

Ahab and Jezebel's murderous joint venture (21:20–24). We should recall here Nathan's rebuke of David (2 Sam. 12:1–15), when David had Uriah killed in order to clean up his messy affair with Bathsheba (2 Sam. 11), because this account is based on the same conception of justice. The prophetic standard leaves no ruler above the law and no commoner below its protection. These stories remain foundational for every culture influenced by the spirit of biblical law.

Poetic justice (2 Kgs. 5). The Iron Age theology discussed in the introduction was imagined by the ancients as having a mathematical precision: "Whatsoever a man soweth, that [precisely, tit for tat] shall he also reap" (cf. Gal. 6:7 KJV). According to their worldview, a moral gravity was operative in the world. Underdog prophets rose and corrupt kings fell. In addition, the Invisible Hand had a deft touch, imbuing the science of cause and effect with poetic qualities.

Narratives throughout the Deuteronomistic History illustrate this. Because the Midianites raid Israel's farms during the wheat harvest, Gideon must hide his wheat in a winepress (Judg. 6:11). At another winepress in the story, the Midianite sheikhs are beheaded (7:25). Abimelech murders his rival princes by beheading them on a stone butchering table (9:5), and he dies when a woman drops a stone on his head (9:53). In the story of Naboth's vineyard, Elijah curses Ahab and Jezebel with the same fate that had befallen their victim, "In the place where dogs licked up the blood of Naboth, dogs will also lick up your blood" (1 Kgs. 21:19; cf. its fulfillment in 1 Kgs. 22:38 and 2 Kgs. 9:30–37). A generation later, Ahab's heir Joram is killed and his body thrown onto the field that had belonged to Naboth (2 Kgs. 9:24–26).

This brings us to the story of Elisha's healing of the Syrian general Naaman from leprosy in 2 Kgs. 5. Elisha instructs Naaman to wash himself in the Jordan River seven times (5:10). When Naaman finally does as he is told, his skin disease is cured: "his flesh was restored like the flesh of a young boy" (5:14).

Poetic justice is not the main theme of the story. The theme of 2 Kgs. 5 is "Who is boss?" Ultimately the Syrian general finds out the Lord is the true God, and the king of Samaria, to whom the princely Naaman was initially directed, finds out that prophets have therapeutic powers that kings can only dream of. A secondary theme in the story is the wisdom of the little people. It is a Jewish slave girl in Naaman's palace who tells him about the prophet in Samaria who can heal him. Later in the story another servant advises Naaman to swallow his pride in Syria's sacred rivers and follow Elisha's prescription that the Aramean enter the spa of the Jordan.

The theme of poetic justice appears in the second act of the story, after Elisha had healed Naaman. The grateful general offers Elisha a gift, but the austere prophet refuses, "As the LORD lives, whom I serve, I will accept nothing" (2 Kgs. 5:16). Meanwhile Gehazi, Elisha's foolish servant, overhears their conversation and cannot resist the prospect of easy money. Note the ironic echo of Elisha's words in the first clause in Gehazi's formulation of his scheme: "*As the LORD lives, I will run after [Naaman] and get something out of him*" (5:20).

Gehazi races to catch up with Naaman's chariot, and reports that, on second thought, while Elisha himself could not accept any gifts, he could be persuaded to accept compensation on behalf of some prophetic guests who arrived at Elisha's house just as Naaman departed. Gehazi receives silver and regal clothing from Naaman and then returns home to his master.

Elisha, ever the prophet, sees through the entire scheme. Elisha, who regularly peers through the mortal atmosphere to glimpse celestial creatures, informs Gehazi that he had supernaturally witnessed the entire transaction on the road to Damascus. Gehazi's crime was receiving a gift from Naaman. For his punishment, Elisha informs Gehazi that he will receive another gift from Naaman: the latter's skin disease.

If we read stories such as this with the kind of sober piety we often reserve for the Bible, we cannot help but be shocked at the cold-blooded glee that its composers and original audiences evidently took in the cruel particulars of how the wicked and the foolish eventually received their comeuppance, their just deserts. Better that we read these accounts as folktales from the underclass, from the prophets and their sympathizers who waited through generations for the reign of peace and justice their tradition promised them, and preserved their hopes in the stories and teachings that would grow into our Bible. The pleasures of these impish narratives about poetic justice may escape us, but for our spiritual ancestors in Ephraim, who were about a century from exile in Elisha's day, the prospect of divine judgment against the high and mighty was one of their few small comforts.

The prophetic repertoire.   To complete this section on prophetic heroism, I offer the following chart that catalogs the powers exhibited by the Ephraimite prophets.

1. Prophets control rain and water
   Elijah terminates and initiates rain in Israel (1 Kgs. 17:1; 18:41–46).
   Elijah parts the Jordan River with his rolled-up mantle (2 Kgs. 2:8).
   Elisha also parts the Jordan River with Elijah's mantle (2 Kgs. 2:13).
   Elisha makes wadis fill with water, even though it has not rained (2 Kgs. 3:14–20).
   Elisha heals Naaman in the waters of the Jordan (2 Kgs. 5:10–14).
   Elisha makes an ax-head float to the surface of the Jordan (2 Kgs. 6:1–7).
2. Prophets control fire
   Elijah makes drenched wood burn (1 Kgs. 18).
   Elijah conjures up "fire from heaven," i.e., lightning (2 Kgs. 1:10, 12).
3. Prophets control wild beasts
   The aged prophet from Bethel controls a lion (1 Kgs. 13:24–26).

An unnamed prophet summons a lion to kill a disobedient peer (1 Kgs. 20:36).
   Elisha controls bears (2 Kgs. 2:23–24).
4. Prophets have visions of the heavenly realm
   Micaiah ben Imlah sees the heavenly court (1 Kgs. 22:19–23).
   Elijah and Elisha see chariots of fire and a divine army (2 Kgs. 2:11–12).
   Elisha allows his fearful attendant to glimpse the heavenly host (2 Kgs. 6:17).
   Prompted by an oracle of Elisha, the Aramean army hears the heavenly host and flees their camp (2 Kgs. 7:6).
5. Prophets have the power to heal and to inflict illness
   A prophet from Judah causes Jeroboam's arm to wither, then restores it (1 Kgs. 13:4–6)
   Elijah resuscitates an apparently dead boy (1 Kgs. 17:17–23).
   Elijah opens the womb of a barren woman (2 Kgs. 2:11–17).
   Elisha resuscitates an apparently dead person (2 Kgs. 4:8–37).
   Elisha heals Naaman from a skin disease (2 Kgs. 5:8–14).
   Elisha transfers Naaman's skin disease to Gehazi (2 Kgs. 5:27).
   Elisha makes the Aramean army go blind (2 Kgs. 6:18–19)
   Elisha's bones heal a man (2 Kgs. 13:20)
6. Prophets perform food miracles
   Elijah multiplies the olive oil reserves of a widow (1 Kgs. 17:8–16).
   Elisha makes foul water drinkable (2 Kgs. 2:19–22).
   Elisha multiplies the olive oil reserves of a widow (2 Kgs. 4:1–7).
   Elisha makes foul food edible (2 Kgs. 4:38–41).
   Elisha multiplies grain (2 Kgs. 4:42–44).

My purpose in listing the full repertoire of the Ephraimite prophets is neither to focus the attention of skeptical readers on the incredible nor to lament with literalists the passing of a race of superhuman prophets from our midst. I simply want to note the significance of these traditions for later biblical, apocryphal, and extra-biblical Jewish and Christian literature. This is the register from which other legends of prophets and acts of apostles will draw. Other motifs, such as the foolish disciple (e.g., Gehazi in 2 Kings), will recur as well.

Freefall (2 Kgs. 14–17)

This section of Kings depicts the end of Ephraim, and here the depressing tone of the scroll as a whole reaches the first and deepest of its two nadirs. The Israelite political state, its capital city of Samaria, and the northern tribes who dwelt so precariously close to the Jordan basin, a northern extension of the Great Rift Valley, fell from history ca. 722 BCE. Israel had its territory ravaged by the army of Nineveh and its population deported throughout the east, or forced to emigrate to Judah, or left to assimilate with other similarly disadvantaged ethnic groups from Western Asia transplanted to Samaria according to Assyrian imperial policy. From this historical crater would emerge legends about wandering Jews and sightings of the lost tribes in Africa, India, and the Americas centuries later.

Beginning in the eighth century BCE, Mesopotamian imperial designs on reaching the harbors of the Mediterranean spelled the end for the state of Israel, the ancient northern kingdom for whom Samaria served as capital from the days of the Omride dynasty in the ninth century. The Assyrian Empire, centered in Nineveh, would reach the apex of its powers in the eighth and seventh centuries before being succeeded by a parade of superpowers who bloodily passed their imperial spoils from one legendary tyrant to another: Assyria fell to Nebuchadnezzar of Babylon in 612 BCE, Babylon fell to Cyrus of Persia ca. 540 BCE, Persia to Alexander of Macedonia ca. 330 BCE, and the Judahite portion of the Hellenistic empire (which enjoyed a century of independent rule under the Maccabeans during this time) to the Roman general Pompey ca. 63 BCE.

Judah had its own share of political instability during the ninth and eighth centuries, but it had a great advantage over the more populous, and territorially and economically richer Israel. Israel was located in the crosshairs of the empires, along the trade routes that linked European Anatolia, Mesopotamian Assyria, and African Egypt. The isolated postage-stamp-size state of Judah had more than the ancient Davidic promises to keep it intact. It was relatively inaccessible, located off the main roads, among the Judean mountains.

The Jehu dynasty reigned in Samaria for four generations (ca. 843–745 BCE) following Jehu's assassination of the Omride Joram (2 Kgs. 9:24). The house of Jehu achieved a measure of stability and prosperity that dwarfed that of contemporary Judah, and the scroll of Kings seems to recognize this in its muted criticism of the dynasty. Jehu had the prophetic support of Elisha, and his great-grandson Jeroboam II had the support of the prophet Jonah ben Amittai, according to 2 Kgs. 14:25 (this is the same Jonah about whom a later prophetic folktale was written). According to the Deuteronomistic perspective, the sins of Israel's first king, the tenth-century Jeroboam I, continued to plague the north. His namesake, Jeroboam II, the last effective Israelite king, receives the standard denunciation (14:24, my trans.: "He did the evil thing in the eyes of the LORD," i.e., allowed families to make holiday trips to Dan and Bethel), but the force of the critique is dampened both by our impatience with the Jerusalem-centric bias that considers such pilgrimages the unpardonable sin, and the scroll's own grudging concession that, for all that, Jeroboam II was an effective protector of his subjects. In language reminiscent of the diction of the book of Judges, the historian concedes that at a time when "the LORD saw that the distress of Israel was very bitter, . . . [the LORD] saved [the northern kingdom] by the hand of Jeroboam" (14:26).

Ironically, the earliest of those prophets whose oracles were collected into eponymously entitled scrolls, Hosea and Amos, both bitterly denounced the Jehu dynasty (Hos. 1:4–5; Amos 7:10–17). Some might hear Hosea's condemnation of Jehu's bloody coup as out of tune with the voice of his Ephraimite predecessor Elisha, who masterminded it according to 2 Kgs. 9. Similarly, though Jeroboam II deserves only a passing glance from the prophetically minded author of Kings (2 Kgs. 14:23–28)—and in those handful of verses, it is noted that the prophet Jonah supported him and that Jeroboam had an Othniel-like competence—the prophet Amos focusing his withering stare directly on him and his shrine at Bethel. But these inconsistencies among prophetic voices indirectly highlight the code that unified all the prophets: their unrelenting critique of anything less than full fidelity to the Mosaic covenant—half-measures would not do—and their bold and risky engagement with the pointed and painful particulars of history. The prophets eagerly drew on those oracles of their predecessors that harmonized with and lent traditional authority to their own jeremiads. But the relevance of past precedent was always contingent upon the moment and subservient to the novel dynamics of the present. Prophets were free to employ the spirit of "You have heard it was said, but I say to you" (cf. Matt. 5). Around the turn of the seventh century, the Judahite prophet Isaiah promised King Hezekiah that the Lord would defend Jerusalem from the Assyrian monarch Sennacherib's siege (2 Kgs. 19:34; Isa. 37:35), but it was the false prophets of Jeremiah's day, a century later, who took their stand on this word of God (cf. Jer. 4:10; 6:13–14; 7:4).

The fall of the house of Israel is sketched in 2 Kgs. 15–17. The house of Jehu fell when Jeroboam II's son Zechariah was killed by Shallum a mere six months into his reign (15:10). Israel floundered under the Assyrian onslaught:

of the six kings who reigned in its final two decades, four were assassinated as the nation veered between appeasement, at the cost of heavy tribute, and rebellion, seeking futile alliances with Syria and Egypt. A sympathetic historian, in retrospect, might conclude that the relatively small ancient kingdom of Israel never stood a chance against the Assyrian army. The fierce ethics and tough love of the Ephraimite prophets insisted to the contrary that, as long as the Lord reigns, the righteous always had a chance and were never at the mercy of the Fates. They make their own luck through their faithfulness or lack thereof to Mosaic torah. This view would not go unchallenged by later biblical writers, but the Deuteronomistic insistence on the rule of moral cause and effect, belied by a thousand exceptions, provided a foundation firm and enduring enough to support the survival of their culture.

The Dynamics of Prophecy and Order (2 Kgs. 18–23)

This penultimate section of Kings marks the zenith of the chronicle of dynastic rule, as the Judahite reigns of Hezekiah (ca. 715–687/686 BCE) and of Josiah (ca. 640–609 BCE) are portrayed as workable and prosperous unions of Mosaic justice and Davidic structure, of Ephraimite prophecy and Jerusalemite order. In two stories from earlier sections of the scroll, the Judahite king Jehoshaphat (ca. 873–849) had properly followed the Deuteronomistic principle that demanded that royal authority be checked by the egalitarian spirit of Mosaic instruction (cf. Deut. 17:14–20). In both cases, the righteous monarch sought the counsel of a prophet.

Before agreeing to a joint attack with Israelite forces against Syria in 1 Kgs. 22, Jehoshaphat insisted that King Ahab of Samaria "inquire . . . for the word of the Lord" (22:5). Despite the fact that Ahab reported back that he had received a favorable oracle from a plurality of prophets, Jehoshaphat was suspicious and pressed further, "Is there no other prophet of the LORD here of whom we may inquire?" (22:7). When another joint campaign, this time against Moab, was faring poorly, Jehoshaphat also called for a prophetic intermediary, "Is there no prophet of the LORD here, through whom we may inquire?" (2 Kgs. 3:11). Jehoshaphat's reliance on the oracular advice of two prophets who cut their teeth on torah, Micaiah ben Imlah in 1 Kgs. 22 and Elisha in 2 Kgs. 3, personified the Deuteronomistic ideal and anticipated the pattern followed by Hezekiah and Josiah.

Hezekiah, who sat on the throne of Judah in the era immediately following the fall of Samaria to Assyria and led a nation that checked and survived Sennacherib's campaign in Judah ca. 700, relied on the Jerusalem prophet Isaiah for mediation with and oracles from the Lord (2 Kgs. 19:1–20:19; cf. Isa. 37:1–39:8). We may suspect that emigrés from Samaria, bearing their Mosaic traditions and Ephraimite prophetic repertoire, had begun to influence Judahite culture because the portrait of the Judahite, temple-centered prophet Isaiah has shadings from northern tradition: like Elisha with Naaman, Isaiah heals Hezekiah from a skin ailment (cf. 2 Kgs. 5) through the application of an elixir of fig paste (2 Kgs. 20:1–7); and like Joshua, Isaiah momentarily arrests the course of the sun (Josh. 10:12–14), causing time to move backward (2 Kgs. 20:9–11).

Josiah's reforms of Judah in the late seventh century, inspired by "the book of the torah of the LORD" (2 Kgs. 22:8, my trans.), had the certification of the sole female prophet recorded in the scroll of Kings, a woman named Huldah (22:14–20). Josiah's reign, though tragically cut short by his death at Megiddo in a battle against the Egyptians (23:29–30), is depicted as a synthesis of Davidic promise and Mosaic fidelity.

By the time we reach this section of Kings, we have already seen most of its theological themes. The king who "clings ["holds fast," NSRV] to the LORD" (18:6)

prospers (18:7) while the two evil kings sandwiched between Hezekiah and Josiah, Manasseh and Amon (chap. 21), doom their children and children's children (including Josiah; cf. 23:26–27) until the third and fourth generations. For the historian who wrote the final version of the scroll of Kings, the resources of gracious divine capital contained in the promises to David were eventually sapped by the enormity of the sins of Manasseh (21:1–16); moral cause and effect demanded that Judah fall to Babylon just as Israel had fallen to Assyria.

Women in the books of Kings. One theme that we have not considered yet is that of the role of women in the scroll, and the prophetess Huldah's prominence in the reforms of Josiah provide us with an opportunity to do so.

There was no golden age of gender equality in biblical history. Prehistoric patterns of a sexual division of labor that impelled men into the public sphere outside compounds and villages to hunt, herd, fight, trade regionally, and perform gross tasks of construction and agriculture, and kept women in the more private spheres of home, town markets, and the fields and wells adjacent to villages in order to bear and raise children, produce the realia of domestic industries, and cultivate and prepare food, had a kind of anthropological inevitability. As in any traditional culture, there doubtless were countless exceptions to these patterns as provisional necessities and the myriad particulars of individual personalities defied written laws and unwritten customs. Let us set aside these generalizations in order to observe the details of how women are portrayed in the scroll of Kings.

Women such as the widows, matrons, and servant girls in the Elijah/Elisha tales were part of the Ephraimite prophetic subculture, as integral to the preservation of this mission as the scores of women who followed and supported Jesus were to the first century CE Christian movement. In the eighteen formulas that summarize the reigns of the kings of Judah throughout 1 and 2 Kings, the name of the queen mother is given fifteen times, testimony to the influence of royal women. Jezebel's power, though vilified and caricatured, confirms that royal women in Israel also wielded considerable clout. Bathsheba ensured that her son Solomon succeeded David to the throne rather than her stepson Adonijah. For a brief period that can be dated to the mid-ninth century (ca. 842–837 BCE), a queen mother who was a member of the Omride house (2 Kgs. 8:26), Athaliah, ruled Judah, the only ruling queen in the recorded history of either state, before she was killed and succeeded by a Davidic descendant, Joash, who was nurtured by his royal aunt Jehosheba (2 Kgs. 11).

These portraits of village women and domestics who supported prophets and courtly women who wielded influence behind and through their sons and husbands hardly redeem the chronicle from the patriarchal bias of ancient literature that overwhelmingly focuses on the world-changing, nature-defying exploits of male action heroes. Aside from Huldah, we do not hear much about the religious activities and practices of women in the era of Kings, but the negative attitude toward them reflected in the references in other biblical literature to such ministrations and mediations as occult (cf. Exod. 22:18; 1 Sam. 28:3–25) were certainly shared by the composers of Kings. This may demonstrate the male bias in traditional articulations of the line between orthodoxy and heresy.

A Theology of Exile (2 Kgs. 24–25)

The books of 1 and 2 Kings began their literary existence as a single scroll of Kings, so it is instructive to note how the entire work begins and ends: "King David was old and advanced in years; and although they covered him with clothes, he could not get warm" (2 Kgs. 1:1). This lukewarm introduction to a chronicle of the dynastic era of two ancient theocracies, Israel and Judah, foreshadows the weary tone that dominates so much of this

priestly history. Walter Brueggemann's quip about the irony of the work's title says it all: "Kings?!?" This miserable succession of mediocre leaders are considered kings?

Even Solomon in all his glory could not redeem the whole sorry roster of monarchs. Rehoboam in the tenth century BCE and his foolish pharaonic conscription of northerners into work gangs on royal projects undid the Davidic-Solomonic union a single generation after its inception (1 Kgs. 12). There was Ahab in the ninth century and his petty rapacity for the traditional homestead of a commoner, Naboth's vineyard (1 Kgs. 21). Ahaz in the eighth century, taking a page from the ninth-century Moabite king Mesha (who had reputedly staved off a foreign attack through occult commerce, a human sacrifice that unleashed "great wrath" upon the invaders; see 2 Kgs. 3:26–27), ritually incinerated his sons in a perversely desperate attempt to gain divine favor for his administration (2 Kgs. 16:1–4). Manasseh in the seventh century erected the statue of a goddess in the temple of the unimaged I AM WHO I AM (2 Kgs. 21:7), despoiling the austere Mosaic mystery of Judah's sanctuary a century before the Babylonian army under Nebuchadnezzar finished the job (2 Kgs. 24). It is a tired chronicle that begins with a geriatric, impotent David (1 Kgs. 1:4) and whose successors are most often memorialized in clichéd historiographic formulas: "For the rest of the deeds of King [fill in the blank], see the Books of the Annals of the Kings [of Judah/Israel]."

Kings? No, they are not the heroes of this chronicle of the dynastic era in ancient Israel and Judah. The prophets are, and it is in those sections of 1 and 2 Kings that feature accounts of the women and men who belonged to this mainly underground subculture of dissent that the narrative pace quickens, the quality of the storytelling rises, and the virtues of this ancient monotheistic religious culture, whose legatees include Judaism, Christianity, and Islam, were epitomized and preserved.

The fierce advocacy of these prophets for Mosaic monotheism and covenantal restrictions on royalty and peasant alike can now be seen as foundational for free societies. The emphasis on the heroism of the prophets in the scroll of Kings democratized the ideal of justice. In ancient Near Eastern culture, the protection of the weak from the strong was everywhere the purview of the king. A just king, Hammurabi was responsible "for the enhancement of the well-being of the people, . . . to make justice prevail in the land, . . . to prevent the strong from oppressing the weak" (*ANET*, 164). The scroll of Kings makes an extraordinary move by decoupling this ideal from the king and placing it with the counselor, the prophet, the religious intermediary. This tempering of royal power by justice, and the informal, traditional institutionalization of the prophetic office among the peoples of ancient Israel and Judah are roots of the doctrine of the separation of powers. The prophetic insistence that even the monarchical office itself be legally circumscribed by Mosaic teaching, the Torah, is a foretaste of constitutional governance.

But neither these prophets nor the priestly composers of the scroll of Kings who revered them were visionary political theorists. These Iron Age activists and historians could not envision a society without a king. The scroll of Judges, a companion work to Kings (a product of the same priestly historians) that sketched the era before monarchy, encapsulated the fractious and violent warlordism of Israel's frontier days in the refrain, "Since there was no king then, every man did whatever he pleased" (Judg. 21:25, my trans.).

Once every century or so, an honest man sat on the throne of Judah, a man sympathetic to the prophets' Mosaic traditionalism: a David, a Jehoshaphat (2 Kgs. 3:14), a Hezekiah (2 Kgs. 18:3–8), and, most of all, a Josiah (2 Kgs. 23:25), the late-sixth-century king of Judah who probably—though not all scholars agree—sponsored the very composition of the scroll of Kings and its prequels,

Joshua, Judges, and Samuel. All these monarchs were members of the Davidic dynasty, which despite its share of corrupt, venal, and weak rulers, remained intact for the entire four-hundred-year existence of Judah.

This brings us then to the end of the scroll of Kings and its curiously underplayed final scene. The Babylonian army conquered Judah by 587 BCE, just as one hundred and fifty years before (ca. 722) the Assyrian army had finished the political state of Israel. Solomon's temple, David's city, the royal palace, the Judahite army, all fell, and the elite citizenry of Jerusalem were forcibly removed to Babylon. The final paragraph of the scroll of Kings (2 Kgs. 25:27–30), the final paragraph of the tetrateuch of Joshua–Judges–Samuel–Kings, a work with conquests and derring-do, with eloquent speechifying and monumental architectural designs, with stories about women who sheltered spies and summoned militias and scolded blood feuders and about men who arrested the orbit of the sun, toppled coliseums, felled pituitary giants, and made it rain, this ancient work of historiography in the grand style ends on a quotidian note about a day in the life of a Davidic prince during the Babylonian exile.

> In the thirty-seventh year of the exile of King Jehoiachin of Judah, in the twelfth month, on the twenty-seventh day of the month, King Evil-merodach of Babylon, in the year that he began to reign, released King Jehoiachin of Judah from prison; he spoke kindly to him, and gave him a seat above the other seats of the kings who were with him in Babylon. So Jehoiachin put aside his prison clothes. *Every day of his life* he dined regularly in the king's presence. For his allowance, a regular allowance was given him by the king, a portion every day, *as long as he lived*.

Compare this text with 1 Kgs. 4:20–21, and its Solomonic measurement of the fullest extent of dynastic grandeur in the united kingdom of Judah and Israel.

> Judah and Israel were as numerous as the sand by the sea; they ate and drank and were happy. Solomon was sover-

eign over all the kingdoms from the Euphrates to the land of the Philistines, even to the border of Egypt; they brought tribute and served Solomon *all the days of his life.*

"Every day of his life," "as long as he lived": in Hebrew these clauses from the end of the scroll are identical to "all the days of his life" in the description of Solomon from early in the scroll. The repetition invites us to compare the respective fortunes of Jehoiachin and Solomon, of their kingdoms and of their subjects, about how the mighty had fallen, and from the plains of Shinar to lament the ruins of yet another fabled city brought low by the judgments of the Lord.

To be fair, the cranky tone of Kings stems from more than theology. It also reflects the values of an ancient culture that venerated the past. The scroll of Kings speaks in the voice of a traditional worldview. If only the people could return to the way it was in the olden days when giants walked the earth and folks lived for centuries, when Moses spoke and Joshua fought and David danced and Solomon presided over cosmogonic pageants on Mount Zion. If only their culture could return to the time when the Lord loved David, and to the brief time early in Solomon's reign and the months during Josiah's time when there was centralized worship in the Jerusalem temple uncontaminated by the goddess Asherah's wooden totems.

But we should decline this invitation to see the final paragraph of Kings as wholly negative. Because the clear sense of this epilogue to the scroll of Kings in 2 Kgs. 25:27–30 is that, as in the final reel of a matinee serial, the hero is preparing a comeback. For Evil-merodach (i.e., Amel Marduk) is not a pharaoh who knew not David, but rather a monarch who, however faintly, has restored the prince's provisions and has given this descendant of David a more exalted place at high table than the other exiled potentates of Western Asia.

If inclined, we might fault the disheartened historian who wrote 2 Kgs. 25 for obscuring his ray of hope with a conclusion so lacking in narrative energy. If inclined, we might appreciate this subtle, sly, final uptick that refuses to bow to the tragic trajectory of the bulk of Kings. Either way, at the end of Kings the walls and citadels of Jerusalem may have fallen, but the prophetic ideals and heroism in the book, and the dream of an ideal city, just king, and covenant society left more than enough foundation upon which to rebuild. The writer of this last chapter of Kings leaves the door ajar for a sequel, though the completion of that task would fall to others. The most stunning and basic theological truth of the scroll of Kings is that ultimately, in the words of a prophet, Isaiah of Babylon, who was still alive even as this final paragraph was inked on animal skin, divine mercy trumps divine judgment.

For thus says the LORD,
who created the heavens, . . .
who formed the earth and made it, . . .
[the LORD] did not create it a chaos.
Isa 45:18

Bibliography

Brueggemann, Walter. *Theology of the Old Testament: Testimony, Dispute, Advocacy.* Minneapolis: Fortress, 1997.

Camp, Claudia V. "1 and 2 Kings." In *Women's Bible Commentary*, edited by Carol A. Newsom and Sharon H. Ringe, 102–16. Louisville: Westminster John Knox, 1998.

Cogan, Mordechai. *I Kings*. AB 10. New York: Doubleday, 2001.

Cogan, Mordechai, and Hayim Tadmor. *II Kings*. AB 11. Garden City, NY: Doubleday, 1988.

Friedman, Richard Elliott. *Who Wrote the Bible?* New York: Perennial Library, 1989.

Nelson, Richard. *First and Second Kings*. Interpretation. Atlanta: John Knox, 1987.

1 and 2 Chronicles

Melody D. Knowles

INTRODUCTION

Beginning with Adam and ending with Cyrus's declaration that the Babylonian exiles may return to Jerusalem in 538 BCE, the books of 1 and 2 Chronicles retell the story of the nations of Israel and Judah. Like all retellings, the books take a particular slant on the nations' past. With their particular focus on the Jerusalem temple, the work of David and Solomon, God's involvement with humanity, and their definition of the nation of Israel, the books reflect and contend for the contemporary interests and programs of the author.

Although long considered the product of the same hand as Ezra and Nehemiah, in recent work scholars such as Sara Japhet and Hugh Williamson have argued for the distinctive authorship of Chronicles. The repetition of Cyrus's edict in 2 Chr. 36:22–23 and Ezra 1:1–3 and a common concern for Jerusalem and its temple should not mask the significant differences between the books with regard to language, style, the definition of the faithful community, evaluation of the northern kingdom, perspectives on mixed marriages, and the practice of religion. The date of composition also seems later than the books of Ezra and Nehemiah—sections of the books are reflected in Chronicles (Neh. 11:3–19 in 1 Chr. 9:2–17), the temple gatekeepers are Levites in Chronicles (as opposed to Ezra 2:42 =

Neh. 7:45 and Neh. 11:19), and the genealogy of David is traced in Chronicles into the fourth century BCE (1 Chr. 3). Although some material was probably added later, the bulk of the book reflects a Jerusalem setting in the late Persian period (ca. 400–325 BCE), during a time in which the city's prosperity and population was limited (but growing). In addition, Jerusalem during this period was the political capital of the province of Yehud, and, in various ways and in varying degrees, the spiritual capital of Yahwists living outside the province throughout the Diaspora.

The large amount of overlap between Chronicles and its biblical sources (i.e., the books of Samuel and Kings as well as Genesis, Exodus, Joshua, etc., although not always in the exact form that underlies our English versions; see Knoppers, *1 Chronicles*, 1:69–71) gives rise to questions regarding the purposes of the author, and the subsequent evaluation of the text by ancient communities. The author presupposes that the readers were familiar with the biblical sources, assuming that, for instance, the reader would know that story behind the brief notice that Saul was condemned for consulting with a medium (1 Chr. 10:13–14; cf. 1 Sam. 28:8–25). It is likely that this presupposition indicates the author was not trying to

145

replace prior histories of the nation. Yet the older texts receive no small amount of reworking such that events central in other texts, such as David's affair with Bathsheba, are not recorded in Chronicles. According to Marc Brettler, the book is best thought of as an attempt not in replacing earlier texts, but rather in "reshaping the known"—presenting a revised or corrective reading of history through which to read the earlier accounts (pp. 21–23). When compared to the biblical sources, it is possible to see a "reshaping" that legitimates current institutions (by emphasizing a Davidic pedigree for the Second Temple and its organization, for example), and buttresses the centrality of Jerusalem in the practice of religion.

Additional perspectives on the book and its purposes can be seen in the titles that ancient communities assigned to the book, which had no title in its original version. In the rabbinic tradition, the book is referred to as "the book of the events of the days" (*sepher dibre hayyamin*), a title relating it to official annals such as "the book of the events of the Kings of Judah" (1 Kgs. 14:19, and cf. 15:7, 23). In the Septuagint, the book is entitled "the things left out" (*ta paraleipomena*), a designation highlighting

the passages in Chronicles not found in other biblical books. Although the title could be interpreted as dismissive (i.e., it contains only those details considered unimportant to the editors of Genesis, Samuel, and Kings), it could also indicate that an ancient community found value precisely in this unique material. Yet the text also presents events already recorded in the books of Genesis through Kings, and it may have been this perceived inaccuracy that led Jerome to designate the book "Chronicle of the Entire Divine History," from which we derive our current title, conveying Jerome's sense of the scope of the work and highlighting the theological perspective that pervades the account. With the reignition of interest in Chronicles in the contemporary academic community, the ancient debate concerning the nature of the book reflected in these different titles (historical record? theological treatise? a rewritten Bible?) is still a lively one today.

Since many of the major themes of Chronicles develop from the first part of the book into the second, readers are encouraged to read the essays on both 1 and 2 Chronicles. When the versification in the English and Hebrew version differ, I follow the English numbers.

COMMENTARY

The Human Community: Redefining Israel

According to the books of Ezra and Nehemiah, the community of Israel is mostly limited to those from the tribes of Benjamin and Judah who returned from the Babylonian exile to the land of Yehud. Chronicles presents a much broader interpretation, and includes the northern tribes united with the southern ones as the ideal manifestation of the kingdom ("all Israel"). To be sure, the author devotes most of the work to the story of the south and its kings, and considers the northern kingdom, with its worship sites outside Jerusalem and non-Davidic monarch, to

be illegitimate. Yet the ideal boundaries of the nation include the north, albeit a north that is united (or reunited) with the south under the authority of the Davidic king and Jerusalem temple.

This issue is dealt with explicitly only in 2 Chronicles (i.e., after the kingdoms have split apart), yet the unity of the north and south is already a theme in 1 Chronicles, expressed in several different ways. In the genealogies that begin the book (chaps. 1–9), the connection of the northern tribes with the southern is telegraphed with the emphasis on common parentage through the lineage of the patriarch Israel (never called Jacob in this text). In addition, the author explicitly records the participation of the entire nation at pivotal points in its history, even when this may contradict the accounts in Samuel and Kings. For example, David is crowned the king of "all Israel" in Hebron (1 Chr. 11:1–3), so that, unlike the account in Samuel, he does not reign first over Judah for several years and then over Judah and Israel (2 Sam. 2:4 and 5:3–5). "All Israel" also participates in temple-related events such as the conquest of Jerusalem (1 Chr. 11:4–5) and the transfer of the ark (1 Chr. 13:2, 5, 6; 15:3, 28), although the Samuel narratives record that these were the acts only of David and his army ("the king and his men" in 2 Sam. 5:6, David and "all the chosen men of Israel" in 2 Sam. 6:1).

Through an emphasis on biological relations and corporate actions, the author redefines the boundaries of the community assumed by the authors of Ezra and Nehemiah. But included in "all Israel" is not only the north and the south: the author also uses shared bloodlines and deeds to incorporate other nationalities into Israel. By beginning the history of Israel with Adam through Noah (1 Chr. 1:1–4), the author indicates that the nation is related to the wider world. Nearer biological ties include those through intermarriage with Canaanites (Judah's wife Bath-shua in 2:3), Ishmaelites (Abigail's husband Jether in 2:17), Egyptians (Sheshan's daughter's husband Jarha in 2:34–35 and Mered's wife Bithiah, daughter of Pharaoh, in 4:17), Geshurites (David's wife Maacah in 3:2), and more. Since many of these unions involve a woman from outside Israel/Judah, it is tempting to see the genealogical record in Chronicles as a response to the forced divorce and expulsion of "foreign wives" in Ezra and Nehemiah (Ezra 9:1–10:44; Neh. 13:23–28). Whereas foreign women are a threat to the "holy seed" in Ezra and Nehemiah, they become the means of expansion in Chronicles. Foreign men are also included in this genealogy (1 Chr. 2:17, 34–35), and, in addition, David's army is made up of "valiant warriors" from other nations such as Ahohites, Hittites, and Moabites (11:12, 41, 46).

By means of this emphasis on the ideal unity of the entire nation and its ethnic diversity, the author can respond to the situation in the Persian period when Yehud was a small province and many Yahwists lived elsewhere. Instead of advocating strict genealogical boundaries (upon penalty of divorce and expulsion), the author emphasizes the nation's ancient ethnic diversity. And, by including the north in key narratives of the nation's life, the author emphasizes a link with Yahwistic communities outside the boundaries of Yehud. This theme will be expanded in 2 Chronicles, but already detectable is the presentation of an "ideal" Israel made up of more than just the southern tribes, related through ancestry and the united support of the Davidic monarchy and the Jerusalem temple.

The Temple: David and Solomon's Endeavor

Religious life in Chronicles revolves around the Jerusalem temple, and in 1 Chronicles David and Solomon are the key figures in the construction of this temple. Concern for the centrality of the temple leads the author to narrate the activities of the kings (i.e., David's securing the throne and achieving victory in battle, and the timing of Solomon's coronation) in light of the temple and its cult. For example, according to the presentation in the book, after David ascends to the throne he immediately captures Jerusalem from the Jebusites (1 Chr. 11:4–7; although see the various flashbacks in 11:10–12:41), contrary to the presentation in Samuel. The capture of Jerusalem is followed by David's transfer of the ark to the capital (chap. 13; 15:1–16:3), as well as his appointment of clergy for the ark's cult in Jerusalem and the cult for the tabernacle temporarily installed in Gibeon (16:4–43). With the strategic insertion of Nathan's oracle in chap. 17, promising David that God will build him a dynasty and that his son will build God a temple, the rest of David's reign is told as an unfolding of the prophet's words: the military success against the Philistines, Moabites, Ammonites, and Arameans secures the peace and tribute necessary for the temple's construction (chaps. 18–20), and David's decision to take a census of Israel results in the divine revelation of the temple's building site (21:1–22:1). Many of the final chapters of the book tell of David's securing materials and workers for the temple and his setting the divisions and duties of cultic officials (chaps. 22–26).

Yet even with all of the emphasis that the author gives to David and his acts relating to the temple, the king and his work are inextricably linked to his successor Solomon. That is, as David's two farewell speeches make clear (22:6–19 and 28:1–29:20, material radically reworked from the parallel in 1 Kgs. 2:1–9 and 5:3–5), both kings need each other— David's work is incomplete without Solomon's efforts, and Solomon's task is based on David's preparations. Like the transition of leadership from Moses to Joshua, the departing leader who has been denied the final attainment of his life's mission charges his successor to conclude his work. After expressing his original desire to build the temple, making initial preparations, and then hearing God's prohibition ("You are a man of battles and have shed blood," 1 Chr. 28:2–3, my trans.), David prays that Solomon would finish the task ("build the temple for which I have made provision," 29:19). This tie between the two kings, the preparation and completion of a single mission, is also emphasized by the repeated assertion of their choice by God. David tells the gathered community that not only was Solomon chosen by God to build the temple but both men were chosen to be king: God "chose me . . . to be king over Israel forever . . . [and] he chose my son Solomon to sit upon the throne of the kingdom" (28:4–5, and see also vv. 6 and 10). As Japhet notes, this explicit designation of divine election, new to the Chronicles account, indicates that "the process of

divine choice is finalized not in David but in his son" (*Chronicles*, p. 488). The link signaled by united mission and divine choice is further demonstrated by David's endowing Solomon with the temple's plan and building materials (28:11–20; 29:2–5). As a final capstone, the author reverses the order of Kings and gives the notice of David's death *after* that of Solomon's coronation, cementing the relationship of both kings to an even greater degree.

Although it may be possible to see in these stories a plea for the restoration of the Davidic monarchy in the Persian period (or even the eschatological future), a more straightforward interpretation is simply the Davidic-Solomonic claim on the temple and its priestly divisions. During a time when the rebuilding and upkeep of present temple (the Second Temple) was associated with the Persian emperor, the author of Chronicles reclaims the edifice for Israel. Cyrus may have instigated the construction (2 Chr. 36:22–23; Ezra 1:1–4), and subsequent emperors may have offered financial assistance (Ezra 6:4; 7:15, 20–22, etc.), yet Chronicles traces its lineage to David and Solomon. And even though Solomon's temple was rebuilt with Persian support, the building site and organization of the Second Temple can still claim a Davidic pedigree. At the site where David originally proclaimed, "This will be the house of the LORD God and this will be the altar of the burnt offering for Israel" (1 Chr. 22:1, my trans.), and where David's organizational structure of Levites and priests were still in place, the nation can see the hand of their earliest kings behind the current support of the foreign emperor.

Religious Life and Practices: Centered on the Temple

According to the biblical texts from the Persian period, the import of the Jerusalem temple was an area of contention. Texts such as Haggai and Zechariah witness to the people's initial lack of enthusiasm for the building project, and Isa. 66:1–2 records a similar sentiment ("Thus says the LORD: Heaven is my throne and the earth is my footstool; what is the house that you would build for me, and what is my resting place?"). Yet Chronicles argues that the temple is the locus of communion between God and humanity, and central to the life of the community.

In 1 Chronicles the pro-temple stance is apparent even though the structure is not built until 2 Chronicles. The temple's close relationship with the Divine is indicated by David's claim that it would be "a house to the name of the LORD my God" (1 Chr. 22:7), "a house of rest for the ark of the covenant of the LORD" (1 Chr. 28:2; cf. 2 Chr. 6:41), and proclamation that God "resides [literally, 'tents'] in Jerusalem forever" (1 Chr. 23:25). In language that becomes more frequent and more clear in 2 Chronicles, 1 Chronicles, with expressions such as these, relates the temple to God's presence with the people.

Further, although God is not contained in the holy precincts, the close link between God and sacred geography or sacred objects in Chronicles is also conveyed through key terms such as "to seek" (*drsh*), which has both religious and geographic aspects. Specifically, "seeking" God can indicate a physical journey to a place where God (or a representative for God, such as the ark) dwells. For example, in 1 Chr. 10:13–14 Saul is accused of "not seeking" guidance from the Lord, preferring instead to journey to a medium to seek guidance. In language that explicitly links "seeking" with the ark, David proclaims to the nation, "Let us bring again the ark of our God to us; for we did not seek it in the days of Saul" (13:3, my trans.); and, during the installation of the ark in the tent in Jerusalem, the Levites sing "seek the LORD and his strength, seek his presence continually" (16:11). In the Chronicler's religious world, obedience and disobedience can have a geographic component, and the faithful are encouraged to enact their piety by attending to cultic objects such as the ark, and, more

explicitly in the later part of the book, worshiping at the temple.

The attention given to the roles and divisions of cultic workers, in texts often unique to Chronicles, also conveys the author's concerns with public center of worship. Throughout the text, the author names and designates people and families to specific duties: Aaronites to offer sacrifice in the Holy of Holies (6:49–53; cf. 24:1–19), and Levites to sing and play instruments (6:31–47;15:16–22; 23:5; cf. "young women" cult musicians in 15:20b), serve as gatekeepers, tenders of cultic furniture, blenders of spices, makers of flat cakes (9:17–34; 23:5; 25:1–19), and additional Levites to "have charge of the work in the house of the LORD," and serve as officers and judges (23:4; and cf. 23:28–32; 26:20–28). These detailed lists demonstrate a concern for the temple and its orderly working, as well as a desire to establish the antiquity and Davidic pedigree of these workings.

For all of the focus on the cult in Jerusalem, the author also records some religious activity outside the city, especially in the form of individual and communal prayer. After the etymology for his name that his mother gives, Jabez is probably outside Jerusalem when he addresses God: "Oh that you would bless me and enlarge my border, and that your hand might be with me, and that you would keep me from hurt and harm!" (4:10). God grants this request, although no reason is given. When the tribes of Reuben, Gad, and Manasseh went out to war, "They cried to God in the battle," and God gave them victory "because they trusted in him" (5:20). Through these accounts, the author can portray a responsive God who is able to hear the prayers of the faithful even outside the geography of the Jerusalem cult.

A God Unbound and Involved

The Chronicler's portrait of this God who hears prayer has sometimes been considered a Divinity that metes out just deserts, so that the actions of humanity elicit immediate and coherent effects from God. As with the response to the prayers of Jabez (4:10) and the fighting tribes (5:20), God in Chronicles sometimes responds with immediate rewards for the good deeds of humanity. In addition to these responses of blessing, God also responds with punishment: Er's wickedness brought him death from the divine hand (2:3), Saul's reign was terminated because of his unfaithfulness (10:13–14), and the north was exiled because God "stirred up" the spirit of the Assyrian king when the people "transgressed against the God of their ancestors" (5:25–26). This theme may also be recognized in parts of 2 Chronicles, and, as such, the book can be read as an encouragement to a life of obedience and repentance. (Indeed, at times the reworking of the narratives from Samuel and Kings shows the author supplying sins for hitherto unexplained punishments [2 Chr. 16:10, 12] or rewards for unrecompensed righteousness [2 Chr. 14:5–7, 11–14, etc.], demonstrating the Chronicler's desire to link causes with effects.) Yet such a reading must be nuanced so that God's moral calculus is free from human prediction, because Chronicles also records unmerited rewards and pun-

ishments. For instance, the divine choice of David and Solomon is, in the Chronicler's account, unmerited by their prior actions, as is God's acceptance of Solomon as "son" (1 Chr. 22:10; or 28:5–7; 29:1). Conversely, seventy thousand men died as a result of David's census (21:14), the unfairness of the situation emphasized by David's proclamation, "It is I who have sinned and done wickedly. But these sheep, what have they done? . . . do not let your people be plagued!" (21:17; and cf. 21:3, where Joab warns the king in the form of the question "Why should [David] bring guilt on Israel?").

In this sophisticated presentation, God is clearly and deeply involved with humanity, responding to their deeds of good and evil. Yet God can also be free from the calculation of humanity, ultimately free to perform God's own purposes. As such, the book teaches some of the same lessons of Job, not through the personal experience of one man, but through the collective experience of the nation. Although it is a call to learn the history of the people for moral edification and education, at the same time it is an acknowledgment that such knowledge has its limitations in light of the possibility of God's unpredictability.

INTRODUCTION TO 2 CHRONICLES

Second Chronicles continues the story of the nation, beginning in the time of Solomon and ending with Cyrus. Along with the continued story line are similar emphases concerning the ideal unity of the

nation and the focus on the temple. (For a basic introduction to both 1 and 2 Chronicles, including remarks about date, author, and purpose, please see the introduction at the beginning of the essay on 1 Chronicles.)

COMMENTARY

The Human Community: Redefining Israel

After the death of Solomon, the northern tribes revolt against his successor Rehoboam, thus dividing the kingdom into two parts (2 Chr. 10). The author understands this move as "rebellion

against the house of David" (10:19), but maintains that the northern tribes are still the people of God and can repent and rejoin the south. Although the book no longer stresses the genealogical links to the extent seen in 1 Chronicles, the two nations are still called "brothers" (11:4; 28:8, 11). In addition, as in 1 Chronicles, in the second part of the book there is an emphasis on the joint acts of the two nations at key points in the historical narrative such as the building and dedication of the temple (2 Chr. 1:2; 7:8) and subsequent religious celebrations in Jerusalem (chap. 30; 35:1–19). In addition, in the speech given by Abijah the author recasts the division as an act perpetrated by only part of the north, namely Jeroboam "and certain worthless scoundrels" (13:6–7). According to the author, the north is apostate, but they are still the people of God who can repent and return. Such "returning" means coming under the authority of the Davidic king and the Jerusalem temple, or, as Hezekiah phrases it in his speech to Israel, "yield yourselves to the LORD and come to his sanctuary" (30:8). Due to the significance of Jerusalem worship for reasons political as well as theological, the remainder of this essay is devoted to this subject.

God and Religious Practices:
Centered on the Temple

The author of Chronicles speaks about God by describing religious practices. That is, the God that the nation serves is revealed by the author through stories and prescriptions about their worship of that God. According to the text, God is moved to act in response to the community's prayers (20:1–29), and worship is often marked by music and joyfulness (1 Chr. 15:28; 2 Chr. 5:11–14; 7:6, 10; 30:25–26), descriptions that indicate that God is responsive, compassionate, and worthy of praise.

As in 1 Chronicles, 2 Chronicles portrays a God who is particularly interested in religious practices that are centered on the temple in Jerusalem. God chose the site (1 Chr. 21:18, 26) and accepted it as the dwelling place for the divine name (2 Chr. 6:10; 7:16). God's connection with this geography means that the secession of the northern kingdom in 2 Chronicles implies not only a rejection of the Davidic monarchy, but also a separation from worship in Jerusalem, and thus true worship of God.

The author emphasizes the significance of Jerusalem worship by claiming that key rituals such as the sacrifice of animals and incense are proper to the temple area alone and illegitimate when practiced elsewhere. In Chronicles this exclusivity of ritual geography serves an inclusive purpose: the worship of God at the Jerusalem temple provides a means for the future reunification of the nation.

As part of its description and prescription for worship in 2 Chronicles, the author confines the practice of animal sacrifice to the Jerusalem temple. This is accomplished via textual suppression and expansion: when compared to the narratives in Kings, Chronicles includes both more references to sacrifice at the temple and fewer references to sacrifice outside Jerusalem. Examples of the additional emphasis on sacrifice in Jerusalem include God's announcement that "I have chosen this place [i.e., the temple] as a house of sacrifice" (2 Chr. 7:12), a designation unique in the Hebrew Bible. In addition to this divine declaration, the book records many accounts of sacrifice in the temple, including those at the Passover celebrations of Hezekiah and Josiah (chap. 30; 35:1–19), passages greatly expanded from or added to the Kings material (2 Kgs. 23:21–23).

The emphasis on sacrifice *in* Jerusalem is also seen in the author's suppression of notices of sacrifice *outside* the city. For instance, when compared to the Kings material, the building of a place for worship and sacrifice (a "high place") outside the city is delayed four generations, moving from the time of Rehoboam in Kings to the time of Jehoram in Chronicles (1 Kgs. 14:22–24 vs. 2 Chr. 21:11). In addition, explicit notices that the people sacrificed at the high places during the reigns of Joash, Amaziah, and Azariah, present in Kings, are absent from Chronicles. Even when Chronicles contains negative assessments of the reigns of Jehoram and Jotham, there is no explicit mention of sacrifice outside Jerusalem (2 Chr. 21:11; 27:2; cf. 2 Kgs. 15:35). In Chronicles, sacrifice outside Jerusalem occurs less often than it does in Kings.

When notices of sacrifice outside Jerusalem are retained (such as during the reigns of Manesseh, Amon, Ahaz, and Asa), the author sometimes makes significant changes to downplay the practice. For instance, 2 Chr. 28 retains the notice from Kings that Ahaz "sacrificed and made offerings on the high places, on the hills, and under every green tree," and the author adds that the king made additional high places throughout Judah (2 Chr. 28:4, 25; 2 Kgs. 16:4). Yet according to Kings, Ahaz also built an altar according to the design of the altar at Damascus, placed this before the Jerusalem temple, and offered "his burnt offering and his grain offering, poured his drink offering, and dashed the blood of his offerings of well-being against the altar" (2 Kgs. 16:10–16). The Chronicler does not include this story, merely recording that Ahaz "sacrificed to the gods of Damascus" (2 Chr. 28:23). By keeping the detail of the foreign altar out of the story, the desecrating object is kept out of the temple area, and the sacred space is not polluted. In addition, although Chronicles repeats that notice that Asa retained the high places during his reign (2 Chr. 15:17; 1 Kgs. 15:14), the passage is preceded with an account of the king's centralizing reform: "he took away the foreign altars and the high places . . . he also removed from all the cities of Judah the high places and the incense altars" (2 Chr. 14:3, 5; cf. 15:8).

When compared to Kings, Chronicles emphasizes centralized sacrifice by adding and expanding accounts of sacrifice in Jerusalem, and by suppressing or modifying accounts of non-Jerusalem sacrifice (or foreign sacrifice in the Jerusalem temple). This emphasis on maintaining Jerusalem (and Jerusalem alone) as the place for sacrifice in Chronicles should be read in light of extrabiblical documents from this time, especially the letters from a Yahwistic community that relocated to Egypt in a settlement named Elephantine (see Porten and Yardeni, *Textbook*, A4, 5, 7, 8, 9, 10). According to this correspondence, the community had a temple dedicated to YHWH, built prior to 525 BCE, and in this temple the community sacrificed animals along with incense and grain. When the temple was burned down by a local rival religious group around 410 BCE, the community first wrote to the Jerusalem temple establishment for help in rebuilding. After waiting three years for an answer, they wrote to the governors of Yehud and Samaria and asked for help in rebuilding the temple in order that they could continue their sacrificial activity. When the political authorities responded, they instructed that worship be reconstituted as it was "formerly," but allowed only for the sacrifice of grain and incense. After this, members of the community itself also wrote a document disallowing the offering of animals in their local religious practice. These texts from Elephantine tell of a great transformation in Yahwistic ritual practice outside Jerusalem in just over three years. At the beginning of this period, they announce to the Jerusalem temple community that they sacrifice animals and need help in reconstructing their worship area so that they can continue. Several years later they explicitly disallow animal sacrifice in their local religious practice. In 2 Chronicles we can hear the Jerusalem side of this issue, a side that emphatically limits animal sacrifice to the temple area alone.

The Elephantine letters also mention the religious offering of incense, a practice, like animal sacrifice, that the Chronicler advocates should be limited to Jerusalem. The author includes removal of incense altars from outside Jerusalem as a laudatory part of the cultic reforms of Asa, Hezekiah, and Josiah (2 Chr. 14:5; 30:14; 34:4, 7). The geographic limitation of incense offerings is buttressed by the author's insistence that only the clerical classes can offer the substance. In a story not found in Kings, Uzziah tries to offer incense at the temple but is smitten by leprosy, providing a cautionary tale for other laypeople (26:16–21). The author's concern to limit the use of incense to Jerusalem was not shared by the Elephantine community, even after they prohibited the local sacrifice of animals. In addition, God's declaration in Mal. 1:11 reflects a similar geographical openness to the practice: "From the rising of the sun to its setting my name is great among the nations, and in every place incense is offered to my name." Although the Chronicler is concerned to maintain the cultic hegemony of Jerusalem through the containment of the ritual use of incense, the texts from Elephantine and Malachi indicate that not all Yahwists agreed on this issue during this period.

Alongside the emphasis in 2 Chronicles on Jerusalem as the sole place for sacrifice, the author permits and encourages communities outside the city to participate in additional practices. For example, the book includes several instances of prayer said outside Jerusalem (2 Chr. 14:11; 20:22). Yet the author also maintains a Jerusalem-centered approach for this practice by specifying the direction of the body during prayer. In the book's reiteration of Solomon's prayer at the temple's dedication (said in the presence of "the whole assembly of Israel"), the instructions to pray toward the temple are retained from the Kings source: "when a foreigner . . . comes from a distant land . . . and prays toward this house"; when the people go out in battle and "pray to YHWH, toward . . . the house that I have built for your name"; and when the people in captivity pray "to you toward their land," Solomon asks that YHWH hear and forgive them (2 Chr. 6:32–39; 1 Kgs. 8:41–50). In this request to God, the king is publicly instructing the people in the posture of prayer, a posture that highlights Jerusalem as the place where prayer is directed. Like Daniel who prayed "facing Jerusalem" (Dan. 6:10), Solomon's prayer incorporates a geographic dimension into private prayer, a direction that prioritizes Jerusalem.

One other practice that the author enjoins upon the faithful outside Jerusalem is pilgrimage to the city. Partially this is done by limiting significant rituals such as sacrifice to the city, with the result that, if one wants to participate in sanctioned sacrifice, one must journey to

Jerusalem. The author also expands and adds additional Passover festivals to the material in Kings, making the inclusion of pilgrims in Jerusalem a commendatory part of the reigns of Josiah and Hezekiah (2 Chr. 30; 35:1–19). In light of the author's portrayal of Hezekiah as a second David (or, due to the emphasis on the unity of the reigns of David and Solomon discussed in the essay on 1 Chronicles, a second David-and-Solomon), Hezekiah's Passover festival can be read as part of this larger theme. Like the first two kings of the dynasty, Hezekiah appointed the divisions of the priests and Levites and contributed to the temple offerings from his own personal wealth (2 Chr. 31:2–3; cf. 1 Chr. 16:37–42; 29:1–5; 2 Chr. 2:4; 8:12–13; 9:10–11). In addition, the king also enacts a reunification of the north and south by including northerners in worship at the Passover celebration in Jerusalem: the "many people" celebrating the Passover in Jerusalem included celebrants from Judah, Asher, Manasseh, Zebulun, Ephraim, Issachar, and resident aliens from Israel and Judah (2 Chr. 30:11–13, 18, 25). In addition to Hezekiah's celebration, Passover was also celebrated during the reign of Josiah, and the worshipers also included people from both Judah and Israel (35:18).

In addition to these several rituals that envision and encourage the participation of those outside Jerusalem in Jerusalem-centered practices, the author also emphasizes that the temple itself relates to ancient traditions, predating the reigns of David and Solomon, to which both the northern and southern tribes can lay claim. Unique to Chronicles is the claim that the temple's site is linked with Mount Moriah, the place of Abraham's near-sacrifice of Isaac (2 Chr. 3:1; Gen. 22). Upon this Abrahamic site is built a temple with design elements that evoke the Mosaic period, including the ark (2 Chr. 5:2–10) and the "veil" or "curtain" (Exod. 26:31–33; 36:35; 2 Chr. 3:14). By emphasizing these elements, the Chronicler not only relates the Jerusalem temple to specific Judean kings but includes the traditions of the entire nation and can thus make the temple a focus for the unity of the separate tribes.

In the descriptions of various religious practices, the text reveals a God who claims a special relationship to Jerusalem, and considers rituals such as sacrifice acceptable only there. Alongside this exclusivity of geography is an inclusivity of communal boundaries: it is precisely this one temple that can serve to unite the entire nation. Whether in sacrifice at the temple or prayers said toward it, the scattered people can be bound together in their common ritual practices and conventions. In the context of the Persian period, when the worship of Yahweh had a large geographic reach, the author strives to include the faithful outside of Yehud in practices that prioritize Jerusalem. It is this aspect of Chronicles that can make the most sense of the very last verses of the book. In addition to seeing Cyrus's edict in 2 Chr. 36:23 as a textual link to Ezra, one can also recognize in it a wish for the future community. Instead of ending the history in exile (as Kings does), the author of Chronicles extends the narrative to the time of Cyrus and his proclamation that God has charged the foreign king to build the temple in Jerusalem, and "whoever is among you of all his people . . . let him go up!" This "going up" to Jerusalem can relate not only to the first returnees, but to the mission of the entire nation during the Persian period: whether as permanent residents or occasional pilgrims, all the nation is called by God to go to Jerusalem and worship together in God's house.

Bibliography

Allen, Leslie C. "The First and Second Books of Chronicles." In *NIB* 3:299–659.

Brettler, Marc Zvi. *The Creation of History in Ancient Israel*. London: Routledge, 1995.

Graham, M. Patrick, Steven L. McKenzie, and Gary N. Knoppers, eds. *The Chronicler as Theologian: Essays in Honor of Ralph W. Klein*. JSOTSup 371. London: T. & T. Clark International, 2003. Includes a variety of articles on theological themes in Chronicles.

Japhet, Sara. *I & II Chronicles*. OTL. Louisville: Westminster/John Knox, 1993.

———. *The Ideology of the Book of Chronicles and Its Place in Biblical Thought*. Beiträge zur Erforschung des Alten Testaments und des Antiken Judentums 9. New York: Peter Lang, 1989.

Knoppers, Gary N. *1 Chronicles*. 2 vols. AB 12. New York: Doubleday, 2004.

McKenzie, Steven L. *1–2 Chronicles*. AOTC. Nashville: Abingdon, 2004.

Porten, Bezalel, and Ada Yardeni. *Textbook of Aramaic Documents from Ancient Egypt*. 4 vols. Winona Lake, IN: Eisenbrauns, 1986.

Williamson, Hugh G. M. *1 and 2 Chronicles*. New Century Bible Commentary. Grand Rapids: Eerdmans, 1982.

Ezra and Nehemiah

Daniel L. Smith-Christopher

INTRODUCTION

It is typical in modern biblical research to study the books of Ezra and Nehemiah together. This makes a great deal of sense, since the same central characters appear in both works, and there is a strong historical link between the events of the two books, even though the precise sequence of those events remains controversial (e.g., who came first, Ezra or Nehemiah?). There are also materials that appear in both books, most notably the list of persons in the community provided in Ezra 2 and repeated almost exactly the same way in Neh. 7. These short books combine different genres, including apparent quotations of royal correspondence, lengthy prayers, descriptions of selected events and political intrigue, and, in the case of Nehemiah, material often referred to as "memoirs."

EZRA

Ezra is the main history-like source in the Bible that addresses the years after the conquest of Babylon by the Persian emperor Cyrus the Great (ca. 539–450 BCE, and likely after this as well), and the resulting return of Judeans who were deported from Palestine by the Babylonians under King Nebuchadnezzar. The Greek work, 1 Esdras, contains material in addition to the book of Ezra, but it is primarily folklore. Prophetic books date from this period, such as Zechariah and Haggai (who are mentioned in Ezra), and some other books (e.g., Malachi) may come from this same era. This prophetic material is not always concerned with description of events in the same manner as Ezra and Nehemiah.

The historical material in Ezra and Nehemiah tends to focus on specific episodes that the writer considered important as an indication of the difficulties facing the community in the generations following the disasters of the Babylonian deportations of 597–587 BCE and the physical devastation of Jerusalem and Judah. One of the main themes of these short books is the importance of vigorous political and religious leadership offered by Nehemiah the governor on the one hand, and Ezra the priest on the other. Some scholars have suggested that the books intended to distinguish the leadership styles of these two individuals.

In this regard, the books of Ezra and Nehemiah emphasize duality of leadership in the postexilic Judean community—a prominent political leader accompanied by a prominent religious leader (see, for example, the extended discussions in the opening chapters of Zechariah that refer to Zerubbabel, the political leader, and Joshua the priest, a religious leader).

Reading Ezra and Nehemiah theologically presents interesting challenges. The books are largely administrative in tone.

Nonetheless, they raise important questions of community life, questions that merit serious consideration in the context of the interpersonal and group dynamics in modern church, mosque, and synagogue life. These issues will be highlighted in the comments that follow.

COMMENTARY

Rebuilding the Temple (Ezra 1–6)

Chapter 1 establishes a major change in circumstance for the people of God, carefully noting that this change is a fulfillment of Jeremiah's prophecy (cf. the "seventy years" of Jer. 29). Cyrus the Persian emperor is responding to the prompting of God and releasing Judean captives in a "new exodus." Cyrus even provides financial assistance and returns the stolen temple implements (1:7–8). Ezra 1 thus maintains the biblical tradition of seeing the hand of God in the circumstances of social and political change. However, it is important to emphasize that God's "hand" or "spirit" is present when God's ultimate purposes are fulfilled—not in any natural or human-inspired phenomenon. It is dangerously simplistic to take this biblical tradition of assigning a religious meaning to specific experiences or events, and take it to be a license to interpret ancient or modern natural disasters, human wars, or crises as having the same sort of religious significance. The events highlighted by biblical writers are relatively rare. Further, biblical writers occasionally interpret the same events and issues differently (e.g., debates among early Christians in the book of Acts).

The famous "Golah List" (*golah* = "exile") in chap. 2 underscores the importance of establishing who belongs to the community. There have been many attempts to understand this list. It is essentially repeated in Neh. 7, where it appears, notably, in quite a different context. Some scholars have suggested that these lists involve issues of inclusion and exclusion.

Certain priests were not allowed to be active in the ritual practices until their membership was clearly established (2:59–63). Lists, by their very nature, reflect administrative concerns and create an atmosphere of "being watched by authorities" throughout these books.

The concern to rebuild the temple is a central matter in chap. 3. This may reflect the not-so-gentle nudging by the prophet Haggai. The emotional response to the building program (vv. 10–13) suggests that rebuilding the temple was symbolic of reestablishing identity, faith, and community for this people. It is easy, in the modern world, to overemphasize the significance of structures as in church building campaigns. Too often, expensive or large buildings are seen as signs of life and stability, rather than faith and action as signs of health. In Ezra, however, the temple represented more than simply signs of life—the temple was a central administrative center for the community—important politically, economically, and religiously. For a population devastated by exile and destruction, this project represented an important focus for communal attention. Perhaps a better modern analogy would be Christian involvement in buildings with wider community significance, and not merely their own membership (e.g., recreational facilities, encouraging small business, community kitchens and homeless shelters—structures that can help rebuild true communities).

Chapter 4 summarizes local opposition to the building project. The local authorities report to the central Persian administration, threatening that the builders of Jerusalem are planning sedition: "They are rebuilding that rebellious and wicked city; they are finishing the walls. . . ." The reference to the walls is important, since siege warfare was prominent in this period. The local authorities are, in effect, accusing the Jewish returnees of planning for war. Furthermore, the local opponents imply that the Persian authorities will lose money: "if this city is rebuilt . . . they will not pay tribute, custom, or toll, and the royal revenue will be reduced." The twin threats of power and money are intended to alarm the imperial authorities. The threats work: the building is stopped.

Again the local authorities intervene to stop the work on Jerusalem. This episode involves heated correspondence with the central Persian administration. In chap. 5, however, the Jewish community under Zerubbabel attempts to provide a full explanation of the events that led them to this point, including the explanation that previous rebuilding attempts had been authorized by the Persians. Throughout this passage, there is a tone of both cautious respect for the authority of *central* administrators and suspicion about the interests of *local* administrators. This is, sadly, a common scenario in modern societies where local minorities (racial or cultural) must often appeal to central authorities for protection against local resentments or violence. The fact that Paul suggests that Rome does not "bear the sword in vain" (Rom. 13:4) does not imply that Paul is somehow pro-Roman, but rather simply advises caution with respect to central powers. Paul counts on the typical tendencies of imperial administrations, which usually do not want trouble or the costs of dealing with growing local conflicts. The operant principle seems to be: "Do not attract unnecessary attention from the authorities!" Ezra 1–6 (much less Rom. 13) does not contain any enthusiastic endorsements of centralized authority. It is much more a cautious counsel to avoid trouble from unpredictable imperial forces. Zerubbabel, like Paul centuries later, is respectful but cautious in dealing with central authorities.

According to chap. 6, when the administration of Darius had the archives searched, it turns out that the returning Judeans did have the permission of the great Cyrus. Hence the rebuilding is resumed. Furthermore, Tattenai, the governor who reported the Jewish project in negative terms, must now not only face the humiliating order from the Persian central authorities to allow the work to continue, but also pay some of the costs of the project from locally collected imperial funds. The author refers specifically to the authority and influence of the prophets Haggai and Zechariah (5:1). The prophets' powerful intervention is celebrated once again in 6:14, immediately after the report of the positive word from Darius, which allows the work to continue. Prophetic authority is honored before secular power. The end of chap. 6 completes the summary of the events leading up to the completion of the Second Temple. The tone is one of joy and celebration. Throughout these chapters, the theme of respectful but cautious dealing with worldly authorities is coupled with understanding the importance of spiritual authority when one lives according to values different from those of the surrounding societies.

The Controversial Priest Arrives (Ezra 7—10)

Chapter 7 establishes a new beginning point, some decades after the events summarized in the opening six chapters. The author introduces Ezra in expansive terms, which certainly reflects a concern with credentials and pedigree typical of the administrative atmosphere of the book as a whole. Although Ezra is introduced as a "scribe skilled in the law of Moses," his precise office has been debated, partly because this passage somewhat strangely mentions that the "king" granted Ezra everything that he asked for. We are not, however, privy to this exchange, and we have little idea what Ezra had asked for—or what he was authorized to do. If we are intended to make a comparison with the longer narrative about Nehemiah's conversations with the emperor, it may well be that the writer presumes that we are reading this material in tandem with reading the story of Nehemiah. If this is the case, we are probably to presume a similar exchange in which Ezra receives the authorization outlined in the following verses. Still, Ezra's instructions seem vague, and amount to "We allow you to do what you think is in keeping with your laws." Ezra is certainly given considerable leeway to engage in ritual and social reforms, many of which involve economic activities connected to the temple.

Chapter 8 reflects both the overall administrative concerns (i.e., the names of those who return with Ezra) and spiritual preparations. The practice of fasting in the postexilic period obviously increased as a spiritual discipline to accompany prayerful appeals to God for protection and assistance (1 Chr. 16; 2 Chr. 11; Esth. 4 and 8; Isa. 56; Dan. 6; Zech. 8; even foreigners in Jonah 3:5). It is likely that fasts emphasized the need for God's assistance in addressing physical hunger and weakness, thus increasing the appeal for power for a powerless people. Furthermore, Ezra's fast and appeal stand in significant contrast to Nehemiah's armed guard (Neh. 2:9). Ezra refused such a guard (v. 22) and appealed to God instead. Ezra's behavior seems consistent with the spiritual encouragement during times of trouble, which was offered by Haggai and Zechariah.

The final two chapters of Ezra are among the most controversial passages in postexilic biblical literature. The format of Ezra's prayer belongs to a set pattern known as "penitential prayers" (see Neh. 9; Dan. 9; Baruch), a unique form of postexilic prayer. Such prayers tend to interpret individual suffering or communal problems as a result of ignoring the Mosaic ethical teachings and the warnings of the prophets, and thus ask for forgiveness and guidance. The general context of the prayer, however, is the cri-sis of mixed marriages in the postexilic community.

Ezra is appalled to discover that many of the returning exilic community (the book of Ezra designates them with the newly minted phrase: "sons of the exile," [NRSV "returned exiles"], 4:1; 6:19–20; 8:35; 10:7, 16) have intermarried with foreigners. Thus they have corrupted the "holy seed" (9:2), another somewhat surprising term found only here.

There is some debate about who these "foreigners" are. Are they Hebrews who were not among those who were deported, or were they non-Hebrews and thus presumably related to those surrounding peoples with whom the earlier returning community was described as having troubles in previous chapters? If, on the other hand, they were "other" Hebrews, meaning descendants of the Hebrews who were left behind in 597 and 587, then Ezra is operating with an exclusionary attitude that wants to preserve certain privileges for a select community. In short, Ezra's in-group consists only of those who descend from the deported population. There is precedent for such crisis communities (one thinks of the Japanese survivors of Hiroshima and Nagasaki, who formed a tight-knit community). If, on the other hand, we are to understand that Ezra is referring to non-Jews who have married into the returning Hebrew communities, then we have further evidence of an interesting debate that appears to have raged in this period—whether non-Hebrews would become part of the community. It seems clear that the book of Ruth, for example, was written as part of this debate (even though the story of Ruth is set in a much earlier period, it was likely written after 539). Passages such as Isa. 56 also speak directly to a debate about including "others" in the community. In times of crisis, or in times of reconstruction and redefinition, there are often debates about whose voices are welcome in the community going through a process of rebuilding. Such debates even occur today, for example, in acrimonious ecclesial conflicts about who has voting rights in certain decisions, who is really one of "us." In such debates, values of hospitality and compassion are often strained or even abandoned.

The results of Ezra's public prayer (really a public demonstration) are that the community gathers together those "offenders" who are willing to repent and disband all their mixed marriages. Clearly some members of the community were not willing to go along with this step, and the consequences appear to be economic as well as social. Ezra 10:8 speaks of losing property and communal membership rights.

Some historians have also argued that there may have been Persian administrative interests in keeping the membership of this community clear (especially if distribution of royal funds is at issue). Part of the debate here is about Ezra's own interests and role. If this is a Persian authorized action, then Ezra may be acting consistent with imperial interests. If, however, Ezra's interests in mixed marriages are more ritual, religious, or even personal, then the mixed-marriage crisis may have caused more local troubles than Persian authorities had authorized, or even wanted, Ezra to deal with.

Typically for the book of Ezra, the work concludes with yet another administrative list, this time a list of the offenders who had repented of their mixed marriage. There is frequent reference to the concept of making "separations" in Ezra—those who "separated themselves" from the surrounding peoples (9:1; 10:11) in order to preserve identity and membership in the "sons of the exile" community, the "holy seed." The contrary view—that foreigners who want to join should be welcomed—is also expressed in this language of "separation" (e.g. Isa. 56:3, "Do not let the foreigner joined to the LORD say, 'The LORD will surely separate me from his people'"). The prominence of such language concerning "separation" surely attests to a serious debate inside the community as it seeks to regain its identity.

There are interesting parallels to the debates in the early Christian community. Here was a community under pressure, worried about attracting too much imperial attention, and yet also attracting interest from a variety of peoples, who also engaged in a heated debate about who is "in" and who is "out." Fear of change "in these difficult times" is always a threat to innovation.

The book of Ezra does speak of the importance of seeking stability, the importance of projects that reflect a communal confidence about the future, and the always important subject of being clear and careful about communal identity. But these are issues that always call for balance—stability must be balanced by openness to necessary change. Symbolic projects that build confidence, for example, ought never to become the primary goal of a Christian community. Such projects can occupy so much time (and budget) that service and fellowship are neglected. Finally, while all Christian fellowships have a responsibility to answer to the unique traditions of which they are a part, faith traditions ought to speak to the times they live in, and be translated to represent the tradition in a new setting. It would be a serious mistake for Methodists to abandon the vision of John Wesley, or Lutherans abandon their emphasis on grace, or Quakers abandon the peace and justice of Fox, Woolman, and Fry—all in the name of change. Still, these traditions must communicate and speak to their times or they will create empty museums rather than vital Christian fellowships. Modern sympathies with the preservationist or traditionalist concerns of an Ezra certainly have a point in an age when churches are often called upon to abandon their traditions wholesale in the name of a simplistic "relevance." Tradition, however, must never shut out a Ruth, a Moabite, nor be allowed to silence the voices of appropriate change in the modern world.

NEHEMIAH

Many scholars think that the book of Nehemiah was constructed in successive layers, some of which began as a set of "memoirs" about the experiences of Nehemiah himself. The book therefore possesses a unique literary style; large sections are written in the first person. The book presents the reflections and adventures of a fifth-century Jewish official of the Persian administration. Added to this material are sections such as Ezra's prayer (Neh. 9), and other history-like material, perhaps by the same hand that eventually finished the work on the book of Ezra. Some of the same concerns of the Judean postexilic community appear in Nehemiah as well as in Ezra, but there are some interesting differences. Nehemiah addresses, it seems, political and administrative concerns in contrast to Ezra's focus on communal and ritual practice, although Nehemiah is concerned about the temple administration as well. Initially, however, Nehemiah highlights the physical infrastructure of the city itself, and this emphasis on physical reconstruction continues throughout the work.

Nehemiah is introduced as a pious Jewish man working for the Persian emperor, and deeply concerned about recent reports coming from Jerusalem. The survivors, he is told, are in "great trouble and shame," and there is further bad news about the physical condition of the walls and gates of the city itself. It is interesting to ask at the outset why it is presumed that such reports should go to Nehemiah—is he some recognized authority in the Diaspora community? Modern suggestions about Nehemiah's possible connections to the royal house of Judah may help to answer this question. Nehemiah responds to these reports by turning to God in the form, once again, of the postexilic standard "penitential prayer" (1:5–11). As noted in the commentary on Ezra 9 (cf. Dan. 9; Bar. 1–2), themes common to this form of prayer include confession and the affirmation that God was in the right for enforcing God's threats with regard to disobeying

the commandments of Moses (and, usually, the teachings of prophets. The prophets are not, however, mentioned in the prayer in Neh. 1). Nehemiah's prayer and fasting focus on his working up the courage to approach the Persian administration. There are interesting parallels to Esther's preparation to approach the Persian emperor as well, including fasting and prayer (Esth. 4:9–17), and one wonders if a similar potential punishment—death—is implied in Nehemiah's concerns. The final verse stipulates Nehemiah's role, "cupbearer."

Nehemiah's role includes carrying wine to the king. It is widely presumed that part of Nehemiah's role would be to ensure the safety of the wine in question as a royal taster. If this is a valid assumption, then the nature of the emperor's question about Nehemiah's "appearance" and his concern that he is not "sick" may come from the emperor's own self-interest as much as any concern for his obviously expendable foreign wine taster. Expositors who claim that the emperor was genuinely concerned for his Jewish servant overlook the otherwise enigmatic phrase that Nehemiah enters into the memoir at the end of Neh. 2:2: "I was very much afraid!"

Appearances before the emperor, whether in Daniel, Esther, Genesis (Joseph), or here in Nehemiah, must all be read as potentially life-threatening episodes. These are feared foreign rulers who can end life instantly—and horrifically! Grisly varieties of execution are mentioned in all these Diaspora books: executions by fire (Dan. 3), by lions (Dan. 6), by impalement (Ezra 6:11). In short, these are not to be read as privileged visits to democratically elected servants of the people. We are better advised to keep in mind the caution even of Jesus according to the Gospel descriptions of his appearances before the brutal Pilate or the maniacal Herod. Minorities learn to be circumspect in the face of overwhelming military power and brutal authority.

There are more parallels between Neh. 1–2 and the Daniel and Esther traditions than are often noted. It is thus wise to be careful when determining whether there are any reliable historical details in such legendary discussions between Jewish captives and Babylonian or Persian emperors. They may be literary works similar to the Athenian plays of Aeschylus, who set his famous drama *The Persians* in the mysterious inner sanctum of the Persian court with an atmosphere not unlike Nehemiah, Daniel, and Esther.

There is interesting speculation that Nehemiah's reference to Jerusalem as "the place of my ancestors' graves" (2:3) may be significant. Only members of the royal line are actually buried within the traditional walls of Jerusalem, and thus there is widespread scholarly speculation that Nehemiah is here implying that he belongs to the royal house. Such a reality would shed new light on Nehemiah's deep concern for the condition of the city itself, his sense of responsibility for issues of infrastructure, and the reports brought to him by travelers in the opening chapters.

The dangerous context is further emphasized by the local opposition to Nehemiah's rebuilding of the walls. Not only did he carefully survey the damaged walls at night, but there is instant suspicion in the reaction to the news that Nehemiah's intentions include restoring Jerusalem in v. 19: "Are you rebelling against the king?" In a time when most war was conducted by siege rather than open-field battle, building walls presumes military intentions.

In chap. 3, primary emphasis seems to be on communal participation in the rebuilding effort. Still, the management style of Nehemiah, who organized this coordinated building campaign, remains impressive. Groups are identified in this chapter not only according to family names but also by locations and villages. This could imply regional participation in the project, though some have suggested that village or place names could identify groups. Blenkinsopp further observed that chap. 3 suggests more work being done on the northern sections of the walls than other parts, which makes sense since the northern walls would have borne the brunt of most attacks from Mesopotamian regimes (e.g., "foe from the north," Jer. 1:14; 4:6). Armies would approach the walls from the only section vulnerable to direct attack by siege engines, the northern section. One of Ezekiel's visions also implies openings and destruction in the northern walls, near the temple, including gaping holes that allowed him to crawl through the wall (Ezek. 8:7–8).

The tone of opposition associated with Sanballat and other local authorities and powerful families in chap. 4 is considerably darker than the suspicions noted from local authorities in Ezra 1–6. The resentment here is bitter; the words are angry and taunting. Little wonder that these reports are followed in vv. 4–5 by a bitter prayer requesting that God curse them.

The conflict between the wall-builders under Nehemiah's leadership and the local officials appears as if it might erupt into open warfare, although what is more likely implied here is random assassinations and violence, tactics today associated with informal violence and resistance. In any case, Nehemiah takes up the role of military strategist as well as engineer. Guards are posted to protect the workers, and the builders are advised to seek shelter inside the completed sections of the wall.

A serious interpretive problem hinges on the relationship between the events described in chap. 4 and those now described in chap. 5. It is traditionally held that chap. 5 raises new issues for Nehemiah to face. He has been so distracted by the work on the wall and infrastructure that he is only now made aware of some of the other economic and social issues facing the Jewish community. Some of the community are apparently complaining about famine and the desperate needs of the people in these troubled times. More disturbing, however, is the implication that some Jewish elite seem to be benefiting from the desperate conditions of impoverished families, who take their protests to Nehemiah himself.

There is, however, another way of reading these complaints. If chap. 5 is a direct continuation of chap. 4, then one might infer that the building project and its military requirements were a major cause of the difficulties of the people. If this is the case, then the complaints of the people that they need help with gathering grain (5:2) and that they are falling into debt because of tax payments would involve the claim that Nehemiah's work details amounted to enslavement. There is certainly precedent for this interpretation. Solomon's heavy taxation and forced work details were at the root of the northern tribal break from Jerusalem after Solomon's death (1 Kgs. 12).

Nehemiah's actions deal primarily with economic enslavement and land distribution. There have been Jewish community leaders who have exploited the terrible conditions of the returning community and shackled them into debt and interest payments that they could not afford. This would then have allowed some of them to confiscate land in lieu of debt payments—precisely the kind of economic oppression that allowed the wealthy in previous generations to "add house to house, and field to field until there is room for no one but yourselves" (Isa. 5:8, my trans.). Nehemiah commits his administration to ending this kind of abuse. Modern readers are reminded of the terrible economic consequences of business fraud and political corruption that have wiped out the life savings of modest-income workers throughout the world. Contemporary workers also long for a political leadership with the will to "shake out their garments" as Nehemiah had done to demonstrate his commitment to general economic recovery.

Nehemiah 5:14–19 reports that Nehemiah made changes unique to his office, admitting that previous administrators had indeed abused their position and exploited the people. This section concludes, as many other sections of the memoir material, with a brief prayer to God to "remember my efforts" (my trans.).

In chap. 6 Nehemiah reports on the many levels of intrigue that began to circulate around the rebuilding of Jerusalem and the potential implications. Local administrators apparently tried to compromise Nehemiah himself, either to ingratiate themselves and be in a position to exploit Nehemiah's success, or eventually to discredit Nehemiah in the eyes of the Persian administration. There is even a vague report that many of the "nobles of Judah"—presumably those who were now losing valuable business privileges because of the new reforms of Nehemiah—continued in their relationships with opponents of Nehemiah, such as Tobiah. "Letters were exchanged" is the suggestive reference in v. 17, which is followed by a report of suspicious family connections. As in every age, privilege ("the nobles of Judah") responds to threat by appealing to other privileged sectors with an interest in maintaining (or restoring) the beneficial status quo. The chapter reports, however, that Nehemiah successfully resists all such solicitations and concentrates on the task of completing the Jerusalem wall and other repairs of the city's infrastructure. The people's successful demonstrations for justice still ring in his ears. At the end of chap. 6, the wall is complete.

When open opposition to social justice appears to be impossible, the privileged sectors of Judean society not only plot among themselves (e.g., "letters are written"), but they also try to "quietly have a word" with Nehemiah himself. This same desperate self-preservation of the elite ("all the kingdoms of the world," Matt. 4:8) appears to function as an implied setting for the famous temptations of Jesus as well. Jesus is alone as the embodiment of unjust power and privilege attempts to have a quiet word in an effort to stop or at least compromise the revolutionary program of change inaugurated by the Messiah.

In chap. 7 the large community list that has already appeared in Ezra 2 is largely copied here (with only minor variations). The context in Neh. 7, however, is quite different. When the attempts to stop or compromise the campaign of change forced on Nehemiah by public demonstrations fails, the Jewish elite and their non-Jewish allies like Tobiah, Sanballat, and Geshem attempt to force the issue. Nehemiah perhaps suspects that he is not the only one who may be subject to temptations and quiet negotiations, and tries to firm up the public resolve. A public reassertion of communal loyalties is implied in the reappearance of the list at this point—virtually a request that Jewish members of the community declare their loyalties: "Are you with us or not!"

In chaps. 8–9 Ezra makes a reappearance, and the subject of Nehemiah's own work shifts more directly to Ezra's overall focus on the ritual as well as material concerns of the community. These chapters describe two main events: a communal reassertion of the importance of celebrating holy days such as the Feast of Booths, and, in most of chap. 9, the fullest and most detailed example of a postexilic "penitential prayer" (cf. Neh. 1). In this long prayer, there is more detail from the history of ancient Israel, and thus more examples of Israel's disobeying of God's commandments. This prayer, then, creates a sense of urgency in asking God for forgiveness and requesting a change of circumstances.

The most controversial part of this prayer, however, is the description (vv. 36–37) of the political and economic circumstances of the people under Persian administration in the mid-fifth (or possibly early fourth) century BCE: "Here we are, slaves to this day—slaves in the land that you gave to our ancestors to enjoy its fruit and its good gifts. Its rich yield goes to the kings whom you have set over us because of our sins; they have power also over our bodies and over our livestock at their pleasure, and we are in great distress." These lines are contrary to the generally held scholarly consensus that the Persian period was largely a positive

time for the Jewish people. Hence many scholars have assigned these words to a much later time, perhaps that of the oppressive Ptolemaic taxation of the Hebrews between 320 and 200 BCE, or even as late as the revolts that broke out under the Seleucid rulers in the 160s culminating in the Maccabean Wars. However, such a late redating of these verses is unnecessary. There is little indication in Ezra and Nehemiah that these were halcyon days for the postexilic Jewish community trying to reestablish itself in the aftermath of the Persian defeats of the Babylonian Empire.

In the final chapters of the book, administrative lists and concerns abound. Chapter 10 repeats the concerns of the community to remain "separate" from the surrounding peoples (v. 28) and to dedicate themselves to the financial survival of the building projects and the ritual life of the recovering community. Among the concerns are economic care for the priesthood. In chap. 11 Nehemiah appears to initiate a repopulation of Jerusalem itself. This has often been taken to indicate the devastation of the city up to the time of Nehemiah—it appears to have required a program of resettlement to guarantee its economic survival. Chapter 12 gives details of the celebrations of the finished wall itself, in terms that are quite similar to the rededication of the temple in Ezra 5–6.

Chapter 13 takes up some further administrative issues, but raises some new concerns as well. Some time has apparently passed, and Nehemiah has requested the Persian emperor for permission to visit Jerusalem again. This visit, however, is reported in far less detail.

The first fifteen verses deal with another episode of mixed-marriage problems, and related to this, corruption among the relatives who have married into the family of Tobiah. Nehemiah reports that he ejects Tobiah himself from privileged quarters in the temple. This act appears to be related to care for the economic well-being of the priests. The chapter then returns once again to the problem of mixed marriages, and concludes with Nehemiah summarizing his reforms: he cleansed the people from "everything foreign," and reestablished the temple economy and the care for the priesthood.

With the book of Nehemiah, the problems of mixed marriages appear more directly related to elite families who have economic motivations for engaging in these liaisons; at least economic changes are implied by Nehemiah's descriptions of his actions. It seems hardly accidental, in other words, that Nehemiah's concerns about trade on the Sabbath are related to his descriptions of mixed marriages between elite families. Once again, one may presume that these elite families are plotting to preserve power and privilege by selective arranged marriages, and Nehemiah attempts to foil such machinations.

Bibliography

Blenkinsopp, Joseph. *Ezra–Nehemiah*. OTL. Philadelphia: Westminster, 1988.

Eskenazi, Tamara. *In an Age of Prose: A Literary Approach to Ezra–Nehemiah*. Society of Biblical Literature Monograph Series 36. Atlanta: Scholars Press, 1988.

Smith-Christopher, D. "Ezra-Nehemiah" in *The Oxford Bible Commentary*, ed. John Barton and John Muddiman, 308–24. New York: Oxford, 2007.

Williamson, H. G. M. *Ezra-Nehemiah*. WBC 16. Waco: Word, 1985.

Esther

Nancy R. Bowen

INTRODUCTION

The book of Esther is a short story set in the Persian court during the reign of Xerxes I (486–465 BCE). The story, located in the Writings in the Hebrew Bible, is one of the five festival scrolls (or Megilloth). As a story that recounts the origin of the Festival of Purim, it is read liturgically during that Jewish holiday. The placement of the story in the Greek Old Testament, following Ezra and Nehemiah, reflects the historical setting. The Greek version differs from the Hebrew text, since the former contains a number of additional passages. Christian canons retain the placement of the Greek, but translate the Hebrew text of Esther. The longer Greek text is retained in the Apocrypha. Issues of ethnic conflict and ethnic identity shape the story and reflect the importance of these issues to the exiled Jewish community, not only in the Persian Empire, but also in the later Hellenistic Empire.

COMMENTARY

Technically there is no theology in the book of Esther. As is the case with the Song of Songs, Esther contains no references to God. God neither speaks nor acts. Nor do other characters refer to God in their speeches. Not even God's absence is noted. The name, Esther, is related to the Hebrew root for "to hide, be hidden," and can be translated as "I will hide" or "I am hiding." Her name becomes a wordplay suggesting that in exile God has hidden God's face (or presence) from Israel. Esther's world is a Godless world, at least in the sense of a God who is actively present with the people. In the absence of divine activity, what is left is human activity. Therefore, ethics replaces theology in Esther. Remarkably, Israel's God appears absent in the face of genocide (3:13; 8:11). It seems that when God is most needed, the people are forced to rely not on God but on one another.

The central issue in Esther is the survival of the Jewish community. In the story the community is threatened by physical destruction. The impetus for their destruction is human maliciousness that seems capricious (3:1–15). Existence is tenuous for a minority community in someone else's empire. Although genocide will cause the disappearance of Jews, another threat to survival is assimilation. To all outward appearances Esther appears to be Persian. Prior to chap. 7, nothing identifies her as a Jew. This too is a form of annihilation. The human activity in the story seeks to defeat these threats.

The primary way the Jews are saved is through solidarity. Esther and Mordechai do things together. Mordechai learns of a plot against the king and informs Esther, saving the king (2:19–23). It is Mordechai who informs Esther of Haman's plot and prods her to action (4:1–17). Esther tells the king of her relationship with Mordechai, and the king honors Mordechai by bidding him to write a counterdecree (8:2–10). In addition to the main characters, the Jewish people also act together. All the Jews join Esther in a three-day fast (4:16–17), and gather to defend themselves against those who sought power over them (9:1–19).

In order to save the Jews, Mordechai demands that Esther petition the king. Esther's obedience requires great courage. First, it means she will have to reveal that she has been living a lie by keeping her Jewish identity hidden from the king. The king is characterized as having a short temper and committing rash actions when angered. That disclosure alone may cost her at best banishment (like Vashti), at worst, her life. Second, no one can go into the king's inner court without first being summoned by the king. Anyone who dares to do so is to be put to death—*unless* the king holds out the golden scepter to that person. The problem is that Esther has not been summoned to the king in thirty days. She can die for daring to approach the king unbidden. Initially, understandably, she is hesitant to accept the risk. Yet after a three-day fast she finds the courage to go forward and put herself at risk for the sake of others. Esther's coming out thwarts the threat of assimilation by asserting her Jewish identity over against her Persian identity.

In addition to Esther's courage, her cleverness or wisdom is a necessary tactic in defense against the destruction of the Jews. She works indirectly. She curries the king's favor through food, which is reassuring and nurturing. She also effectively uses drink, since the king is easily influenced when he is drinking (cf. 1:10–22; 3:15). She seeks the right moment to seize the opportunity to speak directly of herself and her people.

There is also an element of fate or chance to salvation. If Vashti had not just said no, there would be no need for a new queen (chap. 1). If Esther had not been beautiful and pleasing, she might not have found favor with the eunuchs or enjoyed the love of the king, who placed her in a position of power (2:7–9, 15–18). If Ahasuerus had not held out the scepter, Esther would have been killed (5:1–3). If Ahasuerus had been able to sleep, he would have failed to remember and honor Mordechai (6:1–11). If Ahasuerus had not caught Haman in a compromising position, Haman might have succeeded with his plot (7:7–10). Mordechai's challenge to Esther in 4:14 ("Who knows? Perhaps you have come to royal dignity for just such a time as this") does not reveal the hidden, but guiding hand of a provident God, but the need to take advantage of opportunities when they occur.

The book of Esther is idealistic. It claims that through solidarity, courage, wisdom, and a little luck, even the threat of extinction can be averted. History abounds with examples, such as the Holocaust, which mock that belief. Yet, Jews still celebrate Purim every year. The repetition reinforces the ethic: whether or not evil is defeated *this* year, destruction is certain if humans do not act. The book also only considers a violent response to violence. Those who threaten to take the lives of Jews will have their own lives taken. There may be alternatives to violence, but they will require imagination and the telling of other stories.

Bibliography

Beal, Timothy K. *Esther*. Berit Olam. Collegeville, MN: Liturgical Press, 1999.

Day, Linda M. *Esther*. AOTC. Nashville: Abingdon, 2005.

Van Wijk-Bos, Johanna W. H. *Ezra, Nehemiah, and Esther*. Westminster Bible Companion. Louisville: Westminster John Knox, 1998.

Weems, Renita. "A Crown of Thorns (Vashti and Esther)." In *Just a Sister Away: A Womanist Vision of Women's Relationships in the Bible*, 99–110. San Diego: LuraMedia, 1988.

Job

Katharine J. Dell

INTRODUCTION

As part of the Wisdom literature of the Old Testament, the book of Job might be expected to discuss ethical issues in similar fashion to Proverbs. Indeed, we find an airing of the doctrine of retribution according to which the good are rewarded and the wicked are punished, a basic presupposition of the proverbial worldview. We might also expect to find a similar theological outlook, with God primarily as Creator in the wisdom material, but also with a rather behind-the-scenes role as the director of the action rather than as a major character in the story. Perhaps surprisingly, in Job we find God making an appearance as a character in his own right and conveying a message that is far from expected. In many ways, then, the book of Job steps outside the usual ethical and theological confines of the Wisdom literature in order to break fresh ground and challenge the very presuppositions of the tradition from which it came.

The way that the book of Job is constructed is a clue to the challenge that it represents. The book opens with our introduction to a blameless and upright character, Job, whose piety is not in doubt. As a result of a heavenly wager between God and the Satan, that piety is put to the test, and Job's initial reaction seems to be one of acceptance of his fate. The traditional wisdom position is represented by

three friends who come to comfort him and by a fourth friend who appears later in the dialogue. As the dialogue opens, however, it is clear that Job's seeming acceptance masks a much deeper reaction to the injustice of his fate, and Job mounts a challenge to the friends, and hence to wisdom's usual answers, and ultimately to God as the supreme arbiter of justice. God makes an appearance in a whirlwind, ostensibly to answer Job's questions, but those questions are replaced by a set of rhetorical ones that describe the workings of the created world. Although Job ultimately repents and we seem to have a traditional wisdom ending with the righteous man rewarded in the end, there is a feeling of unease with this conclusion, as Job and we are left without direct answers to any of the theological problems raised by the book.

These theological problems concern three major issues. The first is that of disinterested righteousness, the key question raised in the prose prologue by the Satan, "Does Job fear God for nothing?" (1:9). What is our motivation, as human beings, for behaving in a pious manner? Are we in a relationship with God only for what we can get out of it, materially or otherwise? This is an ethical dilemma as much as a theological question—can we ever be morally pure in our motives for doing good actions and for our faith in God?

The second main issue is the doctrine of retribution, which is mainly discussed in the dialogue between Job and the friends and is familiar from the wisdom tradition. The question here is whether those who are righteous are indeed rewarded by God in this life and whether those who behave in wicked fashion are punished. The traditional view is that this is how the world works—Proverbs has the view of life as a path by which the right choices lead to the right outcomes. However, Job's experience of suffering leads him to question this assumption—again it is an ethical assumption that good is always rewarded, but it is treated in a profound theological manner in the dialogues of Job such that the problem of innocent suffering comes to the fore as the main theological theme here, and arguably of the whole book.

The final theological theme is that of the relationship between God and human beings. Can human beings have a relationship with a God who seemingly dispenses justice as he wills and who does not appear to be restricted by human ideas of justice? This is the problem of theodicy: how can one believe in a God who allows suffering in the world? This is perhaps the most profound level of the debate about human suffering and how it can be understood in relation to belief in God. We are presented with God in his role primarily as creator of the world—can we as human beings engage with the Creator in reference to our own small lives? This issue too has an ethical dimension in relation to what God can and does expect of human beings and hence how he might reward that allegiance. The

theological themes and the ethical issues are hence closely intertwined in this book.

The book may be the result of a gradual process of editorial redaction, but the main mind behind its construction is clearly the author of the dialogues and God speeches. This person may have taken an older tale of a pious man called Job and turned it into an airing of the issue of undeserved suffering and how that is to be understood in relation to faith in God. Its date is unknown; the prose tale may be preexilic, and it is set in the patriarchal age, but the main dialogues and God speeches would seem to echo a postexilic situation in which there was a more profound questioning of accepted traditions and more stress on the individual. Within the wisdom tradition the questioning of Job seems to belong most naturally after the book of Proverbs and before that of Ecclesiastes, whose attitude to life is more resigned. However, the nature of the book as a timeless work probably indicates that issues of date, place, and authorship are of secondary interest to an unpacking of its main theological themes, which is the focus of this commentary.

In what follows I will show how the subthemes of the book emerge largely in relation to the portrayal of different characters, and I will treat the book chronologically in reference to these characters. A variety of theologies emerge from the different characters who throw up a number of different answers to the problem of innocent suffering. The way that the author deliberately does this through the characters, raising more questions than answers and providing not one answer but a number, is perhaps the genius of this work.

COMMENTARY

The Prologue

Job, the pious. We are introduced to Job in 1:1 with the words "blameless and upright," a description that leaves us in

no doubt as to the moral purity of his character. Furthermore and perhaps most essentially, he "feared God" and "turned away from evil." It is important to this story that there is no sense in which Job could be seen to deserve the misfortunes that ensue. We are also told (1:5) that Job was concerned that his children should meet these high ethical standards, and so he interceded to God on a regular basis with sacrifices on their behalf too (they might have sinned). This could be seen as overzealousness on his part, although it may function simply to stress Job's extraordinary piety. In the prologue we are also told that Job is a man blessed by ten children and by many material possessions, a crucial part of the good deeds/reward nexus. Job is a slightly bland character at this point; he is in a sense overcharacterized as good in preparation for the fall that is about to take place. The misfortune comes in the form of four disasters, two of them natural ones (fire and wind), two the result of human enemies (the Sabeans and the Chaldeans), the cumulative effect of which is to wipe out Job's children and his possessions. Job's reaction is one of mourning, tearing his robe and shaving his head, acts of identification with the dead. Yet in his prostrating himself to worship and in his words he has clearly not lost his faith in God as the one who may give or take away but who should still be blessed. We are told firmly that at no point does Job sin or blame God. This first test is one of Job's character: can his piety withstand attack? The answer is yes; he does not turn from his allegiance to God despite the terrible losses he has endured. The next attack by the Satan is more subtle—this is an attack on Job's health. While he is not to die, he gets a painful disease (a form of leprosy or other type of skin disease, characterized by "loathsome sores" covering the body), which the Satan believes will weaken his resolve to be pious. Job sits among ashes scraping his body—he has not only lost children, possessions, and health but also status and self-respect, and he can do nothing but sit and scrape. His piety is intact, however, and that, for the present, is all that matters.

Job's children, the feasters. Job's children collectively are rarely seen as characters in their own right. But we do learn a little about them in the prologue. The brothers would hold feasts in one another's houses in turn and would invite their sisters to join the merriment. It is not clear whether the feast days are simply birthdays or other special occasions and hence whether this happens just occasionally or is a regular and rather excessive form of activity. One unusual aspect is that no wives or husbands are mentioned and that the brothers and sisters seem content with the company of their siblings. Nor are Job or his wife mentioned as partakers in the feasts. It may be that this mention of the children's activities is simply to provide the opportunity to speak about Job's great piety, or it may be that we are being told this so that we feel less sorry when, on just such a day when they are eating and drinking wine in the house of the eldest brother, a great wind caused the house to fall upon them, killing them all.

God, the giver of good and evil. Our first introduction to God is in 1:6 in the context of a divine council of heavenly beings, a picture found elsewhere in the Old Testament (e.g., Ps. 82). God is the one to whom all heavenly beings present themselves, including the Satan here. The context then is of a debate between God and the Satan. God uses Job as his example of piety, and again to describe Job we find the words "blameless and upright" alongside "fearing God" and "turning away from evil." Thus here God recognizes Job's piety. This has important implications for the discussion of whether human beings can have a meaningful relationship with God—God is here taking a personal interest in one of God's most faithful servants. The Satan accuses God of being overprotective of Job and argues that once that protection is taken away, Job's piety will melt away. At this point God hands over power to the Satan to afflict Job so as to test this piety. Although the evil deeds are assigned to the Satan, God is also held responsible for delegating the act.

God knows from this point that Job is to suffer and endorses this as part of the test. Is there something rather cold and heartless about subjecting one's most faithful servant to such a cruel test just to win a wager?

We meet God next when the first set of afflictions is past and the Satan asks permission to inflict ill health upon Job. Again we have the scene of the divine council and a certain amount of repetition in the description. God again gives permission to the Satan with the words "he [Job] is in your power" (2:6); once more God delegates the evil but could still be said to inflict it by proxy. God does stipulate, however, that Job's life is to be spared, which is an important proviso in terms of the story, but Job does not always see the sparing of his life as a positive thing.

The Satan, the sower of seeds of doubt. The other major player in the heavenly scene is "the Satan" (with the definite article, which perhaps indicates a role rather than a distinct character). God asks the Satan where he has come from, and his answer is that he has been roaming the earth (there are interesting echoes of God walking in the garden in the cool of the day in Gen. 3:8). The inference is that the purpose of this roaming is to find someone to test. At least that is the implication of God's next question, which is whether the Satan has considered Job as a candidate. The Satan raises the theological question with which this section of the book is most concerned: "Does Job fear God for nothing?" (1:9) He accuses God of putting a fence around Job, of hedging him in with protection, of even limiting his range of experience so that he is more likely to fear God from within those confines. God has rewarded Job in just the way that the wisdom tradition would expect; and as Job would expect as an adherent to that worldview, his work is blessed and his possessions have correspondingly increased. The Satan issues a challenge to God to "stretch out [his] hand

and touch all that he has" (1:11), and it is interesting that the Satan is by these words ascribing the affliction to God even though he will be the one to actually do the deed. In the second encounter the Satan challenges God afresh with the thought that if people are afflicted by illness they will do anything to save their own skin; hence Job will curse God. So God has to respond to the challenge and allow the Satan to do just this. Again the challenge is made to God to do the deed, but the Satan carries out the infliction of loathsome sores.

Job's wife, the curser of God. The Satan's words have always made the point that if Job were afflicted in various ways he would curse God. This reaction would be the antithesis of Job's piety and represent an ultimate rejection of God. At this point in the prologue we meet the character of Job's wife, an unnamed woman, like so many in the Old Testament, with a minor role. The one thing that she does say is important to the theological development of the book, however, because she suggests that Job do just what the Satan wants him to do, "Curse God, and die!" (2:9). Because she echoes the Satan's words, she has received bad press from scholars over the years, being seen as a further temptress to Job in his moment of need. Yet she can also be seen as reacting in a natural way to the loss of children, possessions, and health. She cannot understand the reason for Job's continued integrity. She is revealing her belief in the faith/reward nexus that, when it goes badly wrong, is perhaps to be rejected. She is also suggesting an easy way out for Job—perhaps cursing God and simply dying is a better option than trying to survive amid the turmoil of personal loss and tragedy and a shattered faith. Job is quick to scold her and tell her that she speaks like "any foolish woman" (2:10). We are perhaps reminded here of the contrast between the wise and the foolish found so often in Proverbs. This then provides another opportunity for Job to utter a pious statement: good and bad come alike from God and we need to be ready to receive either (2:10). Again we are reminded that Job did not sin—he was a long way from cursing God at this stage.

The three friends, silent comforters. The three friends come from far away to be with Job in his hour of need. There is a message here about religious community and common humanity in the face of trouble from God. The friends came from afar, making that extra effort to be with Job, and when they arrive they are horrified by what they see—Job is in an unrecognizable state. They are distressed for their friend and adopt mourning rites on his behalf. For a man who has lost so much, comforting words would never be enough, and so they sit in silence with him for seven days and nights out of respect for his period of mourning and need for personal space in which to grieve. This is the way the friends are first presented, so why has the term "Job's comforter" become derogatory? We will go on to see how their comforting silence changes to comfortless quarrelling as Job too changes from pious receiver of good and evil to protesting sufferer as the dialogue opens.

The Dialogue

Job, the rebel. Chapter 3 suddenly introduces a rather different character—no longer is there a certain blandness and one-dimensionality to this highly pious person. Rather the chapter opens with Job cursing, not God, but the day of his birth, sentiments that verge on the blasphemous. Here we have the author of the dialogues presenting a very different picture of the human sufferer who cries out against the injustice of his position and who longs for death, or even for never having existed, as preferable to his current life. There are echoes here of the confessions of Jeremiah (e.g., Jer. 20) and of the psalms of lament (e.g., Ps. 73). Job asks why he did not die at birth or be stillborn or even why he was ever conceived—if either had been the case he

would not have existed in order to suffer this pain. He describes in highly poetic language his longing for death, and he accuses God of fencing him in (an echo of the Satan's accusation to God in the prologue), seen as a negative thing in that Job cannot now escape. Job is not able to rest anymore; both his mental state and his physical body are in turmoil.

Many forget that much of what Job is suffering is the result of severe illness, which arguably leads him to such depths of despair. This raises the issue of human identity in the face of severe physical impairment. Job has lost his appetite and food tastes loathsome to him. His face is red from weeping and his eyes dim. He cannot sleep, and time moves slowly for him because he can no longer occupy his mind usefully. He has no energy. He is also beset by nightmares and strange visions and his calamities keep coming back to his mind and make him relive his despair all over again. This is an interesting subtheme of the psychology of one in a state of despair and physical torment. He also has feelings of physical repulsion and mood swings, at one time longing for death but at another fearing it as it would prevent him from continuing his conversation with God. The dialogues also raise questions of human community in the arguments that go to and fro between Job and the friends. Job becomes quite rude in accusing the friends of "windy words" (16:3) and false arguments. For example, he uses imagery of a fast-flowing river and melting ice to describe the way their friendship has quickly melted away (6:15–16). The friends' attempts to help are simply interpreted by Job as attempts to hinder, and he has lost the sense of their having come from afar to assist him in his troubles. Job becomes self-obsessed and self-pitying, all reactions to the hardships he is enduring. He also becomes obsessed with the need to challenge God face-to-face and justify himself. The friends become sidelined as Job takes up his case with God. Since he has never sinned, he blames God directly for his suffering and for wronging him. He longs at times for a mediator to judge God, because God, as ultimate judge, seems to have turned into the prosecutor.

In the dialogues the doctrine of retribution is the main theological topic under discussion, and the friends in slightly different ways represent the traditional position, claiming that Job must have sinned or else he would not be punished by God in this way. Job's innocence is key here and Job maintains it throughout. But Job is no longer the innocent sufferer who accepts good and bad as it comes; rather he expects more from the God in whom he trusted to reward him as befitted his status. Now his status is nothing and he is jeered at by those who regarded him as a leader of the community whom he helped in their hour of need. How could his former acts of piety have led to his current state? Are the wicked the only ones who prosper after all? At times Job seems convinced of the prosperity of the wicked (e.g., 21:7–16) and is sure that the doctrine of retribution should be turned upon its head. Ultimately, he realizes that only God can answer these questions for him, and so he presents his case perhaps most succinctly in his final lament to God in chaps. 29–31. In chap. 31 he states with a whole string of examples that if he has done wrong then he would understand the punishment, but the point is that he has not done any of these things, so why this suffering? He accuses God of not listening, and though he earlier longed for an arbiter between himself and God, he launches a profound attack on God's justice that shakes the foundations of his faith.

Eliphaz, first friend and visionary. We are presented in the dialogues with three rather verbose friends who are good at presenting arguments and at criticizing Job for his wrongheadedness in seeing his misfortune as anything but the result of sin. Eliphaz treads carefully at first, wishing not to offend Job, and we are prepared for seeing Job in a rather different light as a prickly character. In his first speech Eliphaz reminds Job of how he helped others with words of comfort and advice (good communication skills are a keynote of wise conduct in Proverbs, e.g., Prov. 10:18–21) but sees him as caving in when harsh experiences come his way. He reminds Job to fear God and remember his integrity. His debate then moves on to a more academic plane with the observation that generally in life people reap what they sow.

He also uses the tactic of describing his insights as having come to him in a vision, perhaps a ploy to give his words more authority. He sees a spirit that speaks the words, "Can mortals be righteous before God?" (4:17). This is to raise the issue of theodicy, which will emerge more strongly later in the book, and in many ways this vision of Eliphaz anticipates what is to come when God says in a similar vein that human beings are very small in the general scheme of the world. Here Eliphaz suggests that God does not even trust his angels or see them as blameless, so why should humans expect preferential treatment? Human beings are not without impurities either. He goes on to indicate the transitoriness and frailty of human life. But he still thinks that Job has sinned and that he is therefore being corrected by God. He goes as far as to say that "happy is the one whom God reproves" (5:17) and that eventually God will heal the wounds and be on Job's side again. This reads rather like a prophecy of what does occur: in the epilogue Job is rewarded and the doctrine of retribution seems to be alive and well just as Eliphaz predicts it will be.

Eliphaz in his second speech accuses Job of undermining the fear of God for others—the wise should not engage in unprofitable talk that will hinder others in their contemplation of God. As a leader of the community Job should have known better. Eliphaz chastises Job for his arrogance in thinking that he knows all the answers as well as for his ill-conceived words, and he reaffirms the due punishment of the wicked by God.

In his third speech he accuses Job directly of wickedness and he reiterates God's greatness as well as his justice. He urges Job to receive instruction from God and return to him, and he acknowledges the power of prayer, by which Job will pray and God will hear him.

Bildad, the second friend. Bildad lacks the opening hesitation of Eliphaz, to the point of being blunt. He accuses Job of windy words and reconfirms the wisdom doctrine of just retribution. In his first speech he states that God will restore Job if only Job will seek God and confess his guilt. Bildad explains their death by saying that Job's children must have sinned. He appeals to the experience of former generations; wisdom is very much about passing on knowledge and observation from one generation to another. He characterizes the hope of the godless as short-lived like reeds or papyrus grass with no water. The wicked too are transient; they appear to take root but are quickly uprooted and forgotten by others. He, like Eliphaz, sees hope around the corner for such a blameless one as Job.

In his second speech Bildad is offended that Job treats them as stupid and accuses him of overstated anger (anger was not liked by wisdom writers, who preferred a controlled temper, e.g., Prov. 16:32). He accuses Job of forgetting his smallness in a large universe. He reaffirms God's punishment of the wicked in vivid terms that describe their hunger, illness, and ultimate death.

In his final speech Bildad takes up Eliphaz's point about whether a human being can be righteous before God. No one is pure in God's sight. The inference is that all sin, and even the moon and stars are not perfect. As for mere mortals, described as maggots and worms, they are even less likely to be so. There may be an extra section to Bildad's final speech in 26:5–14, which stresses God's might and power in creation and which reads more naturally as part of a friend's speech than Job's (although the latter possibility is not entirely ruled out).

Zophar, the third friend. The theme of words and babbling reappears in Zophar's first speech, echoing this emphasis in Proverbs. He speaks of Job's endless talk and of the possibility that God might answer to put him right and tell him the secrets of wisdom. He is sure of Job's guilt and states that God is exacting less than his guilt deserves—a strong statement given that Job has lost everything except his life (and his wife!). Zophar again appeals to God's world, the natural world, being much greater than human beings can ever understand. But within that he sees God as a just judge who knows whom to punish and whom to reward. He urges Job to repent so that his life will improve.

In Zophar's second speech he appeals to a spirit beyond his understanding that impels him to speak out and tells him of the inevitable punishment of the wicked despite short-term indications to the contrary. Again he uses vivid imagery to depict their fate at the hands of a just God: the food they eat to excess will be turned to poison and their bellies filled instead with God's anger. Heaven and earth will bear witness to their guilt. Is he trying to frighten Job into submission here?

There is no third speech of Zophar and scholars have tried to reconstruct it from 27:13–23, where a section is apparently attributed to Job but which discusses the punishment of the wicked along similar lines to Zophar's previous speech. It is likely that the heading has been lost and that this may well be Zophar adding to his previous argument. This is followed by a hymn to Wisdom in chap. 28 that is also placed in Job's mouth but is probably an independent poem. In its emphasis on the hiddenness of wisdom within the world of nature, knowledge of wisdom residing only with God and human response of fearing the Lord are of key importance. This hymn fits in with the general tenor of the friends' speeches rather than those of Job.

Elihu, the youngster. These speeches may represent a later addition to the whole book in that Elihu is a fourth friend who does not feature in the book as a character until chap. 32, when he appears from nowhere. According to some, he adds nothing to the arguments already aired by the friends, but this is not entirely true. He explains that he had been hesitant about speaking because of his youth, but that now he wishes to speak out as he has heard nothing from the friends that has convinced Job and so needs to have a turn to do so. He feels compelled to speak in order to find relief from the pent-up frustration of not doing so. He challenges Job head-on. He argues that Job cannot be pure and that God has not made Job his enemy (as Job had maintained). God is greater than human beings and makes use of visions delivered in the night, or pain for chastening, in order to keep people on the straight and narrow. In a sense God is actively promoting righteous behaviour in this description. God will, says Elihu, deliver anyone who is righteous, even at the last minute when death is nigh, and will restore them to fullness. Elihu urges Job to do the same—to repent and to be restored. He claims to teach Job wisdom. He proclaims God's justice in the face of evil deeds. God sees all and will punish and reward according to the principle of the doctrine of retribution. He does not believe that God is not listening and argues that God hears the cries of God's people, listens to the voice of mediation, and gives people second chances. God is good and God is above all, the Creator whose work is beyond comprehension. The end of Elihu's speech anticipates some of the glory of the created world found in God's reply but firmly within the framework of belief in God's justice on behalf of human beings.

The God Speeches

God, the Creator. Finally we meet God, appearing in a whirlwind, a common context for theophanies. God accuses Job of darkening counsel by words without knowledge. God then poses a number of questions to Job that turn out to be unanswerable, rhetorical questions that have

the effect of firmly putting Job in his place. God asks where Job was when God created the world—does he know the measurements of the earth and how the world was constructed? Was he there when God separated sea from land or when God created day? (there are overtones of the descriptions of the creation of the world in Gen. 1 and Ps. 104 here). There is a hint of God's treatment of the wicked when God speaks of shaking them out of the world and withholding light from them (Job 38:13, 15), but in general the emphasis on the creation of the world rather bypasses human concern with justice. It is as if God is simply glorying in the world that God has made, which is one of limits and boundaries imposed by God (including that of life and death). It is not just the created world of nature, but the human mind that God has ordained (38:36). The inference here is that God is much greater than human beings can ever grasp and that God is involved in all of creation, not just in the lives of human beings. Only God knows the full secrets of the world; only God knows the way to the storehouses of the hail and snow (38:32); only God knows the place from which light is distributed (38:24). There is a huge emphasis in these speeches on the animal world, with detailed descriptions of the habits of wild animals and how God knows every detail. The message here is that the world is much more complex than the narrow confines of the doctrine of retribution would seem to allow. Job's wisdom is nothing like that of God, who overcame the great monsters of chaos, Behemoth and Leviathan (of which there are two long and fierce descriptions using the imagery of the hippopotamus and the crocodile, respectively), to create an ordered world and hence whose power is awe-inspiring. How could Job question such a one as this? Here we have the Creator God of the Wisdom literature, but no longer is God simply behind the scenes as a benevolent personage to be feared—God is shown here to be active in the creation and preservation of the world and of all that is in it.

Job, humbled and repentant.

Job responds twice to God. The first time (40:3–5) he acknowledges his smallness in the light of the greatness of God and the world and he says that he will speak no more. However, he does speak again to acknowledge God's power to do anything that God purposes to do. It is not clear whether this is simply a tongue-in-cheek kind of repentance in which Job simply acknowledges God's power rather than God's justice or whether Job is truly humbled by what he has seen and heard. He does distinguish between previously only hearing of God but now seeing God face-to-face. Perhaps the actual encounter is the decisive turning point for Job. He recognizes that he did not fully understand when he spoke out against God and that there are many wonderful things beyond his comprehension. But he never says that he sinned, and so he still holds on to his integrity. He says that he now despises himself and repents, but he is not specific about repenting of anything more than having spoken out of turn.

The Epilogue

The friends, finally humiliated. Contrary to expectation, the friends (represented by Eliphaz) are then rebuked by God for having not spoken right about God as Job did (42:7). One might have expected God to praise their wisdom in maintaining time-honored traditional views. But perhaps here God is rebuking them for being too limited in their understanding, much as Job was too. The difference is that Job sought to understand his situation and was guided by the experience of having suffered knowing that he had not sinned, while the friends supposed that Job must have sinned and could not think outside that reward/retribution nexus. Job is asked by God to sacrifice on behalf of the friends in order to intercede for them, and God accepts Job's prayer.

God the vindicator and restorer. God vindicates Job over the friends, rebuking them for not speaking right of God. This suggests that it is better to question God's justice and seek a deeper relationship with God than to speak in a superficial way of already accepted truths. God restores Job's fortunes such that he receives twice as much of everything that he had before and also a new set of children. We assume that God cures Job's disease too, although this is not explicitly said, and interestingly the figure of the Satan (who inflicted the disasters and disease) does not reappear. This suggests perhaps that it is God who is to blame for the suffering that goes on in the world, as indeed the dialogues and epilogue assume. Furthermore the wisdom blessings of progeny, going on into the future with two further generations, and longevity are given to Job in abundance. However, a question mark may still linger in our minds: can Job ever truly be restored to what he was before having gone through the experience he has? Was the test worth it? Are we always fundamentally changed through the experience of suffering such that we can never go back to how we were before even if our fortunes seem to reverse?

Jemimah, Keziah, and Keren-happuch, the beautiful daughters. A final flourish from the author is the mention of the names of Job's new daughters and of two factors, their beauty and their inheritance. Two of the names relate to makeup items and so have a certain frivolity in the light of all the sufferings that Job has undergone. The beauty of these daughters is legendary, and that they are rich in their own right is highly unusual. It is perhaps most surprising, however, that we are not given corresponding details of the new sons, nor of the fate of Job's wife, although the inference is that they are present and that Job is reintegrated into the community of his family at this point. It is his daughters who, with Job, are given pride of place as the bearers of the next generation, which is the fruit of his inheritance as a final reward for all the troubles he has endured. This seems to put the doctrine of retribution firmly back into the center of the theological debate. The discussion of disinterested righteousness has been proved too—Job has passed that test and he has held on to his integrity. The doctrine of retribution, although somewhat disproved in the dialogues and in God's justification of Job over the friends in 42:7, appears alive and well in the epilogue. The relationship between God and humanity has been given a decisive airing, and we are left feeling that maybe God's answer was a little unsatisfactory in its stress on God's might and power and creative capabilities rather than in providing a direct answer to Job's questions. However, perhaps these capabilities show that God is greater than human comprehension, that human suffering itself is not always to be understood with an easy set of answers, yet that relationship with God, even on rather different terms, is still possible. Indeed, a more profound relationship may in the end be more satisfying.

Bibliography

Clines, D. J. A. *Job 1–20* and *Job 21–37*. WBC 17 and 18A. Dallas: Word, 1989 and 2006.

Dell, Katharine J. *Shaking a Fist at God: Struggling with the Mystery of Undeserved Suffering*. Liguori, MO: Triumph Books, 1995.

Gordis, Robert. *The Book of God and Man*. Chicago: University of Chicago Press, 1965.

Habel, Norman C. *Job*. OTL. Philadelphia: Westminster, 1985.

Newsom, Carol A. "Job." In *NIB* 4:317–637.

Psalms

William P. Brown

INTRODUCTION

The longest book of the Bible, the Psalter is a heterogeneous collection of subcollections of poetic texts designed for liturgy and instruction. As the product of several centuries of ancient Israel's worship life, the Psalms consist of various forms of discourse or genres that include petitions or laments to God, praises or hymns to God, thanksgiving songs for God, and didactic poems or instructions about God and human conduct. The Hebrew title for the Psalter, *Sepher Tehillim* ("Book of Praises" [or "Hymns"]), glosses over this rich variety, in which the laments actually outnumber the praise psalms. Cutting across the various genres, however, is the Psalter's primary object of discourse, God, who is as irreducibly complex as the Psalms are literarily diverse. In the Psalms the God who commands is also the God who sustains. The God of royal pedigree and the God of the "poor and needy," the God of judgment and the God of mercy, God's hidden face and God's beaming countenance—all are profiled in the Psalter. In the Psalms the kinship theology of the personal laments meets the kingship theology of the enthronement psalms.

In addition to its multifaceted focus on God, the Psalter provides an equally thick description of the human self, endowed with glory and honor yet also afflicted and vulnerable. The Psalter has been called the Bible's most introspective book, and appropriately so. To borrow language from John Calvin, the Psalter presents "an anatomy of all parts of the soul," a profile of the human self that plumbs the anguished depths of the heart while scaling the heights of intellectual and spiritual discernment. In short, psalmic poetry is as revealing about the human condition as it is about God. God and the human self, though metaphysically distinct, are existentially bound in the Psalms.

Difficulties abound in any attempt to discern theological coherence in the Psalms. In comparison to most biblical books, which bear some degree of cohesion or plot, the Psalter is a seeming hodgepodge of texts stemming from a variety of social settings and functions. In addition to its eclectic character, the Psalter's very medium—poetry—is by nature allusive and multivalent. The language of metaphor, so prominent in the Psalms, resists conceptual uniformity. Complicating the task also are the differing levels of theological discourse. Certain psalms exhibit a greater degree of theological reflection than others, what could be called "second-order" reflection in distinction from "first-order" discourse, which provides the raw material for more reflective construals of God and the world. "First-order" expressions about God and the human self can be found primarily among the simple laments or petitions, which convey a degree of situational immediacy. "Second-order" reflection, by contrast, has a home in more elaborate and mixed genres, such as the extended hymns of praise, songs of trust and thanksgiving, and psalms of instruction. Such psalms step back from the particular exigencies of life to render a more comprehensive profile of God. Together, these various psalms facilitate a convergence of deep theological reflection and urgent existential concerns. The end result could be called a "practical theology."

Given its diversity in form and content, the Psalter is Scripture's most integrated corpus. On David's many-stringed lyre can be heard almost every theological chord that resounds throughout the Hebrew Scriptures, from covenant and history to creation and wisdom. The complexity of this vast corpus, however, has not dissuaded interpreters from discerning a theological center or focus for the Psalter. A recent proposal is "refuge," a leitmotif that points toward God's sovereign reign over life. But as with any proposal for a single center, it leaves much in the Psalter unaddressed. Another proposal posits the dual focus of "refuge" and "pathway," which recognizes God not only as sovereign and savior but also as lawgiver and guide. One can identify additional theological themes (see below). In any case, it was with good reason that Martin Luther regarded the Psalms as a "little Bible."

Any theological analysis of the Psalter must acknowledge at the outset that the Psalms offer a theology "from below." The Psalms consist primarily of human words to and about God. The human voice, whether in lament or in praise, is the primary vehicle of psalmic discourse. David's name is associated with seventy-three psalms, and later rabbinic tradition attributed the entire Psalter to David (cf. 72:20). If the narrative material of the Bible recounts what God has done and the prophetic and legal literature convey what God has said, the Psalms present, in turn, how the community both yearns for and responds to God's acts and words. The Psalms, as a whole, model the worshiping community's posture before God, and therein lies its prescriptive force. That the Psalter, like the Torah, is divided into five books (1–41, 42–72, 73–89, 90–106, 107–150) suggests that in the Psalms divine discourse and human speech are inextricably bound together (see, e.g., 1:2; 19:14).

The following observations are structured around the various genres or patterns of discourse that constitute the Psalms, with attention given also to the Psalter's overarching shape. Reflecting various social and religious settings, the basic distinctions between genres provide related vantage points for theological discernment. The Psalter, furthermore, evinces a theological movement, albeit spasmodic, that concludes climactically with hymns of praise (146–150). Given the dominance of praise psalms toward the end of the Psalter, the Hebrew title (see above) makes sense. This overarching movement from petition to praise, from an anthropocentric to a theocentric orientation, is readily evident. The laments have more to say about the plight of the human self; the praise psalms, in turn, focus resolutely on God and God's way in the world. The final section of this commentary is devoted to the particular challenge posed by the psalms of vengeance, a subclass of the lament psalms.

COMMENTARY

Laments or Petitions

The individual lament or prayer for deliverance designates those psalms that open with a complaint of distress and typically end on a note of resounding praise or at least with a vow to praise (notable exceptions include 39 and 88). The communal laments, however, are not so typical in this regard (e.g., 44 and 89). Widely attested throughout the ancient Near East, the lament genre was not unique to Israel. Indeed, given their stereotypical language, these prayers speak more about the general human condition than about the Israelite speaker's situation.

Human self.   Whether in the language of self-abasement, penitence, or righteous anger, the pray-er in these psalms speaks as one who is fundamentally in want (contra 23:1). The psalmic self prays from a situation of extreme need both for deliverance and for God. Distress and deprivation set the condition for lament.

The lament psalms describe various forms of distress, from sickness and near death conditions (e.g., 6:2; 38:1–7; 102:3–5) to slander and persecution by unnamed enemies (e.g., 69:5; 71:13; 109). The prayer of the laments depicts life in a world wracked by conflict and dis-ease in all manifestations, from physical to social and spiritual. The language of suffering, though vivid, is stereotypical, allowing for various ways of applying or appropriating the laments. The psalmist's enemies, for example, remain unnamed. Likened to ravaging "lions," the enemies are the wicked who oppress the poor and are filled with pride (10:9; 17:2). They are "greedy for gain" (10:3) and act with impunity, claiming that the Lord is oblivious to their malicious activity (94:7; cf. 64:5–6). When not surrounded by enemies, the psalmist complains of social isolation and loneliness (25:16), "a little owl of the waste places" or "a lonely bird on the housetop" (102:6b–7).

Of all dangers, death presents the ultimate threat and the condition of greatest deprivation. Metaphorically called the Pit, Sheol is the domain of the dead that lies beyond, literally "below," God's direct reign or immediate presence (e.g., 88:4–6). Death is the abode that is devoid of remembrance, a domain "cut off" from God's intervening power ("hand"). Thus

in the pit of Sheol praise to God is impossible (6:5b), or at least highly questionable (88:10–12, but cf. 115:17; 139:8b). Consonant with the metaphor, the psalmist refers to the act of dying as a descent, or return, to the ground: "we sink down to the dust; our bodies cling to the ground" (44:25); "you turn humankind back to dust, and say, 'Turn back, you mortals'" (90:3). Equally vivid is the cry from the watery abyss:

> Save me, O God,
>   for the waters have come up
>   to my neck.
> I sink in deep mire,
>   where there is no foothold;
> I have come into deep waters,
>   and the flood sweeps over me.
>   69:1–2

Such language marks Sheol as the realm of chaos. To cry "out of the depths" (130:1) is to cry from the brink of death. For the psalmist, the threat of death is ever present in manifold ways, constricting human livelihood and existence. Psalm 144, a royal lament, speaks of human existence as a "breath" and a "passing shadow" (v. 4; cf. 39:4–6; 102:11). Finitude and fragility characterize the human condition: "I am a worm, and not human; scorned by others, and despised by the people" (22:6). In the same breath, however, the speaker of Ps. 22 claims that it was God who "took [him] from the womb" and kept him "safe on [his] mother's breast" (v. 9). But this God has now forsaken him (v. 1). In the graphic language of self-abasement and divine abandonment, the speaker acknowledges utter dependence upon the Deity, an indelible mark of the human condition, while at the same time calling God to account.

Any hope of self-sustenance or livelihood *without* God is considered sheer delusion, the root of wickedness. As a taunt against the wicked stands the indictment: "See the one who would not take refuge in God, but trusted in abundant riches, and sought refuge in wealth!" (52:7), in contrast to the righteous one who flourishes as a "green olive tree in the house of God" (v. 8). More than any other genre, the lament acknowledges the self's absolute dependence on God.

The threat that besets the lamenter is frequently described in terms of honor and shame. In a world torn by strife, honor (*kabod*)—the social acknowledgment of God-given dignity—is invariably violated, with shame as the result (e.g., 44:15–16; 69:18–19). Frequent appeal is made to God to vindicate and restore one's honor. "In you, O LORD, I seek refuge; do not let me ever be put to shame; in your righteousness deliver me" (31:1; cf. 25:2; 31:17; 44:15; 69:6–7). The laments aim at restoring not only a person's health and vigor, but also his or her honor in the community (e.g., 26:1; 35:24; 43:1; 54:1).

The psalmist's dependence upon God is expressed in a formula of self-identity like that in the laments: "I am poor and needy" (e.g., 40:17; 70:5; 86:1; 109:22; cf. 74:21). More than economic deprivation is indicated. The psalmist acknowledges his or her essential neediness *before* God and *for* God. Most evocative are the images of the doe and "parched land" thirsting for God (42:1; 63:1; 143:6). Of all objects of desire, from material prosperity to social justice, God is acknowledged as supreme: "There is nothing on earth that I desire other than you" (73:25). On earth, conversely, all "human help is worthless" (60:11).

The human condition as profiled in the laments is marked by distress, deprivation, and vulnerability. The psalmist is a wounded speaker beset by various powers (physical, emotional, spiritual, and social) outside his or her control. Hence the prayers for help acknowledge an essential dependence whose object also lies beyond human or natural means. Self-sufficiency, indeed self-salvation, is a delusion harbored by those the psalmist deems hostile and wicked. The urgent plea to God for help in situations of distress, moreover, constitutes an act of allegiance, a surrendering to divine control, for as often as the pray-er is identified as "poor and needy," he or she is also deemed "servant" (86:1–2; cf. 34:2, 5, 22; 69:17; 143:12).

The "servant" is the one who "trusts," and the one who trusts acknowledges through lament and petition one's dependence on the Divine. But even in this role as God's "servant," as petitioner and pray-er, the psalmist also speaks from a position of power before God, a position of covenantal kinship with God that effectively calls God to account for divine negligence or abuse (see below). Therein lies a paradox: the very act of appeal to divine agency from a state of abject dependence effectively heightens the power of human agency. The human cry for help is itself an affirmation of human dignity, violated yet destined for restoration. The cry of dereliction is not the cry of resignation, but the cry for vindication. The bold language of the laments, in short, rests on an intensely personal, trusting, empowering relationship between God and petitioner, a relationship of covenantal kinship.

God. The God of the lament, and indeed of the Psalms as a whole, is scarcely considered in terms of *abstract* essence or *absolute* attributes (e.g., immutability and eternity). Rather, God is perceived as personally engaged with human beings. First and foremost, God is cast in the role of witness. If psalmic prayer gives testimony to distress, as in the lament, so God takes on the role of active witness to the psalmist's concerns, and not just any witness. The psalms vividly develop the ancient confessional formula that God is abounding in mercy, compassion, and "steadfast love" (*hesed*; see Exod. 34:6–7; Pss. 86:15; 103:8; 145:8). Specific to the lament, God is deemed the (only) one who can fully satisfy and deliver. The laments reflect a personal God who is accessible and even open to argumentation and rebuke: "Why are you so far from helping me?" (22:1b); "Why do you sleep, O Lord?" (44:23); "You have renounced the covenant with your servant" (89:39a). Such bold language challenges and motivates God to respond to human distress: "In my distress I cry to the LORD, that he may answer me" (120:1).

As the object of petition, the God of Israel is deemed the supreme agent of salvation: "You are the God of my salvation; for you I wait all day long" (25:5). Salvation, or more broadly "help" (43:5; 70:5), takes on various forms: deliverance from danger (4:8; 31:20), refuge or protection from the wicked (5:11–12), safe haven from oppression (7:9; 14:6), healing from sickness (38:1–5, 21–22), vindication in the face of slander or false accusation (69:4–5; 109:31), enactment of justice (10:18; 94:14–15), forgiveness of sins (51:1–2; 130:4), strength in the face of adversity (28:7), blessing amid deprivation (3:8b), and breathing room amid dire straits (4:1; 118:5). Various metaphors for God, from the natural to the political, depict God's protective or restorative power for the needy and the victimized: refuge (7:1; 5:11; 14:6), shield (3:3; 5:12; 7:9), stronghold (9:9), rock (28:1; 42:9), fortress (31:2), shelter (31:20), shade/shadow (57:1; 63:7), raptor/wings (57:1; 61:4), light (4:6; 27:1), cup/portion (16:5), healer (6:2; 41:4), king (5:2; 10:16; 44:4), judge (7:11; 9:8), and warrior (7:12–13).

The one in need and the one who saves mark a basic metaphysical distinction between the human being and the Deity.

> Let those who love your salvation
>   say evermore, "God is great!"
> *But* I am poor and needy;
>   hasten to me, O God!
> 70:4b–5

> As for me, I am poor and needy,
>   *but* the Lord takes thought for me.
> You are my help and my deliverer;
>   do not delay, O my God.
> 40:17

The contrast between God and the human self is cast grammatically by the disjunction ("but") and existentially in terms of agency and power. In the laments, human helplessness is met by God's beneficent power. The distinctive-

ness of Divinity is highlighted all the more by the Deity's incomparable nature:

> All my bones shall say, "O LORD,
>   who is like you?
> You deliver the weak from those too
>   strong for them,
>   the weak and needy from those who
>   despoil them."
> 35:10 (cf. 86:8)

Here such incommensurability is matched by an unsurpassable resolve to effect salvation: the resolve to rescue the "weak and needy" (35:10), deliver the oppressed (13:7–9), and vindicate the righteous (71:20–21).

Despite the absolute distinction that Divinity holds over humankind, the psalmist appeals to a quality of relationship without which prayer would not be possible, namely God's responsive concern to human need. The psalmist refers to a solidarity that God exhibits toward the needy: "For he stands at the right hand of the needy, to save them from those who would condemn them to death" (109:31; cf. 12:5–6a). God's power is exhibited in a resolute responsiveness to the cries of the needy. What makes reliance upon God possible, the psalmist affirms, is both preexisting and enduring ("promises" in 12:6a), indeed essential to God's relational character, most frequently defined as *hesed* (NRSV "steadfast love"). Appeals are made to God to act salvifically "for the sake of" or "according to your *hesed*" (6:4; 25:7; 109:26). *Hesed* is the divine impetus for "salvation" (85:7), as well as the divine warrant for the psalmist's deliverance (13:5) and forgiveness (25:7). God is called upon to enact *hesed* as the basis for establishing refuge (17:7). *Hesed* finds in the psalms its semantic partners in "faithfulness" (*'emet*, 25:10; 36:5; 86:10) and "compassion" (*rahamim*, 25:6). The psalmist celebrates the value and vastness of God's *hesed* (57:10), which provides refuge and sustenance for "all people" (36:7–8). Far from being a fleeting emotion or spontaneous act of the will, God's *hesed* is grounded in and bound to the promise of divine initiative:

Has [the LORD's] *hesed* ceased forever?
    Are his promises at an end for all time?
Has God forgotten to be gracious?
    Has he in anger shut up his compassion?
                                        77:8–9

Based on divine benevolence, *hesed* is commensurate with God's sworn word and thus can be relied upon by the petitioner in times of crisis. In addition, the divine covenant (*berit*) with David is rooted in *hesed*, thereby ensuring the covenant's perpetuity (89:28). In this royal context, *hesed* is something sworn by God for David's sake and for the sake of his progeny and kingdom (v. 49). God's *hesed*, freely established for the sake of a people, binds God in benevolent responsiveness to a people. It is fidelity to a people's well-being, fidelity initiated in grace, an essential mark of God's character. As the lament section of Ps. 89 indicates, for God *not* to act in accordance with *hesed* puts God's very integrity in jeopardy.

Even in the laments, God is not simply an instrument of salvation for human beings. Preeminently powerful, God is also preeminently righteous (7:9, 11, 17; 129:4). In light of the competing religions of the ancient Near East, the moral goodness of a deity was no assured fact. Whether Mesopotamian or Greek, the various pantheons of antiquity were populated by deities known sometimes for their fickleness, cleverness, and mischief, not to mention ineptitude. But as for Israel's God, righteousness was considered a sine qua non of divine character: "God is a righteous judge, and a God who has indignation every day" (7:11; see 5:4–6).

As many laments assert, God is not always at the psalmist's beck and call. It is no accident that the laments typically open with a complaint or rebuke (10:1; 13:1). Most anguished is the opening cry of Ps. 22, cited also by Jesus on the cross (Matt. 27:46; Mark 15:34). Other pleas lament God's wrath, rather than absence, as the cause of distress (e.g., Pss. 6:1–2; 38:1–2; 88:7, 16). Rhetorically, such complaints heighten the urgency of the psalmist's situation and direct God's attention to his or her plight. The laments

do not hesitate to implicate God in the particular crises that beset the psalmist and to accuse God of willful negligence and even breach of covenant (44:17; 89:39). Rhetorically, such language places God in the position of accountability to the petitioner. Theologically, the complaints acknowledge that God is elusive and not always available. God is not simply at human disposal. This God, the God of Israel, cannot be manipulated. In the laments, no explanation for God's absence or abstention is given. God's inexplicable absence from the psalmist's situation is met only by more strident cries of complaint, along with greater resolve to wait and hope for God's intervening presence. The laments are thus driven by the hope that God *can* be compelled to pay attention to human plight. Without such hope, the psalmist is without a prayer and God is deemed bereft of *hesed*.

Thanksgiving Psalms and Songs of Trust

Compared to the lament psalms, the thanksgiving psalms and songs of trust offer a different yet related vantage point for theological reflection. Instead of desperate pleas for help, the thanksgiving psalms and songs of trust provide concrete testimony to answered prayer and display unwavering confidence in God's care and power to deliver. Central is the confession: "I sought the LORD, and he answered me, and delivered me from all my fears" (34:4), which becomes generalized in v. 17: "When the righteous cry for help, the LORD hears, and rescues them from all their troubles." God's responsive nearness and the restored state of the human self are the theological markers of the thanksgiving psalms. The songs of trust cultivate the human disposition toward God's responsive nearness, that of humble trust.

Human self. As in the laments, human fragility and suffering are acknowledged in the thanksgiving psalms: "Out of my distress I called on the LORD" (118:5a). But added in the same breath is a testimony of deliverance: "the LORD answered me and set me in a broad place" (v. 5b). Briefer yet is the testimony: "On the day I called, you answered me" (138:3; cf. Jonah 2:2). Most extensive is Ps. 107, which features a litany of various scenarios of distress out of which "they cried to the LORD in their trouble": the plight of refugees in the desert (vv. 4–5), imprisonment (vv. 10–12), sickness (vv. 17–19), and perils on the sea (vv. 23–27). Each disaster is met with concrete deliverance: God guides the refugees to an "inhabited town" (v. 7), releases the prisoners (vv. 14–17), heals mortal illness (v. 20), stills the storm (v. 29), and finds a haven for the endangered (v. 30). In each case, an expression of thanksgiving follows. Other reasons for thanksgiving in these psalms include victory in battle (118:10–16), personal deliverance from enemies (18:3, 17; 92:10; 138:7), agricultural bounty (65:9–13), punishment of the wicked (75:8), and national deliverance (124:7).

In the thanksgiving psalms, the suppliant's lamentable condition is no longer front and center. The language shifts decisively from the psalmist's plight to God's remedy. The transformation of the psalmist's condition gives way, in turn, to the transformation of the psalmist's disposition, as indicated in the songs of trust: "I fear no evil" (23:4); "Surely, goodness and mercy shall pursue me all the days of my life, and I shall dwell in the house of the LORD my whole life long" (v. 6, my trans.). No longer dogged by unnamed enemies, the psalmist is now "pursued" (*radap*) by God's favor. Desperation and fear give way to confidence, joy, and gratitude. The speaker's transformation is consistently ascribed to God's initiative:

> You have turned my mourning
> > into dancing;
> > > you have taken off my sackcloth
> > > > and clothed me with joy,
> > so that my soul may praise you
> > > and not be silent.
> > > > O LORD my God, I will give thanks
> > > > > to you forever.
> > > > > > 30:11–12

In response to God's act of deliverance or restoration, the psalmist dedicates himself or herself to lifelong praise and gratitude.

God. In the thanksgiving psalms, the imperative of petition becomes an indicative; the plea turns into testimony. "Give ear to my words, O LORD!" (5:1) is replaced by "I love the LORD, because he has heard my voice and my supplications" (116:1). Such psalms provide a reflective look back at God's responsive intervention. God is identified as "You who answer prayer" (65:2a), the ultimate source of salvation, as in the laments. The issue of whether God will provide help for those in need is resolved through testimonial assertion in the thanksgiving psalms (34:4, 17). Most confessional is the affirmation: "Our help is in the name of the LORD" (124:8); or "My help comes from the LORD, who made heaven and earth" (121:2). Psalm 136 covers both the cosmic and historical range of divine help, beginning with the work of creation (vv. 4–9) and sliding effortlessly into the events of Israel's journey to the land (vv. 10–22). God both "rescues" from "our foes" (v. 24) and provides "food to all flesh" (v. 25).

Compared to divine agency, *human* help proves consistently impotent: "Better to take refuge in the LORD than to put confidence in mortals" (118:8; cf. 52:7). Though critical of alternative forms of help, the testimony of divine aid is also invitational: "Taste and see that the LORD is good; happy are those who take refuge in him" (34:8). In the same psalm, the testimonial assertion of thanksgiving provides a teachable moment: "Come, O children, listen to me; I will teach you the fear of the LORD" (v. 11; see also 32:8). In the thanksgiving psalms, "fear" of God stands next to gratitude.

The testimony of divine help provides the basis for various statements about God's nature or character: "For though the LORD is high, he regards the lowly" (138:6a). The God whose throne is established in heaven (103:13) proves supremely accommodating for those in need. Indeed, God's compassion bears its own mark of transcendence.

> For as the heavens are high
>   above the earth,
>   so great is his steadfast love (*hesed*)
>   toward those who fear him;
> as far as the east is from the west,
>   so far he removes our transgressions
>   from us.
>
> 103:11–12

The language of cosmic transcendence is ascribed to God's expansive *hesed*. It is in God's nature to be transcendentally compassionate.

Elsewhere in the thanksgiving psalms, God's *immanent* presence takes the fore: "The LORD is near to the brokenhearted, and saves the crushed in spirit" (34:18); "We give thanks; your name is near" (75:1). In the psalms of trust, the individual expresses supreme confidence in God's agency: "[God] alone is my rock and my salvation, my fortress; I shall never be shaken" (62:2). God is claimed as the *only* object of human reliance (vv. 1, 2, 5, 6–7). Human status, whether high or low, is but a "breath" by comparison (v. 9; cf. 103:15–16).

The posture of thanksgiving acknowledges the qualities of divine beneficence, as in Ps. 103, which contains elements of both thanksgiving and praise (vv. 2–5). Whereas certain laments attribute the psalmist's plight to God's wrath, the topic of divine anger in Ps. 103 turns into a theological statement of assurance:

> The LORD is merciful and gracious,
>   slow to anger and abounding in *hesed*.
> He will not always accuse,
>   nor will he keep his anger forever.
> He does not deal with us according
>   to our sins,
>   nor repay us according to our iniquities.
>
> 103:8–10 (cf. Exod. 34:6–7)

Although deeply felt by God, anger does not constitute a divine character trait or disposition. At most, divine wrath is a temporary state. More enduring is God's mercy or compassion, most poignantly depicted in parental imagery: "As a father has compassion for his children, so the LORD has compassion for those who fear him" (103:13). This parental God of compassion, the God of *hesed*, is the God who prompts the psalmist's thanksgiving and blessing.

As a summary reason for thanksgiving, the psalmist lifts up God's "goodness": "O give thanks to the LORD, for he is good; for his *hesed* endures forever" (107:1; cf. 118:1; 136:1). The adjective "good" covers the fullness and constancy of God's gracious outreach toward creation and human beings, embodied in acts of creation, salvation, and provision (136:1–26).

Didactic Psalms

This loose category of psalms covers various types determined more by content than by form, which include the torah psalms (1, 19, 119), so-called wisdom psalms (e.g., 32, 34, 37, 49, 111–112), temple entrance liturgies (15, 24), and historical psalms (78, 105–106, 135–136), as well as several unclassifiable psalms (50, 73, 82, 115, 133). United by their declarative and prescriptive tone, they share the express purpose of providing instruction about the ways of God and of human beings in the world.

Human self. Unlike the prayers, these psalms address the community or individual with instruction, presupposing that human beings are teachable (73:24; 90:12) and thus capable of leading lives of wholeness and integrity. The temple entrance liturgies of Pss. 15 and 24, for example, offer a veritable taxonomy of moral conduct that range from righteousness (15:2) and purity (24:4) to fulfilling oaths (15:4b) and not charging interest (v. 5a). Those who perform such actions "shall never be shaken," established as firmly as the temple itself (v. 5b; cf. 112:6). Like the sage, the psalmist counsels restraint in anger (37:8) and the "fear of the LORD" (112:1), "the beginning of wisdom" (111:10). Such "fear" or heightened reverence for God includes "delight" in God's commandments or obedience (112:1b), care for the poor (v. 9a), generosity (v. 5), and courage against evil (v. 7), as well as the practice of justice (v. 5) and mercy (v. 4). Such qualities mirror God's own character (see 111:4–5, 7). A life of integrity is a life in *imitatio Dei*, literally a godly life formed from following God's "way" or "path" (119:15).

The defining metaphor of human (and divine) conduct, "pathway," is shared also by the Wisdom literature and suggests that a life of integrity is inherently dynamic. To be "blameless" is to "walk blamelessly" (15:2). Those who disobey God "wander from [God's] commandments" (119:21b). The path of the righteous contrasts sharply with the way of the wicked (1:1, 4–6). Whereas a destiny of doom is proclaimed for the wicked (e.g., 1:4–5; 37:15), one psalm in particular, a meditation on theodicy, notes "the prosperity of the wicked" (73:3; see also 37:7, 34). This unsettling discrepancy of the wicked "always at ease" (73:12) questions the legitimacy of leading a morally credible life (v. 13). But the psalmist's despair turns to confidence upon entering "the sanctuary of God," where he "perceived their end" (v. 17). A revelation in the temple renews the psalmist's conviction of leading a life of integrity *before God* (or "near God" [v. 28]) despite present evidence to the contrary.

Perhaps the most evocative metaphor of the human self is the image of the tree in the psalm that opens the Psalter. The righteous one is "like a tree transplanted by channels of water, which yields its fruit in due season, and its leaves do not wither" (1:3a, my trans.). An image borrowed from *asherah* worship, the transplanted tree is rich in religious connotations. In Ps. 1, however, the tree metaphorically designates the righteous human being, rather than a goddess (cf. 52:8; 92:12–13). Transplanted by God, the tree designates the one who takes "delight" in God's *torah* (law or instruction; v. 2a). The one who abides by *torah* is thus secure and efficacious in all her activity. The "tree" is "blessed"

(*ashre*), destined to flourish. The wicked, by contrast, are mere "chaff" blown hither and yon by the wind (v. 4).

When compared with the lament psalms, the didactic (and particularly torah) psalms teach that the matter of salvation is not simply a matter of being saved *from* something, such as calamity or sin, but also that of being saved *for* God. Such psalms claim that human beings belong to God and thereby remain accountable to God through obedience. Put colloquially, "we are not our own"; we are God's, suited for God's glory (cf. 100:3). The God of saving freedom, the God of the exodus, is also the God who gives form to freedom by fitting freedom for the service of God. In the didactic psalms, human beings are called to responsible participation in God's world.

God. From the vantage point of the psalms of instruction, God is cast as guide or teacher. "Graciously teach me your law" is the repeated request in 119:29b (see also vv. 27, 33, 35); "You guide me with your counsel" (73:24a). Consonant with God's pedagogical role is that of judge:

> [God] calls to the heavens above and
> to the earth,
> that he may judge his people. . . .
> The heavens declare his righteousness,
> for God himself is judge
>
> 50:4, 6

As judge, God is the author of justice. Psalm 82 elevates justice as the ultimate criterion of divine power. Within the heavenly council, Israel's God judges the other gods as slackers in implementing justice for the "lowly and the destitute" (v. 3). Consequently, God sentences the other gods to death for their lack of zeal for justice (vv. 6–7).

God's justice, however, does not necessarily involve direct intervention. In an acrostic psalm, the demise of the wicked is cast not as the result of divine intervention but as self-inflicted consequence (37:14–15). Here the wicked are caught in their own devices; their weapons are turned against them. As guarantor of the created order, God has established the world such that the exercise of wickedness becomes ultimately self-defeating (see also 7:12–16).

Related to God the pedagogue and judge is God the lawgiver. As an object of desire and source of delight for the psalmist (1:2; 19:10), the "*torah* of the LORD" is the compendium of authoritative guidance necessary for the community's life and order. "Law" is a gift for the sake of human flourishing, but is by no means the property of any human being or community. The "law" is preeminently God's "law"; it is neither the prerogative of the king nor the product of the community. For the psalmist, the "law" is revelatory; it comes from God's very "mouth" (119:72), like royal decrees, and is established in perpetuity (vv. 153, 160). (The psalms make scarce mention of *mediated* law, as for example by Moses [103:7].) God's *torah* reveals the just and sovereign God. As the direct discourse of the creator, the "law" has a cosmic reach. Psalm 19 relates *torah* to the cosmic manifestation of divine glory, symbolized by the sun, to underline the law's perspicuity: "law" confers wisdom, joy, renewal, enlightenment, and, through God's mercy, purification from sin (vv. 7–9, 12–13). *Torah* is also a medium of salvation. Psalm 119 connects God's "word" or decree (v. 114b) and God's "salvation" (vv. 81a, 166a) as a common object of hope and subject of judgment (vv. 155, 165–166). The psalmist renders the "law" such that it is not confined to its historical manifestation at a particular mountain (Sinai or Horeb) at an appointed time in the wilderness (Exod. 19–Num. 10:10) through the mediation of a human individual. Rather, creation itself bears witness to the divine ordinances (Ps. 19). "The LORD exists forever; your word is firmly fixed in heaven" (119:89). In these psalms, "law" is made transcendentally cosmic.

God's activity in history, which several psalms recount (78, 105, 106, 135, 136), complements God's cosmic commandments. Psalm 78 presents a sweep-

ing narrative of God's mighty acts in order to "teach" the next generation of God's wonderful works (vv. 1–8). In all these psalms, the event of the exodus, complete with various plagues, receives primary attention, but also recounted are God's guidance and provision in the wilderness as well as the gift of the land ("heritage"). As the commandments reveal God's righteousness, so God's acts in history indicate divine forbearance amid a recalcitrant people. Israel's persistent disobedience is matched by God's persistent reticence to disavow Israel. In the face of intractable stubbornness, God exercises restraint and acts with compassion and forgiveness (78:38), while remaining aggrieved over Israel's penchant for putting God to the test (v. 40). In the face of Israel's repeated rebellions,

> Nevertheless, [God] regarded
>   their distress
>   when he heard their cry.
> For their sake he remembered
>   his covenant,
>   and showed compassion
>   according to the abundance
>   of his *hesed*.
> 106:44–45

Highlighted in the recounting of God's marvelous works are God's beneficence and forbearance. Israel is called upon to remember God's mighty acts in history as reflecting God's very character.

Psalms of Praise

As the hymns of praise mark the culmination of the Psalter as a whole (see 146–150), they also offer the culmination of ancient Israel's understanding of God and God's way in the world. As the thanksgiving and didactic psalms mark a further step in Israel's theological work, the extended hymns of praise provide the most panoramic view of God, humanity, and the world.

Human self. In the psalms of praise (and elsewhere), dependency and dignity mark the human condition. However, the language of self-abasement, as found in the laments, is lacking entirely. In its place is a self-abandoning exuberance that focuses resolutely on God yet discovers the proper identity of the human self. Psalm 8, for example, stands out for its high view of humankind. Before God's sovereign status and the vastness of the universe, the psalmist asks plaintively, "What are human beings that you are mindful of them, mortals that you care for them?" (v. 4). Whereas one may expect a negative answer such as one given in response to a similar question in Ps. 144, a royal lament (see v. 4), Ps. 8 invests humanity with elevated status, indeed royal nobility: "You have made them a little lower than the gods, and crowned them with glory and honor" (8:5). The statement resonates with Gen. 1, which describes human beings, male and female, created in God's "image" (1:27), itself an endowment of royal, as well as cultic, identity. Psalm 115, a psalm featuring both proclamation and praise, espouses a similarly high view of humanity: "The heavens are the LORD's heavens, but the earth he has given to human beings" (v. 16). It is humanity's God-given vocation to exercise "dominion" over earthly creation, particularly over the animals (8:6–8), by utilizing and maintaining creation's resources.

The endowment of royal dignity to *all* human beings, as claimed in Ps. 8, opens up the various royal psalms in the Psalter for *general* appropriation. For example, the prescription of proper royal conduct in Ps. 72 is thereby not limited to individual kings but applies to every person; all are called upon to lead lives of justice. The empowering bond between God and God's son that legitimizes the Israelite king's dominion in Ps. 2:7 is now, through the universal claims of Ps. 8, the warrant for every human being.

While certain psalms highlight the dignity and wondrous capacities with which human beings are endowed, several psalms of praise, like the laments, acknowledge humanity's dependence upon the Divine. The "strength" that human beings enjoy and exercise comes entirely from God (46:1; 68:35; 81:1). All forms of sustenance and blessing have God as their source. Dependence upon God is, the praise psalms stress, a feature endemic not just of humankind but of all creation (104:27–28). Most evocative is the reference in Ps. 84 to God's abode as home also for human beings and animals alike (vv. 1–4). God provides a home for swallows as well as for persons, a home that is also God's, the locus of praise (see also 23:6; 68:4).

Dependence on God is nowhere lamented but everywhere celebrated in the praise psalms. As dependence is a feature that pervades all creation, so the capacity to praise the source of all life has universal scope. The range of praise in the psalms is nothing short of cosmic: "All the earth worships you; they sing praises to you, sing praises to your name" (66:4). From babbling infants (8:2) to raging seas (69:34; 96:11; 98:7) and fruit trees (148:9), all creation is called upon to render praise to the Creator. Even the formidable Leviathan is transformed into God's partner in play (104:26). In a similar vein, Ps. 148 provides a roll call of cosmic participants in praise that begins with the citizens of heaven, including the celestial spheres (vv. 1–4), and descends to the denizens of the earth, beckoning "sea monsters," meteorological elements, the terrain, and "wild animals" to render praise (vv. 7–10). Finally, all human beings, regardless of social, gender, and age status, are enlisted (vv. 11–12). The call issued by the speaker of Ps. 148 for all creation to give praise fulfills the call for human beings to exercise dominion over creation given in 8:6 (cf. Gen. 1:28). Human dominion over creation is fundamentally an enabling of all creation to give full, unfettered praise to God.

Compared to Ps. 8, the great creation psalm of Ps. 104 decenters humanity's place in God's cosmic world of praise (cf. Job 38–42). In this extensive litany of God's creative acts, human beings are scarcely mentioned; they are distinguished from the lions (who prowl at night) only in that they take the day shift in their work (vv. 20–23). Plants are available for both cattle and people, though wine and bread, as processed foods, are designated for human use and enjoyment (v. 14).

In praise that is universally performed, universal peace is the end result. The psalms of praise envision a world stripped of conflict (46:9–10) and set for cosmic harmony. Even the "kings of the earth," perhaps the most reluctant to render praise to God, cannot escape the expanding, "edgeless" circle of praise that proceeds to envelop the cosmos. The command "let everything that breathes praise the LORD" concludes the Psalter (150:6). Such cosmic praise is directed toward the God who created the cosmos as an interdependent, variegated whole, a world in which human beings play a significant role but are not alone. In the performance of praise, human beings and animals, mountains and cedars, seas and rocks, all find a level playing field.

God.   The language of praise, varied as it is in the Psalms, shares the common context and purpose of worship. Not so much the response to specific acts of salvation, as in the thanksgiving psalms, the praise psalms rhetorically aim to demonstrate that God alone is worthy of worship. This God is supremely "exalted in the earth" (46:10), enthroned as sovereign of the universe (47:8–9). Indeed, one can speak of a credo of praise: "Great is God and greatly to be praised" (48:1; cf. 89:7; 95:3; 104:1), and the profile of God's greatness bears unmistakably royal contours (e.g., 95:3; 96:4). As king, God is sovereign of the cosmos who elicits praise from all the earth. Praise is not just a response; it is in many praise psalms a command.

Praise of God also bears a polemical edge: it counters the attraction of idolatry. After a litany of God's wondrous deeds in creation and history, from the exodus to the conquest, Ps. 135 concludes with a warning about idols, the manufactured images of other deities (135:15–18; cf. 115:2–8). In comparison to God's power,

idols are lifeless; only God is worthy of worship and trust: "Praise the LORD! . . . Do not put your trust in princes, in mortals, in whom there is no help" (146:1, 3).

In comparison to the thanksgiving psalms, references to divine activity in the praise psalms are cast more as attributes than as historically specific actions.

> Happy are those whose help is the God of Jacob,
>> whose hope is in the LORD their God,
> who *made* heaven and earth,
> the sea, and all that is in them;
> who *keeps* faith forever;
>> who *executes* justice for the oppressed;
>> who *gives* food to the hungry.
> The LORD *sets* the prisoners *free*;
>> the LORD *opens* the eyes of the blind.
> The LORD *lifts up* those who
>   are bowed down;
>> the LORD *loves* the righteous.
> The LORD *watches over* the strangers;
>> he *upholds* the orphan and the widow.
>   146:5–9a

Each clause in the psalm that highlights God's work is signaled by a participle in Hebrew that could be translated as a substantive (e.g., "is creator of," "keeper," "executor," "provider," "upholder"). In the genre of praise, God's creative activity in particular is cast participially, suggesting *ongoing* action on the part of God (e.g., 104:2–10, 13, 14; cf. 148:2–4, 11, 19). Discrete activities, in other words, are cast as divine patterns of behavior, indeed as role categories: creator, healer, judge, provider, delighter, lawgiver. In short, specific acts in history and creation are generalized in the praise psalms as characteristic modes of divine conduct.

It is in the praise genre that God's incomparable status is particularly highlighted: "For I know that the LORD is great; our LORD is above all gods" (135:5); "Who is like the LORD our God, who is seated on high?" (113:5). The psalmist then proceeds to articulate God's freedom of action in creation: "Whatever the LORD pleases he does, in heaven and on earth, in the seas and all deeps" (135:6). This God is not bound, covenantally or otherwise, to anything. God's concern for creation arises out of sheer freedom and delight (see also 104:31b).

The praise psalms come closest to articulating a divine *essence*. As for the divine nature itself, God's "glory" (*kabod*, literally, "weight") comes to the fore. Psalm 29 focuses almost exclusively on this divine attribute:

> Ascribe to the LORD, O heavenly beings;
>> ascribe to the LORD *glory* and strength.
> Ascribe to the LORD the *glory*
>> of his name;
> worship the LORD in holy splendor.
> The voice of the LORD is over the waters;
>> the God of *glory* thunders,
>> the LORD, over mighty waters. . . .
> The voice of the LORD causes the oaks
>> to whirl,
> and strips the forest bare;
> and in his temple all say, "*Glory!*"
>> 29:1–3, 9

The psalm dramatically illustrates God's presence made manifest in the form of nature-disturbing, preternatural power. Attested both visually and audibly, God's "glory" is as much a matter of divine substance as it is a quality acknowledged about God, a property conferred upon the Deity by the worshiping community ("ascribe," "say"; cf. 68:34a). Elsewhere, "glory" is described as an effulgence of light that conveys an overwhelming sense of "majesty" and "splendor" (21:5; 45:3; cf. 104:1b–2a, 31), as well as "power" and "strength" (63:2; 96:7). As in Ps. 29, God's visual manifestation in glory is associated with the temple or tabernacle (see Exod. 40:34; Num. 20:6; Pss. 24:7–10; 26:8; 78:60–61; 96:8). God's "glory" trumps all alternative forms of worship as idolatrous (97:6–7). Originating from "above the heavens" (8:1; 113:4), divine "glory" is a powerful, definitive sign of God's indwelling and inbreaking presence, destined to fill the earth (72:19; 85:9).

Consistent with such emphasis on God's "glory," the language of theophany is prominent in the praise psalms. God's inbreaking presence triggers cosmic convulsions: "Tremble, O earth, at the presence of the LORD" (114:7a; see also 68:7–10; 104:31–32). God's glory renders

impotent all forms of conflict, both human and cosmic (46:9; 76:3). Before God's presence, no element of creation remains intractable. In praise (as opposed to lament), earthly resistance is either erased or transformed into agents of play or praise. Leviathan is now God's playmate (104:26), and the "sea monsters" roar in praise (148:7).

It is in praise that God's transcendence is palpably real yet lies beyond apprehension. Psalm 68, for example, speaks of God as the "rider in the heavens" (v. 33; cf. v. 4) yet also as "father of orphans and protector of widows" (v. 5). God's greatness is ineffable or "unsearchable" (145:3), yet God's hand is "open" to satisfy "the desire of every living thing" (145:16). In the praise psalms, God's transcendent power and providential immanence are held not in tension but in balanced correspondence.

The praise psalms, with their glorious vision of a world united in praise, conclude the Psalms and indicate the Psalter's goal. The ravages of conflict and dis-ease so vividly conveyed in lament have faded away. In the Psalter's overall arrangement, lament makes way for praise, conflict is displaced by peace, enemies fade away, and shalom reigns. For the psalmists, praise of God—the outcome of lament—is the vehicle for such a vision.

The Theological Challenge of the Vengeance Psalms

Perhaps the greatest challenge of the Psalter for readers today is found in the so-called psalms of enmity, a special case of the lament psalms, in which vengeance against enemies is invoked (e.g., Pss. 12, 44, 55, 58, 83, 109, 137, 139). The best-known example is the lament of Ps. 137, which begins with the poignant lyric:

> By the rivers of Babylon—
>> there we sat down and there we wept
>> when we remembered Zion.
>>> v. 1

Yet the psalm concludes with the anger-charged stanza:

Remember, O LORD, against the Edomites,
   the day of Jerusalem's fall,
how they said, "Tear it down! Tear
   it down!
Down to its foundations!"
O daughter Babylon, you devastator!
   Happy shall they be who pay
   you back what you have done to us!
Happy shall be the one who takes
   your little ones
and dash them against the rock!
                                        vv. 7–9

In their brutal honesty, these psalms of vengeance articulate intense feelings of anger and betrayal. For readers who have suffered injustice and abuse, the psalms provide not only an outlet for their outrage but a way of naming the injustices. These most bitter laments do more than simply vent; they redirect (self-)destructive anger to God, transforming lust for vengeance into yearning for justice. In this way, "human wrath" gives way ultimately to "praise" (76:10a). The psalmists do not typically ask for the means to take matters into their own hands. Indeed, they speak from a condition of abject powerlessness. Rather, they invoke the one who is the source of all power by placing their petition squarely upon God's shoulders.

The imprecation psalms articulate a cry from the depths, a cry for justice in the face of human atrocity. Psalm 137 is not so much a call to infanticide as a call for God's judgment to restore a defeated and demoralized people, a judgment that necessarily involves the collapse of hegemonic rule. The anguished cry of Ps. 137 gives voice to the suffering of many colonized peoples in recent history. Being uprooted and forced into servitude is not an experience alien to our modern world. The psalmist of antiquity speaks on behalf of today's refugee, political prisoner, or victim of marital abuse (see Ps. 55). The pray-er has no other means except to beseech God in the fervent hope that the imbalance of power and his or her well-being will be rectified. For many modern readers, particularly those of first world nations, the psalms do not invite prayerful appropriation. Rather, they demand a hearing, for they give voice to the oppressed other, the one crushed by an affliction of which the world's power brokers are knowingly or unknowingly culpable.

Bibliography

Anderson, Bernhard W., with Steven Bishop. *Out of the Depths: The Psalms Speak for Us Today*. 3rd ed. Louisville: Westminster John Knox, 2000.

Brown, William P. *Seeing the Psalms: A Theology of Metaphor*. Louisville: Westminster John Knox, 2002.

Brueggemann, Walter. *The Psalms and the Life of Faith*, edited by Patrick D. Miller. Minneapolis: Fortress, 1995.

Kraus, Hans-Joachim. *Theology of the Psalms*. Translated by Keith Crim. Continental Commentary. Minneapolis: Augsburg, 1986.

Mays, James L. *Psalms*. Interpretation. Louisville: John Knox, 1994.

Miller, Patrick D. *Interpreting the Psalms*. Philadelphia: Fortress, 1986.

Proverbs

Harold C. Washington

INTRODUCTION

Proverbs is a book of keen observation, moral instruction, and theological reflection. Its central premise is that wisdom—human intelligence, exercised with humility, trained in traditional teachings, and shaped by piety—can be a reliable guide to living life well and faithfully. The book has a cosmopolitan quality, showing close affinities in form and content to ancient Egyptian and Mesopotamian wisdom texts, perhaps also some contact with Greek philosophy. But Proverbs grounds its teachings in reverence toward the biblical God of Israel; the motto of the book is: "the fear of the LORD is the beginning of wisdom" (9:10; cf. 1:7; 15:33).

Apart from brief editorial headings, the book is poetry, including extended passages of instruction in second-person address, shorter speeches and poems, and two-line wisdom sayings ("proverbs" proper). Instruction appears in chaps. 1–9; 22:17–24:34; and 30–31, forming an interpretive frame for the collections of wisdom sayings that make up the intervening chapters. The short biblical proverbs create a kaleidoscopic view of the natural, social, and religious realms. Individual proverbs achieve an immediately arresting clarity with very few words, yet they richly repay closer examination and reinterpretation in light of other sayings in the book.

Traditional association with Solomon's renowned wisdom gave authority to the collection (1:1; 10:1; 25:1; cf. 1 Kgs. 4:29–34). Some of the material in Proverbs might date to the Solomonic era (tenth century BCE), but the book in its present form likely dates to the Persian or early Hellenistic period (fifth-fourth centuries BCE). The editorial headings indicate that Proverbs is a composite work of multiple authors and editors (22:17a; 24:23; 25:1; 30:1; 31:1). Ultimately Proverbs derives from countless unnamed sages across the span of ancient Israelite history, from diverse contexts including the royal court, intellectual circles of the urban elite, and the folk wisdom settings of ancient Israelite villages and families.

In biblical antiquity the primary audience of Proverbs appears to have been young Judean men preparing for adult responsibilities. Without exception the book reflects a patriarchal society and an androcentric literary perspective. The basic form of instruction is from father to son. Finding a "good wife" is a key concern (e.g., 12:4; 31:10–31), and warnings against "dangerous" women are frequent. There are, however, some mitigating factors, such as the recognition that mothers, like fathers, also teach wisdom (1:8; 6:20; 23:22; 31:1, 26), the awe-inspiring feminine personification of divine Wisdom in chaps. 1–9, and the strong characterization of the "woman of worth" in 31:10–31.

The religious world of Proverbs differs from most of the Hebrew Bible in its lack of attention to major themes such as the exodus-Sinai tradition, the Davidic monarchy, and temple worship. This does not mean that the sages reject these traditions, only that their emphases fall elsewhere. Wisdom is received not from divine revelation but from the tradition of the elders and experience. Rather than viewing God as Israel's redeemer and covenant partner, Proverbs centers upon God as creator of the world and humanity, and as guarantor of a moral order that structures both the cosmos and human society. For the sages, observation of the world reveals the benefit of being in harmony with this divine order and the detriment of violating it. At times this appears as an immediate, cause-and-effect relationship between acts and their consequences: "Whoever digs a pit will fall into it, and a stone will come back on the one who starts it rolling" (26:27). In other cases it is a matter of divine retribution: "All those who are arrogant are an abomination to the LORD; be assured, they will not go unpunished" (16:5). The act-consequence and retribution doctrines alike insist that human choices matter, and that wisdom means learning to live in accord with the moral order of the world.

A person's character is formed as moral choices become habits on the way from youth into maturity. Proverbs describes this with the metaphor of the "way" or "path," a leitmotif of the book (e.g., 4:10–27). Well-worn paths become fixed, and the further one goes down a certain path, the harder it is to revert to another. Persons, therefore, can be categorized by the paths they choose: the way of the wise and righteous, or the way of the foolish and wicked. The former is characterized by qualities such as honesty, diligence, insight, trustworthiness, self-restraint, prudent speech, concern for the poor, generosity, and avoidance of strife; the latter by deception, indolence, thoughtlessness, inconstancy, self-indulgence, rash speech, injustice, stinginess, and violence. The path of wisdom and righteousness leads to well-being and longevity; the way of folly and wickedness, to disgrace and destruction.

This stark dichotomy would be inadequate to the ambiguities of human experience if applied simplistically. Proverbs, however, recognizes that things are not always what they seem (17:28), and sayings are beneficial only if applied with insight (26:7, 9). Some proverbs appear to contradict each other (e.g., 26:4–5), and many are in tension with other sayings in the book. The proverbs therefore are context-sensitive, within the book and in their relevance to life; they have multiple possibilities of meaning and are not to be applied mechanically. Although religious and ethical norms emerge clearly in Proverbs, the book does not dictate moralistic rules. It offers instead exercises in judicious reading, and in living; it invites the reader into a lifelong discipline of intellectual and moral discernment.

COMMENTARY

Introduction to the Book (1:1–9:18)

These opening chapters are an extended invitation to the pursuit of wisdom, providing a frame of reference for understanding the diverse materials to follow in chaps. 10–31. Most of this material belongs to the instruction genre, following a threefold pattern of (1) introduction, addressing the student as "my child" (e.g., 1:8; literally, "my son"), exhorting him to heed the instruction; (2) teaching proper, urging the student to abide by sapiential values; and (3) concluding summary, sometimes with an illustrative saying. Eleven instructions (1:8–19; 2:1–22; 3:1–12, 21–35; 4:1–9, 10–19, 20–27; 5:1–23; 6:1–19; 6:20–35; 7:1–27) are complemented by four poetic interludes, including three addresses by the personified figure of Woman Wisdom (1:20–33; 3:13–20; 8:1–36; 9:1–18).

Prologue (1:1–7). The title (v. 1) places the entire collection under the authority of King Solomon's fabled wisdom. Next a purpose statement for the book emphasizes the demanding educational process of instruction, or better, "discipline," without which there is no approach to wisdom (vv. 2, 3, 7). This discipline inclines the student not toward personal advantage but to righteousness, justice, and equity. It is a long-term endeavor, commended to the young and simple, and also to the wise (cf. 9:9). Verse 7 states the guiding perspective of the whole book: "fear of the LORD is the beginning of knowledge." "Fear of the LORD" might involve fright at the prospect of divine retribution, but as a mature form of piety it entails reverential awe and trust in God. It results in ethical living and abiding openness to learning and correction.

Instruction: The violent way of the wicked (1:8–19). The first instruction, cast as parental teaching (of father and mother, v. 8), presents the negative example of murderous criminals motivated by greed. In their own words these wicked persons align themselves with the forces of death (Sheol and the Pit, v. 12). They do not realize, however, that their violent plots will bring about their own demise. Verse 17 is a traditional proverb that can apply here to the young student: just as a bird that sees a trap will fly away, so the youth should flee the enticements of the wicked. It can also apply to the criminals, who set their trap in vain as they are only ensnaring themselves. This instruction offers a contrast to a life based in wisdom and fear of the Lord.

Interlude: Wisdom's call (1:20–33). In the first of three addresses (cf. 8:1–36; 9:1–18), Woman Wisdom cries out like a prophet, threatening dire consequences for those who ignore her call. Her address is public (vv. 20–21), not esoteric; and she is

manifest as a vividly realized person, not an abstract concept. She calls to the "simple" (cf. 1:4), callow youths who should be teachable, but are already headed in a bad direction; and to arrogant "scoffers" and incorrigible "fools," whose character is detailed in chaps. 10–29. Wisdom does not threaten punishment, she simply assumes that those who reject her will meet grim ends. As in vv. 8–19, life and death are at stake (vv. 32–33).

Instruction: Wisdom's path (2:1–22). This carefully fashioned poem is a single sentence in Hebrew, arranged in 22 lines according to the number of letters in the Hebrew alphabet. It urges the student to cry out for wisdom (v. 3), echoing Woman Wisdom's call in 1:20–21. Those who seek wisdom ardently, like treasure, will receive it as a gift from the Lord (vv. 3–11). Keeping to wisdom's path, they will be safe from the ways of evil men (vv. 12–15) and dangerous women (vv. 16–19). The "loose woman" or "adulteress" (so NRSV, v. 16), is literally a "strange" or "alien" woman. She looms large in chaps. 1–9 (cf. 5:1–23; 6:20–35; 7:1–27), a negative counterpart to Woman Wisdom.

Instruction: Wisdom and piety (3:1–12). Wisdom and fear of the Lord are inseparably bound in this instruction. In language reminiscent of Deuteronomy (especially chaps. 5–9), the student is enjoined to learn the teaching and commandments by heart (Prov. 3:1; cf. Deut 6:6; cf. also Prov. 3:3 and Deut. 6:8–9); to trust God entirely (Prov. 3:5; cf. Deut. 6:4); and to submit to divine discipline (Prov. 3:11–12; cf. Deut. 8:5). Verses 9–10 contain the only direct instruction in Proverbs concerning liturgical offerings ("firstfruits"; cf. Deut. 26:1–11; Exod. 23:19).

Interlude: In praise of Wisdom (3:13–20). Woman Wisdom is more prized than riches or treasure (vv. 14–15; cf. 8:11). Like the Egyptian goddess of truth and justice, Maat, she is portrayed with long life in one hand, wealth and dignity in the other (v. 16). She is figured as a tree of life, a widespread ancient Near Eastern symbol of longevity and well-being (Gen. 2:9; 3:22); and she is instrumental in God's creation of the world (Prov. 3:19–20; cf. 8:22–31).

Instruction: Wisdom in community (3:21–35). Verses 21–26 describe the genuine confidence that results from holding fast to wise teaching. This sense of security, however, does not allow for self-absorption. Wise living entails kindness and fairness to others (vv. 27–35).

Instruction: Get Wisdom and love her (4:1–9). A father instructs sons to love Wisdom and embrace her as if she were a cherished wife (vv. 6, 8; cf. 5:15–20; 7:4). This ardent love language is designed to capture the imagination of young adult males.

Instruction: The two ways (4:10–19). The figure of contrasting ways, or paths, in life is central to chaps. 1–9 (1:15–16; 2:8–9, 12–15, 18–20; 3:6, 17, 23; 5:5–8, 21; 7:25; 8:13, 20, 32; 9:6); and is important through the rest of the book (10:9; 11:5; 16:17; 20:24; 28:6; 31:3). The present instruction is the most sustained presentation of this motif: the way of wisdom (vv. 11–13) versus the way of the wicked (vv. 14–17). The former leads to life and the latter to death, symbolized here by the contrast of light and dark (vv. 18–19).

Instruction: The straight path (4:20–27). This instruction complements the preceding by urging the student to keep on the straight path. Several parts of the body are mentioned, organs of perception and expression: ear, eyes, heart ("mind"), mouth, and feet.

Instruction: The strange woman (5:1–23). Again the young man is warned against the "strange" or "alien" woman (vv. 3, 20; NRSV "loose woman," "adulteress"), whose identity is unclear. Is she "strange" because she is another man's wife, or a prostitute? Is she "alien" in an ethnic, cultural, or religious sense?

Likely she represents illicit sexual liaisons of various sorts, dangerous diversions from the pursuit of wisdom and from exclusive intimacy with a lawful wife (vv. 15–20).

Instruction: Right conduct (6:1–19). Four lessons in prudent behavior: against standing surety for the debts of others (vv. 1–5), against laziness (vv. 6–11), examples of disreputable characters (vv. 12–15), and a numerical saying about seven vices (vv. 16–19; cf. 30:18–31). Reference to eyes, mouth, hands, feet, and heart corresponds negatively to the bodily language of rectitude in 4:20–27.

Instruction: More dangerous liaisons (6:20–35). The focus is on adultery. Although the prostitute is mentioned (v. 26), her cost is trivial compared to the disastrous consequences of adultery, including the ruthless revenge of the husband (vv. 34–35).

Instruction: The strange woman is lethal (7:1–27). Apprehension about the strange woman intensifies with the chilling narrative of a young man's fatal seduction. The teacher/narrator observes a street scene through a latticed window, typically a woman's circumstance (Judg. 5:28; 2 Sam. 6:16; 2 Kgs. 9:30), raising the possibility that a mother gives this instruction. The predatory woman may be a prostitute (she is dressed like one, Prov. 7:10), yet her proposition is also adulterous (vv. 19–20). With promises of luxury and sexual delight, she draws the youth in like a witless beast to the slaughter. The text portrays her as an archetypal deadly temptress competing with Woman Wisdom's life-giving appeal.

Interlude: Wisdom praises herself (8:1–36). Wisdom cries out in the streets again, this time more in promise than judgment (cf. 1:20–33). Her teaching is more precious than riches and jewels, by her authority kings rule, and she secures the path of righteousness and justice. Woman Wisdom returns to the theme of creation (cf. 3:19–20), praising herself not quite as a goddess, but clearly as one who was with the Lord at the creation of the world, beside God "like a master worker" (v. 30, another possibility is "like a little child"), rejoicing in the world and humanity. She concludes with a call to life rather than death.

Interlude: Two invitations (9:1–18). Woman Wisdom invites the simple to a banquet (vv. 1–6), but the "foolish woman," like the strange woman of earlier chapters, makes a competing appeal (vv. 13–18). Surrounding the book's motto, "the fear of the LORD is the beginning of wisdom" (v. 10; cf. 1:7), are sayings contrasting scoffers and the wise. The seven pillars of Wisdom's house may allude to the pillars on which the earth was founded (v. 1; cf. Ps. 75:3; 1 Sam. 2:8; Job 9:6), evoking Wisdom's cosmic stature in Prov. 8:22–31. The foolish woman's mention of stolen water and bread likely evokes illicit sex (v. 17), enticing gullible young men away from Wisdom's life-giving path.

The Proverbs of Solomon (10:1–22:16). This section comprises two subcollections, 10:1–15:33 and 16:1–22:16. These, along with 25:1–29:27, assemble self-contained, two-line traditional sayings without an overarching literary structure, though there are some meaningful patterns. Chapters 10–15 contain mostly antithetical sayings; 16:1–22:16 is more varied in form. A concentration of proverbs mentioning "the LORD" occurs in 15:33–16:9; and clusters of royal proverbs appear in 16:10–15 and 25:1–7. Smaller groups or pairs of proverbs are sometimes linked by catchwords or theme. Each saying can be taken on its own terms, but also in relation to the surrounding material.

The antithetical collection (10:1–15:33).
10:1–32. The first saying carries forward the parental instruction theme of chaps. 1–9. Thereafter the righteous and the wicked are contrasted, with special attention to their use of speech (vv. 6, 11, 13, 14, 18, 19, 20, 21, 31, 32). Verse 15 is a neutral observation about wealth and poverty; v. 16 adds ethical comment on ill-gotten gain.

11:1–31. Prominent in this chapter is the language of commerce, recompense, gain, and loss. The sayings condemn dishonest and exploitative trade (vv. 1, 26), warn against standing surety for others' debts (v. 15; cf. 6:1–5), yet commend generosity (vv. 24–25). They deem the protection of wealth illusory (vv. 4, 28; cf. 10:15), the wages of the wicked false, and the recompense of the righteous true (vv. 18, 31). One who mistreats a household inherits only wind (v. 29). The startling image of a gold ring in a pig's snout ridicules superficial valuing of women's beauty (v. 22).

12:1–28. This chapter emphasizes antithetical sayings opposing the righteous to the wicked, the wise to the foolish, the diligent to the lazy, and beneficial words to harmful speech. There is concern for finding a "good wife" (v. 4; cf. 18:22; 19:13–14; 31:10–31). Elsewhere generosity and kindness to the poor are urged (e.g., 14:31; 19:17); in v. 10 the concern is kindness to animals (cf. 27:23; Deut. 22:6–7; 25:4).

13:1–25. Chapter 13 upholds the simple view that the righteous are blessed and the wicked suffer (vv. 6, 9, 25), but the rich and poor are here observed with more nuance. Verses 7–8 highlight the ambiguities of wealth and poverty, v. 8 observing ironically that the poor are not threatened as are the rich. Ill-gotten gain does not last (v. 11); sinners fail to bequeath their wealth (v. 22); and injustice can deprive the poor even of their own crops (v. 23). Verse 24 reflects that education and child rearing in antiquity involved physical punishment (cf. 22:15; 23:13–14; 26:3; 29:15, 17). The sages, however, generally counsel restraint; they caution against anger and oppose cruelty, even against animals (12:10). Verse 24b, moreover, emphasizes parental love. This saying should not be taken as license for corporal punishment of children.

14:1–35. In contrast to the preceding chapter, where there is no mention of God, three sayings here uphold the fear of the Lord (vv. 2, 26–27; cf. 15:33–16:9). Here too appear the first proverbs on kingship, which will multiply in later chapters (vv. 28, 35). Verses 20–21 are a proverb pair: v. 20 observes a social reality; v. 21 judges it ethically (cf. v. 31; 17:5; 19:4–7; 21:13; 22:2). Verses 10, 13, and 30 are noteworthy for their psychological insight (cf. 12:25; 13:12; 15:13, 30; 17:22; 18:14; 25:20).

15:1–33. Clemency in speech and moderation of anger are emphasized here (vv. 1, 4, 18, 26b, 28), also sincerity in worship (vv. 8, 29; cf. 21:3, 27). God's all-knowing sovereignty is vividly described (vv. 3, 11). The "better" saying (vv. 16–17) provokes insight through paradox (12:9; 16:8, 19, 32; 17:1, 12; 19:1, 22; 21:9, 19; 22:1; 25:24; 27:5, 10c; 28:6). Verses 16–17 overturn the assumption that luxury is desirable: better is modest means with harmony and piety. This subcollection ends with the book's central affirmation of "fear of the Lord," here combined with humility (v. 33; cf. 1:7; 9:10).

The royal collection (16:1–22:16).
16:1–33. A large number of proverbs here invoke the Lord (vv. 1–7, 9, 11, 20, 33), and several mention kings (vv. 10, 12, 13, 14, 15). The royal proverbs clearly refer to earthly rulers, but together with the "Lord" sayings they also bring to mind the divine Sovereign. It is likely by design that this cluster of theological sayings in chap. 16, also including 15:33, is placed at the center of the book (the exact midpoint by verse count is 16:17), implying that theological concerns are at the center of Proverbs' worldview. The virtues of humility, beneficial speech, and peacefulness also receive emphasis (vv. 5, 13, 18–19, 21, 23–24, 27–28, 32).

17:1–28. This chapter departs conspicuously from the antithetical pattern of chaps. 10–15. A blunt observation about the efficacy of bribes in v. 8 is qualified by the ethical judgment of v. 23. A rhetorical question spotlights the futility of fools'

attempts to acquire wisdom (v. 16). A proverb pair on the ambiguity of silence nuances the usual teaching on refraining from speech (vv. 27–28). An especially rich portrait of fools and their folly appears in these sayings (vv. 7, 10, 12, 16, 21, 24, 25, 28).

18:1–24. The peril and promise of language is a prominent theme here. The metaphor of speech as "deep waters" in v. 4 is ambiguous: words can be profound and life-giving, or dangerous (cf. v. 21). Beneficial words are described in v. 20 (cf. 12:14a; 13:2a). Negative examples include the speech of fools, who speak out of self-conceit, too quickly, and with ruinous results (vv. 2, 6–7, 13); also gossips and the arrogant wealthy, who harm others with their words (vv. 8, 23). Verses 10–11 are a proverb pair: the name of the Lord provides genuine security, while confidence in the protection of wealth may be illusory.

19:1–29. An impressive range of views concerning the rich and the poor appears in this chapter. Some sayings could be taken to reflect the class conceit of the rich and powerful (vv. 10, 14a), or to hold poor persons responsible for their plight (vv. 15, 24). Others observe realistically, perhaps compassionately, the social disadvantage of the poor (vv. 4, 6–7), or contend that poverty is not intrinsically shameful (vv. 1, 22). All these should be read in concert with the commendation of kindness to the poor in v. 17. Other topics are false witness (vv. 5, 9) and family life, where once again the young man's concern in finding a good wife is evident (vv. 13–14, 18, 26).

20:1–30. Several familiar themes reappear here, such as the consequence of laziness (v. 4), respect for parents (v. 20), and the liabilities of surety obligations (v. 16). Sayings describing the power, discernment, and justice of kings (vv. 2, 8, 26, 28) are interlaced with proverbs about the Lord's sovereignty (vv. 12, 22, 24, 27). Honest commerce is at issue in the condemnation of false weights (vv. 10, 23; cf. 11:1; 16:11). There is a humorous notice of the deceitful pretenses that are essential to bargaining (v. 14; cf. Sir. 26:29–27:2). A rhetorical question pointing to the ubiquity of sin sounds a distinctive note (Prov. 20:9; cf. Ps 14:2–3; 51:3–5).

21:1–31. The chapter begins and ends with acknowledgment of divine sovereignty: the motives and judgments of kings are subject to the Lord's authority (v. 1); likewise no wisdom, understanding, counsel, or preparation for war (all the purview of kings) prevails apart from the Lord's providence (vv. 30–31). The intervening sentences are replete with stock characters: the wicked (vv. 4, 7, 10, 12, 18, 26–27, 29), the scoffer (vv. 11, 24), the vexatious wife (v. 9 = 25:24; v. 19), the fool (v. 20), the lazy person (v. 25), and the false witness (v. 28). There are incisive comments on genuine worship (vv. 3, 27) and care for the poor (v. 13).

22:1–16. In this conclusion to the subsection of 16:1–22:16, the rich and the poor are again in view. Verse 7 observes plainly the domination of the poor by the rich. The description of the borrower as "slave" to the lender can be taken literally, as debt slavery was well known in ancient Israel (Exod. 21:2–6; 2 Kgs. 4:1; Neh. 5:5). Generosity to the poor is commended (Prov. 22:9), oppression is denounced (v. 16), all within the understanding that the Lord is the maker of rich and poor alike (v. 2). The lazy person is seen resorting to ridiculous excuses (v. 13); and the strange woman, familiar from chaps. 1–9, appears again in v. 14, her mouth likened to a deadly deep pit.

The Words of the Wise (22:17–24:34)

This section resembles the instruction of chaps. 1–9, with extended units of teaching addressed from parent to child (23:15, 19, 26; 24:13, 21). It is closely related to the Egyptian Instruction of Amenemope (ca. 1100 BCE). Several sayings, especially in 22:17–23:11, are Hebrew adaptations of Amenemope's teaching.

First instruction (22:17–23:11). A prologue invites the student to hear and commit the teaching to memory (22:17–21). Trust in the Lord is the aim of the instruc-

tion (22:19; cf. 23:17; 24:21; 1:7; 9:10). The teacher advocates defense of the poor, especially against theft of their land (22:22–23, 28; 23:10). Wise students will exercise caution in forming relationships, discretion in the company of powerful persons, and restraint in the pursuit of wealth, since wealth is ephemeral.

Second instruction (23:12–18). Discipline is the theme, assuming as elsewhere in Proverbs that corporal punishment is appropriate and beneficial (vv. 13–14; cf. especially 13:24). The affirmative side of discipline here entails speaking what is right and abiding in the fear of the Lord (vv. 16–17).

Third instruction (23:19–21). An admonition against drunkenness and gluttony anticipates the fuller treatment in vv. 29–35. In keeping with other sayings, the apprehension is that a dissolute lifestyle will end in poverty and shame (cf. 21:17; 28:7).

Fourth instruction 23:22–25). Noteworthy here is the emphasis on the teaching of the father and mother alike (vv. 22, 25; cf. 1:8; 6:20; 31:1, 26). The expression "buy wisdom" does not mean that it is literally for sale, but that one should energetically pursue and acquire wisdom (cf. 4:5–7; 16:16; 17:16).

Fifth instruction (23:26–24:12). The teacher takes up the warning against the prostitute and strange woman featured in chaps. 1–9 (cf. 2:16–19; 5:1–23; 6:20–35; 7:1–27). This is followed by a satirical description of the ill effects of drunkenness (vv. 29–35). In 24:1 is the second of three admonitions in this collection not to envy the wicked, presumably because of their superficial success and ill-gotten gains (cf. 23:17; 24:19). The house built by wisdom (24:3) evokes the language of 9:1 and 14:1. Even in warfare, the teacher asserts, wisdom will prevail over strength (24:5–6; cf. 20:18; 21:22). Finally the student is exhorted to come to the rescue of innocent victims of violence (24:10–12). In contrast to 1:8–19 and 24:15–16, where the student is urged to avoid the ways of violent evildoers, here the youth is told to intervene against them.

Sixth instruction (24:13–20). This is a loosely connected teaching on seeking wisdom and avoiding evil. Noteworthy is the admonition not to gloat at the downfall of enemies (vv. 17–18).

Seventh instruction (24:21–22). The concluding instruction admonishes the youth to fear both the Lord and the king, on the understanding that just kings are established by the Lord's authority (v. 21; cf. 16:10–15; 20:28; 21:1; 25:5; 29:14).

More words of the wise (24:23–34). An appendix to the previous collection, this section arranges two thematically parallel sequences of three teachings each. The first theme is the law court: vv. 23b–25 on fair judges corresponds to v. 28 on truthful witnesses. The second theme is helpful versus harmful speech: honest answers in v. 26 are in contrast to vengeful speech in v. 29. Third is labor and care for the land: a positive picture in v. 27 corresponds to the lazy person in vv. 30–34 who neglects the land. Verses 33–34 are a duplicate of 6:10–11.

More Proverbs of Solomon (25:1–29:27)

Like the first Solomonic collection, 10:1–22:16, this one contains two subsections, chaps. 25–27 and chaps. 28–29. The first section favors comparative sayings and images from the natural world; the second features mostly antithetical proverbs concerning the righteous and the wicked, the rich and poor, the king, and justice.

25:1–28. A superscript identifies this collection as the work of scribes in the time of Hezekiah, some two centuries after Solomon. Verses 2–7 address the king's power and prerogatives; vv. 7c–10 advise settling disputes out of court; and vv. 11–14 artfully examine aspects of lan-

guage. The chapter also features memorable psychological insights (vv. 20, 25). Verses 21–22 allude to an Egyptian penitential rite in which coals on the head signified contrition. The sense is that unexpected kindness to adversaries can stir their remorse, even their goodwill (cf. v. 15; 24:17–18, 29).

26:1–28. This chapter has three parts: vv. 1–12 on fools and their folly (the word "fool" occurs eleven times); vv. 13–16 on indolence (the term "lazy person" appears in every verse); and vv. 17–28, sayings on the consequences of antisocial speech and behavior. Verses 4–5 illustrate a key feature of the book of Proverbs: individual sayings make competing claims, and the discerning reader must adjudicate among them. A wise person will determine when it is best not to engage fools (v. 4; cf. 14:7; 17:12; 23:9), and when one must take them to task (v. 5; cf. 24:25; 25:12). The point is reinforced by two sayings to the effect that proverbs are useless to a person who lacks wisdom (vv. 7, 9).

27:1–27. The arrangement of sayings here is almost random, but some pairs and small groups of sayings are thematically linked. Verses 1–2 commend modesty; 3–4 describe vexatious states of mind; and 5–6 examine paradoxes of genuine versus false friendship. Verses 17–19 depict three types of reciprocity among persons. The instruction of vv. 23–27 can be read as practical advice on tending flocks, but the mention of crown and riches in v. 24, and a possible allusion to the motif of the king as shepherd (e.g., 1 Kgs. 22:17; Ps. 23:1; Isa. 44:28) may point to implicit royal advice.

28:1–28. Major topics in this chapter are the contrasts of the righteous and the wicked (vv. 1, 4–5, 10, 12, 28), the rich and the poor (vv. 6, 8, 11, 19–20, 22, 25, 27), and just and unjust rulers (vv. 2–3, 15–16). A new feature emerges in the use of the Hebrew word *torah*, which in Proverbs usually designates the sage's teaching (1:8; 3:1; 4:2; 7:2). Here the term appears to refer to the Lord's revealed law, or Torah (vv. 4, 7, 9, cf. 29:18). This is closer to the usage of Deuteronomy than that of the earlier Hebrew wisdom traditions, and may reflect a step toward the identifying of Torah and Wisdom in the literature of the Second Temple period (cf. Deut. 4:5–8; Sir. 24:23).

29:1–27. This chapter has no clear structure, but is marked as a unit by an alphabetical frame where the first and last lines begin with the first and last letters, respectively, of the Hebrew alphabet. The sayings, chiefly antithetical in form, review the earlier topics of chaps. 25–28, especially kings and rulers, righteous and wicked, wise and foolish. Some sayings partially duplicate or closely resemble earlier proverbs (cf. 29:1b and 6:15b; 29:20b and 26:12b; 29:2 and 28:12; 29:13 and 22:2, 16). In 29:18 the parallel mention of "prophecy" (literally, "vision") and law may refer to the Torah and the Prophets, the first two sections of the Hebrew Bible.

Concluding Teachings (30:1–31:31)

The words of Agur son of Jakeh (30:1–9). Agur, evidently a non-Israelite sage, typifies sapiential humility and piety. He confesses his lack of wisdom and, by way of rhetorical questions, acknowledges that no human being is privy to divine realms (vv. 1–4; cf. Job 38:4–41). Agur professes trust in God's word and offers a modest prayer to be kept from falsehood and from the extremes of abject poverty or excessive wealth (vv. 5–9).

Admonitions and numerical sayings (30:10–33). Four types of sinners are characterized: those who are unfilial, hypocritical, haughty, and rapacious (vv. 11–14). Riddles prompt reflection on insatiability (vv. 15–16), and on four unfathomable "paths" or "ways" in the natural and human worlds (vv. 18–19). The following numerical sayings observe four disruptions of social order

(vv. 21–23; cf. 19:10); four small but instructive creatures (vv. 24–28); and four examples of grandeur (or perhaps pomposity; the comparison with a king might be ironic; vv. 29–31; cf. vv. 27–28).

The words of Lemuel (31:1–9). A royal sage, again apparently non-Israelite, recounts his mother's warnings against women and wine (regarded here as weakening diversions), lest he shirk his obligation to protect the powerless.

The woman of worth (31:10–31). An acrostic poem about the ideal wife, from the husband's perspective (vv. 10–11, 23, 28, 31). The term rendered "capable" (v. 10) can be variously translated as "excellent," "virtuous," "noble," "worthy," or "brave" (of women, cf. v. 29; 12:4; Ruth 3:11). The woman exemplifies strength, independence, courage, kindness, wisdom, and piety. More precious than jewels (v. 10; 3:15; 8:11), she is a human counterpart to the awesome figure of personified Wisdom in chaps. 1–9. This poem, like Proverbs overall, is invested in a patriarchal social order. For all her accomplishments, the wife is still dependent upon her husband for a share in the fruit of her labors (v. 31). Nonetheless, by any account she is a magnificent, redoubtable woman, a portrait of the discernment, faith, and integrity that Proverbs teaches.

Bibliography

Brenner, Athalya. "Proverbs." In *Global Bible Commentary*, edited by Daniel Patte, 163–74. Nashville: Abingdon, 2004.

Clifford, Richard J. *Proverbs.* OTL. Louisville: Westminster John Knox, 1999.

Fontaine, Carol R. "Proverbs." In *The Women's Bible Commentary*, edited by Carol A. Newsom and Sharon H. Ringe, 153–60. Louisville: Westminster John Knox, 1992.

Fox, Michael V. *Proverbs 1–9.* AB 18A. New York: Doubleday, 2000.

Perdue, Leo G. *Proverbs.* Interpretation. Louisville: Westminster John Knox, 2000.

Ecclesiastes

Craig Bartholomew

INTRODUCTION

Ecclesiastes is part of the OT *Writings*, the third portion of the Jewish canon, and with Proverbs and Job is one of the three undisputed wisdom writings. Contemporary scholars remain deeply divided as to whether Ecclesiastes is a deeply pessimistic book or one that affirms life and joy. My view is that Ecclesiastes ultimately affirms life and joy but only as the end result of a ferocious struggle with the brokenness of life.

In the Hebrew Old Testament Ecclesiastes is named after its central character, *Qohelet* (translated as "the Teacher" in the NRSV). Qohelet is presented by the narrator as Solomon (1:1, 12) but this royal fiction is dropped in the course of the book. We know from 12:9–10 that Qohelet was a wisdom teacher, and Ecclesiastes was most likely written in the postexilic period, probably in the fourth century BC. To understand Ecclesiastes, it is important to note that a narrator, whose voice is heard in 1:1, 7:27, and in the epilogue (12:9–14), presents Qohelet's journey and teachings in his own frame narrative.

It is particularly important to read Ecclesiastes against the background of Proverbs, which articulates a character-consequence theology rooted in creation. This theology assumes the rich meaningfulness of life and teaches that the fear of the Lord will in general lead to blessing and prosperity. However, for those living in the postexilic period, the evidence seemed to indicate that Yahweh's purposes had run aground. For an Israelite like Qohelet, such evidence raised acute questions about the meaning of life. Greek philosophy was in the air, and Qohelet draws from Greek thought an autonomous epistemology dependent on reason, observation, and experience, which he uses to explore the question of life's meaning. Thus the big question Ecclesiastes poses is *how* one determines if life is meaningful amid circumstances in which nothing seems to make sense.

Ecclesiastes is a carefully crafted whole but, as befits Qohelet's excruciating search for meaning, the book tracks back and forth as Qohelet explores area after area of life. The tension between his analysis of life—through the grid of his autonomous epistemology that leads him again and again to the conclusion that life is "enigmatic" (cf. 1:2, the NRSV translates Heb. *hebel* as "vanity")—and the positive affirmation of life he knows from his upbringing—as a believing Israelite exemplified in the *carpe diem* passages (e.g., 2:24–26)—combined with the growing irony drive the book forward to its denouement in 11:67–12:8.

COMMENTARY

In 1:1 the narrator introduces readers to *Qohelet* as a Solomon-like figure, an Israelite who is gifted with exceptional wisdom. Nothing therefore prepares one for the summary in 1:2: that everything is "vanity" or, as I prefer to translate the Hebrew word *hebel*, "enigmatic." Life may be meaningful, but if so that meaning is utterly elusive; it cannot be discovered. Verse 3 poses the rhetorical question that the entire book seeks to answer: what do people gain from all their toil under the sun? People work hard, but when Qohelet examines work in the light of his autonomous epistemology, as he does at several points in the book, he finds it utterly enigmatic. The poem in 1:2–11 gives readers a foretaste of the data with which Qohelet will struggle. Both history and nature seem to confirm that nothing is ever settled; the center of the poem that encapsulates his conclusion is found in 1:8: "All things are wearisome!"

Ecclesiastes presents Qohelet's quest for the meaning of life, and in 1:12–18 one hears his voice for the first time as he explains his project. Qohelet stresses that his seeking and searching is "by wisdom" (1:13), but already in this section readers feel his frustration and despair at finding wisdom. Clearly this is a very different "wisdom" from that in Proverbs which makes its starting point the fear of the Lord. As the book develops, it becomes more and more apparent that what he here calls "wisdom" is in fact what Proverbs calls "folly." Irony—saying one thing but meaning the opposite—is a central feature of Ecclesiastes, and already here readers receive a sample of things to come.

A favorite phrase of Qohelet's is life "under the sun," by which he refers to all of life as God has made it. In his quest for solving life's riddle Qohelet ranges across a dizzying variety of areas of life. In 2:1–11 he explores pleasure and the good life, including wine, architecture, horticulture, music, and sex. But none yields the answer he seeks. In 2:12–23 he explores

the problem of death and one's legacy. The enigma of death and the shadow it casts over the question of life surface repeatedly in Ecclesiastes (cf. 9:1–12). In 3:1–13 (a poem) he investigates the problem of time; God has created humans such that they need an overarching story of life, but where is it to be found? In 3:16–22 Qohelet focuses on injustice; in the law courts where one would expect to find justice he finds injustice! In chap. 4 he examines the agonizing problem of oppression (cf. also 5:8–17), the problem of rivalry in work, the problem of individual isolation, and lack of supportive community as well as the problem of bad government (cf. 8:1–9).

The location of meaning in wealth and its pursuit is a major theme in Ecclesiastes. It is connected with oppression in 5:8–17; the vulnerability of wealth is explored in 5:8–17 as well as in 6:1–9; and 10:1–20 culminates in the ironic statement that "money meets every need" (10:19). Although 11:1–6 is about doing everything one can to secure one's wealth, Qohelet concludes in 11:6 that this can never be guaranteed.

Area after area that Qohelet explores with his epistemology of experience, observation, and reason gets him nowhere; again and again he concludes that all is "enigmatic." In 7:13–22 the difficulties such a claim presents surface strongly. If God has made life crooked (7:13), and if the character-consequence theology of Proverbs simply does not work (7:15), then perhaps the answer is to be moderately wise and righteous and moderately wicked (7:16–17). This leads into a reflective section (7:23–29) in which Qohelet looks back on his journey. Against the background of Proverbs one should understand the two women referred to as Lady Wisdom and Lady Folly. Qohelet has apparently conducted his investigation by "wisdom," but it has led him into the arms of Lady Folly (7:26). And although he is an excellent sleuth, he cannot find Lady Wisdom (7:28). The irony of his journey comes strongly to the foreground at this point. In 7:13 he relates what is wrong with the world to God having made it crooked, but by 7:29 the problem is revealed to be not God but humankind.

In the course of Qohelet's journey, readers find not only his negative conclusions about life as enigmatic, but also startlingly positive statements. These are commonly known as his *carpe diem* (seize the day) sayings (2:24–26; 3:10–15, 16–22; 8:10–15; 9:7–10; 11:7–12:7). *Carpe diem* might suggest a form of hedonism by affirming pleasure in response to his despair over discovering life's meaning, but this is quite the wrong way to read them. Israelites, and OT Wisdom literature in particular, strongly affirmed life in all its dimensions as God made it. These passages celebrate the gift of life. They speak of eating and drinking, enjoying one's work, enjoying marriage, and taking pleasure in life as God's gift, and they become stronger as the book progresses. The challenge for the interpreter of Ecclesiastes is how they relate to the decidedly negative conclusions. The answer is that they are deliberately set in *contradictory juxtaposition* with the *hebel* conclusions. Qohelet knows these things to be true, but how are they to be reconciled with what he observes and his analysis through his autonomous epistemology? This is the problem that Qohelet is struggling with, and the juxtaposition of these contradictory views compels readers to enter into the same struggle.

On the one hand Qohelet knows that life is meaningful and good, but on the other he observes everywhere the terrible brokenness of life. Using his epistemology, he concludes that life is utterly enigmatic. This excruciating tension lies at the heart of Ecclesiastes; indeed, by the time one reaches 9:7–10 the juxtaposition is threatening to collapse under its tension. How does one resolve this problem?

The path to resolution comes from two directions. First, as Qohelet's journey progresses it becomes increasingly apparent that his epistemology embraces not wisdom but folly. Key passages in this respect are 5:1–7 and 7:23–29. Some scholars regard 5:1–7 as the center of Ecclesiastes; it urges the reader to approach the temple cautiously in order to listen to God's instruction, and it concludes with the similar exhortation to fear God. The theology of this section is comparable to Proverbs' insistence that the fear of the Lord is the beginning of wisdom. And as noted above, 7:23–29 foregrounds in dramatic fashion that Qohelet's autonomous epistemology has led him right into the arms of Lady Folly. Thus the one way in which resolution comes is in the growing recognition that an autonomous epistemology, which depends on experience and reason, and which does not start with the fear of the Lord, will only place one into deeper and deeper despair when faced with the enigmas of life.

Second, resolution comes through the indication of a better epistemological foundation in 11:7–12:7. The proverb of 11:7 shines out like a firefly indicating that hope and resolution are true possibilities. The two dominating exhortations of this section are "rejoice" and "remember." "Remember your creator" in 12:1 is the second major clue to resolving Qohelet's struggle. Remembrance is far more than a casual reminder; it means that readers should let their perspectives on life be informed by the view that God is creator of everything. This is precisely what has been missing in Qohelet's epistemology; it has all been rooted *in himself*—indeed, one of the great characteristics of Ecclesiastes is the endless use of the first person, "I." The answer to the perplexities of life is to find a way back to that starting point in God as the creator of everything. This does not take one away from the struggles of life: 12:1 is followed by some of the darkest verses in Ecclesiastes as Qohelet describes death, but it puts one in a position to affirm life and its meaning amid the very real struggles.

In 12:8–14 readers hear the voice of the narrator once again. He reports that Qohelet was one of the wise in Israel, that he carefully crafted and edited his teachings, and that, like other sayings of the wise, they goad us into the right way and provide a firm place to stand amid the challenges of life. Verses 13–14 sum up the entire book: all has been heard and the conclusion is, fear God and keep his instructions, for this is the "whole person"—this is what human life is ultimately all about.

Ecclesiastes is a book of great relevance today when so many people struggle with the meaninglessness of life. Ecclesiastes affirms that struggle. Resolution does not come easily in a profoundly broken world but can be found as one works one's way back to a starting point in the recognition of God as the creator and redeemer of the world. The reference to God's commandments in 12:13 as well as to the temple in 5:1–7 remind us that God is not only the creator but also the redeemer, who made the Israelites his people and whose redemptive work culminates in Jesus Christ, the full embodiment of wisdom.

Bibliography

Bartholomew, Craig. *Reading Ecclesiastes: Old Testament Exegesis and Hermeneutical Theory*. Analecta biblica 139. Rome: Pontifical Biblical Institute, 1998.

Crenshaw, James L. *Ecclesiastes*. OTL. Philadelphia: Westminster, 1987.

Seow, Choon Leong. *Ecclesiastes*. AB 18C. New York: Doubleday, 1997.

Towner, W. Sibley. "The Book of Ecclesiastes." In *NIB* 5:265–360.

The Song of Songs

Tod Linafelt

INTRODUCTION

The Song of Songs is a sequence of ancient Hebrew erotic love poems. Although the superscription to the book, "The Song of Songs, which is Solomon's," associates it with King Solomon (who lived in the tenth century BCE), the language of the poetry represents a much later form of Hebrew, making clear that Solomon is not the author. The poems were probably written between the fifth and third centuries BCE, and its author or authors are anonymous. Although many scholars treat the book as an anthology of short poems by different hands, a strong consistency of diction, theme, voice, and poetic technique suggests a single author behind most of the poetry. The book became associated with Solomon perhaps because of his dual reputation as both an extravagant lover of women (1 Kgs. 11:1–3) and a prolific composer of poetry (1 Kgs. 4:32).

Although there is a long history, among both Jewish and Christian commentators, of reading the Song of Songs as if it were a theological treatise, and a significantly shorter history, among biblical scholars, of reading it as if it were a treatise on love or sexuality, the book is neither: the Song of Songs is not a *treatise* of any sort, but is rather lyrical *poetry*. Indeed, the Song of Songs is arguably one of the highest achievements of ancient Hebrew poetry, and to do it justice means to read it *as*

poetry, rather than turning it into something it is not. In reading and appreciating the Song of Songs we should not look for information about or a representation of God's relationship to Israel (it is not theology), or a story with plot and real characters (it is not narrative), or explicit reflection on the sources and nature of love (it is not philosophy). Rather, to appreciate fully the Song of Songs requires that one pay close attention to its poetic art, including the structure of both individual lines and larger poems, word choice, sound play, metaphor, tone, and voice. Some of these elements, most especially sound play, are less obvious or even unavailable in translation, but one can still get a very strong sense of how the Song of Songs works as poetry even in translation.

Like nearly all ancient Hebrew poetry, the Song of Songs makes primary use of short parallel lines, which mostly occur in a couplet form with the second line often heightening, concretizing, or otherwise modifying the first; occasionally a third line is added to complement or extend the image or metaphor. Thus, to the two classically parallel lines in 6:4, "You are beautiful as Tirzah, my love, / comely as Jerusalem," is added a third line, "terrible as an army with banners." Elsewhere the poetry of the Song of Songs exhibits a greater freedom than most ancient

Hebrew poetry in relating the parallel lines. In 2:2, for example, as a male voice describes his female lover, the poet pairs a simile in the first line with its referent in the second: "As a lily among brambles, / so is my love among maidens." Part of the task—and the fun—of reading and interpreting the poetry of the Song of Songs is to ponder and to try to work out the relationship between the lines.

COMMENTARY

The book alternates between a male and a female voice, with occasional interruptions by a female group voice (e.g., 5:9; 6:1) and a male group voice (e.g., 8:8–9). The primary male and female voices represent two young, apparently unmarried lovers, who spend most of the poem expressing their erotic yearnings and describing each other's physical attractions in lush, sometimes hyperbolic imagery. Thus, a quote from the male voice: "Your breasts are like two fawns, / twins of a gazelle, / that feed among the lilies. // Until the day breathes / and the shadows flee, // I will hasten to the mountain of myrrh / and the hill of frankincense" (4:5–6). And from the female voice in 2:3: "As an apple tree among the trees of the wood, / so is my beloved among young men. // With great delight I sat in his shadow, / and his fruit was sweet to my taste." Despite the alternating voices of the lovers, the poetry is not fundamentally dramatic—there is no overarching plot, and little narrative development—but rather remains squarely within the realm of lyric, a form of poetry that works with anonymous voices or personae rather than attempting to represent full-blooded characters. As in the quotes above, much of the imagery is drawn from the natural world, and it often seems to contain double entendres (e.g., "his fruit was sweet to my taste"; or "Let my beloved come to his garden, / and eat its choicest fruits" [4:16]).

One striking consequence of the alternation of female and male voices in the Song of Songs is an underscoring of the egalitarian nature of erotic love with regard to gender roles. The intermingling of voices works against the gender stereotypes that would assign the active role of "lover" to the man and the passive role of "beloved" to the woman. The two voices are given roughly equal amounts of space in the book, each describes the body of the other, and each expresses the desire one feels for the other. This mutuality is exhibited also in the range of imagery with which the lovers are imagined: both lovers (not just the woman) are associated with the beauty and grace of doves, lilies, and fawns or gazelles; and both lovers (not just the man) are described in terms of power and strength, the man being associated with marble columns and cedar trees (5:15) and the woman with ramparts and towers (8:10).

The poetry of the Song of Songs is, for the most part, a positive celebration of the pleasures of erotic love. Yet it does acknowledge, if only briefly, the dangers of Eros—not only those dangers that arise from outside the erotic relationship and threaten the young lovers, but also those dangers that are inherent to the nature of Eros itself. With regard to the former, see especially 5:2–8, where the young woman imagines herself wandering the streets at night searching for her lover, only to be met and beaten by the "sentinels of the walls." With regard to the latter, see 8:6: "Set me as a seal upon your heart, / as a seal upon your arm; // for love is strong as death, / passion fierce as the grave. // Its flashes are flashes of fire, / a raging flame." Though thoroughly rooted in the body, Eros here takes on near-cosmic dimensions. The language of the body, elsewhere in the Song of Songs so positive, teeters in this instance on the brink of obsession.

Given that the Song of Songs is preserved as part of Jewish and Christian Scripture, the question is often asked,

Where is God in all this? In fact, God is never mentioned in the book. Nevertheless, for centuries complex allegorical interpretations of the poetry—in which the two young lovers are taken to be ciphers for God and humanity—have prevailed. In traditional Jewish interpretation, Israel is cast as the female lover and God as the male lover. For Christian interpreters the lovers of the biblical book are taken to refer variously to God and the church, or Christ and the individual soul, or even to Jesus and the Virgin Mary. Modern scholars have tended to dismiss these allegorical interpretations, since they so obviously do violence to the literal sense of the text. It is true that such a mode of interpretation *spiritualizes* the Song of Songs, and thus tames its potentially subversive role in a Bible that has so often been taken as shoring up borders and fencing in sexuality. It is also no less true that such interpretation *eroticizes* theological discourse, with potentially very interesting results for doing theology, especially if one is willing to imagine God as not only an object of desire but subject to its throes as well. Although it seems clear that the poetry was not written with a theological intent, it is worth pondering why later interpreters found the erotic metaphor such a compelling way of talking about God and how the lyrical presentation of Eros that we find in the Song of Songs might contribute to such God-talk.

Although it is true that God is never mentioned in the Song of Songs, there are some close calls, places where the poet seems to come intentionally very near to naming God, without quite doing so. For example, in the twice-repeated oath, "I adjure you, O daughters of Jerusalem, / by the gazelles or the wild does: // do not stir up or awaken love / until it is ready" (2:7; 3:5), there would seem to be a pun or wordplay on two common epithets for God. "Gazelles" in Hebrew is *tseba'ot*, which puns on *YHWH tseba'ot*, or "LORD of hosts." And "wild does" in Hebrew is *be'ayelot hassadeh*, which puns on *'el shadday*, or "God Almighty." By

having her companions swear on these erotically charged animals (gazelles and wild does are frequently associated with the goddess of love in ancient Near Eastern iconography and inscriptions) rather than on a name or title of God, the female speaker both celebrates the natural world as a primary source for erotic symbolism and makes an indirect theological claim. The nature of this claim depends on how one construes the tone of the speaker here. It is certainly possible to take the tone as ironic and intentionally subversive of theological claims, with erotic love pointedly replacing God as ultimate referent. But it is also possible that, rather than subverting piety in favor of love, the poet is vaunting the power of love precisely by associating it with God.

We find the same ambiguity of tone with the second instance of a near-miss in naming God, found in 8:6. This famous verse represents a crescendo of sorts for the poetry, offering for the first time a second-order reflection on the nature of love, even the metaphysics of love, rather than the first-person declarations and descriptions that fill the rest of the book. Here the female voice declares: "love is strong as death, / passion fierce as the grave. // Its flashes are flashes of fire, / a raging flame." We may note how, in a move typical of Hebrew poetry, the second term of each of the three syntactically matched pairs in the first couplet ("love/passion," "strong/fierce," "death/grave") serve to intensify, specify, or concretize the first. The next couplet makes this heightening of terms even more acute with the progression from "flashes" to "fire" to "a raging flame." In Hebrew the final line, translated in the NRSV as "a raging flame," is a single word, *shalhebetyah*. Given the equally weighted lines that precede it and their syntactical parallelism, this abbreviated final line pulls the reader up short, causing one to pause and dwell on the effect of that "raging flame," love. The sense of emphasis on this final line is bolstered by the occurrence here of a fragment of the divine name: –*yah*, the last syllable of the last word of the verse, is a shortened form of Israel's personal name for God, Yahweh, and serves grammatically as an intensifying particle; it is what justifies the translation "a *raging* flame."

The question is whether this fragmentary allusion to God is *only* a grammatical intensifier, or whether it might represent a genuine, if muted, theological claim. If the latter, one still must negotiate the tone of the claim, in the same way as the punning oath in 2:7 and 3:5: is it a theologically subversive replacement of God with erotic love, or an attempt to exalt human love by adding a poetic whiff of divinity? One need not finally decide, of course, since with poetry—unlike theology or philosophy—lack of precision is often a virtue, and the ambiguity may well be intended by the poet.

Bibliography

Bloch, Ariel, and Chana Bloch, translators. *The Song of Songs: A New Translation.* 1995. Reprint, Berkeley: University of California Press, 1998.

Exum, J. Cheryl. "Ten Things Every Feminist Should Know about the Song of Songs." In *Song of Songs*, edited by Athalya Brenner and Carole R. Fontaine, 24–35. FCB 2/6. Sheffield: Sheffield Academic Press, 2000.

Landy, Francis. *Paradoxes of Paradise: Identity and Difference in the Song of Songs.* Sheffield: Almond, 1983.

Linafelt, Tod. "Biblical Love Poetry (. . . and God)." *Journal of the American Academy of Religion* 70.2 (2002): 323–45.

Trible, Phyllis. "Love's Lyrics Redeemed." In *God and the Rhetoric of Sexuality*, 144–65. OBT. Philadelphia: Fortress, 1978.

Isaiah

L. Juliana Claassens

INTRODUCTION

The book of Isaiah offers a rich resource for theological reflection. This multifaceted book in sixty-six chapters constitutes a literary world filled with powerful language and figures of speech where themes imaginatively interact to create a thick description of God and the world in which God chooses to enter. Spanning more than three centuries, several authors (referred to in this essay as the "prophets" to suggest the multiplicity embedded in the figure of the prophet) responded to complex theological questions that grew out of the unique challenges of their time. Employing a variety of rhetorical means to convey an intricate message of judgment and salvation, endings and new beginnings, the book of Isaiah reflects the prophets' struggle to make sense of God and the world in which they live.

The theological potential of this book is evident from the fact that Isaiah has inspired multiple Christian and Jewish interpreters to add their voices to the extensive interpretation history of this intriguing book. And more than any other OT book, Isaiah's influence is felt in the New Testament, particularly with regard to the understanding of Jesus as the Messiah and Suffering Servant. It is thus for good reason that the book of Isaiah has been called "the Fifth Gospel" by John Sawyer.

However, a theological introduction to the book of Isaiah offers a number of challenges. For much of the modern critical study of Isaiah, scholars focused on the complex history of the origin of this book, determining the historical context of individual oracles. Most scholars assume that Isaiah constitutes a composite work that reflects different sociohistorical realities. With regard to a theological interpretation of Isaiah, however, it is a question whether the theological dimension of the text ultimately depends on an accurate reconstruction of the text's original context, particularly in light of the difficulty in determining the exact nature of many of the historical referents in the text. Scholars interested in developing the theological dimension of Isaiah have searched for ways to look with fresh eyes at the rich prophetic material. In addition to a growing appreciation for the literary features of this composite book, scholars now tend to read Isaiah as a whole, being sensitive to the way in which images and themes reverberate throughout the whole book. Moreover, a theological interpretation is attentive to the canonical nature of the biblical text, emphasizing that a text cannot be read in isolation but that one should look for the way in which texts fit into the larger canonical context. Such an understanding holds that the echoes of a given passage may extend throughout Scripture, and for Christian readers, into the New Testament. Finally, a theological interpretation of Isaiah is sensitive to the fact that we are not the first to read these texts; where possible, we should consult voices from Jewish and Christian interpreters to stimulate our theological sensitivities.

A further challenge facing a theological introduction to Isaiah regards the shape of such an undertaking. Should one hold to the traditional division of the book in three parts, typically called First Isaiah, Second Isaiah, and Third Isaiah, treating the theological themes of these units separately? Such a division corresponds roughly to the following temporal and sociohistorical realities: (1) A preexilic, eighth-century context marked by the impending danger of superpowers (Assyria, with Babylon on the horizon), judgment, and an urgent call to repentance; (2) a sixth-century exilic context, which centers around the promised return of the exiles, holding up hopeful visions in the midst of despair; (3) a postexilic context with its challenges of rebuilding a community back home, reflecting the disappointments of delayed promises. Alternatively, should one follow the division held by most commentators that fashions a break between Isa. 1–39 and Isa. 40–66, generally characterized in terms of judgment and salvation, destruction and restoration, exile and homecoming? Although these themes certainly form an important part of a theological interpretation of Isaiah, this distinction is not clearcut: one encounters themes of judgment and restoration throughout the book, often juxtaposed within a singular literary unit.

In light of the tendency to notice greater similarities between the different parts of the book, a theological introduction to Isaiah may be better served by focusing on a number of key themes that

can be developed theologically throughout the whole book. These themes run like a golden thread through Isaiah, finding expression in the various periods reflected in Isaiah, each adding important perspectives to the subject under discussion.

To trace these theological themes in Isaiah shows something of the dynamic nature of the prophetic material, where the prophetic word breaks into the ordinary circumstances of each generation. This process continues throughout the centuries, where the message is updated, added to, and even altered due to changing circumstances. It is powerful to see how each generation dealt with the questions at the heart of these theological themes. So we will see that there is indeed continuity in the theological formulations reflected in Isaiah—the similarities serving the purpose of reinforcing the prophets' message. But we will also see some key differences in the way this composite book treats a certain theme, often managing to hold together contrasting and even contradictory voices. This feature of a theological interpretation of Isaiah makes for a richer, more complex portrayal of reality, which in a world where easy answers reign supreme offers an alternative theological world where there is room for multiplicity, ambiguity, paradox, and nuance.

The ensuing themes are not the only themes present in this compound book, and each of the proposed themes has the potential to be developed in much greater depth. But these themes offer us an entry point into the text to think theologically about the book of Isaiah in light of the challenges our church communities face today. Moreover, this theological introduction may stimulate the reader to delve further into the rich theological resources offered by the book of Isaiah.

COMMENTARY

Facing Reality

A central theme with regard to a theological introduction of the book of Isaiah concerns the world into which the prophetic word is entering. The prophetic oracles in Isaiah do not represent abstract theological formulations, but are very much related to the social and political complexities of the world in which the believers find themselves. In each of the different time periods, the prophets in the book of Isaiah could be considered social and political analysts, visionaries who hold a finger on society's pulse and provide a vision of how God relates to the audience's situation. The prophets face the complex reality of the world, thinking theologically about the external threats and the internal struggles that face the people. Although the details of this analysis may differ depending on the situation of the audience, this prophetic act of naming the current challenges frequently involves truth telling, speaking hard truths that people do not necessarily want to hear.

Moreover, as readers of the prophetic texts, we ourselves live in a world fraught with various complex issues and concerns. A theological introduction to Isaiah offers suggestions of where the prophetic word may become flesh in the particular situations where the theological interpreters find themselves. Although there is a vast temporal and sociocultural difference between our world and the world of the text, there are issues raised by the prophets that are now more relevant than ever.

An analysis of the reality faced by the prophets must be fully aware of the different temporal, social, and political circumstances reflected in this composite book. We are not always certain of the exact details of the respective realities identified by the prophets in each part of Isaiah. However, the language and imagery of the various oracles give us some indication of whether the prophets' reality reflects a preexilic, exilic, or postexilic context—the Babylonian exile being a watershed event that forms the backdrop for much of this book.

The prophets' description of their respective situations involves at least three different questions/issues that each had a significant effect on the theological message the prophets shared with their audience. First, throughout the book of Isaiah a central issue regards the question: How does one live in a complex world dominated by superpowers? Israel, who for most of history was a small, insignificant people, had to figure out how to live in a world where one superpower replaces another, where even though the faces and names may change, the fear and intimidation in the presence of unbridled power remains the same. So we see how the preexilic context is dominated by the Assyrian Empire, which annihilated the northern kingdom and threatened the destruction of Judah and Jerusalem, only to be replaced with the impending danger of a Babylonian invasion that eventually destroyed Jerusalem and the temple and displaced a substantial part of the people of Israel.

Throughout the prophets' description of reality, we encounter glimpses of what superpowers can do. Reading between the lines, we notice something of the suffering brought about by the devastation of war and the imperialist policies that destroy homes and displace people. So we read in Isa. 3 of the humiliation, famine, violence, death, and grief that accompany the destruction of Jerusalem (cf. also 13:12–17, where Babylon is at the receiving end of the carnage). For much of Isaiah, the prophet(s) is thus speaking to people who have experienced terrible violence and devastation at the hand of these powerful nations. So the exilic period in particular is marked by displaced people who have to deal with the loss of everything that has given them certainty: their homes, their city, their temple, their land.

But even though the book of Isaiah reflects an all too harsh realization that superpowers can kill, one also sees how the prophets recognize that power is as alluring as a moth drawn to a flame. So we see in 7:3–9 how the prophet warns King Ahaz against being seduced by these worldly powers, understanding that one runs the risk of being destroyed oneself. In an exilic context, the prophets once more have to warn against the allure of the superpowers and their gods, against being so much settled in their life in Babylon that they forget their true identity as children of God (cf., e.g., the polemic against the other gods in 44:9–20, which responds to the question in v. 8: "Is there any god besides me?").

The external reality of living in a world dominated by superpowers had a profound impact on Israel's everyday life, their religious formation, and their understanding of God. The subsequent theological themes will show how the prophets helped the people make sense of the geopolitical realities of the time in religious terms. Even though we may give different answers to these theological questions, we are to take seriously the process of facing our reality, thinking theologically about the challenges of our time. So the question of how to live in a world dominated by superpowers is before us once again—particularly as many of us live in a nation that is itself a superpower that may threaten the peaceful existence of others. The prophets' description of reality may offer us some incentive to think creatively about the challenges of our own world.

A second issue facing the prophets regards the way the world around the prophets falls short from the ideal they hoped the world to be. The theme of facing a reality of injustice and other societal infractions that is contradictory to a covenantal relationship with God forms a unifying theme throughout Isaiah. Particularly the language of judgment that runs through much of Isaiah invites us to take a hard look at the reality that was responsible for such a response. We see how the prophets repeatedly critique a world where people's greed and self-centeredness reign supreme, where injustice and corruption mar God's ideal for a just society. This failure of people to live up to the ideal of justice is summarized in the clever wordplay in 5:7: God expected justice (*mishpat*), but saw bloodshed (*mispah*); God expected righteousness (*tsedaqah*), but heard a cry (*tsᶜaqah*). Already in the first chapter of Isaiah, Israel is put on trial and accused that their hands are full of blood

(1:15). This indictment is continued all through the book of Isaiah as the prophets highlight a series of infractions that all have to do with the poor and vulnerable suffering injustice. So the leaders of Israel are accused of "crushing my people," of "grinding the face of the poor," of devouring the vineyard, and of harboring the spoil of the poor in their homes (3:14–15). They are indicted for corruption and for not defending the cause of the most vulnerable in society, the widows and the orphans (1:23). We further read about the greed of people who confiscate the property of their vulnerable neighbors and so destroy their property rights and their ability to make a meaningful existence (5:8). The prophets also bemoan a society where there is no justice to be found in the courts that were supposed to protect the poor, the needy, and defenseless (5:23; cf. also 10:1–2). These injustices are not just restricted to a preexilic context; the prophets face the reality of injustice in every part of the book of Isaiah. For example, in 58:3–7 the prophet describes a reality where "the bonds of injustice" and "the thongs of the yoke" press heavy on the oppressed and the despondent. It is a world where there are hungry who need to be fed, where there are homeless who seek shelter, and where there are naked who have to be clothed.

In our world today, issues of justice and righteousness are more relevant than ever. We live in a world where the powerless are exploited; where the rich enrich themselves at the cost of the poor; where greed, corruption, outsourcing, and unjust legal systems have become the norm. Our world is a world where racism, poverty, gender injustice, violence, famine, and HIV/AIDS are realities that need to be faced by all who believe in a world where "justice will dwell in the wilderness, and righteousness abide in the fruitful field" (32:16).

A third issue at the heart of the prophets' theological reflection relates to the question: What is the religious reality facing the prophets in each generation? Frequently we see how the prophets accuse the people of their empty acts of worship, void of justice. This is particularly evident in 1:12–15, where God speaks in the first person, saying that God can no longer endure the people's solemn assemblies, that God's soul hates the people's festivals (cf. also 58:3–7). Without justice, these religious acts mean nothing. Underlying this critique is the concern that Israel no longer knows God, but has turned away from God (1:3–4). For the prophets, the loss of a real relationship with God inevitably results in the series of injustices identified throughout the book.

This reality is further explicated in 2:6–8, in which the prophet describes a world where there is no end to the people's treasures. It is a world overflowing with weapons, including horses and a magnitude of chariots to protect the people against whichever enemy threatens them personally, and especially the riches they have gathered. It is a world where people bow before the works of their own hands, before self-interest and selfishness. In this world, there is no room for God—people focus all their attention on money, power, and idols.

Also in an exilic context, the prophets address the people's religious reality as reflected in the many in-depth questions that grew out of the calamity of the exile. For instance, people asked how one could worship God in a foreign land, in the absence of the temple and a sacrificial system. Reacting to a deep theological crisis, they asked whether the theological formulations of the past still held true. Was God still the powerful God of the exodus? Did God still care about them? Is God present with them in exile? Moreover, their encounter with the gods of Babylon raised serious questions about God's uniqueness and power, asking questions with regard to the relationship of the God of Israel and the other gods.

In a postexilic context where people had to deal with the challenges of building a new community back home, the religion question appears in a different guise when the returning community is struggling with all sorts of questions with regard to religious identity: Who is included in the remnant that the prophets promised shall return (10:19–22; 37:30–32), that was to be regarded as the true, purified believers of God? What should one's relationship be with the other nations, particularly with the foreigners in our midst?

The internal struggle for truth as well as the painful divisions among the believers that mark parts of the book of Isaiah mirror the questions of religious identity and religious truth that are at the forefront of the theological agenda today. Painful divisions among Christians with regard to ethical questions such as abortion, homosexuality, and the war in Iraq call for serious reflection on notions such as truth and discernment. In addition, questions about a closed versus an open identity are becoming increasingly urgent in a post–9/11 world, where we are faced by serious questions as to how one deals with the other and the immigrant in our complex world.

The prophets use a number of striking images to describe their respective realities. We see how images of darkness (5:30; 8:22; 59:9) and barrenness/wilderness (14:17; 27:10; 33:9; 64:10) are powerfully used to capture the mood of the respective realities faced by the prophet(s), realities that are mostly marked by an ominous tone of death, destruction, despair, and the absence of justice and righteousness. Moreover, the prophets frequently use the metaphor of blindness and deafness to describe the people's failure to live up to the ideal of justice and righteousness. The injustice and abuse that mark people's behavior grow out of people's lack of insight, their inability to see whom the God is they are supposed to worship (6:9–10; see also 42:18–25; 56:10; 59:10). In addition, the image of intoxication has a similar function of describing the dulling of the senses that communicates Israel's lack of discernment in 5:11–12 (cf. also 28:1, 7–13; 29:9–10).

As we will see in the following sections, however, there is a distinctive movement from death to life, darkness to life, barrenness to fertility, when the light of a new world, a fertile world, is held up by the prophets as an alternative to the broken, less-than-ideal world faced by the prophets. The image of blindness and sight is picked up once again in an exilic and postexilic context (35:5; 42:7; 43:8), when the prophets issue the call to the servant to help people see the light and enter this alternative reality. These themes are very much related to the next theological theme, a composite portrayal of God that breaks into the reality faced by the prophets.

Imagining God

Growing out of the very real questions and challenges faced by the prophets, the book of Isaiah offers a composite picture of God that serves the function of persuading people to regain their undivided focus on God. A theological interpretation of Isaiah asks how the prophets imagined God in the various parts of this book, and what expectations this portrayal entertains for Israel and its future readers.

A key characteristic of the prophets' portrayal of God is that it is deeply rooted in a description of God's pathos, which grows out of God's response to the reality as identified by the prophets. As Abraham Heschel notes, the God of the Hebrew Bible is not characterized by self-sufficiency but rather is intensely "moved and affected by what happens in the world, and reacts accordingly. Events and human actions arouse in Him joy or sorrow, pleasure or wrath" (*The Prophets*, p. 4).

All through the book of Isaiah, we see compelling descriptions of God's love and anger, compassion and judgment, that mark God's interaction with people. A good example of how these divine emotions work together is in the Song of the Vineyard (5:1–7), which depicts God in terms of a vinedresser who tenderly cares for his vineyard. In this Song, God's passionate love and devotion to Israel is illustrated by the list of actions carried out by the owner with regard to his beloved vineyard: tilling the soil and protecting the vineyard against thieves and scavengers (vv. 2–3). When the vineyard does not yield grapes, however, God's disappointment and sorrow give way to fierce anger, illustrated by a series of violent verbs in vv. 5–6: the owner breaks down the wall, removes the hedge, and destroys the vineyard. This outburst of anger relates to the prophets' interpretation of the violence and destruction by the hand of the superpowers as a sign of God stretching out God's hand against the people and striking them (5:25; cf. also the recurring refrain in 9:8–10:4). It is God's anger that is responsible for the undoing of creation, for laying waste the earth and making it desolate, and for scattering people into exile (24:1–13).

Nevertheless, God's love and compassion are indeed greater than God's anger, for as we see in 43:1–7, God once again acts out of a deep love for God's people. So it is God's love that is responsible for effecting a new liberation, making a way in the wilderness (43:19) to lead Israel back home (40:1–5). It is God's love that is responsible for providing food and protection once again on the journey through the wilderness (49:9–10). And it is God's love that will establish a new creation, creating a new community back home, rebuilding the city and the temple (44:24–28).

These divine emotions find expression in a number of imaginative metaphors that the prophets use to imagine God. Besides the metaphor of an owner of a vineyard (5:1–7) mentioned before, God is said to be a father who begets children (45:10; 64:8), a woman who gives birth (42:14; 45:10), a compassionate mother (49:14–15; 66:13), a midwife who delivers a child (66:9), a scorned husband (50:1; 54:6), a potter who has the power to create a pot (45:9; 64:8) but also to shatter his handiwork if he pleases (30:14), a shepherd who tenderly cares for his lambs (40:11), a powerful warrior who will destroy all that threatens God's people (31:4; 42:13; 63:3–6) but can also fight against Israel (1:24–25; 5:25–30), a lion growling over its prey (31:4), and a bird protecting her offspring (31:5). It seems that the prophets concurred that one image cannot adequately capture the God of Israel.

These metaphors work together to form a multifaceted picture of God, managing to balance images that portray God's anger and judgment with images that denote God's love and compassion, so expressing the themes of judgment and restoration that run all through the book of Isaiah. Quite often, contrasting images for God are held together in close proximity, sometimes even a single sentence. For example, in 30:26 God is said to bind up the injuries of God's people and to heal the wounds that God inflicted by means of God's instruments, Assyria and Babylon. In 40:10–11 we see how images of God's power and mercy are combined when God is depicted as a warrior who comes with might, but also as a shepherd who tenderly feeds his flock.

A theological interpretation of Isaiah seeks to understand the rhetorical function of these metaphors, asking what claims this portrayal of God makes on God's people then and now to live differently. For instance, the image of God's anger in response to a society yielding injustice and bloodshed instead of justice and righteousness makes a forceful claim about God's identity: God is held up as being exalted by justice and sanctified in righteousness (5:16). The portrayal of God as a God of justice who is angered by ethical violations serves as an indictment that the world falls short of the divine ideal, and that God will be exalted by means of instituting a just social order.

Moreover, a theological interpretation of Isaiah recognizes that these metaphors for God may be employed differently throughout the various realities represented in Isaiah, therefore tracing how images are used and reused to rhetorical effect in the different parts of Isaiah. We see, for instance, how new occasions ask for a reinterpretation of the cherished images of the past. So in 8:14, God the Rock, who always signified a source of protection for Israel, now is said to "become a rock one stumbles over—a trap and a snare for the inhabitants of Jerusalem." And a number of times the image of God as warrior who fights on behalf of Israel is overturned to say that God is now fighting against Israel (1:24–25; 5:25–30; 9:11–21).

The prophets' portrayal of God is thus never static but always open to new formulations. Throughout Isaiah, the prophets' reflection is rooted in the past, building upon the rich theological resources of Israel's religious tradition. However, particularly in the exilic and postexilic period, during which time people experienced a complete breakdown in everything that made sense of their reality, the prophets help the people to think anew about God in light of the unique challenges they are facing. Using some of the traditional formulations for God, for example, God as the creator of heaven and earth, or the liberator who delivered Israel out of Egypt, the prophets clothe these formulations in a radically different way and so challenge the people to break through fixed ways of thinking.

Thus in 45:9–11 the prophet uses the images of a potter and a father/mother to expound on the image of God as creator. By bringing together disjunctive images for God, the prophet is creating a new vision of God, forcing the people to think differently about God and the world in which they live. In this text, the prophet is responding to the people's hesitance to see Cyrus, the king of the Persian Empire, who is repeatedly called God's anointed, whom God has called by name, as the means by which God will create a new future for Israel. By using creative imagery for God, the prophet challenges conventional categories, helping the people to be open to surprises—about God and the world.

This multifaceted portrayal of God in the book of Isaiah has the following implications for our own theological reflection. First, the multitude of images, some even paradoxical in nature, that the prophets used to imagine God helps us understand that God is so much more complex than the prophets or we could imagine. This theological point has significant implications for how we think about God and religion in a world beset by simplistic religious formulations.

Second, the prophets' understanding that theological imagination is a dynamic process that should be continued in every generation encourages us in our own theological interpretation to keep on thinking about God and the difficult questions of our faith in light of the multiple challenges facing us in our respective realities. What is more, the new and surprising visions of God imagined by the prophets encourage us to be open ourselves to new formulations about God, which may also affect how we think about the people with whom we share this world.

Finally, a theological interpretation of Isaiah should always maintain a critical appreciation for the metaphors used for God. As theological interpreters of Isaiah, we have the obligation to understand why some of the images for God that grew out of the difficult questions facing the prophets are used in the way they are, even though we may not always agree with their theological conclusions. Many examples from the book of Isaiah warrant further theological reflection, for instance, feminist theological concerns with regard to the image of God as a scorned husband and the violence against the female cities in the book (Isa. 3; 47). I will highlight one example that is particularly relevant in light of the complexities of the reality many of us share.

The notion of God's sovereignty plays a significant role in the way the prophets imagined God. In a preexilic context, the prophets are clear that the looming destruction is due to God's judgment (5:13; 9:11–21), and that the superpowers serve as God's instruments (5:26–30; 10:5–6). As an image of judgment, the notion of God's sovereignty makes an important claim on Israel to change their ways. The prophets remind people who

live as if there is no God that God is a sovereign God who can summon the superpowers of the world and use them at God's discretion.

The theme of God's sovereignty also becomes important in an exilic context, where people harbored serious questions with regard to God's powerlessness and absence (63:11–12; 64:6). As an image of restoration, God's sovereignty serves as a prophetic response to these questions, asserting that God is able to effect the needed change in people's lives, bringing the exiles home, and in the process undoing the powers that destroyed Israel. The superpowers now find themselves at the receiving end of God's wrath (cf., e.g., God placing a hook in the nose of Assyria, who is lead away in shame; 37:29; cf. also 10:12–19).

God's sovereignty is depicted in even stronger terms in the eschatological visions in Isaiah. Here God will definitely destroy all that threatens the survival of Israel. In these visions one sees fierce descriptions of God's violence toward the nations (24:21–23; 26:20–21; 34:2ff.). A particularly vivid apocalyptic image of God who will save the faithful but in the process utterly destroy the enemy is in 63:1–6, where the sovereign God will kill all Israel's enemies in anger, crushing them like grapes in a winepress so that their blood stains God's garments red.

It is true that the image of God's sovereignty exhibits an important rhetorical function in the various periods reflected in Isaiah. So one understands that this imagery is a response of people very much hurt by their surroundings, who use this rhetoric of violence with reference to God to cope in their cataclysmic situation. However, this portrayal of God offers considerable challenges for a contemporary theological reflection. We see how the image in Isa. 63 is taken up in the "Battle Hymn of the Republic": "He is trampling out the vintage where the grapes of wrath are stored." Today we face in our theological interpretation the serious issue of violence in God's name, particularly in light of our violent world, where people increasingly use God's name to execute their own political and social agendas. A theological interpretation of Isaiah seeks to understand these images in context, that is, identifying the liberating power of these images that served the function of lifting up broken people from their situation of despair, helping them to look differently at their oppressive reality. Likewise, a theological introduction has the obligation to warn against an uncritical appropriation of the image of God's sovereignty that may offer considerable problems if uncritically taken over by people who are in positions of power themselves. Then again, the image of the mighty Babylon and Assyria who are like nothing before God (14:3–27; 47) may serve as a notable critique against superpowers who abuse their power, reminding them that before God their power comes to nothing.

Another point where the image of God's sovereignty warrants reflection relates to one of the difficult questions that underlies this prophetic formulation: trying to explain why people suffer and what God's relationship is to this suffering. The prophets perceive the destruction caused by the superpowers, and try to explain this calamity in theological terms. It is important to note that even though we understand the prophetic response to disaster, this does not provide unequivocal answers with regard to our struggle to understand the theodicy question, which reappears every time misfortune strikes on a personal, national, or global level. Once again, a theological interpretation to Isaiah should offer directives of how contemporary readers may appropriate these texts in their theological reflection. In this regard, the prophets' struggle to understand how God relates to the complexities of life should serve as encouragement to keep on wrestling with the theological questions before us with the help of careful theological reflection in light of the rest of Scripture and the resources of our theological tradition.

Imagining an Alternative World

A theme that binds together the various parts of Isaiah is the ability to imagine a world beyond the present reality. Using a variety of images and themes, the prophets create an alternative world that looks very different from the world in which the believers find themselves. Often employing texts with eschatological features, the prophets imagine a world that seems idyllic, even impossible. This world breaks into the "real" world marred by poverty, violence, injustice, and misplaced priorities. At certain key moments throughout Isaiah, the prophets dare to dream of a world that is different, offering a powerful reminder that the current reality is not all there is, that another world may be possible. By reminding people of this world beyond the apparent one, the prophets hope to alter the way people look at their current situation, encouraging them to live differently.

In each generation, this alternative world is pictured differently depending on the challenges faced by the prophets. For example, in a preexilic context with its prophetic critique against societal and religious infractions, the prophets imagine a world where people refocus their priorities and become God-centered, where peace and justice are restored. So we see, for example, in a literary unit like Isa. 1–12, which is very much concerned with God's judgment and the imminent destruction by the hand of the superpowers, how the vision of an alternative world is held up to refocus people's attention on what is really important. At certain key points, visions of hope (e.g., 2:1–5; 4:2–6; 9:1–7) are juxtaposed with descriptions of the reality faced by the prophets (e.g., 1:1–31; 2:6–22; 3:1–26; 9:8–21). This act of imagining a world beyond the current reality is based on a deeply held conviction that God is able to transform a life filled with selfishness and self-interest into a world where people live according to God's will and follow God's word (2:5).

This notion of an alternative world becomes especially important in the exile, where people are living the nightmare of being uprooted, trapped in a situation of hopelessness and despair. The prophets help people who have lost their ability to think of anything beyond their current situation of exile to imagine another world. In this world everything is possible. Deeply rooted in the promises of the past, the prophets remind the audience that God, who does not give up on people, will bring about a new creation, a new exodus, thereby establishing a new community back home.

In a postexilic world where people had to deal with the frustrations of delayed promises, of a temple not yet rebuilt, of living in a world once again tarnished by poverty and injustice in addition to internal strife, the prophetic act of imagining an alternative world once more becomes significant. People are urged to look up and see the light, to see what is not yet there, to believe the fulfillment of God's promise to restore this fledgling community (60:1–5).

This alternative world that the prophets imagine throughout the book has some key features. Each of these characteristics is deeply rooted in the belief that God is able to do the impossible, that God's actions cannot be curbed by what our limited vision deems possible. It is this faith in the unseen that is responsible for helping people look differently at their respective realities.

First, we see that God is ultimately a God who gives life. So a recurring theme in Isaiah recounts the exuberant confession that God is able to create an abundance of water in the wilderness and trees flourishing in a dry land. For example, 41:18–19 states: "I will open rivers on the bare heights, and fountains in the midst of the valleys; I will make the wilderness a pool of water, and the dry land springs of water. I will put in the wilderness the cedar, the acacia, the myrtle, and the olive; I will set in the desert the cypress, the plane and the pine together" (cf. also

35:6–7; 44:3) A key characteristic of this alternative world thus is the potential of life in the most desolate of places. In these texts, water functions as the symbol of life, of God's ability to bring about radical change, to transform a situation of death into one of life.

This transformation is further enacted in the image of Israel's barrenness being transformed into fertility. So we hear in 54:1–3 an invitation to Daughter Zion to sing for joy, for she, the barren one, has been blessed with many children, so much so that she will need a much bigger tent (cf. also 49:19–21).

These images serve as a metaphor of God's resolve to transform Israel's dry existence into one of lush abundance, relating to God's promise of making it possible for the people to return home from exile in Babylon. This commitment is further evident from the image of God making a way in the wilderness, creating a highway for the exiles to return home (35:8; 40:3–4; 43:19; 62:10). God is said to remove all the obstacles before God's people. As 40:4 proclaims: "Every valley shall be lifted up, and every mountain and hill be made low; the uneven ground shall become level, and the rough places a plain" (cf. also 49:11–12). These texts work together to present a picture of an alternative world, and a God who is able to transform a hopeless situation into one of new possibilities.

Second, the prophets imagine a world where the fruits of justice and righteousness fill the earth (27:2). Continuing the theme of life, the prophets hold up the ideal of a world where all people have the opportunity to live unimpaired, where all impediments that restrict quality of life are removed. It is a world where the poor and needy call upon God and are consoled (41:17–20; cf. 25:4). It is a world where the imprisoned are freed and the brokenhearted consoled (42:7; 61:1), where the hungry receive bread, the homeless lodging, and the naked clothes (58:7, 10). It is a world where, as 35:5–6 recounts, the blind can see, the deaf can hear, where the lame not only can walk but can leap like gazelles. As water gives life in the midst of the wilderness, so the poet imagines an alternative world where God gives life to people who are marginalized because of debilitating circumstances. This theme culminates in the eschatological image of God swallowing death, serving as the ultimate expression of the impossible becoming possible (25:7; cf. also 26:19).

Third, in a world epitomized by strife and violence, the prophet is imagining a world where nations live together in peace. This notion of radical peace is evident in 2:1–5, which imagines a world where there is no violence. It is a world of peace, where people no longer take up weapons against one another, but where weapons are transformed into garden equipment, symbolizing a world where every person has the ability to provide food for themselves. It is a world where nobody learns to make war, but where differences are solved by diplomatic means, with God serving as a wise judge.

This notion is powerfully illustrated by the image in 11:6–9: the wolf and the lamb, the leopard and the goat, the calf and the lion shall peacefully live together. The prophet is imagining a world in which relationships in the animal kingdom that are based on fear and hostility are redescribed in terms of God's peaceful kingdom. Serving as a metaphor for the conflict between nations, the prophet imagines a world that is not based on dominion or violence, but where the vulnerable will be safe and able to live unharmed.

Furthermore, in 19:23 one finds the amazing vision of a highway that God will construct between Assyria and Egypt and Jerusalem. In a world where all Israel knew was the misfortune of being threatened and eventually crushed by mighty nations, what could be more impossible than this alternative world where nations live together in peace? But once again this alternative world is rooted in the belief that God is able to do the impossible.

Fourth, in an exilic and postexilic context, the alternative world imagined by the prophets also had the purpose of helping people to think differently about the other in their midst. The prophets envision a radically inclusive community where others are welcomed as an integral part of the returning community. The prophets imagine an alternative world that includes some radical guidelines of how to think about foreigners who are elsewhere sharply excluded from the returning community (Ezra 9:10–10:5 and Neh. 13:23–27), as well as the eunuchs who in terms of a context of holiness did not fulfill the purity laws (Lev. 21:20; 23:1) and accordingly were considered unfit to be part of the faithful. For example, Isa. 56:6–7 states that anybody who keeps the Sabbath should be part of this newly construed community, that they are welcome to worship on God's holy mountain, that God's "house shall be called a house of prayer for all peoples." In this text God is portrayed as the gatherer of outcasts—of Israel, but also beyond Israel's boundaries.

Moreover, that God adopts Israel's former enemies Egypt and Assyria, calling Egypt "my people" and Assyria "the work of my hands" in the same sentence as Israel "my heritage" (19:25) offers a radically different perspective on Israel's relationship to the nations (cf. also the image of the nations streaming to God's holy mountain in 2:1–5).

Nevertheless, one should not romanticize these texts. That Israel found itself in a constant struggle to formulate its relationship with foreigners is clear from the harsh judgment against the "other" that is present alongside visions of a radically inclusive community. So we read in 25:10 that "the Moabites shall be trodden down in their place as straw is trodden down in a dung-pit" (cf. also the final verse of the book, 66:24, where the internal dissidents are harshly judged). Since we live in a world fraught with "others," the prophets' theological formulations serve as a good reminder that we need to continue to think theologically about our relationship to those with whom we share a world.

Vocation as Participation

The ultimate goal of the prophets in the book of Isaiah is persuasion. By means of holding up a composite portrayal of God and imagining an alternative world, the prophets' desire is that people will participate in this alternative world. This act of participation is very much connected to the notion of vocation, to living out the visions of God and the alternative world wherever the believers find themselves. People are thus called not only to imagine this alternative world, but also to live in this world, embodying the vision of God and the world in their societal and religious practices.

So we see throughout Isaiah how believers are presented with a choice to join this world or not. Already in Isa. 6 the prophet is commissioned to go out and proclaim God's word of judgment and salvation. The prophets invite people to become part of this world, to place their trust in God and not to be drawn to the false security offered by superpowers, wealth, or idols (30:15–18). People are invited to walk in the light of God (2:5), to seek God (55:6), to choose the light or end up in darkness (5:30). As 1:17–20 sets up this choice: if people are willing and obedient (v. 19), if they "learn to do good; seek justice, rescue the oppressed, defend the orphan, plead for the widow" (v. 17), they shall live, or as v. 19 says, "eat the good of the land." But if they "refuse and rebel," they "shall be devoured by the sword" (v. 20).

In order to join this alternative world, the people have to accept a new identity as God's people. In 44:1–5 we read how God, who has created and sustained Israel, will give the people a new name that marks them as belonging to God (cf. also 62:2–4). This new name implies that they now look at the world with different eyes, that they become people who can

see new possibilities in a world that seemed to have none.

As children of God, Israel is called to be God's witnesses (43:9–10; 44:7). They are called to testify about God, who creates a world where the impossible becomes possible, where life for all should be the governing principle. But more so, they are called to actively participate in making this impossible world possible, to act as peacemakers, to work for justice and righteousness, to feed the hungry, and to include those whom the world seeks to exclude, the marginalized and the despised (1:17; 58:7, 10).

Throughout Isaiah we see signs of the failure of the leaders to lead the people in this endeavor. For instance, Ahaz is held up as a model of a king who did not believe the sign of Immanuel, that God is with God's people, and as a consequence he placed his trust in worldly powers (8:6–7). Alternatively, Hezekiah serves as a model of a good king, who listened to the prophet's message and chose to rely on God, interceding for his people in the face of the enemy attack (37:14–38). But even Hezekiah fails in 39:8 when, after the king hears the prophetic judgment, he responds by thinking not of the well-being of his people but of his own safety and security.

We thus see gradually how a messianic expectation emerges that stands over against the failure of the leaders. We encounter a growing expectation of the ideal leader, a wise, discerning ruler in 9:6–7 who will help institute this impossible world characterized by peace, justice, and righteousness (cf. also 11:1–9). This leader from the throne of David or, as 11:1 says, "a shoot . . . from the stump of Jesse," will be a light shining in the darkness, who will transform the chaos all around into a world where nobody will "hurt or destroy on all my holy mountain," and where "the earth will be full of the knowledge of the LORD as the waters cover the sea" (11:9). The remarkable language and images used by the prophet(s) to communicate this growing expectation offered multiple opportunities for future interpreters to take this idea of a future Messiah further. So we see how the NT writers saw something of this alternative world realized in the person of Jesus, whose ministry proved to be radically inclusive and based on justice and righteousness for all.

Moreover, the notion of a leader who is called to help people participate in this alternative world is compounded in the figure of the servant of God, who is said to have been especially chosen by God, who experiences God's favor and protection, and to whom God has given God's spirit (42:1). This servant will not break a "bruised reed," and will not quench a "dimmed wick," thus denoting his sensitivity, but at the same time his strength (v. 3). This servant is quiet, not shouting or lifting up his voice, offering a sharp contrast with the noise and the war cries of the superpowers that seek to dominate (v. 2). He is further described as an outcast who is despised and rejected; Isa. 53 offers a moving description of his suffering and humiliation.

However, this servant of God will be exalted and lifted up by God (52:13–14), thereby pointing once more to God's ability to do the impossible. The servant is called to help "sustain the weary with a word" (50:4) and to bring forth justice to the nations (41:1, 3). He is said to be "a light to the nations" (42:6) and is called "to open the eyes that are blind, to bring out the prisoners from the dungeon, from the prison those who sit in darkness" (42:7; cf. also 49:6–10).

The identity of the servant has evoked considerable attention from Isaiah's interpreters. Later, NT writers would identify this servant of God with Jesus of Nazareth, particularly in connection to Jesus being humiliated on the cross and exalted in the resurrection. Jewish interpreters identified the servant as Israel, who are called to be God's servants in the world, who even though being crushed and disgraced should serve as a blessing to the nations. These interpretations are a good example of how a theological interpretation of Isaiah may benefit from viewing the layers in the text and its his-

tory of interpretation not as a hindrance but making for a richer conception of God and what is expected from believers. So it is powerful to think of Israel and future believers as servants in the world, personifying something of this alternative world wherever they find themselves. For Christian believers it may be a source of hope to see this vocation of the servant embodied in the figure of Jesus, who helps to bring about this alternative world. In both instances, though, the Suffering Servant points to God's ability to do something new, to transform the impossible into the possible.

The notion of vocation as participation offers significant implications for our own theological interpretation of Isaiah. The construal of the Suffering Servant encourages us to rethink our perceptions about power. The Suffering Servant advocates a theology of vulnerability, showing that there is strength in weakness. So the notion of the Suffering Servant raises some interesting questions with regard to leadership, deconstructing conventional understandings of what constitutes a good leader. The Suffering Servant powerfully illustrates that God often works through unlikely people in unlikely ways. Moreover, returning to the question of how to live in the midst of superpowers, the notion of the Suffering Servant stands in sharp contrast with the style of the superpowers, Assyria and Babylon, who tend to break those who do not make it; where survival of the fittest, the fastest, and, we could add in our world, the most affluent or popular reign supreme. From these texts we see how this alternative world the prophets imagine is a world where power and prestige do not count, but where there is power in vulnerability. The prophets seek to encourage people to enter this world, choosing to live in a different way. The servants of God are called to hear the cry of the oppressed, to live out God's commitment to the poor, the weak, and the hurt of the world, to work for economic and social justice, and to break the bondage of anything that prevents people from reaching their full potential.

Bibliography

Brueggemann, Walter. *Isaiah.* 2 vols. Westminster Bible Companion. Louisville: Westminster John Knox, 1998.

Childs, Brevard S. *Isaiah: A Commentary.* OTL. Louisville: Westminster John Knox, 2001.

———. *The Struggle to Understand Isaiah as Christian Scripture.* Grand Rapids: Eerdmans, 2004.

Heschel, Abraham Joshua. *The Prophets.* New York: Harper & Row, 1962.

Sawyer, John F. A. *The Fifth Gospel: Isaiah in the History of Christianity.* Cambridge: Cambridge University Press, 1996.

Jeremiah

Carolyn J. Sharp

INTRODUCTION

The book of Jeremiah is a major prophetic work that reflects theologically on the political and religious turmoil of Judah in the late seventh and early sixth centuries BCE. The armies of the Babylonian Empire preyed on many nations in the Near East in the last decades of the seventh century, and Babylon's colonialist eye inevitably fell on Judah. Fear of the Babylonians' imminent approach is palpable in the earliest poetic traditions in Jeremiah. Both pragmatic accommodationist politics and resistance are discernible in the prose material in the book, which scholars usually attribute to the later editorial work of traditionists deemed Deuteronomistic or Deutero-Jeremianic. Vicious infighting characterized the turbulent social world of the Judean leadership during the Babylonian hegemony. The book articulates the anguished reactions of the prophet Jeremiah and the bitter disputes of those around him regarding how best to respond to the looming threat of Babylonian aggression, the disastrous fall of Jerusalem, and massive deportations of Judeans. The final literary shape of the book wrestles with theopolitical problems presented by conflicts among Diaspora communities of Judeans in Babylon and in Egypt and those who had remained in Judah during the time of Babylonian rule. The book of Jeremiah does not present itself as a univocal reflection on those difficult times. Its vivid multivocality indicates that the preservation of differing perspectives on Jeremiah's witness has been understood to be crucial from the earliest formation of the book as Scripture.

The book presents a dynamic mix of poetic and prose traditions. While the distinction between poetry and prose is fluid for ancient Hebrew texts, there are some characteristic differences. Biblical Hebrew poetry tends to be cryptic and semantically open-ended, dense with metaphors, shaped in significant part by conceptual gaps and missing contextual markers that the hearer or reader needs to supply. Biblical Hebrew prose tends to display a fuller and more constrained semantics, showing conceptual connections spelled out with care and a referentiality to context that is heavily semantically determined and sometimes even redundant. Poetry compels a considerable degree of audience agency in making sense of its allusive images and silences. Prose historiography, biographical stories, and didactic exhortations, on the other hand, tend to depict a relatively monologic truth that challenges the audience to assent; this is so even when the prose in question betrays an unusually high degree of ambiguity or multivalence. Poetry and prose in Jeremiah speak in differing vocabularies about God and Judah, and these divergent dictions invite different kinds of responses from the book's audiences. The reader of Jeremiah encounters incoherent cries of the heart and vituperative rants against specific political groups, soaring metaphors of deliverance and pragmatic instructions for accommodation of the enemy. All of these dictions constitute prophetic truth in the book of Jeremiah.

That the traditions about Jeremiah were in considerable flux during the ancient period is evident from the fact that dramatic differences exist between the version of the book of Jeremiah extant in the Hebrew tradition (the Masoretic Text, or MT) and the version of the book based on the earliest Greek translation (the Old Greek, from which derives the Septuagint, or LXX). The Greek text tradition of Jeremiah is fully one-eighth shorter than the Hebrew text. Many single words, phrases, and entire passages within the MT are not represented in the Old Greek, which suggests that scribes reflecting on the Hebrew text continued to add material after the Greek text family had diverged from a common textual ancestor. The Greek text tradition also omitted some words, phrases, and verses due to scribal mistakes and translational choices. Further, the arrangement of some blocks of material differs between the two text types. Most notably, the oracles against the foreign nations are positioned after the first half of Jer. 25 in the Old Greek but after Jer. 45 in the MT. Some scholars have argued that there were two distinct editions of the book of Jeremiah preserved in scribal transmission processes. Others interpret the textual differences as an indication of numerous local changes or errors rather than as coherent evidence for two separate text families. The question of divergent texts should not be dismissed as an abstruse matter of interest only to textual experts. Rather, it is significant for theological reflection on the reception of Scripture in diverse communities over time. In the book of Jeremiah, both in its variant texts and within the complicated final form of the MT, a polyphony of voices was intentionally preserved. Communities of Israelites in Babylon, Judah, and Egypt were separated not only by geographical distance but by distinct cultural and social commitments that influenced their shaping of Jeremiah traditions.

Some have seen the book of Jeremiah as a chaotic welter of diverse traditions, organized in local sections by catchwords or minor themes but governed by no overarching literary structure or theological plot. Older historical-critical work had focused on reconstructing hypothetical sources for Jeremianic materials: the poetic material (called Source A) was thought to contain words authentic to the prophet, these then supplemented by prose biographical additions (Source B), hortatory sermons (Source C), and late oracles of promise (Source D). The value judgments leveled by earlier historical critics that privileged the poetic oracles over the other material are unfortunate, and many leaps in hermeneutical logic bedevil the older source theory. Nevertheless, historically informed literary criticism, performed with hermeneutical sophistication, can be an important means of attending to distinctive voices within the book of Jeremiah. Striking differences of tone, shifts of theological emphasis, and rough transitions between disparate blocks of material would have been quite as obvious to ancient audiences as they are to contemporary readers, yet they were preserved rather than erased or harmonized. This would suggest that honoring those differences is a theologically significant part of hearing Jeremiah as scriptural witness.

Recent literary readings of the book of Jeremiah have argued for various types of coherence in the book, some readers pressing for a dominant movement from judgment to salvation traceable through the book as a whole; and the alert reader can certainly discern coherence of some themes. Reading strategies that honor disjuncture and difference, however, tend to emphasize that centers within the book of

Jeremiah form briefly only to dissolve, that conflicting themes run parallel to each other and spar for the reader's attention, that story lines and diverse voices joust with each other for control of the book's discourse. To read the book as if it were a unitary narrative uttered by a single voice would be to read against that ancient commitment to bear witness to difference. The unruly book of Jeremiah invites its audience to honor the blend and clash of multiple perspectives as testimony to a God who can never be domesticated by a single diction or a monolithic understanding of the divine purpose.

Below, a brief introduction to literary-structural issues will lead into an explo-ration of three major theological themes in Jeremiah: (1) vocation; (2) discernment of idolatry; and (3) the dialogic movement between judgment and restoration in God's purposes for Judah. These three themes animate the book of Jeremiah across all of the distinctions between poetry and prose, earlier material and later traditions, and diverse construals of Judah's theopolitical landscape. The interplay of these themes throughout the book creates a rich theological witness that is like nothing else in Scripture for its rhetorical power both to "to pluck up and to pull down, to destroy and to overthrow, to build and to plant" (1:10), in the name of Jeremiah's God.

COMMENTARY

The diversity of traditions in Jeremiah challenges interpreters to find ways to appreciate coherences within this polyphony of witnesses. Many interpreters find theological coherence in the ways in which various sections are related to one another. Some see the two major literary-structural sections of the book as Jer. 1–25 and 26–52, with the first half of the book focusing primarily on judgment against Judah and the second half focusing on oracles of hope and God's retribution against Judah's enemies. This kind of literary structuring suggests to some the unfolding of a plot that begins with judgment and ultimately yields to restoration. Others resist constructing any such broad narratological theme on the grounds that it fails to attend to crucial dissonances and privileges certain voices within the text at the expense of others.

Certain chapters within Jeremiah play pivotal roles in the theological structure of the whole. Chapter 1 introduces themes that sound throughout the book, setting the stage for the playing out of Jeremiah's vocation as prophet on the national and international fronts. Chapters 25, 26, and 36 are usually identified as structurally important as well. Jere-miah 25 has been seen by many commentators as a kind of hinge, looking back at Judah's history of rejection of the prophetic word (25:3–7) and forward to divine discomfiture of Judah's enemies, including Babylon (the rare word "She-shach," a cryptogram for Babylon, links 25:26 and 51:41). While this reading is plausible, one may instead see the plot of Jer. 25 as moving from divine punishment of Judah to God's devastation of the entire earth ("from nation to nation . . . those slain . . . shall extend from one end of the earth to the other," 25:30–33). This reading makes a much starker theological point: if God's own people must be drastically punished and the temple in which God's holy name resided is to be laid waste, then all the earth shall suffer punishment, for the destruction of God's chosen source of blessing for all the earth (cf. Gen. 12:1–3) is an irrevocable sign of loss of hope for the whole world.

Readers have proposed a number of other literary patterns and linkages within the book. Chapters 27–29 form a unit that focuses on the problem of false prophecy and contests for authority between Judah-based survivors and the Diaspora group in Babylon. Jeremiah 26 and 36 display thematic links having to do with the responses of kings to the prophetic word. These two chapters contrast the example of repentant King Hezekiah (from the time of Isaiah, when Jerusalem was delivered from the Assyrians) with that of insolent King Jehoiakim, whose deliberate destruction of Jeremiah's scroll underlines his recalcitrance and seals the fate of Judah.

Some contend that Jer. 30–31, known as the Book of Consolation, constitutes the theological heart of the book. This is an ambitious theological claim indeed, for the book of Jeremiah arguably holds the promise material at something of a distance, as a dream for future times ("Thereupon I awoke and looked, and my sleep was pleasant to me," 31:26). Further, the bifocal vision of the prose traditions in Jeremiah tends to envision either the privileging of only one group of Judeans (viz., the exiles in Babylon) or, conversely, the destruction of the whole earth by an angry God. Jeremiah 30–31 contains stirring promises of restoration for a unified Israel and Judah, but those promises are arguably contained and ironized by the bitter internecine arguments that continue in the prose (cf. Jer. 38 and 42–44). The visions of hope embedded in the book of Jeremiah unquestionably provide a luminous source of strength for desperate communities, but it is probably too optimistic to suggest that their tenor governs the entire book of Jeremiah. Ultimately, the question of the theological significance of literary structures in Jeremiah depends on the particular criteria and interpretive method(s) used by the interpreter. Those who prefer Jeremiah as a prophet of hope may well privilege the Book of Consolation. Those who emphasize Jeremiah's prophetic mission of warning will muster a different set of interpretive questions to interrogate the structural elements of the book.

We turn now to three major themes that play throughout the book of Jeremiah. The ideal audience constructed by the complex witness of the book is a rereader who already knows the book deeply, as ancient scribal groups undoubtedly did. Each of the following themes, then, can be seen to unfold in a richly complicated multivalence intended for individuals and communities steeped in attentive reading and rereading of Jeremiah.

Vocation

The book of Jeremiah works out the notion of vocation in a number of important ways. One could suggest that variations on this theme constitute the primary melodic structure of the entire book, for the prophet's vocation consists in calling all members of the community back to their vocation as followers of Israel's God. Thus the notion of vocation is worked out in the ways in which various Judean leaders and groups see or fail to see that Jeremiah speaks God's word. Priests, officials, and prophets all have led the people astray (2:8, 26, and passim). Judah's kings come in for scathing indictments. Those who come in for commendation or a special measure of mercy are the Rechabites (Jer. 35), Ebed-melech the Ethiopian eunuch (38:7–13; 39:15–18), and the scribe Baruch (45:1–5). The importance of the roles of these leaders and groups, whether they supported or resisted Jeremiah, underscores the complexity of the prophetic vocation playing itself out in the fraught social interactions of bitterly divided communities.

Vocation, for Jeremiah, involves being known by God, being equipped to proclaim God's will in the public square, being prepared to call others to account, and being fortified to face inevitable resistance. Jeremiah confronts exquisitely high theological stakes as God's chosen people teeter on the brink of destruction, for it is only through his warnings and intermediation that they might remember how to turn to the one who can save them. The emphasis on vocation in Jeremiah throws into sharp relief the destinies of leaders and others—both supporters of Jeremiah (the Shaphanides, Baruch, Ebed-melech), and adversaries (Pashhur, the men of Anathoth, Jehoiakim, Zedekiah). Jeremiah's prophetic proclamation has as its horizon the prospering and defeat of entire nations, even the desolation of all nations in the known world (in 4:23–28 and 25:30–33 the scope of the destruction is unquestionably the entire earth). He dares proclaim that Nebuchadrezzar, whose military aggression has brought Judah to its knees, is carrying out a vocational purpose that earns him the astonishing title of the Lord's "servant" (25:9; 27:6; and 43:10). Jeremiah glimpses the inexorable pull of God's purposes both in the depths of his own soul and in the farthest reaches of global community ("Am I a God nearby, says the LORD, and not a God far off?" 23:23). This prophet, known fully by God even before his conception (1:5; cf. Ps. 139:13–16), has been consecrated "a prophet to the nations," a formulation that underlines the role that Jeremiah will play in international theopolitics. The call of Jeremiah emphasizes the untrammeled power of the prophetic word "to pluck up and to pull down, to destroy and to overthrow, to build and to plant" (1:10).

The theme of vocation may be explored theologically by examining the book's construction of prophetic identity, the Confessions of Jeremiah, and the prophetic sign-acts. First, consider the ways in which the prophetic identity of Jeremiah is constructed in the book. Not only do Jeremiah's inner struggles represent his own resistance to the remarkable demands being made on him, they also incarnate the agony of the people of Judah, for he is one of them—albeit one with a clear vision of the Lord's purposes. Jeremiah's vocation is, at least in part, to live as a faithful embodiment of the encounter between God and humanity. In Jeremiah's tumultuous emotions, and even in his resentment of the prophetic vocation itself, the reader sees where God's purpose meets human pain and confusion, both in Jeremiah's life and in Israel's history as a nation. The destruction of Judah under Jeremiah's anguished gaze may be seen to constitute an unraveling of the story of the exodus. Empowered by the liberating love of YHWH, the

people of Israel had come out of slavery in Egypt under the leadership of Moses and Joshua. Now in Jeremiah's time, the predations of Nebuchadrezzar are empowered by this same YHWH, and the people of Judah descend into the darkness of captivity again.

Indeed, Jer. 1 represents the prophet and his vocation in terms that echo traditions about Moses and Joshua. The commissioning of Jeremiah rings changes on the commissioning of Moses: the call of God is answered by a protestation on the part of the prophet ("Ah, Lord GOD! Truly I do not know how to speak, for I am only a boy," Jer. 1:6; cf. Exod. 4:10). Further, the Lord offers assurances of divine protection in diction evocative of the language of holy war: "Do not be afraid of them, for I am with you to deliver you, says the LORD. . . . They will fight against you; but they shall not prevail against you, for I am with you" (Jer. 1:8, 19). One may read Jeremiah as being figured as a "prophet like Moses" (Deut. 18:18), although one can make a case that the relevant passage in Deuteronomy was influenced by traditions about Jeremiah, so it may be more accurate to suggest that Moses was being subtly figured in postexilic traditioning processes as the original "prophet like Jeremiah." Jeremiah is also a warrior like Joshua: the triumphal claim of the prophet, "The LORD is with me like a dread warrior" (20:11), confirms the way in which holy war tradition has infused representations of this prophet. But a fatal irony reigns here. The plot of this new exodus and conquest runs disastrously in reverse: this prophet is not heeded, it is the inhabitants of Judah who are dispossessed, and God's people, including Jeremiah himself, are taken back into captivity. Theologically, Jeremiah is more an antitype of Moses and Joshua, a prophetic warrior-leader who is tragically helpless to stop the destruction of the promised land and the reenslavement of his people.

The anguish of attempting an impossible prophetic task is revealed in dramatic terms in the Confessions of

Jeremiah. Jeremiah not only struggles with the horror of what he sees and the resistance of the people. He also is constrained by prohibitions placed on his role by God. He is repeatedly forbidden to intercede on behalf of Judah (7:16; 11:14; 14:11), and he is forbidden to mourn the destruction of his people (16:5–9). In the Confessions, Jeremiah's trust in God's salvation (11:18–20) is shaken by his alarm concerning the apparent prospering of the wicked and the treacherous (12:1–6). The sufferings of the prophet are exacerbated by his uncertainty as to whether God is truly on his side (15:10–21). His pleas for healing and vindication (17:14–18; 18:18–23) yield to passionate anger at God and deep despair (20:7–18). The most graphic representation of the coercion that Jeremiah feels is the image of violation that he employs in his accusation, "O LORD, you have enticed me . . . you have overpowered me, and you have prevailed" (20:7). The verbs there, taken together, suggest a semantic range not only of deceit generally but of sexual seduction of the less powerful by the more powerful (Exod. 22:16 [15 Heb.]), and possibly even rape (cf. Deut. 22:25).

The prophet's rhetoric is riven by sharp cries of pain: "My anguish! My anguish! I writhe in pain! Oh, the walls of my heart!" (Jer. 4:19); and, "My joy is gone, grief is upon me, my heart is sick. . . . For the hurt of my poor people I am hurt. . . . O that my head were a spring of water, and my eyes a fountain of tears, that I might weep day and night for the slain of my poor people!" (8:18, 21; 9:1 [8:23 Heb.]). The prophet's pain gives way to a desperate weariness mirroring God's own weariness at Israel's recalcitrance. God has tirelessly sent God's "servants the prophets" to the people of Israel and Judah since the time of the ancestors (7:25; 25:4; 26:5; 29:19; 35:15; 44:4), but the people have stubbornly refused to heed. Now God is "weary of relenting" (15:6). Jeremiah, compelled to speak the horrors of judgment, cannot resist his divinely ordained vocation: when he tries to

refrain from speaking God's word, he becomes "weary with holding it in" and cannot (20:9).

The prophetic vocation is also represented in the sign-acts that Jeremiah is instructed to perform. In these embodied actions, one may trace a kind of vocational plot as the life of the prophet mingles with and textures the life of the people of Judah, performing God's perspective in their midst. First are two vision reports, which both convey a message and authenticate Jeremiah's prophetic "seeing": a branch of an almond tree and a boiling pot suggest that God is watching over the divine Word in order to perform it and a dread enemy is on the march (1:11–16). Next, Jeremiah is commanded to go and "stand in the gate of the LORD's house and proclaim" a word (7:2). Jeremiah's physical presence in the gate of the temple is an integral part of the temple sermon that he delivers, which focuses on the Lord's promise to continue to abide there if Judah amends its ways (7:3) and underlines the divine presence in the temple as witness to abominations (7:9–11).

In another sign-act, Jeremiah dons a clean linen loincloth, then buries it at the Euphrates, digging it up later to find it ruined: they who once clung to the Lord in obedience now have refused relationship with God and are ruined as a result (13:1–11). In another sort of performance, Jeremiah must remain unmarried (16:2) and father no children in Jerusalem. His living in isolation, without wife and children to rejoice his heart and guarantee the survival of his family name, signals the horrific death that will overtake Judah on a scale so vast that the dead will lie unburied and unlamented (16:4). In the last sign-act before the narration of the fall of Jerusalem, Jeremiah is commanded to "stand in the court of the LORD's house" to proclaim God's word (26:2). Here the prophet's reception becomes a significant aspect of the overall message, as "the priests and the prophets and all the people" roughly crowd him with the intention of doing him harm (26:8), the contrastive positions of two kings regarding prophecy are underlined (26:17–23), and Jeremiah is saved from the threatening mob by Ahikam the Shaphanide. Here the way in which Jeremiah's embodied message is received or rejected is demonstrated to have profound consequences for differing groups within Judah.

Following are a number of sign-acts directed to urgent questions facing Judah after the fall of Jerusalem, among them how long Judeans will remain in captivity in Babylon (Jer. 28) and how to adjudicate rival claims to authority among different groups of Judeans in Babylon, Egypt, and back in Judah. For example, Jeremiah stages the refusal of the Rechabites to assimilate (Jer. 35). Their refusal is commended: not only have they honored the command of their ancestor, they have steadfastly resisted all pressure to assimilate. Here may be pointed instruction from traditionists who disagreed with the dominant Deutero-Jeremianic advice to submit to Babylon, build houses in exile, and eat the produce of the foreign land (29:4–7). The Rechabites have a vocational purpose, for themselves as a kinship group and now as an object lesson for other Judeans; Jer. 35 is of central importance for the notion of vocation writ broadly as a matter of community ethos and identity. In another rhetorical performance, the prophet is commanded to bury stones in front of Pharaoh's palace at Tahpanhes as a foundation for the throne of the king of Babylon, who is coming to conquer Egypt (43:8–13). This sign-act is performed against Egypt for the purpose of contesting the political authority of the Judeans in diaspora there. The final sign-act in Jeremiah brings closure to the entire book, confirming the initial call of the prophet to "pluck up and pull down" nations and kingdoms. Jeremiah writes "in a scroll all the disasters that would come on Babylon" and commissions a Judean official to read those words aloud there, then weight the scroll and throw it into the Euphrates so that the scroll may perform the sinking of Babylon as its final signifying act (51:59–64). All of these sign-acts, taken together, enact an embodied narrative of prophetic vocation as Jeremiah engages his cultural context.

The second major theme running through the book of Jeremiah is the discernment and condemnation of idolatry.

Discernment of Idolatry

Idolatry is fundamentally the most serious charge that any ancient Israelite could face. In the book of Jeremiah, the accusation evolves into a potent metaphor for misbehavior and wrong thinking of all kinds. Jeremiah wrestles with the urgent problem of how to discern and proclaim God's truth to a people who have looked for truth in the wrong places and have heeded the wrong leaders. Leaders and people alike have forgotten the mighty deeds of the God of Israel: "My people have forgotten me, days without number" (2:32). Idolatry proper (worship of false gods) and false prophecy are the two chief problems with which the book of Jeremiah is concerned here. Intimately bound up with those two issues is the question of how Judah is to position itself politically in the international landscape: military alliances with other nations constitute an idolatry of sorts, both because Judeans might look to the supposed strength of their allies' gods and because their pragmatic reliance on military rescue by an ally could displace trust in Israel's God as the only guarantor of security. False prophecy may be either prophesying by Baal—speaking a word attributed to a false deity—or prophesying a misleading message that did not come from Israel's God. The idolatrous word against which much of the book fulminates is the false message of *shalom*, a Hebrew concept connoting peace, freedom from aggression, and prosperity. False prophets are promising that disaster will not come upon Judah and, later, that the exile will be of short duration. Contesting this dangerous thinking is a major rhetorical purpose of the book of Jeremiah.

Idolatry is portrayed in Jeremiah as fruitless seeking, as a stubborn, generations-long refusal to remember the

God of Israel, as false confidence that God does not see the political and moral corruption of the people, and as callous indifference to the Law. The Lord's exasperation is patent: "What wrong did your ancestors find in me that they went far from me, and went after worthless things, and became worthless themselves? . . . They have forsaken me, the fountain of living water, and dug out cisterns for themselves, cracked cisterns that can hold no water" (2:5, 13). Judah's religious leaders come in for blistering critique: "The priests did not say, 'Where is the LORD?' Those who handle the law did not know me; the rulers transgressed against me; the prophets prophesied by Baal, and went after things that do not profit" (2:8); false prophets and priests "ply their trade throughout the land, and have no knowledge" (14:18). The absurdity of idolatrous worship prompts biting sarcasm directed at those "who say to a tree, 'You are my father,' and to a stone, 'You gave me birth.' For they have turned their backs to me, and not their faces. . . . Where are your gods that you made for yourself? Let them come, if they can save you, in your time of trouble; for you have as many gods as you have towns, O Judah!" (2:27–28).

False prophets earn a particularly heavy indictment because they mislead the people into believing that God intends something that God does not, thus fatally undermining any earnest attempt on the part of the people to seek God's truth and live faithfully according to it. The false prophets have not taken seriously the gravity of Judah's disobedience to God, even though acknowledgment of that sin and subsequent repentance are the only steps that can save Judah: "They have treated the wound of my people carelessly, saying, 'Peace, peace,' when there is no peace" (6:14; 8:11). The metaphor of adultery is used for both the people's idolatry and the falsity of priest and prophet: "they commit adultery and walk in lies; they strengthen the hands of evildoers, so that no one turns from wickedness. . . . From the prophets of Jerusalem, ungodli-

ness has spread throughout the land" (23:14–15). Jeremiah's dramatic confrontation with the prophet Hananiah (Jer. 28) shows that a great deal was at stake for the people of Judah in the issue of discernment of God's truth. A false prophet could muster important political support for an agenda that ran counter to God's purposes, with catastrophic results.

The book of Jeremiah uses another literary technique to combat idolatry and redirect its audiences to the truth of God: the inclusion of doxologies that identify YHWH as the Creator God who has power over all the earth. The identity of Israel's God is crucial for the construction of community identity in matters of cultic practice and theopolitics. Consider the divine claim that comes immediately after a horrific oracle of judgment against Zion ("human corpses shall fall like dung upon the open field," 9:22). Jeremiah 9:24 exhorts, "let those who boast boast in this: that they understand and know me, that I am the LORD; I act with steadfast love, justice, and righteousness in the earth, for in these things I delight." This powerful claim reinforces for Jeremiah's audience what is required of them: knowledge of the Lord will allow the community to experience God acting with steadfast love, justice, and righteousness. In Jer. 10 a doxology is placed in a literary position that allows it to respond fluidly to diction of warning, judgment, and plea. The chapter opens with a warning not to learn the idolatrous ways of other nations; then follows a majestic hymn praising God's sovereignty as "King of the nations" and as "the living God" at whose "wrath the earth quakes . . . the nations cannot endure his indignation" (10:7, 10). The doxology underlines the futility of idol worship and emphasizes that Israel alone "is the tribe of his inheritance" (10:16; so also 51:19). In highlighting both God's power and God's covenantal care for Israel, the doxology serves a crucial purpose in preparing the book's audience for another oracle of judgment (10:17–18). Finally, the prophet appeals to the covenant relationship, begging God to pour out the divine wrath on nations other than Jacob (10:25). Often in the book of Jeremiah, the divine epithet "LORD of hosts" is used of God, a doxology in miniature that acclaims God as Divine Warrior leading the heavenly armies into battle. Occurrences of this title for God are seen in the oracles against the nations, where the assertion of God's power as warrior is especially appropriate rhetorically (particularly noteworthy there is a repeated formula, "the King, whose name is the LORD of hosts," 46:18; 48:15; and 51:57). These claims serve both to instruct the idolatrous Judah about the identity of God and to proclaim God's power. "See, I am the LORD, the God of all flesh; is anything too hard for me?" (32:27) works rhetorically both to encourage and to teach. The oppression of Israel and Judah will be ended when they learn that "their Redeemer is strong; the LORD of hosts is his name" (50:34).

The title "LORD of hosts" is deployed often in Jeremiah to point to the power of Israel's God to create, to destroy, and to redeem. The tensive movement in the book of Jeremiah between threats of judgment and promises of restoration springs, then, not only from Judah's own sinful behavior and capacity for repentance, but from the identity of Israel's God. Profound indeed are the theological tensions that arise from the interplay between judgment and salvation, the third major theme to be explored here.

Dialogical Movement
between Judgment and Restoration

Some have argued that the book of Jeremiah moves along a plot trajectory from judgment to restoration. While there are local dynamics within certain blocks of text that might suggest this kind of "plot" movement from terror to hope, the text of Jeremiah overall is far too complex and turbulent to be mapped along any simple story line of that sort. Jeremiah celebrates God's power both as one who punishes sin and as one who can restore the devastated

fortunes of Judah. The book contains two discrete collections that may be said to focus on hope: the Book of Consolation (chaps. 30–31, to which some would add chaps. 32–33) and the oracles against the nations (chaps. 46–51), the latter argued by many to constitute hope for Judah because Judeans would naturally rejoice at divine retribution on their enemies. But the book seethes with warnings of division, oracles of judgment, and narratives of destruction from Jer. 1, where Jeremiah is fortified as a warrior to face resistance from fellow Judeans, to Jer. 52, which renarrates the capture of Jerusalem, the maiming and execution of Judah's royals and other officials, the desecration of the temple, and deportations of Judeans into slavery. The final vignette shows Judah's only remaining royal, Jehoiachin, receiving favor at the table of Babylonian king Evil-merodach (52:31–34). Interpreters wanting to read this as a muted sign of hope must overlook the devastating pathos of this passage. King Jehoiachin is shown a negligible sign of favor by his captor, and that only in the thirty-seventh year of his exile. This gesture of elevation is virtually meaningless politically, for Jehoiachin simply remains in captivity until "the day of his death." Passages offering effervescent hope are indeed present in the book of Jeremiah, and they continually engage the rhetoric of destruction in a dynamic dialogue. But it would be difficult to argue convincingly for a large-scale plot unfolding from judgment to salvation in the book. The prophetic diction of chaos, terror, divine fury, and grievous loss controls the tenor of the book from beginning to end.

The fullness and horror of judgment are expressed in the Jeremiah traditions by means of a number of images. God is imaged as the Divine Warrior fighting against Judah, and the inescapable scope of God's retribution is portrayed using images of a plague triad, a divine cup of wrath from which all nations must drink, and a catchphrase, "terror-all-around." These are worth exploring in some detail.

The idea of God as Divine Warrior fighting against God's own people emerges with chilling clarity in Jer. 21: "I am going to turn back the weapons of war that are in your hands. . . . I myself will fight against you with outstretched hand and mighty arm, in anger, in fury, and in great wrath" (21:4–5). God's mustering of human invaders as instruments of the divine purpose is likewise clear. "I will prepare destroyers against you, all with their weapons" (22:7), the Lord says. In the MT of Jeremiah, the idea that God deputizes other nations is taken to a rhetorically hyperbolic extreme with the designation of Nebuchadrezzar as God's "servant" (25:9; 27:6; 43:10). Through this locution, Nebuchadrezzar's status approaches that of YHWH's prophets ("my servants the prophets" serves as an organizing motif in the book's recital of Judah's rebellious history). The illustrious ancient warriors Caleb and Joshua, too, were called YHWH's servants in Israel's ancient traditions. Comparisons with Moses himself may have been evoked for the shocked Judean listeners (Moses is named as servant of the Lord in Num. 12:7, 8; Deut. 34:5; and very often in Joshua). And this new Babylonian "servant" is stronger than Moses: God declares that even Moses and Samuel themselves, towering heroic figures and paradigmatic intercessors on behalf of God's people, would not be able to avert the punishment that Nebuchadrezzar will be carrying out (Jer. 15:1). Most alarming for the book's audience may be the alignment of Nebuchadrezzar's ruthlessness with God's own ruthlessness. In 13:14 God says, "I will not pity or spare or have compassion when I destroy them," and the text later says of Nebuchadrezzar almost exactly the same thing (21:7), thus rhetorically constructing a virtually seamless identity between God and God's brutal servant, Nebuchadrezzar.

That this judgment on Judah and all the nations is inescapable is brought home with three different figures for far-reaching catastrophe. A triad of means of destruction is cited repeatedly in Jeremiah: sword, famine, and pestilence will stalk the earth, eventually exterminating every last survivor (14:12; 21:7; 24:10; 27:8; 42:17; and passim). A second image is the cup of wrath that God will make all the nations drink, including Babylon (25:15–29; 48:26; 49:12; 51:57): all will stagger and be rendered helpless in the face of God's fury. The final image used to evoke the scope of destruction is the catchphrase "terror-all-around." The phrase is used variously: it is the bone-crushing fear experienced in Jerusalem at the onslaught of the enemy (6:25); it becomes a mocking nickname for an adversarial temple official who will incur God's wrath (20:3) as well as a taunt hissed by those with whom Jeremiah is in conflict (20:10); and it is to be the portion for foreign nations (Egypt, 46:5; Kedar, 49:29). There is no escape: the image evokes the siege surrounding the city, with all possible avenues of escape cut off and Terror itself at the gates.

This discourse of utter destruction and the inevitability of doom is interrupted throughout the book of Jeremiah by luminous expressions of hope. A muted and tenuous hope may be perceived in the conditional diction that suggests that the people may yet "turn from their evil ways" or "amend their ways and their doings" and thereby avert the looming disaster (7:3, 5; 25:5; 26:3, 13; 35:15; cf. also poetic passages such as 4:4). A second, oblique sort of hope the book of Jeremiah offers is the promise of God to destroy Judah's enemies. Relevant here are 25:12–26 and the oracles against the nations. Also worth noting in this regard is a promise to thwart specific enemies of Jeremiah (e.g., 11:21–23). Lyrical indeed are the divine promises of healing and deliverance for a future time after the destruction of Judah and Jerusalem. Here are some of the most sublime promises of restoration and peace in all of Scripture. These are occasionally conditional on repentance (e.g., 3:12–14) but usually have to do with an act of salvation on God's part unmerited by the people. God will give

Judah "shepherds [i.e., kings] after my own heart," and all nations will stream to the throne of God in Jerusalem (3:15–17; cf. 17:24–26; Isa. 2:2–3, and Mic. 4:1–2). The language of promise often draws on the imagery of Jeremiah's commissioning in 1:10, sometimes for a unified Israel and Judah (e.g., 31:27–28), and sometimes in ways that privilege one group over others (24:5–10). Life will be characterized by joy and abundance (31:1–14). A new age of everlasting covenant faithfulness will dawn: God will write the law on the heart of every Israelite, and "they shall all know me, from the least of them to the greatest" (31:33–34). God the incomparable, all-powerful Creator will never allow Israel to be annihilated (31:35–37).

Words of judgment and hope continually displace each other in a fluid and charged dialogical dynamic throughout the book of Jeremiah. Sometimes passages of judgment give way to promises of healing, but beautiful passages of restoration also yield to intense threats of inescapable destruction. An eloquent promise of salvation in terms reminiscent of the exodus (16:14–15; cf. 23:7–8) is framed by some of the most brutal judgment material in the book: "I will hurl you out of this land into a land that neither you nor your ancestors have known . . . for I will show you no favor" (16:13), and the Lord will dispatch malevolent "hunters" who will ruthlessly track down all survivors, "because they have polluted my land with the carcasses of their detestable idols and have filled my inheritance with their abominations" (16:16–18)—terror all around, indeed. The sublime hopes expressed for a unified Israel and Judah in Jer. 30–33 are contained and perhaps even fatally ironized by powerful words of judgment and bitter internecine polemics clashing in huge swaths of material before and after them. Rather than offering a synchronic narrative of gradually unfolding hope, the book of Jeremiah insistently holds together visions of suffering and promises of deliverance. It is in this tension born of pain and hope, exhortation

and indictment, that readers of Jeremiah may find the truths of a God who speaks to every heart and every lived context. The rhetorical purpose underlying both the judgment and the promise material has to do with changing the hearts of those who hear (and read). For untold generations, Israelites and Judeans have "walked in the stubbornness of their evil" hearts and wills (3:17; 7:24; 9:14; and passim). Their recalcitrance was as deep as their very being: "the sin of Judah is written with an iron pen; with a diamond point it is engraved on the tablet of their hearts" (17:1). Judeans will receive the gift of a unified new heart to know God (24:7), per Jeremiah, only when they face the truth of their idolatry unflinchingly and trust in their Redeemer alone.

Conclusion

The prophet Jeremiah does not speak "shalom" lightly. His book leaves its audiences inspired, troubled, and convicted of their own idolatries. In the conceptual realm of idolatry arises a particularly difficult problem for contemporary readers: images that gender sin in terms of female sexual behavior. Figures of adultery, prostitution, and nymphomania abound in the passages that decry idolatry. Underlying this metaphorization is the cultural view that the female body is appropriately owned by the males of the family and that unending shame comes from female sexuality breaking free of strict male control. Judah's sin is likened to the indiscriminate sexual desire of a young female camel in heat, the overt sexual overtures of a female prostitute, and the infidelity of an adulterous wife (2:23–25, 33; 3:1, 20; and passim). Idolatry narrated as female willfulness comes in Jer. 44, where the prophet denounces the cult of the Queen of Heaven as being under the leadership of unrepentant women in the Judean Diaspora in Egypt.

Appropriate power (even divine power) is portrayed in terms of phallic aggression, and male warriors are shamed by having their fear in battle likened to the pain of a woman in labor (e.g., 4:31; 6:24; 22:23). Images of the military ravaging of "daughter" Zion combine the notions of earned punishment and the rape of young girls in warfare: "It is for the greatness of your iniquity that your skirts are lifted up, and you are violated" (13:21–22). Perhaps most disturbing in this metaphorical rhetoric of rape-as-just-deserts is the verse that portrays retribution as sexual violence premeditated by God himself: "This is your lot, the portion that I have measured out to you, says the LORD. . . . I myself will lift up your skirts over your face, and your shame will be seen" (13:25–26).

Only two positive images of women's agency exist in Jeremiah. The role of women as professional and private mourners is obliquely affirmed as an important ritual part of communal life (9:20–21; 31:15–17), and in 31:22, an elusive phrase, "female encompasses warrior-male," is used as a figure of hope or encouragement. This phrase has not yet been fully understood by interpreters. Given that it follows an image of divine compassion for Ephraim as "my dear son" and "the child in whom I delight" (31:20), it may be signaling that divine maternal compassion will "surround" (i.e., besiege) and trump Israel's militaristic male heroism in the restoration that God has planned. Be that as it may, metaphors gendered in the feminine remain overwhelming negative in the patriarchal diction and conceptual world of the book of Jeremiah. This gendering of sin and recompense has serious implications for how readers of Jeremiah construe the possibility of repentance. In ancient Near Eastern societies based on phallocentric notions of honor and shame, a female body once defiled can never be purified anew. Further, these metaphors have significant power to shape (and misshape) the imaginations of those who encounter them, in ways that readers might not even recognize. This, then, is one of three major ethical prob-lems raised for contemporary readers by the book of Jeremiah.

Two other ethical issues in Jeremianic rhetoric require attention: the way in which accountability for sin is cited throughout the book as a just reason for martial atrocities committed against entire peoples (whether Judah or foreign nations), and the way in which ruthless scapegoating and polemical infighting are enshrined in the prose traditions (cf. especially Jer. 24 and 42–44) as revealing God's favor for one political group of Judeans and utter contempt for others. Here the promise material in Jeremiah may prove a valuable resource for readers who are resistant to the prophet's message. Radical expressions of hope may be mustered to interrogate the book's misogynist metaphors, harsh rationalizations of suffering, and vicious internecine polemics. Jeremiah hopes for the healing of an incurable wound (15:18; 30:12, 15); so too we may await the healing of human cultures' incurable wounds of xenophobia, militarism, and phallocratic violence. Jeremiah hopes for a unified Israel and Judah (30:3; 31:27; 33:7); so too we may look for an end to the divisions that rend our communities. Jeremiah hopes for the restoration of some of Judah's most intractable enemies (46:26; 48:47; 49:6, 11 [unless this pastoral word to Edomite widows and orphans is sarcastic], 39); words of hope spoken to the despised Egypt, Moab, Ammon, Edom, and Elam may offer us the seeds of a fuller hope, that no "other" will remain beyond the reach of God's healing love.

The public and highly political nature of theological proclamation can be readily discerned in the book of Jeremiah. Its combustible mix of politics and prophecy points to a Word of God that is dynamic, contextually responsive, and stubbornly resistant to commodification by any one group or ideology. Jeremiah proclaims a truth not only for private meditation but for the public discourse of communities struggling to walk in faith. The book of Jeremiah inscribes the life of the faithful along a thin line between the pain of judgment and the grace of restoration, exhorting its audience to acknowledge the magnificent power of God for weal and for woe.

Bibliography

Brueggemann, Walter. *A Commentary on Jeremiah: Exile and Homecoming*. Grand Rapids: Eerdmans, 1998.

Diamond, A. R. Pete, Kathleen M. O'Connor, and Louis Stulman, eds. *Troubling Jeremiah*. JSOTSup 260. Sheffield: Sheffield Academic Press, 1999.

Perdue, Leo G. *Reconstructing Old Testament Theology: After the Collapse of History*. Minneapolis: Fortress, 2005. See especially his sections on feminist, African-American liberationist, and postcolonial interpretations of the book of Jeremiah.

Stulman, Louis. *Jeremiah*. AOTC. Nashville: Abingdon, 2005.

Weems, Renita J. *Battered Love: Marriage, Sex, and Violence in the Hebrew Prophets*. Philadelphia: Fortress, 1995.

Lamentations

Carleen Mandolfo

INTRODUCTION

The book of Lamentations, placed after the book of Jeremiah in the Christian canon, consists of five chapters or poems (the first four are alphabetic acrostics), each of which is most simply categorized as a type of lament. In the Jewish tradition, the book is placed at the end of the canon among the Writings and is recited in the Jewish liturgical calendar on the ninth of Ab, which commemorates the destructions of the First and Second Temples in 586 BCE and 70 CE, respectively. The poems of Lamentations were probably composed soon after the destruction of the First Temple by the Babylonians, and the subsequent exile of the elite members of Judean society. The poems seem to commemorate (perhaps liturgically) the experiences of those left behind, who were struggling to survive in the midst of the devastation.

COMMENTARY

Chapter 1, featuring two voices—one narratorial and one prayerful—focuses on the city of Jerusalem, figured as a woman (subsequently identified as "Daughter Zion"), a once-upon-a-time princess, now diminished to widowhood and bereft of her children (1:1). The metaphor of the city as widow harks back to the prevalence of the marriage metaphor in many of the prophetic books, in which the relationship between God and the people is figured as a marriage that is in danger of dissolution because of the wife's infidelity. Lamentations, however, is less concerned with guilt and blame and more concerned with the experience and expression of suffering.

The choice of gendered imagery in chaps. 1–2 is theologically significant and recognizes that women and men experience suffering in different ways. In the book of Lamentations, women suffer as wives and mothers—the loss of a husband meant the loss of prestige and security in ancient Israel; the loss of children meant then what it means now, perhaps the ultimate hardship a woman can endure, and thus a particularly effective way for the poet to express the magnitude of suffering experienced by the people, a strategy that is used to even greater effect in chap. 2.

Five times throughout chap. 1 the absence of a comforter for Zion is mentioned (vv. 2, 9, 16, 17, 21), a theme that is picked up and reversed by Second Isaiah (Isa. 40:1). There has been much speculation as to the identity of the comforter, but it is clear from the level of despair and hopelessness conveyed by the poet that Daughter Zion's only possible comforter is God; and that God seems utterly deaf to Zion's cries in spite of this is the real tragedy of the book. God is held responsible for Zion's misery, but both of the poem's speakers acknowledge that Zion's sins (never specifically identified) triggered God's actions (vv. 8, 14, 18, 20). Still, one should not assume that Lam. 1 upholds a standard biblical doctrine of retributive justice—clearly the poet sees Zion's torment as surpassing her deserts.

Chapter 2 focuses even more forcefully on divine culpability. Here the voice of the poet joins that of Zion in its indignation. In vv. 1–9a the verbs used to describe God's actions toward Zion are relentlessly harsh: God "casts down," "lays waste," "ravages," "slays," "destroys," "rejects," and so on. The theme of mothers and babies is raised again with devastating poignancy as children are described as perishing on their mothers' bosoms as they plead for food (vv. 11–12). Thoughts of Zion's guilt are pushed into the background, mentioned only briefly in the context of holding her prophets responsible for leading her astray (v. 14). The poet acknowledges the hopelessness of her situation and the irreversible absence of a comforter (v. 13), but then urges, as the only option available, that she cry out to God. As hopeless as it may seem, the lives of her children demand no less (v. 19). Zion's response is to rage at, rather than beseech, God (vv. 20–22). Her last words in the chapter (and the book) include a reference to God as "my enemy" (in contrast to the reluctance of the poet to say so earlier in the chapter [vv. 4–5]). Of note, however, is that Zion brings her anger to God, a sign of their ongoing intimacy.

Chapter 3, an individual lament, continues the theme of unmitigated suffering, this time expressed by a male voice, but seems concerned to counter the troubling theology of the first two chapters. The theological thrust of the central portion of the poem contradicts that of the first section by focusing on God's mani-

fold goodness (vv. 21–39). Its placement at the heart of the chapter, and thus the heart of the book, suggests an editorial hand that wants to centralize Israel's normative theology—"the LORD is good to those who trust in him" (v. 25, my trans.)—that celebrates God's ultimate goodness and justice, and insists on the meaningfulness of suffering (vv. 31–38). One must be careful, particularly in a post-Holocaust world, that these potentially clichéd expressions of trust in the Lord not justify suffering at the expense of victims. Of real benefit to victims, however, is this poem's insistence that stubborn, even defiant and angry faith is sometimes the only viable option to despair (v. 50).

Chapter 4 contains no prayer element, but is rather one monologue, the tone of which is reminiscent of the poet's voice in chaps. 1–2. The theme of suffering children is renewed here, with a twist. Society's cruelty toward its children demonstrates the depths to which these people have sunk. Cruelty in this case is not remonstrated against, per se, but is one more manifestation of their victimization (vv. 1–4, 10). This poem is less overtly theological, but the notion of justice haunts its rhetoric, as it does the other poems. Its value lies primarily in its description of how "common" people are often the principal victims of the powers-that-be, domestic and external.

The final chapter is a prayer of the people, a communal lament, which bemoans the dissolution of civic order and institutions (5:2–16). In direct address, the speaker implores God to take note of their disgrace, a request also made in chap. 1, but this poem ends with an explicit request that God not only see but act to restore their fortunes. The poem has traits in common with the penitential psalm tradition in its unequivocal acknowledgment of human wrongdoing (vv. 7, 16), but unlike most prayers in the Psalter it ends on a note of despair. Belief in God's unending glory and ability to redeem persists, however (vv. 19–20), in spite of so much evidence to the contrary. The book of Lamentations ends largely how it began, with unrequited cries of anguish to God.

The book of Lamentations insists that extreme suffering is never justified, and is properly raged against. For the most part, the poet(s) resists the temptation to justify God's actions and for that reason the book should be considered a kind of anti-theodicy. The idea that God responds to this rage with tenderness in Isa. 40–55 supports its legitimacy as a theological response of faithful persons, much like God's preference for Job's discourse over that of the friends. In fact, hope in the midst of Lamentations' suffering is kept alive through the perseverance of a dialogic relationship, no matter how thorny that relationship becomes.

Bibliography

Berlin, Adele. *Lamentations: A Commentary.* OTL. Louisville: Westminster John Knox, 2002.

Dobbs-Allsopp, F. W. *Lamentations.* Interpretation. Louisville: Westminster John Knox, 2002.

Gottwald, Norman. "Lamentations." In *Harper's Bible Commentary*, edited by James L. Mays et al., 646–51. San Francisco: Harper & Row, 1988.

Linafelt, Tod. *Surviving Lamentations: Catastrophe, Lament, and Protest in the Afterlife of a Biblical Book.* Chicago: University of Chicago Press, 2000.

O'Connor, Kathleen. *Lamentations and the Tears of the World.* Maryknoll, NY: Orbis, 2002.

Ezekiel

Stephen L. Cook

INTRODUCTION

Ezekiel and his theology are often neglected in contemporary communities of faith. It is not just that Ezekiel's prophecies are intricately woven writings, full of baroque, bizarre, and even offensive images. Ezekiel's priestly and hierarchical world is just plain foreign to the modern mind. Today we find it hard to appreciate this prophet's theology of God's burning holiness.

Modern ways of thinking are highly secular, and Ezekiel was a Jerusalemite priest, immersed in the thought forms of cult and ritual. His theology centers on *holiness*, an idea that feels unattractive to most of us in Western society. Holiness, for modern people, is about grimness and solemnity. We think of it as a value of puritans or authoritarians, who lack humor and the ability to enjoy life.

The problems with Ezekiel's book do not stop there. Ezekiel was not just any priest, but a member of the Zadokite priesthood, the highest ranking of Israel's sacral orders. This is off-putting. Modern people generally steer clear of sanctimonious officials, afraid of being told, "Keep your distance! I'm holier than thou!" They are wary of priests' tendency to assert their status in order to secure their own advantage. Our cynicism traces back to critics such as Thomas Hobbes, who

sketched a skeptical picture of the motivations and character of society's priests.

To judge Ezekiel's theology fairly, we must delve into his thinking and its sources and try to appreciate the true attraction of holiness as he understood it. For Ezekiel, human beings never fully apprehend or possess holiness, but may glimpse its beauty and feel echoes of its power. Our inmost longings resonate with such echoes, and our souls thirst for more. If such echoes should ever swell into an epiphany of holiness itself, we would immediately recognize it as the object of our deepest desires.

This is not to say that holiness is a safe or cozy thing. Quite the contrary, it is more scorching than "burning coals of fire," more unnerving than a lightning storm (Ezek. 1:13). Before the meridian blaze of this spiritual sun, the human self shrinks in awe, prepares for surrender, and opens to transformation. The soul becomes a hollow mold, ready to receive the hot, molten metal of holiness for which it was always meant. It becomes ever more willing to receive this metal's bright, stinging influx.

Ezekiel's theological system leaves no doubts about the transformative, sanctifying power of divine holiness. His ideal is a proximate, tangible dwelling of God's

241

glory in the center of Israel, which would mean the ennoblement of every human community and individual arrayed around it. It would mean the realization of Lev. 20:26, where God proclaims to all Israel: "You shall be holy to me; for I the LORD am holy, and I have separated you from the other peoples to be mine."

To be fair to Ezekiel's theology, we must not only rethink the meaning of holiness but also try to appreciate the idea of hierarchy. Ezekiel's hierarchical thinking is highly developed and claims distinct theological advantages. It is based on a theology of holiness laid out in one of the several sources of the Pentateuch, a recently perceived strand called the Holiness Source (the HS strand).

The Zadokite theology of the HS strand assumes that God's glory properly dwells amid the worshiping community. Specifically, the divine glory—the visible sign of God's holy presence—resides in the temple on Mount Zion, in incredible proximity to the congregation. The glory of the Lord had ranged freely outside both the sanctuary and the land of Israel in times past (cf. Exod. 16), but has intentionally settled in Israel's midst (cf. Ezek. 9:3; 10:4; 11:23; 20:40; 35:10; 37:27–28; 43:7; 48:35). It now *dwells* there in the temple (see especially Exod. 25:8; 29:45–46; Lev. 26:11, all HS; also cf. Exod. 40:34). Indeed, God now has personal attachments to Jerusalem's shrine, calling it "my sanctuary" (Lev. 19:30; 20:3; 26:2, all HS; Ezek. 5:11; 9:6; 23:39; 37:28).

God's people, in Ezekiel's ideal world, emulate the holiness in their midst (see Lev. 11:44; 19:2; 20:7, 26, all HS; Ezek. 37:27; 43:9). At the same time, from the midst of Israel, God radiates the divine holiness out to the entire land and to every sector of society. For details see the HS strand at Exod. 31:13; Lev. 22:32; Num. 5:3; 35:34; and cf. Ezek. 37:28.

For Ezekiel, the Lord's divine intent is to sanctify the entire community of faith as well as the land on which they live. Speaking of God's people, God proclaims, "I the LORD sanctify them" (Ezek. 20:12). Just so, in Lev. 21:8, God exclaims,

"I the LORD, *I who sanctify you*, am holy" (emphasis mine; cf. Lev. 20:8; 22:16, 32).

Ezekiel's hierarchical thinking reckons with both the danger and the sensitivity of holiness, its searing threat to mortal life and its volatile incompatibility with anything profane or unclean (see, e.g., Num. 16:38; 17:13, both HS; Ezek. 42:14; 44:19; 46:20). Fixed gradations of holiness within the temple and land safeguard the people with God's burning glory so near. At the same time, Ezekiel's system keeps all things anathema to holiness at arm's length from the divine presence.

The center and periphery of the Zadokites' system are linked in dynamic communion and interconnectivity. Not just the land's center, but the entire territory of Israel becomes sacred—God's own land (Ezek. 36:5; 38:16; cf. Lev. 25:23, HS). Every corner of the land becomes ceremonially pure (Lev. 18:25; Num. 35:34, both HS; Ezek. 39:12, 14–16). Successful communication and interaction flow up and down tiers of holiness in a way that empowers both individuals and groups.

No one is left out (Ezek. 34:4, 16). In HS theology, God values the worth and holiness of all God's people (see especially Lev. 19:2). For this conviction, Ezekiel is directly indebted to the HS strand (Ezek. 20:12; 37:28; 43:9).

Ezekiel's theology of a *hallowed land* strongly promotes the full humanity of all persons, including their economic and material well-being (e.g., Lev. 25:10, 23–24, 42). The whole of the land is God's holy possession, according to Ezekiel, and God has allotted it to the members of families, kin groups, and tribes for their own local benefit. Relying on HS traditions, Ezekiel's ideal blueprint for the future guarantees each family permanent tenure on their ancestral homesteads, thus ensuring their ongoing economic viability. Not even the people's princes should have the power to evict them from their ancestral farms (Ezek. 45:8–9; 46:18; cf. 22:27).

Ezekiel's unique theological emphases were of great service amid the horrendous political, social, and religious crisis of his times: the subjugation and destruction of Judah by the Babylonian Empire. Ezekiel prophesied as an exile, a deportee forcibly removed from Jerusalem by King Nebuchadrezzar of Babylon and his forces in 597 BCE. A decade after coming to Babylonia, he received word that Babylonian troops had returned to his Judean homeland and wreaked the ultimate catastrophe. They had destroyed both Jerusalem and God's temple.

This eventuality raised disorienting questions for Ezekiel's community. How could God have abandoned Jerusalem and the temple? Was there to be any future for God's people? Ezekiel's hierarchical theology provided him and his fellow prisoners of war with profound answers. It helped them find their way in an overturned world.

Hierarchical environments are known to be vulnerable to overthrow through the spread of impurity. Such structures may well collapse when new, threatening nuclei of power form and challenge the system's traditional center. The rise of multiple centers in a pyramidal system creates instability, which may spread like cancer across the structure's web of interconnectivity.

Ezekiel's theological sources depict God's holy land as possessing this very sensitivity to impurity. They use the image of God's territory as a sensitive stomach to drive home the point. Israel could have expected to have been evicted from God's land, if only they had grasped the import of this metaphor. The land tends to vomit out any people who dare defile it (see Lev. 18:24–30, HS; cf. Ezek. 36:16–19).

Though incredibly threatening, the land's ability to spew out impurity has a positive side. It means the land has resiliency, and may recover and heal during the people's exile in Babylonia. It may become a new homeland for them once again (Lev. 26:42–43; Ezek. 36:8–11, 33–34).

The hierarchical system of the HS strand clearly entails Israel and God sharing a *conditional* relationship, a vassal covenant with severe curses for any disobedience from Israel. This theology avers, however, that the covenantal curses are offset by specific unconditional promises of God. For one thing, God has made a perpetual covenant with the people's earliest ancestors (Gen. 17:7; Lev 26:42–45, both HS; Ezek. 16:60, 62). This ancestral commitment is unilateral and irrevocable.

For another, God is intensely, even patriotically, devoted to the land of Israel and its sacral center, the temple (Lev. 25:23, HS; Ezek. 7:22; 34:26; 35:10; 36:5). Israel's mountain heights are the true home of the Lord's glory (Ezek. 9:3; 20:40; 37:26; 43:7). Israel is the center of the nations, the earth's navel, and God's fiery hearth (5:5; 38:12; 43:15). The glory can depart from there for only "a little while" (11:16).

Even though Israel must go into exile, God will remain true to God's everlasting allegiances and commitments. Ezekiel's audience can rest assured that God will ensure that God's land is healed and that the Babylonian exiles are restored to it.

COMMENTARY

The book of Ezekiel is carefully organized, and proceeds logically along a clear trajectory. It moves from judgment and punishment to promise and salvation. Finally, there is a utopian vision of peace, security, and sanctification for all God's people.

Prophecies of judgment form the first part of the book, pronouncing doom on Judah because of the people's evil. The theological aim is to awaken the audience to their false sense of security and their complacency and to convict them of their total need of God.

A middle section of the book consists of prophecies directed against foreign nations. This section includes the themes of both judgment and salvation, since judgment on Israel's enemies is both a punishment of their hubris and, at the same time, an act of deliverance of God's people.

Beginning with chap. 33, Ezekiel's book offers prophecies of Israel's restoration from exile. The prophecies right the wrongs of the past, envision a new, exodus-like beginning for Israel, and address specific spiritual problems that have long plagued God's people.

After Ezekiel's prophecies of the destruction of Jerusalem are fulfilled in 586 BCE, many of the exiles lapse into a debilitating state of despair. Convinced of their total loss, the exiles become emotionally and spiritually paralyzed. Echoing the saying "a downcast spirit dries up the bones" (Prov. 17:22), they verbalize their inner state of dejection and hopelessness (Ezek. 37:11).

At this juncture, the tone and goal of Ezekiel's messages change dramatically. Now the prophet works to overcome the people's self-abnegation. His prophetic word now points to God's grace, affirming God's radical *yes* to creation and to humanity. The aim is spiritual renewal and regeneration. God wills to communicate God's holiness to the entire people, forever sanctifying them.

Part I: The Call of Ezekiel (1:1–3:27)

Superscription (1:1–3). From the superscription we learn several key facts about the prophecies to follow. First, as the collection begins, the year is 593 BCE and Ezekiel is already in Babylonian exile with other Jerusalemite officials, including King Jehoiachin. Jerusalem's final destruction and the capture of its last king, Zedekiah, still lie in the future. Second, we are told that Ezekiel is not only an official of Jerusalem but also a central priest of the city. Third, we discover that God is about to seize him, exercising divine control over his person, showing him supernatural visions.

In his visions, Ezekiel will peer beyond the veil of normalcy and encounter divine glory. The glory of YHWH is divine holiness made present, tangible, and accessible. It is the revealed character of Israel's God, which the Lord's people long to receive and internalize. It is their divinely appointed role to receive this holiness, be transformed by it, and then reflect it back to God, thus demonstrating their loyalty to their divine sovereign. This is the theology of the HS strand in a nutshell.

Tellingly, when Ezekiel beholds the divine glory, he will fall on his face (1:28; 3:23). In the presence of the numinous, that which is utterly, unspeakably *other*, every human being shrinks in reverence. Figures from across human cultures report such a feeling of being a creature of finitude and mortality in the presence of the holy. They grasp for language to express their awe. After encountering the *Other*, Yen Yuan, a Confucian student, spoke of being dwarfed by that which appeared to rise sheer above him.

The throne-chariot vision (1:4–28a). Immediately, we encounter the divine glory, the manifest presence of God's holiness. As here, the glory is usually a brilliant, fiery effulgence (e.g., Exod. 24:17; 40:38; Num. 16:35, all HS). It is a phenomenon central to Ezekiel's book. The prophet's various visions of the glory of YHWH and its movements across the Fertile Crescent structure his prophecies. They help to divide the book thematically, and they provide it with a specific eschatological trajectory moving from judgment through salvation to the promise of a secure, holy future. Key references to the glory's movement in the book include the following: Ezek. 1:28; 3:23; 8:4, 6; 10:1–22; 11:22–23; 43:2–5; 48:35.

At first, neither Ezekiel nor the reader perceives the true identity of the glory of YHWH. Time is needed to understand this inaugural vision, for at least two reasons. First, God appears to Ezekiel enthroned high atop a huge, multistory throne-chariot. Its undercarriage alone fills the viewer's entire field of vision. All that Ezekiel is able to see at first is the glow of metal in the midst of a fireball, darting movements of monstrous creatures, and four immense wheels with rims circled with eyes. God's presence is removed from the prophet by a graduated, spatial system of tiered holiness with wheels, monsters, and a crystalline expanse demarcating the storied levels.

Second, the thought that God's throne could appear in Babylonia, over five hundred miles from God's holy city of Jerusalem, must have required a major psychological adjustment for Ezekiel. The temple on Mount Zion was supposed to be where one encountered the Great King, not Babylonia at the other end of the Fertile Crescent. As the psalmist recites, "The LORD has chosen Zion; he has desired it for his habitation" (Ps. 132:13; cf. Pss. 48:1–2; 68:16; 76:2).

Key traits of Ezekiel's theology are already apparent from this initial vision of Ezek. 1. We can see that Ezekiel shares with the HS strand some daringly anthropomorphic images of God. He actually views the appearance of God, beholding what looks to be a "human form" gleaming like "amber" and "fire" (1:26–27). Although God is fully *other* in Ezekiel's theology, God also wills to be present to humanity, to be accessible.

Although God wills to be unusually close to humanity, there can be no simple, easy contact between the holy and the profane. In particular, note the careful description of the holy in 1:28. The prophet uncovers the divine glory by peering through four distinct degrees of removal between him and the Lord. He sums up his vision: "This was (1) the appearance of (2) the likeness of (3) the glory of (4) the LORD."

A third point concerns God's sovereign freedom, including the territorial and spatial freedom of the divine glory. God's election of the Holy Land as the locale specially chosen for manifesting divine holiness never implied God was parochial. The immense wheels that Ezekiel sees beneath God's throne denote a mobility and incursion of God's glory that extend to the four corners of the cosmos. Ezekiel's God is not limited to any particular locale or territory.

Ezekiel's commissioning (1:28b–3:27). Throughout Ezekiel's commissioning God addresses him as "mortal" (2:1, 3, 6, 8; 3:1, 3, 4, 10, 17, 25), as happens a full ninety-three times in the book. The idiom stresses how God and Ezekiel belong to two different tiers of existence within a storied cosmos. To constantly call Ezekiel "mortal" emphasizes that in this book the holy realm of God and the profane realm of creatures have wondrously come into contact.

Israel was used to interacting with its prophets in a hearty give-and-take relationship. There was supposed to be an opportunity to respond to a prophetic message, and a prospect that God would relent from threatened judgment. Central to Ezekiel's commissioning, however, is the physical act of swallowing a scroll whose contents will inexorably determine Ezekiel's prophetic work (2:9–3:3). Ezekiel's prophetic message has already been inscribed in a document, becoming fixed and inevitable. Ezekiel's task is to digest it, internalize it, and radically embody it.

How striking! God's present message of impending judgment for Judah will allow no give-and-take. It is a matter of scriptural record, archived and treasured in books such as Habakkuk (Hab. 1:5–11). There is presently only hope for individuals to save themselves amid the coming crisis (see Ezek. 3:21; 14:16; 18:32). Scripture as a theological force to be reckoned with emerges here before our eyes in the book of Ezekiel.

At 3:22–27 we learn that the prophet is constrained not only by a written scroll but also by a God-imposed speechlessness. Ezekiel's speechless state requires some theological wrestling, since texts such as 11:25 show that the prophet did engage in verbal communication with his audience, and informed them about the Lord's visions. We must probe the meaning of his speechlessness as a metaphor.

Very likely, the prophet's bridled speech is related to the strange, new prophetic commissioning given him. Ezekiel's speechlessness refers especially to the traditional prophetic role of representing the people and their rights before the Lord (e.g., Exod. 32:11–14; Num. 14:13–19). Ezekiel must not side with the people in this traditional manner, but merely let the doomful scroll that he has swallowed reach its fulfillment.

The metaphor of speechlessness helps to structure the progress of Ezekiel's book. God bridles Ezekiel's tongue only in the first twenty-four chapters of the book, where the judgments of the scroll that Ezekiel has swallowed work themselves out. As the book's prophecies against the foreign nations begin, God announces Ezekiel's impending release from this constraint (Ezek. 24:25–27; cf. 29:21). This release becomes a reality at the start of the following major section of the book, containing Ezekiel's prophecies of Israel's restoration (33:21–22).

Part II: Prophecies of Doom against Judah and Jerusalem (4:1–24:27)

Ezekiel's God is devastated by the people's immorality and social injustice, by their false worship and idolatry. Abominations are desecrating God's land, driving God's glory from the temple (5:11; 8:6; 10:18). Divine judgment inevitably follows in the wake of its egress. Jerusalem will be utterly destroyed and its remaining inhabitants suffer exile.

From Ezekiel's theological perspective, there is no worse punishment for Israel than exile. To be in exile is to find oneself shut out from God's holiness. It is to be alone in a strange land, the land that Bernard of Clairvaux calls "the land of unlikeness," where nothing and no one emulates God.

To counter the tragic, alienated state of the people, God's *prevenient grace* emerges as an essential element in Ezekiel's theology. Jerusalem's destruction is inevitable, but that is not the end of the story. God's stubborn, irresistible grace will eventually triumph over the people's current ineluctable state. To begin to appreciate the full reality of human alienation from God is at the same time to begin to marvel at the inexplicable power of grace.

Ezekiel's message of judgment takes several forms. Symbolic actions portray the coming siege of Jerusalem. Visions of apostasy in Zion depict the departure of the Lord's glory from the temple. Ringing denunciations confront false prophecy and idolatry; disputation sayings counter false beliefs and claims. In several memorable passages, Ezekiel outlines Israel's history of faithlessness using daring allegorical depictions and bold theological schematizations.

In all of this, Ezekiel's prophecies repeatedly emphasize a focal divine purpose. God's work of judgment aims to evoke knowledge of YHWH. In the understanding of the HS strand, God has intervened in history on behalf of Israel, drawing them into direct knowledge of God's life. God is in the business of making Israel holy, and nothing is more important than for Israel to get in tune with this work (see, e.g., Exod. 10:2; 16:32; Lev. 23:43, all HS).

Symbolic actions describing the coming siege of Jerusalem (4:1–5:17). The symbolic actions of Israel's prophets amounted to a sort of street theater. Their dramatics helped them drive home urgent messages from God. Symbolic acts were common among Ezekiel's predecessors, but in his book we see this type of communication develop in extreme, puzzling ways. Ezekiel loses his speech (3:26); he lies immobilized for months, first on his left side (4:5) and then on his right (4:6–8).

When one reads of such behavior, one is tempted to imagine that Ezekiel was traumatized by his exile or afflicted with psychological illness. But then one realizes that the persona of Ezekiel is, to a significant extent, more of a literary construct than a simple figure of history. Ezekiel is a character within the book's prophetic narratives, associated with stupendous outflows of holy power in the manner of an Elijah or an Elisha.

The stories about Ezekiel's life, like the legends of Elijah and Elisha in the books of Kings, intend to invigorate our spiritual imaginations. They make one think outside the box, inviting people to envision the world as a place where divine holiness may be at work, a place where God's glory wants to dwell. As Martin Luther maintained, the market is sacred as well as the sanctuary; there does not remain any work or place that is profane. Similarly, Martin Buber understood that there is no true human share of holiness without the hallowing of the everyday.

Just as the symbolic actions depicting Ezekiel are not literal or empirical, their significations are far from straightforward. Ezekiel's prophecies are often nonmimetic, entailing much more than simple representation of the observable world. They collapse varying realities from across time into compressed, baroque presentations.

Ezekiel's sign-acts point not only to the miseries of the coming siege of Jerusalem in 586 BCE but also to the impurities of exile that will follow it. They allude to the complex nature of the covenant curses described in the HS strand. The curses of the HS covenant are first played out in the land of Israel before intensifying into the threat of foreign exile (4:5; cf. Lev. 26).

Within this section depicting Ezekiel's symbolic actions, God first makes clear the central purpose of God's coming intervention and judgment against Jerusalem. God is about to act so that the people may know that God is the Lord—God is YHWH (5:13). This is recurring, fixed language in Ezekiel: the prophet's celebrated *recognition formula*. What is its theological import?

For Ezekiel, God's identity as YHWH signals that God is sui generis—one of a kind in character, power, and claim on people's lives. To recognize God as YHWH is to know that no one else accomplishes things as this Deity does. God's thoughts, words, and deeds are irrepressible. "I am the LORD; I have spoken, and I will perform," declares Ezekiel's God (Ezek. 17:24 NASB; cf. 24:14).

Before the time of Ezekiel's writings, the same recognition formula found here occurred in the HS strand (e.g., Exod. 6:7; 7:5; 10:2; 16:12; 31:13). There, as here, recognition of YHWH is deemed spiritually crucial. Knowing that God intervenes in history in irrepressible acts of judgment and blessing is what allows God's people total confidence in faith. Only such confidence permits them to let go of their pride and self-reliance and throw themselves upon God. This freedom is their salvation.

It is also their sanctification. Ezekiel's God is a self-revealing, self-giving Deity, intent on releasing God's presence, fidelity, and emancipation into the world. Such a God's holiness is eminently available to God's people. If one orients one's being toward such a Deity, one allows God's holy presence so to transform oneself that one finds complete fulfillment in communion with the Lord. This is the genius of the HS theological system.

The temple visions (8:1–11:25). Ezekiel's theological traditions placed extremely high value on the sanctuary at Jerusalem as Israel's sacred space of worship and the dwelling place of God's glory. The temple was the all-important fulfillment of God's programmatic command at Mount Sinai, "Have them make me a sanctuary, so that I may dwell among them" (Exod. 25:8, HS). Israel's sacral leaders who drew near to the Lord in service at the sanctuary bore tremendous responsibility. They had the duty of maintaining and protecting the holiness of the shrine and of drawing the people to it in safety.

The holiness of the sanctuary was not to be taken lightly. Those who were careless about it risked being devoured by fire (see Num. 16:35, HS). So also desecration of God's land and the sanctuary at its center threatened the people's continued existence. The holiness of God cannot coexist with what is unholy or unclean, and this means that Israel's continuing life within the Holy Land is subject to certain vulnerability.

Given the significance of the Jerusalem shrine, one can only imagine Ezekiel's dismay at what he witnesses in his vision of wickedness in the temple (Ezek. 8:1–18). God reveals "great abominations" that must "drive me far from my sanctuary" (8:6). Intensifying the horror, the visionary experience collapses time, unearthing atrocities from across Israel's history.

The departure of the Lord's glory from the temple (10:1–22 and 11:22–25). Ezekiel's visionary experience reveals the unthinkable, the ultimate tragedy that Israel could possibly suffer under the HS covenant. God's glory is in the process of forsaking Israel and departing the temple. With the divine glory absent, holiness will no longer infuse the people and they will become completely ordinary. What is more, with God absent they will be left exposed, open to judgment for their abominations.

Ezekiel 10:1–22 illuminates the problem of the wrath of God, helping us come to terms with this dimension of the divine nature, at least as it is understood by Ezekiel. It is particularly instructive that according to this passage the burning of Jerusalem originates from the coals of fire between the cherubim guarding God's divine holiness (10:6–7). A central role of the cherubim in Ezekiel is to surround this supernatural fire, containing it, preventing its uncontrolled release into the world.

The fire of the temple's altar coals represents the holy—the numinous presence of God. Blaise Pascal memorialized an experience of God on November 23, 1654, by sewing a paper with the following words into the lining of his coat: "From about 10:30 at night until about 12:30. *Fire*." Pascal experienced holiness as fire. Released into the world, this holy fire has a necessarily ambivalent character just as mundane fire may both warm and scorch. It is two-edged, capable as much of horrible devastation as of unspeakable good. Humanity needs to prepare carefully to encounter God's blazing holiness.

God's fiery holiness is experienced as divine wrath when it is encountered by those enmeshed in sin, bloodshed, or impurity. Only precious metals are not consumed by the ravishing heat of a smelter's fire. In like manner, irresponsibility and obduracy prove fatal before a manifestation of the glory of YHWH.

Can we bring ourselves to appreciate, or even treasure, God's fiery holiness? Perhaps we can, if we remember to associate it with the intensity of God's consuming jealousy for God's people (cf. Ezek. 6:9; 16:8; 36:5; 38:19). It burns passionately against any dross that contaminates and overthrows the covenant relationship. It flames up at the people's betrayal, but its burden and goal is the everlasting renewal of the HS covenant.

God's fire consumes, but the faithful devoutly *long* for such consummation. Powerful expressions of this sort of theology appear in many lines of the poetry of John Donne, such as the following: "Burne me o Lord, with a fiery zeale / Of thee and thy house, which doth in eating heale" (Holy Sonnet #5).

The allegory of the unfaithful wife (16:1–63). The intense desire of God for Jerusalem in this passage resonates with the much later spiritual language of Catherine of Siena: "O fiery abyss . . . O mad lover! . . . Have you need of your creature? It seems so to me, for you act as if you could not live without her, in spite of the fact that you are Life itself."

Though filled with divine emotion and passion, Ezek. 16 is admittedly disturbing. Not only vulgar and grotesque (particularly in the Hebrew), it also confronts us with ugly time-conditioned views of marriage. It is appropriate to wish that Ezekiel had more carefully considered how later female ears would likely hear his words.

A responsible hermeneutic must recognize the time-conditioned background of this passage and, in particular, decry any use of it to sanction violence against women. One must understand the text (i.e., its tenor) as pointing away from any sort of domestic violence toward a theological truth: divine holiness has a scorching, lethal effect on the arrogant and the cruel—of whatever gender (see 10:2; Ps. 18:10–13; Rev. 8:5).

Similarly, the careful expositor will emphasize that the tenor of Ezek. 16 has little to do with the stripping of women as a means of male titillation or domination. (Literal adultery was punished in ancient Israel by stoning, not stripping; 16:40.) In their arrogance, Assyria and Babylonia humiliated their enemies by leading them away stripped (cf. Isa. 20:3; 2 Chr. 28:15; Job 12:19). The males of Ezekiel's audience would have envisioned their own fate in that of the female Jerusalem and felt horror, not arousal, at the shame in store for them.

Being accountable (18:1–32). Ezekiel 18 has often been misunderstood. The passage does not deny sin's long-term consequences for the corporate community. Indeed, elsewhere Ezekiel affirms this long-standing and obvious truth (16:44). Rather, it contests the validity of a key defense that sin often builds up against God: the defense of fatalism.

Ezekiel insists that his fellow exiles can turn from sin and choose life amid the coming judgment. Their current alibi (18:2) will not hold up. They will not get away with what John Calvin called "shuffling"—handing off blame to someone else. No treasury of accumulated evil from the past is preventing the exiles' conversion.

God is squarely on the side of life (18:23, 32; 33:11) and does not mete out death indiscriminately. The Lord is neither capricious nor absent, far from sinners. The way forward for the exiles, according to Ezekiel, is to get themselves out of the judge's seat, take responsibility, realize God's nearness, and seize life.

There is no moral or theological innovation here. Rather, God's statement that "all lives are mine" (18:4) strongly recalls Num. 16:22 (HS), which affirms that the Lord is the source of all life, the "God of the spirits of all flesh." Such a Lord wills for each individual to choose life; God does not lock people into a fixed destiny.

In Ezek. 18, as in Num. 16, those Israelites who separate themselves from all offenders against God's holiness will surely find salvation amid God's judgment (Num. 16:24 HS; cf. Deut. 24:16).

Ezekiel 18 gives us fulsome insight into the entire range of sin—moral as well as ceremonial—that is condemning Judah to certain chastisement. The God of HS theology is committed to both ritual and ethical righteousness. Idolatry is forbidden, but defiling a neighbor's spouse is just as grievous a fault (18:6; cf. Lev. 18:20, HS). One must worship God in truth, but also refrain from oppression (Ezek. 18:7; cf. Lev. 25:17, HS), robbery (Ezek. 18:7; cf. Lev. 19:13, HS), and loan-sharking (Ezek. 18:8; cf. Lev. 25:36, HS). The courts must execute true societal justice (Ezek. 18:8; cf. Lev. 19:15, HS).

Ezekiel's theological traditions of the HS strand staunchly emphasize that holiness involves more than just the proper service of God in the realm of ritual. Holiness in this type of theology is a much broader matter that must include everything from social organization to agricultural life. For this theology, to grow in sanctity is increasingly to live into God's character and will in *all* areas of human life.

Israel's pattern of rebellion (20:1–44). Ezekiel 20 represents some of the prophet's most intense theological reflection on God's ways with God's people. He reviews Israel's history in a manner that is fundamentally theological in nature. Schematizing the history into a series of periods, he argues that in each era God preserved the people in spite of repeated rebellion. Israel has repeatedly failed to know YHWH, appreciate YHWH's holiness (20:12, 20, 26), and demonstrate this holiness before the world (20:9, 14, 22, 39, 41).

The occasion for this historical review is the appearance at Ezekiel's domicile of a group of Israel's elders who want him to ask the Lord questions for them. The book's ongoing motif of Ezekiel's speechlessness comes to the fore again as the

Lord refuses their request. God exclaims, "Why are you coming? To consult me? As I live, says the Lord GOD, I will not be consulted by you" (20:3; cf. 20:31).

In addition to the prophet's speechlessness, another key emphasis of Ezekiel now emerges. For the first time in his book, we learn that Ezekiel's God has an intense concern with the honor of the divine name. At 20:9, 14, 22, 39, and 44, God stresses that God's actions on behalf of Israel throughout the people's history have always been primarily for the sake of the divine name.

The motif of God's concern for God's holy name comes straight from the HS strand (see Lev. 18:21; 19:12; 20:3; 21:6; 22:2, 32). It is repeated by Ezekiel here and at Ezek. 36:20–23; 39:7, 25; 43:7–8. The tone of the motif seems highly problematic at first glance. Can God's primary motivation in interacting with the world really be evoking honor? Does this not make God less than caring, perhaps even egotistic?

Far from an egotist, Ezekiel's God is more gracious than at first appears. The prophet is using shocking rhetorical language, not face-value language. He is driving home the mystery of God's grace over against Israel's fossilized heart (cf. 2:4; 3:7; 20:33; 36:26). The members of his audience need to learn that the universe does not revolve around them. It revolves around God, and God's intention to infuse the world with divine holiness. In Ezekiel's theology, holiness must extend itself to all earth's peoples (20:41; cf. 28:22, 25; 36:23).

Ezekiel's harsh language of theological depravity pushes his audience to see that the status quo is far from acceptable, that they are not presently pleasing and lovable to God. It is only God's *prevenient* (proactive, radically persistent) grace that has preserved Israel in the past and that gives the people hope for the future. God must act in a manner set by God's character, not based on how humans make God feel.

One day, of course, God's people truly will please God because God is in the business of making them holy (see 20:12). When God acts, they will recognize their loathsome condition. They will open themselves to transformation once God's holiness and glory have their rightful, central place in Ezekiel's hierarchical world.

That is precisely the goal to which Ezekiel points with his rhetoric of keeping God's name hallowed (see Lev. 22:32, HS; Ezek. 43:7). To hallow God's name is to acknowledge that God, God's self, *is* holiness. It is to recognize that the world must align itself with such holiness if it is to thrive and foster all persons' full humanity.

The sign of the death of Ezekiel's wife (24:15–27). Two signs mark the end of the judgment section of Ezekiel's book: the death of the prophet's wife, and the announcement of the prophet's release from speechlessness.

The death of Ezekiel's spouse signals the people's loss of the Jerusalem temple and their own children (24:21). The prophet's suppression of normal human grief at her demise is a sign that a stifling discernment of judgment must now overcome the people, replacing their skepticism. Awestruck, shuddering in dismay, they will experience the sort of submergence that humans commonly undergo before an epiphany of the holy (see esp. Aaron's silence in Lev. 10:1–3). Clearly, God will not rest until the divine jealousy has penetrated the heart of the exiles. They simply must come to know "that I am the Lord GOD" (Ezek. 24:24).

Up until this point in the book Ezekiel has been "speechless," but with Ezek. 24:25–27 we glimpse a new phase in his ministry. Now the people fall silent in awe and Ezekiel's tongue is released. The prophet may now begin to represent their cause.

Part III: Oracles against the Nations (25:1–32:32)

Throughout the book of Ezekiel the Lord acts with the same overriding purpose: vindicating the divine holiness. This purpose now takes the form of judgment upon the nations surrounding Israel for their gross hubris. To know the nature of true holiness is to forsake such hubris, to abandon ostentation and pretense. It is to confess instead that humanity is puny, vulnerable, and easily self-deceived.

In Ezekiel the deeds of the Lord always have knowledge of YHWH as their central concern. God wants to be known as God is, by the name denoting the divine holiness, as "I am YHWH." This is no less true with reference to the nations as it is when the focus is on Israel. Sixteen times within Ezek. 25–32, God stresses the importance of the nations knowing that "I am YHWH."

For earth's nations to know "I am YHWH" means for them to recognize God's cosmic prerogative and humble themselves before God. It means for them to acknowledge YHWH by name and to fall prostrate in reverence. It does not, however, necessarily mean their conversion and inclusion within the strictures of the HS covenant.

Ezekiel nowhere calls the nations to become holy, to undergo sanctification in the manner of Israel. Apparently, their proper place for now is to recognize the centrality of God's holy temple and the leading role of Israel in reflecting God's holy character.

Yet this may not be the complete story. Ezekiel does not state it explicitly, but, logically speaking, such recognition should eventually lead the nations to join willingly with Israel in the worship of YHWH. God's holy presence is irresistibly magnetic, drawing all tribes and tongues around God's throne in worship and praise. Should we not deduce that eventually it must draw in all earth's peoples?

Oracles against Tyre (26:1–28:19).   Among the most fascinating of Ezekiel's prophecies against the foreign nations are his oracles against the Phoenician city-state of Tyre. Ezekiel's metaphorical and mythological portrayals of Tyre cut to the heart of its inmost self, its motivating force. He knows Tyre's self-conception to

be delusional, an affront to God and a threat to Israel, and his verbal artistry brilliantly exposes this delusion.

Among the oracles against Tyre, the most compelling is the prophecy against the king of Tyre in Ezek. 28:11–19. The passage describes Tyre's king by comparing him to a mythical cherub whose hubris caused him to fall from heaven. This understanding is clearest in translations such as the NJPS, NJB, NLT, and NIV.

As we know from Ezekiel's descriptions of God's throne-chariot, the cherubim are the wondrous guardians of God's throne. Arrayed about this volatile center, they keep its holiness contained and facilitate its safe journey into the world. Apparently, however, cherubim are rather untamed and unpredictable. If overcome by lust, they can become demonic in the worst sense.

At Tyre, to conceive of oneself as a cherub was a positive thing. One magnificent Phoenician ivory from the ninth century BCE depicts a monarch as a semidivine cherub. Ezekiel deftly shows, however, that the king of Tyre has been ambitious and reckless in bearing the cherub role. The results will be catastrophic.

Tyre's king has not appreciated the terrible risk of a position so interconnected with the numinous. Trespassing across the threshold of the cosmos's holy center, he has sealed his fate (cf. 28:2). He has attempted to seize prerogatives that belong exclusively to God but is too puny to manage them (28:17). Thus he is destined to be overwhelmed and swallowed up by the terrible heat of the numinous (28:18).

Part IV: Prophecies of Israel's Restoration (33:1–39:29)

After the fall of Jerusalem, the focus of Ezekiel's prophecies shifted away from judgment toward the theme of salvation. Ezekiel announced that God was reversing all the past wrongs that had impacted negatively on God's holiness and led to the people's exile. God would gather the exiles back to the promised land in a new exodus and settlement.

With the people safely resettled in God's land, God would see to it that the HS covenant was never broken again. The people were to be miraculously transformed and God's sanctuary was to be permanently set among them. God's perpetual dwelling in the midst of the people would have a constant sanctifying effect on them that would bring lasting honor to God's holy name among the nations.

Release from speechlessness (33:21–22). Judah's judgment was inevitable— already recorded in a scroll that Ezekiel swallowed whole (3:1–3). Correspondingly, from the start of his prophetic work, Ezekiel had labored under a strict speechlessness by which he was prevented from standing up for his fellow exiles before God (3:22–27). At the occasion of the death of his wife, however, God informed Ezekiel that he would be freed from his speechlessness upon hearing of Jerusalem's fall (24:27). Now that prediction comes to pass.

It is hard to read Ezekiel's terse note of January 585 without emotion: "The refugees from Jerusalem came to me, saying, 'The city has been taken'" (33:21, my trans.). Judgment has come upon Jerusalem; God's dear city and temple are gone (cf. 2 Kgs. 25:8–11). Clearly, a watershed has been reached in Ezekiel's prophetic career.

With their false hopes and cultural pride dashed, the people are finally in a position to see their total dependence on God. Ezekiel's prophetic task changes. Now he is vindicated as God's true prophet. Now he is able to act as arbiter and reconciler. Strikingly, as the people receive a new, everlasting covenant, Ezekiel's prior speechlessness is transferred to them (cf. Ezek. 16:63).

The shepherds of Israel (34:1–31). The neglect and abuse of Israel's rulers had victimized the people and exposed them as prey for invading nations. To right this wrong, Ezekiel announces that God,

the Good Shepherd, will now personally tend the people, bringing them into their own land, caring for their interests, giving the flock's weakest members special attention (34:11–16).

Furthermore, a future Davidic shepherd, the Messiah, will caringly tend the sheep on God's behalf (34:23–24). God sets him over the people, declaring him God's own "servant."

The chapter ends in 34:25–31 with an announcement of future blessedness using the language of the HS source. God is creating a secure new future for Israel, without the threat of wild animals (34:25; Lev. 26:6, HS), with blessings flowing down from Zion ("my hill," Ezek. 34:26), with the rain coming in its season (34:26; Lev. 26:4, HS), and with the bars of the people's yoke broken (Ezek. 34:27; Lev. 26:13, HS). The people will live in safety, and no one will make them afraid (Ezek. 34:28; Lev. 26:5–6, HS).

God's honor as the cause of the restoration (36:16–38). The radical holiness and irresistible grace of God shine brilliantly through this oracle. Here God steps back and reexplains the root causes of the exile. God is determined to reverse these causes, thus securing the sanctification of God's people.

Two very similar verses bracket Ezek. 36:22–32, forming a set of bookends highlighting the jarring theme of the section: "It is not for your sake that I will act, says the Lord GOD; let that be known to you. Be ashamed and dismayed" (v. 32). The *inclusio* makes clear that Israel's restoration is not anything deserved. The grace of God is truly not merited. The Reformation dictum, *sola gratia*, finds one of its firmest scriptural supports in this text.

Ezekiel's point is not that the Lord is uncaring. Ezekiel's God is the Good Shepherd, committed to care for even the weakest of the flock (34:11–16). His point is that Israel has lost any right to sympathy. What is more, they are stuck in a mystifying intransigence.

The people have hit rock bottom, yet amazingly even this has not brought about their repentance. Time and again, Ezekiel's calls to repent have fallen on deaf ears (see 14:6; 18:21, 30–31; 33:10–20).

Israel appears incapable of moving toward restoration (cf. 20:8, 13, 21), but God determines that grace will triumph anyway. Israel's restoration will redound to God's glory no matter what, even if the people are merely passive, and remember their evil ways and deeds only after restoration, not before it (36:31; cf. 20:33–34, 43). The impetus for the restoration is now totally out of the exiles' hands. Not even their repentance is required; God's grace is now revealed as purely prevenient.

When the exiles come to realize their utter unworthiness, they will be "ashamed and dismayed," a reaction akin to what Martin Luther called "God-pleasing despair." Such despair is pleasing to God because it signals a spiritual condition where one finally admits one's need of God.

Once restored to their land, a radical new creation will be needed by the people. They must not fall back into the endless cycle of sin and retribution that entrapped them before (see Ezek. 20). Creating them anew, the Lord will remove their stone heart and give them a sensitive, responsive heart. Their new transplanted hearts will be completely God-willed, not self-willed (36:26; cf. 11:19–20; 18:31).

This language goes beyond even the radical depictions of a new covenant in Jer. 31:33 and Deut. 30:1–6. Ezekiel wants to be crystal clear on the need for fundamental human transformation. Once restored to their land, the people must be supernaturally and dramatically changed. Only then can they be counted on to obey consistently the HS covenant, and their restoration be guaranteed as permanent (cf. Lev. 26:3–4, HS; Ezek. 16:60; 37:23, 26).

Vision of the valley of dry bones (37:1–14). Perhaps Ezekiel's most memorable vision, chap. 37 has long captured readers' imaginations. The prophet provides an engrossing vision of the resurrection of a huge mass of skeletal remains. He leads us step by step through his participation in the bones' regeneration, an experience replete with deafening noises and rushing winds. As living persons slowly reemerge from the dead, we are drawn into the reality described. Our minds reconfigure and our spirits find themselves renewed.

Such spiritual renewal is precisely the experience needed by Ezekiel's first audience, what Karl Barth emphasized as God's *yes* to creation and above all to human beings. Ezekiel 37 vividly communicates such a yes. It restages creation as it is described in Gen. 2:7, with bodies re-formed first and then reanimated with God's vivifying breath.

The exiles were afflicted with a theological malady that the desert ascetics called *accedia. Accedia* is a toxic combination of despair, self-shrinking, unresponsiveness, and dull, hidden anger. It may be considered a case of extreme spiritual depression. Ezekiel's audience was *stuck.* But Ezekiel's God, passionately desiring not death but life, is determined to reverse their fate.

God's intervention leaves us exhilarated. God causes the valley of dry bones to throb with divine power. God summons the four winds from the corners of the cosmos to rush through the valley. God acts as God, dramatically overturning the people's *accedia.*

The Gog of Magog oracles (38:1–39:29). The oracles against Gog of Magog have always stood out from the rest of Ezekiel's book. The idioms and style of these chapters match the rest of Ezekiel, but the ideas and images are radicalized, close to the end-time visions of Joel 3, Zech. 14, and Rev. 19–20. As in these comparable passages, an apocalyptic imagination emerges here. This fact belies the commonplace claim that apocalypticism is a religion of dissidents and peripheral figures. Ezekiel 38–39 is emergent apocalyptic literature from the pens of central priests, Zadokite temple officials.

In Ezekiel's little apocalypse, evil takes on mythic proportions, appearing incarnate in a monstrous northern horde (Gog's Mob), which swarms down on God's people safely resettled in the Holy Land (38:9, 16). They do not realize their doom is foreordained. From beyond the veil separating earth and heaven, God intervenes to destroy evil's forces with hailstones, fire, and brimstone (38:22; 39:6).

After the battle, Israel enters a wondrous new era. Now, at last, the people truly know the Lord (39:22) and have God's spirit poured out upon them (39:29). A great shaking of the earth and a collapse of the mountains separates the present age and the new era of salvation (38:19–20).

Ezekiel's apocalyptic theology bears clear marks of his priestly HS background. According to the HS strand, divine holiness should flow out from a sacred center—the temple mount—and permeate the land and people of Israel, even those at the periphery. Ezekiel's apocalypse reverses the past desecration and disruption of this ideal hierarchical system of holiness.

In the end times, the nations will again attack God's system for releasing holiness. They will again assault God's holy center, just as they did in 586 BCE, but this time God will reveal Zion's true nature as God's cosmic mountain (38:12). On doomsday God will display God's fiery glory in an incontestable manner, before the entire world (38:16; 39:13). Gog's Mob—evil incarnate—will be forever vanquished.

The presence of Gog's corpses within Israel risks defiling the land, where God's glory dwells in Israel's midst. As the HS strand insists, corpses cannot be allowed to desecrate such a special place. Israel must not "pollute their encampments, in the heart of which I dwell" (from Num. 5:2–3 NJB; cf. Num. 19:11–13, also HS). Taking this theology seriously, Ezek. 39:11–16 describes elaborate, intensive efforts at ensuring the ceremonial cleanness of God's land. (Ezekiel's term "cleanse" here, used three times, is the same Hebrew verb used in Num. 19:12, HS.)

Part V: Blueprint for the Restored Temple and Land (40:1–48:35)

In the final section of Ezekiel's book, a heavenly being leads the prophet through a floor plan of a new ideal temple in Jerusalem, established in the midst of a restored land. The new temple's utopian design is less a prophecy of the future than a literary summary and embodiment of Ezekiel's theology. It includes radical new features, many of outrageous proportion, designed to prevent the wrongs of the past that led to the disaster of the people's Babylonian exile from ever happening again.

These chapters contain more than simply a floor plan. They also challenge the reader with an ideal new polity and torah for Israel. They bring the eschatological trajectory of the book to a finale, with a climactic description of the return of the glory of YHWH from exile: "And there, the glory of the God of Israel was coming from the east; the sound was like the sound of mighty waters; and the earth shone with his glory. The vision I saw was like the vision that I had seen when he came to destroy the city, and like the vision that I had seen by the river Chebar; and I fell upon my face" (Ezek. 43:2–3). This is the hope that has inspired the faithful down through the ages. Believers have continually dreamed of the day when the glory of YHWH will dwell among the gathered community, bringing holiness and blessing to both great and small (43:7).

In accord with the theology of the HS strand, Ezekiel's blueprint provides for God's glory to dwell in Israel's midst, so that God's holiness can encompass the entirety of the settlements and people of Israel. The temple functions as an organizing center of this holiness (43:12), and its new structures permanently safeguard God's indwelling presence there (43:7; 44:1–3; 48:35).

Gated walls, narrowing entrances, and rising terraces demarcate zones of graded holiness in the new Zion. The tiered zones extend out from God's central presence, mediating God's fiery power both to those who draw near to the Lord and those on the periphery. The system also allows the people and their leaders to come safely to the Lord in worship and to learn God's ways.

Within the schema, Levites and Zadokite priests are specially consecrated, belonging to God in a unique way. Their role is extremely challenging. Taking special responsibility for holiness, they protect the people from its scorching burn and encourage them to benefit from its sanctifying power. Ezekiel's blueprint for the restored priesthood of Israel is found in 44:6–14, a text that sets right Israel's past failures in guarding the temple's sanctity, especially as they are encapsulated in the HS strand in Num. 16–18.

Ezekiel's theological emphases and spiritual values are knit into the very fabric of the vision of restoration. Now, in this new ideal arrangement, God deals concretely and materially with the oppressive realities of societal injustice and sin that have long plagued both Israel and humanity as a whole. Ezekiel's blueprint embodies God's ideal identity for Israel. The chosen people are destined for dynamic communion with God, for continual growth in ethical and ritual holiness, for ever-increasing support of the dignity and liberty of each individual.

Promoting the humanity and economic independence of all society's members is paramount. Relying on the HS strand (e.g., Lev. 25:10, 23–24, 42), Ezekiel's plan ensures that all families will dwell in perpetuity on their own homesteads. Unlike the past, princes will no longer have the power to evict subjects from their ancestral plots of land (Ezek. 45:8–9; 46:18; cf. 22:27).

This is a radical provision. In the social world of ancient Israel, guaranteeing the tenure of families on their ancestral lands would effectively establish local justice and fellowship. Specifically, it would block any process of the rich getting richer and the poor getting poorer so that property is continually being bought up and concentrated in the hands of the few. It would foster sacrificial, other-centered life on the land, rather than selfish exploitation of people and nature.

Although Ezekiel's blueprint enforces a hierarchical and restrictive view of Israel's cult, it involves no hostility toward strangers. Quite the opposite, Ezekiel's eschatological program is stunningly generous in welcoming outsiders into Israel. Care for the alien is as important for Ezekiel as care for widows, orphans, and the poor (cf. 22:7, 29).

Specifically, Ezekiel's final chapters offer foreign sojourners within Israel's borders the unprecedented provision of a permanent allotment of family land alongside native Israelites (47:22–23). This guarantees them full enjoyment of the spiritual rights and benefits of the faith community. In the reign of God, foreigners will no longer have to live in constant dependence and vulnerability.

In effect, Ezekiel has radically extended the theological norm of the HS strand for the treatment of resident aliens. He takes the force of Lev. 19:34 to its logical conclusion: "You shall love the alien as yourself" (cf. Lev. 24:22; Num. 15:29). Here, as elsewhere in biblical literature, God's eschatological ideal for humanity is the inclusion of all willing nations and peoples into the reign of God.

The book of Ezekiel closes with a glorious emphasis on God's eschatological renewal of nature and the environment. In God's promised future, a river of life will flow forth from the new temple, now indwelt by the glory of the Lord. Flowing down into the world, the river transforms creation into a veritable Eden. In the theology of this final vision, the physical world is of incalculable value to God.

Bibliography

Block, Daniel I. *The Book of Ezekiel*. 2 vols. NICOT. Grand Rapids: Eerdmans, 1997–1998.

Cook, Stephen L., and Corrine L. Patton, eds. *Ezekiel's Hierarchical World:*

Wrestling with a Tiered Reality. SBLSymS 31. Atlanta: Society of Biblical Literature, 2004.

Knohl, Israel. *The Sanctuary of Silence: The Priestly Torah and the Holiness School.* Minneapolis: Fortress, 1995.

Levenson, Jon D. *Theology of the Program of Restoration of Ezekiel 40–48.* Harvard Semitic Monographs 10. Missoula, MT: Scholars Press, 1976.

Wells, Jo Bailey. *God's Holy People: A Theme in Biblical Theology.* JSOTSup 305. Sheffield: Sheffield Academic Press, 2000.

Daniel

Carol A. Newsom

INTRODUCTION

The book of Daniel contains two quite different literary genres. Chapters 1–6 are a cycle of stories, whereas chaps. 7–12 consist of a series of four apocalypses. The stories concern the fate of four young Jews, exiled to Babylon when Nebuchadnezzar captures Jerusalem, who rise to power in the courts of the Babylonian, Median, and Persian kings. It has long been recognized that these stories are fictional narratives: short stories with historical settings. The careful plots, folkloristic motifs, and historical errors indicate their character as fiction. This in no way diminishes their theological value, however, for narrative is a powerful tool for theological reflection. These narratives probably originated in the fourth or third century BCE in the eastern Jewish Diaspora, that is, among Jews who lived in Syria or Mesopotamia, and the stories explore themes of particular concern to such Jews. The tales tend to be optimistic about the possibilities for Jews to succeed in the Gentile world, though they acknowledge the vulnerability of Jews who might be caught in a conflict of allegiance between God and the Gentile king. Thus the overriding theme of the collection is the nature of royal or state power in relation to the sovereignty of God.

Chapters 7–12 are not stories but apocalypses, that is, revelations about heavenly mysteries concerning the future course of history, communicated to Daniel in dreams, visions, and angelic visitations. In contrast to the narratives, which were critical but ultimately optimistic about Gentile kings, the apocalypses see Gentile power as irredeemably evil and destined for ultimate destruction by God. The difference in perspective reflects the different historical context in which the apocalypses were written. They were composed in Palestine between 168 and 164 BCE during the time of the persecution of the Jews by the Seleucid king Antiochus IV Epiphanes and the revolt led by Judah the Maccabee. Although the historical references in Daniel to this period of time are clear, the mysterious and veiled style in which the apocalypses are written encouraged later interpreters to perceive in them allusions to their own times.

COMMENTARY

The Narratives

Although most readers tend to think of Daniel and his three friends as the heroes of the stories in chaps. 1–6, the real focus of the narratives is on the character of the kings and whether they are capable of

257

recognizing the sovereignty of God. The first four chapters concern Nebuchadnezzar and trace his slow and painful growth toward recognition of the power of God.

The first story (chap. 1) not only introduces the major characters but also sets up the theme of the irony of power. Nebuchadnezzar thinks he is a powerful monarch because he has captured Jerusalem; but the narrator tells the reader that the real author of events is "the LORD [who] let King Jehoiakim of Judah fall into his power" (1:2). An apparently gracious as well as practical monarch, Nebuchadnezzar orders that the most capable of the captured Jewish youths be specially trained for posts in his royal court, providing them with rich food and wine from the king's own table. The story expresses well the tensions between the advantages of participation in Gentile society and the concern to preserve Jewish identity and faithfulness to God. Daniel and his friends express no anxiety about being trained in Babylonian language and literature, receiving Babylonian names, or serving the king. But the food from the king's table is perceived as defiling, leading Daniel to request that they be allowed to eat vegetables and water instead. Whether Daniel's concern reflects an early form of Jewish kosher food laws is debated, but food clearly functions symbolically in the story. The question "Who feeds you?" is a way of understanding both the source of one's support and the object of one's loyalty and devotion. Moreover, in most cultures rich food and wine are considered power foods, whereas vegetables and water are symbolically associated with weakness. Yet here the values are reversed and Daniel and his friends, though ostensibly eating the poorer foods, "appeared better and fatter" than those who ate the king's food (1:15). Similarly, although Nebuchadnezzar would assume that the superior performance of Daniel and his friends is due to the training he provided, the reader knows that it was "God [who] gave knowledge and

skill" to these youths (1:17). Nebuchadnezzar lacks knowledge of the true source of power and of the ultimate allegiance of Daniel and his companions.

The following chapter contains the familiar story of Nebuchadnezzar's dream of the statue of four metals, which is shattered by a rock that grows to become a mountain. The Jewish audience of the tale would recognize the symbolism immediately as referring to a succession of Gentile kingdoms that will be succeeded by a lasting Judean kingdom that manifests God's sovereignty on earth. But Nebuchadnezzar's distress suggests that he suspects the dream is a portent of his own personal destruction. His suspicious and volatile character is expressed through his demand to have his dream experts not only interpret the dream but to do so without his telling them the content, an apparently impossible condition. Here, as in chap. 4, the failure of the Babylonian dream interpreters serves as a foil for the God-given success of Daniel and develops the theological message of the stories: that God alone is the source of both knowledge and power.

The characterization of Nebuchadnezzar in Daniel's interpretation of the dream is strikingly positive. Not only does Daniel identify him with the head of gold in the dream but also describes him as a monarch to whom the God of heaven has given unprecedented power (2:37–38). This characterization of Nebuchadnezzar as a royal servant of God was first developed in the book of Jeremiah in order to persuade Judeans that it was God's will that the nation submit to the Babylonians rather than to revolt (Jer. 27:1–11). For the Jewish Diaspora readers of Daniel such a view of Nebuchadnezzar helped to reconcile what would otherwise be a theological problem. How could one believe that the God of Israel was sovereign when a succession of Gentile empires had continued to rule for centuries? The stories in Daniel go further than Jeremiah, however, in imagining that Nebuchadnezzar did come to recognize and honor the God of Israel as the source of his own power. The narratives also have some fun at Nebuchadnezzar's expense, by depicting him as dense and unperceptive. Although at the end of chap. 2 he seems to acknowledge the power of God as "God of gods and Lord of kings" (2:47), the succeeding events show just how far from understanding he still is.

Chapter 3 opens with Nebuchadnezzar erecting a giant golden statue. Although the story never says exactly what the statue represents, its similarity to the statue with the "head of gold" (chap. 2) and the fact that he requires all of his subjects to bow down to it suggest that it is an image of his own royal power. Moreover, when Shadrach, Meshach, and Abednego refuse, Nebuchadnezzar frames the conflict in terms of a struggle with their God: "who is the god that will deliver you out of my hands?" (3:15). As in chap. 2, a display of God's power (here the miraculous deliverance of the three youths from the fiery furnace) appears to convince Nebuchadnezzar, for he blesses "the God of Shadrach, Meshach, and Abednego," who delivered them when they disobeyed the king's command (3:28). But his understanding is still flawed, for he issues a decree threatening to use his royal power to punish anyone who blasphemes God, as though God needed the king's protection (3:29).

Only the humiliating events that Nebuchadnezzar himself describes in his letter of testimony in chap. 4 lead him to true recognition of the sovereignty of God and an understanding that his own royal power is a trust from God. As in chap. 2, the events are presaged by a troubling dream that Daniel interprets to Nebuchadnezzar. The symbolism of the dream is crucial to the theology of kingship embedded in Dan. 1–6. In the dream, Nebuchadnezzar's kingship is represented by a great tree at the center of the earth, stretching to heaven, which provides food for all from its fruit, nesting places and sheltering shade for wild creatures, and beauty for all who behold it. The imagery evokes the symbol of the tree of life, which was often used in Near East-

ern art as a symbol of royal power. The cosmic dimensions of the tree were traditionally understood to represent the king's role as the mediator between the gods and his people. In Dan. 4, however, the phrase "its top reached to heaven" also has a negative connotation, for height is often used as a symbol of arrogance in the Bible. More specifically, the phrase echoes the description of the tower of Babel in Gen. 11:6. Thus Gentile kingship, as represented in the figure of Nebuchadnezzar, is depicted as an institution willed by God and so essentially good. But kings who do not recognize that their power comes from God are corrupted by arrogance and subject to judgment. The following two chapters repeat these themes with contrasting characters, the arrogant but weak Belshazzar, and the good-hearted but easily manipulated Darius.

The Apocalypses

If the story cycle paints a critical but ultimately optimistic picture of Gentile kingship, that is not the case in the apocalypses, composed during the persecution by Antiochus IV Epiphanes. In these chapters Daniel is no longer the interpreter of dreams but the recipient of mysterious dreams and visions that an angel interprets for him. Although communicated through different images, all four revelations deal with the same historical and eschatological scenario. Four successive empires dominate the world: the Babylonians, the Medes, the Persians, and finally the Greeks. The Greek Empire divides into rival kingdoms, the Ptolemaic kingdom in Egypt and the Seleucid kingdom in Syria. During the years of their struggle, a particularly arrogant king arises, Antiochus IV Epiphanes, who defiles the Jerusalem temple and attacks the faithful Jews. When at the height of his power he challenges heaven itself, however, he will be destroyed according to the decree of heaven. The most detailed version of this scenario is presented in chap. 11.

Chapter 7 picks up the four-kingdoms schema introduced in chap. 2, but here the imagery is more negative. Instead of representing the kingdoms as parts of an imposing but ultimately fragile statue, chap. 7 represents the kingdoms as beasts rising from the sea. Traditionally, in ancient Near Eastern mythology and in the Bible, the sea and the sea monsters that reside in it are symbols of the chaos that the Creator God defeats in battle (Job 7:12; 26:12–13; Pss. 74:13–17; 89:9–10; Isa. 27:1; 51:9–10). Thus, implicitly, the claim is made that the Gentile kingdoms do not rule with God's authorization but spring from a source of evil and so threaten God's order. The restored kingdom of Israel is represented as a human figure (traditionally translated "one like a son of man," Dan. 7:13) in contrast with the monstrous animals that figure the Gentile kingdoms. The early Christian community reinterpreted this symbol in messianic terms and applied it to Jesus.

Although the Babylonian exile nominally came to an end with the decree of Cyrus the Persian in 539 BCE, the continuing rule by Gentile empires caused many Jews to feel as though the exile had never ended. Thus prophetic texts originally written in relation to that earlier crisis were reinterpreted and applied to later events. In chap. 9 the exilic Daniel is presented as reading the book of Jeremiah, which in 25:11–12 and 29:10–14 predicted the end of the exile after seventy years. Although the passages are clear and straightforward, here they are reinterpreted as having a hidden meaning. The duration of the time of distress for Jerusalem will not be seventy years but seventy weeks of years, that is, 490 years. Like Jeremiah's original words, these are symbolic figures and do not quite fit the chronology of events. But this passage shows how, during the second century BCE, Scripture was being read in a new way, as containing predictions for a distant future which those who knew how to interpret them could uncover. A

similar approach to Scripture interpretation was practiced by the Jewish community responsible for the Dead Sea Scrolls that flourished between ca. 150 BCE and 68 CE.

Corresponding to this new approach to Scripture is a new understanding of history. In most of the Hebrew Bible history is understood to be an open process, developing through the free interaction of people and God. Beginning at the time of the exile (see Isa. 46:8–10; 48:3) and increasingly during the Persian and Hellenistic period a more deterministic view of history came to be developed. This new view of history was a response to the theological dilemma described above. How could Jews affirm the sovereignty of God in a world that seemed to be dominated not only by Gentile empires but by those who oppressed the Jewish people and even defiled the temple? To believe that the events of history, however mysterious they might seem, were part of a preordained plan of God was the theological solution proposed by some Jews, including those responsible for Dan. 7–12. Not all adopted this perspective, however. The books of 1 and 2 Maccabees, also written in response to the Antiochean crisis, continue to view history as presided over by God but not strictly determined.

Bibliography

Fewell, Dana Nolan. *Circle of Sovereignty: Plotting Politics in the Book of Daniel.* Nashville: Abingdon, 1991.

Goldingay, John E. *Daniel.* WBC 30. Dallas: Word, 1988.

Gowan, Donald E. *Daniel.* AOTC. Nashville: Abingdon, 2001.

Seow, C. L. *Daniel.* Westminster Bible Companion. Louisville: Westminster John Knox, 2003.

Smith-Christopher, Daniel L. "The Book of Daniel." In *NIB* 7:19–152.

Hosea

Julia M. O'Brien

INTRODUCTION

The superscription of the book of Hosea sets the prophet within the eighth century BCE, when the Assyrian Empire dominated the ancient Near East. While occasionally addressing Judah, Hosea's message targets Israel and its capital Samaria, insisting that the nation will suffer military defeat as punishment for its sins. Hosea describes at length the nature of Israel's transgressions. People, prophets, and priests are accused of swearing, lying, murder, adultery (4:2); of failing to trust God alone; and, most consistently and harshly, of idolatry.

Specifically, Hosea accuses the people of worshiping "the Baals." *Baal*, which literally means "master," was a title used for one or more gods worshiped in the ancient Near East. Documents from the ancient city of Ugarit describe Baal as "the rider of the clouds," controlling not only thunder but the fertility of the earth. Hosea accuses the Israelites of attributing agricultural prosperity to Baal rather than to Yahweh (2:5) and of calling Yahweh "Baal" (2:16). The rhetoric of Hosea implies that many within the society combined worship of Yahweh with that of Baal, an implication also drawn from archaeological finds from the time period.

Even though Hosea and other biblical books draw a sharp distinction between Baal and Yahweh and demand worship of Yahweh alone, much biblical literature uses Baal imagery to describe Yahweh. Throughout the prophetic books, the image of Yahweh as Divine Warrior is lined to that of a storm god: "His way is in whirlwind and storm, and the clouds are the dust of his feet" (Nah. 1:3); and, just as in the Ugaritic texts Baal battles against and defeats the Sea, so too in the Bible Yahweh "split open the sea by your power; you broke the heads of the monster in the waters" (Ps. 74:13, my trans.). In ancient Israel as well as in current religious expressions, visions of "pure" religion are influenced by the cultural environment in which they are shaped.

COMMENTARY

Idolatry as "Whoredom"

Throughout the book, Hosea calls the worship of deities other than Yahweh "whoredom" (NRSV). While in English this term suggests a professional prostitute, the Hebrew word is used elsewhere in the Old Testament for a wide range of sexual activities considered off limits for women. Used to refer to both premarital sex as well as extramarital sex, it is generally synonymous with promiscuity. Hosea equates Israel's failure to be loyal to Yahweh alone to a woman's failure to remain loyal to the male who owns the rights to her sexuality.

In ancient Israel, marriages were not ones in which equal parties made mutual promises to one another. The Pentateuch clearly reveals that while women had some rights within marriage, access to a woman's body was controlled by her father before marriage and by her husband after marriage. The penalty for the rape of a virgin, for example, is payment to her father (Exod. 22:16); and the penalty for causing a woman to miscarry is restitution to her husband (Exod. 21:22).

Equating idolatry with a woman's willful defiance of these limits on the expression of her sexuality serves Hosea's theological message in multiple ways. It casts God's anger against Israel as the response not simply of an emotionally wounded spouse but, even more so, as the righteous indignation of one whose honor and authority have been challenged. The severity of God's punishment becomes "reasonable" as well; like a promiscuous woman, Israel deserves death.

The opening of Hosea introduces the "idolatry as whoredom" analogy through a story about the prophet's life. God tells Hosea to take a "wife of whoredom" in order to symbolize the nature of the relationship between God and Israel. In this marriage metaphor, as it is usually called, every stage of the prophet's relationship with his wife, including the naming of the couple's children, reveals some aspect of God's relationship with Israel. The prophet's actions mirror God's actions.

The equation of the prophet's actions with those of Yahweh becomes especially problematic in chap. 2, in which the prophet/God announces the punishment that awaits the unfaithful wife/Israel. Feminists have insisted that the treatment the wife receives in this chapter follows the classic pattern of domestic violence. A jealous husband charges his wife with unfaithfulness and threatens to strip and kill her; his threats also extend to her children. Although the cessation of violence in 2:14–23 is often seen as a "happily ever after" ending to the story, it also reflects all too painfully the honeymoon phases of some abusive relationships.

When readers take seriously the threats of chap. 2 and the equation of God's actions with the actions of a human husband, Hosea's image of God the husband becomes in contemporary terms an image of God the batterer. The woman in Hosea's metaphor is not "married" in the modern sense of the term; she is a domestic prisoner of war. For those who insist that God is not a batterer and a batterer is not God, "God as husband" has no role as a title, in liturgy or elsewhere, where it is isolated from the context of study and conversation. In the contexts of Bible study, counseling, spiritual direction, and prayer, however, study of the metaphor can invite reflection on the vast differences between ancient and modern concepts of marriage and on the way in which God is known—and distorted—in human relationships.

"Sacred Prostitution?"

While subsequent chapters move beyond the description of the prophet and his wife, they abandon neither the language of "whoredom" nor the prophet's insistence that Israel must be punished. In Hos. 4, the catalog of the people's sins echoes the commandments of Moses; they swear, lie, murder, steal, and commit adultery (4:2), and even prophet and priest forget the law of God (4:4–6).

The primary crime of the people, however, remains "whoredom." In most cases, the literary context in which the term appears suggests that it refers to the worship of other gods. The NRSV translation, however, implies that men also sacrifice with "temple prostitutes" (4:14) and indulge in "sexual orgies" (4:18). While earlier generations of scholars maintained that Canaanite religion practiced sacred prostitution, in which male worshipers engaged in sexual intercourse with temple priestesses, contemporary interpreters are more likely to understand Israelite use of sexual language for Canaanite religion as pejorative rather than as descriptive of actual practices. Separating metaphorical from nonmetaphorical language in Hos. 4 is nearly impossible.

International Politics

Idolatry for Hosea is clearly a religious matter. The worship of other gods, even when it includes worship of Yahweh, compromises the exclusive covenant relationship and dishonors the Deity. Several verses in Hosea, however, also link the adoption of foreign deities to eighth-century BCE Israelite political policies. Intertwined with the criticism of idolatry are criticisms of military alliances with Assyria (5:13) and Egypt (7:11, 16). In 8:9–10 the charge that "Ephraim has bargained for lovers" stands in parallel to "they bargain with nations," and 14:3 is clear that "Assyria will not save us; we will say no more, 'Our God,' to the work of our hands." Hosea's harangue against idolatry, then, may have had political overtones in the ancient world; in trusting international diplomacy rather than Yahweh alone, Israel had shown itself unfaithful.

Hosea's censure of international diplomacy could be interpreted as xenophobic and isolationist. But it also can be valued for highlighting the danger of staking one's safety on the goodwill of political leaders. For example, Jews who considered themselves assimilated into German society in the early decades of the twentieth century, having cast their lot with the German people, learned swiftly and brutally with the rise of Nazism that savior could turn executioner.

Hosea's Images for God

Yahweh as battering husband is but one of many images for God in the book. The Deity is compared to a lion, a leopard, and a bear robbed of her cubs (13:7–8); to maggots and rottenness (5:12); to dew (14:5); and to an evergreen cypress (14:8). In 11:1–9 God is a compassionate father who recoils from executing the punishment that his son deserves.

The diversity of these images serves several functions. First, it highlights that the metaphor of God the husband, while central in Hosea's thought, is not sufficient for describing God, even within the worldview of an ancient prophet: God's character is so complex that no single image can do it justice. Second, the oddness of the images chosen suggests that they were intended to shock readers into new insight rather than to provide static depictions of God. In calling Yahweh "maggots" and "rottenness," the writer of Hosea depends upon the freshness of the image to communicate his message. Were these images of God to be regularly included in worship, they would lose much of their effectiveness.

The recognition that metaphors for God can become dead, as once-surprising metaphors lose their power when they are reduced to simple names, encourages readers of the Bible to pay special attention to its less-common metaphors, pondering what value strange images such as "God as maggot" might have for religious understanding. It spurs readers, too, to discover what may have once been shocking about God images that are now comfortable and safe. Which aspects of common images of God continue to surprise and challenge?

Judgment and Salvation

Hosea's dominant theme is that of punishment for Israel. He bluntly announces that the king of Israel will be cut off (10:15) and that Samaria will fall by the sword (13:16). As noted above, most of its images for God are ones of destructive power.

Like many other prophets, however, Hosea nonetheless calls people to return to Yahweh. Chapter 14 provides the words by which people may petition

God, encouraging them to ask for forgiveness and to admit the folly of turning to Assyria and to idols. God's words of forgiveness and love are reported as well. Yahweh, who once had been like maggots and rottenness (5:12), will become like dew to Israel (14:5) and like an evergreen cypress (14:8).

While some have argued that Hosea's concluding promise of salvation must be the work of a later hand, added after the fall of Israel to provide hope for the future, the interplay of judgment and forgiveness is characteristic of Hosea and of the prophets in general. The prophets agree that God does not spare the guilty but also is merciful and gracious (Joel 2:13; Exod. 34:6–7). In the words of Hosea's conclusion, "the ways of the LORD are right, and the upright walk in them, but transgressors stumble in them" (Hos. 14:9).

Bibliography

Mays, James L. *Hosea*. OTL. Philadelphia: Westminster, 1969.

Weems, Renita. *Battered Love: Marriage, Sex, and Violence in the Hebrew Prophets*. Minneapolis: Fortress, 1995.

Yee, Gale. *Poor Banished Children of Eve: Woman as Evil in the Hebrew Bible*. Minneapolis: Fortress, 2003.

Joel

Julia M. O'Brien

INTRODUCTION

The book of Joel begins with a harrowing description of a locust plague: "What the cutting locust left, the swarming locust has eaten. What the swarming locust left, the hopping locust has eaten, and what the hopping locust left, the destroying locust has eaten" (1:4). In 1:6, however, the book turns abruptly to description of a military invasion: "For a nation has invaded my land, powerful and innumerable." This shift complicates our understanding of Joel: does the book refer to two separate catastrophes or one? If one catastrophe, are locusts being described as an army or an army as a horde of locusts?

Rather than settling these questions, the book proceeds to announce a yet bigger catastrophe on the horizon. The locust/army invasion is but the prelude to the impending Day of the Lord, when God will appear as a Divine Warrior to fight God's enemies—a day of reckoning both for other nations and for the covenant people. Joel sees the events of his own time as a prelude to God's greater act of judgment.

COMMENTARY

The devastation that Joel surveys appears total. Crops are destroyed, food is cut off, watercourses are dried up, even the animals cry. "The day of the LORD is great and very terrible; who can endure it?" (2:11, my trans.).

In the midst of a thoroughgoing communal trauma, however, Joel 2:12–17 issues a call to repentance. All people—the aged and infants, even bride and bridegroom—should fast and repent, and priests should issue prayers on the people's behalf. Even though God seems intent on destroying the community, Joel holds out a slim possibility for hope: "Who knows whether he will not turn and repent, and leave a blessing behind him, a cereal offering and a drink offering for the LORD, your God?" (2:14, my trans.). Joel stands in a long tradition of Israelite and Judean leaders who admonish the people to return to God in the hope that repentance will elicit divine compassion. Salvation is neither guaranteed nor perhaps even merited; the only basis for the people's hope lies in God's merciful nature: "Return to the LORD, your God, for he is gracious and merciful, slow to anger, and abounding in steadfast love, and repents of evil" (2:13, my trans.; Exod. 34:6–7).

Joel 2:18 marks an abrupt shift in verbal tense and tone. It reports that God heard and responded to the people's petitions, or at least to Joel's call to repentance, and voices God's promises to send food, turn back armies, and pour out God's spirit on all flesh (2:28). In Joel repentance provokes a change in God's intentions.

The Revised Common Lectionary designates 2:1–17 as a reading for Ash Wednesday. In ending the passage before God's change of heart, it treats 2:14 as a real, open-ended question: who truly knows what God will do? On Ash Wednesday the lectionary invites worshipers not to rush to resolution of Joel's question but rather to sit with human brokenness and the brokenness of the world.

Throughout, Joel voices the pain of— and hope for—not only humans but also the broader world. Joel 1:18–20 movingly depicts the suffering of animals; and 2:21–22 calls to animals and to the soil itself to rejoice in God's restoration. Joel fits well with contemporary ecological concerns, reminding readers that humans are not the only ones whose suffering matters to God.

Messages of hope for people and the earth in Joel 2 are followed in Joel 3 by an extended vision of the judgment of the nations. The Day of Yahweh, seen as judgment of Judah in Joel 2, is in Joel 3 a time of judgment for the nations. Strikingly reversing the image of peace voiced by Isaiah and Micah, Joel 3:10 calls the people to take up weapons: "Beat your plowshares into swords, and your pruning hooks into spears; let the weakling say, 'I am a warrior.'" The glorious future of Judah is strongly linked with the desolation of other nations.

While contemporary readers may value Joel's willingness to critique his own community as well as others, they may also wish to expand Joel's vision of the future. In addition to the gender, age, and status inclusivity of Joel 2:29, they might hope—and work—for the future well-being of all nations and peoples.

Bibliography

Barton, John. *Joel and Obadiah.* OTL. Westminster John Knox, 2001.

Crenshaw, James L. *Joel.* AB 24C. New York: Doubleday, 1995.

Amos

Julia M. O'Brien

INTRODUCTION

During the twentieth and early-twenty-first centuries, many Christians heard a clear voice for social justice in the book of Amos. In Amos's scathing critique of the wealthy who "trample the head of the poor into the dust of the earth" (2:7) and in his fervent call that "justice roll down like waters, and righteousness like an ever-flowing stream" (5:24), Martin Luther King Jr. and Latin American liberation theologians found biblical precedent for the church's role in combating systems of oppression. In Amos's harangue against the Israelites' worship, "I hate, I despise your religious feasts; I cannot stand your assemblies" (5:21), interpreters have also found grounds to challenge the role of religious ritual.

These aspects of Amos's message are clear and appropriately challenge the church. But Amos's message is also complicated by the injustices that it does not address and by the confidence it invests in the the affirmation that God works justice in the course of human history.

COMMENTARY

Amos and the Oppressed

The speeches of chaps. 1 and 2 belong to a genre of prophetic literature known as oracles against the nations, which announce Yahweh's punishment on countries other than Israel and Judah. While other prophetic books contain oracles against the nations, Amos is distinctive in identifying the crime of the nations *not* as mistreatment of Israel or Judah but as mistreatment of *one another*. In holding all nations accountable to standards of just behavior, Amos may be seen to support the idea of universal human rights.

When Amos's critique turns to that of Israel in 2:6, his focus remains almost exclusively on the economic sins of the wealthy—taking the garments of those who default on loans (2:8), assessing fines (2:8), taking levies of grain (5:11), and luxuriating in expensive homes while ignoring the needs of others (6:4–6; cf. 3:15). Absent from Amos are the diatribes against the worship of other gods that characterize Hosea.

Amos clearly presents mistreatment of the poor as a fatal, not a minor, flaw. With bold hyperbole he describes the wealthy as "selling the righteous for silver" (2:6), and in humiliating caricaturization, he calls the wealthy women of Samaria "cows of Bashan" (4:1). Amos also clearly presents the consequence of the wealthy's behaviors: the nation of Israel will be destroyed (3:11); Israel will come to an end (8:3; 9:8).

Understandably, Amos's message resonates well with liberation theologians, who argue that faithful Christians should be concerned not primarily with life after death but more importantly with the real conditions in which people live now. Amos's claim that Israel will be destroyed for individual and structural economic injustice also finds common cause with liberation theology's call for active resistance and even revolution against oppression.

One scholar, however, has highlighted the limitations of Amos's critique. Judith Sanderson argues that, in targeting the women of Samaria as "cows" destined for slaughter, Amos participates in rather than challenges the oppression of women: "Amos specifically condemned wealthy women for oppressing the poor (4:1) but failed specifically to champion the women among the poor" ("Amos," pp. 218–19).

Amos is certainly not unique in falling short of a truly inclusive vision of justice: both the American Revolution and the abolitionist movement subordinated the fight for women's property and voting rights to the struggle for other causes; the feminist movement of the 1960s did not address matters of race and class; and many who fight discrimination against African Americans do not find common ground with activists for gay and lesbian causes. Amos might best be read, then, as a theological grounding for Christian commitment to the material conditions of people's lives rather than as an exhaustive description of what universal justice might entail.

Amos and Religious Ritual

Amos also directs harsh words to those participating in religious ritual. Amos 5:21–25 claims that Yahweh does not want the people's offering—perhaps that Yahweh never did. In the late nineteenth century, many German biblical scholars read such verses in Amos as calling for an end to the formal worship practices of ancient Israel; prophets like Amos, they argued, identified true religion as morality rather than ritual. Some scholars in the 1960s read Amos in a similar way, as a voice against institutional religion.

Surely the spirit of the age in which both sets of interpreters worked influenced their view of Amos. The German scholars in question were Protestants challenging Roman Catholicism, and the scholars of the 1960s shared the era's anti-establishment sentiments.

Current interpreters, also influenced by their contexts, are more likely to understand Amos's language about worship as hyperbole created for the sake of persuasion. In keeping with Amos's style of overstatement and shocking rhetoric, Yahweh's words about sacrifice were intended not to abolish the sacrificial system but to stress the greater importance of the demands of justice.

Amos and "God in History"

Amos clearly argues that for its mistreatment of the poor, Israel will fall in war. The people are repeatedly threatened with exile (5:27; 6:7), the forcible relocation of inhabitants by a conquering army. Israel's national security depends less on the effectiveness of its military than on the will of God.

Similarly, Amos draws a direct line of causation between "natural" events and divine intention. In 4:6–10, for example, God is said to orchestrate blight, mildew, and drought in order to capture the people's attention. Clearly, Amos assumes that the material well-being of the nation of Israel depends on its morality. God is understood to work the divine will in the course of human events.

Many readers accept Amos's words as fact and retell the history of Israel in such terms, claiming, for example, that "Israel was destroyed because of its sins." Hearing such claims in a modern context, however, highlights their problematic nature. When commentators claimed that the terrorist attacks of September 11, 2001, or the 2004 tsunami devastation in Southeast Asia were acts of God, sent by God to punish and/or instruct human behavior, many Christians protested. Blaming God for events caused by flawed human beings and by earth's natural forces, they responded, draws too clear a connection between individual behaviors and the broader unfolding of human history.

For the present as well as for Amos, then, attempts to discern how God works in the world are better understood not as facts but as theological judgments—judg-

ments that can be discussed, corroborated, or refuted. The holy task in such judgments is to avoid two extremes: denying that God cares about the world or claiming inappropriate knowledge about God's involvement.

Bibliography

Carroll, R., and M. Daniel. *Amos: The Prophet and His Oracles: Research on the Book of Amos.* Louisville: Westminster John Knox, 2002.

Sanderson, Judith. "Amos." In *The Women's Bible Commentary*, edited by C. A. Newsom and S. H. Ringe, 218–223. Rev. ed. Louisville: Westminster John Knox, 1998.

Obadiah

Julia M. O'Brien

INTRODUCTION

Like the book of Nahum, the book of Obadiah is devoted exclusively to God's judgment of one of Israel's enemies. Other prophetic books include such oracles against the nations, but Obadiah's single-minded focus on God's destruction of Edom focuses attention on the theological merits of vengeance, as well as on the political dimensions of theological discourse.

COMMENTARY

Many Christians publicly disapprove of the sentiments expressed in the book of Obadiah, viewing its eye-for-an-eye mentality of v. 15 ("As you have done, it shall be done to you; your deeds shall return on your own head") as contradicting Jesus' call to "turn the other cheek" and to "pray for those who persecute you." The delight that the book takes in announcing Edom's pending punishment is considered unchristian.

But many readers also would admit, if only privately, that like they, like Obadiah, find revenge to be sweet. The popularity of movies in which villians eventually suffer physical retribution, as well as international outcries for retribution against terrorists, suggest that the desire for the wicked to be punished is strong in the human spirit.

As discussed in other entries on the Minor Prophets, this insistence on justice is characteristic of the prophets. They insist that humans are accountable for mistreatment of others and that God cares about—and will respond to—injustice. Obadiah's condemnation of Edom may certainly be understood as an affirmation of God's stance against human suffering. But the charges that Obadiah brings against Edom demonstrate also the complications of justice, how identifying enemies and their just recompense all too easily can become self-interested and political—how tempting equating our enemies with God's enemies can be.

Obadiah 11–14 claims that during the Babylonian destruction of the temple in Jerusalem in 587 BCE, neighboring Edom gloated over Judah's fall, entered the gates of Jerusalem and looted the city, and handed over fleeing Judeans to the enemy. Historians and archaeologists, however, debate the accuracy of these charges. In the sixth century, Edom was a relatively poor and weak country and was in no position to defend its brother nation with military force. While a few biblical passages echo the claims of Obadiah, no nonbiblical evidence points to Edom's participation in the sack of Jerusalem or to collaboration with the Babylonians.

Evidence from the time period, however, does attest to territorial disputes between Judah and Edom, especially in the Negev, in southern Judah along their common border. Obadiah's charges that Edom collaborated with the enemy may, then, have served as justification for Judah's reclaiming of land from Edom, a possibility strengthened by the fact that Obadiah ends with a promise that Judah not only will reclaim the Negev but also will enlarge its borders in every direction: west to the land of the Philistines; north to Ephraim and Samaria; northeast to Gilead and Phoenicia; and, of course, south to Edom/Mount Esau itself.

The case of Obadiah calls Christians to an appreciation of justice but also to holy skepticism about motives that drive people and nations to call for retaliation against enemies. Faithful reading and faithful living require that we acknowledge not only the self-interests of biblical authors but also of ourselves and our societies.

Bibliography

Barton, John. *Joel and Obadiah*. OTL. Louisville: Westminster John Knox, 2001.

Mason, Rex. *Micah, Nahum, Obadiah*. Old Testament Guides. Sheffield: JSOT Press, 1991.

Raabe, Paul R. *Obadiah*. AB 24D. New York: Doubleday, 1996.

Jonah

Julia M. O'Brien

INTRODUCTION

The short book of Jonah fits uneasily in the Minor Prophets. Although the book twice uses the prophetic phrase, "the word of the LORD came to . . . ," the book as a whole concentrates not on the prophet's speeches but rather on stories about him—what he does, where he travels, how people respond to him. In this way, the book's style parallels more that of the books of Kings than that of the other Latter Prophets.

Yet, the book remains unique. It employs an exaggerated, even comic style—Jonah is rescued from the sea by being swallowed by a large fish, and a tree grows over his head in a day; the cattle of Nineveh join humans in repentance and wearing sackcloth. Consistently, too, the character acts in ways uncharacteristic of biblical prophets. When Isaiah is confronted by God in Isa. 6, he responds, "here I am, send me," but when the Lord tells Jonah to go to Nineveh, he immediately flees in the opposite direction. When God shows Amos visions of Israel's fall, the prophet appeals to God for mercy, but when God is merciful to the Ninevites, Jonah grows angry with God's compassion.

Indeed, the message of the book seems designed to question the views of its primary character. Jonah is portrayed as a comical, misguided figure, and his resentment over God's forgiveness of the Ninevites is a viewpoint that the author of the book wishes to challenge. The reader is led to recognize that the prophet Jonah is not hero but antihero.

COMMENTARY

In Jonah, true piety is demonstrated by foreigners. In chap. 1 the sailors are more righteous than Jonah: while he runs from Yahweh, they are reluctant to throw him into the sea, and, having seen this Deity's power, they offer sacrifices and vows to Yahweh. While, in Joel, the prophet calls the people to repent even in the face of pending judgment, since "Who knows whether he will not turn and relent?" (Joel 2:14), in Jonah it is the king of Nineveh who calls for repentance, since "Who knows? God may relent and change his mind; he may turn from his fierce anger, so that we do not perish" (Jonah 3:9). While the Ninevites respond wholeheartedly to Jonah's call to repentance—from the greatest to the least—Jonah's heart never changes.

Many biblical scholars claim that Jonah was written in the postexilic period as a reaction to the reforms of Ezra and Nehemiah, which banished non-Jews from the Jewish community. Jonah, they maintain, was written to challenge nationalism and exclusivism, advancing instead an inclusive vision of the Jewish community. Following this line of interpretation, the book is often contrasted positively with the book of Nahum (both books concern Nineveh). While both Nahum and Jonah end with a rhetorical question, their sentiments toward Nineveh clearly differ. While Nahum delights in the suffering of Nineveh, the book of Jonah portrays its salvation.

Such an interpretation, however, fails to recognize the complex political situation of postexilic Judah—the way in which Ezra's reforms were not formulated in a vacuum but within the political realities of a province controlled by the Persian Empire. Such interpretations of Ezra's reforms are also problematic in that they often have fed stereotypes of Judaism as narrow and exclusivistic— stereotypes often perpetuated by Christians who cast Jesus' message of widespread welcome as a radical challenge to his own religious background.

A more fruitful line for interpreting Jonah takes its cue from the dialogue between Jonah and God at the book's close. When God asks Jonah if he is justified in his anger over Nineveh's escape, Jonah does not respond but rather leaves the city to sulk. When, after both growing and destroying a tree to shade Jonah, God asks Jonah if he is justified in his anger regarding the plant, Jonah responds yes. God then asks why Jonah should care about the plant but not about the scores of women, men, children, and even cattle who live in Nineveh.

The great irony of God's final rhetorical question is that Jonah does not care about the plant any more than he does about the inhabitants of Nineveh. Throughout this book, Jonah cares only about himself. In chap. 1 he jeopardizes all onboard the ship in order to avoid a task he refuses to accept. In chap. 4 his concern appears to be his reputation: he credits his refusal to go Nineveh to his awareness that God might relent from carrying out the very punishment Jonah had announced. In the same way Jonah's care for the plant is not for its own well-being but for what it offers him. In satirizing the character of Jonah, the author satirizes not simply national self-interest but self-interest in all its forms. The book also demonstrates the importance of human action and God's freedom to act. Even Nineveh, described as evil in other prophetic books, can escape judgment through the action of its people. And a merciful God can choose to cancel intended punishment. When people act in faith, who knows what God may do?

Bibliography

Sasson, Jack. *Jonah.* AB 24B. New York: Doubleday, 1990.

Trible, Phyllis. "Jonah." In *NIB* 7:463–529.

Micah

Julia M. O'Brien

INTRODUCTION

The superscription of the book of Micah sets the prophet early in the eighth century BCE, before the fall of Samaria to the Assyrians. Much of the book fits well into such a historical setting—envisioned in the future are an Assyrian invasion (5:5–6) and the fall of Samaria (1:6). Other passages, however, address the "remnant" of Judah (5:5–7) and the rebuilding of the walls of Jerusalem (7:11), suggesting an exilic or postexilic date. Scholars debate whether the book is primarily a preexilic composition to which later, postexilic additions were made, or rather a postexilic document that utilizes earlier material. In either case, however, Micah is the product not of a single person or even a single community, but rather a repository of theological responses to different periods of Judean history.

The book shifts, too, between messages of rebuke and of hope. Micah includes both some of the most direct language of judgment in the prophets ("you who eat the flesh of my people and tear the skin off them," 3:3, my trans.) and also some of the most captivating visions of the future ("they shall beat their swords into plowshares . . . nation shall not lift up sword against nation," 4:3). Although the juxtaposition of judgment and hope has often been explained as the result of the book's historical growth, these two themes stand in creative tension within Micah and within the rest of the prophetic literature.

COMMENTARY

Social Justice

Micah is often seen, along with Amos, as one of the Bible's clearest voices for social justice. Its famous rhetorical question places treatment of the neighbor at the center of religious faith: "He has told you, O mortal, what is good; and what does the LORD require of you but to do justice, and to love kindness, and to walk humbly with your God?" (6:8). Micah criticizes the wealthy who cheat others (6:11–12) and also all leaders of an unjust society—rulers, chiefs, priests, and prophets (3:5–11). Like Amos, Micah claims that ritual cannot substitute for justice.

Micah does not, however, disparage traditional Israelite worship practices. The book's challenge of idol worship (5:10–15) indicates that, for Micah, the call to justice and the call to faithful worship are not mutually exclusive.

Visions of the Future

The image in Mic. 4 of nations at peace, no longer needing to manufacture weapons or train armies, has fed the imaginations of many working to end violence. "Swords to plowshares" became a popular image of efforts for international peace in the twentieth century, and a statue of a muscular man in this very act stands in the North Garden of the United Nations. This passage appears not only in Mic. 4:1–5 but also in Isa. 2:2–4, suggesting this articulation of hope for the future was just as captivating in the ancient world.

Utopian visions have functioned in various ways. At times, they have spurred communities to action; seeing alternative possibilities for a warring world can encourage people to act to change the present. At other times, however, they have fed complacency, as believers wait for God's intervention in the world. Readers, then, are responsible for using such images in ways that motivate action rather than simply reassure the faithful.

Readers do well to recognize, too, that even the most elaborate scenarios that humans imagine for the future are limited by our own experiences and historical contexts. In the case of Mic. 4, while the author can imagine a world without war, he apparently cannot imagine a world in which men and women are equally strong and equally valued. Micah 4:6–5:5 consistently uses feminine forms to describe the weakness and vulnerability of the people and city, while rescue comes in the form of the male: in the future, Yahweh will rule Daughter Jerusalem and kingship will return. A man's safety on his own property (while the NRSV of 4:4 uses plural forms, the Hebrew uses masculine singular) is a privilege of gender in a society in which women do not own property. Readers, too, do well to recognize the limitations of their own hopes for the future and the need for communities to talk to one another about what is good, just, and hopeful.

Judgment and Hope

In the final form of the book of Micah, neither judgment nor hope stands alone. The future that Micah promises cannot happen without judgment, without change, without justice: whatever stands in the way of truth must be overcome in order for the world to be as God intends it. Judgment, at least sometimes, is a precondition to peace.

The ending of Micah integrates both aspects of God's response to humans. Micah 7:8–20 acknowledges that the people's punishment is deserved, but it also insists that God is compassionate and forgiving. God's judgment, while necessary for justice to be done, is not God's last word.

Bibliography

Hillers, Delbert. *Micah*. Hermeneia. Philadelphia: Fortress, 1984.
Mason, Rex. *Micah, Nahum, Obadiah*. Old Testament Guides. Sheffield: JSOT Press, 1991.

Nahum

Julia M. O'Brien

INTRODUCTION

After reporting that its words are directed against Nineveh, the capital of the Assyrian Empire in the eighth century BCE, the book of Nahum opens with an image of God as a warrior charging onto the earth for vengeance. It alludes to the traditional affirmation that Yahweh is "merciful and gracious, slow to anger, and abounding in steadfast love and faithfulness . . . forgiving iniquity and transgression and sin, yet by no means clearing the guilty" (Exod. 34:5–7), but, by stating three times that Yahweh is vengeful (Nah. 1:2–3), it clearly focuses on the concluding portion of the Israelite creed.

The nature of Yahweh's vengeance against Nineveh is graphically, even gleefully, described in chaps. 2 and 3: "piles of dead, heaps of corpses, dead bodies without end—they stumble over the bodies!" (3:3). Throughout, Nahum resolutely refuses any empathy or care for those about to be destroyed: "Nineveh is devastated; who will bemoan her?" (3:7); "All who hear the news about you clap their hands over you" (3:19). Nineveh's devastation is portrayed as a sexual assault in chap. 3. Nineveh, already having been portrayed as a woman in the book, is here called a prostitute whose skirts will be lifted up and whose nakedness will be uncovered. The one who will carry out this assault is none other than Yahweh himself. For obvious reasons, Nahum's insistence on revenge and its celebration of multiple forms of violence disturb readers committed to peace and justice.

COMMENTARY

Acknowledging just how ethically problematic Nahum can be is a significant step toward an honest reading of the Bible. While Nahum is ignored by the Revised Common Lectionary and often dismissed as just ancient poetry, it has been preserved within the Christian canon alongside Isaiah, the Psalms, and the Gospels. It is part of the Bible that many Christians describe as their "only rule of faith and practice." Taking the violence of Nahum seriously requires Christians to find honest ways to describe the Bible and its authority in their lives: those who refuse to accept Nahum as a valid guide to the faithful life clearly make discernments in reading the Bible that simplistic descriptions of the Bible (such as "The Bible says it. I believe it. That settles it.") do not reflect.

Denigrating Nahum as ethically inferior to our own values, however, is misguided and dangerous. Wilhelm Wessels, a South African biblical scholar, has provocatively compared Nahum to the resistance poetry produced in South Africa during the apartheid years, which sought to give oppressed people the confidence that justice will one day come. Nahum, Wessels argues, is less a call to violence than a call on the imagination to believe that apparently overwhelming evil can be overcome. Wessels's reading reminds interpreters that the target of Nahum's words was a resource-hungry, brutal empire whose kings advertised their ruthfulness in art and celebrated their cruelty in written texts. Some have compared "Assyria" in Israelite memory to "Nazi" in contemporary imagination. Reading Nahum as the voice of the oppressed suggests that, like other prophets, Nahum is concerned with justice.

Over a generation ago, the Jewish theologian Abraham Heschel insisted that God's anger against injustice is a sign of God's goodness, that a God who cares about humanity must be angered at its suffering. An angry God is not the opposite of a loving God but rather the opposite of an apathetic God. In this understanding, the affirmation of God's goodness in Nah. 1:7 belongs with the insistence that God will not clear the guilty.

As in the case of other prophets, however, Nahum's concern does not extend to all oppressed people. It stereotypes women as either vulnerable (Judah) or deserving of sexual assault (Nineveh); and it voices no protest at human suffering.

Most adults well know that few people or institutions are wholly good or wholly evil. Recognizing what is good about parents, employers, friends, partners, or neighbors does not require overlooking or explaining away their abusiveness. In a similar way, a thoughtful response to Nahum, as to other prophets, is one of discernment, of finding ways to recognize the power of anger to mobilize resistance to oppression while refusing to substitute one form of oppression for another.

Bibliography

Heschel, Abraham J. *The Prophets.* New York: Harper & Row, 1962.

O'Brien, Julia Myers. *Nahum.* Readings. New York: Continuum, 2002.

Wessels, Wilhelm. "Nahum, an Uneasy Expression of Yahweh's Power." *Old Testament Essays* 11/3 (1998): 615–28.

Habakkuk

Julia M. O'Brien

INTRODUCTION

The opening of Habakkuk arrests readers with its challenging claims: "Justice never prevails. The wicked surround the righteous—therefore judgment comes forth perverted" (1:4). Although within the book "the wicked" are the Babylonians, the question of God's justice in the face of suffering is also a contemporary one. If God is all powerful and all-loving, why does God not intervene in human history for the sake of the oppressed?

COMMENTARY

Habakkuk does not solve the issue of theodicy (the technical term for such theological questioning), but the book does suggest avenues for Christian responses to human pain. Each avenue, however, can be both promising and problematic.

Patience

Habakkuk 2:4 is perhaps the best-known verse of the book. For Martin Luther "the righteous shall live by faith" was a crucial affirmation that God accepts sinners based not on their own merit but on the merit of their reliance on the saving power of Jesus Christ. Within the context of the book, however, the verse calls the prophet to wait on God's response to his complaint about injustice. Indeed, the Hebrew word is better translated as "faithfulness" rather than "faith," because it refers to steadfastness, endurance, loyalty. The literary context of the verse, 2:1–4, also may suggest that the "faithfulness" resides in the vision itself: the prophet should wait for God's response because, while it is delayed, it is trustworthy.

Many find the insistence on God's justice, even while it is delayed, to be hopeful and good news. In times of distress, believers may be assured—despite evidence to the contrary—that God cares about their plight and will act in God's own time. Others, however, consider such a message dangerous because it discourages Christians from taking concrete action against injustice. For these Christians, injustice calls not for patience but for human agency.

Protest

The style of the book, however, suggests that Habakkuk does not counsel quiet

279

acceptance of suffering. The book is constructed as a series of dialogues—arguments, perhaps—between the prophet and Yahweh. In chap. 1 the prophet voices his complaint about injustice in 1:2–4; Yahweh responds in 1:5–11; and the prophet protests again in 1:12–17. In 2:1 the prophet challenges God to answer his complaint, and Yahweh offers an extended response in 2:2–20, announcing the punishment of the wicked.

Clearly then, the book of Habakkuk joins other biblical literature such as the psalms of lament, the book of Job, and the book of Lamentations in challenging God. Assuming throughout that God is powerful and able to act, the prophet repeatedly asks why God does not intervene. While God's responses do not always satisfy the prophet, the book as a whole models the ability—and duty—of believers to complain about the pain of their world, to petition God to act on behalf of the oppressed.

Alternative Vision

The final chapter of the book turns from the dialogue format to an extended vision of God as a warrior, marching on Judah's behalf. This image of the Divine Warrior, controlling and overwhelming the natural world, is a common one in the Bible and has many parallels in the mythologies of other ancient Near Eastern cultures. In using this language, the prophet underscores God's raw power. The chapter is entitled a "prayer" and shares many features with psalms, including the ending instructions to the choirmaster. Like some psalms, the memory of how God

acted in the past both awes and comforts those who seek God's action in the present: God, who marched against the rivers and the sea in the past, can be trusted to march again against Israel's enemies.

The depiction of Yahweh as the Divine Warrior in Hab. 3, on the one hand, provides good news: both in the past and in the present, God is not powerless in the face of evil. This image, on the other hand, also poses ethical questions. Does envisioning God as a warrior against evil encourage readers to envision their own enemies as God's enemies and their own battles as divine? Does the violence inherent in the image truly reflect God and God's intention for human activity?

A response, if not an answer, to these questions may be found in the book's affirmation of both the Divine Warrior and also the prophet's complaints. Habakkuk suggests that believers faced with the realities of human suffering should not only trust that God will act but also assume their responsibility to raise voices of protest—even and perhaps especially to God.

Bibliography

Hiebert, Theodore. "Habakkuk." In *NIB* 7:623–55.
Roberts, J. J. M. *Nahum, Habakkuk, and Zephaniah.* OTL. Louisville: Westminster John Knox, 1991.
Sanderson, Judith. "Habakkuk." In *The Women's Bible Commentary*, edited by Carol A. Newsom and Sharon H. Ringe, pp. 237–39. Rev. ed. Louisville: Westminster John Knox, 1998.

Zephaniah

Julia M. O'Brien

INTRODUCTION

Zephaniah is in many ways a microcosm of the prophetic books. Not only does it share language with other prophetic literature, but its generic accusations against Judah and other nations also appear to draw on stock prophetic vocabulary. Most importantly, however, its sharply contrasting statements of unmitigating judgment and promises of a hopeful future spotlight the interplay between judgment and hope that is characteristic of the prophets.

COMMENTARY

The voice of God in Zeph. 1 is scathing, and the punishment announced is total. Not only kings and the wealthy are targeted, but, in a reversal of creation, humans, animals, birds, and fish will be swept from the face of the earth. A litany of devastation in 1:14–16 (the basis for the *Dies irae*, long part of the Roman Catholic Mass for the Dead) characterizes the day of God's reckoning. Chapters 2 and 3 reveal that nations other than Judah also will face the full force of God's wrath.

Faint notes of hope can be heard amid this booming theme, however. Zephaniah 2:2–3 calls for the repentance of the humble, raising the possibility that they might yet escape destruction. Zephaniah 3:9–13 also suggests that a remnant might be spared and live in peace. The book closes with a happily-ever-after image: Daughter Zion is rescued like a damsel in distress by Yahweh the mighty warrior and king, who, according to the NRSV of 3:17, expresses his love. Some scholars maintain that the happy endings of prophetic books were added by later generations of believers, in hopes that God's punishment of their ancestors was not God's last word for Israel; but even without its final verses Zephaniah typifies the prophetic tension between judgment and hope.

Some readers of Zephaniah focus only on the hopeful aspects of the book. Offended by the image of an angry, punishing God, they give priority to its profession of love and peace. But in the book of Zephaniah, and the prophets in general, God's punishment and God's love belong together. God's care for humans does not preclude, and in fact may require, God's action against oppression and wrongdoing. As discussed in the commentary on Nahum, a compelling case can be made for the ethical necessity of God's anger, God's stance against injustice. A moral God cares about what happens to the world. Yet, even though the book insists that Judah deserves God's punishment, Zephaniah leaves open the (slim) possibility that repentance might alter God's decrees.

Zephaniah joins other prophets in insisting that Yahweh will judge other countries: Judah's neighbors are targeted in chap. 2; 3:8 reveals that Yahweh will pour out indignation on the nations; and 3:19 promises that Yahweh will deal with Judah's oppressors. Such thinking could lead to nationalism and self-congratulation, but Zephaniah's insistence that only a remnant of Judah may survive and its vision of a day in which all people may one day call on the name of Yahweh (3:9) lead to another conclusion: that all nations, including Judah, are held accountable by a God who is righteous but also merciful.

Bibliography

Mason, Rex. *Zephaniah, Habakkuk, Joel.* Old Testament Guides. Sheffield: JSOT Press, 1994.

Roberts, J. J. M. *Nahum, Habakkuk, and Zephaniah.* OTL. Louisville: Westminster John Knox, 1991.

Haggai

Julia M. O'Brien

INTRODUCTION

Haggai's focus on a specific moment and issue makes appreciating its theological value difficult. Much about the book roots it solidly in the past: long date formulas; direct address to named individuals; discussion of ancient priestly rulings on ritual cleanness; and, most importantly, the book's insistence that Judeans in the Persian period should rebuild the temple destroyed by the Babylonians almost two generations earlier. Reflection on how an ancient prophet understood God's working in his own day, however, might allow us to consider God's work today.

COMMENTARY

Temples in the ancient world functioned on both religious and political levels. In preexilic Judah, the temple not only served as God's "house," the proof of God's presence for the nation, but it also served to legitimate the monarchy, as reflected clearly in linking of temple and kingship in 2 Sam. 7. In the Persian Empire the rebuilding of ancestral temples not only restored the honor of local gods but also may have been used to administer Persian policies and to collect Persian taxes. A restored temple in Jerusalem would symbolize Yahweh's presence with the people but also may have advanced Persian interests.

Haggai's particular understanding of the temple, however, implicitly critiques Persian control. By stressing the importance of the temple's glory and by linking its completion with a cosmic shaking that will topple kingdoms (2:6–9), Haggai stresses the sovereignty of God over all human institutions. The ultimate power is not the Persian king Darius, whose control is acknowledged by the date formulae that punctuate the book, but the God whose temple Haggai places at the center of the community.

The ultimate sovereignty of God over all other powers is stressed, too, by the final verses of the book, which envision an exalted role for Zerubbabel, whom the Bible elsewhere traces to the line of David. While some have seen the beginning of messianic hopes in this portrait of Zerubbabel, Haggai makes clear that Zerubbabel's importance is subordinate to that of Yahweh: he is God's servant, the ring on God's hand.

Several features of the book further underscore Haggai's concern with God's honor and power. In 1:12–15, for example, God proclaims to the people, "I am

283

with you," *before* they begin work but *after* they "fear." The completion of the temple appears less important than the people's obedience to the divine word as communicated through Haggai. God stirs the people's spirits to work only after they obey God and God's prophet. Hence, while the book of Haggai greatly emphasizes the rebuilding of the temple, it nonetheless places even greater importance on the people's proper attitude and reverence for God.

At times Haggai appears to draw a direct correlation between pleasing God and material success. The people's hesitance to work on the temple is blamed for their lack of agricultural and financial success (1:6–11; 2:15–19), and 2:19 promises that when the people work on the temple God will bless them. While such a perspective is not unique among the prophets, such clearly drawn lines of cause and effect fail to honor the complexities of human living and the natural world. The sovereign God, whom Haggai so clearly portrays, surely works in ways less transparent than Haggai suggests.

Bibliography

Meyers, Carol. "Temple, Jerusalem." In *Anchor Bible Dictionary*, edited by David Noel Freedman, 6:350–69. New York: Doubleday, 1992.

Meyers, Carol L., and Eric M. Meyers. *Haggai; Zechariah 1–8*. AB 25B. Garden City, NY: Doubleday, 1987.

Petersen, David L. *Haggai and Zechariah 1–8*. OTL. Philadelphia: Westminster, 1984.

Zechariah

Julia M. O'Brien

INTRODUCTION

Although much of the book of Zechariah is typically "prophetic"—complete with chronological formulas, language such as "thus says the LORD," and oracles of judgment and hope—perhaps Daniel is the only prophetic book that can challenge Zechariah for the title "most enigmatic." A montage of rich yet puzzling images and sayings, Zechariah often leaves its readers bewildered.

For at least two centuries, scholars have attributed some of the book's disjointedness to multiple authorship. Chapters 1–8 are often labeled "First Zechariah" and dated to the Persian period; chaps. 9–14, which differ markedly in style from earlier chapters, are called "Second Zechariah" or "Deutero-Zechariah" and dated to the Hellenistic period. Determining the precise historical background of any particular part of Zechariah, however, is difficult.

Scholars debate whether one or both sections deserve the label "apocalyptic," a description usually reserved for biblical materials such as Daniel and Revelation in which secrets to the future are given in symbolic visions and in which the future is seen to mark a radical break with the present. Some interpreters have suggested that the book as a whole provides evidence of developing apocalypticism in the Persian period, while others argue that the visions of Zechariah fit well within the range of classical prophecy, more akin to the visions in Amos 7–9 than to Daniel.

COMMENTARY

First Zechariah

The theme of First Zechariah is summarized in 1:12–17. When asked how long Jerusalem will remain in ruins, Yahweh declares the end of Jerusalem's punishment and the beginning of the rebuilding of city and temple: "The LORD will again comfort Zion." While the book of Haggai calls on humans to undertake temple construction, Zechariah focuses on what God is doing on behalf of the temple project: the restoration of Jerusalem is not the cause of God's favor but rather its result.

The eight visions that follow support this theme of God's forgiveness and goodwill toward Jerusalem. They depict rather than narrate the scattering of Judah's enemies (1:18–21), the complete security of the restored Jerusalem (2:1–13), the cleansing of the priesthood (3:1–10), the return to the leadership of priest and Davidic heir (4:1–14), the reestablishment of the rule of Torah (5:1–4), and the banishing of idolatry (5:5–11). Throughout, First Zechariah seeks to convince readers that although Jerusalem was rightfully punished for its sins, it is now forgiven and stands ready for transformation. Fasting in memory of the past destructions should now end (7:1–7), as the people anticipate a joyful future—in which old and young will thrive (8:4–23).

First Zechariah's vision for the future is not naive, however. In chap. 3 the high priest Joshua is challenged by an adversary. The NRSV translation "Satan" suggests the cosmic evil one who appears in the New Testament, but the term here is better translated "the adversary," as in the NRSV footnote, since the Hebrew word includes the article "the." In the Old Testament "the adversary" is not a supernatural opponent of God but rather one within God's court whose role is to challenge humans (as in Job 1). In Zech. 3 the adversary exposes the challenges that must be overcome in order for the high priest to be restored to his proper role, recognizing that restoration faces obstacles.

First Zechariah's message cannot be separated from its style. The book demonstrates that trusting in God's forgiveness and care is not simply a matter of the intellect and will—it is a matter of the imagination as well. Glimpses of God's future transform suffering communities in ways that arguments cannot. Those who wish to extend Zechariah's message into the present, to convince people of God's care and the goodness of God's future, are encouraged to create wherever and whenever possible real-life tableaux of grace and transformation that can provide intimations of a hopeful, though difficult to imagine, future.

Second Zechariah

Even though the single label "Second Zechariah" is often given to chaps. 9–14, this material does not cohere. New headings begin at 9:1 and 12:1, and the material introduced by them is complex and uneven.

In general, however, these chapters extend, in dramatic and often disturbing ways, the themes of First Zechariah. Second Zechariah shares with earlier chapters a commitment to the restoration of Jerusalem, to challenging Judean behaviors and attitudes, and to announcing punishment of the nations who have harmed Judah. Its amplification of these themes, however, goes to extreme lengths, arresting the reader with over-the-top depictions of Jerusalem's splendor, God's anger at Judah, and the subjugation of the nations.

The resulting images of Yahweh are bold and disturbing. The march of the Divine Warrior in Zech. 9—charging onto the earth intent on spilling the blood of the nations in order to save the people—develops imagery found in other prophetic books. The intensification of the imagery in chap. 14, however, is dramatic: Yahweh stands with feet firmly planted on the Mount of Olives, which splits underfoot to provide an escape route for inhabitants of Jerusalem. Those who fight against Jerusalem will die gruesome deaths, but Jerusalem will enjoy continuous daylight and year-round abundance of water.

In both chapters the violence of Yahweh against nations is cast as good news for Jerusalem. In chap. 9 the Divine Warrior defends Daughter Zion with power and might, and in chap. 14 everything in Jerusalem will become holy. Hearing Zech. 14 as good news today, however, is difficult. While most would affirm that its insistence on God's care and power can be good news for those who despair over the injustice of the world, the sheer violence of the image can subvert its message of hope. A parallel to the danger of overexaggeration might be *Uncle Tom's Cabin*: while Harriet Beecher Stowe sought to convince readers of the evils of slavery, her exaggerated caricatures of childlike Negroes fed paternalistic attitudes toward freed slaves rather than attempts toward African American empowerment.

That biblical interpretation should be—and is—informed by the convictions of its readers can be seen clearly in the way in which the writers of the Gospels gave new meaning to passages in Zechariah. In chap. 9 the king who enters Jerusalem to save the city is likely either Yahweh himself or an agent of Yahweh in the Persian period. Matthew 21, however, interprets Jesus' triumphal entry into Jerusalem as the fulfillment of Zechariah's words. Similarly, the one who throws thirty shekels of silver into the temple (Zech. 11:12–13) is, in the context of the passage, the prophet himself; in Matt. 26–27 the one who throws silver is Jesus' betrayer, Judas.

The significance of Zechariah, like that of other great literature, music, and visual art, is not exhausted by any single interpretation. But faithful people bear responsibility for the impact of their interpretations: does a given reading of Zechariah contribute to a world characterized by widespread holiness and peace or to a world governed by violence and self-interest? Readers who work for international peace and justice are encouraged to take responsibility for reading in ways that provide hope to the oppressed without calling for greater bloodshed and revenge.

Bibliography

Meyers, Carol L., and Eric M. Meyers. *Haggai; Zechariah 1–8*. AB 25B. Garden City, NY: Doubleday, 1987.

O'Brien, Julia M. *Nahum, Habakkuk, Zephaniah, Haggai, Zechariah, Malachi*. AOTC. Nashville: Abingdon, 2004.

Petersen, David L. *Haggai and Zechariah 1–8*. OTL. Philadelphia: Westminster, 1984.

Malachi

Julia M. O'Brien

INTRODUCTION

Many Christians have encountered only bits of the book of Malachi: verses devoted to tithing (3:10) or divorce (2:13–16), or, during the singing of Handel's *Messiah,* the promise of a coming messenger of the covenant, who, like a refining fire, will purify the sons of Levi and restore worship that is pleasing to God (3:1–5). These issues deserve attention, but so too does Malachi's depiction of God as a scolding, authoritarian father.

COMMENTARY

God the Father

Throughout the book of Malachi, God's relationship to the people is compared to that between a father and a son: in 1:2–5, where Yahweh favors one son over another; in 1:6, where Israel's failure to honor Yahweh is failure of a son to honor his father; in 3:17, where God promises to spare Israel as "a man spares a son who serves him"; and in 4:6, where the Day of the Lord will restore proper relationships between fathers and sons (even though in thse texts the NRSV reads "parents" and "children," the language in Hebrew is masculine in gender). While many Christians find "father" language for God comforting, the way in which Malachi uses the metaphor is striking. Here God is not a comforting, warm father, but one who demands respect and who threatens humiliating punishment for erring sons (see, e.g., 2:3).

The harshness of this father image is intensified by the argumentative, even combative, style of the book. The attitudes of the people are caricatured with impudent speech: ("'What a weariness this is,' you say"—1:13) and God's retorts are equally harsh. Tellingly, the book ends with reference to God's curse.

Malachi calls attention to the dark side of many of our cherished metaphors for God, the ways in which they both dishonor God and support dangerous assumptions about proper parenting. Those who support a model of parenting in which both mothers and fathers share authority equally, in which value is placed on nurturing children rather than on their obedience, and in which physical punishment is avoided, may need to challenge rather than assent to Malachi's view of God as father.

Divorce

In most modern translations, God's pronouncement in 2:16 is unambiguous: "'I hate divorce,' says the LORD, the God of Israel." The verse in Hebrew is not so clear, however. In Hebrew the verb reads "he hates" and the noun is literally "sending." Modern translations "correct" the verb to the first person and assume that "sending" refers to sending away a wife in divorce, though some scholars have argued that "sending" is a shortened form of an idiom meaning "treachery." Indeed, "divorce" does not appear in most translations of the verse prior to the twentieth century, as seen in the KJV, "For the LORD, the God of Israel, saith that he hateth putting away."

In suggesting that some passages are clearer than they really are, modern Bible translations often prevent us from realizing how difficult the Bible can be to understand, and even more difficult to apply to our daily lives. Clearly, theological or ethical positions that rely on the English translation of isolated verses such as 2:16 stand on shaky ground.

Bibliography

O'Brien, Julia M. *Nahum, Habakkuk, Zephaniah, Haggai, Zechariah, Malachi*. AOTC. Nashville: Abingdon, 2004.

Petersen, David L. *Zechariah 9–14 and Malachi*. OTL. Louisville: Westminster John Knox, 1995.

The New Testament

Matthew

Stanley P. Saunders

INTRODUCTION

The Gospel of Matthew presents Jesus as the definitive expression of God's presence and power in the world. After the Romans destroyed Jerusalem in 70 CE, Jews and Christians alike grappled with foundational theological questions: How and where was God's presence to be discerned? Had God abandoned God's people? Were the prophetic promises of restoration and liberation misplaced? Had God's power gone over to the Romans? Was the empire of Rome really the manifestation of divine will and destiny? How were God's people to understand and engage anew the traditions and institutions and especially the God they knew from experience and through the biblical writings? How could faithful vision, hope, and practice be nurtured under the brutal and violent dominion of a world power that proclaimed itself the embodiment of "salvation" and "peace" (the *pax Romana*)? For Matthew, God's presence and power are not discerned in association with human forms of power—whether Jewish elites or Roman emperors—but in Jesus of Nazareth, to whom all power in heaven and on earth has been granted. The crucified and risen Jesus is present among disciples as "God with us" (Matt. 1:23; 28:18–20). As the incarnate presence of God and the agent of God's power, Jesus breaches the boundaries between the human and the divine,

between heaven and earth. Matthew's story trains audiences for faithful ways of living in the transformed time and space that is the "empire [or "kingdom"] of heaven."

Matthew's Gospel was meant to be performed orally in its entirety within the worshiping assemblies of the early Christians. Some reconstructions locate the production of this Gospel within a cosmopolitan setting such as Antioch in Syria, others within one of the larger, hellenized cities of the Galilee. Both proposals presuppose a mixed population of Jews and Gentiles, where relations with the leadership of both emerging, post–70 forms of Judaism and the Roman imperial order, including the imperial cult, would be in play. Matthew contests the rule of Rome and the Jewish elites, who are linked together in exploitation, violence, and resistance to God's rule.

After the destruction of Jerusalem, Jews and Christians alike looked to Israel's Scriptures and traditions to define themselves and confirm their respective worldviews. Matthew, however, also makes Jesus himself the defining figure around which Israel's traditions and institutions are interpreted. The sacred space of God's presence, for example, is no longer the temple, but wherever "two or three" gather in Jesus' name (18:20).

Matthew confirms that Jesus "fulfills the law" (5:17–20) even as his teachings and practices radicalize and stretch it. Matthew presents Jesus as a figure like Moses and as the fulfillment of prophetic vision and hope, especially that of Isaiah and Jeremiah, but always in ways that break the mold. Matthew's presentation of Jesus' conflicts with the scribes, Pharisees, and leaders of Israel may also represent the conflicts between Matthew's own community and the leaders of Judaism after 70.

While Jesus' conflict with the Jewish leaders is much more prominent in Matthew than his engagement with imperial authorities, the Roman order nonetheless touched virtually every dimension of life both in Jerusalem and Judea and in Galilee where Jesus conducted most of his ministry. Herod the Great, who seeks to murder Jesus at his birth (Matt. 2), ruled over and exploited the Jewish people as a "client-king" in service to Rome, as did his son, Herod Antipas, who has John the Baptizer beheaded (Matt. 14:1–12). Pilate, the governor who presides over Jesus' execution, is a member of the Roman equestrian order. Even the chief priests and leaders of the Jews exercise their power in collaboration with Roman rule. Roman control of land, political and religious office, military authority, taxation, legal systems, economic structures, and even religion gave rise to widespread poverty, alienation, humiliation, and suffering. Rome styled its rule as the manifestation of divine order and destiny—a dominion without spatial or temporal end. Caesar himself was hailed as king, "Lord," "savior," and even "son of God." Rome claimed to bring justice (or "righteousness") and plenty to those it ruled, and demanded faith (*fides*) in exchange for peace and security (salvation). Announcements of Caesar's deeds and commandments were called "good news" (gospel). The imperial order thus looms over the Gospel's landscapes as the demonic embodiment of a distorted theology.

Matthew's story of Jesus provides a sharp alternative to foundational elements of Roman "theology." Matthew juxtaposes the language of the imperial cult with Jesus, in order to help audiences imagine an alternative world—"the kingdom [or "empire"] of heaven." Both John the Baptizer and Jesus begin their ministries in Matthew with the announcement that "the empire of the heavens is at hand" (3:2; 4:17). Jesus, not Caesar, is named "God with us" and "Son of God." Jesus describes and embodies in his ministry the kind of justice that God is calling forth, renewed and restored relationships characterized by mercy, forgiveness, and love even for enemies. Jesus' disciples are to make peace (5:9) by means of self-sacrifice and identification with the least ones (25:31–46) rather than by violence or domination. Matthew's resignification of imperial power is most evident in the story of Jesus' death on the cross. For Rome (and the Jerusalem leaders) the cross manifests the power of coercion, terror, and death, while for Matthew it is the defining expression of God's love for and identification with the victims of human domination. Roman theology views the cross from the perspective of those who wield the power of life and death and thus see themselves deserving of worship and obedience as representatives of the divine. Matthew regards the cross from the standpoint of the victim; divine power resides not with the executioner, but with the one crucified. For Rome, the crucifixion of Jesus is another successful pacification. For Matthew, the cross is the turning point of history, the definitive revelation of God's true identity and character.

Because the crucified and resurrected Jesus is present in power on earth as well as in heaven, the earthly realm itself is being transformed. Matthew's story invites its audience into this new world, where death is no longer the ultimate barrier, in which the boundaries between heaven and earth are breaking down, and where divine power is indeed loose in the world among humans, albeit not with those who practice domination and violence. In Matthew, humans now possess, like Jesus, the power to forgive sins (9:8), to cast out unclean spirits, heal disease, cleanse lepers, and even raise the dead (10:1, 8). Like Jesus, Matthew's disciples can even walk on water (14:28–32). Matthew democratizes divine power, but the disciples are not to use this power for their own sake, or to "lord it over" others, as do the rulers of the Gentiles (20:25–28). They are not to be called "rabbi," "father," or "master," or to exalt themselves or seek public honor, as do the scribes and Pharisees (23:2–12). Instead, divine power is expressed in servanthood and humiliation, in being slaves to one another (20:26–28; 23:11–12).

The Gospel of Matthew employs a creative mixture of literary conventions and cues in order to present Jesus as a life worthy of emulation (biography), as the culmination of Israel's story and the one who redirects human destiny (history), and as a revelatory figure whose life and ministry cross the boundaries between heaven and earth, inviting hearers into the mysteries of God's presence in and purposes for the world (wisdom and apocalyptic). Matthew also incorporates multiple, overlapping structural patterns. Five times in Matthew the formula "and when Jesus had finished these sayings . . ." marks a transition from one of Jesus' five major speeches to a narrative section recording his deeds (7:28–29; 11:1; 13:53; 19:1; and 26:1). Matthew uses yet another transitional formula ("from that time Jesus began to . . .") at 4:17, when Jesus begins his ministry in Galilee, and at 16:21, when he turns toward Jerusalem, where his suffering, death, and resurrection will occur. Recurrent themes and motifs suggest to some that Matthew is arranged as a series of parallels that fold back on themselves (a "chiasm"), with the parables of chap. 13 as the hinge. Modern audiences should resist the temptation to choose among these alternative structural patterns, which are based on differing but not exclusive criteria. Matthew is an integral, organic, and complex whole. This commentary employs the following outline: (1) The Ancient Origins of a New World, 1:1–4:16; (2) Jesus' Ministry to Restore Israel, 4:17–11:1; (3) Jesus' Ministry Generates Conflict and Crisis, 11:2–16:20; (4) The Journey to Jerusalem, 16:21–20:34; (5) The Clash of Powers in Jerusalem, 21:1–25:46; and (6) God with Us, 26:1–28:20.

Matthew's overlapping generic and structural cues enhance the sense of creative tension that pervades the whole Gospel. From beginning to end, Matthew juxtaposes themes, images, and motifs that many modern readers find contradictory or paradoxical. The most prominent tensions in Matthew involve christological assertions, relations with Israel and the law, the nature of Jesus' saving activity, and the persistent juxtaposition of judgment and mercy. Matthew's tensions mirror the tumultuous setting in which the Gospel is produced and performed, but offer no simple, one-sided resolutions. Faithfulness is realized within the tensions, where Matthew's community continues to live. By posing issues and questions in terms of tensions that remain unresolved, the evangelist calls forth a community of active interpreters.

The christological titles Matthew uses most prominently demonstrate the Gospel's creative tensions: Jesus is both Son of God and Son of Man (or "the human one")—at once the manifestation of divine rule and the representative of common humanity. Matthew's depiction of Jesus as both Son of God and Son of Man takes on comical expression in the story of the triumphal entry into Jerusalem (21:1–11), where Jesus rides not one but two animals—a donkey and a colt—that together symbolize Jesus' identity as king and servant. As Son of Man, Jesus is both the human Christ—rejected, homeless, and marginalized—and the heavenly judge anticipated in the apocalyptic tradition since Daniel. As the Son of God, Jesus demonstrates both divine power and complete trust in and obedience to God. Jesus is also the Son of David, but as one who heals and saves his people, rather than merely a political ruler. Jesus fulfills Israel's messianic hopes associated with each of these titles, but at the same time breaks the molds. In this way, Matthew establishes Jesus as a figure who is at once continuous and discontinuous with Jewish expectation. This in turn allows the Matthean audience itself to claim an identity that is both old (continuous) and new (discontinuous).

Matthew's depiction of the relationship between God, Jesus, and the people of Israel is yet another key tension. Matthew designates Jesus as the one who "will save his people from their sins" (1:21), but leaves the audience to wonder, by the end, whether God has abandoned Israel in favor of the church (see, e.g., 21:33–46; 27:20–25) or, in profound irony, saved the very people who call for Jesus' death. Who are "his people"? Matthew's story is about Israel's Messiah who comes to heal, gather, and restore, but at the same time is the cause of division. The relationship between God, Israel, and Jesus is set forth as an interpretive puzzle that Matthew's audiences must resolve for themselves.

COMMENTARY

The Ancient Origins of a New World (1:1–4:16)

Matthew announces itself as "an account of the genealogy of Jesus the Messiah, the son of David, the son of Abraham." "Account of the genealogy" (NRSV) may also be translated "the book of origins" or "book of genesis," which echoes the Greek version of Gen. 2:4 (cf. also Gen. 5:1). These words serve as a title for the whole Gospel. Matthew is the story of the genesis of a new world that encompasses both "the heavens and earth." As "Messiah, son of David," Jesus fulfills messianic hopes for a king who will restore and bring salvation to the nation. But it is the common people—the blind (9:27; 20:30–31), the Canaanite woman (15:22), the crowds (21:9), and the little children in the temple (21:15)—who will hail him as Son of David, while Israel's leaders will resist his rule. Jesus, the son of Abraham, also announces and embodies in his life, death, and resurrection the promises God made to Abraham, not only for the sake of Israel, but for all the nations of the earth (Gen. 12:3). Matthew's opening line thus locates Jesus among the founding figures in Israel's history and associates him with God's creating, covenant making, and blessing of Israel and the people of earth.

The genealogy (Matt. 1:2–16) establishes two seemingly contradictory impulses: Jesus is at once the continuation and fulfillment of Israel's story and the beginning of a definitively new reality. Matthew creates a storied space in which even women and outsiders have their place in bringing God's blessings to the world. The genealogy also begins training the audience to expect the unexpected. The monotonous structure of the genealogy contains some surprising departures from the norm, especially the inclusion of women—Tamar, Rahab, Ruth, "the wife of Uriah," and finally Mary the mother of Jesus. The stories of these women recall moments in Israel's history when God's purposes were accomplished through ordinary people, the disenfranchised, non-Israelites, the marginal, and by those who cross boundaries. The inclusion of these characters dislocates the audience from their everyday expectations about the origins of God's anointed one.

The sense of dislocation is strongest when the genealogy arrives at the birth of Jesus, where a shift to the passive voice verb signals divine agency in the birth (1:16). Matthew also presents the birth of Jesus as a riddle for the audience to solve: Matthew states that each segment of the genealogy has fourteen generations (1:17), but the last one turns out to be defective (from Shealtiel to Jesus is thirteen generations). Is this a mistake? Is Jesus to be counted twice, as Jesus and as the crucified and resurrected Christ? Is God the implied but missing generation?

Matthew does not resolve the puzzle for us, but compels the audience to become active interpreters who must determine what to make of this one who continues and fulfills Israel's history, while radically disrupting it.

The story of Jesus' birth reveals that the Holy Spirit is the primary agent in Jesus' conception (1:18); Jesus is both a "Son of God" and a "new Adam," a wholly new human generation. Joseph, who is the husband of Mary but not the birth father of Jesus, becomes the conduit of divine communication and the model of one who acts righteously—not according to conventional expectation—in his dealings with Mary. Joseph claims Jesus as his own when he follows the angel's directive in naming him "Jesus, the one who will save his people from their sins" (1:21). Matthew's use of titles to define Jesus' identity culminates in the designation "Emmanuel," whose importance Matthew signals by interrupting the narrative to make sure that the audience knows its meaning: "God with us"" (1:23).

Matthew peppers the early stages of the performance, and key points thereafter, with fulfillment quotations (e.g., 1:22–23; 2:15, 17–18, 23; 4:14–16; 8:17; 12:17–21; 13:35; 21:4–5; 27:9–10), which provide interpretive frameworks for the narrated events. While these citations appeal to Jewish expectations, they also surprise. The first of these citations (1:22–23) affirms that the birth of Jesus fulfills Isa. 7:14, which speaks of a "virgin" (following the LXX) who will bear a son, whose name shall be called Emmanuel. While great attention has been focused on the term "virgin," the primary function of the citation is to remind the audience of God's promise of deliverance and the threat of judgment if the promise is refused. The birth of the child was to be a sign of God's faithfulness when Judah was threatened by both Syria and the northern kingdom. King Ahaz, however, refuses to heed this prophetic vision, refuses to trust God, and suffers God's punishment at the hands of Judah's enemies. Jesus' birth brings hope and judgment.

The world in Matthew's story belongs to the God of Jesus Christ, who is reordering the creation. Even though God is not formally on stage in these chapters, God is nonetheless active in each scene, in the birth of Jesus, securing Jesus' life from risk, directing the travels of the magi, and bringing the family back from Egypt after Herod's death. Matthew's story of the magi and Herod's attempt to kill Jesus paints a picture both surprising and realistically violent. Outsiders, "wise men from the east," are the first to recognize Jesus as king. Their announcement of God's messianic blessings is not welcome news to Herod and Jerusalem, and generates a spasm of violence and terror. Matthew's account of the slaughter of the innocents (2:16–18) casts the story of Jesus as a clash between divine will and the violence of human power.

The flight of Joseph, Mary, and Jesus to Egypt is an ironic twist on the stories of the patriarch Joseph (Gen. 37–50) and the exodus from Egypt. While Gentiles come to pay honor to the new king, his own people force him to flee, back to Egypt, where God's people had once been enslaved. Matthew's second fulfillment citation (2:15) is drawn from Hos. 11, which recalls both the exodus from Pharaoh's enslavement and the failure of the people to live justly with one another. The God of Hosea and Matthew is full of mercy, yet also abhors the violence of God's people (Hos. 11:5–7). The third fulfillment citation (Matt. 2:17–18) draws from a passage that couples judgment and lament with the vision of a "new covenant written on the heart" (Jer. 31:15; 31:33). Again, Matthew stands judgment and promise side-by-side.

The Messiah, who is forced to flee into exile and to live at the margins in Galilee, has a forerunner, John the Baptizer, who preaches in the wilderness east of Jerusalem. John's wilderness setting, call to repentance, clothing and diet, and attacks upon the Pharisees and Sadducees are all prophetic signs that associate him with Elijah, who also preached repentance to the kings and religious leaders of his day. John's ministry represents a vote of no confidence in Israel's leaders, who fail to "bear fruit worthy of repentance" or to produce the kind of justice that fits God's reign.

Jesus' baptism signals his embrace of the reign of God John has been proclaiming. As John notes, Jesus will baptize with both the Holy Spirit and fire, denoting the eschatological tenor of salvation and judgment that Jesus embodies. God's reign requires a complete break from the world's obligations, debts, and order. Jesus repents of all these in order to align himself with God's coming reign. At the very moment Jesus arises from the water the heavens are opened and the Spirit descends upon Jesus, signaling the correspondence of divine power and presence with Jesus. The voice from heaven announces that Jesus is God's Son. The descent of the Spirit and the words "well pleased" recall Isa. 42:1 (cf. also Ps. 2; Matt. 12:18–20), when God anoints the chosen one "to bring forth justice to the nations." The opening of heaven and the descent of God's Spirit to earth are apocalyptic signs of God's re-creation of the world. Amid these signs of divine power, God's Son also demonstrates his humility and obedience.

Immediately the Spirit leads Jesus away into the wilderness to be tested. Jesus' temptations mirror Israel's temptations in the wilderness on the way to the Holy Land. Jesus fasts for forty days and nights, which recalls Israel's time of wandering (Exod. 16:35), as well as Moses' fasting on Mount Sinai (Exod. 24:18; 34:28) and Elijah's sojourn to Mount Horeb (1 Kgs. 19:8). The number forty also echoes the length of the flood during the time of Noah (Gen. 7:4, 12, 17), which signified both judgment and new creation. The first temptation sets the agenda for the whole series of tests: "If you are the Son of God. . . ." Will Jesus use his divine power for his own purposes, or trust God to supply what is needed? In answer, Jesus cites Deut. 8:3 (cf. Exod. 16), where Moses reminds the people that God let them experience hunger so that they might learn to trust God. Jesus will trust God to provide what he needs.

Then the devil places Jesus on the pinnacle of the temple in the "holy city," the axis point between heaven and earth. Will Jesus provide a dramatic public display of his messianic power in association with the central symbols of Jewish identity and hope? Citing Deut. 6:16, Jesus affirms God's faithfulness in providing the people with everything necessary to take possession of the land. Jesus will not test God's faithfulness, as Israel did at Massah (Exod. 17:1–7). This temptation also foreshadows the passion account, where Jesus refuses the aid of angels to escape the cross (26:53) and resists the call of the onlookers to "save himself" if he is "the Son of God" (27:40). In Jerusalem Jesus will indeed provide a dramatic sign of his true identity and obedience to God: the cross itself.

The final temptation takes place on a very high mountain, where Jesus can see "all the kingdoms of the world and their glory" (4:8, my trans.). Satan offers Jesus power over all of these empires if Jesus will worship him. Satan controls the whole world by means of such human empires—they are his to give. But Jesus would then rule and be ruled by the violence of human power. God's empire, on the other hand, unites heaven and earth and focuses on inclusion, mercy, and justice. This temptation juxtaposes fundamentally different kinds of power—human and divine—between which Jesus must choose. Jesus trusts that God's power, which he embodies, will indeed prevail even when his own life will be taken by the powers of this world. He dismisses Satan with the citation of Deut. 6:13: Jesus will worship and serve God alone.

Jesus has now been baptized by John and endured Satan's attempts to divert him from his calling. When John is arrested, Jesus withdraws to "Galilee of the Gentiles," where his ministry brings light to those in darkness (Matt. 4:15–16, citing Isa. 9:1–2). This citation recalls the time when the Assyrians occupied Samaria and Judah, a time not unlike the present moment in Jesus' ministry, when God's people are exploited by the Romans and their own leaders. Isaiah 9 also looks forward to the time when the rod of their oppressor will be broken (9:4), and the messianic king will establish the kingdom with justice and righteousness (9:6–7). In Jesus, God's long-awaited reign is at last at hand.

Jesus' Ministry to Restore Israel (4:17–11:1)

Jesus proclaims the same message as had John the Baptizer: "Repent, for the kingdom of heaven has come near" (Matt. 4:17; cf. 3:2). His teaching and actions focus on gathering and restoring Israel, the messianic harvest (9:37–38). He calls his first disciples, who immediately leave their nets and their families to "fish for people" and begins teaching and healing in Galilee and Syria. His healings point to the reality of God's power over every form of human disorder and disease.

The Sermon on the Mount is a manifesto of God's powerful empire (5:3, 10, 19, 20; 6:10, 33; 7:21). The sermon describes an alternative world, already being realized in the midst of this world, where God's power and presence define human perceptions and relationships. The sermon's images, case studies, warnings, and calls illustrate the nature of God's reign and describe those who participate in it. At the heart of Jesus' sermon is the Lord's Prayer (6:9–13), which articulates the essential relationship between humans and God, from which springs faithful participation in God's reign. Above all, the sermon describes who God is, how God is at work in the world, and how disciples live in conformity with this reality. As the audience notes, the sermon itself is an expression of extraordinary power (7:28–29).

Jesus begins with nine pronouncements of divine favor upon the subjects of God's empire and the ways they embody God's power in a broken world. They are "salt," a "city set on a hill," and "light" (5:13–16), because their lives preserve and

purify the world and provide a beacon by which others may find their way to God. The Beatitudes do not describe individual virtues, but practices nurtured and sustained in the community of Jesus' disciples. The first four beatitudes (5:3–6) echo the imagery of Isa. 61. Those who experience poverty and grief, who trust God in the face of brutality and violence, and who yearn for relationships restored and made whole, experience God's eschatological rule and the reversal of injustice. The next four beatitudes (5:7–10) describe practices that conform to the reality of God's presence and power: mercy, purity in heart (i.e., integrity of thought and action), peacemaking, and persecution for the sake of justice. The final beatitude (5:11) suggests that Jesus' disciples can expect the same ridicule and opposition, even persecution, that the prophets faced.

Jesus' teachings point to God's presence and power in the world and thus fulfill the law and the prophets (5:17–20). By means of six case studies (antitheses) Jesus demonstrates the ways in which his commandments go beyond the law and human traditions to create social space for restoration and reconciliation (5:21–48). In each case, the actions Jesus describes overturn expectations and open the door for the transformation of relationships. These cases reach their most forceful expression in the call to love enemies and to pray for persecutors; in this way the disciples are made "perfect" (or "mature" and "whole"), as God is perfect (5:43–48).

Jesus then focuses on three foundational religious practices—almsgiving, prayer, and fasting—that can be distorted by human self-interest (6:1–18). In every case Jesus warns against acting so as to be seen by others or to gain honor among humans, for such actions do not lead to justice, restoration, or reconciliation. Instead, the disciples should act so as to be seen by "your Father who sees in secret."

At the center of the sermon stands the Lord's Prayer (6:9–13), which also provides the foundation for the material that follows in chaps. 6 and 7. The prayer simultaneously recognizes and pleads for God's reign to come on earth, with a corresponding transformation of relationships. It presumes and calls for the kind of trust, forgiveness, and deliverance from the powers of this world that confirm God's presence and power here and now, as well as in the future. The first half of the prayer invites God to breach the boundaries between heaven and earth and to realize on earth the intention and effects of God's heavenly rule. The petitions that follow (6:11–13) call upon God to supply what is needed each day (as God supplied manna for Israel in the wilderness), to forgive debts (i.e., not just sins, but the bonds associated with debt and obligation in the world of patronage), and to preserve the disciples from the allures and threats of the evil one. Each petition looks expectantly for signs of God's presence and power. Only the petition focused on forgiveness (6:12) explicitly calls for human action, which makes forgiveness a primary locus of sacramental experience, in which God and humans act in concert with one another. As if to underline the point, as soon as the prayer is finished, Jesus reasserts the integral relation between forgiving the trespasses of others and our own experience of God's forgiveness (6:14–15; cf. 9:1–8; 18:21–35).

God's empire is both free of debts and built upon trusting relationship with God in every aspect of life (6:19–34). In God's empire there is no need to worry even about physical needs. The disciples' focus is to be on "heavenly treasures," not just "spiritual rewards," but the justice that attends God's presence and power in this world. Primary orientation toward God's reign is incompatible with the pursuit of worldly possessions or treasures (6:24). God's justice also requires that humans resist the inclination to stand in judgment of others (7:1–5). A series of warnings against following the broad, popular way, and against false prophets, brings the sermon to its end (7:15–27). Echoing John, Jesus affirms that a tree is known by its fruit; our actions betray our real commitments (7:15–20). Yet even those who do mighty deeds in the name of Jesus may not enter the empire of heaven, but only those who "do the will of the Father" (7:21). The issue is not just the demonstration of power, but power that comes from and serves God.

Matthew 8–9 records stories of healings and miracles, interspersed with teachings on discipleship, meant to further define the nature, locus, subjects, and dimensions of God's powerful empire. Jesus gathers and restores the marginal, heals the sick, liberates those possessed by demonic power, and crosses physical and social boundaries, except those imposed by the lack of faith. The healing of a leper (8:1–4) demonstrates that God's power cannot be contained within the boundaries between clean and unclean, but is more contagious than the leper's uncleanness. Jesus' encounter with the centurion whose slave (or child) is paralyzed (8:5–13) turns on both the navigation of social boundaries between Jesus and the Gentile and the recognition that God's power has no spatial limitations. As the centurion notes, Jesus does not need to come to his house to accomplish the healing, but can bring it about by means of a word. Jesus also heals Peter's mother-in-law, the sick, and many who are possessed by demons (8:14–17), thereby fulfilling yet another Isaianic Servant Song (8:17; cf. Isa. 53:4): like the servant, Jesus gathers and restores those who were in exile, but the servant's way also leads to suffering.

The stories that focus on the demands of discipleship also retain spatial aspects. Following Jesus means leaving behind the obligations and securities of this world for a life of homelessness (8:18–22). Jesus demonstrates power over the chaos of the sea by rescuing his disciples from a storm (8:23–27). Then he takes them across the sea to the Roman-occupied territory of the Gadarenes, where two demoniacs meet them. Jesus is pushing back the boundaries of his disciples' imagination; no space—and no person—is beyond the reach of God's redemptive power (8:28–34). When Jesus returns to Galilee, he is met by people carrying a paralyzed man. Rather than simply heal the man, Jesus offers to forgive his sins, which the scribes regard as a blasphemous arrogation of divine privilege. But Jesus uses the paralytic's healing as verification for his assertion—as Son of Man—of the divine power to forgive sins. The crowds praise God, who has given this kind of (divine) power to "human beings" (9:8). They perceive that God's power is being democratized.

Boundaries are again the primary issue when the Pharisees challenge Jesus' inclusive table practices (9:10–13), and when John's disciples wonder at the fact that Jesus' disciples do not fast. Jesus states that fasting is appropriate to the time when "the bridegroom is taken away" (9:15), but not for the time when the groom is present. Jesus breaches the boundary of death itself when he heals Jairus's daughter, and the healing of the hemorrhaging woman confirms that faith itself crosses boundaries (9:18–26). Boundary-crossing faith restores community, sight, and the capacity to hear and speak (9:27–33). But God's liberating power also elicits polarized responses: the crowds marvel at expressions of power they have never before seen in Israel, while the Pharisees assert that Jesus' power comes from Beelzebul (9:33–34), foreshadowing the coming clash over the nature and source of Jesus' power.

Jesus' compassion for the "harassed and helpless" crowds, whose shepherds have not been faithful (9:36), leads him to prepare his disciples to join him in "the harvest," which denotes both gathering and judgment. The disciples receive the same powers Jesus has demonstrated, including authority over unclean spirits and power to heal the sick, raise the dead, and cleanse lepers (10:1, 8). Like Jesus and John before him, the disciples are to announce the presence of the kingdom of heaven to "the lost sheep of the house of Israel"—not the Gentiles or the Samaritans (10:5–6). Jesus' messianic mission first concerns gathering and restoring

Israel, which is to be a sign for the nations (cf. 10:18). The disciples conduct their mission by means of "sign-acts"—taking no gold or silver, no bag, no extra clothes or sandals, nor even a staff for protection (10:9–10)—a form of proclamation that also causes division (10:11–15, 21–25, 34–39). They invite and enact radical trust and dependence upon God.

This mission entails risk: they will be delivered to councils, flogged in the synagogues, and dragged before governors and kings (10:17–18), as will Jesus himself. But however dire the circumstances, there is no need to be anxious, for God will speak through them (10:19–20). Human authorities have power only to kill bodies (10:28); the one who wields ultimate power is taking care of the disciples. The disciples fully represent both Jesus and "the Father who is in heaven" (10:32–33, 40); their reception or rejection is the basis for salvation and judgment. The revelation of God's power, whether through Jesus or his disciples, threatens human power and as a result incites division and violence (10:34–36), even among the disciples' own families. Those who are "worthy of Jesus" will "take up the cross" and "lose their lives" (10:37–39).

Jesus' Ministry Generates Conflict and Crisis (11:2–16:20)

The Mission Discourse has made clear that God's empire brings healing and division within Israel. The stories and parables in Matt. 11–13 highlight the growing rifts. First, John the Baptizer sends his disciples to determine whether Jesus is really "he who is to come" (11:3). Jesus simply names the fruit of his mission: the blind see, the lame walk, lepers are cleansed, the deaf hear, the dead are raised up, and good news is proclaimed to the poor (11:5). Those who take no offense at these irruptions of divine power are blessed (11:6; cf. 5:3–12). Jesus regards John himself—Elijah announcing God's reign—as a sign of God's presence and power. But regardless of the different means by which the pipers (Jesus and

John) have piped, the people have not danced (11:17). Judgment now looms over those cities that did not repent (11:20–24). Why? God's presence and power have been revealed to "babes" rather than the "wise and understanding" (11:25). Those who receive Jesus recognize God's presence and power at work in him, while those who reject Jesus' demonstrations of power are rejecting God (11:27–30). The two Sabbath controversies (12:1–14) demonstrate one reason for the rejection of Jesus and the impending judgment: the collusion between religion and human power. Jesus reiterates God's call for mercy rather than sacrifice (12:7; cf. 9:10–13). But rather than show mercy, the Pharisees use the man with the withered hand to entrap and accuse Jesus (12:10). Jesus, the Son of Man who is Lord of the Sabbath (12:8), demonstrates God's mercy by restoring the man's hand. The Pharisees in turn begin planning his destruction. Despite rejection and division within Israel, God's servant "brings justice to victory" and is a sign of hope for the nations (12:18–20, citing Isa. 42; cf. Matt. 3:17).

The conflicts over power continue. Another healing of a blind and dumb demoniac leads the crowds to wonder whether Jesus is the Son of David, while the Pharisees again attribute Jesus' power to demonic origins (12:24; cf. 9:34). Jesus' response lays bare the Pharisees' distorted logic: if Jesus casts out demons by the power of Satan, Satan's house is divided. If, on the other hand, Jesus casts out demons by the Spirit of God, then rejection of Jesus is nothing less than blasphemy against the Spirit (12:25–32). Both he and his opponents are known by—and will be judged by—their fruit (12:33–37). When the scribes and Pharisees then ask for climactic proof of his divine power, he offers only the cryptic sign of Jonah, a veiled allusion to the cross and resurrection, a greater sign than even Jonah's stay in the belly of the sea monster (12:38–42). Jesus had warned his disciples that God's reign would even divide families (10:21–22, 34–37). Now, as his mother and

brothers stand at the door, Jesus redefines his family as "whoever does the will of my Father in heaven" (12:50). The rule of the heavenly Father trumps all other obligations and relationships.

In the face of mounting opposition Jesus begins speaking in parables. Matthew's parables speak the language of "the harvest"; they name and engender division, judgment, and salvation. The parables mark a division between the disciples, to whom have been given "the secrets of the kingdom of heaven," and those to whom they have not been given (13:11). Hearing or seeing is not the question, but "understanding," "perceiving" (13:13–15, 19, 23), and "bearing fruit" (13:8, 23). Isaiah 6:9–10 provides the model: God abandons to their own blindness and deafness those who reject clear demonstrations of God's power and presence. But even as the parables are instruments and expressions of judgment, they also are meant to disturb the everyday rationality of their audience and lead those who will listen to a place where they may discern what God is doing. Jesus' parables thus hide the reign of God from those who see but reject it, even as they reveal to those who listen "what has been hidden since the foundation of the world" (13:34–35).

Each of the parables in Matt. 13 admits multiple readings; what the audience understands depends on who and where they are. The story of the sower contrasts the failure of much seed—snatched by the evil one, scorched by distress, or choked by the world—with the astonishing production of seed that falls on good soil (13:3–9, 18–23). Yet surprisingly, even weeds sown by an enemy are allowed to grow up amid the wheat, so that the wheat will not be uprooted until the harvest (13:24–30, 36–43; cf. also 47–50, the harvest of fish). Many of the shorter parables in this chapter deal with "hiddenness" (13:33, 44), the surprising abundance or value of what seems small or insignificant (13:31–33, 45–46), and the crazy logic of "selling all" in order to gain what is of ultimate worth (13:44–46).

The story of Jesus' visit to his home town highlights the rejection of God's chosen one by God's own people (13:53–58). Matthew describes their failure of imagination as "faithlessness," which in turn sets the boundaries on Jesus' capacity to perform the works of God there. An integral link exists between faith-filled perception and the manifestation of God's transforming presence and power. For those who will not see, there is nothing to be seen, or what is seen is reckoned as demonic. But vistas of God's abundant power in the world await those who put their faith in God.

The disciples have been given the secrets of the kingdom of heaven, but they still do not comprehend the dimensions of divine power in their mission, and they are not yet ready to face the brutal opposition of human powers, which Herod's murder of John the Baptizer powerfully illustrates. Herod, the agent of imperial violence, is himself caught in its web of blindness and manipulation (14:3–11). Herod perceives Jesus' power, but misconstrues Jesus as the reincarnation of John (14:2). In light of the threat Herod poses, Jesus again withdraws, but he cannot escape the crowds, upon whom he continues to lavish his compassion. Matthew's two stories of miraculous feedings (14:13–21; 15:32–39) emphasize the importance of meals as the locus of God's presence, power, and abundance. By the second episode, however, it is still clear that the disciples perceive neither their own resources nor God's power. Their vision is hindered by an earthbound imagination of scarcity. God is able to supply even more than what is needed, enough baskets for each of the tribes of Israel (14:20).

Divine power is again the focus when Jesus comes walking on the sea to the disciples as they are being "tormented" by the storm (14:22–33). Jesus identifies himself as "I am," the divine name (14:27), and does what God can do—control the chaos of the sea—once again blurring the boundaries between the human and the divine. Matthew's version of this story includes the distinctive element of Peter's walk with Jesus on the sea. As Peter observes Jesus' manifestation of divine power, he wonders whether he too might participate in such power. Peter indeed takes a few steps before he is overwhelmed by his perception of the wind. Matthew again is democratizing divine power, but Peter and the disciples remain those of "little faith" (14:31; cf. 8:26) who stand in two places at the same time (the same term describes the disciples when they encounter the risen Jesus in 28:16–17). Still, the disciples are able to name the divine power at work in Jesus (and Peter): they confess that Jesus is "Son of God" (14:33). Vision, faith, and participation in God's power form an integral whole.

Earlier in the Gospel, people came out of Jerusalem to hear John and Jesus announce God's coming rule (3:5; 4:25), but now the Pharisees and scribes come out to challenge Jesus. They are concerned that Jesus' disciples do not wash themselves ritually before they eat. Jesus reminds the disciples that what comes out of the mouth, from the heart, not what goes in, is the source of defilement (15:11, 17–20). In contrast to the tradition-rooted opposition of the Jerusalemites stands the faithful persistence of a Canaanite woman, the only person in the Gospel to best Jesus in a verbal contest (15:22–28). Her great faith compels Jesus for a moment to loosen his focus on the people of Israel, so that her daughter can be healed. Again, faith crosses boundaries, even Jesus' boundaries, and leads to the manifestation of God's liberating power.

Jesus continues to offer signs of the power of "the God of Israel" by healing great crowds of lame, maimed, blind, and dumb people (15:29–31). Yet neither these demonstrations of power nor the second feeding sign (15:32–39) satisfies the Pharisees and Sadducees, who again ask for a "sign from heaven" (16:1). As in 12:38–42, Jesus offers only the "sign of Jonah," a riddling reference to the cross and resurrection. The "leaven of the Pharisees and

Sadducees" (16:5–12) continues to threaten to permeate the imagination not only of the people but of Jesus' own disciples. Yet when Jesus quizzes them about his identity, Peter names Jesus as the Messiah, "the Son of the living God" (16:16), a confession that Jesus identifies as a revelation that comes not from "flesh and blood" but from "my Father in heaven" (16:17).

The Journey to Jerusalem (16:21–20:34)

The disciples have confessed that Jesus is God's chosen Son, but they are not yet ready for what this means. Jesus now must prepare his disciples for the path the Son of God will take toward the definitive expression of God's power, the cross and resurrection (16:21). The cross is the inevitable, ultimate contest between human and divine power, between the powers of death and life. Like Jesus, the disciples must relinquish the life of this world and take up the cross (16:24–28). Those who do so will not taste death before they see the Son of Man coming in power as eschatological judge and resurrected Christ, God with us (cf. 28:16–20).

Jesus takes some of the disciples with him to a mountain, where they witness his divine transformation and confirmation (17:1–8). As at Jesus' baptism, a heavenly voice confirms that Jesus is God's Son and enjoins the disciples to "listen to him!" (17:5). Even after this epiphany, however, the disciples still lack the power, or faith, to heal an epileptic boy (17:14–20). They are distressed when Jesus again warns them of his impending death by "human hands" (17:22–23). The story concerning the payment of the temple tax (17:24–27) is meant to offer reassurance. The first fish (a symbol of God's bounty) yields a coin that pays the tax for both Jesus and Peter. God's power is sufficient to meet the demands that human rulers place on Jesus and his disciples; God's power will be sufficient to meet the demands of the cross. Jesus has no obligations or debts to the powers of this world, but will nonetheless pay the debts of humankind.

Jesus' fourth great discourse focuses on the kind of community and practices the disciples will need to sustain their distinctive witness in a world beset by debt, domination, and violence (18:1–35). Jesus highlights the surprising values and practices that define the community's life: caring for "the little ones" (18:6, 10, 14), seeking the lost sheep (18:12–14), and carefully pursuing peace even with recalcitrant members of the community (18:15–17). These are the primary ways by which the community lives in and manifests God's power in the world. Jesus calls for limitless forgiveness (18:21–22) and warns that those who refuse to live in forgiveness will find themselves back in a world of impossible debt and ultimate judgment (18:23–35). Divine presence and power are mediated communally, wherever even two or three gather in Jesus' name (18:19–20) and fix their vision on the little ones and on forgiveness.

The stories in Matt. 19–20 all address dimensions of the disciples' question, "Who is the greatest in the kingdom of heaven?" (18:1); this question suggests that they are still shackled to human notions of power and honor. Jesus first redefines greatness in terms of a child (18:3–5), one who is dependent, vulnerable, and lacks the rights and power of adult males. Matthew continues this line of argument in stories that turn typical household models of power on their head. Jesus' teaching about divorce (19:3–9) emphasizes God's intention that marriage be a locus of reconciliation and unity, and effectively removes from males their "right" to divorce their wives. Eunuchs, those who lack or renounce typical male status (19:10–12), and again children (19:13–15) provide models for the disciples to imitate. Jesus calls upon the rich man to sell his possessions, give to the poor, and then follow Jesus, in order to be "perfect" or whole (19:16–22). The parable of the workers in the vineyard (20:1–16) provokes foundational questions about the nature of power and status within the human community. The "greatest" in the empire of heaven do not exercise their power as do the "rulers of the nations" or "their great ones," but by being servants of one another (20:20–28). Divine power restores life and relationship.

The Clash of Powers in Jerusalem (21:1–25:46)

Jesus and his disciples arrive in Jerusalem—the center of religious, social, economic, political, and ideological power for Jewish people—during Passover, the holiest season of the year, which commemorated and looked forward to God's liberation of Israel from slavery. Jesus' triumphal entry into Jerusalem signals that God's anointed—the Son of David, Son of Man, and Son of God—is ready to extend God's rule. "Triumphal entries" were high imperial dramas in which kings, emperors, and liberators displayed their power. Jesus, too, enters the city in triumph, but in parody of these human dramas of conquest and power. His entry is celebrated not by the leaders but by the crowd that has been following him from Galilee. He rides no war horse, but sends two of his disciples to borrow not one but two animals, an ass and a colt, which symbolize Jesus' dual identity as king and commoner.

Jesus goes immediately to the heart of Jewish identity and hope, the temple, where he does not offer sacrifice, but disrupts the commerce that supported the sacrificial system and takes possession of the temple. He declares it once again "a house of prayer" (21:13). All the wrong people—the blind, the lame, the children, who were not ordinarily permitted in the temple—come to him there for healing (21:14). He continues effectively to hold possession of the temple until he pronounces God's judgment upon it (23:37–39; 24:1). Jesus' cursing of the fig tree as he returns to the temple the following morning (21:18–22) is another prophetic, symbolic action that represents God's judgment against the temple and the leaders, who have failed to "bear fruit" (cf. 3:7–10; 12:33–37).

Jesus' ironic expression of authority in seizing control of the temple compels the leaders to attempt to discredit and dislodge him (21:23–22:46). As soon as Jesus again enters the temple, the chief priests and elders of the people challenge his authority. Their two-part question—by what authority do you do these things, and who gave you this authority (21:23)—defines what is at stake in the ensuing conflict: the nature of Jesus' power and its source. The death and resurrection of Jesus are for Matthew the definitive resolution of these two questions. But Jesus' first response focuses on John the Baptizer: was his baptism from heavenly or human origins? The Jewish leaders know they cannot answer without affirming the ministries of both John and Jesus or risking public disfavor. The parable of the two sons (21:28–32) creates yet another embarrassing trap: the son who says he will work in the vineyard (a common symbol for Israel), but does not, represents the authorities, while the tax collectors and harlots who repented because of John's (and Jesus') preaching represent the second son, who, the authorities admit, "did the will of the father."

In the parable of the tenant farmers the leaders again pronounce their own condemnation. Because the leaders were themselves the wealthy landowners of their day, they identify with the owner, and announce that they would "put those wretches to a miserable death and let the vineyard to other tenants who will give him the fruits in their seasons" (21:41, my trans.). From the Gospel's perspective, however, it is the tenant farmers—who usurp the owner's (God's) authority, fail to produce the fruit of the harvest, and murder the son—who represent the Jewish leaders. The story raises key theological questions for the audience to resolve: Will God's kingdom be taken away from "them" (the Jewish leaders? Israel?) and given to "a nation" (the Gentiles? the church?) that will produce appropriate fruit (21:43)? Has the God who calls for unlimited forgiveness run out of forgiveness for Israel? Most important, does God act as the Jewish leaders would? The ways in which audiences answer these questions in turn determine how they will hear the whole Gospel and how they will see God.

The story of the king and his son's wedding feast (22:1–14) also seems to offer an allegory of salvation history from a Christian perspective. Despite repeated invitations, those invited to the wedding feast dishonor and even kill the king's servants (22:6)—signs of rebellion against the king's authority. So the king sends troops to destroy and burn their city. He then invites people from the streets, good and bad alike (22:8–10) to the feast. But this allegory should also leave us wondering: does God in fact behave like an oriental king? Does God's story duplicate on a grand scale the scripts of imperial life and politics?

The chief priests and Pharisees realize that Jesus' parables speak about them (21:45), but their fear of the crowds prevents them from arresting him immediately. Instead the elites stage a series of challenges to his authority, knowing that any victory on their part will diminish his authority and put an end to the threat he represents. But in each case Matthew's Jesus outmaneuvers his adversaries. The Pharisees and Herodians, who held opposing positions on the question they pose, ask Jesus about paying taxes to Caesar. Jesus demonstrates that they, not he, carry the coins that bear Caesar's image, and so must fulfill their obligations, to whatever powers they stand in submission (22:21). Jesus' response to the Sadducees concerning the resurrection focuses on the claim that Israel's God is the God of the living, not the dead (22:23–33). He affirms that the greatest commandment entails both loving God and loving neighbor (22:34–40). Finally, Jesus turns the tables and asks his adversaries a question about the Christ as Son of David (22:41–46), which can be resolved only by recognizing Jesus' own messianic identity. Their silence at the end of this story (22:46) indicates that their verbal challenges to his authority have come to an end. Jesus' victory in these contests seals his fate.

Jesus then delivers the last of his five great sermons in Matthew. While the material in chap. 23 has a different setting and focus than what follows in chaps. 24–25, these three chapters nonetheless form a coherent whole. Just as Jesus' entry into the temple was a prophetic action, his departure from it is a sign of its desolation and coming destruction (23:37–24:2). The judgment against the temple and Holy City leads to the material in chaps. 24–25, where Jesus prepares his disciples for the chaos, upheaval, and violence of the coming time.

The sermon begins in the temple, where Jesus calls his disciples to be a community of integrity, equality, and service (23:1–12), in contrast to the scribes and Pharisees, who are singled out for their hypocrisy (23:13–36). The woes against the scribes and Pharisees first attack the burdensome and destructive effects of their behavior on others (23:13–15), their focus on casuistry at the expense of justice, mercy, and faith (23:16–24), and the lack of integrity between their public behavior and inner lives (23:25–28). The woes reach their climax in Jesus' implicit identification of these leaders as children of Cain, who resort to violence and murder to preserve and sanctify their disobedience (23:29–36). As a consequence, Jerusalem's house will be forsaken and desolate (23:38). But again Jesus appends a word of hope, a citation of Ps. 118:26 (cf. Matt. 21:9). While the immediate context in Matt. 23 suggests that the citation refers to Jesus' return in judgment, Ps. 118 celebrates God's faithful love for and deliverance of the people. The saying thus looks forward to the day when "Jerusalem," even its leaders, will bless rather than reject the one who comes in the name of the Lord (23:39).

As Jesus leaves the temple, he proclaims that not one stone will be left standing on another (24:1–2). The eventual destruction of the temple, which Matthew's community looks back upon, is both a sign of the integrity of Jesus' prophetic word and a prominent symptom of the violence and disruption that will mark the time between Jesus' death and resurrection and his return. The messianic woes of chap. 24 encompass events past, present, and future—including the destruction of Jerusalem—that accompany continued human resistance to God's rule (24:3–8). The cataclysms of this age are actually the "birth pangs" of God's reign. Judgment and blessing continue beside one another.

The assertion of human power in the face of God gives rise to sudden flight, intense suffering, and false messianic hopes. Rome, which is the agent of God's judgment against the temple and Holy City, will itself fall subject to judgment and destruction, as have all human empires throughout history. At the very moment of deepest suffering, at a time no one expects (24:36–44), the Son of Man will appear in power to judge the nations and gather the elect from the ends of the earth (24:29–31). Because no one can anticipate when the Son of Man will come, and because of the intense opposition of human powers, the disciples must be constantly ready and watchful (24:44). This is the theme of six parables that conclude this final sermon (24:37–25:46). As in the days of Noah, or when a householder sleeps at night without knowing that a thief is about, there is no room for business as usual (24:37–44). God blesses the servants who work and are ready even when the master is away (24:45–51). The parable of the wise and foolish maidens illustrates that the sudden coming of the bridegroom brings division and both judgment and reward (25:1–13). Those who faithfully increase the resources entrusted to them, even while the investor is away, receive still more to invest, while the servant who battens the hatches and lives in fear, producing nothing, loses all that he had (25:14–30).

But what produce does Jesus expect from his disciples? The story of the sheep and the goats (25:31–46) addresses this question. When all the nations are gathered before the Son of Man, they learn that he has been among them—among the "least ones"—all along. Judgment turns on whether those gathered before the throne attended to the needs of the hungry, the thirsty, strangers, the naked, the sick, and those in prison. These least ones are the victims of human systems of oppression, exploitation, and violence. Their afflictions are symptoms of the conflict between human and divine power (cf. 23:34–36; 24:6–10, 16–21). The goats ignore the plight of these least ones because they presume a world dominated by human order rather than by God's power and presence. The sheep also did not know that the king was among the least ones, but nonetheless produced fruit worthy of the empire of heaven. This final judgment scene thus identifies the locus of divine presence, describes the threshold between heaven and earth, and sets forth the terms by which the disciples' watchfulness, readiness, and service come to expression.

God with Us (26:1–28:20)

Jesus' last sermon concludes with the image of the nations gathered in submission before the throne of the king/Son of Man, but before this vision can be realized the Jewish leaders and the emissaries of Rome must reexert their power in a spasm of violence, the final contest between human and divine power. From the human perspective, the cross is the definitive expression of imperial power, a sacred liturgy meant to restore order to the world. Matthew also sees the cross as the locus of divine power, but from the perspective of those who are its victims, from the perspective of God's own Son. For Matthew the cross and resurrection are a single event that shakes the foundations of the world and shatters the boundary of death, thereby robbing death—and the imperial order—of its power (27:51–53).

The chief priests and the elders gather at the palace of Caiaphas—as if in response to Jesus' final word concerning his impending death (26:2)—to plot his arrest and murder (26:3–5). At the same time, Jesus is in Bethany at the house of Simon the leper, where a woman anoints him. Her action acknowledges that Jesus is the true king, but she is also preparing him for burial (26:6–13). Jesus' rule as God's anointed will be manifest in his crucifixion. Jesus' Passover meal with his disciples is the occasion for yet another prophetic, symbolic action, which juxtaposes betrayal with redemption (26:17–30). The Lord's Supper is the defining ritual—an alternative to both the temple sacrifice and Roman crucifixion—that constitutes the community of disciples.

Jesus predicts that the disciples will all be scattered and betray him, but also promises that he will be present with them after the resurrection (26:31–32). Yet, even in Gethsemane, where Jesus repeatedly calls the disciples to the eschatological disciplines of "watching" and praying, they are unable to remain awake with him (26:36–46). The betrayal scene concisely portrays the distinctive character of the powers engaged in this conflict. Judas approaches with a crowd from the chief priests and elders, armed with swords and clubs (26:47), while Jesus, who could call upon twelve legions of angels (26:53), stands defenseless. When one of Jesus' own followers draws a sword and cuts off the ear of Caiaphas's slave, Jesus responds by healing the slave, a symbolic action that fulfills his own teaching about loving enemies and demonstrates the effect of divine power. The disciple's action is of the same kind as those who come to arrest Jesus and thus is the second betrayal depicted in this scene. God's power is not manifested by means of the sword (26:51–53). Consequently, the disciples abandon Jesus and flee (26:56). Their continuing acts of betrayal are recounted thereafter through the story of Peter (26:69–75).

The most compelling testimony during Jesus' trial comes from two witnesses who report that Jesus had spoken of destroying the temple of God and rebuilding it in three days (26:61). The irony is lost on the jury. When the high priest demands that Jesus tell them whether he is the Christ, the Son of God (26:63), Jesus speaks of the "Son of Man seated at the right hand of Power [cf. Ps. 110:1], and coming on the clouds of heaven" (Matt. 26:64; cf. Dan. 7:13–14). For Caiaphas and the council this is blasphemy; they demand his death and begin to mock their victim (Matt. 26:65–66). Before Pilate, Jesus again does not defend himself; he has no need to plead for his life. Pilate's form of justice includes releasing whichever prisoner the crowd chooses. The choice between Jesus and Barabbas may symbolize the eventual choice between the way of the cross and armed resistance to Rome (27:15–23). Despite Pilate's reluctance, the crowd, whipped into a frenzy by their leaders, demands the crucifixion of Jesus (27:18–26), the one who "will save his people from their sins" (1:21). Pilate washes his hands but is no less guilty. As in the case of Herod's execution of John (14:1–12), those who wield human power are also controlled by it.

The epithets hurled at Jesus as he is being crucified—"King of the Jews" (27:29, 37), "Son of God" (27:40, 43), savior, and "King of Israel" (27:42)—are all ironically true, but blindness prevents perception by those who stand on the human side of the cross. The leaders invite Jesus to demonstrate his kingship and saving power by abandoning the cross, but Jesus had already withstood this temptation at the hands of Satan (4:5–9). The cross is for the moment still the symbol of imperial power, but God's power is also soon to be revealed in it. As Jesus is being crucified, darkness covers the whole land, like the primordial darkness that preceded creation. Jesus' cry of abandonment (27:45) is a citation of Ps. 22, which looks to God to redeem and vindicate the righteous suffering one.

After three hours on the cross, Jesus cries out in a great voice and "breathes his last" or, more literally, "releases the Spirit" (27:50). The moment of death coincides with the movement of God's

Spirit into the world—the realization of Israel's eschatological hope. Jesus' death corresponds with the return of light (27:45) for those who sit in the darkness of death (cf. 4:15–16). Matthew signals the apocalyptic (revelatory) and eschatological (world-ending, world-renewing) nature of Jesus' death by immediately piling up signs of divine power and creation. The tearing of the temple veil from top to bottom (27:51) signifies both judgment against the temple and the movement of God into the world. The world shakes and the rocks split, classic signs of God's apocalyptic power. The raising of the saints signals the defeat of death and the democratization of resurrection power, even though Jesus himself has not yet been raised (a problem the evangelist addresses by means of a literary sleight of hand, 27:53). God vindicates Jesus and affirms the divine power he embodies at his crucifixion. This cosmic, architectonic shift in power is evident even to the Roman soldiers present at the cross, who, in terror, confess that Jesus is "Son of God" (27:54). God's power has overwhelmed the imperial power of death.

The authorities, however, believe and continue to act otherwise. Pilate permits Joseph of Arimathea to take charge of the body, preparing it and placing it in a rock tomb, sealed with a "great stone" (27:57–61). The chief priests and Pharisees nonetheless worry that there will be no body and ask Pilate to seal the stone and place guards at the tomb (27:62–66). To the end, Matthew portrays the leaders as manipulative schemers bent on distorting or denying the demonstrations of divine power taking place before their eyes (28:11–15).

During his ministry, women have demonstrated deep faith and special insight into Jesus (cf. 8:14–15; 9:20–22; 15:22–28; 27:19). They have remained at the cross (27:55–56), watched as Joseph of Arimathea buries Jesus (27:61), and are the first witnesses of the empty tomb (28:1). The sons of Zebedee have disappeared, but their mother, who once asked Jesus to grant her sons seats of honor in God's empire (20:20–21), has remained. Like the other women—and the women of the genealogy—she models faithful discipleship (27:56). But "Mary Magdalene and the other Mary" are the two primary witnesses of all these events, without whom the disciples would not learn of Jesus' resurrection and his command to go to Galilee (28:10). The second earthquake and the descent from heaven of an angel of the Lord (28:2–3) are eschatological signs of God's continuing power and presence in these events. As the women run from the tomb to tell the disciples what has happened, Jesus himself meets them. They take hold of his feet—a sign of his physicality—and worship him (28:9–10).

When the eleven disciples meet Jesus on the mountain in Galilee (28:16–17), they too worship, but their worship is mingled with "doubt" (cf. 14:31). Jesus has chosen precisely these broken betrayers to announce the gospel to the nations. The disciples' mission rests on the claim that Jesus has been given "all authority in heaven and on earth" (28:18). His rule and power are complete, encompassing both the divine and human realms. Jesus has been blurring the boundaries between heaven and earth throughout his ministry, and now he fully embodies God's rule and power in both. The disciples are called to announce, name, and participate in God's reign wherever they go. God's power and presence, manifested in Jesus' life, ministry, death, and resurrection, continue to restore and re-create the world. The crucified and resurrected Jesus—"God with us"—is the power and the space, amid heaven and earth, within which the mission of Christ's disciples takes place.

Matthew's Theological Landscape

Like the Roman imperial cult, Matthew perceives divine power at work in the world and among humans. The realized eschatology of the imperial cult locates divine power with the emperor, proclaims Caesar's actions and will as "good news," and sanctifies Roman dominion—domination, exploitation, and violence—as the realization of the divine order. Matthew's Gospel also discerns God's presence and power in the world, but in Jesus of Nazareth, who proclaims and brings to fruition God's rule. The differences between imperial rule, whether Jewish or Roman, and God's rule come to definitive expression over the meaning and significance of crucifixion, which for Matthew reveals that God's power is not only superior but of a different order: God's power gathers, heals, restores, overwhelms death itself, and creates communities of equality, mutual service, sharing, reconciliation, and restored relationships. Matthew's story renders illegitimate all human expressions of power in community that effectively deny God's presence and rule in mercy and restoration.

The empire of heaven, which Jesus proclaims and embodies, brings both judgment and salvation, which are persistently juxtaposed in Matthew. God's presence and power bring judgment upon human institutions and structures that serve the forces of domination and violence. Trusting in human political and economic arrangements, even those that are clothed in the guise of divine order, means embracing idolatrous misunderstandings of reality. Those who look for salvation in human systems of power thereby refuse the rule of God, and live inevitably into the judgment brought about by their own convictions and practices. Participation in God's empire, on the other hand, yields the fruit of its convictions in transformed relationships and communities.

The blurring of the boundaries between the human and the divine, between heaven and earth, and especially the dissolution of the boundary of death, means that divine power is present not only with Jesus, but among his disciples and with those who in faith participate in God's empire. Matthew's God changes the foundational structures and assumptions of the world in order to restore right relationships. Human institutions and structures that pass for enduring reality are shown to be plastic. Only God's power endures, manifested among the little ones and least ones and among those whose faith enables them to cross the boundaries imposed by this world's order. Matthew's theological vision remakes the landscapes of human reality and perception, inviting audiences to perceive themselves within a world in which mercy, forgiveness, and restoration—rather than domination, violence, and death—are the normative experiences.

Bibliography

Aune, David E., ed. *The Gospel of Matthew in Current Study: Studies in Memory of William G. Thompson, S.J.* Grand Rapids: Eerdmans, 2001.

Carter, Warren. *Matthew and Empire: Initial Explorations.* Harrisburg: Trinity Press International, 2001.

———. *Matthew and the Margins: A Sociopolitical and Religious Reading.* Maryknoll, NY: Orbis, 2000.

Luz, Ulrich. *Studies in Matthew.* Translated by Rosemary Selle. Grand Rapids: Eerdmans, 2005.

Riches, John K. *Conflicting Mythologies: Identity Formation in the Gospels of Mark and Matthew.* Edinburgh: T & T Clark, 2000.

Mark

Joanna Dewey and Elizabeth Struthers Malbon

INTRODUCTION

This brief commentary seeks to highlight the theology of the Gospel of Mark, the particular message the Gospel aims to convey to its hearers and readers, then and now, through its story of God's action in Jesus' life, death, and resurrection. We have no certain knowledge about the Gospel's origins other than what we can infer from the text itself. Most scholars agree that it is the earliest narrative of Jesus we possess. The Gospel itself is anonymous, probably composed by someone named "Mark," a person otherwise unknown to us, whom we shall continue to call Mark. Although scholarship is divided, we believe it was composed somewhere in the Eastern Mediterranean, in Syria or Galilee, shortly after the end of the Roman-Jewish war and Rome's destruction of the temple in Jerusalem in 70 CE. It appears to be addressed to a rural peasant audience, those who are the poor, living at a subsistence level. The Gospel originally ended at 16:8, with other verses added later, after the writing of the Gospels of Matthew and Luke.

The Gospel of Mark is first of all a narrative—a story whose meaning is conveyed through plot, characters, settings, and rhetoric, that is, through how the story is told. While Mark uses traditional lore about Jesus, his primary aim is *not* to provide factual information about Jesus to his hearers but rather to proclaim his understanding of the good news through his construction of the story, his narrative of the Markan Jesus. Mark's aim is to convince his hearers to become or remain faithful to the good news, not to believe in certain things. He does not present a systematic theology. He does use terms that have become theological titles, Messiah (or Christ), Son of God, Son of Humanity (we use "Son of Humanity" rather than "Son of Man" since it more accurately reflects the Greek term *anthrōpos* and emphasizes that it is Jesus' humanity, not his maleness, that is theologically significant), but they gain their meaning not as theological concepts brought to the story but through the events and characters by which Mark shows us God's activity in and through Jesus. Mark's theology is a narrative theology and a theology focused on God (Gk. *theos*).

The Gospel presents its theology primarily through three interacting plot levels of theological conflict. The first level is the *cosmic conflict*, the conflict between God and Satan, along with Satan's representatives, the demons and unclean spirits. As Mark tells the story, the audience knows from the beginning that God will be the sure victor. This level, though often fading into the background as the narrative progresses, is foundational for the

311

entire story. If the hearers reject the premise of God's victory, the story will be unconvincing. The second or middle level is the *authorities' conflict*, the conflict between Jesus and the political, social, and religious establishment. Jesus proclaims and enacts the rule of God on earth. (We use the phrase "rule of God" rather than "kingdom of God" to stress that it is God's ruling activity that is intended rather than a particular place.) Those presently in power, the empire of Rome and the local secular and religious authorities, reject the rule of God and ultimately crucify Jesus, its agent. The third level is the *followers' conflict*, conflict between Jesus, on the one hand, and the disciples and the broader group of those who welcome Jesus and the rule of God, on the other. The disciples' successes and difficulties in understanding and remaining faithful to Jesus are a means to engage the hearers in the story and to instruct them about the rewards and challenges of being part of the rule of God. This level of the plot is constructed to encourage the audience to be faithful followers of Jesus.

In addition, Mark is a particular type of narrative, an oral narrative that was performed and heard, not a manuscript read individually in silence nor read aloud to groups of listeners. In the first-century Mediterranean world only about five percent of the population was literate, primarily elite males. Few Christians could read or write; most would have told and heard stories. The Gospel of Mark takes approximately an hour and a half to perform in Greek, quite short in terms of ancient oral performance. Thus the entire Gospel would be heard at one time; it is the Gospel as a whole that would impact the audience, not individual episodes.

Oral narrative style is additive rather than subordinate, simply adding one phrase, sentence, and episode to another, rather than relating them in causal or analytic ways. It is episodic in order to give the audience aural clues to identify the beginning and ending of narrative units. It is repetitive with variation: the picture of Jesus as healer is created by telling one healing episode after another; the emphasis on Jesus' coming execution is created by the repetition of the passion-resurrection predictions. Most important, the logic of this additive style is an inclusive, both/and logic: Jesus is *both* this *and* that. If we read Mark as a modern novel, then the stress on Jesus' healings early in the narrative gives way to an emphasis on Jesus' suffering and death in the second half. Heard in oral performance, however, the narrative stresses *both* Jesus' healing power *and* persecution for following the way of God. Both are true and equally important. To understand the theology of Mark, we need to "hear" the Gospel in its entirety as an oral narrative. In the following commentary, we treat sections of the Gospel as discrete for convenience; as in typical oral style, however, there are no clear breaking points but episodes echo what comes before and hint at what is to come.

COMMENTARY

Prologue (1:1–13)

The opening verses establish the foundational cosmic conflict between God and Satan, Jesus as God's agent in the conflict, and God's sure victory. Verse 1 functions as a title announcing to the audience the story of the good news of Jesus, God's Messiah. Then Hebrew Scripture is cited to prophesy that God's messenger is coming. Immediately John the Baptist appears and prophesies that a greater one will come who will baptize with the Holy Spirit. Immediately Jesus appears and is baptized by John. Jesus sees the Holy Spirit descend on him and hears God's voice telling him that he is God's beloved Son. While the theology is far from the formal doctrine of the Trinity formulated in later centuries, the three "persons," God, Jesus (the Christ), and the Holy

Spirit, are present. The Gospel opens with God firmly in control and Jesus established as God's chosen agent.

Conflict is also established, first by the very necessity for God to send an agent, and second by the Spirit sending Jesus into the wilderness to be tested by Satan. Jesus triumphs: the wild beasts, Satan's creatures, do not harm him, and God's angels serve him. In the conflict between God and Satan, God is acting anew through Jesus to defeat Satan.

The Coming of God's Rule (1:14–8:26)

In these chapters Mark portrays the rule of God taking root and growing in Galilee, the place of God's new revelation, and two responses by people to God's rule: the establishment authorities rejecting God's rule (the authorities' conflict) and the followers welcoming it (the followers' conflict).

Summary (1:14–15). The Markan Jesus opens his ministry in Galilee by proclaiming a summary of his message: "The rule of God has arrived. Turn and trust the good news." (All translations are the authors' own.) God's rule is breaking out on earth. Mark presents an apocalyptic understanding of time. First, there is the created order, the "old age" or "this age" temporarily controlled by Satan, which began with creation and will run to the end of history. Second, there is the rule of God, "the new age," which has begun with Jesus' public ministry. In some ways, God's rule is to be fully experienced here and now; the new age has begun. But the old age has not yet ended—and will not until God's rule comes in power as indicated later in Mark (9:1; 13:1–37; 14:62). So people live in a time in which the two ages coexist: the blessings of God's rule are real, but so is the power of the old age.

These two verses not only continue the cosmic conflict, but they introduce the other two conflicts as well. The rule of God is not only in contrast to the rule of Satan (cosmic conflict) but also would be

heard by those in the first century as opposed to the rule of Caesar, the Roman Empire (the authorities' conflict). Normal political terms are used. Jesus calls the audience to turn away from the rule of Satan and Rome and trust the good news that God is acting on earth. To the extent that hearers believe this message, they become followers who will struggle with its implications for their lives (the followers' conflict).

Characteristics of God's rule (1:16–45). This series of episodes describes the blessings of God's rule now present. The section begins with the call of four disciples, the first members of the new community of God's rule on earth; the rule of God both demands and creates community. The Markan Jesus does not presume to spread the word of God's rule alone but calls coworkers. Jesus is presented as teaching with authority, and he performs a variety of exorcisms and healings. (In antiquity, possession by a demon or unclean spirit was considered to be caused by evil powers under Satan, while other illnesses or disabilities were caused by the sin or impurity of oneself, one's group, or one's ancestors.) That God's rule includes the marginalized is indicated in the choice of healings: a man with an unclean spirit (1:21–28), a woman dependent on her son-in-law (1:29–34), and a leper who is an outcast (1:40–45).

Opposition to God's rule (2:1–3:6). This section consists of an elegant concentric arrangement of five episodes that shows forth *both* the blessings of God's rule available already in this age *and* the rejection of God's rule by the establishment. The first two stories, the healing of the paralytic (2:1–12) and eating with tax collectors and sinners (2:13–17), deal with sin. In the first, the Markan Jesus proclaims forgiveness of sins to the paralytic. In the second, Jesus calls a sinner engaged in a sinful occupation (Levi, the tax collector) and then eats with tax collectors and other sinners. It should be noted that, in Mark's theology, forgiveness of sins is associated with Jesus' bringing God's rule in his public ministry and not with the crucifixion. The last two episodes deal with Sabbath practice; fundamental to Jewish law was abstaining from work on the Sabbath. In 2:23–28 the disciples pluck grain on the Sabbath, and in 3:1–6 Jesus heals on the Sabbath, both instances of working. Here Jesus asserts that serving human need is more important than following religious demands. Furthermore, the Markan Jesus asserts his authority over both sin and Sabbath: the Son of Humanity has authority to forgive sins on earth and is lord of the Sabbath. The Markan Jesus—but neither other characters nor the Markan narrator—uses "Son of Humanity" in speaking of himself; the term gathers various meanings as the story progresses. In these first uses, it stresses Jesus' earthly authority.

Crossing the sin/Sabbath theme in the five episodes is the theme of healing—eating—healing. The first and last stories are healings; the middle three each include eating in some way: eating with the wrong people, eating at the wrong time (2:18–22), and preparing food at the wrong time. In Mark's (and Jesus') peasant subsistence communities, health and food are scarce commodities and are blessings indeed. Thus Mark describes the present blessings of God's rule: sin is overcome; human need takes precedence over religious law; people's needs for health and sustenance are met. Not surprisingly, the crowds following Jesus continue to increase (2:2, 15; 3:7–8).

At the same time, these five stories set forth the opposition of the establishment authorities to God's rule and Jesus as God's agent. The scribes (legal experts) and the Pharisees (religious authorities) take offense. They consider Jesus' forgiving sins as blasphemy, usurping what God alone can do. They question why he does not obey the normal regulations about when, where, and with whom to eat. They take offense at his disregard of the Sabbath, watch to see if they can accuse him of working on the Sabbath, and finally plot with the Herodians, the local secular political authority under Rome, to destroy Jesus. The Markan Jesus has affirmed for the audience that he will indeed be destroyed: the bridegroom will be taken away (2:20). The authorities believe the customary religious understandings to be God's will and Jesus to be flouting God's will—and claiming his ways as God's will. It is important to note that this conflict is not *between* Christian and Jewish understandings of God. Jesus himself is Jewish. Rather it is a conflict that occurs in many ages between religious practitioners and the religious authorities *within* any particular culture or faith.

In 2:1–3:6 the Gospel has set forth both the characteristics of the rule of God available in this age and the implacable resistance of the authorities of this age to God's rule. In good oral style, Mark has set forth for the audience the conflict between Jesus and the authorities and indicated its outcome—Jesus' death. Mark is now free to continue with Jesus' public ministry; he returns to the plot against Jesus only much later in the narrative.

Followers (3:7–35). Having established the cosmic conflict and the conflict with the authorities, Mark now turns to the followers. More and more people keep coming to Jesus from the regions around Galilee (3:7–12). Out of this large group, Jesus names twelve to be with him and to share his power to proclaim the good news and cast out demons (3:13–19). Then, when his own family comes to try to restrain him, he defines his new family (or fictive kinship group) as those with him who are doing God's will (3:20–21, 31–35). Thus the followers include persons with various levels of commitment: the huge crowds who come after him, often seeking healing or exorcism; the small group of twelve disciples specially chosen; and the larger group around him who are his new family. Following is not limited to the Twelve; many participate.

Other conflict levels are also present. Demons, part of the cosmic realm, recognize Jesus as the Son of God, and Jesus orders them to keep silent. Here Mark speaks to the audience over the heads of the story characters: the audience has been told at the beginning that Jesus is the Son of God, and they are now reminded of this. The followers in the story do not yet recognize Jesus' status. The authorities, this time scribes from Jerusalem, accuse Jesus of healing by the power of Satan. Jesus retorts that Satan's rule is coming to an end, and that they are guilty of an eternal sin for naming what is good as evil (3:22–30). This section of the Gospel expands the groups of followers embracing God's rule and aligns the authorities with satanic powers in the cosmic conflict rather than with God.

A collection of parables (4:1–34). Jesus teaches the crowd in a series of parables or riddles that show what God's rule is like. If the audience is expecting images of power and glory, this is not the rule Jesus describes. Rather, the kingdom of God is like seeds, many of which fail to grow at all, but a few yield grain in abundance (4:3–9, 14–20). It is like seed that is planted and grows we know not how but eventually leads to the harvest (4:26–29). It is like a tiny mustard seed that grows into a great big bushy weed (4:30–32). This is not the rule of God in power in the age to come; it is the rule of God present in this age while the authorities of this age still rule, present for those who welcome it. Jesus tells the followers (those around him with the Twelve) that to them has been given the mystery of God's rule (4:10–11). They are participants in God's realm, but even they have trouble understanding (4:13), a theme that will be greatly expanded as the story moves on.

Those who are not followers do not understand; they are even depicted as being prevented from understanding. The allusion to Isa. 6:9–10 reminds the hearers of the long pattern of God sending messengers who are not heeded (Mark 4:10–12). Outsiders only hear parables that are not explained to them (4:33–34). Mark loves contrasts, loves to juxtapose material to encourage thought.

So in the middle of the parables, the Markan Jesus asserts that lamps are to give light, that the hidden is to be proclaimed (4:21–23). In the present age, only Jesus' followers, those who have turned and trusted the good news (1:15), participate in God's rule, and even they find it problematic. Yet God's rule is to come to light, is to be proclaimed to all "who have ears to hear." Only insiders participate, but all are invited to be insiders.

Acts of power and hints of trouble (4:35–6:52). This section (and the next) is punctuated by Jesus' bringing God's rule in the present with acts of power. It contains the first two boat scenes, the stilling of the storm (4:35–41) and Jesus' walking on water (6:45–52), and the first feeding story, the feeding of five thousand in the wilderness (6:30–44). These nature miracles echo God's actions with Israel, the exodus from Egypt through the Red Sea and the giving of manna to feed the people wandering in the wilderness. Jesus is portrayed doing the acts of God. There were other human healers and exorcists, but it is God who controls water and gives food in the desert. These stories are powerful examples of God's activity in Jesus.

These stories also develop the followers' conflict. In all three of them the disciples do not trust God's power for good that is active in Jesus. In the storm they fear drowning and are nearly as alarmed when Jesus quiets the storm (4:38, 41). In the desert, they want Jesus to send the crowd away to buy food; when Jesus tells them to feed the crowd they expect to have to go buy food themselves. Jesus tells them to see what they have—five loaves and two fish. Jesus blesses and breaks the loaves, and with this the disciples feed all five thousand and take up twelve baskets of leftovers. The disciples did not expect God to provide.

In the second boat scene, as the disciples row against the wind, Jesus comes walking on the water; they are again terrified and astounded when Jesus joins them and the wind drops. The storyteller observes they did not understand about the feeding and their hearts were hardened (6:52). The disciples do not trust in God's abundant gifts. The section, however, also shows the disciples' success in following. Jesus sends out the twelve called earlier (3:13–19) two by two; they go through the villages inviting people to turn to God and casting out demons and healing the sick (6:7–13). They stay in the houses of others, receiving meals, and offering healing.

Three exceptional healings follow the first boat scene. First a violent demoniac in Gentile territory is exorcised; his demons are named "Legion," and Jesus gives them permission to enter some pigs, who race into the lake, which Mark calls the Sea of Galilee, and drown (5:1–20). Jews considered pigs unclean animals; perhaps more important, "legion" is a large unit of the occupying Roman army. So this exorcism not only shows the defeat of Satan's minions in the cosmic struggle but also hints at the defeat of the Roman Empire in the authorities' struggle. Next comes the healing of the woman with the flow of blood (5:24–34) embedded within the story of the raising of Jairus's daughter (5:21–23, 35–43). It is the power that goes out from Jesus that heals the woman, not her faith. Her trust that healing can happen is necessary for the healing, but it is God's power, not her faith, that heals (see also 6:5–6). Her faith does serve as a model for the faith Jairus—and all followers—will need.

This section abounds primarily in the powerful acts of God through Jesus and portrays the disciples' inability to trust that power. But it also hints at a darker fate for Jesus. He faces rejection in his hometown (6:1–6). Herod Antipas, the ruler of Galilee, has John the Baptist executed, which points ahead to the execution of Jesus (6:14–29). Jesus' enactment of the rule of God is not without political danger to himself. As what happens to John foreshadows what happens to Jesus, so what happens to Jesus foreshadows what his followers may expect for themselves.

Pushing the boundaries (6:53–8:26). The action continues in Jewish Gennesaret, not in Gentile Bethsaida, where Jesus had directed his disciples to go before him (6:45). First, everyone brings their sick to Jesus at Gennesaret for healing (6:53–56), much like the crowd healing scenes of 1:34 and 3:10. Then there is another debate between Jesus and Pharisees and scribes over eating practices (7:1–23), echoing the controversies of 2:13–28. Jesus responds to the query of why his disciples do not follow the traditions of the elders with an attack on the Pharisees—that they abandon the way of God to follow their own traditions (7:6–13). Jesus is not criticizing Judaism per se, but rather the Pharisees, the first-century religious authorities who are imposing rules on economically marginalized Jews who have neither the time nor the resources to follow such rules. The Markan Jesus stresses this teaching by repetition: first he calls the crowd and tells them that nothing outside a person can defile a person; and then, for further emphasis, he instructs the disciples that it is what comes out of persons (theft, murder, adultery, etc.) that defiles them. The storyteller summarizes—and extends—this teaching for his own audience: "thus he declared all foods clean" (7:14–23).

With the food laws put aside, the way is open to include Gentiles. The Markan Jesus then leads his disciples to Gentile territory by a land route north to the region of Tyre (7:24). Although Jesus tries to keep his presence hidden, a Syrophoenician woman comes to him begging him to cast the demon out of her little daughter. Jesus responds rudely, "Let the children [the Jews] first be fed; it is not right to throw the children's food to dogs [Gentiles]"! The woman does not argue with Jesus' premise but responds that dogs do get the crumbs from under the children's table. Jesus replies that her daughter is healed because of *her word*. The Markan Jesus has been portrayed as able to do what only God can do in forgiving sins and controlling nature. In this episode he is portrayed as fully human, needing to learn from another human being—a Gentile woman at that. In this, Jesus serves as a model for the disciples, who also need to learn about the expansive nature of the rule of God.

Although the geographical markers are confusing at 7:31, the next healing story, of the deaf man in the region of the Decapolis, the Ten (Greek) Cities (7:31–37), reiterates the lesson that there is enough of God's healing power in Jesus to share with presumed outsiders. Thus it should not surprise the audience that there is also enough bread to share. Jesus teaches a large crowd of Gentiles and then feeds them in the desert with seven loaves, and with seven baskets left over (8:1–9). As twelve stood for Israel, so seven stands for Gentiles. The good news of God's rule is also for Gentiles; the dogs have gotten an abundance of crumbs. Yet the disciples are surprised: even after they have experienced the feeding of the five thousand (6:30–44), they do not expect such an event to happen again. They ask, "How can one feed these people with bread here in the desert?" (8:4). They have not learned to trust in God's power for good.

Upon returning to the Jewish (western) side of the sea (8:10, Dalmanutha), Jesus is met by the Pharisees, coming to request a sign from heaven. It might appear that feeding four thousand with seven loaves of bread is an adequate sign; but, by placing the request at this point, the narrator implies that they are asking Jesus to give them a sign from God that God approves of feeding Gentiles. Jesus refuses. The Markan Pharisees want God's revelation on their own terms, in their own time. The Markan Jesus wants people simply to trust the good news.

Again Jesus and the disciples set out across the sea. Again a scene is narrated on the sea (8:14–21). No nature miracle happens this time; rather Jesus lectures them on the two feeding stories. Do they not yet understand about God's abundance? Do they not yet trust the good news? The question is not answered by the characters; it is forwarded to the audience. The audience has accompanied Jesus as he led the disciples on an over-land detour on the way to Gentile Bethsaida (6:45; 8:22). There he heals a blind man—but in two stages (8:22–26), just as he has moved in two stages to heal the disciples of their blindness to the expansion of the rule of God to Gentiles and has repeatedly tried to help them grasp the abundance of God.

The Cost of Participating in God's Rule (8:22–10:52)

In chaps. 1–8 Mark has established Jesus as God's agent bringing God's rule to Galilee and its Gentile environs. In this section Mark turns to teachings on the cost of following God's rule in this age and to instructions on discipleship, to the themes of persecution and service.

Structure of 8:22–10:52. This section, a journey from Galilee south to Jerusalem, is carefully structured. It begins and ends with a miracle of sight. The first, that of the blind man of Bethsaida, is a difficult two-stage healing (8:22–26); the one at the end, that of Bartimaeus, is easy, and Bartimaeus immediately follows Jesus on the way (10:46–52). Both stories function as healing miracles and as signals that the enclosed teaching is difficult. Next comes Peter's recognition of Jesus as the Christ (8:27–30). Then three times Jesus predicts his passion and resurrection; each prediction is followed by a misunderstanding of the disciples and Jesus' teaching on discipleship. The three sets of prediction/misunderstanding/discipleship instruction are separated by interludes of related teaching and events.

First passion-resurrection teaching unit (8:27–9:1). The Markan Jesus asks the disciples who they say he is, and Peter replies, the Messiah (the Christ). The disciples, internal characters in the narrative, have finally realized what the audience was told at the beginning. Using the title "Son of Humanity," Jesus prophesies that he will undergo many things, be rejected by the official authorities, be killed, and rise from the dead, thus adding a new level of meaning to both "Son of Humanity" and "Messiah." The Christ was expected to be a triumphant figure, defeating Israel's enemies, not to be executed by them. When Peter protests, Jesus calls him Satan. The Markan Jesus does not explain his fate to the disciples; instead he immediately tells them it is to be their fate as well (8:34–9:1). Jesus issues an invitation to all (crowd and audience) to become followers and stresses the cost: if you want to follow, you must deny yourself (your family, your status), take up your cross (your means of execution), and follow. Using the two-age framework, Jesus issues a threat—whoever rejects him now will be rejected by the Son of Humanity in the age to come—and a promise—the rule of God in power will come soon, ending the present age.

Thus the narrative has shifted radically, from emphasizing the blessings of God's rule available already in this age to emphasizing the cost of participating in God's rule while this age still lasts. It is important to note that it is *not* suffering per se that is the way of Jesus and followers. Much present suffering is indeed ended by the healings, feedings, and new community. Rather, participating in the rule of God now in this age results precisely in persecution by the powers-that-be of this age. People like Oscar Romero and Martin Luther King Jr. were assassinated for challenging the status quo. So also Jesus and his followers risk persecution. Participating in the rule of God brings both blessings and persecution. In order to enjoy the gifts of God's rule now, one must also risk being persecuted. It comes with the territory.

First interlude (9:2–29). The story of the transfiguration affirms that Jesus is indeed God's agent (9:2–8); the unlikely message of 8:31–9:1 is true. The disciples are again enjoined to secrecy (9:9–13). They are not to proclaim Christ's glory without also understanding the inevitability of persecution and the way of lowly service. The disciples do not understand what rising from the dead means, once more underscoring their difficulty comprehending the power of God. Finally this section ends with Jesus' dramatic exorcism (with resurrection language) of the boy with the unclean spirit after the disciples fail, with related teaching on faith and prayer (9:14–29). The father's cry, "I believe, help my unbelief," suggests that even the intention of having faith or trust is enough to enable Jesus or God through Jesus to work the miracle. Jesus' explanation for the disciples' failure, that prayer is needed, suggests the disciples do not have adequate connection to God's power through prayer.

Second passion-resurrection teaching unit (9:30–49). Again Jesus prophesies his execution, "the Son of Humanity will be handed over to humans." God's agent is rejected by the powers of the world, whether they be Jews, Romans, or today's rulers. After the first prediction, the teaching about the cost of discipleship was addressed to all potential followers. The teachings after the second and third predictions are addressed to the disciples and describe the service required of followers. As usual, the disciples do not understand and debate among themselves which one of them is the greatest. Jesus tells them if they wish to be first they must be last of all and servant of all. *Diakonia* is ordinary service—waiting on table, taking care of children. The male disciples are called upon to do what then was considered women's work. We are all called to serve those with *less* power than ourselves. Jesus gives an example, placing in their midst a child, the one with the least status, as the one to be welcomed. But the disciples' misunderstanding continues: they try to stop an exorcist who is not part of their group from healing in Jesus' name (9:38–41). Jesus rebukes them: they are not to exclude people. They are instructed not to be a stumbling block to little ones and to keep peace among themselves (9:42–50).

Second interlude (10:1–31). In this section, the focus is instruction on the nature of the new community as it challenges the status quo. As often in oral narrative, examples are given of how *not* to behave. In a discussion with the Pharisees, Jesus affirms that a man is not allowed to divorce his wife, and if either the man or woman divorces and remarries, he or she commits adultery. The man and the woman are equal in the relationship (10:1–12). Still not getting the ideal of service to those of less status, the disciples try to prevent children from bothering Jesus. Jesus affirms children as close to God's rule (10:13–16). Then a rich man asks about eternal life—the life of the age to come. Jesus suggests that he sell all and follow him, and the man departs grieving (10:17–22). The disciples assume wealth is an asset for entering God's rule. Jesus, in contrast, states that it is a major hindrance, but that all things are possible with God (10:23–27). In the new household under God's rule, men are not valued above women, adults above children, or the rich above the poor.

The new community of God's rule, then, is to welcome outsiders, serve the most vulnerable, and fully include women and children. Wealth is likely to be a stumbling block. At this point the audience (but not Jesus) may have almost given up on the disciples: they want to be the greatest and keep control of who is inside. They are not models of service; they are, however, still following. Peter says, "We have left everything and followed you." Jesus affirms their rewards in this age and the next: having left behind fathers, mothers, children, houses, and fields (that is, family and economic livelihood—but not spouses), they receive again in this age family and economic livelihood in abundance, along with persecutions, and eternal life in the age to come (10:28–31). The blessings and cost of participating in the rule of God are reaffirmed; the disciples are still on the way.

Third passion-resurrection teaching unit (10:32–52). The third passion-resurrection

prediction is the most detailed: Jesus will be handed over to the Jewish authorities, who in turn will hand him over to the Gentile, that is, Roman, authorities, to be killed, and he will then rise (10:32–34). The audience, by now anticipating the disciples' incomprehension, is not disappointed. Immediately James and John ask Jesus to let them be the greatest in the age to come (10:35–40). They have understood that they are not to seek power or reward in this age, so now they seek it in the age to come! Jesus asks them if they can stand firm in the face of persecution, drink his cup, be baptized with his baptism. They say they can. The audience may be reassured that the disciples do understand that persecution is a consequence of following God's rule now. But Jesus does not give them what they ask; persecution in this age brings no reward in the next. The Markan Jesus instructs all the disciples once again on service (10:41–45). In contrast to the world, where great ones lord it over others, among Jesus' followers the great ones are to serve others, to serve those with less power and status than themselves. Jesus uses himself as the example: "the Son of Humanity came not to be served but to serve, and to give his life a ransom for many" (10:45). "Ransom" is a technical term for securing the release of a hostage or a slave. Thus the Markan Jesus does not present his death as a sacrifice for sin, but as a continuation of his service for others. It is in the context of service that Jesus' death in Mark is to be understood. His whole life, his ministry of proclaiming and enacting God's rule and his faithfulness to it, even to death, are Jesus' service.

The Implications of Participating in God's Rule (11:1–15:47)

The narrative now turns to the larger conflicts, chaps. 11–12 and 14–15 returning to the conflict with the authorities, and the embedded chap. 13 returning to the cosmic conflict. The audience knows that Jesus will be executed in Jerusalem. The mood of the narrative, however, changes;

in these chapters the audience is made to reflect on the paradoxical nature of the power of the Markan Jesus and of the rule of God.

Jerusalem, temple, and prayer (11:1–25). Jesus enters Jerusalem in triumph, riding on a colt, accompanied by huge crowds hailing the coming of David's kingdom (11:1–11). On the way into the city the next day, Jesus curses a fig tree, a symbol of Israel, then enters the temple, casts the sellers and buyers and moneychangers out of the temple courtyard, and prophesies the coming destruction of the temple (11:12–19). The temple is the political and economic as well as religious center of Jerusalem. The issue is not corruption or the presence of commerce in the temple: the provision of animals for sacrifice and the proper coinage to pay the temple tax were necessary services for carrying out temple worship. Jesus' allusion to Jer. 7:11, that the priests have made the temple "a den of robbers," suggests that the temple is where the bandits hide out after robbing others elsewhere, and that God will once again destroy the temple. (Since at the time of Mark's composition the temple had likely been destroyed by the Romans, this "prediction" would be comforting; the destruction of the temple is given theological meaning.) The narrative portrays an intra-Jewish conflict between a popular Jewish prophet and the temple authorities. The authorities understand the challenge to themselves—they seek a way to destroy Jesus.

The finding of the withered fig tree the next day confirms that Jesus was prophesying temple destruction. The storyteller then turns briefly to the followers' plotline in order to instruct the disciples and audience on prayer (11:20–25). In antiquity a temple was understood as the dwelling place of the god; thus the destruction of a temple raised a serious question: how can one communicate with a god who has no dwelling on earth? The Markan Jesus assures the disciples that if they pray trusting that God will act, their prayers will be answered. God can move mountains, that is, do the impossible. At the same time, Jesus' own prayer in Gethsemane, that he not be crucified, is not answered (14:32–42). Once again, the narrative presents a both/and: *both* prayers will be answered *and* suffering happens. Mark will not limit the power of God or the reality of persecution in this age. The destruction of the temple increases the importance of prayer rather than destroying it.

Conflict with religious authorities (11:27– 12:44). The Jerusalem scene of conflict with religious authorities echoes the Galilean scene at 2:1–3:6. The audience is made aware, however, of a shift in perspective. First, Jesus no longer has the home field advantage; the temple is the religious authorities' center of power. Second, Jesus does not claim authority in connection with the temple; sitting is the position for authoritative teaching (4:1; 13:3), but Jesus is "walking" in the temple. This section opens with the chief priests, scribes, and elders asking Jesus by whose authority he acts—is he a true prophet or just another troublemaker? The Markan Jesus adroitly avoids answering by questioning them about John the Baptist's authority (11:27–33) and moves to the attack in the parable of the wicked tenants in the vineyard (12:1–12). The vineyard stands for Israel, and the story echoes earlier Jewish traditions that they have rejected God's true prophets. The parable culminates with the rejection of the "beloved son," echoing the baptism and transfiguration (12:6; cf. 1:11; 9:7). The vineyard is given to others, perhaps the Jewish peasants who have been economically exploited by the priests and Rome.

The series continues in quick succession with questions from Pharisees, Sadducees, and a scribe. The Pharisees endeavor to trap Jesus concerning paying taxes to Rome, a trap Jesus again avoids by saying: "give to Caesar, Caesar's, and to God, God's" (12:13–17). Of course, it is understood by all that everything really belongs to God! Then the Sadducees, the high priestly aristocracy, test Jesus, who clearly affirms the resurrection (12:18–27). Finally, a friendly scribe asks Jesus about the great or fundamental commandment (12:28–34). Jesus affirms the basic Jewish understanding: to love God and neighbor. While generally Mark presents the authorities as opposed to Jesus and God's rule, there are exceptions. This scribe acts like a follower, "not far from the rule of God." Like having wealth, being part of the establishment presents difficulty in participating in God's rule; it does not, however, preclude the possibility. These controversies in Mark 12 show Jesus' agreement with dominant Jewish views on taxes, resurrection, and the basic demand of God, unlike 2:1–3:6, which shows Jesus' difference from dominant Jewish perspectives in regard to Sabbath and sin, healing and eating. The Markan Jesus has shown he is a good Jew, thus perhaps a legitimate prophet. So the authorities dare not question him further. Jesus returns to the attack: questioning the Davidic (high status) descent of the Messiah (12:35–37), denouncing the scribes for hypocritical behavior (12:38–40), and praising the (low status) poor widow for exemplary behavior, giving her "whole life" (12:41–44).

The apocalyptic transition of the ages (Mark 13). Throughout the narrative, Jesus has brought God's rule in the present age, bringing for participants both blessings and persecutions, and has promised fulfillment in the near future (9:1). In Mark 13 the Markan Jesus tells the inner core of the disciples—and the audience—about future events of the cosmic struggle and God's ultimate victory. For this authoritative speaking, the Markan Jesus sits on the Mount of Olives. The section uses common Jewish apocalyptic imagery of the birth pangs of the new age: war, famine, general disasters. It warns against false prophets and false messiahs of the last days. It warns the followers that they, like their leader, will be persecuted by both religious (Jewish) and political (Gentile) authorities but assures them that, precisely in

the context of trials, the Holy Spirit will speak through them. Finally, no one but God, not even the Son, knows *when* the end will come, but then the Son of Humanity, who has been shown to embody both authority and costly service, will come with power and glory to gather all God's elect, all participants in God's rule. The timing is uncertain, but God's victory is certain.

Escalating conflict with religious authorities (Mark 14). Chapter 14 picks up the plot where chap. 12 left it. Chapter 13 is an embedded speech of the Markan Jesus on the transition to the age to come, similar to the embedded parable discourse disclosing the surprising blessings of God's rule in the present age (4:1–34). Both speeches remind the audience of the central point of the good news: the rule of God has broken into history. Not even the growing conflict of Jesus with the authorities, with its increasingly inevitable result, changes that affirmation. The Markan Jesus' ability to predict the near future—the colt for the entry into Jerusalem (11:1–6), the upper room for their Passover meal (14:12–16), Judas's betrayal (14:18–21), the disciples' flight and Peter's denial (14:26–31)—enhances the audience's confidence in the reliability of the predictions of chap. 13 as well as stressing the present events of the narrative.

When the Markan Jesus began his ministry in Galilee, everything seemed to happen "immediately." Now, as Jesus' passion approaches, time slows down and references to time become more specific (e.g., 14:1, 12). The storyteller is signaling to the audience the significance of the unfolding events. Another Markan rhetorical device for emphasizing significance is juxtaposing contrasting stories. An unknown woman anoints Jesus beforehand for burial with expensive nard (14:3–9) while a disciple betrays Jesus for money (14:10–11). During Passover the religious authorities seek a way to kill Jesus (14:1–2), while Jesus and the disciples seek a way to celebrate Passover (14:12–16).

The narration of that Passover meal, the Last Supper in the Gospel of Mark, does not institute a ritual for the future. There is no command to "do this in memory of me." Rather the shared meal affirms the meaning of Jesus' life and coming death for the new community, the community anticipating with Jesus drinking the cup "new in the kingdom of God" (14:25). The pairing of the terms "body" and "blood" for the bread and wine suggest not sacrifice or atonement to a first-century audience, but rather martyrdom. In the hearing before the Jewish authorities that night, the Markan Jesus is first silent in face of accusations, and then affirms "I am" when the high priest asks if he is the Messiah (14:55–65). Jesus' "I am" echoes God's "I am" to Moses in Exod. 3:6, giving clear grounds for the capital charge of blasphemy (see Mark 2:1–12). The Markan Jesus sees his coming execution, but he does not seek it; he has no martyr complex. In prayer at Gethsemane he asks God three times that this cup be removed (14:32–42). Yet he reaffirms his commitment to the will of God, speaking to God as an obedient son to his father, *Abba* (14:36). Again the Markan storyteller affirms *both* the coming of God's rule *and* its implication—persecution in the present age.

Throughout the passion narrative, Mark uses irony to convey his meaning to the audience: being anointed by a stranger and betrayed by a friend (14:3–12); the kiss of friendship as a sign of betrayal (14:43–50); the desertion of Jesus' followers—even unknown, mysterious ones (14:51–52); Jesus' initial silence before the high priest, but even more Jesus' breaking silence in a way that assures his condemnation to death (14:60–63); the taunting of Jesus to "prophesy" (14:65) at the moment his prophecy of Peter's denial is being fulfilled; Peter's denial of his identity in the courtyard below in order to save his life at the moment when Jesus confirms his identity to the high priest in the palace above (14:53–54/55–65/66–72). Irony signals the ultimate both/and of the situation to the audience.

Conflict with political authorities (Mark 15). In the morning the conflict moves to the secular authorities, those with real political power, the Romans. Their representative is Pilate, Roman prefect or governor of Judea. What is at stake politically is clear in Pilate's first question to Jesus, "Are you the King of the Jews?" (15:2). Since the Roman emperor was considered the king of all peoples, any other contender would be an insurrectionist. The Markan Jesus' only answer, "You say so," is ambiguous. According to Mark, Pilate offers the crowd the release of Barabbas or Jesus (15:6–15). From our knowledge outside the Gospels, this offer of release is unlikely to be historical; more likely it is a later Christian attempt to shift blame for Jesus' death away from the Romans, where it properly belongs. What is clear is that Jesus was crucified, a horrible and humiliating Roman (not Jewish) punishment reserved for low-status persons accused of direct challenges to the empire. What is equally clear from Mark's perspective is that Jesus was innocent of such charges.

The audience would grasp the irony of Pilate's charge and the soldiers' mocking (15:16–20); they understand that Jesus claimed not to be king himself but that the kingdom (or rule) of God has broken into history. Of course, to proclaim that God is king is dangerous in the presence of those who consider themselves the gods' agents on earth. The Markan Jesus' statements about the inbreaking kingdom (rule) of God are thus not apolitical or purely spiritual; his claims are indeed a challenge to the political status quo of the overbearing empire of his day.

The imperial power of Rome is manifest in the way the crucifixion is carried out. Everything is done to maximize humiliation of the accused: flogging (15:15), mocking (15:16–20), stripping of clothes (15:24). This imperial power even applies to innocent bystanders: Simon of Cyrene is compelled to carry the cross (15:21). Crucified with Jesus are two other accused insurrectionists ("bandits" in the sense of those attacking manifestations of Roman power). Earlier James and John asked to be at Jesus' right and left; he told them they did not know what they were asking (10:35–40). Now those at Jesus' right and left are crucified with him. The cost of participating in the rule of God—always at least an implicit challenge to the rule of empire—is clear.

The taunting continues almost to the end, delivered by passersby (15:29–30) and the chief priests and scribes (15:31–32). Jesus' cry from the cross, "My God, my God, why have you forsaken me?" (Ps. 22:1), is open to various interpretations. The internal characters hear "*Eloi, Eloi*" ("My God, my God," in Aramaic) as "Elijah" (Mark 15:34–36). Some external interpreters hear total devastation; others hear not just the first verse of Ps. 22 but an allusion to the entire psalm, which ends with assurance and a vow to "proclaim [God's] deliverance to a people yet unborn" (Ps. 22:31). How audience members interpret will affect their understanding of the story's meaning.

At the very end, after Jesus gives a loud cry and breathes his last (15:37), two incidents are narrated in succession that show Mark's understanding of where true power resides. The first involves the cosmic level, the second the level of the authorities' conflict. First, the curtain of the temple is torn in two "from top to bottom" (15:38). Scholars argue over which temple curtain is intended, but the symbolic reference to the temple's destruction is clear. Also clear is the cosmic nature of this event in Mark's story. Both curtains were huge; only God's power could tear one from top to bottom, just as only God's power could cover the whole land with darkness at noon (15:33). Second, the Roman centurion, seeing how Jesus died, says, "Truly this man was God's Son!" (15:39). Whether we interpret the centurion as sincere or sarcastic, his words are ironic in their Markan context. It is ironic that the official carrying out Jesus' execution is the only human

character in the narrative to call Jesus God's Son. To be a son of God is to be obedient to God—regardless of the consequences. To proclaim God's rule in the face of human rule is to risk one's life, perhaps even to lose it in order to save it (see 8:34–35).

The disciples have all fled; they have betrayed, denied, and abandoned Jesus. While they have understood that following involves risk to their lives—they have promised to die with Jesus (14:29–31)—they are unable to live it out. At this point, Mark tells us that there are women followers as well, and they are still following. Having watched the crucifixion from afar, they observe where Jesus is buried (15:40–41, 47). These women used to follow and serve Jesus in Galilee; they come up to Jerusalem with him. Three are named, but there are many others. "Follow" and "serve" are discipleship words in Mark. How challenging of gender stereotypes that it is women followers who follow to the end!

So also Joseph of Arimathea challenges the stereotype of Jewish authorities who reject God's rule (15:42–46). He requests the body of Jesus from the Roman authorities in order to bury it in dignity—a privilege not usually granted for those crucified. Joseph of Arimathea is described as both "a respected member of the council" and as "waiting expectantly for the rule of God"—a Markan plea to the audience not to judge by status and role alone. Joseph provides the tomb and the linen shroud, but the women, after the Sabbath rest, provide the spices to anoint the body.

Epilogue (16:1–8)

The story of the empty tomb presents reversals on all three levels of theological conflict in Mark's story. On the cosmic level, life overturns death, good outlasts evil, God conquers Satan. On the level of the authorities' conflict, the seeming victory of both the religious (Jewish) and political (Roman) powers-that-be is reversed. The crucifixion is not the end of Jesus or of the inbreaking of God's rule. Finally, on the level of the followers' conflict, resolution is implied. First, the women are still following to the empty tomb. When told to "go, tell," they flee in terror, amazement, and silence (16:7–8), but clearly the story gets told or there would be no Gospel of Mark. Second, the story assures forgiveness for the male disciples—even Peter—and the women for failures in following. The young man at the tomb reaffirms the promise of the Markan Jesus that he still goes ahead of them to Galilee (14:28; 16:7) in spite of their denials and abandonment. There is an opportunity for a new start back where it all began, in Galilee, with Jesus proclaiming and enacting that the rule of God is near—is here. The question is before Markan audiences, then and now: Will they be faithful followers, perhaps failing like the characters in Mark's story, but accepting forgiveness and continuing to embrace God's rule?

Conclusion

Because the Markan Jesus' proclamation and his ministry in life and death are centered on God and the inbreaking of God's rule, theology, not Christology, is foundational for the narrative theology of the Gospel of Mark. The orality of the Gospel of Mark decisively informs this narrative theology, since the story is intended to be performed, heard, and responded to. Mark's audience, with more complete knowledge than any characters throughout the story, is intended to continue the gospel story in its life, in its communities, and in the face of the powers-that-be in its world. Along with the characters, Mark's audiences must face the risk that serving others entails, but they also share the assurance that with God nothing is impossible.

Bibliography

Dewey, Joanna. "Mark." In *Searching the Scriptures: A Feminist-Ecumenical Commentary*, edited by Elisabeth Schüssler Fiorenza, 2:470–509. 2 vols. New York: Crossroad, 1994.

Donahue, John R., S.J. "A Neglected Factor in the Theology of Mark." *Journal of Biblical Literature* 101 (1982): 563–94.

Dowd, Sharyn. *Reading Mark: A Literary and Theological Commentary on the Second Gospel*. Macon, GA: Smyth & Helwys, 2000.

Malbon, Elizabeth Struthers. *Hearing Mark: A Listener's Guide*. Harrisburg: Trinity Press International, 2002.

Rhoads, David, Joanna Dewey, and Donald Michie. *Mark as Story: An Introduction to the Narrative of a Gospel*. 2nd ed. Minneapolis: Fortress, 1999.

Luke

O. Wesley Allen Jr.

INTRODUCTION

The Gospel according to Luke was written ca. 80–95 CE as the first half of a two-volume narrative often referred to by contemporary readers as Luke–Acts. This narrative tells the story of the origins, ministry, death, resurrection, and ascension of Jesus Christ in the first volume (Luke) and the beginning of the postresurrection church in the second volume (Acts of the Apostles), which focuses especially on Peter and the Twelve in the first half and on Paul in the second half. Although tradition asserts that the narrative was written by Luke the physician (from Col. 4:14), a companion of Paul (see the use of first person plural pronouns in Acts 16:10–17; 20:5–21:18; 27:1–28:16), there is no real evidence to support this claim. As with the other Gospels, the identity of the author of Luke–Acts is simply unknown, but the traditional name ascribed to the author continues to be used for ease of reference.

While the author does not offer his own identity, he does specifically name his addressee in the prologue—Theophilus (1:1–4; see also Acts 1:1). Since, however, this name literally means "God-lover," it is unclear whether Theophilus is a real person (e.g., the patron of the publication) or simply a way to refer to any implied reader. Regardless, that the name does mean "God-lover" and is Greek in origin

instead of Aramaic hints that Luke is writing to Gentile Christians. Luke is not writing to convert people who are hearing the story of Jesus for the first time. Instead, he is writing to (re)interpret elements of the faith to those already within the faith. He is describing a certain time period in the past (the origins of the Christian faith) to shape the faith and theology of his late-first-century church.

Luke makes clear in the opening verses of the Gospel that his purpose in writing is not to introduce something entirely new to the reader but to present such a narrative that the reader "may know the certainty concerning the things about which you have been instructed" (v. 4, my trans.). The "certainty" that Luke wishes to offer his audience is set over against other narratives that are available for reading (v. 1). That Luke claims to have researched these narratives, as well as reports from eyewitnesses and servants of the word (presumably second-generation preachers) that informed those narratives (v. 2), implies that Luke offers his two-volume story as a corrective to traditions currently available to his audience. Scholarship generally holds that in his research and writing of the first volume, Luke used Mark as a main source (more than 50 percent of Mark's material is found in Luke) along with Q (a hypothetical sayings source used independently by Matthew and Luke—material from which makes up nearly 25 percent of Luke's material) as well as other written and oral sources used only by Luke (material found neither in Mark or Matthew makes up nearly 25 percent of Luke). While Luke valued these sources enough to build much of his first volume using them, he also critiqued them theologically by freely omitting parts of their work, significantly editing other parts, and adding a great amount of material to them.

Luke signals at the beginning of his writing that the genre of narrative is a key element of his theological method; he offers an "orderly account" (v. 3). Luke's theology is to be found not just in this saying of Jesus or that miracle story or certain patterns of use of vocabulary but also (or better, primarily) in the overarching plot—in the way that scenes, themes, and characters build over the course of the whole of the narrative to construct, a piece at a time, a specific but broad Christian worldview. Before we focus on individual characteristics of Luke's theology as exhibited in the Third Gospel, we must get a sense of their narrative context, the way Luke constructs his theological plot across both volumes of Luke–Acts.

Salvation History and Wider History

The cornerstone of Luke's theological plot is salvation history—the understanding that God's salvific work is found in the way that God has acted (and thus continues to act) in the course of history. In presenting his view of salvation history, Luke directs the readers' view beyond just the events narrated from Luke 1 to Acts 28. Luke connects his narrative to wider history in two significant ways. First, Luke writes in such a way that his story of the Christ/church event is a continuation of the history of Israel as found in Scripture. Luke is a master of Greek style. The style of his writing shifts throughout the narrative to fit the occasion he is describing (e.g., contrast Paul's speech to Jews in Acts 13:16–41 with his speech to Greek

philosophers in 17:22–31). Luke's opening prologue (Luke 1:1–4) is one long, complex sentence that matches the best Hellenistic writing of his day. But in the scenes that immediately follow and tell of the conception and birth of John the Baptist and of Jesus, Luke's style imitates that of the Septuagint, the Greek translation of the Hebrew Scriptures. This literary technique has the effect of giving the reader the experience that the story of Jesus begins in and continues the history found in Israel's Scriptures. In addition, Luke has Jesus claim explicitly that his life, death, and resurrection are a fulfillment of these Scriptures. While he does on occasion present this fulfillment theme in a manner similar to Matthew's prophecy-fulfillment model of individual proof texts from the Hebrew Scriptures (especially in apostolic sermons in Acts), Luke has Jesus claim himself as the fulfillment of the whole of Scripture (Luke 18:31; 24:25–26, 44–45; cf. 16:29–31; Acts 28:23).

The second way Luke connects his theological narrative to wider history is by locating his story in the context of world history (Acts 26:26), that is, in the Gentile world. In the very chapters where Luke's style is most septuagintal, he repeatedly links the narrated events to the broader political world of the Roman Empire by referencing rulers and events outside the narrative proper (Luke 1:5; 2:1–3; 3:1–2). These opening references form a sort of *inclusio* with the fact that Paul is awaiting trial before the emperor at the end of Acts. In his genealogy of Jesus, Luke traces Jesus' lineage not only back through Israel's history but also to the beginning of world history by ending the genealogy with "the son of Adam, the son of God" (3:23–38). Thus, unlike Matthew, who traces Jesus' lineage back to Abraham, hence relating Jesus' story to that of Israel, Luke presents Jesus' story as related to the story of all humankind.

At stake in connecting Luke's narrative to these two wider views of Israelite and Gentile history seems to be the question: How is the Gentile church that has grown out of the Christ event and spread across the world a fulfillment of God's promises to Israel (see Luke 1:54)? While it is in Acts that Luke must deal explicitly with the existence of the Gentile church, already in the Gospel Luke presents Jesus' mission as extending to the Gentiles (2:31–32; 4:23–27; 7:1–10; 8:26–39; 9:52–56; 10:33–37; 17:11–19; 24:46–47). In the unity of the two-volume work, Luke brings together the story of Israel and the story of all children of Adam. In Jesus and the church, there is salvation for all the world. But Luke does more than offer a series of cause-and-effect events that unfold into a story moving from Israel to the Gentile church. Luke claims that everything that unfolds in the narrative is in accordance with God's providential plan and will (Luke 7:30; 22:22, 42; Acts 2:23; 4:28; 5:38; 13:36) and therefore was necessary (see the use of the Greek verb *dei* [translated variously as "it is necessary," "must," should"] in Luke 2:49; 4:43; 9:22; 13:33; 17:25; 21:9; 22:37; 24:7, 44; Acts 1:21–22; 3:21; 4:12; 9:6, 16; 14:22; 19:21; 23:11; 25:10; 27:24).

The Periods of Salvation History

In addition to these references to God's plan, Luke offers a subtler ordering of the narrative plot of the Christ event resulting in the Gentile church to show the unfolding of divine providence. For example, some scholars have found in Luke's theology, especially as named in Luke 16:16—literally, "The law and the prophets were until John; since then the good news of the reign of God is proclaimed, and all force their way into it"—and then borne out in the narrative, a division of salvation history into three periods. The threefold division would look like this: The first period is that of Israel and extends into the time of Luke's narrative to John the Baptist. In this period God's salvific will and work are known through the law and the prophets. After this, the proclamation of the dominion of God becomes primary. There is scholarly debate as to whether John belongs to this first period or to the sec-

ond. The second time period is that of Jesus. In this sense, Jesus stands between the first and third periods as a hinge. The third period is that of the church. Some scholars follow this basic schema, but think Luke's narrative divides salvation history into only two phases: first, Israel; then, Jesus and the church. Regardless of which division is more convincing, the point is clear: God is doing something new in Jesus and the church.

The Prophetic Pattern of Salvation History

It must be noted that these schemas overemphasize the discontinuity between historical periods in Luke–Acts. In Luke's claim that God's plan concerning Jesus' life, suffering, death, and resurrection is revealed in the law and prophets, Luke seems to assert that the events and teachings he narrates are in continuity with salvation as it has unfolded in Israel's story as opposed to indicating a complete break with the past. Indeed, Luke's central characters are presented not as over against the prophets of the past but as typologically shaped in the likenesses of Abraham, Moses, and Elijah. These central Lukan characters, and many minor characters in the narrative, are viewed as Spirit-filled prophets standing in line with the prophets of old (see especially Acts 3:18–26; 7:37; but also Luke 1:15–17, 26, 35, 41–42, 46ff., 67ff.; 2:25–38; 3:3–4; 4:14–15, 17, 18, 24, 27; 6:23; 7:16, 26, 39; 9:7–8; 11:47–51; 12:11–12; 13:33–34; 20:6; 24:19; Acts 1:2, 8; 2:3–4, 17–18; 4:8, 31; 5:32; 6:9–10; 8:39; 9:17; 11:22–24, 27, 28; 13:1, 9; 15:32; 19:6; 21:10). This prophetic characterization leads to a recurring plot structure in Luke–Acts that follows the same orderly pattern Luke finds in Israel's story. The prophet who brings God's word is rejected by the people and suffers at the hands of persecutors. God responds by redeeming/rescuing the prophet, but in the process the prophet steps aside from being the central character in the story. God then deals with the persecutors, and the next prophet steps up to continue the work of God's reign.

See how this pattern unfolds in Luke–Acts: Jesus preaches the reign of God only to be rejected and crucified; but God raises him from the dead and he ascends into heaven (Luke 24; Acts 1:6–11); Judas, who betrayed Jesus into the hands of the authorities, dies a death that fulfills Scripture (Acts 1:18–20); God's promise of the Holy Spirit comes upon Peter and the apostles (Acts 2). Peter and the apostles proclaim the good news of Jesus Christ; after they suffer various persecutions (e.g., Acts 4:1–22; 5:17–42), Herod beheads James the brother of John and imprisons Peter (Acts 12:1–5); the angel of the Lord leads Peter out of prison, but as a fugitive he leaves center stage of the narrative (Acts 12:6–11, 17); the angel of the Lord strikes down Herod so that he is consumed by worms (Acts 12:23); with the Twelve dismantled, James the brother of Jesus becomes head of the church in Jerusalem and Paul becomes the central prophetic figure in the narrative. (The martyrdom of Stephen follows this pattern as well, Acts 6:1–8:3.)

Paul preaches in synagogues and to Gentiles throughout the empire and encounters rejection and persecution to the point of being arrested in Jerusalem (Acts 20:22–23; 21:27ff.) and facing trial before the emperor in Rome (Acts 25:10– 12, 21; 26:32; 27:24; 28:19). The narrative ends with Paul awaiting this trial. Indeed, that Luke consistently chooses not to name this emperor (Acts 25:8–12, 21; 26:32; 27:24; 28:19; cf. Luke 2:1; 3:1; Acts 18:2) even though he has named lower rulers with whom Paul dealt during his final imprisonment (Claudius Lysias, Felix, Festus, Agrippa; Acts 23–26), shows that Luke's concern is not with the specific emperor who executes Paul, but with Caesar as the highest ruler in the land. Those who read the whole of Luke's narrative are to be certain that God's salvific pattern exhibited in history is mightier than the greatest human threat to God's prophetic church. They know that when Paul is martyred, God will bring retribution on the persecutors and raise up new prophets so that the church will increase and continue to fulfill the plan of God (e.g., Acts 2:41–42; 4:4; 12:24).

In sum, then, Luke views history as linear with something new occurring in the Christ/church event. This seeming discontinuity is portrayed, however, through the use of the prophetic patterning of the plot, as continuous with God's salvific work through the prophets of Israel. Thus the Gentile church is indeed a providential fulfillment of God's promise to Israel. To read Luke–Acts theologically is to keep this historical discontinuity and continuity in tension.

COMMENTARY

The Gospel's Salvation Narrative

While Luke presents Jesus as one character among many in the prophetic pattern through which he views salvation history, the evangelist certainly does not view him as a prophet among equals. In his first volume, Luke offers Jesus as the *paradigm* of the repeating prophetic pattern for the church. He is the center of salvation history (in terms of God's salvation effected in the past) and the model for how and the hope for why the church lives out its salvation—its eschatological life in the Spirit—in ongoing history. By virtue of his resurrection, his ascension, and Pentecost, he is still present in that ongoing history through the Holy Spirit (see Acts 16:7, which refers to the Holy Spirit as "the Spirit of Jesus"). Thus we now turn our attention from Luke's broad view of salvation history as laid out in both volumes to his narration of the story of Jesus in the Gospel and how it portrays God's salvation in orderly fashion.

Prologue (1:1–4). As discussed above, Luke opens with a declaration of his intent to offer his readers certainty concerning the faith they have been taught by providing them with an orderly account of the Christ/church event.

Beginnings (1:5–3:38). Luke's opening chapters tell of Jesus' conception, birth, growth, and baptism. The closing genealogy divides this section from the next. Unlike Mark, in which Jesus becomes Messiah at his baptism, and unlike John, in which Jesus is the incarnation of the preexistent *logos*, Luke (similar to Matthew) has a Christology in which Jesus is born as the Messiah.

One of the major emphases of this section is to present Jesus as superior to John the Baptist. Their birth stories are told in parallel fashion, but with each parallel John is subordinated to Jesus as forerunner to the Son of God. Luke pushes this aspect so far that he tells of the end of John's ministry with his arrest before he narrates Jesus' baptism (3:18–22). In addition to presenting Jesus as superior to John, in this section Jesus is also distinguished from all the other "prophets" who are in the narrative (see above). While many in Luke's narrative are filled with the Holy Spirit, Jesus alone is *conceived* by the Spirit (1:35) and receives the Spirit *in bodily form* at his baptism (3:22). Moreover, Luke's basic understanding of the theological uniqueness of Jesus is set forth in this section with the introduction of numerous christological titles and descriptions: heir to the Davidic throne (1:27, 32, 33, 69; 2:4, 11; 3:31), Son of God/Most High (1:32, 35; 2:49; 3:22, 38), savior (1:69–71; 2:11, 31, 38), Christ (2:11, 26; 3:15), Lord (1:43; 2:11; 3:4), light for Gentiles and glory for Israel (2:32), one who baptizes with the Holy Spirit and fire (3:16).

Jesus' ministry in Galilee (4:1–9:50). Whereas Mark and Matthew present Jesus' temptation as flowing forth from his baptism, Luke separates the two scenes with his genealogy (3:23–38). The temptation story initiates Jesus' ministry of confronting evil in the world instead of concluding his preparation for ministry.

Instead of being paired with the baptism, the temptation is coupled with Jesus' inaugural sermon in Nazareth. As in the temptation Jesus rejects the worldly approach to gaining power, so in the scene in the Nazareth synagogue Jesus declares that his ministry is oriented toward those without power (see below). Throughout this narrative section, that orientation is affirmed in healings and exorcisms, in conflicts with religious authorities, in table fellowship with sinners and crowds, and in calling and commissioning the apostles to preach the good news and to heal. Near the end of the section, it becomes clear that this type of ministry will result in Jesus' crucifixion (9:22, 44). That this execution fits into the prophetic pattern discussed above is highlighted near the end of this section in the story of the transfiguration. When Jesus' appearance changes and his clothes become dazzling white, Moses and Elijah, two prophets of old who appear in glory, speak with him about his "exodus" (*exodus* is the Greek word in 9:31 but is often translated in too neutral a way as simply "departure").

Jesus' ministry on the way to Jerusalem (9:51–19:28). The Lukan narrator indicates a major narrative transition by opening this section of the story with the words, "When the days for him to be taken up [for the Greek verb form of this word referring to the ascension, see Acts 1:2, 9, 11, 22] were fulfilled, he resolutely set his face toward Jerusalem" (9:51, my trans.). In the travel narrative that follows, a theological geography is established in which Jerusalem is the center of Luke's narrative world. In the Gospel, God's providence leads to Jerusalem (2:38, 41ff.; 4:9; 9:31, 51, 53, 13:32–35; 17:11; 18:31; 19:11; 23:5), and in Acts God's providence flows forth from Jerusalem (Acts 1:8; cf. Luke 24:46–47).

But not only is the destination of Jerusalem significant. The journey itself is a theological metaphor for Luke. As Jesus travels on the way/road to Jerusalem in accordance with God's plan

(Luke 9:57; 19:36), so he sends his disciples out to minister on the way (9:3; 10:4; 14:23), and indeed the Christian movement itself is called "the Way" (Acts 9:2; 18:25, 26; 19:9, 23; 22:4; 24:14, 22). Moreover, whereas Mark refers to Jesus as one who teaches with authority without providing his readers much content of Jesus' teaching, and Matthew primarily collects Jesus' teaching into five main discourses, Luke offers the bulk of Jesus' teaching along the way to Jerusalem. In other words, in this section readers travel into discipleship, learning what it means to follow Jesus and to participate in the reign of God. Thus, for example, Luke fills the travel narrative with Jesus' parables (9:30–37; 12:13–21, 35–48; 13:6–9, 18–20, 24–30; 14:15–24, 28–35; 15:1–32; 16:1–8, 19–31; 18:1–14; 19:1–27).

As Luke showed in the previous section that the kind of ministry in which Jesus engaged in Galilee would lead to the crucifixion, so in this section does the imminence of Jesus' death become all the more evident (11:53–54; 13:31–35; 18:31–33). Whereas in the Galilean section religious leaders were constantly challenging Jesus (e.g., 5:21, 30, 33; 6:1–2, 7, 11), in the travel narrative Jesus challenges them (11:37–54; 12:1; 13:14–17; 14:3, 7; 15:1ff.; 16:14–17; 18:9–14). In this section Jesus levels charges against and calls for repentance from many groups (10:13–16; 11:29–33; 12:13–15, 54–59; 13:1–9; 18:22).

Jesus' ministry in Jerusalem (19:29–21:38). In this section, Luke presents Jesus as entering Jerusalem triumphantly, cleansing the temple, and teaching the crowds there daily during his last days (see 19:47; 21:37–38). Here Luke follows Mark fairly closely in terms of structure and basic content, but some small changes in language indicate significant theological differences. For instance, Luke must deal with the paradox of having Jerusalem as the geographical center of his narrative world—a structure, as we have seen, with significant theological import— while in the world of Luke's audience (80–95 CE), the city and the temple had

been destroyed by the Roman army years earlier (70 CE). He does this by having Jesus explicitly predict the destruction as judgment for rejecting his coming (see 19:41–44; cf. 13:34–35). Whereas Mark presents Jesus as speaking to the disciples about the destruction of the temple and retreating to the Mount of Olives to unpack what he meant with the eschatological discourse about the coming of the Human One (Mark 13), Luke presents Jesus as making this speech publicly in the temple and adds to it explicit descriptions of the fall of Jerusalem (Luke 21:5–36; especially cf. vv. 20–24 with Mark 13:14–17).

The rejection of Jesus is intensified in this section in that even as the crowds are enamored with his teaching, the religious leaders are seeking all the more to arrest him and turn him over to the Roman authorities as quickly as possible (19:39–40, 47–48; 20:19–20, 26). Because of his popularity, however, the authorities are unable to fulfill their desires publicly (see 22:53).

Jesus' passion (22:1–23:56). The leaders' chance to get their hands on Jesus privately arises when Satan enters Judas (22:3; see 4:13, where Satan leaves Jesus after the temptation until "an opportune time"), leading him to betray Jesus into their hands. This narrative signal that Jesus' death is at hand opens the door for Jesus' concluding teaching of his disciples, preparing them for their leadership role in the church after he is gone. At the Last Supper Jesus institutes the meal that would constitute the church's fellowship (22:14–20; cf. Acts 2:42); defines the type of servant-leadership required of those in the reign of God (22:24–30); identifies Peter as the one who will strengthen the other disciples after his denial and Jesus' crucifixion thus foreshadowing his dominant role in Acts 1–12; and instructs them that while the evangelistic missions before were peaceful (9:1–6; 10:1–12), the mission that lies ahead will be full of strife (22:35–38). Luke presents the disciples as ready for this mission. Whereas

Mark describes the disciples as completely abandoning Jesus at his arrest (Mark 14:50), Luke omits this line and has them falter (exemplified in Peter's denial) but ultimately remain faithful and near to Jesus (Luke 22:28; 23:49).

Luke also changes Mark's presentation of Jesus' trials and execution in theologically significant ways. Mark's Jerusalem narrative is an ironic coronation of Jesus—he enters the city and the temple in a less than triumphant manner (Mark 11:1–11); has his head anointed not by the high priest but by a woman (14:3–9); hosts a messianic banquet (14:17–25); is robed in royal garb by the guards mocking him (15:17–19); and is enthroned in glory on the cross (see 10:35–40, where Jesus foreshadows the cross as his seat of glory with those who sit on his right and left already chosen—i.e., the thieves), at which point he is mockingly declared King of the Jews, Messiah, and King of Israel (15:25–32). Luke omits some of these elements—the reference to coming into his glory along with those seated at his right and left, the anointing (cf. a very different story of anointing of Jesus' feet in the Galilean section of the narrative, Luke 7:36–50), and the robing scene. And Luke changes others, for example, in narrating Jesus' trials before the Sanhedrin, Pilate, and Herod, Luke increases Mark's emphasis on Jesus' innocence (22:66–23:25; notice especially the ambiguous [22:67–70; 23:3, 9] and false testimony [23:2, 14] as well as the explicit declarations of innocence [23:4, 14–16, 22, 47]).

These changes do not mean that Luke refutes the understanding of Jesus as a kingly messiah. They do mean, however, that the crucifixion is not the point at which that messiahship is theologically emphasized and defined. Jesus dies *because of* his messianic ministry, not to effect his messianic ministry. In other words, for Luke the cross is not the locus of salvation. He makes this clear in two ways. First, Luke omits the Markan Jesus' claim that he dies to give his life as a ransom for many (Mark 10:45). Second, in the sermons in Acts, the contrast is repeatedly offered that humans killed Jesus and God raised him (Acts 2:23; 3:15; 4:10; 5:30; 7:52; 10:39–40; 13:28–30). In Luke Jesus' death is not so much that of a salvific sacrifice (see, however, Luke 22:19–20; Acts 20:28) as that of an innocent, prophetic martyr. We must be careful, however, not to overstate this claim, since (as we have seen above) Jesus' death was a *necessary* part of God's providential plan as revealed in Scripture. The cross plays an essential role in salvation, it is simply not the center of salvation.

Jesus' resurrection and ascension (24:1–53). Instead, for Luke, the resurrection is the axis of God's salvific action in history. Whereas Mark has a parabolic, seemingly failed ending to his narrative (Mark 16:1–8), Luke presents the resurrection as the event from which his whole second volume (i.e., from which the Spirit-filled life of the church) flows. Instead of a young man at the tomb (Mark 16:5—reminiscent of the young man who fled at Jesus' arrest, 14:51–52), Luke has two men in dazzling clothes appear in the epiphany at the empty tomb (Luke 24:4—reminiscent of the language surrounding the appearance of Moses and Elijah at the transfiguration when they discussed Jesus' "exodus," 9:29–31; see the reappearance of these two men at the ascension in Acts 1:10–11). Instead of the women fleeing from the tomb and telling no one what they had seen and heard and thus leaving the story to end on a note of fear (Mark 16:8), Luke presents the women as faithfully witnessing to what had occurred (Luke 24:8), leading to a chain of events so that the story ends on a note of joy (24:52–53).

But more than changes to the Markan material Luke inherited, the additions that are found in Luke alone signify the centrality of the resurrection for Lukan theology. These additions indicate that, for Luke, it is through the resurrection that Jesus continues to be revealed to and present with the church in a salvific manner. The story of Jesus being made known in the breaking of the bread in Emmaus (24:28–32) reaffirms the importance placed on the Lord's Supper in 22:17–20 but also reinterprets it in the sense that the church's meal is a place where Jesus is continuously revealed, not just an occasion to remember his martyrdom. And while Mark points to and Matthew narrates Galilee as the place where the resurrected Jesus appears to the disciples, Luke has the resurrection appearances occur in and around Jerusalem, even to the point that Jesus' appearance on the road to Emmaus results in the two disciples who left town returning to Jerusalem (24:33). This element, along with Jesus' instruction for the disciples to remain in Jerusalem (24:49), opens the way for the Holy Spirit to be given in Jerusalem in order to continue Jesus' presence with the disciples and to empower the mission of the church (24:47–49).

Having foreshadowed the plot of his second volume, Luke concludes the Gospel narrative with Jesus' ascension (24:50–53). While the time line for the ascension is different in the Gospel than it is in Acts (see Acts 1:3), the theology is the same. In the church's experience of God in history, the stories of resurrection and Pentecost describe *God's imminence in Christ* while the story(s) of the ascension is sandwiched between them not just to remove Jesus from the narrative but to hold in paradoxical tension with this claim the recognition of *Christ's transcendence in God*.

Luke's Salvation of Reversal

To recognize that Luke's broad understanding of the Christ/church event is shaped by a view of salvation history is not to exhaust the whole of Lukan soteriology. Having examined ways that Luke plots out salvation in his orderly narrative, it is important to see as well how the evangelist unfolds the concept of salvation thematically in the Gospel.

Luke uses the range of Greek cognates of salvation much more than Mark or Matthew (1:47, 69, 71, 77; 2:30; 3:6; 6:9;

7:50; 8:12, 36, 48, 50; 9:24; 13:23; 17:19; 18:26, 42; 19:9–10; 23:35, 37, 39; Acts 2:21, 40, 47; 4:9, 12; 7:25; 11:14; 13:26, 47; 14:9; 15:1, 11; 16:17, 30–31; 27:30–31, 34; 28:28). Among the Synoptics, Luke alone refers to Jesus as savior (2:11; Acts 5:31; 13:23; cf. Luke 1:47). This vocabulary of salvation is used in a wide variety of contexts, indicating that salvation for Luke is not a narrowly defined theological topic. There are, however, some core understandings about salvation that appear in the narrative in terms of prominence of placement and repetition.

A passage that draws together a common thread from many of these different references to salvation is the scene of Jesus' inaugural sermon in Nazareth (4:16–30). Luke takes this story from Mark 6:1–6 but moves it from the middle of the Galilean ministry to its beginning and edits it so thoroughly that a new story is born. As Jesus' first public proclamation, the speech offered here is paradigmatic for the rest of Jesus' ministry in Luke. Jesus begins by reading from Isa. 61:1 and 58:6—"The Spirit of the Lord is upon me, because he has anointed me to bring good news to the poor. He has sent me to proclaim release to the captives and recovery of sight to the blind, to let the oppressed go free, to proclaim the year of the Lord's favor." He then declares to those gathered at the synagogue, "Today this scripture has been fulfilled in your hearing." Unlike in Mark where the crowd immediately rejects Jesus for his teaching, in Luke's version of the scene the crowd praises Jesus. But he, in a surprise turn, rejects them, accusing them of wanting him to use his power for their benefit and reminding them of the stories of Elijah and Elisha being sent to Gentiles. The crowd responds this time with anger and seeks to kill Jesus, but he escapes miraculously.

One of the first and most important things to notice in this passage is that, for Luke, salvation is reversal of the status quo. The use of the eschatological prophecy from Isaiah points to an overturning of the situations of the poor, the ill, and the oppressed. This salvific reversal is emphasized in many other places in Luke, for example, the Magnificat (1:46–55), the Beatitudes and Woes (6:20–26), and the parable of Lazarus and the rich man (16:19–31). Thus salvation is social, not simply spiritual. It is less something that happens to an individual and more the overturning of social structures that keep some downtrodden while others lead a life of privilege and advantage. In Luke there is a recognition that the oppressed cannot be lifted up as long as the oppressors remain in power, and the poor cannot be lifted up without the rich being brought down.

Luke's salvific preference is for those who are socially, economically, ritually, and physically marginalized. Before we turn to look at some individual examples of those who experience this kind of salvation as reversal in the Gospel narrative, consider the lists Luke repeatedly uses to present the whole of those in need. In the Nazareth scene, the Isaiah quotation mentions the poor, the captives, the blind, and the oppressed (4:18). In the Beatitudes Jesus blesses the poor, the hungry, those weeping, those hated and excluded (6:20–23; see, by contrast, the woes about the rich, the full, those laughing, and those about whom others speak well, vv. 24–26). When John sends messengers to ask whether Jesus is the "one to come," Jesus' answer lists those whose situation his ministry has reversed: "the blind receive their sight, the lame walk, those with skin disease are cleansed, the deaf hear, the dead are raised, and the poor have good news brought to them" (7:22). While Matthew's version of this scene is similar (Matt. 11:2–6), in Luke this answer clearly echoes back to Jesus' sermon in Nazareth. At the dinner in the Pharisee's home, Jesus instructs his host not to invite those who can return the favor of hospitality but the poor, the crippled, the lame, and the blind (14:13). This instruction is reiterated in the parable that follows when the one preparing a banquet invites the poor, the crippled, the blind, and the lame after the initial invitees

reject the invitation (14:21). These lists are not static. While there is overlap among them, there are also differences. Therefore, the lists should be read as representative of those who are marginalized and need the salvation of reversal instead of as an exhaustive list. However, we must be careful not to take this generalization too far. It is still important to recognize specific patterns in Luke's representation of different groups.

Luke and the poor. Of high significance for Luke's theology is the salvation of the poor. In the lists mentioned above, the poor are always listed at either the beginning or end of the list. Indeed, Luke refers to the poor (and the rich) more than any of the other Gospels. Thus, while Luke is concerned about reversal of the oppressive status quo in general, he has a special concern for the poor. After all, Jesus is born in a stable to parents temporarily relocated at the whim of the emperor, and his birth is proclaimed not to the emperor but to night-shift shepherds (2:1–20). Or to hear the concern come straight from Jesus' mouth, Luke has Jesus explicitly address economic disparity by saying, "Blessed are you who are poor" (Luke 6:20), whereas Matthew's version of the Beatitudes presents a spiritualized, "Blessed are the poor in spirit" (Matt. 5:3).

Jesus not only proclaims consolation to the poor, but also warns the rich of the danger of possessions. At the beginning of the Sermon on the Plain, Jesus curses the rich in the same breath that he blesses the poor (Luke 6:24). In a theology of salvation as reversal, the two cannot be separated— the concern for the poor is expressed in terms of lamenting the rich. Indeed, the danger of wealth and the call to use possessions for the good of others are common themes in Luke's parables (8:14; 10:29–37; 12:13–34; 14:15–24; 15:11–32; 16:1–3, 19–31; 18:9–14; 19:11–27). Wealth can be a barrier to being a disciple of Jesus. Jesus repeatedly instructs those who follow and those who wish to follow concerning the peril that wealth represents. At one point, Luke has Jesus explicitly state, "None of you can become my disciples if you do not give up all your possessions" (14:33; see also 6:30; 7:25; 9:3; 10:4; 11:41; 12:33–34; 14:12–14; 16:13–14; 18:18–30; 22:3–6). Luke, however, does offer a positive example of relinquishing possessions for the sake of discipleship in Zacchaeus. When he gives half of his possessions to the poor and pays back fourfold to those he has defrauded, Jesus announces, "Today salvation has come to this house" (19:1–10). That Zacchaeus does not give up all of his wealth, however, shows that Luke is not entirely consistent in his claims about the rich. What remains clear about Luke's view is that economics cannot be separated from God's salvation.

Luke and women.   This kind of theological inconsistency is also found in Luke's treatment of women. While women do not appear in the lists of those whose situations need reversing, they were certainly oppressed in the first-century, patriarchal, Mediterranean world. Luke addresses their need for reversal by giving them more prominence than is found in any of the other Gospels. Over against Matthew, who places Joseph as the main parental character in the infancy narrative, Luke presents Mary as the lowly servant of God who is divinely favored and lifted up and who speaks prophetically about God's reversal (1:26–53). Women follow Jesus and financially support his ministry (8:1–3). Martha's sister Mary is presented as sitting at Jesus' feet and listening to his teachings (10:38–42). Women who followed Jesus from Galilee are included among those faithfully witnessing the crucifixion (23:49). And women are the first witnesses to the resurrection (24:1–11). Moreover, Luke often pairs references about men with parallel references to women (e.g., the prophetic speeches of Mary and Zechariah, 1:46–55, 67–79; the presence of Simeon and Anna in the temple, 2:25–38; Jesus' reference to the widow in Zarephath and Naaman the leper in his inaugural sermon, 4:25–27; the healing of the centurion's servant and the raising of the widow's son, 7:1–17; Sabbath healings of the bent woman and the man with dropsy, 13:10–17 and 14:1–6; the man who plants the mustard seed and the woman who takes leaven, 13:18–21; the man who searches for the lost sheep and the woman who searches for the lost coin, 15:4–10). Luke is concerned to present women as participating in God's promise of salvation for all.

It must be said, however, that for the prominence and quantity of material Luke dedicates to women, he does not present Jesus as fully reversing the patriarchal situation under which women are oppressed. Luke has women support Jesus' ministry but does not portray them as giving all to become disciples and evangelists sent out by Jesus. While individual (and presumably significant) women are named in the Gospel, they are not named in the same lists with male disciples as equals. Jesus ministers to women and women support Jesus' ministry, but women do not share in Jesus' ministry as do males. Or to give a specific example, Jesus heals Simon's mother-in-law, but this reversal of her health situation only allows her to rise and serve "them" (presumably Jesus and the male disciples, 4:38–39). Luke lifts up women and presents this lifting up as part of God's providential salvation, but he does not lift them up far enough to escape the mire of patriarchy.

Luke and the ill.   Unlike the inconsistency in Luke's treatment of the poor and of women, the healing miracles in the Gospels offer a straightforward view of Jesus' salvific work. Luke, like the other Gospels, is filled with stories of healings and exorcisms. However, the inclusion of the blind and the lame in the lists discussed above gives them a distinct purpose in the Third Gospel. Instead of simply demonstrating Jesus' power or his compassion for those in need, the healings also serve as the most concrete example of salvation as reversal in the Gospel. Whereas Luke presents only

Jesus' closest disciples (5:11, 27–28; 18:28–30) and Zacchaeus (19:1–10) as escaping the perils of possessions, over and over again Jesus saves people from illness and demon possession. Their recovery and health are representative of God's providential will for the salvation of all whose situations need to be reversed (see 7:50; 8:36, 48, 50; 17:19; 18:42, where Jesus specifically refers to individual's healings as being "saved," although some English translations simply translate the Greek as "healed").

Luke and the lost.   Finding the lost is an important metaphor for Luke's understanding of Jesus' salvific ministry. Chapter 15 of the Gospel consists of three parables with this theme: the lost sheep, the lost coin, and the lost son. Viewed broadly, the metaphor of having been lost and now being found can be understood to encompass salvation as reversal in general. But for Luke it also has a narrower context related to forgiveness of sins. The reason Jesus tells these three parables is that religious authorities are complaining because tax collectors and sinners are gathering to listen to Jesus, who "welcomes sinners and eats with them" (15:1–2). Indeed, Jesus has already made clear to religious authorities that this is not simply the way he operates; this is the very purpose of his ministry. When a paralytic is brought to Jesus, he forgives his sins and then heals the man to prove that he indeed has the authority to forgive sins (5:17–26). Immediately after this forgiveness-healing scene, Jesus calls Levi the tax collector to follow him and then eats at his house with tax collectors and sinners. When the religious authorities complain, Jesus says, "Those who are well have no need of a physician, but those who are sick; I have come to call not the righteous but sinners to repentance" (5:27–32; cf. Jesus' words that followed his proclamation that salvation had come to Zacchaeus's house: "The Human One came to seek out and save the lost," 19:10). Not long after this, Jesus forgives the sins of the woman who

anoints his feet in the house of the Pharisee, again raising for the religious authorities the question, "Who is this who even forgives sins?" (7:36–50). Central to Jesus' mission is the forgiveness of sins, and likewise the resurrected Jesus instructs the disciples to proclaim the forgiveness of sins to all nations (24:45–49). Luke shows that this is a central theme of the church's proclamation in Acts (Acts 2:38; 3:19; 5:31; 10:43; 13:38–39; 22:16; 26:18).

That forgiveness of sins plays such an important role suggests that readers should not overemphasize the social nature of Luke's understanding of salvation to the point of excluding the individual, spiritual character of salvation. On the other hand, for Luke, forgiveness of sins is not without social implications. Sinners are forgiven and repentance is invited, so that that which is lost is found *and* returned to the community. One way that this is evident in the Third Gospel is Luke's emphasis on table fellowship. Jesus always seems either to be eating or peppering his teaching with references to eating (5:29–39; 6:1–5; 7:34, 36–50; 8:55; 9:3–4, 12–17; 10:7; 11:3, 5–13, 37–41; 12:22–31, 36, 42, 45; 14:1–24; 15:16–30; 16:19–21; 17:7–10, 27–28; 22:7–38; 24:28–32, 41–43). It is often when Jesus is at table or in relation to his eating habits that we hear the charge concerning his association with sinners and tax collectors (5:29–32; 7:31–35; 19:7). Likewise, it is while at table with Pharisees that he forgives the sinful woman who anoints his feet (7:36–50); chastises the religious authorities for seeking honor to the point of neglecting justice and placing burdens on people (11:37–52); and heals a man with dropsy on the Sabbath, instructs guests to quit seeking the places of highest honor, instructs the host to invite those who cannot repay his hospitality, and tells the parable of the great banquet where the poor, the crippled, the blind, and the lame get invited (14:1–24). It is after the second of these table scenes that the religious authorities begin to conspire against Jesus (11:53–54).

In the context of the ancient Mediterranean world, sharing food (especially at formal occasions) was symbolic of social bonding. Jesus' eating with tax collectors and sinners, therefore, crossed over accepted social boundaries. For Luke, it signified forgiveness of sins, a reversal of social systems of exclusion and inclusion, a finding of the lost in which the lost are brought back into community. The institution of the Lord's Supper (22:14–20) and the meal at Emmaus (24:28–35) carry into the life of the church this significance of meals as communion that breaks down boundaries (see, e.g., Acts 2:41–42, 44–47).

Luke and the reign of God. Although Luke replaces the proclamation of the advent of the reign of God with the claim that Jesus is the fulfillment of Isa. 61:1–2 and 58:6 as Jesus' paradigmatic proclamation (Luke 4:16–21; cf. Mark 1:14–15; Matt. 4:17), the reign of God, the institution of God's providential purpose for the world, is nevertheless an important concept for Luke. Jesus still travels from town to town proclaiming God's reign (Luke 4:43; 8:1; 9:11; 16:16) and sends his disciples to do likewise (9:1–2, 59–60; 10:8–11). Wherever God's salvation of reversal is proclaimed, effected, and lived out, there is the reign of God. When demons are cast out and those who are ill are healed (9:1–2, 6; 10:9; 11:17–20), when the downtrodden are lifted up (6:20; 18:15–16), when oppressive authorities are challenged (13:17–18), when table fellowship that crosses societal boundaries is established (13:29; 14:15–24), the reign of God is evident. Indeed, Luke changes much of the eschatological tone of the proclamation of the reign of God found in the other Synoptic Gospels. When the Pharisees ask him when the reign of God is coming, Jesus responds (in a statement unique to Luke), "The reign of God is not coming with things that can be observed; nor will they say, 'Look, here it is!' or 'There it is!' For, in fact, the reign of God is among you [plural]" (17:20–21). While different interpretations are possible, the significance of "among you" (or "in your

midst") is best understood by hearing the phrase as similar to Jesus, after having read the eschatological vision in Isaiah, declaring to those in Nazareth, "Today this scripture has been fulfilled in your hearing" (4:16–21). As Jesus then claimed to be the fulfillment of the prophecy of salvation by reversal, so here with the Pharisees he claims that he is the manifestation of the reign of God. Jesus' ministry *is* the advent of God's dominion and this reign is a present reality (see also 9:27; 10:9, 11; 12:32; 16:16).

However, this sense of realized eschatology in Luke can be, and often has been, overstated. For instance, it is often asserted that Luke would not have written a church history if he were expecting the Parousia to occur any day. Indeed, we have already seen that Luke's concern in his two-volume narrative is with a pattern of salvation history that extends into the time of the reader. This, however, does not necessitate the loss of all eschatological emphases. In some passages Luke is quite willing to speak of God's reign as still coming (11:2; 13:28–29; 19:11ff.; 21:29–31; 23:51; also Acts 1:6–7). Moreover, immediately after Jesus tells the Pharisees that the reign of God is among them, he tells his disciples about the future revelation of the Human One (Luke 17:22–37). This theme of the Parousia yet to occur reappears in Luke's version of the eschatological discourse (21:5–36; cf. Mark 13:1–37; Matt. 24:1–44). Even though Luke historicizes the discourse he inherits from Mark by making more explicit references to the destruction of Jerusalem in 70 CE (see Luke 21:20//Mark 13:14; and Luke 21:23b–24), he still has Jesus claim that "they will see 'the Human One coming in a cloud' with power and great glory." Then Luke adds, "Now when these things begin to take place, stand up and raise your heads, because your redemption is drawing near" (21:27–28). As we have seen in other aspects of the Gospel's soteriology of reversal, Luke is comfortable with some level of ambiguity. The Gospel writer is quite willing to hold in tension the already and the not yet aspects of God fulfilling God's providential will. Luke's view of salvation history does not only connect Luke's church with God's providential action in the past, nor does it only promise God will act in a consistent providential manner in the future. Luke also holds that God will act providentially in the end.

Participation in God's Salvation

In the Gospel of Luke, participating in God's providential purposes and responding to God's gift of salvation is manifested in a number of ways. Some of these have already been noted (e.g., giving of possessions to the poor, an ethic of orientation toward the marginalized, and being brought into the fullness of community). Others merit further discussion.

Repentance. Repentance is a major theme for Luke. It is part and parcel of the proclamation of forgiveness of sins offered by John the Baptist, Jesus, and the church (1:16–17; 3:3, 8; 5:31–32; 11:27–32; 13:1–9; 15:7, 10; 16:27–31; 17:3–4; 24:45–48). One must be careful, however, not to view this repentance simply as an interior, attitudinal turning (although it does include this as well, 18:9–14). For Luke repentance is evidenced in one's turning toward an ethical life of discipleship that accords with God's salvation of reversal (6:43–49). When John preaches a baptism of repentance, the crowds ask what they must do (cf. Acts 2:37). John instructs people with two coats to give away one, tax collectors to collect only that which is appropriately owed them, and soldiers to extort no money from those under their power (3:10–14). When Simon Peter sees the miraculous catch of fish, he falls on his knees confessing his sinfulness. Jesus responds by calling him to "catch people," and Peter leaves all behind to follow Jesus (5:4–11). The prodigal son returns to his father with the posture of a slave, ready to serve (15:17–21). Zacchaeus repents by giving away half his possessions and making restitution for his fraudulent dealings (19:1–10). Jesus instructs Peter that, after he repents for denying Jesus, he must strengthen the other disciples (22:31–32).

In addition to offering examples of appropriate forms of repentance, Luke's narrative shows that there are dire consequences for those who do not welcome the good news and fail to heed the call to repentance and a life aligned with God's justice (6:24–26; 8:11–15; 9:5; 10:10–15; 11:42–52; 12:35–48; 13:1–9; 18:18–25; 19:41–44; 20:9–19). Nowhere is God's retribution in relation to the failure to repent more strongly narrated than in the parable of Lazarus and the rich man, in which the rich man is condemned to Hades for failing to share his possessions in accordance with the law and the prophets. Indeed, his brothers will share the same fate, for, as Abraham makes clear, not even a resurrection could persuade them to live otherwise (16:19–31).

Discipleship. The line between the call to repentance as a radical turning in obedience to God's salvific purposes and the call to discipleship is blurry at best in Luke. Indeed, at times the two are synonymous (5:4–11, 27–28; 9:57–62). But discipleship involves more than just repentance. The primary metaphor for discipleship in Luke is *following* (5:11, 27–28; 9:23, 49, 57–62; 14:27; 18:22, 28, 42; 23:49, 55). As noted earlier, the journey motif in Luke is one in which disciples are portrayed as following and learning from Jesus along the way. This following entails leaving house and hearth to be with Jesus continually, being shaped by his life and ministry, sitting alongside him at table with sinners, being challenged by opponents because of him, and risking persecution to the point of death. In a word, to be a disciple involves self-denial and daily cross-bearing in response to God's redemptive will (9:23–27).

But following Jesus leads to being *sent out* by Jesus. To be a disciple is to join in Jesus' mission. Thus Jesus sends out the Twelve (9:1–6) and the Seventy (10:1–20) and commissions the church to continue this mission after his death and resurrection (22:35–38; 24:44–49). Jesus' ministry of proclaiming the good news to the poor, the release of the captives, the recovery of sight to the blind, the liberation of the oppressed, and the year of the Lord's favor (4:18–19) becomes the ministry of the church.

Prayer. For Luke, an important element of being equipped for this mission is a life of prayer. The Gospel portrays Jesus as modeling such a commitment to prayer (5:16; 11:1; 22:32). Indeed, when the narrator notes that Jesus is praying, it signals to the reader that an important event in Jesus' ministry is occurring (baptism, 3:21; appointing the Twelve, 6:12; Peter's confession, 9:18; transfiguration, 9:28–29; Gethsemane, 22:41, 44–45). Thus for Luke prayer, which by definition depends on God's faithfulness (11:5–13), is closely associated with God's providential actions (see also 1:10–13).

Jesus not only models prayer for the disciples, but also teaches them to pray. He instructs them to pray for their abusers (6:28). He offers them a prayer—Luke's version of the Lord's Prayer—which relates to the major themes of the Gospel: the advent of the reign of God, trusting in God and not possessions, forgiveness of sins, and eschatology (11:1–4). He taught them to pray with perseverance (18:1–8)

and humility (18:9–14). He critiqued the practice of saying long prayers for the sake of appearance (20:47). He told them to pray in the face of coming tribulations (21:36; 22:40, 46).

In the opening scenes of Acts, Luke makes clear that the church has adopted Jesus' practice of praying (Acts 1:14, 24; 2:42; 3:1; 4:31; 6:4), thus indicating that they will be faithful disciples in fulfilling Jesus' mission of proclaiming God's salvation of reversal for all the world.

Bibliography

Bovon, François. *Luke the Theologian: Fifty-five Years of Research (1950–2005).* 2nd ed. Waco: Baylor University Press, 2006.

Buckwalter, Douglas. *The Character and Purpose of Luke's Christology.* Cambridge: Cambridge University Press, 1996.

Green, Joel B. *The Theology of the Gospel of Luke.* New Testament Theology. Cambridge: Cambridge University Press, 1995.

Levine, Amy-Jill, ed. *A Feminist Companion to Luke.* London: Sheffield Academic Press, 2002.

O'Toole, Robert F. *The Unity of Luke's Theology: An Analysis of Luke–Acts.* Wilmington, DE: Michael Glazier, 1984.

John

David Rensberger

INTRODUCTION

The Gospel of John, more obviously than the other NT Gospels, makes specific theological claims about Jesus. Perhaps for this reason John has often been used to introduce people to Christian faith; but Johannine theology is deep and complex enough to challenge even long-time believers.

John offers a distinctive understanding of Jesus and his relationship with God. In this understanding, what is to be known about God and received from God is fully present in Jesus, because Jesus himself is the divine Word made flesh. Yet this divine Son of God remains fully human, eating and drinking, weeping and dying. This is John's point: God entered the world as a human being, and those who recognize and accept this radically new divine act receive the eternal life God is offering through him. John's Christology is not a fixed item of dogma but a paradox that can be expressed only in symbolic and ironic language and grasped only by believing, by entering into a trusting relationship with Jesus that includes a willingness to learn surprising things from God and to live with and in paradox and mystery.

John's message is about the salvation of the world, but it was probably first addressed to the needs of a particular Christian community, one still largely of Jewish origin, but now alienated from its roots because of its beliefs about Jesus. This alienation is expressed by repeated references to believers being "put out of the synagogue" (John 9:22; 12:42; 16:2), an occurrence not mentioned in any other ancient Christian or Jewish text and not at all likely to have happened in Jesus' day. Those who do this "putting out" are identified as "the Pharisees," or simply "the Jews," an expression that usually refers to specific religious authorities in the days of the Gospel's writer. The Gospel of John bristles with hostile statements about "the Jews," which readers today must be careful to understand not as condemnations of Judaism but as the hazardous expression of a first-century religious controversy.

Traditionally this Gospel's author has been identified as John the apostle, the son of Zebedee. However, the Gospel itself speaks of an anonymous "disciple whom Jesus loved" as responsible for its writing (21:24); and even this may refer simply to someone responsible for the Gospel's formation, or even to a purely symbolic figure. Both ancient tradition and modern scholarship generally hold that John was the last of the NT Gospels to be written; it may date to the year 90 or so.

COMMENTARY

Prologue (1:1–18)

The prologue to John introduces the Gospel's basic theme and some of its usual terminology, but it also contains an emphasis found only here, the Greek term usually translated "Word" (*logos*). This term had a range of meaning covering aspects of intelligence as well as verbal expressions of intelligence, and it had acquired a specific use among philosophers to refer to the divine intelligence or wisdom that gives order to the world. In some Jewish philosophies, the Word in this sense was identified with God's Wisdom as the agent through whom God created the universe (cf. Prov. 8:22–31; Sir. 24:1–12; Wis. 7:22–8:1). Since John begins by echoing the first verse of Genesis, then speaks of the Word as that through which all things came into being, this usage of "Word" is surely in view here. The prologue makes two basic statements: the Word was the divine agent in the creation of the world, and this Word "became flesh."

Christians may be more likely to think of Jesus as our redeemer and teacher than as creator of the world. Our reflections take on a new dimension, however, when we recall that "all things came into being" through the Word, the one whom we also embrace as teacher and redeemer. If we regard Jesus' divinity as a mere doctrinal truth or piece of theological obscurity, opening ourselves to this cosmic claim about him may renew our sense of the mystery at the heart of Christian faith. This mystery is expressed here in the paradoxical statement that "the Word was with God, and the Word was God." Rather than trying to reconcile these opposing assertions of coexistence and identity, the author seems to invite readers to live with them, to ponder and explore them.

We encounter mystery again when the prologue speaks of the incarnation. The Word through whom God created the world has made a special entrance into the world, something different from its constant life- and light-giving presence. This entrance is called "becoming flesh," a statement so radical as to be almost incomprehensible, given the dualistic background that the prologue presupposes. In that dualism, the Word, divine reason, was simply incompatible with flesh, human weakness and desire. To speak of the Word becoming flesh was genuinely revolutionary, in a way that has become difficult to imagine for us who hear this phrase as a regular part of Christian tradition.

The theological claim that the Word became flesh—ultimately to be crucified—bears with it an image of social transformation as well. In antiquity, spirit and intellect were associated with free males of the governing classes, while matter and flesh were associated with the lower classes, slaves, and women. In this system the spiritual must not descend to intermingle with the physical any more than the inferior may rise up to challenge the superior. To see the glory of the Word in the flesh of Jesus implied a rejection of hierarchy, a rejection portrayed elsewhere in John when, for example, an ignorant beggar instructs the learned authorities (9:24–34).

In one further paradox, John adds that the Word's own creation failed to recognize it. Not the entire creation, though: "He came to *what* was his own, and his own *people* did not accept him" (1:11, italics added). Human beings, and no other creatures, failed to know their creator. It is this double paradox, the Word made flesh and then recognized only by a few, that the rest of the Gospel will portray in relentless detail. Ultimately, human rejection of the offer of divine life will lead to a third paradox, that the gift of life is made through the death of the life-giver.

The Forerunner and the First Disciples (1:19–51)

John differs from the other Gospels in having Jesus call his first disciples from among the followers of John the Baptist. These first disciples come to a progressively higher recognition of Jesus as they associate with him and follow him. They first address him as "Rabbi," then recognize him as Messiah, and finally as Son of God. This pattern is found elsewhere in John (in chaps. 4 and 9, for example), and suggests that the Gospel's readers are also expected to deepen their understanding of Jesus' identity as they deepen their acquaintance with him.

As Lamb of God, Jesus "takes away the sin of the world." Lambs were not used as sin offerings (but see the comments on Jesus as Passover lamb in the crucifixion, at 19:16–42). Jesus confronts the world's sin of rejecting its Creator by entering the world and presenting it with a new possibility of accepting the Creator's gift of life (see also 3:16–21). As Son of Man, Jesus promises that his disciples "will see heaven opened and the angels of God ascending and descending" (cf. Gen. 28:12). "Son of Man" thus does not refer to Jesus' humanity in John, but is another of his divine titles, used in relation both to his heavenly origin (3:13; 6:27, 62) and to his redemptive suffering (3:14; 8:28; 12:23, 34; 13:31).

The First Sign in Cana (2:1–12)

The Gospel of John calls Jesus' miracles "signs," and the first two are numbered (2:11; 4:54), suggesting to many scholars that the seven miracle stories in John 2–20 derive from a "signs source." In any case, miracles are treated not simply as wondrous deeds but as pointers to Jesus' identity and so to belief in him (see 6:30; 7:31; 12:37). Jesus' disciples believe as a result of this first sign, but he sometimes seems skeptical about such faith (2:23–25; 4:48; see the comments there). The few miracles John relates are almost all distinctively *life-giving* acts. These signs point to Jesus' relation to God, and so also point to God's own character as compassionate giver of life.

Besides his mother and his disciples, only the servants, those lowest on the social scale at the wedding, know what Jesus has done. That the water jars were meant for Jewish purification rites perhaps symbolized, for the Gospel's Jewish Christian first readers, that the loss of their Jewish roots did not leave them without access to life from God, but that Jesus offers divine life abundantly, that God has "kept the good wine until now." Jesus seems reluctant to act, even at his mother's urging (2:4), before the "hour" of his glorification, that is, his death and resurrection (see 7:30; 8:20; 12:23, 27; 13:1; 17:1). Yet he does act, and so reveals his glory already. Thus Jesus' glory, his identity as divine life-giver, is disclosed here in his powerful provision of sustenance and subsequently in his shameful crucifixion.

The Action in the Temple (2:13–22)

John differs dramatically from the other NT Gospels in placing Jesus' action in the temple near the beginning of his mission instead of just before his death. In this way the conflict between Jesus and the religious authorities begins just after he first reveals his glory (2:11), establishing both the dominance of the crucifixion motif in John and the connection between Jesus' crucifixion and his glorification. The writer overtly links this story to Jesus' death with the reference to the destruction and resurrection of "the temple of his body." This is the first of a number of instances in which other characters in the story fail to understand Jesus' words, but the readers are given the clue (or assumed to have it already). This superior knowledge shared by the readers, the narrator, and Jesus creates the irony so typical of John. Irony is essential to John's conception of the divine revelation in Jesus, for "he was in the world, and the world came into being through him; yet the world did not know him" (1:10).

Nicodemus, John the Baptist, and Jesus (John 3)

The use of the plural pronouns "you" and "we" (3:2, 7b, 11–12), intermingled with the singular "you" and "I," suggests that this dialogue between two individuals represents a conversation between two groups or communities: the Johannine Christians represented by Jesus, and Christians hoping to stay within the synagogue represented by Nicodemus. Nicodemus is presented as a Jewish religious authority who believes that Jesus is a teacher from God because of his signs—just the kind of faith Jesus does not trust in 2:23–25. In later appearances (7:45–52; 19:38–42) Nicodemus seems to be on Jesus' side, but never with complete openness. His covert faith resembles that of other highly placed people unwilling to risk the social stigma of open confession (see 12:42). The Gospel's writer may have hoped to encourage such Christians to grow into full belief.

Those who would believe in Jesus must recognize his heavenly origin and be willing to acknowledge him publicly, even at the risk of expulsion from the synagogue (9:22; 12:42; 16:2). There is a connection here among theology, spirituality, and communal identity. To be "born from above," to choose light over darkness, means not only personal faith but confessing the Son of God openly in company with other believers, despite their marginal status. The Nicodemus Christians prefer maintaining their social position over the downward mobility of new birth. Being "born of water" refers to baptism, the mark of membership in the believing community, the boundary line between those outside the community and those who have "come to the light." As the mark of being "born of the Spirit," baptism symbolizes both a new communal identity and an inner transformation given by God. To be "born from above" is to accept this transformation, and so to begin a new life in every respect, individual and collective, spiritual and social. To reject this new birth is to align oneself with deeds of evil and oppression rather than with acts of love and of justice toward the marginalized.

The concluding dialogue of John the Baptist continues the same themes, using much of the same language. This time it is followers of the Baptist (who continued as a separate group after Christianity had begun) who are encouraged to be born not only of water, through the Baptist's ministry, but of the Spirit, which only Jesus can give (1:32–34). Together, the two dialogues present the need for full belief in Jesus as more than a teacher like Nicodemus or a prophet like John the Baptist. His gift of eternal life is received by those who acknowledge that he has indeed come from heaven testifying to what God has given him to speak.

The Samaritan Woman (4:1–42)

After the failure of (male) religious insiders to grasp Jesus' identity and the gift that he brings, someone unexpected—an outsider, a woman—recognizes him, receives his gift, and presents him to others. By NT times Jews and Samaritans had developed a deep mutual hostility, though both groups (descended from the ancient Judeans and Israelites) claimed the same ancestry and worshiped the same God. Now Jesus, though he declares that "salvation is from the Jews" (since he, the Savior, is Jewish), abandons the Jewish claim to the superiority of Jerusalem over "this mountain" (Gerizim; see Deut. 11:26–30; 27:12–13; Josh. 8:33–35).

Jesus' dialogue with the woman begins like many others in John, in that she at first fails to understand the deeper meaning of what he says. But unlike many, she progresses to an ever deeper realization of Jesus' identity (cf. 1:19–51): a Jew, a prophet, Messiah. Jesus' invitation to call her husband is the turning point; it brings to mind other scenes where men and women meet at a well, resulting in a marriage (Gen. 24:10–61; 29:1–20; Exod. 2:15–21). Thus she represents the bride of John 3:29, and the focus is not on her multiple husbands (which may reflect a status more as victim than as sinner) but on her insight that draws her to Jesus.

Worship that unites Jews and Samaritans is in spirit and truth (and Jesus is

Truth, 14:6). Creating this new worshiping community is the work from God that is Jesus' food. But it will be his followers who complete it, gathering a harvest prepared by the labor of others—in this case, perhaps the Samaritans' own religious leaders. This validation of Samaritan religion alongside Judaism as a basis for Christian faith is a further radical departure from traditional taboos. Correspondingly, when the Samaritan villagers build on the woman's apostolate by encountering Jesus for themselves (always essential for John), they offer him the highest title in the Gospel so far: Savior of the world.

The Royal Official's Son (4:43–54)

The story of Jesus' second sign (see on 2:1–12) raises the question how signs relate to faith. As in 2:23–3:3, Jesus seems dubious about faith based on seeing signs. Perhaps in response, the royal official believes Jesus' word without yet having seen anything. Yet it is only when the miracle has happened that he is said to *believe*, that is, to believe fully in Jesus. There seems to be a concession to or even a positive evaluation of the human need to see some evidence that God is present and acting. Certainly those who see and fail to believe are considered remiss (6:36; 12:37); yet John seems inclined to place the highest value on those who believe without having seen (20:25–29).

The Sabbath Healing at Bethzatha (John 5)

Jesus' first two signs had only brief dialogues attached to them. Most of the rest are accompanied by more substantial discourses, which unfold the meaning of the signs. Here Jesus' healing of a disabled man, giving him new life, is interpreted by a discourse concerning Jesus as giver of eternal life, attested by his deeds and by Scripture.

John 5:6–7 does not criticize the disabled man for not taking the initiative to be healed. He is sick, poor, and friendless—truly marginalized. Now, however, he finds healing not in the water but in one who sees his need and meets it immediately. He does not have to wait and get into the pool, just as those who believe in Jesus receive eternal life now, without awaiting the final judgment (5:24). This reflects the realized eschatology of this Gospel, the way in which the blessings of the last days are already made real in Jesus: the Messiah, resurrection, judgment, eternal life, restored social relations (see also 11:25–26; 13:34). Jesus' words to the healed man in 5:14 need not imply that his illness was the result of sin. They do suggest that those who receive new life must also accept a transformed life*style*.

The healing is both an example and a symbol of how Jesus does the works of the Father: he gives life in this world, and gives eternal life to those who believe. In this way he reveals God, showing who God is by showing what God does. How this makes him "equal to God" is explored in the discourse. He is not independent of God as a second deity. He does not come to reveal himself or to glorify himself, but comes in God's name to do God's work and so to make God known, remaining obedient to God and dependent on God; and in all this he is God's Son. Yet precisely in this role he must have the same honor as God, so that God may be rightly honored. Ultimately, though, "equal to God" is not John's way of thinking about Jesus; instead we read that Jesus is one with God and is in God as God is in him (John 10:30, 38; 14:10, 20; 17:11, 21–23).

Belief in Jesus can be sparked by various witnesses—John the Baptist, the Scriptures—but especially through God's witness, the works of God that Jesus does. In these works God testifies to Jesus' identity as the Son. God, who cannot be seen or heard (5:37; also 1:18; 6:46), "appears" in the works of Jesus (14:7–11). Those who miss this testimony also miss the testimony of Scripture. To be occupied with Scripture as an end in itself, expecting to find life there, while failing to come into relationship with the Giver of life, is to miss the point of Scripture.

Feeding the Five Thousand, Walking on the Sea, and the Bread of Life (John 6)

The feeding of the multitude is the only miracle story found in all four Gospels. In all of them it shows signs of connection with the Eucharist. In John this is brought out by Jesus' giving thanks (Gk. *eucharisteō*), by the references to Passover and manna, and especially by the startling allusion to eating Jesus' flesh and drinking his blood.

Jesus is presented here as the generous provider of life. In contrast to the other Gospels, he feeds the crowd himself. He incorporates earlier figures, events, and signs of divine deliverance and life-giving: Moses, Passover, manna, Elisha (the barley loaves echo 2 Kgs. 4:42–44; also compare the walking on the sea with Ps. 107:23–31). The feeding miracle also represents the messianic banquet, a symbol of the abundance of God's reign in the last days. The people whom Jesus has fed come looking for him because of this sign; but they fail to understand its full meaning. In the discourse that unfolds this meaning, Jesus points them toward eternal life as the true gift of God, and himself as the true bread. Like the manna, he directs attention away from material supplies to God on whom all life depends (see Deut. 8:3); and John 6:33–35 declares that the divine power (the Word) that constantly brings life from God into the world is now uniquely focused in Jesus.

The life that is in Jesus is imparted to "everything that the Father gives" to him, that is, to "all who see the Son and believe in him." There is a dialectic between human and divine choice here (see also 10:27–29; 12:37–41; 17:6–12). God has given and drawn people to Jesus, and yet they must come and see, hear and learn, believe. From the believers' point of view, there is a real decision to believe in the one whom God sends even though he comes in an unexpected way. In the Gospel's historical context this question of divine and human responsibility arose not as a philosophical abstraction but as a reflection on why some do not believe.

For the Johannine Jewish Christians, separated from the synagogue and its holy days, Jesus replaces the Passover bread with something better, the Bread of life; eating the living bread symbolizes believing in Jesus. But the shocking statements about eating his flesh and drinking his blood present the Eucharist also as new bread for Christians. This "flesh" and "blood" gives life because it is Jesus' flesh, the flesh that is the Word, in whom life came into existence (1:3–4, 14). What is called for is to "eat" Jesus, to appropriate his giving of life by faith. To eat the Eucharist without believing that Jesus is the life-giver would not bring life. It is the word of Jesus, the message of faith in him, that is spirit and eternal life, not the "flesh" of the eucharistic elements themselves.

The Eucharist symbolizes open adherence to the community's claim that Jesus is the source of life and so (as with baptism in chap. 3) helps to define the Christian community and mark its distinction from the world. Although the Gospel writer has placed the eucharistic discussion here rather than at the Last Supper, he has signaled the connection between the two by using language that occurs again in the discourses that are unique to his Last Supper narrative (cf. 6:56–57 with 14:19–20; 15:4–10; 17:18, 21–23). Solidarity with Jesus, abiding in him, is closely connected there to solidarity within the community, loving one another.

Divisions in Jerusalem (7:1–52)

After John 6 Jesus never returns to Galilee, but remains in Jerusalem and elsewhere in the south. The Festival of Booths (Sukkot), with its rituals of water and light (see Zech. 14:7–8, 16), forms the background at least through chap. 9. Throughout chaps. 7 and 8 there is a continuous process of decision about Jesus, separating those who accept him from those who do not, with criticism even of some who believe. Jesus makes increasingly stark assertions that provoke sharp divisions among the people and increasingly hostile and violent responses from the authorities. Their attempts fail "because his hour had not yet come": Jesus' death can happen only as God wills it; but the thought of it is frequent from John 5 onward.

In chap. 7 various groups make comments about Jesus and about one another: the crowd, the people of Jerusalem, the authorities, the chief priests, the Pharisees, and "the Jews." Given that *everyone* here is Jewish, we are reminded that "the Jews" in John does not refer to the entire people but probably to religious authorities. However some of these groups may be related to one another, only some of the "crowd" comes to believe in Jesus, and in the end they are condemned by the Pharisees. Faith is thus associated with the margins of society rather than with its central powers.

"Anyone who is without sin" (7:53–8:11)

Manuscript and other evidence makes clear that this short passage was not originally part of John, but was an isolated tradition that still circulated orally after the Gospels were written. Fortunately, copyists kept it from being lost by inserting it at various points in John and Luke; this location in John was the most popular of these points, even though it interrupts the flow of John 7–8. Its picture of Jesus compassionately defending someone unfairly singled out as if she alone had sinned remains a valuable contribution to our understanding of his way of lovingly restoring people to fellowship with God.

The Light of the World and Those Who Fail to Believe (8:12–59)

Jesus' declaration that he is the light of the world and offers his followers the light of life (see 1:3–4) provokes a debate over proper testimony and Jesus' origin and destination, which only underscores the ignorance of his opponents about all these things—implying also their ignorance of God, who is his origin, destination, and witness (cf. 5:30–39). Unwittingly, how-

ever, they correctly identify his fate as a self-empowered (though not self-inflicted) death (see 10:17–18). His even bolder assertion "I am he" leaves them mystified, since this is a direct reference to the God they do not know. Isaiah 43:10–11, 25; 52:6, along with Exod. 3:14 and other texts, provide the basis for the use of "I am (he)" as a name of God. Jesus has already employed it (John 4:26; "it is I" renders the same Greek in 6:20), and he will do so even more dramatically at the end of this chapter: "before Abraham was, I am" (see also 13:19; 18:5–8). John qualifies even this claim to divine identity, however: God is indeed completely present with Jesus and completely revealed in him, because Jesus is completely *obedient* to God. The ultimate act of obedience, and so the ultimate revelation of divine presence, will come when Jesus is "lifted up," that is, raised on the cross and so, in the deepest of all ironies, exalted back up to God by this most degrading form of death (see also 3:14; 12:32–34).

Jesus' words in 8:28–29 do at last bring some to belief; yet surprisingly Jesus disputes with them even more bitterly than he has with those who oppose him. The reason seems to be that they do not really accept his word, do not admit their need for him to free them; they want to claim ancestral religious privilege without acknowledging that their ancestry also included oppression from which God had liberated them. Jesus offers to free them through knowledge of the truth; this statement has nothing to do with information but refers to *Jesus* as Truth (see 14:6), the reality of God that undergirds all things and is revealed in him.

Rather than doing what Abraham did, responding to God's unexpected calling and leaving his former world behind (Gen. 12:1–4), the would-be believers want to remain on their current ground. Perhaps they stand for Christians whom the Gospel's writer considers halfhearted. In response, he puts on Jesus' lips a terrible denunciation of them as children not of God but of the devil. We may be able to understand this as the result of heated debate about deeply held convictions in an environment where harsh polemic was permissible. But we can hardly accept its demonizing of the enemy as a model for Christian dialogue. The later effect of this text, when Christians came to power and could base anti-Jewish theologies and practices on it, shows that even when spoken from the underside such dehumanizing language inevitably exacts a price from its users and its objects.

The Light of the World and Those Who Believe (John 9)

The repetition of Jesus' claim to be the light of the world connects this miracle story to 8:12, which suggests that the discourse interpreting the sign includes not only the dialogues of chap. 9 but also those of chap. 8. There no one seemed to believe successfully in Jesus. Here the blind man not only believes but defends his belief against Jesus' opponents. Like the Samaritan woman in chap. 4, he comes to full recognition of Jesus' identity only gradually. He does so in the process of confrontation with those who would deny the divine origin of his healer and his healing. In this confrontation he takes the place of Jesus (who is absent from the story for a long period) and also represents the believing community, exemplifying tenacious assertion of Christian belief. Against the learning of the authorities he can set only his own experience of what God has done for him: "One thing I do know, that though I was blind, now I see." The blind man locates God in active mercy, not in faithfulness to tradition. He represents those who are willing to "be taught by God" (6:45), to drop their presuppositions and let God be God, however unanticipated the result.

The question the disciples posed, "Who sinned?" is implied in different ways throughout the chapter. Was it the blind man, his parents, Jesus himself? Jesus refuses to associate suffering with sin. In the end, Jesus attaches sin to the Pharisees. Neither the sufferer nor the

Sabbath breaker but those at the center of religious tradition and authority are exposed in sin as Jesus gives sight to the blind and blinds those who think they see.

This story offers a profound challenge to people who find their strength in religious tradition. It suggests that it may not be the things that we have long heard and held onto that are the markers of divine presence, but new experiences consonant with God's power, justice, compassion, and love. It may not be those with the accepted credentials of knowledge and authority who recognize what God is doing, but people considered "blind." God may even be at work in someone who seems to be sinning. And one may need to be willing to stand up for such new things under prolonged duress in order to come to the deepest understanding of who Jesus is. It is the blind who see: this is wonderful grace, but also a serious problem for the sighted.

The Good Shepherd (John 10)

The transition from chap. 9 to chap. 10 is abrupt; Jesus is apparently still speaking to the Pharisees. The comments about strangers, thieves, bandits, and hired hands, then, may be partly aimed at them, as well as at other Jewish leaders known to the Gospel writer (including violent revolutionaries, perhaps represented by the bandits). Jesus is presented as an alternative to these leaders.

This chapter begins with the closest thing to a parable in John. The "parable" is then interpreted by a symbolic identification of Jesus with two of its elements, the gate and the shepherd. Both of these are images of safety, protection, and reliability, but the result is oddly inconsistent: Jesus is both that by which the sheep go in and out and the one who leads them in and out, both the means of access to safety or salvation and the guide to this means. This resonates at a deep level with John's presentation of Jesus as both the revealer and the one revealed. As shepherd, he leads the sheep through no other gate to salvation than himself.

He also assures his sheep's safety by giving up his own life, something that he is uniquely empowered to do (cf. 8:22; 18:4–8; 19:28–30). As in chaps. 5 and 8, John emphasizes Jesus' obedience to God, an obedience that is part of his intimate relationship with God as Son to Father. There is a similarly intimate relationship between sheep and shepherd, a loving knowledge of one another that is deep and lasting, and likewise leads to the obedience of following. (Such paralleling of relationships is typical of this Gospel; see 6:57; 15:9; 17:18; 20:21.)

The shepherd imagery is drawn from the Jewish Scriptures. Both Jer. 23:1–6 and Ezek. 34:1–24 present a denunciation of bad shepherds, God's promise to be shepherd, and the coming Davidic king as good shepherd. John identifies Jesus as the fulfillment of these promises, both as king and as God tending the flock (see 10:30, 38). In the Gospel's historical context, this would bolster the community members' willingness to follow Jesus (to whom, indeed, God has given them) rather than other Jewish leaders and movements. More broadly, it is a reminder that God's people are always at risk from self-serving leaders, and that Christian leadership (symbolized by shepherding in 21:15–17; see also Acts 20:28; 1 Pet. 5:1–4) must constantly renew itself by taking the self-sacrifice of the Good Shepherd as its model.

The Raising of Lazarus (John 11)

This story presents a number of difficult puzzles. Why does Jesus wait two days, until it is too late to heal Lazarus? What does it mean when he says that those who believe in him will live even if they die, but also that everyone who lives and believes in him will never die? How can Lazarus come out of the tomb with his head, hands, and feet still wrapped up? These and other difficulties remind us that this account of restoring the dead to life offers us a *mystery*, a glimpse into that which is beyond our everyday understanding.

The puzzles noted above have no easy solutions. For instance, the Greek text, often obscured in English translations, suggests that Jesus delayed going to Lazarus *because* he loved him. We should resist the temptation to rationalize this or simplify it. Hard as it is, the text may reflect circumstances familiar to the Gospel's first readers—and to us. We know of Jesus' love, yet find ourselves dying. Jesus' absence is real for believers, and he does not rebuke the sisters for their grief. The story offers hope that Jesus' love and power are such that "though we die, we will live," and encourages faith in him even when he seems absent and unwilling to help. If Lazarus's illness is for God's glory and the glorification of God's Son, we must remember that Jesus' glorification comes through his crucifixion (7:39; 12:23–25; 13:31–32; 17:1). This glory can be seen only through faith (11:40), and so it is that Jesus can be glad that his absence will lead to such believing (v. 15).

If Jesus' male disciples fail to understand his actions and words, Lazarus's sisters seem to do better. They both say the same thing to Jesus; he responds to Martha in words and to Mary with action, John's familiar coordination of discourse and sign. The little discourse is one of the puzzles of this story. Jesus' words seem logically indecipherable, and his "Do you believe this?" almost a challenge. But Martha does not try to sort out the logic or formulate correct doctrine about life, death, and resurrection. Instead she confesses her faith in Jesus himself. The mystery is not supposed to be resolved but to be inhabited in faith. Belief is not the end of confusion, but is to be exercised *through* all the confusions.

We may distinguish between the physical death that all must experience and the spiritual death that believers escape; or between Jesus as resurrection, assuring believers that they will live after death, and as life, assuring them that they will never die. We should certainly note that Jesus creates a new world here, where death is not abolished but overcome and given new meaning. Moreover, as "resurrection" he draws the end of all things into the present moment (since he is the Messiah, the bringer of eschatological redemption); and as "life" he places himself at the ultimate beginning and draws it also into the present (since he is the Word in whom life came into being; see 1:3–4). But Martha's response remains the best—faith not in a doctrinal explanation or philosophical affirmation but in Jesus himself.

The raising of Lazarus enacts Jesus' words in 5:25, 28–29. That he emerges still in his grave wrappings keeps us on the level of paradox and encourages us to look beyond physical miracle to deep mystery. Jesus' opponents, aware only of the miracle, begin setting the final mystery in motion by plotting his death.

The Anointing at Bethany (12:1–8)

The author makes the transition from Jesus' public ministry to his passion, and uses a series of concluding incidents to facilitate this. John gives added point to the anointing story, found in other Gospels as well, by locating it at the house of Mary, Martha, and Lazarus. It is Mary who anoints Jesus, as if in gratitude for the raising of her brother. This connection makes the reference to Jesus' coming burial even more poignant, highlighting the giving of his life for Lazarus's as the plotting against both of them intensifies.

The Triumphal Entry (12:9–19)

The continuing references to Lazarus likewise give deeper resonance to this story, common to all the NT Gospels. Jesus' "triumph" as royal Messiah is set in a context of growing hostility from the authorities and acclaim from crowds who are coming to a belief that is still untested. Jesus' disciples are present, but the Gospel writer says candidly that they did not reach understanding or see a fulfillment of Scripture here until after his glorification—that is, his crucifixion, resurrection, and ascension.

Jesus Anticipates His Glorification (12:20–36)

A final incident now allows Jesus, in his last public discourse, to speak of this coming glorification. The interest of non-Jews in Jesus indicates that "the hour has come" to give his flesh for the life of the *world* (6:51). In words similar to Mark 8:34–35 and Matt. 10:39, Jesus links his destiny to that of his followers: if we wish to be with Jesus, we must be with him everywhere, including the cross. Then, in language that the other Gospels associate with the agony in Gethsemane (John uses the garden scene for other purposes), Jesus considers but immediately rejects evading the purpose of the "hour." His purpose remains God's glory, which will be achieved when he is "lifted up"—on the cross—and draws everyone to himself. John 6:44 seems to limit the number of those who will be drawn to Jesus, but here the scope is universal. After a final invitation to the light (see 8:12; 9:4–5; 11:9–10), Jesus puzzlingly goes into hiding. There are moments of opportunity for faith, and we must not miss them.

Concluding Summary of Jesus' Public Ministry (12:37–50)

Quotations from Isa. 53:1 and 6:10 provide a theological framework for understanding why some do not believe in Jesus, a framework also seen in John's references to those whom God gives or draws to Jesus (6:36–40, 44–45, 65; 10:27–29; 17:2, 6). Failure or refusal to believe lies beyond simple human difference or stubbornness for John; it too is mystery, and has its roots in the will of God. Yet it involves human will also, including the desire for honor ("glory"), a primary value in ancient society. The Gospel writer sees unwillingness to risk dishonor as a chief reason why highly placed people refuse to make their belief public; and he considers a private, unacknowledged belief as little better than no belief. The closing sentences summarize the nature, purpose, and effect of Jesus' coming: his transparency to God and his mission of light and salvation, which nevertheless results in judgment for those who reject it, since the word they reject is the word of God, whom Jesus perfectly reveals by his perfect obedience.

The Footwashing at the Last Supper (13:1–30)

The solemn opening of this section signals the beginning of the passion narrative. Jesus knows that the "hour" of his death has come, knows where he is going, and is in control of the events. John has no Lord's Supper at the Last Supper, no institution of the Eucharist (see instead 6:52–58). Instead we find the symbolic narrative of Jesus washing his disciples' feet. This action is interpreted by the dialogues that follow, in two directions: first as a symbol of Jesus' sacrificial service, and then as a model to imitate. The footwashing symbolizes Jesus' death on behalf of his followers. Jesus' surrender of dignity in this act may seem insignificant to us, but in that culture a man's honor was his life. Hence the act of humble service is an appropriate symbol for the life-renouncing and life-giving service that Jesus undertakes for those who believe in him, and which believers are to imitate toward one another. The sense of Jesus' obscure exchange with Peter seems to be that, however incongruous it might seem for the Son of God to serve others, this service, and only this service, is the essential requirement for them to "share" with him. The second dialogue is more straightforward, but no less challenging: as he has served them, so they must serve each other, without claims of superiority.

Introduction to the Farewell Discourses (13:31–38)

After the departure of Judas and the note that "it was night," Jesus begins a series of dialogues with his disciples that are unique to this Gospel, and partially resemble the "testament" genre of deathbed instructions. The closure implied in 14:30–31 leads many scholars to suggest that chaps. 15–17 were added in a second edition of the Gospel.

The Farewell Discourses concern the disciples' lives after Jesus' departure, and they express the results of the Word having become flesh to bring life to the world, having suffered rejection, and through that rejection having completed his life-giving work and returned to God. Jesus is going where his disciples cannot yet come. Only later, when he has prepared the way by his sacrifice and when they themselves are willing to walk in that way and lay down their lives, will they follow (cf. 21:18–19). Jesus' commandment to them is what they will need for that walk: to love one another as he has loved them (see 13:1; 15:12–17). It is a "new" commandment (despite its roots in Lev. 19:18) because it is the commandment that characterizes the new age inaugurated by the Messiah Jesus. It is notable, though, that the commandment here is for believers to "love *one another*," in contrast to the commandments to love one's neighbor and even one's enemies (Mark 12:28–34; Luke 6:27–29). This is congruent with the Johannine community's more sectarian, inward-turning response to their persecution. Yet even in this limited way, the commandment to love as Jesus loved, if it were carried out, would be a revolutionary witness to the reality of his messianic work. To be known as his disciples in this way is what led the early church to follow where he had gone—to the cross.

The First Farewell Discourse: Jesus' Departure and Return (John 14)

This discourse explores what it means for Jesus to go away and come again. His return is understood in several ways. Most obviously, v. 3 suggests Jesus' second coming at the end of time. In a sense, though, Jesus returns in the ongoing lives of the disciples themselves, who do his works and more. His return is, in another sense, his resurrection, and in yet another, the coming of the Holy Spirit to the disciples, carrying on Jesus' work of presence and teaching. John sees Jesus' going away to God (his crucifixion and ascension) and his return (his resurrection, gift of the Spirit, and second coming) as a single event, and the discourse elaborates on this event.

In the opening thematic statements, Jesus' departure, his crucifixion, *is* his preparation of a dwelling place for his disciples in God's house (heaven, the heavenly temple, or simply God's presence). Jesus' dialogue with Thomas and Philip explains how he is the way to this place. He is Truth (1:14, 17; 4:23–24; 8:31–32; 17:17–19; 18:37) and Life (11:22–26). He is the way to God, and his way is the way of the cross, which is also the way that his followers must take (12:24–26; 13:31–38). The exclusive formulation in 14:6, which many today find troubling, is a forceful reply to the forceful rejection of the community's belief in Jesus. It could be (re)interpreted to mean that the Word, the Truth, incarnate in Jesus, is indeed the divine way by which all travelers reach God, whatever their particular paths. Only his way of suffering love truly reveals God and the way that people who seek God must take. That Jesus' disciples will do even greater works than his implies that they will make God even more widely known in this same way. They pray confidently in his name (cf. 15:7, 16; 16:23–27; and Matt. 7:7–11), and their prayers continue to reveal God; but to pray in the name of the crucified Revealer must surely affect what they pray for!

The parallels between what is said about the Spirit in John 14:15–17 and about Jesus in vv. 19–21 suggest that the coming of the Spirit is seen as one manner in which Jesus comes again. "Paraclete" is used as a title for the Holy Spirit only in John (vv. 16, 26; 15:26; 16:7; see also 1 John 2:1). It means a "helper" in a variety of senses, most significantly as an advocate, sponsor, or intercessor with powerful figures in court. Like Jesus, the Advocate sets believers apart from the world and brings them divine presence.

The return of Jesus himself in 14:18–24 seems no longer to mean his second coming but an intimate divine abiding with his followers. As believers exercise their discipleship by keeping Jesus' commandments and maintaining his revelation of God, they enjoy divine presence now, and this presence of the risen, living Jesus is the source of their life. In this way Jesus' resurrection, gift of the Spirit, and return are seen under a single aspect.

The identification of the Spirit with the return of Jesus means that Jesus' role as teacher can continue in a new way. The Spirit will not only recall Jesus' words but will give new teaching, beyond what Jesus said (so also 16:12–15). There are Christian beliefs (including much in this Gospel itself) that are not part of Jesus' own teaching, and the Gospel claims that these beliefs also are God-given and valid (cf. v. 12).

The Second Farewell Discourse: Abiding and Bearing Fruit (15:1–17)

In the Hebrew Bible the vine is used as a symbol of God's people Israel (Ps. 80:8–16; Isa. 5:1–7; 27:2–6; Ezek. 15:1–6; 17:1–10; 19:10–14). As often happens in John, Jesus fulfills and displaces Jewish traditions: the identity and hope of Israel are realized in him, and his followers share in this realization. They bear the expected fruit if they "abide" in him, remain faithful to their intimate believing relationship with him and to his way of love. They may have to endure "pruning" or "cleansing" (as the Johannine community suffered persecution), which is necessary for remaining fruitful; but those who do not abide (in the confession of Jesus as the Word made flesh) are cut off altogether.

"Bearing fruit" symbolizes several things, notably answered prayer and discipleship, particularly works of love (cf. 13:34–35; 14:12–14), and perhaps also successful evangelism. As in 13:20; 15:18–25; 17:18; 20:21, the relationship between Jesus and his disciples parallels that between God and Jesus; here the focus is on obedience and love. The obedience needed to abide in Jesus' love does not consist of a multitude of duties, but simply of extending Jesus' love to other believers (despite the NRSV translation, vv. 12 and 15 are essentially identical). The result is not mere spiritual job satisfaction but utter joy.

The Third Farewell Discourse: The World's Hatred (15:18–16:4)

Here we are reminded of the context within which John's Jewish Christian community was to abide in their confession of Jesus and their love for one another. Exclusion from the synagogue (see the introduction, and 9:22; 12:42) left them to build a new religious and social world around Jesus and their fellow believers. The sayings here return to themes from 13:12–20 but focus on persecution (similar sayings are also found in Mark 13 and Matt. 10). As the mission of Jesus' followers is a continuation of his own (14:12), so their treatment will be like his. Indeed, John often seems to project the community's experience back into Jesus' lifetime, so that his representation of God's will in works of love, his perseverance, and his isolation from the world become models for their own mission. The deep irony of John is that those who speak for the Creator cannot be sure the human creation will receive them favorably, since they disclose how far from the Creator's love people have strayed. The language of hatred and murder is extreme and may seem exaggerated; but it is a reminder that the witness of Christian love is not always a matter of nice people encouraging other nice people to keep on being nice.

The Fourth Farewell Discourse: Recapitulation (16:4–33)

This section takes up a number of themes from chap. 14, in ways not always consistent with it. After the transitional 16:4, Jesus speaks again of the coming of the Paraclete, the Advocate, who has two roles here, one in relation to the world and one in relation to believers. The exact significance of the former is not very clear. The Advocate is to convince the world it is wrong (or perhaps simply reprove or refute it) about sin (presumably the world's own), righteousness or innocence (apparently that of Jesus), and judgment or condemnation (evidently that of the devil). If this is related to the testimony that both the Spirit and the disciples give (15:26–27), then this work of convincing may be carried out through the words and deeds of believers. In any case the Advocate continues Jesus' work of testifying against the world. With regard to the believers themselves, the Spirit carries on Jesus' work of teaching them and goes beyond it (see the final comments on chap. 14).

Jesus compares the disciples' grief at his absence to labor pains, an agonizing experience that nevertheless ends in the joy of new life. Jesus will return (at his resurrection, in the gift of the Spirit, and/or at his second coming; see the opening comments on chap. 14). Though they are puzzled now, then they will plainly understand what Jesus will plainly say (perhaps through the Spirit). They will pray in his name in the confidence that God (as in 15:16; contrast 14:12–14) will answer them. When the disciples mistake the present moment for that ultimate clarity, they become overconfident of their own belief. Yet in spite of all that they must suffer now, they can live in courage and peace because Jesus— in the very moment of his isolation and crucifixion—has conquered the world that is hostile to God and to them. John's readers, it seems, lived both in the time of confusion and pain during Jesus' absence and in the time of clarity and joy following his return. Surely they were not the last believers to do so.

Jesus' Prayer (John 17)

In this prayer John presents Jesus' wishes for his followers as he prepares to return to God by means of the cross. Despite a few echoes of the Lord's Prayer ("Holy Father, protect them in your name"; "protect them from the evil one"; see also Matt. 11:25–27), it reflects the theology of this Gospel and the community for which it was written. Thus the entire prayer, not just vv. 20–23, is for the church beyond the days of Jesus' immediate disciples, and it looks back on Jesus' work (including his crucifixion and resurrection) as completed.

By making God known, Jesus has made eternal life available to those who believe. He has given to his disciples what God gave him; and he prays that in his absence this revelation will keep them safe and unified in the world that hates them, but into which they are sent as he was.

These disciples were given to him by God, who must now protect them in Jesus' absence. As in 6:36–40, 44–45, 65; 10:27–29; 12:37–41, the answer to the question why only some accepted Jesus as Messiah was that it lay in God's will and gift. "Predestination" (like the believers' "not belonging to the world") arises as an explanation of this mystery. It does not eliminate human responsibility for believing and keeping Jesus' revealing word as a word from God. Such enduring belief separates Jesus' followers from the world that rejects him. Their risk-filled mission parallels Jesus' own (see 13:16–20; 15:18–16:4; 20:21–23). We must be careful about generalizing from such sectarian language; yet such language reminds us that it is the oppressed and marginalized whom God chooses.

Jesus and God share all things in a unity of love, including the believers themselves. Jesus' prayer is that these believers will enjoy a similar unity, not only for their own sake but so that the world may come to believe (cf. 13:34–35). Both the unity and the protection of believers come through the divine name that Jesus has given them (expressed in his own "I am"; see, for instance, 8:24, 28, 58; 13:19; 18:4–8). This name is the presence and being of God, the divine glory and reality, revealed in Jesus as his loving unity with God. This revelation is what his followers have believed, so it is this name, this revelation of divine unity in love, that will protect them and make them one.

The Arrest of Jesus (18:1–11)

After the lengthy discourses and prayers at the Last Supper, the passion narrative unfolds with few of the speeches or symbolic scenes that express John's distinctive theology. One exception is the arrest in the garden. There is no agony here (but see 12:27–28). Jesus has full knowledge and control (see 10:17–18; 13:1, 3; 19:28); he practically has to order the soldiers and temple police to arrest him. The question "Whom are you looking for?" is one that leads to revelations of Jesus (see 1:38; 20:15), and Jesus' self-identification "I am he" is a disclosure of the divine name (see 8:24, 28, 58; 13:19; and cf. 6:20). The theophany overwhelms those who have come to arrest him, and demonstrates that Jesus makes his climactic revelation of God in the hour of his suffering. For this reason he prevents Peter from fighting to defend him (see 18:36).

Jesus' Hearing before the High Priest and Peter's Denial (18:12–27)

In contrast to the other Gospels, John has no formal Jewish trial and condemnation of Jesus, nor any Jewish beating or mockery. Motifs of arrest, testimony, and judgment abound in Jesus' earlier dialogues with Jewish authorities; their verdict against him has already been given (5:16–18, 31–40; 7:19–32, 45–52; 8:13–18; 10:24–39; 11:47–57). The hearing at this point serves simply to showcase Jesus' defiance, perhaps as a model for Christians in similar situations (and in stark contrast to Peter's denial).

Jesus' Trial before Pilate (18:28–19:16)

John places responsibility for Jesus' condemnation to death on the Roman governor Pilate. The trial is carefully arranged into seven scenes, with Pilate alternately addressing the Jewish authorities outside his headquarters and Jesus on the inside. Both theological and political themes are present, suggesting that John sees the two as interwoven. The word "king" occurs twice as often in John's account as in any of the other Gospels, and John seems interested in exploring whether Jesus is indeed the "king of Israel" (1:49; 12:13) and what kind of king he is.

Commentators usually see Pilate as a sympathetic figure, wanting to let Jesus go but unable to overcome the hostility of the Jewish authorities. But most of Pilate's statements read more naturally as sarcastic and sneering than as sincere. He shows no interest in Jesus' mission (not waiting for the answer to his question "What is truth?") or in his innocence. In Roman law a prisoner was flogged only after being sentenced to death (as Jesus is in the other Gospels). By transferring Jesus' flogging to the center of the seven scenes, John shows Pilate as unconcerned about whether Jesus is innocent or guilty. The transfer also allows Pilate to exhibit Jesus twice to the Jewish authorities as a bloodied mock king, ridiculing Jewish sovereignty. The pagan governor is momentarily alarmed that Jesus might be a divine being with access to power "from above" (a power that overrides the authority Pilate imagines he has over Jesus). But on the whole, his interest is (as a Roman official's naturally would be) in getting the occupied people to acknowledge the dominion of the emperor—which he succeeds in doing.

The Jewish authorities try once to interest Pilate in a charge of blasphemy, but when this fails they insist on the political accusation of seeking kingship. The depiction of the humiliated and beaten Jesus as "King of the Jews" horrifies them. This is not the king they desire (they prefer the bandit/revolutionary Barabbas), and they call for the mockery to be done away with. In the end, at the hour when the Passover lambs are being slaughtered (and as if in parody of a Passover hymn that acclaims God alone as Israel's king), they profess no king but the emperor, thus acknowledging their status as a nation without sovereignty.

Neither Pilate nor the Jewish authorities want Jesus to be king, but in John's irony Pilate's pronouncement "Here is your King!" is one of those statements that tells more truth than its speaker is aware (see, for example, 4:12; 11:49–52). Jesus is a king unlike any in this world, whether Caesar or Barabbas: his throne is a cross and his followers refuse to fight. Yet he is a king, and for John's Jewish Christian readers in the years between two uprisings against Rome, Jesus represented not only a new spiritual alternative but a new political one as well. There are no nonpolitical messiahs. The claim that Jesus was Messiah meant that God's long-anticipated redemption had appeared in a radically unanticipated way, a revelation of God in human flesh, bringing healing and life. If God had taken the downward plunge into human life, if the Messiah had given his own life without taking anyone else's, then human politics of hierarchy, oppression, and violence cannot serve God's purposes. The politics of John's Jesus, like his revelation of God, stand the world's values and expectations on their head.

The Crucifixion (19:16–42)

With economy of language, John relates the climax of the revelation of God in Jesus, the Word made flesh. One final exchange between Pilate and the Jewish authorities confirms Jesus' ironic enthronement on the cross as King (see the preceding section). Jesus' clothes, which the soldiers divide, may include the purple robe from 19:1–4, reinforcing the royal theme. Ultimately, however, it is not Pilate but God who has "written" this about Jesus, and John works at showing how the crucifixion of the Messiah, so completely contrary to all expectations, fulfills the Scriptures and therefore is indeed the will of God. (The other Gospels do the same, but John emphasizes Jesus' conscious and deliberate intention.) Thus the division of

Jesus' garments refers to Ps. 22:18. Jesus' thirst, quenched with sour wine, relates to Ps. 69:21, and the piercing of his side to Zech. 12:10. The business about his legs not being broken (a measure meant to hasten death by making it impossible for the victim to push up on his feet so as to breathe) seems to combine references to Exod. 12:10, 46; Num. 9:12; and Ps. 34:20. Even the odd reference to hyssop (a small plant completely unsuited to lifting a wet sponge up to a crucified man) may have in mind Exod. 12:22.

Jesus is thus portrayed as the righteous sufferer depicted in the Psalms, and as the Passover lamb. Consistently with this, John emphasizes that the crucifixion took place on the day of preparation for Passover, when the lambs were slaughtered, not on Passover itself as in the other Gospels. The Passover lamb was not a sin offering, but it was connected with God's saving of the Israelites' lives and with their redemption from slavery (Exod. 12:1–27). According to John 8:31–36, Jesus liberates people from the slavery of sin; perhaps for that reason he is called "the Lamb of God who takes away the sin of the world" (1:29).

The scene in which Jesus entrusts his mother and the disciple whom he loves to each other has inspired many interpretations, none of them certain. Is it simply an act of filial piety? An allegory of synagogue and church? A symbol of the loving relations that Jesus' death makes possible? Some connection with the first sign in Cana, where Jesus' mother and disciples figure (2:1–11), is conceivable.

Jesus' last word from the cross is not simply an expression of finality, much less a groan of despair, but a cry of triumph: the work of God that he came to do has been completed (see 4:34; 17:4). Some exegetes see in this moment Jesus not simply "giving up the ghost" but "handing over the Spirit" to those who believe in him. The text would allow that understanding, and the flow of blood and water from his side might also symbolize the Spirit (cf. 7:37–39), or have a sacra-

mental symbolism, or simply represent the gift of life through Jesus' death. John's symbolic method is flexible enough to include any, all, or none of these. What is certain is that for this Gospel Jesus' death is his glorification, the supreme moment of his revelation of God and the hour of his return to the Father (7:39; 12:16, 23–28; 13:1–3, 31–32; 17:1–5). The paradoxes of John all revolve around this: that the only true God can be seen most clearly in a naked man dying a horrible death at the hands of a cruel superpower for the sake of those he loves.

The crucifixion scene ends with two types of "witness" to Jesus' death. The one whose "testimony is true" is not named, though traditionally understood to be the Beloved Disciple (cf. 21:24). What he attests may be not simply the events themselves but their fulfillment of Scripture. The other witnesses are Joseph of Arimathea and Nicodemus. The latter is mentioned only in John. Here in his third appearance (see 3:1–15; 7:45–52) he seems at last to make an open profession of his allegiance to Jesus; yet he does so only when Jesus is safely dead. The quantity of burial spices he brings, though fit for a king, seems to preclude any future for Jesus. Nicodemus remains an ambiguous sort of believer, and this is accentuated by John's unique note that Joseph was a secret, fearful disciple (see 7:13; 9:20–22; 12:42–43).

The Empty Tomb (20:1–18)

John's resurrection narrative combines materials related to all three of the other Gospels with stories unique to itself, resulting in some awkward transitions. Mary Magdalene is a central figure (though the "we" in v. 2 is a reminder of the other women present in the tradition; see Mark 16:1–8; Matt. 28:1–10), and it is she who first encounters the risen Lord and bears the good news to others, becoming an "apostle to the apostles."

Peter and the disciple whom Jesus loved (who may represent ideal discipleship) are the first to examine the empty tomb (cf. Luke 24:12). The Beloved Disciple "believes," yet his belief is qualified by the remark that the two men still did not understand the Scriptures, and thus has an ambiguous quality. It is certainly unfruitful, as they simply go home without a word and leave Mary weeping at the tomb. For the writer of this Gospel, personal encounter with Jesus is always the ultimate step in coming to belief. Such encounter is superior to any form of testimony, however valuable the latter may be (see 4:39–42; 5:39–40; 9:35–38; 17:20–24). Thus neither the male disciples nor the angels can bring Mary what she needs; it is only her experience of meeting Jesus that does so. By the same token, though she brings the good news back to the disciples, they remain fearful behind closed doors until Jesus comes to them; and Thomas, though given the Easter message, cannot believe until he himself sees Jesus. Similarly, the Beloved Disciple's belief based on seeing the empty tomb remains precarious until he meets the risen Christ.

The encounter between Mary Magdalene and Jesus is among the most vivid and moving scenes in the Bible. Jesus' question "Whom are you looking for?" harks back to the beginning of the passion narrative in 18:4, and to the beginning of the Gospel in 1:38; as in those places, that question leads to a revelation of him. Mary recognizes Jesus only when he calls her by name (cf. 10:3–4, 27), when he reaches out to her deepest identity and draws her to him. She must not cling to him (cf. Matt. 28:9), probably not because of the "untouchability" of his present condition, but because he desires no delay in his ascension or in the mission that Mary is to undertake. She must not linger in devotion but deliver the message, inform his brothers that they *are* his brothers. John has not referred to God as the disciples' Father until now: it is only in the hour of Jesus' glorification (of which his resurrection and ascension are part) that it becomes fitting. This is the

great, glad, and profound meaning of Easter for John, that believers are children of God as Jesus is Son of God, brothers and sisters to the Word made flesh (see also John 1:12–13). Accordingly, though Thomas will soon hail him as "my God," Jesus here makes the disciples' God his God as well.

Jesus Commissions His Disciples (20:19–31)

When Jesus appears at last to the still-frightened disciples (cf. Luke 24:36–40), they receive a mission from him as he had from God (see 17:18–23; and cf. 6:57; 13:20; 15:9–10). It is the same mission, to take away the sin of the world (1:29). Like Jesus, they do not condemn the world, but their message awakens the world's potential for condemning itself by rejecting those whom God sends (3:17–21; 8:21–24; 9:39–41; 12:46–49; 15:22–24). John brings not only Jesus' ascension but the gift of the Holy Spirit into the Easter narrative; for this Gospel it is all one "hour." The Spirit, representing the ongoing presence, testimony, and teaching authority of Jesus (14:15–17, 26; 15:26; 16:7–15), enables Jesus' followers to carry out their mission. Forgiving and retaining sins, therefore, is not a function of an institutional authority vested in the church, but the work of the Holy Spirit bearing witness to Jesus through the mission of his followers in the world.

Jesus' appearance to "doubting" Thomas brings the resurrection narrative to a close. Thomas seems to be chided for needing to see in order to believe (in contrast to the Gospel's readers, who believe without seeing). Yet, as noted above, his encounter with Jesus is part of a pattern throughout John. Perhaps it is his resistance to believing at the testimony of others and not his need for personal encounter that is criticized. In any case his confession of Jesus as Lord and God is a fitting climax to the Gospel.

In what was likely the conclusion to the Gospel's first edition, the writer indicates a purpose: that readers may believe and have life. A one-letter difference between Greek manuscripts leaves it uncertain whether it is that they may "come to believe" or "continue to believe"; the latter has better textual support and seems better suited to the nature of this Gospel. Those who like Nathanael, Martha, and Thomas (1:49; 11:27; 20:28) believe Jesus to be the Messiah and Son of God need sustenance for their faith in a world that questions it constantly. Belief, like eternal life, is not something that is once done and accomplished, but something that *continues*, and in its continuation we *live* our eternal life. The paradoxes and symbols of the Gospel of John are meant to sustain this living, to lead us toward deeper encounter with the crucified and risen Word.

Epilogue (John 21)

The evident finality of John 20:30–31, along with differences in the language and style of chap. 21, lead many scholars to conclude that this is an epilogue, added in a second edition of the Gospel but sharing its general characteristics and outlook (like chaps. 15–17).

In chap. 20, as in Luke 24, all the appearances of Jesus were near Jerusalem; here, as in Mark 16:7 and Matt. 28, we read of an appearance in Galilee. The fishing story (cf. Luke 5:1–11) has an aura of mystery similar to many other stories in John. The scene on the lakeshore is vivid, realistic, and miraculous all at once. This makes it hard to know whether to take it simply at face value (but what is the face value of a story about a man raised from the dead feeding his friends breakfast by a lake?) or seek some symbolic meaning, for instance about Jesus sustaining the believers or sending them "fishing" for people (cf. Mark 1:16–20). That he feeds them with fish and bread echoes the miracle in John 6:1–13, with its accompanying discourse on Jesus as the Bread of life (see the comments there). Many suggestions have been made for a

symbolic interpretation of the number 153 (interestingly, it is the sum of the numbers from one through seventeen); perhaps the large number symbolizes the expansion of the church, but even this is uncertain.

Jesus' dialogue with Peter is no less mysterious (21:15–17). Is there some significance in the use of two different Greek words for "love"? Jesus' first two questions use *agapao*, the standard term for Christian love in the New Testament, while the third question and Peter's three replies use *phileo*, a word sometimes said to represent a lesser type of love, akin to friendship. Is Peter hurt because Jesus asked him three times, or because the third time Jesus used the lesser term? In John the two words are used interchangeably: *phileo* in 11:3 and *agapao* in 11:5; *agapao* in 14:21; 15:9; *phileo* in 5:20; 16:27; *agapao* in 13:23; 19:26; 21:7, 20; and *phileo* in 20:2, so that even here we cannot be sure there is any special meaning in the variation. Peter's threefold profession of his love parallels his threefold denial (18:15–18, 25–27). Now we learn that he will indeed follow where Jesus has gone, which he could not do before (13:36–38)—a shepherd following the Good Shepherd in laying down his life for the sheep (10:11–18), in a death that glorifies God (cf. 12:23–28).

Peter plays a significant role in this Gospel, though somewhat less so than in others, since John's passion and resurrection narratives also feature the "disciple whom Jesus loved," traditionally identified with John the son of Zebedee. The Gospel does not make this identification, however, and the Beloved Disciple might be a symbolic figure standing for ideal discipleship or the community for which the Gospel was written. The narratives at the end of chap. 21 may be meant to encourage this community to acknowledge Peter's leading role, or to contrast Peter's martyrdom with the "abiding" of the Johannine community's leadership, or to defend that leadership in a rivalry with Christians centered on Peter. In any case both figures seem to be honored in this epilogue.

Bibliography

Lee, Dorothy. *Flesh and Glory: Symbol, Gender, and Theology in the Gospel of John*. New York: Crossroad, 2002.

Miranda, José Porfirio. *Being and the Messiah: The Message of St. John*. Translated by John Eagleson. Maryknoll, NY: Orbis, 1977.

O'Day, Gail R. *Revelation in the Fourth Gospel: Narrative Mode and Theological Claim*. Philadelphia: Fortress, 1986.

Rensberger, David. *Johannine Faith and Liberating Community*. Philadelphia: Westminster, 1988.

Smith, D. Moody. *The Theology of the Gospel of John*. New Testament Theology. Cambridge: Cambridge University Press, 1995.

Acts

Matthew L. Skinner

INTRODUCTION

The Acts of the Apostles, the traditional title of this originally untitled and anonymous book, inadequately expresses the book's content and theological message. As a literary summary of a narrative that spans twenty-eight chapters, the title obscures that the full range of Acts is really quite unconcerned with the activities of the twelve apostles. For one thing, only one apostle, Peter, plays a prominent role. The lack of attention given to the remaining eleven is about the only thing that makes them conspicuous. Although Acts occasionally notes the apostles' collective importance, especially in the first half of the book, their specific individual deeds remain shielded from readers. As for Paul, the other human character who receives sustained attention, the narrative regularly refrains from ascribing the title *apostle* to him (the only exceptions are Acts 14:4, 14). Moreover, many additional nonapostles make significant appearances in the narrative's spotlight, creating the impression that the stories of people such as Barnabas or Priscilla are somehow more worthy of notice than those of such virtually invisible apostles as Bartholomew or Matthew.

A theological analysis of the Acts of the Apostles further reveals the book's title to be inadequate, for the story's predominant focus falls upon the God who empowers believers to continue the ministry that bears witness to God's plan of salvation in Christ, not upon any of the people who proclaim Jesus Christ. The actions and words of God's people in Acts consistently point toward God and identify God's involvement in all periods of human history. Acts presents its account of the genesis and expansion of the church as a thoroughly theological story. The deeds and speech of believers stem from and point back toward the God who acts, the God who initiates and guides the adventures of the earliest Christians.

God hardly speaks without intermediaries in Acts, but many authorized representatives (including human beings, angels, Jesus, and the Holy Spirit) consistently speak for God and interpret Jesus' and the church's stories as part of God's plan. Acts emphatically declares the reality and certainty of God's intentions for the world's salvation, but it makes this point in ways that acknowledge subtle and elusive aspects of God's interactions with the world. This is a complex narrative, full of twists, turns, and redirected expectations, resulting in a complex, broad, and multifaceted testimony about God and God's involvement in the work of the church. Such complexity prohibits interpretations that offer either simplistic characterizations of God or reductionistic paradigms that claim to extrapolate normative models for humanity's encounters with God. Acts does not present a template for the church's structure, mission, or leadership in any age. Nevertheless, in characters' varied attempts to discern and respond faithfully to God's initiatives, readers of Acts find a story of God purposefully engaged with the world. In Acts, God fulfills promises insofar as Jesus' followers participate in God's work by offering inspired testimony as divinely empowered witnesses (e.g., Luke 12:11–12; 21:12–15; 24:45–49; Acts 1:8).

Many commentators characterize Acts as a book about journeys, observing that the narrative describes people on the move in a story of crossing borders and entering new terrains. Twists in the plot ferry characters and readers into new and sometimes unexpected locations (geopolitical, ethnic, cultural, and theological locations) in which believers both proclaim and discover the Christian gospel's implications for the world. While individual characters enter and exit the narrative stage with few hints about their origins or ultimate destinations, the principal journey traced in Acts belongs to the word of God, the message of the gospel. The story traces the impact of the word of God on the world once it becomes unleashed through the power of the Holy Spirit beginning in Acts 2. From that point forward, the servants of the word journey to keep pace with the word's movements, responding to God's impulses and proclaiming God's fidelity. Human social networks serve as channels for the word to travel, and through these channels it finds a hearing in all sorts of venues. Not surprisingly, such adventures provoke and encounter risks, for the first generation of Jesus' followers bears witness to Christ even in the face of great opposition. God's involvement in the endeavors of Jesus' followers does not safeguard them from all hardship. The word of God travels difficult routes.

The centrality of God, the efforts of believers to interpret and proclaim theological realities, and the persistent movement of the gospel message into new cultural contexts most deeply shape the book's theological outlook. These themes converge to assert that Acts is first and foremost a story about the ongoing proclamation of the kingdom of God, which was inaugurated by Jesus Christ and confirmed through his resurrection from the dead. Acts tells a story about *the perseverance of the word of God.*

The expression *word of God* (also *word of the Lord*) appears frequently in Acts to denote the message of the gospel of Jesus Christ (e.g., 13:44–49), which extends and delivers salvation to its hearers, and the proclamation of this message. Because this "word" unites and guides people of faith, the expression *word of God* also refers to the society or communities created by the gospel (e.g., 12:24). Continually God, through the work of the Holy Spirit, empowers these communities to proclaim and minister on behalf of the word despite all manner of opposition, setbacks, and challenges that arise as the word journeys across an array of cultural boundaries. Obstacles occasionally take serious tolls on the people who proclaim the message. Sometimes hardships appear to render the word ineffective. But they do not finally derail the word's ability to find an audience. This manner of determined *perseverance* is hardly synonymous with unchecked progress or guaranteed, triumphal enlargement; the word's perseverance reflects the book's conviction that God has an unwavering commitment to enable means of communicating the gospel to the world, despite opposition or rejection. Even when the word does not attract new converts, still it perseveres when Christians are able to function as Christ's witnesses because of the word's capacity to infiltrate any social or cultural context. This perseverance reconfirms that God has vindicated Jesus Christ and that God's plan of salvation is operative.

Authorship, Date, and the Gospel of Luke

Because there is no doubt that the same author is responsible for both the Gospel of Luke and Acts, it has become conventional to use the name *Luke* to indicate the author of each. Neither the Gospel nor Acts, however, includes any mention of who wrote them. Traditions ascribe authorship of Luke–Acts to one of Paul's travel companions, but discrepancies between Paul's story in Acts and the details gleaned from Paul's own letters cast strong doubt on this supposition. The first-person narration sprinkled throughout Acts 16, 20–21, and 27–28 reflects ancient literary conventions and by itself does not require the conclusion that these passages came directly from someone who was an eyewitness to the events described. The rhetoric of Luke–Acts suggests that its author was well educated, a Christian, and very familiar with Jewish biblical writings.

Acts was almost certainly composed after the Gospel of Luke, during the decades following the destruction of the Jerusalem temple in 70 CE. The most reasonable hypotheses date Acts in the late 80s. A number of the book's theological concerns—especially those that relate to Jewish rejection of the gospel, Gentiles' acceptance into the church, and the potentially volatile status of Christians navigating the Roman political climate—speak to that historical context.

Those who read Luke and Acts as a coherent two-volume work discover the theological perspectives of both books relating to one another in a dynamic, mutually informing way. Each strongly emphasizes that, in Christ, God unfolds a plan of salvation prefigured in the Jewish Scriptures. Believers in Acts proclaim the kingdom of God, just as Jesus does in Luke. Each book likewise understands Jesus' ministry as rooted in God's prior commitments to Israel; in Acts this same ministry continues, present now in the work of Jesus' followers, his "witnesses"

(1:8). While the books share significant continuity, Acts also exhibits its own theological concerns that do not duplicate the message of the Gospel. These concerns, many of which are described in the commentary below, reflect the demands posed by the social, political, and religious contexts in which the word of God is proclaimed in Acts. For example, several speeches of Peter, Paul, and others devote attention to the status of the resurrected and exalted Lord Jesus Christ and to the legitimacy of the church's evangelization of Gentiles. While concerns like these are hardly at odds with the theology of Luke's Gospel, their prominence in Acts reflects that first-century Christians encountered new theological questions and opportunities as their devotion to the word propelled them into new circumstances for proclamation and discernment. (For additional reflection on the relationship between Luke and Acts, see the entry on Luke in this volume.)

Acts as a Theological History

The two-volume work of Luke–Acts offers itself as a project of pastoral theology (see Luke 1:1–4; Acts 1:1–2), endeavoring to nurture faith by highlighting God's role and fidelity in the stories it tells. Acts presents a history that is interpreted through a theological lens, amplifying the theological significance of the lives and witness of certain figures in the early church. Such theological concerns shape the entire drama of the narrative, making themselves known in the episodes it recounts and in the general architecture of the plot. On one hand, this theological outlook requires readers to make nuanced assessments of the historical claims of Acts and to put Luke's account into conversation with other sources when reconstructing the history of the first decades of Christianity. (Indeed, acute differences between the particular theological perspectives of Paul's Epistles and those communicated by Paul in Acts make it very difficult to reconcile these two portraits and histories of Paul.) On the other hand, the relentless theological focus of Acts makes it a provocative source for Christian theological reflection, as a first-century expression—and an enduring expression—of God's commitment to create, commission, and sustain communities of faith through the persisting proclamation of the word throughout human history.

COMMENTARY

The theological vision articulated in Acts presents God as thoroughly involved in human history and in the events or forces that directly affect nations, people, and the dissemination of the gospel. This active theological emphasis comes to light especially through the book's depiction of the perseverance of the word of God; through assertions and suggestions about God and God's activity in the world; and through material describing Jesus Christ, the Holy Spirit, humanity's conditions, and the life and work of Christian communities.

The Word That Perseveres

Although Acts does not identify Jesus Christ himself as "the Word," as does the prologue of John's Gospel, nevertheless it does locate the salvific power of "the word of God" in Jesus. The narrative is less interested in delineating the precise content of "the word of God" in the message that believers proclaim, but much more interested in depicting the *effects* of this divine word as the message that accomplishes salvation. "The word" encompasses the preaching and ministry of Jesus and, by extension, the witness made by the communities of the risen Christ's followers whom the Spirit empowers. *Word*-language in Acts includes both propositional speech and effective action, depicting God addressing humanity in the story of Jesus Christ with a message of peace (10:36), salvation (13:26), and grace (14:3).

The word perseveres in Acts, not because it automatically or always draws new members into Christian communities (which, in fact, it does not), but because it propels the church to extend its witness across the Roman world, claiming new cultural landscapes in which it can be proclaimed. Geographical expansion and cultural extension do not necessarily ensure an appreciable increase in the numbers of believers. Although Acts offers periodic summaries about the word gaining adherents (e.g., 6:7; 12:24; 19:20), and the church does spread at least as far as Rome, the narrative scarcely guarantees consistent additions to church membership. While the story begins with accounts of massive growth in the church (2:41; 4:4), later in Acts rejection becomes more common than acceptance. The last clear report of a conversion comes in 19:17–20 (although 28:24 may indicate another positive response). What does increase as the narrative progresses is persecution against believers and opposition from various populations and their leaders. Nevertheless, believers continue to find opportunities to proclaim the word. Even as the final quarter of Acts depicts Paul held in Roman custody, still he bears witness (see 23:11) as he defends his faithfulness to God's calling. In Acts 21–28 Paul the prisoner is still Paul the missionary; only the word he speaks has now found new locations to gain a hearing.

The proclamation of the word perseveres despite apparent setbacks because it is God's word, not because of charismatic or resourceful preachers (see 4:29). Believers are the word's "servants" (see Luke 1:2), and so any instance of the word's persistence through either favorable or adverse circumstances points to God's ongoing influence. Although it may be tempting to view the primary human protagonists in Acts (especially Paul, Peter, and Stephen) as clever and heroic, the narrative regularly counters such perceptions with indications that the gifts, status, or energies of individual human witnesses are not vital to the ongoing journey of the word. For example, immediately after a summary announcing increased church membership (6:7) Luke reveals that the heretofore predominant apostles are not the only ones "serving the word"; Stephen leaves off his assigned task of waiting on tables and ministers in public. Of course, his death likewise eliminates any impression that the word's future *requires* his particular efforts. Likewise, the final verses of Acts (28:30–31) do not dwell on what happens to Paul, but are concerned with the ongoing proclamation that emanates from his dwelling. Acts concludes with the message, not the messenger, still at center stage.

Luke's portrayal of the perseverance of the word, therefore, glorifies neither church growth nor "successful" evangelism as much as the indefatigability of the good news and the fact that God will ensure that the word will infiltrate human society. Acts celebrates the witnessing church as God's instrument to promulgate the word, and through the steadfastly confident depiction of the perseverance of the word Acts also reconfirms and celebrates God's comprehensive plan for salvation.

God and the Plan of God

Luke's theological vision describes more than groups of believers experiencing God's empowerment of their ministry and communal life. Acts also affirms God's involvement with humanity on a much greater scale. The God of Acts is the God of Israel, the same God who played an active role throughout the histories of the ancestors and the nation (see, e.g., Stephen's speech in Acts 7:2–53 and Paul's in 13:16–23). The connections between Luke and Acts also assert that this God continues to be a force in the world, affecting the course of human history and committed to the redemption of Israel and the salvation of all (cf. Luke

1:46–55, 68–79; 2:29–32). God remains in Acts the "Father" of Jesus, yet with the exception of Acts 2:33, no one but Jesus calls God by this name (see 1:4, 7). Likewise, only rarely does Acts refer to Jesus as God's "Son" (9:20; 13:33). Nevertheless God's intimate connection to Jesus is reaffirmed through the deep extent that Jesus stands as the full expression of God's commitment to accomplish salvation (4:12; 5:31; 13:23). That God has engineered this plan of salvation is a particular accent of the book of Acts.

Acts presents the whole scope of God's salvific action as unfolding according to God's own purposes, from the promises recorded in the Jewish Scriptures, to God's activity wrought through the deeds of Jesus Christ (2:22; 10:38), to God's momentous act of raising Jesus from the dead, and into the narrated events describing the witness of Jesus' followers. Luke views Jesus' death and resurrection as part of a divine "plan" (or "purpose"), known to God in advance (2:23; 3:18; 17:3). God controls overarching elements of human history and destiny (5:38–39; 10:42; 13:48; 14:16–17; 17:26, 31). God's will likewise imparts a necessity to certain situations or developments (1:16–22; 19:21; 23:11; 27:24); occasionally Acts implies God's intentions with the words *must* or *necessary*.

At the same time, such affirmations of divine sovereignty do not negate all traces of human agency or accountability. Frequently, especially in discussions of Jesus' passion, statements about God's resolute plan and human culpability sit side-by-side. A prominent example comes when the apostles pray to God, "in this city, in fact, both Herod and Pontius Pilate, with the Gentiles and the peoples of Israel, gathered together against your holy servant Jesus, whom you anointed, to do whatever your hand and your plan had predestined to take place" (4:27–28; see other instances in 3:13–18; 13:27). Human beings conspired to kill Jesus, but this too was part of God's design. On another occasion, Peter's Pentecost sermon contrasts the human deed of killing Jesus with the divine deed of his resurrection, all "according to the definite plan and foreknowledge of God" (2:22–24). God's foreknowledge does not eliminate human guilt, as seen when Peter condemns his listeners and exhorts them to repent (2:36–38). Acts also pairs statements of divine initiative and human agency in contexts describing the witness of believers. For example, Paul and Barnabas declare, "the Lord has commanded us, saying, '*I have set you* to be a light for the Gentiles, so that *you may bring* salvation to the ends of the earth'" (13:47, emphasis mine; see also 20:22–23; 23:11; 26:16–23). God creates opportunities for the church to act, but still people must themselves participate by giving testimony in those opportunities.

What modern readers might encounter in Acts as a tension—perhaps even a contradiction—where divine causality intersects with human agency does not seem to create a problem for Luke. The narrative never attempts a precise explanation of the interaction between divine and human acts; it affirms both while placing primary emphasis on God as the Lord of history. The theological implications of this portrait of God are strongly informed by the way in which Acts reads as a work of pastoral theology. The author's stated purpose in writing Luke–Acts—to build up readers' faith (Luke 1:4) and perhaps to encourage the late-first-century church's ongoing mission—discloses that the narrative makes its theological claims as a means of offering pastoral support, encouragement, and maybe even amusement to Christian readers. Various theological statements and storytelling conventions support Luke's pastoral efforts insofar as they proclaim God's sure control over all kinds of apparent obstacles or setbacks (such as imprisonments, storms at sea, and even death). These claims make a celebratory or doxological statement that God and the dissemination of God's word are not at the mercy of history or countervailing forces. God's salvific intentions will be vindicated. The book of Acts insists that some will resist the word of God, authorities will

persecute the church, evil spiritual powers will attempt to thwart the gospel (5:1–11; 8:4–25; 13:4–12), and the Jewish people will respond to the gospel in various ways. Yet the theological claims of Acts also insist that history is not out of control, and no powers or circumstances can ultimately thwart God's overarching intentions (see 5:38–39).

The means by which Acts relates the unfolding work of God in human history also have implications for the narrative's comprehensive theological outlook. When Acts declares God's interventions in human affairs, usually these declarations come from characters enmeshed in the story who interpret events in which they participate as directly influenced by God (e.g., 2:14–21; 11:18; 12:11; 14:27; 15:6–10, 14, 28; 27:24). The primary mode by which Acts makes its theological claims, then, is the interpretation offered by God's people. Naming God's presence in and influence upon the church's and world's affairs is a constitutive aspect of what it means for believers to bear witness. Acts thereby offers its readers a model of theological discourse, that they themselves might interpret events in their own experience with eyes that identify God's influence and with the confidence that God accomplishes God's purposes through the efforts and witness of the people of God.

Jesus Christ

Many interpreters have rightly observed that Acts does not offer a uniform or static depiction of Jesus' nature and significance. The book does not aim to give an exhaustive or systematic account of *how* Jesus accomplishes God's purposes, yet it insists *that* he does. Various sermons delivered in Acts speak about Jesus' importance in ways that fit the demands of preachers' particular contexts. The consistent centerpiece in Luke's overall portrait is that Jesus is the Christ, Israel's promised Messiah. What exactly it means for Jesus to be Christ is much less explicitly developed. Acts discusses the Christ from various perspectives, including his identity as the prophet like Moses (3:22; 7:37; see Deut. 18:15); his fulfillment of divine promises about a descendant of David (Acts 2:30; 13:23, 32–37); the necessity of his suffering (3:18); and his identity as "Lord" (see especially 10:36), a title used frequently in Acts for both God and Jesus. The resurrection of Jesus represents a particular pivot point in Acts, because it was a moment of vindication and recognition that prompts Jesus' followers to declare his exalted status, accomplished by God. Acts regards the resurrection as an act of God that declares who Jesus is: the Christ (2:25–32), one more powerful than death (2:24), the source of salvation and forgiveness of sins (4:10–12; 5:30–31; 10:43; 13:32–39), judge (10:42; 17:30–31), and the pledge of humanity's future resurrection (23:6). Salvation comes through Jesus—his life, death, resurrection, and exaltation—but Acts does not understand the crucifixion as the *central* locus of divine redemption or revelation, as do John's Gospel, Paul's Epistles, or the book of Hebrews.

Although Jesus ascends out of the physical realm of human history in Acts 1:9, his direct influence persists throughout the narrative. Stephen glimpses the ascended Lord in 7:55, and Jesus speaks to Saul/Paul on at least three occasions: in 9:4–6 (which is followed by Jesus' communication with Ananias in 9:10–16), in 18:9–10, and in 23:11. Luke also suggests a close though unspecific connection between the ascended Jesus and the activity of the Holy Spirit by mentioning Jesus' role in pouring out the Spirit (2:33; see also Luke 24:49) and by once referring to the Spirit as "the Spirit of Jesus" (16:7).

Jesus' ongoing relationship to believers also emerges in passages that mention "the name of Jesus" (or "the name of the Lord"). In Jesus' name people are baptized (2:38; 8:16; 10:48; 19:5), experience healing (3:6; 4:30; 16:18), and receive salvation and forgiveness (2:21; 4:12; 10:43; 22:16). The name of Jesus relates to the church's proclamation of the word. To speak or act in Jesus' name is to operate as Christ's representative, one who bears the power to declare boldly (4:17–18; 5:28; 8:12; 9:15, 27–28; see also Luke 24:47). Finally, part of the church's witness is to suffer hardship for the sake of this name (Acts 5:41; 9:16; 21:13). These potent associations with Jesus' name underscore believers' identification with Jesus and their membership in a community defined by him. As people bound to and empowered by his name, they operate in close relationship to him and continue in the ministry he began during his life. The church's ministry is Christ's ministry.

Jesus serves as a model for believers' ministries in an additional way. Luke describes the public deeds of Peter and Paul in ways that recall aspects of Jesus' activity in the Gospel of Luke. These literary parallels forge strong associations among these three major figures, suggesting that Peter and Paul's experiences echo and imitate Jesus'. For example, all three raise people from the dead (Luke 7:11–17; 8:40–56; Acts 9:36–43; 20:7–12) and perform healings that bear similarities in both general terms (Luke 6:17–19; Acts 5:12–16; 19:8–12) and specific details (Luke 5:17–26; Acts 3:1–10; 14:8–18). Likewise, each of them is seized by and encounters rejection from certain Jewish groups (Luke 22:54–71; Acts 4:1–18; 21:27–22:29). This repetition unites Peter's and Paul's ministries to Jesus', suggesting that their work is a direct outgrowth or continuation of his, and that God empowers the witness of Jesus' followers just as God previously empowered Jesus (Acts 10:38).

The Holy Spirit

The activity of the Holy Spirit forms a central piece in the theology of Acts, for people receive divine power through the filling of the Holy Spirit (see the connections between "Spirit" and "power" in Acts 1:8; 10:38; also Luke 1:35; 4:14; 24:49). This power exercises itself in believers' acts of ministry, enabling them to speak the word of God with boldness (4:31) and wisdom (6:10). The Holy Spirit places people into circumstances that allow them to bear witness—sometimes suddenly (e.g., 8:29, 39), sometimes as a result of calls issued to communities of believers (e.g., 13:1–4). In this the Spirit repeatedly inaugurates new or renewed opportunities for Christian ministry and community. Both the Gospel of Luke and Acts emphasize that the Spirit serves as the source and effective power of Christians' spoken and embodied witness (Luke 12:11–12; Acts 4:8, 31). Acts frequently portrays the Spirit clearly leading through communication with people (e.g., 10:19; 16:6–7; 20:23; 21:11), but the narrative does not dwell on precisely how believers experience these messages.

Acts includes strong expressions of the Spirit operating to nurture Christians, as seen in the conclusion of the Pentecost story, where the Spirit's coming and the sudden increase of believers creates a community of impressive fellowship, unity, and charity (2:41–47). The Spirit's presence fuels the worship of Jesus' followers (2:47; 10:46). The Spirit benefits the communal life of the church also in 6:1–6, when the Jerusalem believers address shortcomings in hospitality and justice through the help of people who are "full of the Spirit and of wisdom" (compare also the Spirit's role in accompanying church leaders in 20:28). In a startling passage that implies the Spirit's vigilant guardianship of the church, Ananias and Sapphira's corrupt attempt to deceive fellow believers is described as lying to the Spirit and triggers severe consequences (5:1–11). When Peter equates their lying to the church as lying to the Spirit, he suggests that the community of faith mediates the Spirit's actual presence, and that the Spirit defines the community. Additionally, other close connections between the Spirit and the corporate life of believers come to light when Christians receive and interpret divine leading. Luke describes these occasions of discernment as the church acting in concert with the Spirit (see 13:1–4; 15:28). In one passage (21:3–6), apparently unresolved disagreements about how to interpret the Spirit's leading still conclude with a moving expression of unity.

Acts regards the Holy Spirit as the same spirit that spoke through Israel's prophets (4:25; 7:51; 28:25), that accomplished Jesus' conception through Mary (Luke 1:35), and that empowered Jesus' ministry (Luke 3:21–22; 4:1, 14, 18; Acts 10:38). The coming of the Holy Spirit to believers is the result of God's promise (2:33, 39; also Luke 24:49); it is described as a gift (Acts 2:38; 5:32; 10:45; also Luke 11:13) that is conferred through a spiritual "baptism" (Acts 1:5; 11:16; also Luke 3:16), which decisively signals a person's entrance into the community of faith. Jesus' followers sometimes participate in these inaugural bestowals of the Spirit through laying hands upon people (Acts 8:14–17; 9:17; 19:6). Other times, however, the Spirit comes without warning, leaving observers to interpret the occasion as a divine act (10:44–47; 11:15–18; 15:8–9). In all this the Spirit remains beyond humanity's ability to contain or exploit, as Simon the magician discovers when he attempts to purchase the power to bestow the Spirit (8:9–24).

The Pentecost narrative of chap. 2 is a foundational depiction of the Spirit in Acts. While the Spirit gives its recipients a newfound ability to manifest miraculous signs (2:2–11), these displays are not the focus of Peter's Pentecost sermon. The startling ability to speak in various languages permits believers to offer their witness on Pentecost, but Peter concentrates instead on the Spirit's role as the source of Christian prophecy, or as the means by which believers can name God's intervention in the world (2:17–18; see also 19:6). Drawing from and slightly refashioning the oracle of Joel 2:28–32, Peter proclaims the coming of the Spirit as a new development, as God's gift to people of all sexes, ages, and social classes. The coming of the Spirit—at this point in time, which Peter defines as "in the last days" (Acts 2:17)—heralds the commencement of an era in which salvation is near at hand and the people of God are spiritually empowered to "prophesy," meaning that they announce this impending salvation as God's doing. Peter's sermon provides an example of prophetic speech, as he draws upon the living promises of Scripture to interpret God's hand at work in the events of the day. From this introductory explanation, Peter moves to speak about Jesus. His proclamation is also prophecy—not in the sense of foretelling future events, but in attesting to God's involvement in the life, death, and resurrection of Jesus the Christ.

The gift and enduring presence of the Holy Spirit, therefore, hardly serve as merely ends in and of themselves. Believers emerge as utterly dependent upon the Spirit for their ability to perform their work as Christ's witnesses through spoken proclamation and corporate life. Through the ways in which Luke correlates the activity of the Spirit with the activity of God (e.g., 5:3–4, 32), the Spirit stands as a means by which God directly supports and guides Christian life and ministry. The Holy Spirit's presence and activity are God's presence and activity.

Acts repeatedly establishes intertwined relationships among the activities of God, Jesus Christ, and the Holy Spirit (e.g., 2:33; 5:32; 7:55; 10:38; 20:28; cf. Luke 24:49). The book does not delineate these threefold associations with enough detail or precision to suggest an understanding of the Trinity that approximates the terminology and distinctions that Christians would formulate in later centuries. Still the close connections that Acts does posit contributed substantially to the material from which Trinitarian theology would eventually arise.

Eschatology

Characters in Acts understand their location in God's design as within "the last days" (2:17), insofar as they stand in the period between Jesus' exaltation and his return. This period, evidenced by the gift of the Spirit and the prophetic proclamation it empowers, permits and calls for repentance prior to the time when God will consummate all things, as reflected in this statement by Peter: "Repent therefore, and turn to God so that your sins may be wiped out, so that times of refreshing may come from the presence of the Lord, and that he may send the Messiah appointed for you, that is, Jesus, who must remain in heaven until the time of universal restoration that God announced long ago through his holy prophets" (3:19–21; see also 5:31). Compared to the Gospel of Luke, Acts rarely mentions events associated with the end of history; nevertheless the Spirit's active involvement through the course of the narrative steadily reaffirms the Pentecost message that the eschatological age is at hand. Although eschatological convictions hardly dominate the content of Christian preaching in Acts, they are always the assumed precondition of that preaching, the basis of believers' urgent appeals to turn to God.

When questioned by his followers about the restoration of Israel, Jesus responds, before being taken up into heaven, "It is not for you to know the times or periods that the Father has set by his own authority" (1:7). Just after Jesus disappears from their sight, two angelic figures disrupt the onlookers' idle and speculative staring into space by repeating the promise that Jesus will return (1:10–11). This scene lays a foundation concerning future expectations: Jesus will return at an unknown time. Proclamation in Acts recalls that basic eschatological tenet when preachers describe Jesus' return as involving humanity's judgment (10:42; 17:30–31; 24:25; also implied in 2:20–21, 40; 24:15). Acts declares the certainty of Jesus' return, with no hints about the details or timing of this event. Nothing indicates that this return is either particularly close at hand or substantially delayed. Instead, the perseverance of the word intimates that God's promises about the future are reliable and securely kept in God's hands.

Turning to God

Acts employs numerous terms to describe or call for a positive response to the proclamation of the word, including "repentance," "turning to God" (or to "the Lord"), "belief," and "welcoming [or accepting] the word." Some audiences are moved by proclamation (e.g., 8:12), some by miracle (e.g., 9:35, 42), and some receive the Spirit apparently before they can will themselves to respond (10:44). Varied accounts of conversion or transformation (physical and spiritual) imply that there is no single normative order or experience by which a person's salvation and incorporation into the church occurs.

Acts consistently states that salvation comes through Jesus (see 4:12). While this salvation includes forgiveness of sins, healing, and belonging in the community of faith, the book ultimately refrains from offering an exhaustive definition of salvation. Correspondingly, Jesus' followers exhort different hearers to embrace God's salvific intentions in different ways. Proclamation to Jewish audiences in Jerusalem throughout Acts 2–7 highlights their complicity in Jesus' rejection and execution. These people are exhorted to recognize their error and acknowledge Jesus as the Christ and Savior sent by God. Other Jews hear that Jesus brings a freedom from sins that the law could not accomplish (13:38–39). Later in Acts the gospel seeks to move Gentiles from their idolatry (14:11–18), ignorance (17:29–31), or bondage to Satan (26:17–18) toward recognition of God's work in Christ. When the imprisoned Paul speaks to Jewish assemblies in Acts 22–26, he contends that, through the gospel, God has brought salvation to Gentiles and reaffirmed the Jewish hope of resurrection from the dead. No uniform vocabulary or manner of appeal encompasses the whole range of salvation and its benefits, as Acts presents it.

Gentiles, Israel, and the Promises of God

The status of Gentiles in Christian communities—both the possibility and the conditions of these people's inclusion—constitutes a major concern of Acts. The importance of this topic is clearly sig-

naled by the long description of Peter's encounter with Cornelius (10:1–11:18), the decision reached in Jerusalem about not impeding Gentile converts (15:1–35), Paul's repeated frustrations with unresponsive Jewish audiences (13:36–47; 18:5–6; 28:25–28), and Paul's attempts to convince Jewish audiences of his call to evangelize Gentiles (22:21; 26:16–18). Paul's commission by Jesus to "bring my [i.e., Jesus'] name before Gentiles and kings and before the people of Israel" (9:15) and Peter's recognition that "God shows no partiality" (10:34; cf. 15:9)—a truth that James locates in Scripture (15:14–18)—are pivotal landmarks in the theological cartography of Acts, even as they recall an older promise made early in Luke's Gospel, that Jesus will be "a light for revelation to the Gentiles and for glory to your [i.e., God's] people Israel" (Luke 2:32).

The enthusiasm for this new direction in the journey, however, is offset by anxieties concerning the results of missionary efforts to Gentiles (e.g., 21:20–24) and by diminishing returns from the word's ongoing proclamation to Jewish audiences. Although incredible numbers of Jews respond to the gospel in 2:41 and 4:4 (and they remain part of the church, as seen in 21:20), momentous scenes such as these quickly become exceptions to a familiar pattern of rejection. When Paul indicts a group of Roman Jews, he interprets their resistance to his message as a reiteration of the recalcitrance that Isaiah also faced (28:25–27, citing Isa. 6:9–10). This idea of a proclamation of good news that is in continuity with Judaism yet manages to divide Israel recalls the foreboding statement from the beginning of Jesus' life, that Jesus "is destined for the falling and the rising of many in Israel, and to be a sign that will be opposed" (Luke 2:34). The story of Acts represents one way in which first-century Christians sought to make sense of the painful and potentially embarrassing gradual cleaving of Christianity and Judaism. From Luke's perspective, some Jews' disappointing refusal to embrace the gospel must be part of God's plan; at the same time, other Jews do respond positively, and God never gives up on Israel.

The Church and Its Leaders

The structure and activity of the church in Acts is dynamic, insofar as energy and variation characterize the communities that God's word creates and employs in its service. Groups of believers organize themselves and make decisions in numerous ways, usually as circumstances require. The church does not act or insist upon its own authority, but exists to participate in the journeys led by God's word.

A measure of ambivalence accompanies Luke's treatment of the twelve apostles. The replacement of Judas (1:12–26) reaffirms that the constituting of the Twelve signifies God's intentions concerning Israel's place in God's kingdom (see Luke 22:28–30). More obvious, these men provide noteworthy yet still undifferentiated leadership to the church in the first half of Acts, which connotes their high degree of authority (see 2:42–43; 4:33; 5:12; 6:1–6; 8:14–17; 9:26–27; 15:1–6, 22–23). But other parts of Acts attenuate the sense of the apostles' uniqueness, thereby suggesting that the Twelve's early prominence implies neither their centrality nor their indispensability. For example, although Peter emerges as the chief apostolic figure in Acts 1–12, his sudden disappearance from the story in 12:17, followed only by a brief cameo in 15:7–12, reminds readers that his efforts are not essential for the word to "gain adherents" (12:24). Moreover, when other characters arise and participate in the ministry of the word in ways that resemble the apostles' work (e.g., Stephen's and Philip's Spirit-led deeds in Acts 6–8; Ananias's call to lay hands on Saul in 9:10–19; Paul's ministry in chaps. 13–28; elders appointed to oversee new churches in 14:23 and 20:17, 28; Priscilla and Aquila's ability to instruct in 18:26), they reveal that the apostles do not necessarily exercise exclusive leadership functions. The apostles' primary role is to serve as Jesus' appointed emissaries, just like other believers in Acts.

Early in Acts readers find subtle acknowledgment of and support for women involved in the leadership of the early churches. Jesus' mother and additional women huddle with the apostles and other followers just after Jesus' ascension (1:14; cf. Luke 8:1–3; 23:49, 55–56), and the Joel citation in Peter's Pentecost address prominently notes that God gives the Spirit to men and women (Acts 2:18). As the story progresses, however, little more is said about women's roles. Although a handful of snapshots of potentially influential churchwomen dots the narrative (e.g., Tabitha/Dorcas in 9:36–41; Priscilla in 18:2–3, 18–19, 24–26; Lydia in 16:13–15, 40; Damaris in 17:34; Philip's four daughters in 21:8–9), Acts discloses very little about them or the countless other women who—as other historical sources, including Paul's Letters, reveal—exercised public leadership among the first generations of Christians. Because of this relative silence, Acts falls far short of clearly commending women's ecclesial leadership. At the same time, the statement of Acts 2:18, the work of Priscilla, the pattern in Luke–Acts of God empowering various people for prophecy and service, and the assertion that "God shows no partiality" (10:34), all create an ingrained, weighty countercriticism to an otherwise persistent focus on men and their activities. Since the word of God perseveres, and since the Holy Spirit empowers both men and women to announce this word of salvation, one well concludes that the bold witness and effective leadership of Christian women should also rightly persevere, despite the unbalanced presentation of Acts.

The Witness and Life of the Church

The structure and leadership of Christian communities are only incidental concerns in Acts. The narrative speaks with a much louder voice about the identity and role of believers: they are witnesses to Jesus and his resurrection. In a programmatic statement in Acts 1:8, Jesus declares that his followers will receive power from the Holy Spirit and will be his witnesses. Language of *witness, bear witness,* and *testify* appears frequently in Acts, stressing that the church is to make public affirmation about its experiences concerning Jesus Christ. The focus of this witnessing activity consistently is Christ, and the forensic character of the notion of testimony implies that Christian witness involves identifying and confirming truths that have already been manifested, not possessing secret knowledge or specialized abilities. The prophetic dimensions of the Holy Spirit's work, reiterated by Peter in 2:16–21, empower this kind of witness.

The witness of Christian communities assumes many forms in Acts, as believers engage in evangelism, healing, worship, prayer, table fellowship, compassion, and generous sharing of resources. Even prior to Pentecost the company of Jesus' followers prays together (1:14), and right after the arrival of the Spirit the narrative depicts a corporate life marked by numerous practices (2:42–47). Although the hyperbole in this and another (4:32–37) sketch of the believing community borders on unrealistic idealism, still Acts refuses to insinuate that the church forms a perfect community. The tale of Ananias and Sapphira's deception in 5:1–11 counterbalances the immediately preceding episode of 4:32–37 and declares that the "church" (the first appearance of this term in Luke–Acts comes in 5:11, directly in the wake of Ananias and Sapphira's deaths) should not expect to be without faults (see other potentially embarrassing behavior in 6:1; 15:38–40). Taken as a whole, 4:32–5:11 reveals the best and worst of the church's potential—charity and justice on one hand, hypocrisy and corruption on the other. Likewise, even though Christians exist as God's agents, they are often slow to discern God's work in their midst (see 10:9–17; 12:11–15).

The Church in the Roman Empire

As the word of God journeys and impacts human societies from Jerusalem, into sur-rounding lands, and ultimately into Rome, several scenes make suggestions about the cultural implications of the gospel. Episodes involving various members of the Jewish and Roman cultural elites (e.g., the council of Jewish elders and chief priests, Gamaliel, Sergius Paulus, magistrates in Philippi, Gallio of Achaia, officials in Ephesus, Claudius Lysias, Felix, Festus, and Agrippa) and related controversies permit Acts to address the matter of Christianity's relationship to institutions of political authority and the wider Roman imperial atmosphere. Acts sets the stage for a precarious relationship, for almost all of the narrated encounters between Christians and these high-ranking figures come as a result of serious accusations levied against the believers. The proclamation of the word does not leave a cultural system untouched or unchallenged, and guardians of a culture often retaliate (e.g., 9:1–2; 13:50; 16:19–21; 17:5–9; 18:12–13; 19:23–29; 24:5–6).

Within this charged climate, Acts makes some conciliatory gestures that may attempt to defuse perceptions of the gospel as a threat to imperial law or authority. There are frequent instances of Roman authorities or believers expressing the absence of wrongdoing (e.g., 16:35–39; 18:12–16; 19:35–41; 23:29; 24:10–21; 25:8–20; 26:30–32; 28:17–19). At the same time, the book scarcely suggests that the gospel is harmless to the Roman order. Human political authority is far from absolute in light of this gospel (see 5:29; 12:21–23; 16:35–39), and the word of God, by persevering despite frequent and concentrated attempts to restrict those who proclaim it, refuses to acquiesce ultimately to the dictates and priorities of the world's sociopolitical structures. While Acts comes across as much less aggressive toward the imperial order than the book of Revelation does, nevertheless it insists that the word of God will not yield to construals of political power that attempt to obstruct it. Instead, the word can manipulate those structures to serve its own purposes.

Paul's extended detention under the Romans in chaps. 21–28 subtly demonstrates that the physical and social restrictions of Roman incarceration actually open up possibilities for him to speak about the gospel to new, sometimes influential audiences (e.g., 23:1–10; 24:10–26; 26:1–29) and to minister to others (e.g., 28:7–10, 13b–14a), as long as God continues to guide his steps (see 23:11). Paul's ability to continue his efforts as a witness to Christ, even while held captive under imperial authority, intimates that God is able to manipulate and incapacitate Rome's ostensible power to limit the ministry of the word. The final verse of Acts, underscoring Paul's freedom to proclaim the kingdom of God "with all boldness and without hindrance," even while captive, likewise suggests that the word of God is capable of making use of or overcoming mechanisms of sociopolitical control. Acts does not depict an outright revolutionary gospel, but a gospel that will find venues for its proclamation despite any forces—political or otherwise—that threaten to restrict it.

Bibliography

Gaventa, Beverly Roberts. *The Acts of the Apostles.* Abingdon New Testament Commentaries. Nashville: Abingdon, 2003.

Jervell, Jacob. *The Theology of the Acts of the Apostles.* New Testament Theology. Cambridge: Cambridge University Press, 1996.

Marguerat, Daniel. *The First Christian Historian: Writing the 'Acts of the Apostles.'* Translated by Ken McKinney, Gregory J. Laughery, and Richard Bauckham. Society for New Testament Studies Monograph Series 121. Cambridge: Cambridge University Press, 2002.

Wall, Robert W. "The Acts of the Apostles." In *NIB* 10:1–368.

Romans

Michael Joseph Brown

INTRODUCTION

Paul's letter to the Roman church is among the better known and most popular writings in the New Testament. Very few other documents in the canon have influenced the development of Christian thought as much as Romans. The longest of the surviving Pauline Letters, Romans is the standard against which the authenticity of all other letters attributed to Paul is measured. Its theological depth and presentation constitute the most complete exposition of Paul's gospel. It is little wonder, then, that this letter has received more scholarly attention than any other Pauline epistle.

Although a few individuals in past centuries questioned the authorship of the letter, no one in recent years has succeeded in challenging the epistle's authenticity. Its acceptance as a genuine letter of the apostle Paul is beyond question in modern biblical study. As with the other Pauline Letters, this work derives its name from the recipients of the letter. According to 1:7a, the apostle addressed this letter to "all God's beloved in Rome" (NRSV). Although a few ancient manuscripts lack the phrase "in Rome" in 1:7, the weight of the evidence favors its inclusion. Its omission in these texts probably arises from a desire on the part of later editors to raise the universal appeal of the work.

In the current arrangement of the NT canon, Romans follows immediately after the four Gospels and the Acts of the Apostles. In its present position, Romans is the first epistle in the New Testament as well as the first of thirteen letters in the New Testament written by or attributed to the apostle Paul. The ordering of the Pauline Letters appears to follow two principles: (1) they are arranged roughly from longest to shortest; and (2) they are subdivided into letters addressed to churches (Romans through 2 Thessalonians) and letters addressed to individuals (1 Timothy through Philemon). The position of Romans indicates to the reader that it is Paul's longest surviving letter to a church. As such, it serves as an introduction to Pauline thought. Moreover, it follows immediately after the Acts of the Apostles, which focuses on Paul's missionary career and ends with Paul in Rome (Acts 13–28).

Romans also occupies an important place in the career of the apostle. Many believe it was written late in his missionary career. In the letter Paul indicates that he has completed his missionary journeys in the eastern Mediterranean. According to the apostle, "from Jerusalem and as far around as Illyricum I have fully proclaimed the good news of Christ" (15:19). A few verses later, Paul tells the Romans that he is heading to Jerusalem with financial aid for the believers in that region (15:25). With this as a point of reference, we can construct a relative chronology of Paul's writings. A collection for the Jerusalem church was inaugurated at the apostolic council described in Gal. 2, when Paul agrees to "remember the poor" (Gal. 2:10; see also Acts 15). Paul introduces this collection to the Corinthians in 1 Cor. 16:1–4, where he provides instructions to that congregation for collecting the money. In 2 Corinthians Paul exhorts the congregation to complete what they have begun (2 Cor. 8:6, 10; 9:1). When Paul writes Romans, he is ready to travel to Jerusalem to deliver what he has collected (Rom. 15:25–26). Thus, before his writing of Romans, Paul had already written Galatians, 1 and 2 Corinthians, 1 Thessalonians (believed to be Paul's earliest letter), and possibly Philippians as well.

The theological arguments and themes found in Romans represent a careful reflection upon ideas first presented in Paul's earlier writings. Among the topics addressed in Romans are justification by faith and not by works of the law (Gal. 3–5; Phil. 3; Rom. 1–4), the fatherhood of Abraham (Gal. 3; Rom. 4), Adam as the head of the old order of humanity and Christ as the head of the new order (1 Cor. 15:21–22, 45–49; Rom. 5:12–19), the church as the body of Christ composed of diverse elements (1 Cor. 12; Rom. 12:4–8), and the need to claim and exercise personal freedom with consideration for the limitations or consciences of others (1 Cor. 8–10; Rom. 14–15). These themes are not just reiterated. Romans demonstrates clearly that Paul has reflected on and refined his major theological premises during the course of his apostolic career.

Although it is not addressed in Paul's own writings, the visit to Jerusalem that Paul announces in Rom. 15:25 results in his arrest (Acts 21:27–23:30). After being taken into custody in Jerusalem, Paul was transferred to Caesarea, where he remained in prison for no less than two years (23:31–26:32). As a citizen of the Roman Empire, Paul appealed to Caesar for a hearing, and so is conducted to Rome (25:11; 27:1–28:16), where he remained in custody for another two years (28:17–31). Tradition says that Paul was executed at the imperial capital around 62 CE, a few years before the persecution by Nero in 65–68 CE. Keeping these details in mind, we can estimate that Paul's letter to Rome was written at the height of his apostolic career, around 55–57 CE.

This letter was most likely written from the city of Corinth. In 2 Cor. 1:16 Paul tells the Corinthians that he intends to depart from Corinth for Judea once the collection of the offering is complete. When Paul tells the Romans of his impending trip "to Jerusalem with aid for the saints," the collection is already complete (Rom. 15:25, my trans.). He names the Roman province of Achaia (whose capital is Corinth) as a prominent contributor (15:26). Moreover, Paul's commendation of Phoebe of Cenchreae (one of the seaports of Corinth), a deacon, to the Romans appears to confirm the capital of Achaia as the place of the letter's composition (16:1–2, although some doubt that chap. 16 was part of the original epistle). In short, it is most likely that Paul composed his letter to the Romans during his three-month stay in Corinth not long before his departure for Jerusalem (see Acts 20:2–3). This means that Paul's letter to Rome is his final epistle as a free man, one coming late in his missionary career.

Romans stands alone among the undisputed Pauline Letters because it is the only surviving letter written by Paul to a church he did not found. More astonishing, Paul wrote this letter to a church he had not even visited before (see, e.g., Rom. 1:10). Unlike his letters to the Corinthian church, Romans is not a response to specific questions addressed to the apostle, nor is it an account of a troubled relationship with one of his communities. Unlike Galatians, Romans is not a reaction to an alternate Christian teaching at odds with Paul's own theological views. Unlike Paul's other letters, Romans does not appear to be an "occasional" writing. It is not clear that Paul is writing to this community to address specific problems or situations that confront its life. Nevertheless, although it is the longest and most complete explanation of Paul's gospel we have, Romans is not the equivalent of a Pauline systematic theology. Notice, for example, certain important Pauline themes like the Lord's Supper (1 Cor. 11) and his somewhat detailed chronology of the end (2 Thess. 2) are missing.

What constitutes the heart of the message in Romans has been much debated. For some, it is Paul's theology of justification by faith and not by works of the law. For others, it is the mission to the Gentiles and God's plan for universal salvation. To reduce Romans to a single theme, however, even one as important as justification by faith, is to oversimplify a complex and often subtle argument. My suggestion of three central theological themes (alienation, judgment and justification, and salvation) is to be seen as only one avenue into Paul's argument in the letter. My reading of Romans also suggests the following proposition: there is only one God, the creator of all, who acts in history for the salvation of all.

COMMENTARY

Slavery as a Metaphor
for the Human Situation

Paul begins his letter to the Romans by calling himself a "servant" (literally, "slave") of Jesus Christ (Rom. 1:1). For modern Christians, the metaphor of slavery as a form of self-designation, especially when it comes to our relationship with God, is disturbing, to say the least. The ugly history of slavery throughout human civilization, one that continues to this day in various parts of the world, makes us recoil in disgust. The idea of slavery in Paul's day was more nuanced.

During the period of Paul's missionary enterprise, society consisted of roughly three types of people: freeborn persons, freed persons, and slaves. Elsewhere Paul makes reference to these three categories of people: "For whoever was called in the Lord as a slave is a freed person belonging to the Lord, just as whoever was free when called is a slave of Christ" (1 Cor. 7:22). Although the concept of the "freeborn" probably needs no explanation, and the concept of "slave" is most likely clear as well, the concept of the "freed person" may need some clarification. A freed person was a manumitted slave. Although no longer technically a slave, a freed person was not the same as a freeborn person. A freed person still had obligations to his former master. She was required, for example, to take the family name of her former master. Notice that Paul in 1 Cor. 7 calls the former slave "a freed person belonging to the Lord." Freed-person status was better than slave status, but it was not absolute freedom. The point in Corinthians appears to be that all disciples, of whatever initial status, are now under obligation to the Lord. Likewise, by calling himself a slave in Rom. 1:1 Paul is saying that his relationship to Christ involves certain obligations, a renunciation of a considerable degree of personal freedom. Slaves, in fact, were under the complete control of their masters.

The metaphor of slavery has a long history in Western civilization, particularly in our philosophical tradition. Most of its understanding of slavery has been negative. The idea of being a "slave to one's passions," for example, means that one is negatively controlled by one's emotions. This understanding of slavery is that of a person who has inappropriately renounced her rational capabilities to become a creature less than human. By contrast, another idea of slavery is not as negative. For instance, when someone, usually a poet, speaks of being a "slave to love," we understand that it involves a loss of freedom as well, but we are to consider the advantage that love offers as an acceptable exchange for unlimited freedom.

The question of advantage is at the heart of determining the acceptable or unacceptable nature of slavery. The apostle Paul understands this distinction as well. When he calls himself a slave of Christ, he is saying that the advantage of slavery to Christ is such that it is an acceptable loss of personal freedom. When Paul speaks of advantage in Romans, he is asking his readers to consider the advantage of their service, whether to God or to someone or something else, and the necessary loss of freedom such service entails. This discussion of slavery and its advantage comes to a head when the apostle says,

> When you were slaves to sin, you were free in regard to righteousness. So what advantage did you then get from the things of which you now are ashamed? The end of those things is death. But now that you have been freed from sin and enslaved to God, the advantage you get is sanctification. The end is eternal life. For the wages of sin is death, but the free gift of God is eternal life in Christ Jesus our Lord. (6:20–23)

Thus we see that slavery is one of the salient metaphors used by Paul to describe the human situation. Instead of a purely negative understanding of slavery, Paul advances a more nuanced understanding of slavery that raises the central issue of advantage as a means to determine the acceptability of service.

Paul's Slavery as a Vehicle for the Liberation of Others

Paul opens his argument in Romans with a bold thesis statement: "For I am not ashamed of the gospel; it is the power of God for salvation to everyone who has faith, to the Jew first and also to the Greek. For in it the righteousness of God is revealed through faith for faith; as it is written, 'The one who is righteous will live by faith'" (1:16–17). Paul's service to the gospel, the power of God, is not con-

sidered the sort of service that brings about shame. In other words, the advantage of this service is one that brings honor, although it requires a certain loss of freedom on Paul's part, as opposed to the service others may render (see, e.g., 6:21, quoted above).

Three key theological terms are presented in this thesis: power, salvation, and righteousness. They are elaborated throughout the letter, but their importance here needs to be highlighted because they serve as an apt introduction to Paul's description of the human situation (1:18–3:31). Paul calls the gospel "the power of God." Too often, we read this statement and interpret it to mean that the gospel is the message about God's power. In doing so, we obscure the brilliant subtlety of the apostle's statement. The gospel is not simply the message *about* the death and resurrection of Jesus. It *is* this event. In the death and resurrection of Jesus, the power of God has been revealed. The demonstration of God's power in the Christ event is to effect (or bring about) salvation.

The meaning of the term "salvation" in Romans has been debated by Christians through the centuries. The reason for this continued concern undoubtedly has to do with its central position in the letter and Paul's theology (see, e.g., 5:9–10; 8:24; 9:27; 10:1, 9–10, 13; 11:11, 14, 26; 13:11). Salvation can be understood in the letter to pertain to individuals and their eternal destinies—whether they will experience eternal life or eternal damnation. By contrast, others have understood Paul's use of salvation here as something social and pertaining to an experience one has in the present. This understanding is bolstered by Paul's reference to "the Jew first and also to the Greek," since they refer to ethnic groups rather than simply individuals. Both readings, however, do not have to be mutually exclusive. Individuals and groups are relative categories. Neither exists in absolute independence from the other. Individuals are who they are because they exist and operate within particular historical contexts that bring them into relationship with other individuals and groups. Persons create their individuality by influencing and being influenced by others (whether individuals or groups). Likewise, groups exist because they consist of individuals who share, debate, define, and redefine their common life in relation to one another within a particular historical context. For example, I am an American because I was born into and continue to operate in a context that says I am a member of this national group by virtue of my birth. My relationship and identification to the larger group of individuals called Americans is influenced by members of the group both past and present who contributed and continue to contribute to group self-definition. Likewise, my understanding of being an American influences present and future awareness of what it means to be a member of this group. A choice of one or the other understanding of salvation is not entirely necessary. Both options point to something more integral in the concept of salvation than has been discussed thus far.

Salvation is about the character of a relationship. Whether understood in individual or more social terms, salvation has to do with the character of one's relationship with God and with others. It is the positive appraisal of the network of relationships that one has with God, with nature, with others, with work, and so on. Salvation resides in the recognition that the good of the self depends on the quality of these relationships. When these relationships are mutually enhancing, the good of the self is realized. Concern for the character of these relationships is indicative of God's righteousness.

Paul's use of the concept of righteousness is another subtle aspect of his argument in Romans. In one sense, by "righteousness" Paul means the character or virtue of God that demonstrates that God is "just" or "fair." Indeed, God's "fairness" is an important part of Paul's argument, spelled out primarily in terms of God being "without favoritism" in judg-

ing human beings (see 2:11; 3:22; 11:33–36). In another sense, God's righteousness refers to God's will to "do justice" by intervening in human affairs to establish right relationships where they do not exist (see, e.g., Pss. 98:4; 118:40). In still another sense, God's righteousness may be understood in explicit relation to the quotation of Hab. 2:4, in which case Paul could be saying that God's righteousness is revealed "through [the] faith [of Jesus] for [the] faith [of Christians]" (Rom. 1:17). That is, Jesus' faithful response to God enables our faithful response as well. In this case, in the gift of the Christ event God empowered us with the means to respond in the same way (see 5:18–19). In his thesis statement Paul tells us that the gospel is the "power of God" because it reveals or demonstrates something about God, in terms of both nature and activity. In the gospel we see that righteousness is an aspect of God's nature as well as a work to which God is committed.

Slavery and Alienation . . . the Human Situation

Paul follows his bold thesis statement with an equally bold and symmetrical statement regarding the human situation: "For the wrath of God is revealed from heaven against all ungodliness and wickedness of those who by their wickedness suppress the truth" (1:18). The explicit parallelism between 1:17 and 1:18 forces the reader to pause and reflect. If the "righteousness of God" is revealed through the gospel's power to effect salvation, then how does the "wrath of God" reveal itself? By analogy, we may assume that this "wrath" is revealed through another power, one that brings about something other than salvation. To be more explicit, Paul appears to believe that—when viewed in light of the gospel's power—the other power that reveals itself in the world is one that enslaves and degrades human beings and their relationships.

As a theological phrase, "the wrath of God" has a history that goes back to the time of the prophets (see Jer. 6:11; Hos. 13:11; Zeph. 1:15). Moreover, prophetic pronouncements regarding the folly of idolatry are also age-old (e.g., Isa. 44:9–20). Paul's emphasis then is to be understood in relation to his prophetic predecessors. The wrath of God is not indicative of God's psychological state as much as it is a widely used OT symbol for the retribution that follows the human decision to turn away from God. The wrath of God is symbolic of the destruction that humans bring on themselves by rebelling against the truth. To put it another way, if the righteousness of God effects salvation, then the wrath of God is effected by human alienation.

Alienation may appear to be an odd way to describe the human situation. More traditional theological language would speak of human sinfulness. It is used purposefully here because Paul does not introduce the idea of sin until Rom. 2:12, and it may rob the apostle's argument of its brilliance by introducing it too early in our discussion. However, some explanation of the concept appears to be in order. By "alienation" I mean a negative form of belonging. It involves some sort of distancing, whether between persons or between individuals and God. More importantly, it involves a special kind of relationship, one that is inherently contradictory. Alienation is a relationship in which people are caught in a pattern of behavior contrary to their own good. Paul points to this kind of behavior when he says, "Claiming to be wise, they became fools; and they exchanged the glory of the immortal God for images resembling a mortal human being or birds or four-footed animals or reptiles" (1:22–23).

Through the practice of idolatry, human beings engage in behaviors that degrade their relationship with God and with one another. It is not that they can or do sever completely their relationship to the Creator; rather they pervert it: they exchange "the truth about God for a lie and [worship] and [serve] the creature rather than the Creator" (1:25). It is a misplacement of devotion, taking the mani-

festations, objects, experiences, and such that point to God and mistaking them for an adequate understanding of God. The outcome for such misguided understanding and practice is idolatry—alienation. Moreover, since human beings are in a network of relationships, embracing such a fallacy about God influences negatively all other relationships human beings have.

Paul demonstrates how destructive these relationships can be through a vice list that builds and builds until it reaches its crescendo in the term "ruthless" (1:31). The most vexing problem, from Paul's perspective, is that human beings are unmerciful. Paul attributes this pervasive predicament to the power of sin (see 2:9–18). Notice that Paul's emphasis in this list of human vices falls on those that are antisocial—those that degrade relationships (1:28–31). The list avoids behaviors that arise simply from human weakness, such as lust. Instead, Paul wants to emphasize that the patterns of behavior that we often associate with strong-willed individuals—practices that emphasize and promote conflict—are emblematic of a degraded divine-human relationship. The final term, "ruthless," is particularly interesting because this is the only place in the entire New Testament where this word appears (aside from a textual variant of Titus 1:9). In contrast to human behavior, God acts in a manner that seeks to overcome human alienation. Paul makes this most explicit when he says, "But God proves his love for us in that while we still were sinners Christ died for us" (5:8).

Another interesting aspect of Paul's description of the human situation is that he does not equate idolatry with polytheism. Idolatry is not just a problem for the so-called pagans. It is a thoroughgoing human problem. Paul makes this clear when he turns his attention away from the problem of Gentile idolatry to the individual who believes he is superior and unaffected by the human situation: "Do you imagine, whoever you are, that when you judge those who do such things and yet do them yourself, you will escape the judgment of God?" (2:3). Self-righteous judgment arises from the same impulse that misperceives God's nature and action as does pagan idolatry.

Judgment and Justification

With this shift to the self-righteous individual, Paul moves the theological emphasis from alienation to judgment, from humanity's response to its Creator to the Creator's reply. The self-righteous individual is just as alienated as the pagan she condemns. The judgment of the self-righteous is emblematic of human alienation because it is also an act of "insolence, haughtiness, boastfulness" (1:30). He who stands in judgment on the morality of another claims a superior status and is, in truth, engaging in a form of self-aggrandizement. Paul will return to this issue of judgment later on in the letter with the same prohibition (see 14:1–23).

The balance of Paul's discussion of judgment focuses on the just and impartial nature of God's judgment (2:6–11). He argues that God will repay every person for what he or she has done. People ultimately receive what they deserve, either reward or punishment (2:7–8). Individuals are judged not on some perceived "status," but on what they do. This is fundamental to Paul's argument because it deflates the ability of the self-righteous person to presume God's mercy for himself while denying it to others. With the assertion, "For God shows no partiality," Paul relativizes the status of all human beings. He goes on to make this clear when he focuses specifically on the Jew (2:17–29). As he concludes, "For there is no distinction, since all have sinned and fall short of the glory of God" (3:22b–23).

In this shift to God's judgment Paul has described the impartiality that characterizes it and is indeed an expression of God's righteousness. God is absolutely just in nature and action, and will judge everyone by what he or she does. Such reward or punishment is not based on ethnic background or any other per-

ceived special status. Yet Paul does not appear to believe that God's judgment is to be feared.

Divine judgment is a difficult concept for Christians who believe that it is inconsistent with the idea of a loving God. Judgment, however, is a necessary experience, especially when it comes to the practice of love. Unlike the self-righteous person, God does not use judgment simply as a tool for condemnation. Let me draw upon another text to illustrate. We are familiar with John 3:16, but very few of us continue and read 3:17: "Indeed, God did not send the Son into the world to condemn the world, but in order that the world might be saved through him." God uses judgment as a means to reestablish relationship with human beings. God's judgment does not seek to perpetuate or enhance human alienation. It seeks to overcome it. As creator, God alone is in a position to "judge the secret thoughts of all" (Rom. 2:16).

When understood in context, God's judgment is actually a liberating theological concept. Alienated humanity struggles with the fear of never being truly known. Yet Paul asserts that our Creator knows us utterly. In fact, this is what God's judgment means: God knows us thoroughly. Still, Paul tells us that the final word to humanity is one of mercy, not condemnation (11:32; 15:9). God's mercy, however, would be meaningless if God did not know us in all of our frailty. God's salvation would be empty if God did not judge sin.

Paul shifts the theological conversation again at 3:21 with another bold declaration, "But now, irrespective of law, the righteousness of God has been disclosed, and is attested by the law and the prophets" (my trans.). God's reply to humanity is not simply judgment. God has also revealed a way of reestablishing a healthy relationship with humanity that does not hinge on human behavior, a pattern of divine behavior consistent with how God has acted in the past as well. Paul characterizes this relationship—justification—as one of "grace as a gift" (3:24). Thus, if human beings are justified through faith, then there can be no distinction between this group or that group. God is the creator of all and, therefore, the God of all (3:29).

Citing the example of Abraham, an individual who spans the divide between Jew and Gentile, Paul argues that Scripture demonstrates that faith—the deep human desire to be in relationship with God—has always been the basis upon which God has acted to overcome human alienation (4:1–15). Paul then goes on to show in 4:16–25 that Abraham's faith is a type of Christian faith. As the apostle says, "he is the father of all of us" (4:16). Abraham's response to God's reply to human alienation, although it occurred chronologically before the death and resurrection of Christ, is pivotal because it demonstrates conclusively that God has always acted outside human deeds to reestablish and cultivate relationships with human beings. The emergence of the Christian faith is just the most recent example of God's activity.

According to Rom. 1–4, both Jew and Greek are alienated from God—under the power of sin—and both are liberated from sin through faith in Jesus Christ. Because distinctions between groups are overcome by God's act in Christ, the following discussion of Christian life in chaps. 5–8 omits mention of Jews and Greeks. Not until chaps. 9–11 does Paul return to the topic of Jewish-Gentile relations.

Slavery as salvation. Paul opens chap. 5 with a statement reminiscent of the conclusion he reached in 3:28, saying that justification brings with it a renewed relationship with God characterized by "peace" and "access" (5:1). Paul emphasizes that this relationship was at God's initiative: "For . . . while we were enemies, we were reconciled to God through the death of his Son" (5:10). He goes on to compare Christ with Adam. Adam was the head of the old creation, which was in bondage to sin and death since Adam's act of disobedience. Christ, by contrast, inaugurates a new reign of God's grace—an act that "leads to justifi-

cation and life for all" (5:18). He then concludes the chapter with two bold assertions, the first about the law and the second about sin (5:20). These two assertions occupy the discourse of the next two chapters. In 6:1–7:6 Paul addresses the problem of sin, while in 7:7–25 he addresses the law.

Paul's discussion of sin begins a shift in the discourse from justification to salvation. He initiates this with the question, "Should we continue in sin in order that grace may abound?" (6:1). His response is an emphatic no. He goes on to explain that believers are no longer controlled by sin, because they have "died to sin" (6:2). Through baptism believers are united with Christ in his death so that they are no longer enslaved to sin (6:3–6). The apostle then uses two analogies to demonstrate that sin and the law have no power over this renewed experience of justification. Drawing again upon the slave analogy Paul asserts that a slave is bound to a single master for life, but death destroys this servitude. Believers are now free to serve a new master, as Paul does (6:15–23). In the following marriage illustration, the apostle notes that a wife is legally bound to one husband for life, but that death again discharges this relationship. She is then free to marry another (7:1–6).

Paul's move to salvation becomes full-blown in 8:1 when he says, "There is therefore now no condemnation for those who are in Christ Jesus." Life in Christ is life in the Spirit. Paul shows that possession of the Spirit has a twofold function. First, the Spirit makes us aware that we have yet to experience the fullness of ourselves and our relationships to others, including God (8:12–27). Second, the Spirit assures us that God is still active, working with us and the entire creation, which "groans" for the fullness and consummation of this relationship (8:28–39). Indeed, Paul's doxology in 8:31–39 is an apt summation of the entire argument in chaps. 1–8. As the apostle says, "If God is for us, who is against us?" (8:31b).

This, by implication, raises again the topic of Judaism. The solemn beginning to this section contrasts sharply with the conclusion of the last (9:1–5). Paul recognizes here, however, that the unbelief of Israel and the implication of Paul's message that God has turned toward the Gentiles potentially undermines the credibility of God's faithfulness. After all, God made promises to Israel (9:4–5). Will God now abandon Israel? Was God unable to initiate and sustain a relationship with Israel that would lead to its salvation? These are among the questions Paul must answer.

He begins his response by saying, "It is not as though the word of God had failed" (9:6). He argues that even though "not all have obeyed the good news," God continues to work to bring about the salvation of Israel (10:16–21). Thus, to the question, "Has God rejected his people?" Paul emphatically announces, "By no means!" (11:1) Rather he demonstrates that the rejection of Israel is partial, temporary, and serves a deeper purpose (11:1–36). The stumbling of Israel has brought salvation to the Gentiles, which in turn will "make Israel jealous" (11:11). Realizing that his argument here is empirically weak, the apostle fends off a possible rebuttal by saying, "I want you to understand this mystery" (11:25). The salvation of Israel is as much a statement of faith on the part of the apostle as it is a proposition supported by Scripture. Further, Paul employs the metaphor of the olive tree to dismiss any notion of supersessionism among his listeners. If they had any impulse to think that they are the "new Israel" (as some later Christian thinkers will contend), Paul responds, "That is true. They were broken off because of their unbelief, but you stand only through faith. So do not become proud, but stand in awe" (11:20).

Paul concludes this section on salvation with another hymn of praise (11:33–36). Here he maintains that God's ways of dealing with humanity are "unsearchable" and "inscrutable," far surpassing the ability of humans to understand immediately (11:33). God is indebted to no one, so there is no limit to God's ability to save. Thus Paul assures his readers that God's faithfulness extends to those who may now have rejected God's actions: "And so all Israel will be saved" (11:26).

Salvation transforms the relationship between human beings and God and also transforms the relationships between human beings themselves. Paul maintains that this transformation arises out of gratitude for "the mercies of God" (12:1). The discourse falls into two distinct sections. The first section contains more generalized exhortations punctuated by an emphasis on the ethic of love (12:3–13:14). The second section involves a more detailed discussion of relations between the strong and the weak in which believers are asked to do more than simply tolerate one another's various practices (14:1–15:13). Believers are to place their concern for others above mere self-interest. Their aim is to be one of inclusion that leads to mutual affirmation and self-creation, as Paul says, "Let us then pursue what makes for peace and for mutual edification" (14:19, my trans.).

The preceding reading of the apostle's famous letter is unconventional, yet it avoids the unnecessarily thorny questions that arise when one attempts to put new insights into old categories. For example, the category of alienation shares much with previous understandings of the term, but it differs here in that it does not presuppose any sort of "ingroup/outgroup" scenario. Rather it presupposes that all humanity (as well as the entire universe) belongs to this great creative enterprise. The only distinction is between positive and negative forms of belonging. Yet such a presupposition changes the entire orientation of the theological conversation. If Romans is not understood as an explanation of how to bring the "outgroup" in—which is usual in discussions of justification—but as a way of transforming and integrating those who already belong in a positive way, then salvation is not a choice between the individual and the universal but of individuals-in-community.

In this brief overview of Paul's Epistle to the Romans, I have attempted to demonstrate how the apostle has constructed a subtle theological narrative that provides the foundation for some of his most memorable and complex theological convictions, repeatedly using the metaphor of slavery to give it coherence. The movement from alienation to salvation is only one avenue into Paul's theological argument. The usefulness of this orientation is that it avoids premature and unnecessary choices among equally complex and subtle theological arguments that can obscure the necessary relationships between such ideas as justification, sanctification, God's righteousness, the relationship between Jews and Gentiles, and so forth. It is only when Paul's argument is seen as a whole that its full power can be understood adequately.

Bibliography

Barth, Karl. *The Epistle to the Romans*. Translated by Edwyn C. Hoskyns. Rev. ed. Repr. Oxford: Oxford University Press, 1968.

Boers, Hendrikus. *The Justification of the Gentiles: Paul's Letters to the Galatians and Romans*. Peabody, MA: Hendrickson, 1994.

Grieb, A. Katherine. *The Story of Romans: A Narrative Defense of God's Righteousness*. Louisville: Westminster John Knox, 2002.

Johnson, Luke Timothy. *Reading Romans: A Literary and Theological Commentary*. Macon, GA: Smyth & Helwys, 2001.

Käsemann, Ernst. *Commentary on Romans*. Translated and edited by G. W. Bromiley. Grand Rapids: Eerdmans, 1980.

1 Corinthians

Brad R. Braxton

INTRODUCTION

Corinth was the capital of the Roman imperial province of Achaia and a cross-roads of culture, commerce, and politics. One can imagine why Paul spent much time and energy preaching the gospel and establishing a congregation in Corinth. The city's commercial activity ensured a large and diverse audience. Additionally, Corinth's political connections to imperial and senatorial leadership provided Paul an intriguing and risky context to proclaim his anti-imperial gospel—a gospel declaring that true power resided not in the empire but rather in the hands of Jesus Christ, whom the empire had executed.

Many scholars date Paul's arrival in Corinth to the fall of 50 or the spring of 51 CE. According to Acts 18, Paul remained in Corinth for eighteen months, laboring as a leatherworker and preacher. If Acts 18 is historically accurate, Paul sparked controversy during his Corinthian sojourn. Yet his extended stay may also indicate that he enjoyed missionary success.

After leaving Corinth, Paul traveled to Ephesus, and from there he began a fascinating literary exchange with the fledgling Corinthian congregation. Some of this exchange is now lost, but fortunately history has preserved much of it. In this exchange, Paul refers to an earlier letter that he had written to the Corinthians (5:9). Although the contents of this letter are unknown, Paul offered ethical admonitions in it.

Possibly, in response to Paul's letter, certain Corinthians wrote Paul a letter, asking questions about Christian belief and behavior. Additionally, Paul received an oral report concerning events in Corinth from family members or slaves of Chloe, presumably an influential woman in the Corinthian congregation (1:11).

Paul then responded to the Corinthians' concerns by composing another letter. This response is 1 Corinthians. Though Christian history has entitled this letter *1 Corinthians*, it was neither the first letter Paul had written to this congregation, nor would it be the last.

First Corinthians presents the reflections of an apostle passionately concerned about a community he founded. By the letter's conclusion, Paul has: (1) explored communal life under Christ's cross, (2) provided lessons on Christian leadership, (3) discussed Christian sexuality, (4) promoted a communitarian ethic based on concern for the neighbor, (5) offered directives on Christian worship, and (6) engaged in theological reflection about the resurrection and the future of believers.

COMMENTARY

A Community of the Cross (1 Cor. 1–2)

Paul outlines certain themes of the letter in the introduction (1:5–9). He notes the Corinthians' abilities in speech (*logos*) and knowledge (*gnosis*). Also, he mentions their spiritual gifts (*charismata*) and the fellowship (*koinonia*) of the community. Though Paul mentions fellowship last in the introduction, he treats this topic first in the body of the letter. God, through Christ, has created a special community that should strive for a common, divine purpose.

Paul has received distressing news about the community (1:10–17). Excessive allegiance to certain Christian leaders threatens to corrode the congregation's unity. Paul turns to the cross to correct the harmful effects of factions. The message of the cross does not boast in human achievement but rather glories in the divine demonstration of "power through weakness" in Jesus' crucifixion (1:18–31). Divisions in a church—especially those based on social status and favoritism toward leaders—represent a fundamental misunderstanding of the message of the cross.

The cross judges the incessant quest of humans to achieve. The drive to acquire prestige and material wealth and be better than one's neighbor creates communities where competition and fragmentation rule the day. By emphasizing what God has done through human weakness, the message of the cross neutralizes the desire for one-upmanship. Thus, for Paul, communities of the cross should exemplify cooperation, not competition; fellowship, not fragmentation.

Paul uses ethnic relationships to demonstrate how the cross creates unity where one might expect disharmony. Interpreters often ignore the socially radical statement that the cross unites Jewish and Gentile believers (1:24). There was a long history of social hostility between Jews and Gentiles in the ancient world. Paul's yoking together these two estranged social groups—"both Jews *and* Greeks"—would have seemed strange. Yet the cross mysteriously traverses social boundaries that often create bitter resentment and misunderstanding.

Paul personified God's power through weakness (2:1–5). Fearing that the Corinthians were emphasizing the rhetorical aptitude of preachers instead of the power of the gospel, Paul teaches them that human weakness does not dilute divine potency. Even though humans proclaim the gospel, the gospel is ultimately a divine accomplishment. In Paul's estimation, the Corinthians' preoccupation with human messengers indicates a lack of trust in the message of the cross.

Lessons on Leadership (1 Cor. 3–4)

Paul addresses the relationship between Christian leaders and the church in chaps. 3 and 4. Having alluded to the cliques forming around preachers (1:10–17), Paul revisits these schisms, noting that jealousy and strife are inappropriate for Spirit-led people.

There is exasperation in Paul's language (3:1–4). He derogatorily refers to the Corinthians as "infants." The Corinthians' partisanship demonstrates immaturity and a refusal to ingest the substantive food of the gospel. In a vexed tone, Paul exclaims, "Even now you are still not ready [to eat solid food]" (3:2).

Paul next launches a barrage of provocative images aimed at correcting the Corinthians' perceptions of leadership. Agricultural and architectural metaphors govern chap. 3. Slavery and familial metaphors are prevalent in chap. 4.

In chap. 3 Paul likens himself and Apollos, his apostolic colleague, to gardeners who plant and cultivate. Though Paul planted the Corinthian congregation (3:6), he quickly acknowledges Apollos's assistance. Paul and Apollos's efforts would have been in vain, however, had it not been for God's germinating influence.

Paul instructs the Corinthians on interdependence in ministry through these agricultural metaphors. Unless the planter sows, the one watering has nothing to water. Unless the one watering irrigates the seed, the planter's work will wither under the weight of drought. These apostolic gardeners are not in competition with each other but are connected to and dependent upon each other in a common purpose (3:8).

Switching to architectural metaphors in 3:10, Paul is the "master builder" in the Corinthian congregation. The term translated "master builder" (*architekton*) gives us the English derivative "architect." In antiquity the *architekton* was involved in both the design and construction of a building.

Paul alludes to his theology of leadership with these architectural metaphors. Unfortunately, the NRSV translation of 3:10, "skilled master builder," diminishes this allusion. The Greek word translated "skilled" (*sophos*) should receive its more usual meaning, "wise." Thus Paul refers to himself more literally as a *"wise* master builder." Paul demonstrates divinely inspired wisdom by recognizing the appropriate foundation for the community—the crucified and risen Christ. Christ, not human personality or ability, is the sure foundation of the church (3:11).

In 4:1–5 Paul appeals to a slavery metaphor to instruct the Corinthians on the proper identity and role of the Christian minister. He exhorts the Corinthians to consider Apollos and him as "servants" and "stewards." Frequently, slaves fulfilled the role of stewards in Greco-Roman culture.

Though ancient Greco-Roman slavery was violent and dehumanizing, slaves of well-to-do people (e.g., slaves of business managers and imperial bureaucrats) occasionally wielded power and enjoyed limited social prestige. Often these well-positioned slaves fulfilled important business duties on behalf of their masters, supervising the day-to-day affairs of the master's household. There was much incentive for slaves to be loyal to their masters as well as faithful managers of the master's business dealings.

By alluding to himself as a "steward [i.e., a slave] of God's mysteries," Paul acknowledges the parameters of his leadership. As a slave of God, he possesses authority, but of a delegated nature. His authority is a gracious gift from God, not the consequence of personal ability or status. Likewise, any praise or blame for his ministry will ultimately come from God.

Furthermore, Paul is not free to do as he pleases; nor can he allow himself to be buffeted by the Corinthians' evaluations of his ministry. All human evaluations of Christian ministers, whether favorable or unfavorable, are always penultimate. Ministers should not court the applause of people but instead seek the ultimate affirmation—God pronouncing them "faithful" on the day of judgment. Ultimately, faithfulness, not human wisdom or rhetorical ability, commends one to God.

In 4:14–16 Paul employs a parental metaphor to recall his unique role in creating the Corinthian congregation. Paul's claim to be the Corinthians' father has drawn criticism from various interpreters. Some scholars consider this claim and Paul's call for imitation to be overt patriarchy meant to establish an oppressive authority. But the indictment of patriarchy in 1 Cor. 4 may be ill-founded.

First, familial metaphors serve as bookends around 1 Cor. 3–4. Paul opens chap. 3 with a *maternal* metaphor, likening himself to a mother who suckles children (3:2). Paul concludes chap. 4 by referring to himself as a father who begat children (4:15). Here and in other letters (e.g., 1 Thess. 2:7 and Gal. 4:19) Paul does not employ exclusively paternal imagery in his familial metaphors.

Second, although teachers might assume a significant role in the rearing of children, the father in an ancient Greco-Roman family was chiefly responsible for the education, and especially the moral instruction, of children. Paul's assertion of paternal status is not a manipulative power play but rather a passionate appeal to the Corinthians to be more concerned about their conduct.

Paul's call for imitation is an expression of parental responsibility. As the first Christian leader the Corinthian family ever knew, Paul presents himself as an ethical model. His model celebrates God's power through weakness, the indispensability of mutuality, and ultimate accountability to God—hardly the staple qualities of a patriarchal mind-set.

Community Membership and Sexual Ethics (1 Cor. 5–7)

Paul turns his attention more fully to ethics in these chapters. His ethical admonitions are not simply focused on the individual (What should I do?). They concentrate primarily on the communal (How do believers' actions affect the broader Christian community?).

There are four major sections in 1 Cor. 5–7. First, Paul comments on an inappropriate sexual relationship within the church (chap. 5). Second, he chastises the Corinthian proclivity for taking internal church disputes before "pagan" law courts (6:1–11). Third, he addresses another instance of immorality, the sexual union of believers with prostitutes (6:12–20). Finally, Paul discusses how the call to be a Christian affects persons in various social relationships, many of which involve sexual matters such as celibacy, marriage, being single, being widowed, or being divorced (chap. 7).

Paul first addresses the troubling news of sexual immorality (*porneia*) in the church (5:1). Apparently, a Corinthian Christian is having sexual relations with his stepmother. While this improper sexual activity horrifies Paul, certain members of the community celebrate the relationship between this man and woman. The Corinthians' "boasting" about the relationship may reflect adoption of the values of the culture where sexual activity outside marriage was not a source of shame for men.

Paul strongly urges the Corinthians to expel this man from the community and to hand him over to Satan for the destruction of his body but the salvation of his spirit. The word Paul uses for "body" is *sarx*, not the more usual term, *soma* (5:5). *Sarx*, which is commonly translated "flesh," is a characteristic Pauline term connoting a life dominated by sin. Paul considers this communal discipline restorative, not punitive. He hopes that the shame engendered by this excommunication will prompt the man to change his behavior, thereby restoring both the man and the health of the church. Given Paul's silence about the woman in this relationship, some interpreters assume that she was not a member of the Corinthian church or was not responsible for her actions because she was a slave and was coerced into the relationship.

Though details surrounding this incident and Paul's response to it remain unclear, the straightforwardness of Paul's approach to sexuality is striking. Two impulses have characterized attitudes about sexuality in many modern cultures. One impulse has been sexual obsession—the pursuit of sexual pleasure at all costs. The other impulse has been sexual repression—the denial of sexual pleasure or ignoring of sexuality.

The pendulum has swung decidedly toward repression in many discussions of sexuality across Christian history. Yet Paul demonstrates that the frank discussion of sexuality is a matter of ecclesial discernment and should not be delegated to families and cultural institutions alone. The church must overcome its reticence to address sexual matters and openly teach about sexuality.

In addition to Paul's forthrightness about sexuality, he provides another vital lesson, the importance of restoration. Christians must vigilantly seek the restoration and healing of the victims of sexual misconduct, as well as the restoration of the church's integrity when the misconduct has involved Christians.

Also, the gospel, which promises unmerited forgiveness for those who seek it, mandates believers to restore to the Christian community the perpetrators of sexual misconduct.

Paul next rebukes the Corinthians for taking certain disputes (possibly involving sexual matters) to pagan law courts. In these courts believers allow pagan judges to adjudicate their sacred business. Moreover, these secular judicial proceedings frustrate attempts at fellowship among believers. By inciting hostility, an apparent legal victory of one believer over another is actually a defeat for the involved parties and the entire congregation (6:7–8).

Paul then chastises the Corinthians for another occasion of sexual immorality (6:12–20). Presumably, certain Christian men are frequenting prostitutes. Again, this immorality may indicate how thoroughly some Christian men had adopted the mores of the wider culture. Paul's response to this immorality amplifies the theological significance of the human body.

As a Jew, Paul did not subscribe to the soul-body dualism of Greek philosophy that deemed the human body a prison from which the eternal soul sought release. Paul believed that believers' bodies would be the location of God's transforming power in the resurrection. The future would involve not the saving of souls but instead the transformation and resurrection of bodies. He appeals to the resurrection of Christ's body as evidence that bodies will play a role in God's future (6:14). Moreover, God has made human bodies dwelling places of the Holy Spirit even in the present (3:16–17).

Human bodies are not autonomous but are joined to Christ's body. Thus, when believers have improper sexual relations, they replace the holy union shared with Christ's body with an impure union. Paul's positive perspective on the body is meant to curb sexual immorality. Also, the theological significance he places on the human body has implications for topics ranging from genetic cloning to health care for persons with various diseases. Regardless of the positions that Christians advance on these complex issues, our bodies are not simple objects for science but instead subjects in God's redemptive process.

Finally, in 1 Cor. 7 Paul affirms his own preference for celibacy, while offering a variety of opinions to the married, the unmarried, and persons in "mixed marriages" (i.e., one partner is a Christian while the other is not). His instructions demonstrate enormous flexibility. Contrary to one popular portrayal of Paul as an authoritarian, Paul willingly accommodates a variety of spiritual gifts and dispositions regarding sexual matters (7:7). Rather than establishing rigid apostolic decrees, in many instances he offers opinions, fully aware that the preferences of others may win out. This portrait of the flexible Paul provides an important counterbalance to the more definitive stances he takes in chaps. 5–6.

The Relinquishment of Rights (1 Cor. 8–10)

Paul's concern for communal ethics continues in chaps. 8–10. If sexual immorality has threatened the community's health in chaps. 5–7, disdain for the welfare of fellow believers is the peril in chaps. 8–10. There is a growing controversy over the appropriateness of Christians eating food sacrificed to idols in pagan temples. The deeper issue is elitism produced by knowledge.

Corinth was home to a number of religious temples and shrines honoring Greco-Roman deities such as Apollo and Aphrodite. In religious celebrations at these temples and shrines, meat would frequently be sacrificed to various deities and then eaten by guests. In addition to their religious function, these banquets provided a forum for important cultural and commercial networking.

Apparently, upper-class members of the Corinthian church were attending these banquets and freely eating meat in the temples. They had no qualms eating the meat since they had "knowledge" that the idols to whom the meat was sacrificed did not exist (8:4). Their knowledge liberated them, so they thought, from the problematic religious implications of eating the meat, and they eagerly welcomed opportunities for contact with the wider Corinthian society.

While dining in these temples did not damage the religious sensibilities of the "enlightened" Christians, it could defile the consciences of certain Christians, the so-called weak, who still associated this food with idols (8:7). Some members of the Corinthian church were recent converts from pagan religions. If these "weak" Christians (for whom idols were still real forces) witnessed other influential Christians dining in these temples, the "weak" might be encouraged to enter the temples and possibly be tempted to return to idol worship (8:10). Far from being a simple social occasion for "enlightened" Christians, these pagan banquets might serve as a catalyst for the destruction of another Christian's faith.

Responding to this crisis, Paul remarks, "Knowledge puffs up, but love builds up" (8:1). Interestingly, Paul agrees with the "enlightened" Christians' assertion that idols do not exist (8:4–7). Yet he reprimands the "enlightened" Christians for their preoccupation with a "liberating" knowledge that actually enslaves fellow believers.

This knowledge has "puffed them up," creating in them an elitist disdain for fellow Christians. Paul has used the verb "to puff up" (*physioō*), which carries the connotation of human arrogance, on other occasions (4:6, 18–19; 5:2). Knowledge can lead to an inflated obsession with one's own interests. Love, however, eagerly seeks to edify the neighbor, even if it involves the relinquishment of one's rights.

Paul demonstrates his willingness to relinquish rights for others. After establishing his right to financial support as an apostle (9:1–14), Paul recants that right

(9:15–18). Due to the Corinthians' inclination toward elitism, Paul is leery of accepting their financial support. Through financial patronage, the Corinthians might claim "ownership" over Paul. By refusing payment, Paul remains free from their "ownership." Yet, returning to the slavery metaphor, Paul reminds them that he is God's slave, having been commissioned as a "household steward" (9:17–18).

In chap. 10 Paul reflects extensively on the dangers of idolatry—the wrongful attribution of ultimate status to something or someone not ultimate. In his prohibitions against idolatry, he appeals to Jewish Scripture, offering very imaginative interpretations. Furthermore, he boldly declares that these biblical texts were not written exclusively for ancient Jews but also for Paul's present community (10:6, 11). Paul unashamedly reads biblical texts for their contemporary religious value, not simply for ancient historical accuracy.

Instructions about Worship (1 Cor. 11–14)

Behavior in worship is the theme connecting the disparate discussions in chaps. 11–14. Paul treats four main issues. First, he deals with certain women in the church prophesying with their heads "uncovered" (11:1–16). Second, he speaks about social divisiveness when the community shares the Lord's Supper (11:17–34). Third, he examines the role of spiritual gifts in Christian worship (chaps. 12–14). In the midst of discussing spiritual gifts, Paul inserts a compelling "hymn to love," which contends that love is the proper context for all spiritual gifts (chap. 13). Finally, he addresses the matter of certain women speaking in public worship services (14:34–36).

A worship dilemma troubling Paul emerges in 11:5: "Any woman who prays or prophesies with her head unveiled disgraces her head." Apparently, certain Christian women prophets have broken with prevailing social custom by either removing their head coverings or loosing their hair and letting it down while prophesying in worship. Paul is concerned that people inside and outside the Corinthian church might realize that these women have shamefully disregarded gender distinctions symbolized by "appropriate" hairstyles. Additionally, people might mistake these women for members of suspect social groups whose women also let their hair down in frenzied prophetic utterances. While assuming women's vital leadership roles in Christian worship, Paul cannot endure the shameful implications of their actions and mounts three basic arguments. He argues on the basis of culture codes in vv. 4–6, the Genesis creation stories in vv. 7–9, and finally "nature" in vv. 14–15.

Paul reveals his own doubt about the persuasiveness of these arguments. In frustration he remarks, "We have no such custom [for women prophesying with their hair down]." A paraphrase of Paul's socially conservative plea might be: "Do as I have urged because this is the way we have always done it."

Paul's words are riddled with patriarchal assumptions. The avoidance of social disgrace is Paul's motive in 11:1–16. He uses some form of the word "disgrace" or "shame" three times in vv. 4–6. Earlier in the letter, Paul's theology of the cross stressed that the church finds its honor in what the world calls shameful (1:18–31). It is hypocritical for him to suddenly become concerned that outsiders might heap shame upon the community. How can Paul place the cross at the center of his ministry and be worried about social respectability?

Additionally, Paul employs a patriarchal method when reading the creation stories in 11:7–9. No amount of interpretive maneuvering can rescue him from the charge of chauvinism here. His assertion that a woman brings glory to a man and not directly to God gives to women a derivative, second-class status. Finally, Paul suggests in vv. 14–15 that it is contrary to "nature" for a woman's head to be uncovered. By "nature" he appears to mean prevailing cultural customs defined by patriarchal assumptions. Verses 1–16

serve as a cautionary tale of how easily well-intentioned church leaders can perpetuate the sin of patriarchy.

In 11:17–34 Paul returns to the theme of schism that governed earlier portions of the letter. Class inequities are at the root of these schisms and manifest themselves at the Lord's Supper, the sacred meal of the early church symbolizing the community's common history and destiny. More specifically, as the community gathers for the Lord's Supper, certain wealthier members also bring elaborate dinners and eat them in front of the poorer members, who lack resources for such meals. As in the case of meat offered in pagan temples (chap. 8), this flaunting of class differences demonstrates an inexcusable lack of concern for the community.

In chaps. 12–14 Paul explores the use of spiritual gifts in worship. Clues in the text reveal that Paul has at least two objectives. First, he wants to de-emphasize speaking in tongues, an ecstatic language that believers employ when praying to God. Christian worship in Corinth is apparently a lively affair. Yet the prevalence of speaking in tongues and a disregard for order in worship threaten the effectiveness of the worship services (14:13–19). Second, Paul wants to emphasize the variety of ways that the Holy Spirit equips believers.

The de-emphasis on speaking in tongues and frenzied worship begins as early as 12:2. There Paul appeals to the Corinthians' former involvement with idol worship. In their pagan religious rituals, they occasionally were carried away in religious frenzy. Paul contrasts their former religious ecstasy with the correct confession of Jesus' lordship, which the Holy Spirit inspires (12:3). The work of the Holy Spirit is supremely manifested in instructive speech that builds up the community (i.e., prophecy), not in frenzied speech that potentially edifies only the individual (i.e., speaking in tongues).

Paul also emphasizes the diverse ways that the Holy Spirit empowers believers for the common good of the church. He repeats the word "variety" (*diaireseis*) three times when discussing the media through which God's power flows (12:4–6). Additionally, he returns to the body metaphor to underscore that the proper functioning of the body of Christ (i.e., the church) depends on diverse parts carrying out their responsibilities (12:12–31).

Paul's promotion of love—the self-transcending attention to and concern for the other—reaches full maturity in his famous hymn to love in chap. 13. In its literary context, Paul's hymn is not an abstract speculation about love but rather a concrete pastoral insight that the use of spiritual gifts must spring up from the soil of love.

At the conclusion of chap. 14 Paul addresses another divisive issue concerning speech in worship. In a notorious passage he seemingly urges certain women in the congregation to be silent (14:34–35). Interpreters have advanced at least three positions concerning this passage: (1) Some believe it is an interpolation inserted into the letter by a later copyist. (2) Some consider it to be Paul's authentic words and note the unfortunate patriarchal perspective. Yet they emphasize Paul's affirmation of female ecclesial leaders in other contexts. (3) Some read vv. 34–35 as a slogan of persons in the Corinthian congregation, which Paul quotes. Then, in v. 36, Paul rejects the slogan with his question: "Did the word of God originate with you [who believe that women should not speak in worship]?" In other words, Paul is not silencing women but disagreeing with those who want to silence them.

Paul demonstrates great concern about the importance of worship throughout chaps. 11–14 as he engages this wide range of issues with which the Corinthian community struggles as it builds its communal identity.

The Resurrection Reexamined (1 Cor. 15)

Paul tackles possibly the most pressing dilemma in the Corinthian congregation in chap. 15. Apparently, certain believers are denying the prospect of future bodily resurrection. In Paul's estimation they misunderstand the significance of Christ's resurrection. Thus Paul attempts to reestablish the link between Christ's bodily resurrection in the past and their bodily resurrection in the future.

Paul does not immediately attack the faulty premises of these believers. Instead, he creates common ground, recalling his initial preaching among them (15:1–11). He reminds them that the death and resurrection of Jesus were the bedrock of his proclamation, which they eagerly accepted. Paul then cites multiple appearances of the resurrected Christ to confirm that the resurrected Christ had a body that other people could physically experience.

In the remainder of the chapter, Paul's arguments reveal more clearly the problematic positions of these Corinthians. On the one hand, they fail to connect Christ's resurrection in the past and their resurrection in the future (15:12–19). On the other hand, they do not believe that the resurrection is bodily (15:35). Paul's involved arguments address these issues.

He employs agricultural metaphors to instruct the Corinthians that Christ's resurrection and their future resurrection are inextricably linked (15:20–23). He likens Christ's resurrection to the "first fruits." In Judaism persons sacrificed the initial produce of the harvest (e.g., Exod. 23:19). This "first fruits" sacrifice symbolized both the greater harvest to come and God's sovereignty.

Christ's resurrection exemplifies the symbolic realities of the "first fruits" and is the beginning of a greater future harvest—the resurrection of all believers (1 Cor. 15:23). Additionally, Christ's resurrection signals God's sovereignty over other contending powers (15:24–28). Even death, that ancient and persistent foe, will eventually succumb to God. Paul then provides agricultural and cosmological examples to persuade the Corinthians that resurrection is always a bodily phenomenon (15:35–57). Yet Paul admits that in the resurrection human bodies will undergo a mysterious transformation.

Paul's arguments provide useful guidance for theological discernment about the resurrection. First, Paul teaches that the proclamation of the risen Lord is essential to the church's identity (15:3–4). Christ is central not because he was a good teacher or a moral exemplar, but because he is the risen Lord of the church! Second, since Christ's resurrection is the opening, not closing, act of God's eschatological drama, the celebration of the resurrection cannot focus solely on Christ. It must also celebrate the resurrection's implications for all Christians. Finally, the prognostication of death's defeat should always fan the flames of Christian hope—the unswerving assurance that God has a glorious future for believers and the whole creation.

Parting Words (1 Cor. 16)

In chap. 16 Paul provides instructions about the "collection for the saints." He encourages this congregation to contribute to a relief fund to support Jewish Christians in Jerusalem who have fallen upon financial difficulties (Gal. 2:10). Paul believes that the acceptance of this offering by Jewish Christians in Jerusalem might signal the unity between the Jewish and Gentile wings of early Christianity, since the Pauline congregations contributing to this fund are largely Gentile.

Intending to visit with the Corinthians soon, Paul also sketches his future itinerary. Yet, as the reader of 2 Corinthians learns, Paul's travel plans undergo serious alterations. New controversies in Corinth challenge Paul to present even more persuasively his understanding of God and the gospel.

Bibliography

Braxton, Brad Ronnell. *The Tyranny of Resolution: I Corinthians 7:17–24*. SBLDS 181. Atlanta: Society of Biblical Literature, 2000.

Hays, Richard B. *First Corinthians*. Interpretation. Louisville: John Knox, 1997.

Martin, Dale B. *Slavery as Salvation: The Metaphor of Slavery in Pauline Christianity*. New Haven: Yale University Press, 1990.

Polaski, Sandra Hack. *A Feminist Introduction to Paul*. St. Louis: Chalice, 2005.

Schottroff, Luise. "A Feminist Hermeneutic of 1 Corinthians." In *Escaping Eden: New Feminist Perspectives on the Bible*, edited by Harold C. Washington, Susan Lochrie Graham, and Pamela Thimmes, 208–15. Sheffield: Sheffield Academic Press, 1998.

2 Corinthians

Brad R. Braxton

INTRODUCTION

Like a movie sequel, 2 Corinthians allows readers to trace the continuing relationship between the apostle Paul and the fledgling Corinthian congregation. The cast of characters includes persons from 1 Corinthians such as Paul and his evangelistic comrade, Timothy. Also, new characters surface: Titus, another of Paul's missionary colleagues; and a group of antagonists referred to as the "super-apostles."

In this letter, as in 1 Corinthians, Paul attempts to influence the Corinthians' perspectives on topics such as authority and honor. Yet, by the writing of 2 Corinthians, accusation, bitter confrontation, public humiliation, and formidable rivals have impinged upon the relationship between Paul and the Corinthians, creating a charged atmosphere.

At the conclusion of 1 Corinthians, Paul informed the congregation that he would stay in Ephesus until the next spring. He planned to leave Ephesus for Macedonia and then for Corinth, where he would spend the winter (1 Cor. 16:6). From Corinth he would journey to Jerusalem to deliver the financial collection for impoverished Jewish Christians. However, congregational crises in Corinth altered Paul's travel plans.

Timothy, whom Paul had dispatched earlier to Corinth as an emissary, found Paul in Ephesus and told him that congregational life in Corinth was deteriorating. Due to this troubling development, Paul changed his itinerary. He journeyed directly to Corinth to rectify the situation, instead of first visiting Macedonia.

Stringent opposition met Paul in Corinth. A member of the congregation offended and humiliated Paul before the church. After this wounding episode, Paul proceeded to Macedonia and eventually returned to Ephesus. So hurtful was this impromptu visit to Corinth that Paul later referred to it as the "painful visit" (2:1).

Rather than return to Corinth, Paul wrote a letter to the Corinthians in order to prevent the downward spiral of their relationship. Scholars call this letter, which history has not preserved, the "letter of tears," since Paul experienced emotional outbursts when composing it (2:4). Titus delivered the "letter of tears" to Corinth.

Eventually, Titus conveyed to Paul the hopeful news that the "letter of tears" had created contrition among the Corinthians (7:6–13). The community disciplined the person who offended Paul. Still, Paul sensed that his relationship with the congregation needed much healing. To effect further reconciliation, Paul wrote yet another letter in approximately 55 CE. This letter is 2 Corinthians.

Paul pursues an expansive theological agenda in 2 Corinthians. He attempts to: (1) mend a previously fractured relationship with the congregation; (2) defend himself against charges of duplicity; (3) instruct the Corinthians about authentic Christian ministry; (4) bolster financial support among the Corinthians for the Jerusalem collection; and (5) address the dangers posed by rival preachers in the community.

COMMENTARY

The Restoration of a Relationship (1:1–2:13)

Paul begins with his customary salutation and greeting and cites Timothy as the cosender. After naming the Corinthians as the addressees, Paul mentions "all the saints throughout Achaia" (1:1). Achaia was the Roman imperial province (present-day Greece) whose capital was Corinth. By referring to Timothy and the saints in Achaia, Paul announces a major theme of the letter: relationships.

Presumably, Timothy was in Corinth when the congregational crisis erupted, and the Corinthians may have imposed their dissatisfaction with Paul upon Timothy. Thus the early reference to Timothy may be Paul's vote of confidence for his colleague, a prominent leader whom the Corinthians should respect.

Also, Paul's allusion to other Christians in Achaia contains a subtle message. Though geographically the Corinthian congregation was on a peninsula, by no means theologically was it an island unto itself. This congregation was part of a larger constellation of believers throughout the province; thus its members were accountable to other believers, and especially to Paul.

Paul highlights another crucial aspect of relationships, reciprocity. He emphasizes reciprocity with the word "consolation" (*paraklēsis*). Some form of the word "consolation" occurs ten times in 1:3–7. *Paraklēsis* connotes an individual who stands beside a struggling person to offer encouragement (cf. the person of the Paraclete in the Gospel of John). God is the supreme provider of consolation (1:3). Having benefited from God's consolation in perilous moments, Paul is obligated to console others.

Next, Paul rehearses significant moments in his relationship with the Corinthians (1:8–2:13). Paul recalls a desperate moment in his ministry, which depleted him and his companions of their ability to contend with it. The situation seemingly imposed upon them a "sentence of death" (1:9). To Paul's utter surprise, he and his companions did not meet death. Their survival manifested a fundamental conviction: God's ability to bring life from death. God had decisively demonstrated this capacity in Christ's resurrection. By rescuing Paul from this perilous circumstance, God again displayed resurrection power—this time in Paul's life.

The death and resurrection motif is central to Paul's ministry. He interprets his suffering for the gospel as a sharing in the suffering and death of Jesus. Similarly, he understands God's power that shines through his weakness and tribulations as a manifestation of the resurrection.

In 1:12–24 Paul broaches a contentious topic: his conduct. Some in the congregation regard Paul's repeated change of travel plans as a symptom of his vacillating character, and they doubt whether Paul can be trusted. Paul's carefully chosen words reveal how seriously he takes the Corinthians' accusation. With God's empowerment, he had conducted himself frankly and sincerely among the Corinthians. Paul urges the community to place the changes in his itinerary in a broader, divine framework. While he values reciprocity with the Corinthians, he must ultimately answer to God, not to them.

Paul narrates the events of the "painful visit" in chap. 2. The frank words of discipline in the "letter of tears" (see introduction) demonstrated Paul's love for the Corinthians and spurred the community's repentance (2:4).

Paul assesses the theological implications of the "painful visit" (2:5–13). The hurtful actions directed toward Paul were actually an offense against the community. In the "letter of tears," Paul likely advocated some form of community discipline for this perpetrator. Heeding his recommendation, the Corinthians exercised discipline upon the offender, possibly removing community rights or even expelling the person from the community momentarily. Convinced that the discipline had run its course, Paul urges the Corinthians to forgive that person, since a failure to forgive might permit Satan to orchestrate further harm in the community (2:11). Paul implies that Satan constantly searches for opportunities to ambush believers. By actively forgiving one another's trespasses, Christians avoid these demonic snares.

A Ministry Approved by God (2:14–7:16)

Paul mounts an elaborate defense of his ministry in this central section of the letter, and especially responds to accusations of duplicity. An implicit question brings coherence to his various arguments: What characterizes a ministry approved by God? The continuation of his relationship with the Corinthians may depend on whether Paul and the Corinthians can agree on the answer to this question.

For Paul, a ministry that bears God's approval: (1) allows its work to speak for itself; (2) realizes the inescapability of suffering; (3) engages the present in light of God's future; and (4) strives to be a channel of God's reconciliation.

First, a God-approved ministry is authenticated by its work. Paul points to the Corinthian congregation as the validation of his ministry (3:1–3). In the Greco-Roman world, proof of credentials was important, and letters of recommendation assisted persons in establishing their social identities. Unlike other ministers (e.g., Paul's rivals in Corinth) who seek validation through letters of recommendation from outsiders, Paul avoids this practice, declaring that the Corinthian converts are his credentials.

Second, a ministry that bears God's approval recognizes the inescapability of suffering. In 2 Cor. 4 Paul presents the hardships that attend apostolic ministry. These hardships, however, do not dampen his enthusiasm for ministry or cause him to lose courage (4:1). Indeed, his apostolic sufferings create the conditions for a marvelous display of divine strength.

Were it not for hardships, Paul suggests that ministers might arrogantly assume proprietorship of God's power, instead of humbly serving as channels of that power. God deposits the treasure of the gospel in ordinary "clay jars" in order to reveal more prominently the extraordinary power of God (4:7). Human fragility is not a prohibition for, but a prerequisite of, authentic ministry.

Paul's hardships constantly remind him of his fragility (4:8–12). Yet in every hardship God's grace sustains him. Paul neither willingly invites suffering into his life, as if there is an inherent value in all suffering; nor does he vigorously flee from suffering. As a representative of a Savior who suffered, Paul courageously endures the hardships that proclamation of the gospel brings. While suffering is a central feature of Paul's theology, he would surely reject the reprehensible use of his words as scriptural sanction for the abuse and victimization of persons on the margins of power or for a theology that simplistically names suffering as "God's will."

Third, a ministry that bears God's approval engages the present in light of God's glorious future. Believers can be of good courage during hardships because those hardships will eventually give way to God's future. Paul develops a dichotomy between the transitory tribulations of the present age and the eternal extravagance of the age to come (4:17–5:10). If believers weigh their burdens in relation to the impending blessings of the future, the blessings excessively outweigh the burdens.

Paul's emphasis on the future may be a corrective to the claims of his rivals in Corinth who contend that they experience God's glory fully in the present. Thus, while asserting the importance of the future, Paul teaches the Corinthians that God's future has yet to be consummated. In the future, God will conclude the transformation of the world begun in the life, death, and resurrection of Jesus Christ.

God provides believers the Holy Spirit as a guarantee that God will finish what has been started (5:5). The word translated "guarantee" in 5:5 (*arrabon*) refers to a down payment or earnest money given to secure a financial transaction. The Holy Spirit ministers to believers in the present and constantly reminds them of the future—a future on which God has placed a considerable down payment.

Impatience for God's future causes persons to focus inappropriately on the outward appearance of present existence. Paul maintains that the realities that are visible with the physical eye are ephemeral features of the present age. Spiritual vision is necessary to comprehend eternal realities (4:18). Paul contrasts spiritual insight with physical sight in 5:7, which literally reads, "Through faith we walk, not through appearance." The impressive outward appearance of ministers can be deceptive. The ability to discern God's authentic representatives requires faith, which is a life properly oriented toward God.

Finally, a ministry that bears God's approval participates in God's reconciliation toward the world. In 5:11–6:13 Paul develops two interrelated themes: God's reconciling action toward the world, and the need for the Corinthians to be reconciled to Paul. The metaphor of reconciliation refers to the overcoming of hostilities that estrange family members.

For Paul, humanity's decision to live contrary to God's will creates a deep chasm between God and humanity. God has graciously bridged the chasm in the death and resurrection of Christ, affording humanity the possibility of another kind of existence (5:17). Persons can now live "in Christ" by utilizing Christ's death and resurrection as the compass for their existence. Paul believes that God has entrusted to him and his colleagues a "ministry of reconciliation" (5:18). He urges the Corinthians to demonstrate their desire to be reconciled to God by being reconciled to him and implies that the Corinthians' rejection of him would be equivalent to rejecting God's grace (6:1).

Paul's theology of reconciliation in chaps. 5–6 possesses strength and a potential problem. Its strength lies in its grounding of theological truths in human relationships. Certainly, reconciliation involves a vertical dimension, transforming the relationship between God and believers. But it also involves a horizontal dimension, seeking to transform the relationships among believers. The vertical relationship with God and the horizontal relationship with one's neighbors are not independent but interdependent.

Nevertheless, Paul's equation of his wishes with God's action is potentially problematic. Paul declares that in order to be in a right relationship with God the Corinthians must be in a right relationship with him. By establishing this tight correspondence, Paul has created a potentially oppressive structure that labels disagreement with him as disobedience toward God. Readers should be aware of the dangers of claiming to act in the name of God. To identify one's intentions and actions with God's will can be a genuine act of piety. It can also be an act of power meant to further one's agenda. An even-handed treatment of Paul neither accuses him of impure motives nor affords him a sacrosanct status.

Paul's intricate responses to the question—what constitutes a ministry approved by God—reveal how much he values his relationship with the Corinthians. He struggles passionately to restore his standing with these believers and concludes this section confident that his arguments have aided his efforts (7:16).

A Call for Generosity (2 Cor. 8–9)

In this section Paul hopes to renew the Corinthians' commitment to the Jerusalem collection. At a meeting of church leaders several years earlier, Paul had agreed to collect funds from his congregations for the relief of Jewish Christians in Jerusalem who were experiencing economic difficulty (Gal. 2:10). In addition to the pragmatic benefits of this relief effort, Paul attaches enormous theological significance to the collection. Since Paul's congregations consist primarily of Gentiles, he hopes that the acceptance of this offering by Jewish Christians in Jerusalem will symbolize a spiritual unity amid the ethnic diversity of the church.

Paul's previously strained relationship with the Corinthians has placed a damper on their commitment to the collection. Some of the Corinthians may have inquired, "Why should we entrust Paul with our money if we doubt the genuineness of his character?" While persuading them of the uprightness of his character, Paul seeks to instruct the Corinthians on their connection to a wider network of Christians. Nothing will signal more convincingly the revitalization of the Corinthians' trust in Paul than their willingness to contribute to this collection.

First, Paul attempts to incite "holy jealousy" by telling the Corinthians of the enormous generosity of Macedonian Christians in cities such as Philippi, Thessalonica, and Beroea. Their example is impressive because the Macedonian believers gave generously to the collection in spite of their extreme poverty (8:2). Second, Paul grounds his exhortation for giving in Christology—his understanding of the significance of Christ's actions (8:9). Christ provides the supreme manifestation of sacrificial giving. In his preexistent state, Christ shared the riches of God's divinity. For the sake of humanity, Christ forsook those riches and became "poor" by identifying with humanity. Christ's willingness to experi-ence "poverty" created the conditions for humanity to experience the riches of salvation.

Through the Jerusalem collection, Paul reveals the interconnection between the material and the spiritual in his theology, affirming that the gospel calls believers to financial generosity. Generosity of the most concrete kind demonstrates believers' allegiance to Christ.

Moreover, Paul's commitment to the Jerusalem collection stands as a critique of Christian insularity. Paul does not allow this local congregation to become so consumed by its own circumstances that it loses sight of the vast needs of others throughout the world. To be Christian is to have more than a personal relationship with Christ. It is also to enter into an extensive, even global, set of relationships with fellow believers. To that ancient question—am I my brother's and sister's keeper?—Paul resolutely replies in these chapters, yes.

Strength in Weakness (2 Cor. 10–13)

In this final section of the letter, Paul mounts his most impassioned arguments to reclaim the Corinthians' affection and to persuade them of his apostolic perspectives. Paul's increased emotional intensity in these chapters has given rise to partition theories—the belief that chaps. 10–13 are a different letter written later, which an editor stitched to chaps. 1–9. However, one can explain Paul's increased passion by ancient rhetorical theories, which often called for an intensification of emotions as a letter or speech concluded. Furthermore, there are important connections between chaps. 1–9 and 10–13, including Paul's defense of his apostleship and his commitment to a theology of the cross.

Paul's use of military metaphors in 10:1–6 reveals his intention to go on the offensive. A war is waging. The combatants are Paul and his ministerial rivals in Corinth, whom he later calls "false apostles" and "deceitful workers" (11:13). By attempting to steal the Corinthians' affection, these rival preachers have committed a spiritual offense against God. In order to combat this offense, Paul assumes the weaponry of spiritual warfare.

In 10:3 a play on words discloses Paul's battle plan: "We live in the flesh (*en sarki*), but we do not wage war according to the flesh (*kata sarka*)" (author's trans.). Paul's designation "in the flesh" (*en sarki*) is a neutral term designating human existence in the world. However, to live "according to the flesh" (*kata sarka*) is a negative term connoting a life not oriented toward God. While Paul is enmeshed in this world, he employs methods of warfare from another world—the realm of the Spirit. Paul's spiritual weapons are able to tear down strongholds (10:4).

Paul responds to the charges of his critics in the remainder of chap. 10. He concedes that he may have boasted too much about his apostolic authority and reminds the Corinthians that believers should boast only about God's deeds (10:17). Moreover, any attempt to commend oneself in this life is premature. The self-commendation of Paul's rivals demonstrates their fraudulent nature. True commendation will come from the Lord on the day of judgment.

Paul attempts to present the grounds for legitimate apostolic boasting in chaps. 11–12. In the ancient Mediterranean world, boasting or self-promotion was an expected social phenomenon, especially among rhetoricians and philosophers. Performed in the proper amount and the right context, self-promotion alerted others to one's importance and honor. Presumably, Paul focuses on boasting because his rivals have called attention to their ministerial prowess while denouncing Paul.

Scholars have constructed from chaps. 11–12 a basic portrait of his rivals. In 11:5 he sarcastically calls his rivals "super-apostles," possibly referring to their tendency to boast about their impressiveness. These "super-apostles" may be skilled rhetoricians (11:6). They eagerly receive financial support from the Corinthians for their ministerial services (11:7–9). Also,

they proudly claim their Jewish heritage (11:22). Moreover, they may have boasted of their ecstatic religious experiences (12:1). Their approach to ministry is triumphalistic—the validation of spiritual authenticity by charismatic or ecstatic performance.

From Paul's perspective, his rivals' boasting in their abilities manifests their sinful orientation. In a masterful display of irony and wit, Paul decides to play momentarily the game of his opponents by boasting "according to human standards." He repeatedly acknowledges the foolishness of such "human" boasting (11:16–23). Yet he condescends to the level of his opponents. Paul says in effect, "Opponents, I will play the boasting game with you, but such boasting profits nothing." Instead of boasting of any marvelous exploits, Paul provides embarrassing examples of his vulnerability and weakness (11:23–12:10). For example, Paul was once smuggled out in a basket to avoid capture by a ruling official (11:32–33). In this instance he was hardly a model of courage!

Perhaps the most telling example of Paul's apostolic weakness occurred during his trip to "third heaven." In the first-century Mediterranean world, people assumed that individuals could journey to heavenly realms and receive secrets concerning God's plans. "Third heaven" connotes that Paul ascended as far into heaven as possible. According to human standards, ascending to the highest level of heaven would conclusively attest to a person's ecstatic powers. Paul notes that his trip to third heaven and the revelations he received were outstanding (12:7).

Yet, in an ironic twist, Paul experiences a debilitating humiliation during his supposed exultation in third heaven (12:7). He receives a "thorn in the flesh." The nature of this thorn remains unspecified. Interpreters have speculated that it is spiritual or sexual temptation, a physical illness, or even a reference to Paul's opponents. Paul's three protestations do not compel the Lord to remove the "thorn." Paul implies that the thorn comes from Satan, but it accomplishes a divine purpose in Paul's life.

The Lord responds to Paul, "My grace is sufficient for you, for power is made perfect in weakness" (12:9). God teaches Paul that divine power works most effectively through human weakness. Humans, in their diminished and weakened state, become marvelous channels of the only true power, God's power. The acceptance of weakness, not the avoidance of it, is the context for a person's legitimate boast. Boasting in their "strength," Paul's rivals indicate their commitment to worldly wisdom. Boasting in his weakness and thus in God's strength, Paul reveals his commitment to God's foolishness—a foolishness displayed most decisively in the cross of Christ. A theology of the cross opens the Corinthian correspondence (1 Cor. 1) and propels it along to a dramatic conclusion (2 Cor. 12–13).

In the letter's concluding chapter, Paul marshals a number of final warnings and imperatives aimed at securing the Corinthians' allegiance. Many of his hopes for them are encapsulated in 13:11: "Finally, brothers and sisters, rejoice, aim for restoration, encourage each other, be united in your thoughts, live in peace, and the God of love and peace will be with you" (author's trans.). We can only speculate how effective 2 Corinthians was in restoring Paul's relationship with the Corinthians. Yet Paul composes the last letter of his ministry (as far as we know)—the Letter to the Romans—from Corinth (Rom. 16:23). The renewed hospitality and fellowship that Paul eventually experienced in Corinth must have made his previous struggles with this congregation worthwhile.

Bibliography

Bassler, Jouette M. "2 Corinthians." In *Women's Bible Commentary*, edited by Carol A. Newsom and Sharon H. Ringe, 420–22. Rev. ed. Louisville: Westminster John Knox, 1998.

Furnish, Victor P. *II Corinthians*. AB 30A. Garden City, NY: Doubleday, 1984.

Manus, Ukachukwu Chris. "2 Corinthians." In *Global Bible Commentary*, edited by Daniel Patte, 455–62. Nashville: Abingdon, 2004.

Matthews, Shelly. "2 Corinthians." In *Searching the Scriptures*, vol. 2: *A Feminist Commentary*, edited by Elisabeth Schüssler Fiorenza, 196–217. New York: Crossroad, 1994.

Murphy-O'Connor, Jerome. *The Theology of the Second Letter to the Corinthians*. New Testament Theology. Cambridge: Cambridge University Press, 1991.

Galatians

Sandra Hack Polaski

INTRODUCTION

The term "Galatia" denotes a region of Asia Minor, rather than a particular city, so it is not entirely clear who the addressees of the Letter to the Galatians were. Somewhat clearer is the situation that prompts Paul's writing of the letter. Paul founded the Galatian church and remains its spiritual "father," at least in his own estimation. Since he left the congregation, though, other traveling evangelists have arrived and told the Galatian Christians that Paul delivered only part of the message of Christ. What Christ really came to do, the new missionaries likely told the Galatians, was to make it possible for Gentiles to become part of the people of God—that is, the Jewish people. The Galatians should therefore take on the law proclaimed in Scripture, including the practice of circumcision. The congregation apparently received this message gladly and began moving toward a life regulated by Jewish law.

When Paul hears of this innovation in the Galatian church, he responds with a fiery missive that addresses many issues central to the gospel of Christ. Primary among these is the notion of freedom, specifically, what it means to be free in Christ. Paul defines freedom not only in contrast to the Galatians' previous polytheism but also in contrast to "the law," by which he means primarily the law given by God to Israel in Scripture. The Galatians' experience of the Spirit demonstrates that they need not be followers of the "law" in order to be followers of Christ. Yet that very same Spirit is given by God to guard the Galatians from falling into sin, so that in the Spirit the law's true purpose is accomplished. Paul summarizes the social implications of freedom in Christ, and eloquently describes the work of the Holy Spirit in the life of believers. All of these make Galatians one of Paul's most familiar and most quoted letters.

COMMENTARY

Paul Defends Himself and His Gospel (1:1–2:14)

Paul's ministry was not without controversy, and opponents often attacked his person as well as his message (see, e.g., 2 Cor. 10–13). In Galatians Paul foregrounds his self-defense, tying his personal reputation inextricably with the truth of the message he preaches. The prescript of the letter, usually a place simply to state the letter's author and addressees, becomes Paul's opening salvo in his argument: he is literally, "Paul Apostle," then immediately he defends his claim to apostolic status as being not of or by human action, but directly by God (1:1). He will take second place to no one, just as he will defend his gospel as being complete, sufficient, and authoritative.

Right away he states the reason for his urgent tone. He has learned that the Galatians are "turning to a different gospel" (1:6). Immediately Paul corrects himself—of course there is no other gospel that can be truly so called. But he knows that there is another message circulating, one that the Galatians have taken for the gospel. He uses the strongest possible theological language to decry this message, saying that anyone who preaches it is to be *anathema*, accursed.

Having briefly stated his purpose for writing, Paul returns to his self-defense, giving us along the way the fullest autobiography that we see in his letters. The reason Paul needs to prove himself is quite logical. He was not one of Jesus' followers during the earthly ministry, and came to faith only some time after Jesus' crucifixion and resurrection. How, then, could his message possibly be as authoritative as that of Jesus' own followers or those whom they personally commissioned?

Paul's answer is succinct: revelation. He received his gospel, he states, by revelation of Jesus Christ (1:12). To bolster his argument, he recites a history hardly commendable by the standards of the community: he was a zealous Jew, to the point of persecuting the church. Paul's self-presentation of his revelation contrasts with the story of his conversion found in Acts. Instead of a detailed narrative (Acts 9:1–22; 22:4–16; 26:9–18), Paul mentions his revelation of the risen Christ in passing. When he received his revelation, he immediately went away, far from the Jerusalem apostles. Paul acknowledges that he did spend fifteen days with Peter, three years later, and also met James (Gal. 1:18–19). Yet by this time, Paul implies, he had already shaped his revelation into a proclamation of the gospel.

A gap of fourteen years separates the visit with Peter from Paul's next trip to Jerusalem, a meeting of equals regarding the proclamation of the gospel to Jews and to Gentiles. Again, Paul begins the story with revelation, this time a revelation in response to which he makes the journey (2:2). The event is told rather differently in Acts 15, although the basic outline is the same. In Paul's version, he lays his gospel before the "acknowledged leaders" (Gal. 2:6, or translated more literally, the "ones supposed to be something.") Although some opponents seek to make trouble, the Jerusalem authorities agree that Paul's gospel is true and complete, require nothing of him, and send him and Barnabas on their way with "the right hand of fellowship" (2:9). Almost as an afterthought, Paul mentions that he has agreed to "remember the poor" (2:10), presumably referring to the Jerusalem collection for which he appeals frequently in his letters (Rom. 15:25; 1 Cor. 16:1; 2 Cor. 8:4; 9:1).

Throughout this self-defense, Paul emphasizes both his freedom from the Jerusalem authorities and the grace given directly to him by God. God's call to him is by grace, beginning before he was born (Gal. 1:15), and does not require human confirmation. Paul's detractors at the Jerusalem consultation are unable to take away "the freedom we have in Christ Jesus" (2:4). Paul and Peter are equals, with apostolic commissions from God for Gentiles and Jews, respectively (2:8). Paul leaves Jerusalem with the "acknowledged" leaders' recognition that grace has been given to him.

The next chapter of Paul's story, the conflict with Cephas (Peter) at Antioch (2:11–14), ties into the current situation at Galatia that has led to Paul's letter. The church at Antioch is apparently either Gentile or a mixed Jewish and Gentile congregation; in any case, when Peter visits Antioch he (and presumably Paul as well) shares table fellowship with Gentiles, although such practice was against Jewish law strictly interpreted. Later a group of Jewish Christians arrives at Antioch, apparently from Jerusalem (Paul says that they are "from James"), who practice separation from Gentiles at meals. Peter's consideration for their qualms, if we could hear his side of the story, might be phrased as "concern for the weaker brother," not unlike Paul's own argument regarding meat offered to idols (see 1 Cor. 8 and commentary). But we do not hear Peter's side, and Paul sees this issue as not open to compromise. Paul vehemently opposes Peter's stance and his actions, claiming that Peter's behavior is inconsistent with "the truth of the gospel" (Gal. 2:14). To Paul, Peter is attempting to "compel the Gentiles to live like Jews" (2:14). It is not merely a refusal of table fellowship nor a failure of hospitality that offends Paul. Rather, Peter's act seeks to impose a requirement that Paul rejects: law observance (in this case, kosher law) by Gentile Christians. This is also the problem in Galatia.

Not Law but Faith (2:15–5:12)

Paul's theological argument is woven so seamlessly into his reported speech to Peter that scholars disagree on where one ends and the other begins. (Quotation marks, added in most English versions, do not appear in the Greek manuscripts.) In one sense, the entire rest of the letter could be read as Paul's response to Peter, and all those who would impose Jewish legal requirements on their Gentile brothers and sisters.

Paul's unfolding of his position proceeds by interweaving a number of arguments and metaphors. First, he lays out the issue in terms of justification, a metaphor he will later expound on at length in the Letter to the Romans. Here he states: "we know that a person is justified not by the works of the law, but through faith in Jesus Christ" (2:16). Nearly every term in this sentence is theologically significant. Justification, a legal metaphor, refers in Paul's theology to a person's standing before God, a

standing that God has the power to determine. "Works of the law," often shortened simply to "law," is related both to human effort and to the divine requirements set forth in the Torah; but exactly how to understand what Paul means is difficult to determine. We should not think that Paul is making a distinction between the law's moral requirements and the ritual practices that the law commands. Such a distinction may be popular in contemporary interpretations, but it would go against the ancient understandings of the law. Paul never makes such a distinction, nor does Paul suggest that God stands ready and eager to condemn those who break one of the thousands of laws. The law does not require us to live in fear of God's condemnation; the law shows us how to live rightly even when we cannot do it ourselves. Indeed, Paul shares with first-century Jews and Christians a deep belief in both divine justice and divine mercy.

What, precisely, does Paul mean by "faith in Jesus Christ"? Traditionally, particularly following the Lutheran tradition, this phrase has been interpreted as the single requirement for being a Christian: placing one's belief in Christ. Yet the phrase Paul uses, *pistis Iēsou Christou*, can be read grammatically either as "faith in Jesus Christ"—our faith with Christ as its object—or "Jesus Christ's faith[fulness]"—the faithful act of Christ in dying on the cross, in which we are made participants by God's grace. The former reading has the weight of Christian tradition, and particularly of Reformation tradition with its emphasis on the responsibility of the believer. The latter keeps even faith from being an "act" by emphasizing Christ's faithfulness and God's grace rather than our own initiative. It fits well with the participatory theology of such claims as "I have been crucified with Christ, and it is no longer I who live, but it is Christ who lives in me" (2:19–20). Scholars have made strong cases for both readings. Perhaps the best way forward is to hold both possibilities open, continuing to explore what "faith in/of Christ" means for Paul in Galatians.

Just as Paul makes the case for his own authority by appeal to personal experience of divine revelation, he also urges the Galatians to recall their own experience of faith and of the Holy Spirit. They should know that they do not need the law, Paul says, because they have already experienced salvation outside the law. They have begun well, Paul says; to turn from the Spirit to the "flesh," which he equates with "works of the law," would be a "foolish" venture (3:3).

Reference to salvation preceding law immediately reminds Paul of one of his favorite biblical examples, Abraham. Abraham, the celebrated forefather of the Jewish people, becomes in Paul's arguments an example of faith preceding all the markers of Jewish ethnic identity: law, circumcision, and table fellowship. Furthermore, the blessing to all nations through Abraham (Gen. 12:1–3) serves Paul as evidence that Abraham is intended as the forefather not of the Jews but of all who believe (Gal. 3:9). Paul returns to the Abraham theme twice later in the letter, once to reinforce the equality of believers as offspring of Abraham (3:29), then again to develop an allegory on the story of Abraham's two wives, Sarah and Hagar (4:21–31). This allegorical reading further turns the traditional Jewish understanding of Abraham on its head. Not only are believers in Christ the true children of Abraham, but since they are "free" and not "slaves," they are the true children of Sarah, while the "slave" children of Hagar "correspond . . . to the present Jerusalem" (4:25).

One of the most confusing aspects of Galatians is its apparent equation of the law with slavery and curse, particularly since Paul elsewhere goes to significant lengths to deny that he views the law in a negative light (e.g., Rom. 7:12: "So the law is holy, and the commandment is holy and just and good"). In his passionate Letter to the Galatians, though, Paul throws nuance to the wind. Not only were human beings enslaved by the law; even Christ

was under its curse, since "Cursed is everyone who hangs on a tree" (Gal. 3:13, citing Deut. 21:23), that is, his crucifixion was evidence of his being under divine curse according to Torah. Yet Christ's death, Paul proclaims, is our redemption from the law's curse, because by participating in Christ's death we are no longer bound to the law. The law cannot make alive, but can only imprison those who sin (Gal. 3:21–22). Those who seek to take the law's requirement upon themselves (in the Galatian instance, particularly by becoming circumcised) enslave themselves to a whole law that is impossible to keep (5:3). In ironic and startlingly graphic terms Paul characterizes circumcision as "cutting off" from Christ and "falling away" from grace (5:4).

In keeping with Hellenistic rhetorical style, Paul incorporates personal references into his argument to remind his readers of the relationship they share. Paul first evangelized the Galatians during a time of personal physical weakness; he refers to his "physical infirmity" (4:13) and says that they would have given their eyes to him (4:15). But he also reverses the dynamic of dependence when he addresses the Galatians as "my little children" (4:19) and scolds in a parental tone. Interestingly, he images himself not as father but as mother to the congregation, "again in the pain of childbirth until Christ is formed in you" (4:19).

Paul also uses the metaphor of the minor child who is to become the heir of the estate. This image works for Paul on a number of levels. For many members of Paul's congregations from the lower social classes, the idea of being an heir would be beyond their experience. Yet they would well have understood the basics of inheritance law: that a ratified will guaranteed that an inheritance would come, that a child in line for an inheritance would receive his wealth and influence once he became of age, that an heir could be either a natural or an adopted child. Through this metaphor, then, Paul assures the Galatians that, though they may have seemed like slaves and not members of the family, they are in fact God's adopted children and heirs (4:7). Their divine inheritance is sure (3:17). The law has served as a disciplinarian for a child, but the child who has reached the age of majority needs supervision no longer (3:25).

Paul moves from the metaphor of inheritance as equal standing before God to another topic that is one of the most famous in this letter. Drawing his imagery, and probably his language, from the Christian act of baptism, Paul speaks of those who are members of Christ as having "put on" Christ. Early Christian practice was that the candidates for baptism would take off their own clothes (with whatever status symbols they carried), be baptized naked, and then dress in plain, identical white robes to symbolize both purity and community. Most likely the words Paul uses here come from a baptismal liturgy:

> There is no longer Jew or Greek,
> there is no longer slave or free,
> there is no longer male and female;
> for all of you are one in Christ Jesus.
> (3:28)

The social equality these words imply, including gender equality, and the use Paul intended to make of them in his message to the Galatians have been extensively debated. As the liturgical words of inclusion into a community, they imply the obliteration of all race, class, and gender distinctions within the Christian fellowship, and may well have been meant to bring about a community in which the patriarchal institution of marriage was no longer observed. Would this, then, have meant a celibate community? Or is it possible that egalitarian Christian communities existed in the first century—and if they did, what became of them? Paul's comments on gender elsewhere in his letters seem to make clear that he does not understand membership in Christ to mean the obliteration of sexual difference. The echo of "male and female" from Gen. 1:27 (notice the difference from the "or" formulation of the other two pairs) can be understood to point to the distinct curses for the man and the woman, after the fall; the implication may be that membership in Christ undoes the curse of Genesis. In any case, the narrow interpretation of this text, that it implies only an equality of standing before God and has no implications for societal relationships, is untenable in this letter's context. Whatever "all of you are one" means in Galatians, it certainly points toward a community that lives out their theological commitments in changed relationships with one another.

Live by the Spirit (5:13–6:18)

For Paul the very heart of Christian freedom is the community that is shaped by that freedom. We cannot be certain that the Galatians had been celebrating freedom in libertine or licentious ways, although such problems may have been one drawing point for the missionaries who preached the restraining power of the Jewish law. For Paul, though, libertine practices are not freedom at all, but fleshly desires that demonstrate a lack of the Spirit.

Paul's lists of "works of the flesh" (5:19–21) and "fruit of the Spirit" (5:22–23) have a great deal in common with virtue and vice lists of Hellenistic philosophy, whether of Jewish or pagan origin. Several groupings or orderings have been suggested for Paul's vice list, but none seems self-evident. Indeed, the chaotic structure may be meant to reflect the disorder that fleshly desire wreaks in human life. The list is interesting for its scope. Violations of person and property are prominent, as is sexual sin and religious transgression; but also featured are a number of actions that tear at the fabric of community, such as quarrels, dissensions, and factions (5:20). These, no less than fornication and idolatry, are the result of the power of evil.

Notably, Paul refers to the evidence of the Spirit in believers' lives as "fruit" rather than "works," a term that in this letter carries a negative connotation. "Fruit," by contrast, suggests that which happens naturally, without special effort on the part of the individual, when the Spirit is in control. Like the vice list, most of these fruit are not specifically Christian virtues. Love, the primary Christian virtue, heads the list, however. The final place is occupied by self-control, the chief virtue of most Greco-Roman philosophy of the day.

The life of the Spirit results in specific practices in the community. Believers are to be involved in one another's lives in constructive ways, "restoring" those who have transgressed and bearing one another's burdens—while at the same time being concerned for their own work rather than that of their neighbor (6:1–4). The believing community is to act so as to gain high regard in the community: "let us work for the good of all," but "especially for those of the family of faith"—charity begins at home (6:10).

At the very end of his Letter to the Galatians, Paul returns to the themes that occasioned his writing. The rival missionaries who "try to compel you to be circumcised" (6:12) do not have the Gala-tians' best interests at heart, but only their own reputation. Paul is the congregation's true model of suffering and faith. By following the gospel he has preached, and living in the Spirit they have received as a result of that gospel, the Galatians will continue in God's grace.

Bibliography

Betz, Hans Dieter. *Galatians: A Commentary on Paul's Letter to the Churches in Galatia*. Hermeneia. Philadelphia: Fortress, 1979.

Cousar, Charles. *Galatians*. Interpretation. Atlanta: John Knox, 1982.

Gaventa, Beverly Roberts. *Our Mother Saint Paul*. Louisville: Westminster John Knox, 2007.

Hays, Richard B. *The Faith of Jesus Christ: The Narrative Substructure of Galatians 3:1–4:11*. 2nd ed. Grand Rapids: Eerdmans, 2002.

Polaski, Sandra Hack. *A Feminist Introduction to Paul*. St. Louis: Chalice, 2005.

Ephesians

Sze-kar Wan

INTRODUCTION

Cast in the form of a Pauline letter, Ephesians is at heart a theological treatise. It summarizes the teachings of Paul even as it draws them to their logical conclusions. Its theme revolves around the church, "built on the foundation of the apostles and prophets, with Jesus Christ as the cornerstone" (2:20). Gentiles were separated from the commonwealth of Israel, but they are now fellow heirs with the Jews and fellow sharers of the promise through the gospel (3:5–6). This is the eternal mystery that was hidden for generations but is now revealed first to Paul and through him to all. Gentiles and Jews have been brought into one people by the blood of Christ, the peace that reconciles the two previously warring factions and makes them into a new human being (2:13–16). In Christ the church grows into a new organism, a dwelling place of God (2:20–21).

Members of this new community become what has been called the "embodied Christ" (Yoder Neufeld). There is a diversity of gifts, but there is only one body of Christ. This body must leave behind childish things and mature into Christ from whom the whole body is joined together and made into a unified building in love (4:1–16). Though there is no confusion in Ephesians between the role of Christ and that of the members of the body, the church nevertheless must carry on the mission of Christ on earth. As children of the light, they must not engage in behaviors that belong to darkness (5:3–14), but rather live a life in the light, as a model household of God (5:15–6:9).

The body of Christ is not a world-denying sect but a living and breathing organism called to continue the work of Christ in engaging the evil forces of the world. Just as Christ engaged principalities and powers, the church is enjoined to engage these and any evil forces that threaten the peace of Christ by taking up the "whole armor of God" (6:10–20).

Ephesians bears a striking resemblance to Colossians on a number of points. Even though it never cites Colossians directly, Ephesians echoes it in about a third of its material and even draws conclusions from what is only hinted at in Colossians. The Christology of Ephesians is based on the Colossian Hymn (Col. 1:15–20), but whereas the preeminence of Christ is the focus of Colossians, in Ephesians this preeminence is shifted to the church (Eph. 1:20–23). The Household Code of Ephesians is adapted from Colossians (Col. 3:18–4:1), but in Ephesians the relationship between husband and

All quotations from Scripture in this chapter are the author's translation.

wife is vastly expanded to symbolize the relationship between Christ and the church (Eph. 5:22–33). These and other considerations spawn the suspicion that Ephesians was composed by a later disciple of Paul.

COMMENTARY

Ephesians follows the usual Pauline division of theology and ethics. An exposition of the nature of the church as the body of Christ (1:3–2:22) is followed by an extended exhortation on how to behave within the body (4:1–5:20). The center section (3:1–21) presents Paul as a mystagogue (3:2, 9, etc.) and his writings as a *via media* to the mystery of Christ (especially 3:3). All this is introduced by a blessing to God (1:3–14) and an apostolic prayer (1:15–23), which set the tone for the rest of the discussion.

Paul customarily begins a letter with a thanksgiving prayer, but on at least one occasion (2 Corinthians) he uses a blessing to God instead. Ephesians also opens with a blessing (1:3–14), followed by an apostolic prayer (1:15–23). The blessing in Ephesians announces the major themes, as in a Pauline thanksgiving prayer, but it also establishes the theological foundation for a church that is centered in God's election of the believers through Christ's redemptive work.

While a Pauline thanksgiving prayer often stresses the well-being of the recipients and their past and anticipated accomplishments, a blessing by its very nature highlights God's attributes and actions. In the Ephesian blessing, God is the subject of every major statement, the prime actor responsible for putting the plan of salvation into motion. It is God who bestows blessings on the people, elects the saints for adoption in Christ, and reveals the mystery of ages past to all. The people, on the other hand, are the object of God's actions, recipients of God's grace. They act only insofar as they reflect on and respond to the blessings of God. The reflexive nature of the people's action is stated in the opening line of the blessing: "*Blessed* be the God and Father of our Lord Jesus Christ, who has *blessed* us with every spiritual *blessing* in the heavenlies in Christ" (v. 3). The tenses of the verbs make clear that God's blessing is the prior act that calls forth the human blessing of God. We are in a position to bless God, because we were first blessed by God. The opening sentence establishes a pattern for the rest of the blessing and introduces a theological motif for Ephesians: God is the prime actor who takes the initiative to elect the saints, while the elect act in response to God's grace. But at every turn God acts through Christ the mediator to fulfill the preordained purpose of creation and salvation.

God the Prime Giver

The blessing of Ephesians portrays God as a giver of free gifts, three in particular: the election of the people for adoption, saving grace, and knowledge of the mystery. First, election is part of the eternal plan of God that began even before the creation of the world, before the beginning, as it were: "God elected us in [Christ] before the foundation of the world—to be holy and blameless before him in love" (v. 4). Election is therefore part of the original design of creation, and its purpose is that the elect be holy and blameless and that they might praise the Creator: "God foreordained us for heirship through Jesus Christ for himself, according to the pleasure of his will, for praise of his glorious grace" (vv. 5–6a).

Second, while "glorious grace" is the object of praise, it is also the basis of salvation, for the author immediately continues with, "[God] bestowed *grace* on us through his Beloved, in whom we have redemption through his blood, the forgiveness of trespasses, according to the richness of his *grace*" (vv. 6b–7). "Grace" in this context is the divine favor shown in Christ, "his Beloved," for the purpose of redemption and forgiveness. If election is the design of creation, grace is the realization of that plan in salvation, the new creation.

The full plan of salvation by grace is laid out in detail in 2:1–10. The passage begins in typical Jewish fashion with the rebellion of human beings, who were misled by powerful forces "of the air" while they lived in the passions of the flesh (vv. 1–3). It then describes God's grace (using two synonyms, "mercy" and "love") as liberation (vv. 4–7): "We have been saved by grace" (v. 5; also v. 8). "To save" (*sōzō*) literally means "to rescue" or "to make whole," and it is used here to describe God making those who have been dead in trespasses alive with Christ. The image of rising with Christ and being seated in Christ (v. 6) comes from the baptismal theology of Col. 2:11–12, except that the author of Ephesians omits dying and burying with Christ and singles out rising with Christ. In so doing, Ephesians takes Paul's understanding of baptism to a new level. While Paul thought resurrection with Christ to be a hope for the future in the eschaton, in Ephesians the resurrection is seen as an accomplished event. Thus Paul's dynamic *"justification by faith"* is replaced by Ephesians' *"salvation by faith"* (vv. 5, 8).

The third gift God imparts to the elect, according to the opening blessing, is wisdom and insight through which they are revealed "the mystery" (vv. 8–9). *Mystery* (*mystērion*) in first-century apocalyptic Judaism was a secret from ages past that God had kept hidden from generations of seekers. Its contents were to be revealed not through human ingenuity but only by God to the initiated at the divinely appointed time. In apocalyptic circles (e.g., the Qumran covenanters) secrets of the mystery were revealed only to the privileged few (e.g., the Teacher of Righteousness). In Ephesians, by contrast, knowledge of the mystery has been made public and is now available to all: "In former generations [this mystery] was not made known to humanity, as now it has

been revealed to his holy apostles and prophets by the Spirit: namely, the Gentiles are coheirs, members of the same body, and cosharers of the promises in Christ Jesus through the gospel" (3:5–6). The special knowledge now available to the Gentiles is that they are part of the elect through the hearing of the gospel (1:13) and that they have been given an inheritance as part of an eternal plan of God (1:11), even though they were formerly enemies of God. What makes all this possible is that all things have been gathered up in Christ (1:10). As a result, Christ now maintains a relationship with the church as intimate as that between husband and wife (5:19).

Christology

The author of Ephesians speculates little on the nature of God outside the work of salvation effected through Christ. While God remains the prime actor, Christ is the necessary mediator. Twelve times "in Christ" or its equivalent appears in the opening blessing. However the expression is understood, it highlights Christ's constitutive role of mediation in this cosmic drama. In Christ we obtained an inheritance (1:11). In Christ we have the redemption and forgiveness of trespasses (1:7). In Christ we are granted grace (1:6). In and through Christ we have been elected and foreordained for adoption (1:4–5). Even our ability to bless God owes its existence to the mediation of Christ (1:3). Indeed, Christ appears so frequently in the blessing and his actions are so closely identified with God's that the author seems intent on merging the two together. While God is ultimately the author of redemption, owing to "the riches of his grace," God achieved it "in Christ" and "through his blood" (1:7). While God predestined believers for inheritance, the plan was executed "according to the plan of the one who energizes all things according to the counsel of his will" (1:11). Modern readers might identify "the one who energizes all things" as Christ, who works out God's counsel and will and who is distinct from

God, but it does not seem to be the intention of the author to do so. After all, it is God who vested Christ with God's good pleasure in order to execute God's plans (1:9; cf. 1:5). God acts as Christ acts.

This close relationship between God and Christ, especially in giving Christ prominent roles in both creation and redemption, owes its pattern to early Jewish Wisdom speculation. Thus election takes place *in Christ* before the foundation of the world (1:4), an acknowledgment of Wisdom's role in creation (see Prov. 8:22), which means plans for the formation of the church were made long ago, at creation, in Christ (Eph. 3:11). In the redemptive plan, Christ is the peace that reconciles warring factions of Jews and Gentiles by abolishing the hostility between them and by re-creating them into one new human being (2:14–18) and giving them a new identity (2:15; 4:24). As such Christ is the head of the new body (1:23; 2:16; 4:11–16; 5:23). God or Christ lavishes on us "in all wisdom and understanding" (1:8), a reference to Wisdom seeking receptive human beings for enlightenment. Even the romantic union between Wisdom and the righteous described in the Wisdom of Solomon is paralleled by Christ's relationship to the church allegorized as husband and wife, except the genders of the two are now reversed (5:25–32). As a fitting précis to the Christology of Ephesians, Christ is appointed for the "administration [*oikonomia*; not just "plan" of NRSV] of the fullness of the times, gathering in all things in him, things in the heavens and things on earth" (1:10). Christ the Wisdom is preeminent over all creation.

Another biblical motif that informs the Christology of Ephesians is that of the Divine Warrior, who intrudes into human time and space to vindicate the oppressed and protect the weak, sometimes through violence. In this tradition, God is warrior, judge, and liberator. Frequently the agent through whom God prosecutes the divine plans is a messianic emissary (see Isa. 11). In Ephesians, Christ was raised from the dead and installed above, while God subjected all things under him (1:20–22). But this peaceable "warrior" accomplished this world "domination" through defeat and suffering, "killing enmity" to reconcile warring factions into one (2:16).

Cosmology

Time in Ephesians is not *khronos*, which is linear time, but *kairos*, loaded time, the divinely appointed time when the cosmic plan of God is put into effect. It is used in the plural, "times" (so correctly NIV and KJV) in 1:10. "Fullness of times" therefore refers not just to the timeliness of God's actions through Christ in history but especially to the transtemporal, transhistorical, even transspatial realm that Christ fills to its overflowing completion. The emphasis is not on some distant future date in a faraway place but on the here and now Christ has transformed into a special time and space.

There is therefore some truth to the observation that Ephesians extends classical Pauline eschatology. While Paul modifies Jewish apocalypticism to maintain a tension between this age and the age to come, it is almost exclusively a temporal category. Ephesians, on the other hand, while retaining the temporal dimension of Pauline eschatology, places the emphasis on the present. The language of election and predestination pervades the blessing, especially 1:4–5, 11–12, and it is used to convey the understanding that we were chosen in Christ "before the foundation of the world" (v. 4). Before the beginning, at creation, the eternal plan of salvation in Christ—redemption through the blood of the cross and forgiveness of trespasses, inheritance, hope—was preordained according to an eternal plan established by the will of God, a plan that stretches from the beginning to the end (1:10). But in Ephesians the temporal tension that characterizes much of Paul's eschatology is transmuted into a cosmic conflict. The battle is waged between the fleshly and the spiritual, between the children of light and the children of darkness, between the church, the bodily envoy of Christ on the one hand, and on the other hand evil forces that threaten the peace of the world. The battlefield is the heavenly realm.

The phrase, *en tois ouranois*, literally, "in the heavenlies" and often translated as "the heavenly places" (so NRSV), is found in the New Testament only five times, all in Ephesians (1:3, 20; 2:6; 3:10; 6:12). The heavenlies are where Christ is, where at the resurrection God enlivened and raised him and seated him far above all rulers and authorities and powers (1:20–22). While Ephesians retains the tension between this age and the age to come (1:21), it uses Ps. 110:1 to describe Christ's subjugation of all things as an event of the past (1:22). By contrast, the Paul of 1 Cor. 15:24–28 is at pains to explain why the past tense of "subjugated" in Ps. 110:1 actually refers to the future (especially 1 Cor. 15:27). But the heavenlies are also where rulers, authorities, world dominators, and other spiritual forces of evil reside, and the heavenlies are called "this darkness" (Eph. 6:12; see also 3:10). If so, the heavenlies represent the spiritual realm, the cosmological space where the spiritual warfare between Christ and evil powers is joined. While Christ is seated "higher up," other disrupting forces of the rebellion occupy the air below. The saints, on the other hand, have been raised up to the heavenlies with Christ as a consequence of baptism (2:6) but are also enjoined to engage the evil forces that occupy the air below (3:10; 6:10–20). While God places the elect alongside Christ, God also enlists them for active duty in the current conflict. Baptism has an ethical impetus, and ethics in Ephesians is engaged within the context of the church.

Ethics

The closing of the blessing recasts the saints in an active role, but only as a response to the primary initiatives of God. "In [Christ], you hear the word of truth" and "in [him] you believe," but hearing and believing are none other than an appropriate response to and acceptance of God's proffering of "the truth, the gospel of your salvation," to the believers and hearers (v. 13). When the elect are called out of their old hideouts to form an assembly, therefore, their work is born out of God's bestowal of gifts.

The church is described in the apostolic prayer as the "body of Christ," a designation that has plenty of Pauline pedigree (Rom. 12:4–5; 1 Cor. 12:12–27; Col. 1:18, 24; 2:19; 3:15), with Christ being its "head" (Eph. 1:22b–23). These two originally independent metaphors, combined for the first time in Colossians, enrich the relationship between the church and Christ with ambiguity. While v. 22b could be read as "God made [Christ] the head over all things *for the church*" (so NRSV), the sentence can also be translated as "God gave [Christ], the head over all things, *to the church*," meaning that Christ the cosmic Lord has been given to the church as a gift. A third possibility is to translate it as "God made Christ the head *through the church*," thus vesting the church with a powerful impetus to bring Christ's headship to realization. All three possibilities have support in the text, and all three might well be meant by the author.

The church as the body is also described as "the fullness (*plērōma*) of him who fills all in all" (1:23). In Colossians *Christ* is called God's fullness, meaning that Christ represents God to the fullest; in Ephesians this divine fullness is transferred to the church. In Eph. 3:19, likewise, the author prays that the saints might get to know the love of Christ, so that they "may be filled with all the fullness of God." The church in this connection is the new creation of Christ, his resurrected body. In place of the hostility between Jews and Gentiles, Christ abolishes the law and its commandments to "create the two into *one new human being* in him." This "new human being" is nothing short of the resurrected Christ himself, for it is the result, according to 2:15–16, of his death on the cross. He "killed enmity," thereby making peace and reconciling the two formerly warring factions into "one body." If so, the ecclesiology of Ephesians is an explicit working of Paul's second Adam Christology (Rom. 5:12–21; 1 Cor. 15:21–22, 45–47). Christ's resurrection inaugurates him as the new Adam, from and in whom a new humanity issues. This "new human being" is identified as the church in Ephesians.

Both metaphors of body and fullness tie the church to the headship of Christ, who himself is the full manifestation of God. What is true for Christ is therefore also true for the elect, what is at work in Christ is also at work in the church, and whatever the task of Christ might be is also the task of the church. But if Christ's task is the administration of the world and the ingathering of all things, to claim the church as the body of Christ is to claim that it is the also the church's task for the gathering of all things. This cosmic responsibility of the church is already implied in the formulation of the church as "the fullness of him who fills all in all" (1:23). The prime actor remains God, who fills the church with God's fullness (see also 3:19); but because this is the same God who fills "all in all," God's fullness also pours out into the cosmos through the church.

But the close connection between Christ and the church also makes a statement about the church's relationship to the world. As Christ is the head over all things as well as over the church, the author is claiming that all things and the church are somehow related. In the felicitous words of one commentator, "in Ephesians the *church* is already what *all things* are in the process of becoming. As Christ's body, the church is the reconciled or gathered-up cosmos in embryonic form" (Yoder Neufeld, p. 80).

The relationship between Christ and the church is not just a matter of hierarchy, as the head is over a body, but it is also a matter of identification. The saints identify with Christ, but Christ also represents the goal toward which the saints must strive and the perfection it must emulate. Thus the church must "grow into the maturity [literally, *perfect man, anēr teleios*] of Christ, to the measure of the full stature [literally, *fullness, plērōma*] of Christ" (4:13). While the church *is* the fullness of Christ, it must also work toward growing into the fullness of Christ. This is the tension between the already and not yet that determines the ethical imperative of Paul. In other words, the church must become what it is. While the church has been given the identity as the body of Christ, the saints must "grow up in every way into him who is the head" (4:15). Reverting to baptismal language in 4:21–24, the author sums up by reminding the readers that they have been taught to put away "the old human being," hopelessly corrupted by passion, and to renew their mind and put on "the new human being."

It would be a mistake, however, to take this "new human being" in the individual sense, which is encouraged by the common translation as "new self" (so NRSV). In Ephesians as in Paul, the body is a community of saints who embody a variety of gifts (4:7–12), but the saints belong to the same body under the same Spirit (4:4–6). Unity stands in tension with the variety of individual gifts, but all must work individually and together to accomplish the same goal. Each part of the body has its function, but all must work properly before they could grow, as a single entity, "into the head, Christ" (4:15–16).

But there is more to growing into Christ's headship than collective narcissism. Many translations read 4:15 as NRSV does: "We must grow up in every way into him who is the head, into Christ." But another possible translation reads: "Let us make all things to grow into him, who is the head, Christ." If so, to maintain unity of the body includes taking part in Christ's task of gathering all things into him (1:10). Unity is understood as *both* adhering to the same Lord in whom the new body is created (2:15) *and* participating in their head's ingathering of all things unto himself

(1:10). To mature as a body of Christ, the earthly representatives of Christ need not just an inward gaze but also an activist spirit of call to Christ's headship, to engage as Christ does the principalities and powers of the world (6:10–20), and to convey to them as Paul does Christ's wisdom (3:8–11)—so that all may be gathered into one.

Bibliography

Barth, Markus. *Ephesians.* AB 34. 2 vols. Garden City, NY: Doubleday, 1974.

Lincoln, Andrew T. *Ephesians.* WBC 42. Dallas: Word, 1990.

Yoder Neufeld, Thomas R. *Ephesians.* Believers Church Bible Commentary. Scottdale, PA: Herald, 2002.

Philippians

Sze-kar Wan

INTRODUCTION

Philippians is an intensely personal letter. It gives us a glimpse of an imprisoned Paul facing affliction and the threat of death and feeling anxious about his young congregation in Philippi. While Paul is never one to hold back from recounting his adversities (e.g., 2 Cor. 11:22–33), what distinguishes Philippians from his other letters is how intimate his reflections are here. He confesses to his readers his wish to depart to be with Christ (1:21–23), his continual striving for perfection (3:13–14), his personal ideal of living in contentment above hardship (4:11–13), his love for the Philippians and theirs for him (1:7–9; 2:1–4; 4:1), his affection for his fellow workers (2:20–22, 27) that extends even to his detractors (4:3), and so on. Even in his polemics against his opponents (3:2–6), a frequent feature in his other letters, Paul ends not in bitterness but in defiance (3:7–11). Throughout the letter, Paul appears tender, concerned, dignified, upbeat, even joyful. Though he remains his boastful self when he perceives threat, only in Philippians does he appear magnanimous to his competitors and detractors (1:15–18).

More than any of his other letters, Philippians rhapsodizes about Paul's sufferings. Elsewhere Paul uses suffering as a demonstration of his self-sacrificial labor for the gospel and firm proof of his apostleship (e.g., 2 Cor. 4:8–12). In Philippians he sees suffering not only as a tool for advancing the gospel (1:12–14) but also as a portal to full union with Christ (1:23). Suffering means identification with Christ's death and is the basis for the resurrection hope (3:10–11). Suffering is so essential to a life in Christ that Paul regards it as a gift graciously granted to believers (1:29). Since suffering joins the Philippians to him, Paul asks them not only to accept it but indeed to share with him in it (1:30).

Paul's appeals for the Philippians to imitate him are distributed throughout the letter. He asks them to share his joy even as his life is being forfeited (2:17–18). He asks them to become imitators of him (3:17; 4:9) and to establish a fellowship with him so closely that they actually share in his ministry (1:5) and in all that entails—including imprisonment and the defense of the gospel (1:7). Paul, however, is not asking the Philippians to attach themselves to him, as was the wont of first-century teachers of philosophy. Rather, he urges his charges to follow his example of striving to attain Christ (3:12–16) and to conduct themselves in keeping with the "commonwealth of heaven" whose

All quotations from Scripture in this chapter are the author's translation.

"savior" is Christ (1:27; 3:20). Above all, Paul wants the Philippians to live a life of self-sacrifice, to follow the supreme example of Christ, who divested his own divine prerogatives for the sake of others (2:1–11). In counting others as better than themselves, the community of Christ realizes its true identity. This deeply personal letter, in the final analysis, is about the proper behavior of being a community.

The work as it stands in the canon is a possible composite of several letter fragments, which would explain abrupt shifts in topic and in tone. One section appears to be a recommendation for two coworkers, Timothy and Epaphroditus (2:19–30); another reads like a thank-you note for a gift from the Philippians (4:10–20). While the different sections are unified by such themes as joy, perseverance, humility, and sacrifice of the individual for the common good, these might well have been familiar topics in Paul's correspondence.

COMMENTARY

In the opening thanksgiving prayer (1:3–11), Paul uses his imprisonment to forge a bond with the Philippians. He uses suffering not merely as an empathetic vehicle but as a shared experience that makes his readers into full participants of the gospel. In 1:7 he writes, "you hold me in your heart" or "I hold you in my heart." It is not necessary to resolve the verbal ambiguity, since the context has room for both meanings. Paul shapes a close relationship, even identification, with the Philippians, by making them his "partners of grace" (see also 1 Cor. 9:23; Rom. 11:17), who share "both in [his] imprisonment and in the defense and confirmation of the gospel" (Phil. 1:7). Just as the Philippians took part in the sharing (koinōnia) of the gospel from the first days (1:5), so now they work alongside Paul and experience with him the travails of ministry. To Paul, his identification with the Philippians is so profound and complete that they take part even in his imprisonment and suffering. Indeed, suffering is a necessary characteristic of Christian life. Just as grace and faith are gifts from God, suffering for the sake of Christ too is a prerogative divinely given to the believers. And just as the Philippians witness Paul's struggles from a distance, now they experience it firsthand. The Philippians' struggles are Paul's and Paul's struggles are theirs (1:29–30). They are equal partners for the sake of the gospel.

This move allows Paul to make the Philippians into an extension of himself. As a result, he could exhort them as he would himself and project onto them his experience of elation and despair. This is a standard strategy for Paul, who often universalizes his own experiences into theological claims. But Paul goes a step further here: he makes his readers into his cosufferers, so that his own choices become theirs and his own sacrifices are emulated and reproduced in them. Paul's autobiographical statements in Philippians are intended as normative assertions.

Paul's imprisonment leads him to reflect on the viability and continual significance of his lifework, the preaching of the gospel. He first makes room for his competitors, who plow his field in his absence, even if he thinks they conduct their ministry with impure motives. As long as the gospel is preached, he could rejoice (1:15–18). Regarding his own ministry, he is confronted with a dilemma, a choice between personal wish and the greater good of his congregation. "For me," Paul says, "to live is Christ, and to die is gain" (1:21), because death means departing from this world to be with Christ, which is Paul's own desire (1:23). He conceives of death as a passage to full union with Christ, of which his daily identification with Christ in this life is but a foretaste. Paul clearly still maintains the imminent resurrection of all in the end time, as he repeats several times in the letter (3:10–11, 21; 4:5), but the cosmic implications of Paul's apocalypticism in Philippians give way to existential and personal thoughts about his impending death.

Enticed as he is by the "far better" alternative of being with Christ right away, Paul nevertheless chooses life. He tells his readers that he hopes to be restored to them through their prayers, so he may continue his work (1:24–26; cf. v. 19). In the choice, Paul reaffirms his affection for the Philippians, but he makes clear that he is modeling for them an example of self-sacrifice. He is to give up what he holds dear in his heart, which is to depart this life to be with Christ, in order to stay behind for the sake of the Philippians' salvation. Likewise, the devotion of Timothy and Epaphroditus to the welfare of the Philippians (2:19–30), with Epaphroditus nearing death, exemplifies the same self-sacrifice. On the other hand, Paul's opponents (1:28; 3:18–19) and the squabbling Euodia and Syntyche (4:2) are motivated by selfishness. Sacrificing one's self-interests for the sake of others is a constant refrain in Philippians.

The supreme model for self-sacrifice is Christ. Paul advances this idea using an existing hymn (2:6–11). The hymn depicts the cosmic drama of salvation in three acts. In the first, the preexisting Christ, resisting the temptation to be equal to God and renouncing the "form of God," voluntarily empties himself of divine nature to become a mortal (vv. 6–7a). In the second act, Christ's self-sacrifice takes a step further as he humiliates himself by becoming a slave, even to the point of dying a slave's death, the crucifixion (vv. 7b–8). In the final, triumphant act, however, God vindicates Christ, elevating him above all others, giving him the name "Lord," which all tongues must confess and before which all knees will bow (vv. 9–11).

The hymn retells the story of Christ after the Genesis story of the primordial fall with contribution from first-century Wisdom speculation. Unlike Adam, who took the forbidden fruit in an attempt to become God's equal, Christ does the opposite. He divests his own divine nature to become a human being and furthermore becomes a slave to die on the cross. This act of self-humiliation is rewarded with a glorious end that Adam never dreamed of attaining. Thus told, Christ is the second Adam who reverses the primordial curse and raises creation to unimaginable heights (see, e.g., Rom. 5:12–21; 1 Cor. 15:21–22, 45–48). First-century Wisdom speculation provides a similar pattern. God sends his consort Wisdom down among mortals in search of the wise. Disappointed in finding no lovers of wisdom to dwell in, she returns to heaven. Basic to Wisdom speculation is an up-and-down pattern of descent to earth followed by ascent to heaven, which the hymn writer uses to depict Christ's humiliation and exaltation. This hymn gives us a glimpse of Paul's central understanding of the incarnation and its implied ethics: it is in giving up one's life that one gains it, and it is in self-denial that one realizes oneself.

The Philippian Paul exemplifies this line of thinking. His renunciation of personal desires for the sake of his congregation is modeled after the incarnation, even as he puts his own action forward as an example for the Philippians to emulate. This is why Paul talks at great length of his identification with Christ. Union with Christ means for him both a personal aspiration and a paradigmatic act. In letting go of his personal claims and private ambitions, including his past achievements as a Pharisee (3:4–6), Paul grasps the surpassing worth of knowing Christ: "I regard all as loss because of the superiority of the knowledge of Christ Jesus my Lord, on account of whom I have lost all things. And I regard them as dung in order that I might gain Christ and be found in him" (3:8–9). Knowledge of Christ means more than just an abandonment of external accomplishments, however; knowledge means a first-person identification with Christ's suffering and death. Renunciation of all external accomplishments is not an end in itself but the by-product of "knowing him," that is, to share in Christ's sufferings and to conform to the likeness of his death (3:10).

In using religious language that had common currency in the first century, Paul nonetheless uses "knowledge" (gnōsis) in a way radically different from his Hellenistic contemporaries. For the latter, gnōsis represents a form of privileged knowledge of the divine that results in identification with the deity. Because it singles the knower out from above his or her peers, it inevitably invites perfectionism, conceit, and ultimately elevation of the individual above the community. Paul's gnōsis, by contrast, always has as its direct object Christ, or more accurately Christ's sufferings and his death. While it is clear that Paul has a high view of Christ's lordship (2:9–11), he redefines the gnōsis of Christ in terms of identifying not with his glory and exaltation but with his sufferings, even his death. Hence, for Paul, entrance into the cosmic drama of incarnation takes place at the identification with the human Christ.

The language of conforming to the likeness of Christ's death anticipates Paul's interpretation of baptism as "baptizing into Christ's death" in Romans (6:1–11). If that is the case, Paul suggests here that the ongoing identification with Christ's sufferings and death logically and chronologically begins with baptism. Life in Christ means nothing less than self-denial and dying with Christ, which is a daily undertaking. No one has yet become perfect, but since believers have been claimed by Christ, they must strain toward the goal with ever-vigilant efforts (Phil. 3:12–16).

In speaking of knowing Christ as "a sharing" (koinōnia) of his sufferings and death in 3:10, and by asking the Philippians to imitate himself and those living according to his example (3:17; 4:9), Paul hints at a second reason why he raises the topic with such urgency: to build a community of Christ based on self-sacrifice. In the thanksgiving prayer, Paul asks the Philippians that, since they have already taken "a share in" (koinōnia) the gospel in the early days (1:5), they now become partner, or "cosharers" (synkoinōnoi), of Paul's grace (1:7). As Paul strives to imitate Christ, he asks the Philippians to imitate his endeavor to identify with Christ, and it is in this context that the Philippian hymn is set.

Just as he himself sacrifices his personal wish of union with Christ for the sake of the collective good of the Philippians (1:20–26), he now asks them to put others' interest ahead of their own. Just as Christ emptied himself of all divine prerogatives in humility, his followers should likewise emulate his example by putting others' interests above their own (2:1–4). Paul exhorts the Philippians "to think the same thing," a common expression meaning "to be in agreement and to live in harmony" (v. 2). This means concretely to act in humility regarding others as better than oneself and looking out not for one's own interests but for those of others (vv. 3–4). In so doing, the Philippians have the mind of Christ: "consider this in you that which also was in Christ Jesus" (2:5).

In the next section (2:12–18), Paul drives home the conclusion that the Philippians must exert efforts in realizing their true identity as a community of Christ. "Salvation" (v. 12), which the Philippians are asked to "achieve" or "produce" in fear and trembling, is often read individualistically, as if to ask the reader to achieve his or her own perfected end. In the context of the community, however, it seems clear that Paul is asking his readers to realize the unity of the community by following the example of Christ's ultimate act of sacrifice and treating one another in humility and in gentleness. The challenge is not that personal salvation can be obtained by exertion but that authentic living in communal unity must be conscientiously achieved by all members.

Such a community is characterized by joy. He uses his own example to reinforce this point. In suffering and in hardship, in want or in plenty (4:11–12), Paul learns to be content and to rejoice, and he enjoins the Philippians to do likewise. But this rejoicing is not merely a willful disregard of adversity, a bravado that has no anchor in reality. The Philippians are asked to rejoice always "in the Lord" (3:1; 4:4, 10). The inner source of joy is the authentic identity in Christ, which marks the community for glorious transformation, for "the Lord is near" (4:5). Joy in Christ is real, because the future breaks into the present and affords those mired in affliction a glimpse of the possibility of freshness.

Ethics in this context becomes ineluctably communal. If not even intense sufferings, such as Paul's and Jesus', are merely individualistic or private, then all personal conducts must affect the corporate life of a community. Behind this is a view that members of the community are stamped with a common identity, and they collectively form a "citizenship" or "commonwealth" (*politeuma*). This commonwealth is in heaven, whence "we expect a savior, Lord Jesus Christ, who will transform the body of our humiliation to conform to the body of his glory" (3:20–21). This commonwealth is opposed by the "enemies of the cross of Christ," whose "end is destruction" and whose "minds are set on earthly things" (3:18–19). To the ears of the citizens of Philippi, the Roman colony, this earth-heaven contrast could not but constitute a criticism of the earthly empire. It designates the Philippians as belonging to an otherworldly power, under the sovereignty of another lord. The contrast is also between the present and the future, since the transformation of our bodies still has to take place in the future (cf. 1 Thess. 1:9–10).

What distinguishes the commonwealth of Christ is that this Lord suffered and died. Instead of defeating his enemies, he was crucified on the cross. Like the Lord, the citizens of this commonwealth must accept sacrifice and suffer-ings, and death if necessary. The suffering Lord gives the citizens a communal identity that rises above the individuals. It is *both* the Philippians' understanding of their own special status based in heaven *and* their conduct toward each other that Paul appeals to when he exhorts them to become worthy of the gospel. Only in so doing do the Philippians "conduct themselves as citizens (*politeuesthe*) in a manner worthy of the gospel" (1:27–30).

If the Philippians persevere until the end, they could uphold and fulfill this heavenly identity. Christ's own passage is again paradigmatic: just as Christ retains his divine nature and fulfills it by giving up his prerogatives, a community of Jesus' followers fulfill their identity, a heavenly commonwealth, only through mutual humility. In this context, the body subject to transformation in the end time refers not just to the physical entities of each individual but also, reading this in light of Paul's discussion of the "body of Christ" in 1 Corinthians, to the corporate identity that is the community of Christ.

Bibliography

O'Brien, Peter. *The Epistle to the Philippians: A Commentary on the Greek Text.* New International Greek Testament Commentary. Grand Rapids: Eerdmans, 1991.

Witherington, Ben. *Friendship and Finances in Philippi: The Letter of Paul to the Philippians.* New Testament in Context. Valley Forge, PA: Trinity Press International, 1994.

Colossians

Sze-kar Wan

INTRODUCTION

In spite of the epistolary form and exacting admonitions, Colossians is an exposition of ethics or, more properly, of the ethical demands placed on those who have been baptized into the church. Colossae is explicitly named in the prescript (1:2), but details about its congregation are wanting in the rest of the letter. The sender, ostensibly "Paul" (with Timothy in 1:1; by himself in 4:18), remains in the background. His personality is traceable in two passages that recount in typical Pauline fashion his concerns, struggles, and hard work on behalf of his charges (1:24–25; 2:1–5), but otherwise does not factor in the theology of the letter. The concluding greetings (4:7–17) lend the work the look and feel of a Pauline letter but read more like an afterthought. In the last analysis Colossians is a well-structured exposition on postbaptismal ethics that could have been addressed to any congregation in Asia Minor, and its author could have been Paul or a close student.

The theological underpinning of the work is that baptism carries with it clear ethical imperatives for the newly initiated, because it signals a passage from one mode of existence to another, a "transference" from the power of darkness to the kingdom of Christ (1:13). This stark demarcation between the two realms means the baptized must leave behind worldly standards and human traditions in order to seek the heavenly realm of Christ, who is before and above all principalities and powers, in whom the fullness of God dwells, and through whose blood on the cross all things have been reconciled to God (1:15–20). The mystery hitherto hidden from the world is now revealed to the Gentiles, to whom has been granted knowledge of this divine mystery (1:26–27). In this final age, Christ is the head of his body, the church, whose members are "circumcised with a circumcision made without hand" (2:11) into Christ. With this new identity, the initiates must put to death their mortal selves by renouncing earthly things (2:20–23; 3:5–11) and seek heavenly things that befit their resurrected identity (3:1–4, 12–17). Colossians is the product of a church coming into its own and becoming increasingly conscious of its own identity and obligations. In this church, the conflict between Jewish and Gentile followers of Jesus, which receives much attention in Galatians and Romans, is no longer the burning issue.

Given the slightly different understandings of such traditional Pauline

All quotations from Scripture in this chapter are the author's translation.

concepts as mystery, baptism, body, as well as the growing self-consciousness of the church reflected in the letter, Pauline authorship of Colossians is disputed. If Paul himself wrote the letter, he would have done so late in his life when the Jewish-Gentile conflicts in the early Christian movement had receded into the background. In that case he wrote the letter to counter a perceived heresy threatening his congregation. If Paul was not the author, a close disciple must have written it in the name of his master to address religious syncretism. He did so by fully developing Paul's teachings on Christ and the church using an epistolary form that had become favored in the Pauline movement.

COMMENTARY

Colossians is divided neatly into theology (1:9–2:19) and parenesis (ethical exhortation; 2:20–4:1). The theological section is anchored by a hymn (1:15–20) that parallels the Philippian hymn (Phil. 2:6–11). Both are integrated into a didactic context, both extol the person of Christ in lyrical language, and both borrow liberally from Jewish wisdom tradition in praise of Christ. Unlike its counterpart in Philippians, however, the Colossian hymn does not rely on a descent and ascent pattern that was typical of Wisdom speculation. Christ is depicted in vv. 15–17 as the preexistent Wisdom, the "image of the invisible God, the firstborn of all creation," who took part in creation (cf. Prov. 8:22–31). Christ is before all and sustains all. This theme of preeminence continues in Col. 1:19–20, where he is said to embody the "fullness" (*plērōma*) of God (cf. 2:9). "Fullness" is Hellenistic religious language that describes full divine essence; here it gives the hymn writer a category to elevate the divinity of Christ.

The hymn continues with a reference to all things being reconciled through Christ, who made peace through the blood of the cross (1:20). But little in the preceding context makes reconciliation necessary, since there is no mention of enmity between creation and God. One would have to read Christian redemption into the hymn. Indeed, except for references to the church (v. 18a), the resurrection (v. 18b), and the blood on the cross (v. 20), there is nothing specifically Christian about the hymn. There is good reason to suggest, therefore, that the composer adapted a hymn in praise of Wisdom to the Christian narrative, perhaps using the Philippian hymn as a model.

The result is a triptych presenting Christ on the first panel as leader of the created order (vv. 15–17) and on the third as reconciler of the world (vv. 19–20), with the pivotal middle panel depicting Christ as the head of the church through the resurrection (v. 18). As leader of creation, the preexistent Christ takes over the attributes of Wisdom—as image of the invisible God (v. 15a) and as instrument (v. 16) and sustainer of creation (v. 17b). As the visible manifestation of God and agent in creation, he is before all creation, in chronology and in status (vv. 15b, 17a). For all practical purposes, Christ *is* the Creator.

As reconciler of the world, Christ also assumes an instrumental role. The full divinity that dwells in Christ effects reconciliation of the whole creation to God's own self through death on the cross. Assumed in this presentation is an act of rebellion that caused alienation between God and the created order, but this has been reversed by the cross. The nature of the implied atonement is left cryptic, but the cross remains central to cosmic reconciliation.

It is the cross, more properly the cross and resurrection as an indivisible whole, that constitutes the middle panel of the christological triptych (v. 18), around which Christ the creator and Christ the reconciler revolve. At the resurrection, Christ becomes "the firstborn from the dead" (v. 18b), the firstborn of all who are dead but are to be raised in like manner. But the ultimate purpose of the resurrection is that Christ would "become first in all things" (v. 18c), Christ would become the leader of the whole cosmos. In all likelihood, the hymn writer interprets the resurrection as the moment the fullness of Divinity dwells in Christ (v. 19). The thought here is decidedly Pauline, harking back to Christ as the "first fruits" pioneering and heralding the general resurrection for all (1 Cor. 15:23).

In contradistinction from the nuanced language of Rom. 6:5–11, in Colossians resurrection is not deferred to an indefinite future but is a present, accomplished reality for the baptized. At baptism believers are buried with Christ but are also raised with him (Col. 2:12). It follows that Christ "is the head of the body, the church" (v. 18a), for the church is a collection of the baptized, the resurrected, raised in the same manner as Christ. When Christ becomes the firstborn of all who are to be raised through the resurrection, he lays the foundation for the church.

If the preexistent Christ who preceded and took part in creation ends up dying on the cross in order to accomplish cosmic reconciliation, this must have happened with forethought and planning. This is the "mystery" of Colossians, a word used four times in the letter (1:26, 27; 2:2; 4:3). The term in Jewish apocalyptic and Pauline usage means a divine secret from aeons ago being revealed to the privileged few at the end time. In Colossians the term retains its classical meaning of a secret revealed but also refers to a specific revelation to all the saints: Christ is in the Gentiles (1:26–27). While the sentiment remains Pauline, the term loses its apocalyptic urgency.

Correspondingly, the way to appropriate the mystery, Christ, is by way of "knowledge." This special knowledge is not a static object but the result of a process that begins with an intellectual grasp of Christ the mystery (likened to discovery of new riches in 2:2), and bears the fruits of spiritual understanding and wisdom (1:9–10). The ultimate goal of this specific knowledge is daily renewal and total transformation into the image of Christ (3:10). There is also a sense that the continual quest for transformation itself is the very knowledge. If Christ is the preexistent Wisdom, to know Christ is to attach oneself to him in order to gain understanding, spiritual maturity, and wisdom.

Like many concepts in Colossians, the church as the body of Christ has a Pauline pedigree. Paul uses the metaphor to describe a community of multiple functions that are all manifestations of the Spirit (1 Cor. 12–14). The author of Colossians takes the metaphor a step further by giving it ontological substance. As the body whose head is the resurrected Christ (Col. 3:1), the church is the lower portion of a cosmic being that spans heaven and earth. Only with this notion of body in mind can we understand how the Colossian Paul can claim boldly that he makes up for "the deficiencies of Christ's afflictions" by his own suffering in the flesh (1:24). He thinks so because he toils for Christ's body, the church. Thus not only does the cosmic Christ span spatially over heaven and earth, he also spans time, extending beyond the historical Jesus into the life of the church. It is with justification that such a church is called a "mystical body."

As a self-conscious institution, the church establishes a clear demarcation between insiders and outsiders, with the boundary being crossed through baptism. The realm outside the church is "the authority of darkness," while the church represents "the kingdom of the Son" (1:13), and baptism transfers a person from one realm to the other. Even though our author does not espouse a mechanical view of baptism or imbue it with magical properties, he comes close to it when he calls baptism "a circumcision made without hands" (2:11 NRSV mg.). The expression in early Judaism was used to distinguish the real from the counterfeit. According to Philo, the word of God, only spoken to Moses but never written down by hand, is the "real" Scripture, while the written codes are but copies that, even if perfectly executed, are derivative none-theless. Colossians applies the same distinction to circumcision. True circum-cision, one made without hands, is the authentic "circumcision of Christ" (2:11) that has the power to excise the "uncir-cumcision of the flesh" with its trespasses (2:11–13). At baptism, the initiate is "buried with" Christ (2:12a).

Here the author of Colossians is dependent on the classical Pauline for-mulation of Rom. 6:3–11, but he goes beyond it by adding that through bap-tism one is also resurrected with Christ (v. 12b). Romans 6 cautiously distinguishes the pastness of identification with Christ's death and burial at baptism from the futurity of the resurrection, which remains an item of faith to be realized only eschatologically (Rom. 6:5, 8). For Paul the tension between death with Christ and hope for future resurrection is the very basis of his ethical imperatives. Colossians makes explicit the ethical implications implicit in Romans by mark-ing the two distinct modes of existence before and after baptism. Because bap-tism is understood as resurrection with Christ, a fait accompli done once and for all, the future is telescoped into the past. And the resurrection, instead of marking a dynamic, imperatival strain toward self-realization, now becomes an identity marker. Baptism is the all-important rite of passage marking the abandonment of life outside the church for the embrace of life within.

It would be inaccurate to say that Colossians has lost its futuristic outlook, since it does expect the revelation of Christ in the eschaton, when those who have died and whose lives are hidden with Christ will be revealed in glory with "Christ our life" (3:3–4). But the author transforms the eschatological tension of Romans into ethical demands in the maturing institution. In Colossians the old and new selves are precise roles iden-tified with and by the church that one must "take off" (cf. 2:11; 3:9; cf. 2:15) or "put on" (3:10, 12). Stripping off the old self implies no longer following old reg-ulations such as "Do not handle, do not touch," for these are all human com-mands and traditions that belong to "the elemental spirits of the universe" that oppose Christ (2:8, 21–22). Correlatively, it also means forsaking vices (3:5–9), because the baptismal resurrection sets one's mind "on things that are above, not on things that are on earth" (3:2).

Regeneration of the new self is a daily, continual exercise: "putting on the new that is being renewed" (3:10). The redun-dancy of this injunction stresses the new as both a status and a reality. In putting on the new self, its newness is itself being renewed every day, and it is directed toward gaining the "knowledge of the image of its creator," total transformation into the image of Christ. Just as taking off the old self implies adopting a specific code of conduct and disavowal of partic-ular vices, however, putting on the new self entails acquiring new virtues, such as compassion, kindness, humility, meek-ness, patience (3:12–17), but "above all, clothe yourselves with love, which binds everything together in perfect harmony" (v. 14). In this connection, the author follows the Pauline trajectory of ethical behaviors in making extensive use of catalogs of vices and virtues. The only difference is that he grounds these behav-iors explicitly in baptism, which forms the basis for new demands. But since baptism is now contextualized in an insti-tutional setting, so are its ethical implica-tions, which among other things include behaviors deemed proper to roles in a household.

In the household code (3:18–4:1), rela-tionships between wives and husbands, between children and parents, and between slaves and masters are co-opted by the church, seemingly reinforcing rather than challenging hierarchical roles traditionally defined in Roman society. Wives are to "be subject" to their husbands, and husbands are to love their wives (3:18–19). Children must "obey" their parents, and fathers are not to provoke their children (vv. 20–21). Most jarring to modern sensibility is the slave-master relationship, according to which slaves are to obey, submit, and be faithful in their tasks, while the masters retain their social preeminence over their slaves.

It therefore seems reasonable to conclude that the Colossian household code is designed to temper the radical egalitarianism of Galatians, "In Christ there is no Jew or Greek, no slave or free, no male and female, for we are all one in Christ" (Gal. 3:28). The Colossian version is based on the Galatian proclamation but also makes crucial changes to it: "There is no Greek or Jew, circumcised or uncircumcised, barbarian, Scythian, slave, free, but Christ is all and in all" (Col. 3:11). The first relationship, on ethnic difference, is retained but the order is reversed, "There is no Greek or Jew." The second, on class distinction, comes after further expansion on ethnic differences and is then formulated not as a parallel pair but as items on the list, "There is no . . . circumcised or uncircumcised, barbarian, Scythian, slave, free." The third, on gender relationship, is altogether omitted.

Even if the household code falls short of the Galatian egalitarian ideal, it ultimately upholds the dignity of the householders. It is framed in love, "which binds everything together in perfect harmony," and in peace (3:14–15), and it is introduced by a call to come together for teaching and worship (3:16). In short, it appeals to everyone in the worshiping community as acting subjects with full moral agency. This is in marked contrast to Greek and Hellenistic moral writings, in which codes governing households invariably appeal only to the stronger parties, while assuming subordinates have no capacity for reciprocity. Colossians starts with the basic assumption that everyone in a community united in the new baptismal identity is equipped for moral action. Both parties, the weak and the stronger, must therefore bear the responsibility of upholding harmony within the household, the church.

For subordinates, their responsibility is directed primarily to the Lord, only secondarily to their human superiors. Thus wives in the Christian household are to subject themselves to their husbands, "as is fitting in the Lord" (3:18). Children are to obey their parents, because that would ultimately please the Lord (3:20). Slaves are to obey their earthly masters not because they fear them but because they fear the Lord, for they ultimately serve the Lord and not human beings (3:22–24).

These injunctions can be open to abuse, as they indeed have been abused in subsequent generations. One need only compare the Colossian code, the earliest of its kind, to later versions found in Ephesians, the Pastoral Epistles, 1 Peter, and Ignatius of Antioch. One does well to keep in mind, however, the contextual character of Colossians, whose purpose is to draw up a blueprint not to change society at large but to appraise how social roles brought in from the outside—Greek, Jew, barbarian, slave, free—should be reshaped inside the burgeoning church. The household code is formulated at the intersection between roles assigned by society outside the church and roles within. It is part of the church's involvement with society, and it represents the church's wrestling with social expectations imposed on its communal ethos. The result is the emergence of a new household that owes its origins to a temporal appropriation of the Hellenistic household.

Bibliography

Lohse, Eduard. *Colossians and Philemon: A Commentary on the Epistles to the Colossians and to Philemon.* Translated by William R. Poehlmann and Robert J. Karris. Hermeneia. Philadelphia: Fortress, 1971.

Schweizer, Eduard. *The Letter to the Colossians: A Commentary.* Translated by Andrew Chester. Hermeneia. Minneapolis: Augsburg, 1982.

1 Thessalonians

E. Elizabeth Johnson

INTRODUCTION

First Thessalonians may well be the earliest extant letter written by Paul and thus the oldest Christian literature we possess, from perhaps the late 40s of the first century CE. It opens a revealing window on some of the first Christians and their relationships with God, with one another, and with the world around them. The most common theological use of this letter refers to Paul's discussion of the last things and the return of Christ in 4:13–5:11, even though that comprises less than one-fifth of its content. The true center of gravity in 1 Thessalonians is less the cosmic future than the present life of the church. Paul's repeated references to the Parousia, the appearing of the risen Lord (1:9–10; 2:19; 3:12–13; 4:15; 5:23), function to shape the congregation's faith, hope, and love (1:3; cf. 1 Cor. 13:13). Each mention of the Parousia stands at a critical turning point in the letter's structure. The first three mark transitions within the thanksgiving—Paul's gratitude for the Thessalonians' faithfulness to the gospel (1 Thess. 1:2–8), his gratitude for their faithfulness to the apostolic mission team (2:1–18), and his prayer for their continued faithfulness (3:1–10)—and the fifth initiates the letter's concluding benediction (5:23–28). Only the fourth mention of the Parousia, at 4:15, occurs in the discussion of the end times. This recurring image of the Lord's appearing serves as the letter's heartbeat, the steady rhythm that moves it from beginning to end, a persistent reminder that the risen Christ is both the source and the guarantor of the church's faithfulness.

In 1 Thessalonians Jesus' Parousia carries at once the reality of God's election and the promise of redemption. Jesus is the one through whom the Thessalonians bring their faithful work, loving labor, and hopeful endurance into the very presence of God (1:3); who "rescues us from the impending wrath" (1:10, my trans.); who makes the faithful church a crown of apostolic boasting (2:19); who pours into believers' hearts his own love such that their love becomes known beyond their own fellowship (1:8; 3:12; 4:10); who sanctifies the church, assuring its holiness in the presence of the holy God (3:13; 5:23); and who will gather his church to himself at the last trumpet (4:16; cf. 1 Cor. 15:52).

Paul assumes that God's certain redemption of the cosmic future already transforms the human present. The apocalypse—the Greek word means "revelation"—that constitutes his gospel is the cross of Jesus Christ. His gospel discloses the character of the church's life under the impact of Jesus' death and resurrection as well as its destiny in the triumph of God. The Christian community is cruciform, "cross-formed," shaped by the revelation that Jesus' death manifests God's love for the world. The cross redefines love in terms of itself: it is self-giving, power-renouncing, death-denying. The life brought into being by the gospel of Christ crucified is the corporate life of the church that God has loved so decisively that the church is able to lay down its own life for the world God loves. Earlier discussions of the function of Paul's apocalyptic language explained it largely in terms of ethical warrant: righteous living will be rewarded and wickedness pun-

ished at the last judgment (cf. 1 Thess. 1:10; 4:6). Most of this letter, however, reflects the apocalypse of Christ that reorders the present life of the church. It results for believers in the reversal of prevailing cultural values, the dismantling of the social economy of honor and shame, the replacement of conventional morality with the radical claims of the gospel, and the empowerment of Christian proclamation. These matters are emphatically this-worldly, a helpful reminder that Paul's apocalyptic gospel by no means speaks only of the future.

COMMENTARY

The thanksgiving, a conventional part of letters in Greco-Roman antiquity, is unusually long in 1 Thessalonians (1:2–3:13) as compared with Paul's other letters. In 1:2–10 he rehearses with gratitude the Thessalonians' loyalty to the gospel despite hostility from their neighbors. In 2:1–3:10 he gives thanks for their faithfulness to the apostolic mission in the face of alternative models of leadership. In 3:11–13 he prays that their faithfulness will endure and increase. He refers to himself and his missionary colleagues as the brother (1:4; 2:1, 9, 14, 17; 3:2, 7), the infant child (2:7; the adjective "gentle" in some translations reflects a textual variant on the noun "infants"), the nursing mother (2:9), the father (2:11), and the orphan (2:17) of the church in Thessalonica. These kinship metaphors—with the exception of the infant and the orphan—are relatively common among first-century teachers. Wet nurses are models of gentle instructors who take account of listeners' frailties; philosophers assume paternal responsibility for their students; and several religious communities use sibling language to describe themselves. Only Paul, though, claims the roles of both the newborn and the mother, both the father of the church and its orphaned child. The apostolic mission takes on the astonishing weak-

ness of a newborn and the precarious vulnerability of an orphan, the tender love of a nursing mother and the encouraging guidance of a father, because that mission is cruciform in character, shaped by the love and vulnerability of Jesus Christ. Although the gospel entrusted to the apostles could give them authority to "throw [their] weight around" (2:7; NRSV "make demands"), it instead shapes ministry in the image of Christ. This is a fundamental reordering of the pursuit of honor and avoidance of shame that structure ancient life.

In 2:13–3:5 Paul interprets the violent reception the gospel mission encounters in the work of the apostles and the lives of Christians. Just as Jesus was crucified, so his believers are persecuted. Persecution is indeed the church's destiny (3:3), not an accident of history or an invalidation of its message. The church inevitably suffers for the gospel because that gospel challenges the values of the world and replaces them with its own. The gospel strengthens believers to endure, to withstand the temptation to capitulate to a hostile culture, and to remain faithful to God, who calls them into the very glory of God's presence. Some interpreters have chafed at the anti-Jewish sound of 1 Thess. 2:14–16, comparing it with Paul's affirmation in Rom. 9–11 of God's abiding faithfulness to Israel. In his indictment of the church's enemies in 1 Thessalonians, however, Paul speaks not of the whole covenant people but specifically of those who hinder the Christian mission.

Throughout 1 Thessalonians Paul highlights the normative function of Christian proclamation. He variously calls that proclamation "the word," "the word of the Lord," or "the word of God" (1:6, 8; 2:13 [bis] 4:15, 18), "the gospel" (1:5; 2:2, 8, 9; 3:2, 6), "exhortation" or "comfort" (2:3; cf. 2:12; 3:2; 4:1, 10; 5:11), "command" (4:2, 11), and "prophecy" (5:20). He customarily uses verbs of speaking and hearing with the word "gospel," as he does in 1 Thess. 2:2, 9. The gospel, however, is more than the specific words Paul speaks or his listeners hear. God entrusts the gospel to Paul and his coworkers (2:4) and they in turn hand it over to the Thessalonians (2:8). Nowhere is there such a clear picture of the preacher as servant of both God and of the church. The only use of the verb "preach the gospel" in 1 Thessalonians describes Timothy's report that the Thessalonians stand firm in the faith despite opposition and suffering (3:6). The safety and well-being of the church are gospel to the apostle, because "we now live since you stand firm in the Lord" (3:8, my trans.). Paul thanks God that the gospel comes "in power and in the Holy Spirit and with complete conviction" rather than in word alone (1:5). The Thessalonians receive the word with both joy and tribulation (1:6; 2:13) and it "sounds forth" from them (1:8). The apostles deliver to the church not only the gospel but also their own lives (2:8). The word of the gospel thus is never entirely circumscribed by the words uttered by human preachers, even though they are God's coworkers (3:6), because the word originates with "God, who gives you his Holy Spirit" (4:8).

In 4:1–12 the apostle reprises ethical exhortations that were part of his initial preaching in Thessalonica, apparently because those exhortations have become controversial. Christian morality seeks to

please God and to love the family of faith, he says, and that requires holiness in domestic (4:1–9) as well as community life (4:10–12). The metaphor "to acquire one's own vessel" in 4:4 is ambiguous and has been variously rendered "to control one's own body" and "to marry one's own wife." Although either traditional interpretation suits the context, it is also possible that Paul advocates here the ascetic standard he endorses in 1 Cor. 7:36–38, encouraging those who are able (in 1 Thess. 4:4, those who "know how") to maintain celibate marriage relationships that exhibit holiness pleasing to God and that avoid compromising the holiness of others in the community (4:3–8). Obviously such unconventional domestic unions are likely to arouse suspicion among outsiders, so Paul urges the church to shore up its communal boundaries, maintain behavior that is beyond public reproach, and refrain from imposing on its neighbors, demonstrating love for one another that is "God-taught" (4:9–12).

The discussion in 4:13–5:11 comforts Christians who await the Lord's Parousia with the promise that no one will be abandoned on the Day of the Lord. Not only are believers who have died assured a place with Christ in glory, they will actually precede the living when the trumpet blasts. Here again, it is the least honored in society who take precedence in the Christian community. Paul's assurance that the Day of the Lord will come suddenly empowers the church's distinctive life in the midst of the world. As heirs of the day (5:5) they are equipped by God's own protective armor (5:8) to live as well as to die in the confidence that God's faithfulness to them takes on flesh and blood in their faithfulness to God. The concluding exhortations in 5:12–24 call believers to nurture one another, particularly the least among them, admonishing, encouraging, helping, and being patient with the weak, even as they honor those who proclaim the gospel among them.

Bibliography

Collins, Raymond. *The Birth of the New Testament: The Origins and Development of the First Christian Generation*. New York: Crossroad, 1993.

Cousar, Charles B. *Reading Galatians, Philippians, and 1 Thessalonians: A Literary and Theological Commentary*. Macon, GA: Smyth & Helwys, 2001.

Donfried, Karl, and I. Howard Marshall. *The Theology of the Shorter Pauline Epistles*. New Testament Theology. Cambridge: Cambridge University Press, 1993.

Gaventa, Beverly Roberts. *First and Second Thessalonians*. Interpretation. Louisville: John Knox, 1998.

2 Thessalonians

E. Elizabeth Johnson

INTRODUCTION

Second Thessalonians purports to come from the author of 1 Thessalonians and to be addressed to the same readers. Numerous questions have arisen, however, about its authorship. The virtual identity of several parts of 2 Thessalonians to 1 Thessalonians, from its salutation and thanksgiving to concluding benediction, suggests that the earlier of the two served as a model for its successor. Whereas 1 Thessalonians anticipates the Lord's Parousia (his coming in glory) in the very near future and without warning, 2 Thessalonians says instead that a series of historical events must occur before the Day of the Lord. An emphatic warning against pseudonymous letters (2:2), a reminder of an earlier letter from Paul (2:15), and verification of Paul's signature (3:17; cf.

Gal. 6:11) suggest a measure of self-consciousness on the part of an author who takes up the apostle's role in a later period of the church's life, perhaps during its second generation, to address new situations that have arisen, notably continued hostility to the church and concerns that the Parousia has already occurred. Despite differences between 1 and 2 Thessalonians, there are many similarities as well: thanksgiving for the church's faithfulness to the gospel in the face of persecution (1:3–4; 2:13), prayer that believers become and remain worthy of God's call (1:5, 11), interpretation of present suffering in light of God's vindication of them at the last judgment (1:6–7; 2:1–12), and exhortation for the church to imitate the apostles' self-support (3:7–9).

COMMENTARY

Second Thessalonians begins and ends with prayer for peace. The initial greeting, "Grace to you and peace from God our Father and the Lord Jesus Christ" (1:2), is mirrored in a concluding benediction, "May the Lord of peace himself give you peace at all times in all ways" (3:16). Between these bookends, the letter's three sections (1:3–12; 2:1–3:5; 3:6–15) address conflict and chaos that

threaten the church from outside and disorder that unsettles life within the community. The letter promises that God in Christ is the source of peace who will restore peace and give the people rest.

The first section outlines the cosmic vengeance God is poised to wreak on the enemies of the church. God's vindication of the church and punishment of those who oppress it are nothing less than

God's "justice" (1:6), a word that in other Pauline letters is translated "righteousness." The character of God is vindicated when God balances the scales of justice, rewarding those who remain faithful and punishing those who oppress God's people. The passage begins and ends with the hope that the church will remain "worthy" of God's advocacy (1:5, 11), urging loyalty to the gospel and empowerment for "every desire of goodness and work of faith" (1:11, my trans.).

The timetable in 2:1–12 responds to the false claim that the Day of the Lord has already arrived. Any number of ideas might have prompted such a claim: an experience of religious ecstasy that some consider evidence of heavenly reality no longer rooted in mere human life (cf. 1 Corinthians), a misinterpretation of 1 Thessalonians that alleges God's trumpet has already sounded (1 Thess. 4:16) and that some Christians have not in fact joined Jesus in the air, or simply an awareness that the vindication of persecuted believers, once thought very near, has been postponed or even cancelled. In the midst of continuing persecution and social ostracism, it is easy for Christians to wonder if God has abandoned them. The author responds that God's promise of redemption is still trustworthy, that the present life of the church is far from redeemed when it is beset by idolatry and violence, and that before the end a series of events must take place. All this is according to God's own plan:

- "First" there will be a rebellion against God (2:3; cf. 1 Tim. 4:1; 2 Tim. 3:1–5; Jude 17–19).
- Someone called "the restrainer" hinders the revelation of someone else called "the lawless one," although his influence is already felt in "the mystery of lawlessness" (2 Thess. 2:3–7), until
- the appearing (parousia) of the Lord Jesus (2:8), at which time
- the restrainer will be removed (2:6) to make way for
- the appearing (parousia) of the lawless one (2:9), an agent of Satan who will

deceive people by means of a widespread delusion that is—ironically— sent by God (2:11).
- Finally, the Lord Jesus, the agent of God, will destroy the lawless one, condemn the wicked, and reward the faithful (2:8, 12).

This sequence of historical events promises the Thessalonians that God remains faithful to them despite the apparent ascendancy of idolaters who persecute Christians. Much like the Revelation to John, the scene is full of cryptic symbols and invitations to read between the lines ("you know," 2:6). As in other apocalypses of the day, the picture in 2 Thess. 2:1–12 abounds with biblical language and imagery. The lawless one is depicted in language from Isa. 14:13–14; Ezek. 28:1–10; and Dan. 11:21–45. The Lord Jesus is described with the image of God's servant whose breath slays the wicked (Isa. 11:4). God sends a powerful delusion upon people, as in 1 Kgs. 22:23; Isa. 6:10; and Ezek. 14:9, a claim that preserves God's integrity against the charge that Satan could thwart God's saving purpose.

The letter's third section encourages continued faithfulness to the traditions on which the church is founded. The distinctive lifestyle of believers stands out in a pagan society, and the author urges vigilance in maintaining that lifestyle. They are to hold fast to their Christian confession, love one another, and separate themselves from unruly people who disrupt the church by presuming on its hospitality and abusing its communal bonds. Those who do not work to contribute to the common good of the community not only take advantage of brothers and sisters but fail to follow the pattern of life set before them by the apostles, who work with their hands "night and day" so as not to burden those to whom they preach (3:8; cf. 1 Thess. 2:9). Some interpreters draw a causal connection between anxiety that the Day of the Lord is past and the disruptiveness of those who do not work. If the new age is upon them, they reason, there is no longer reason to work. Others suggest that "busybodies" (3:11) are instead the poor or unemployed who have no work and have become accustomed to being cared for by the church. In either case, the author points to the self-sufficiency of the church's founders to call all members to mutual caring and responsibility.

Bibliography

Bassler, Jouette M. "Peace in All Ways: Theology in the Thessalonian Letters: A Response to R. Jewett, E. Krentz, and E. Richard." In *Pauline Theology*, vol. 1: *Thessalonians, Philippians, Galatians, Philemon*, edited by Jouette M. Bassler, 71–85. Minneapolis: Fortress, 1991.

Donfried, Karl, and I. Howard Marshall. *The Theology of the Shorter Pauline Epistles*. New Testament Theology. Cambridge: Cambridge University Press, 1993.

Gaventa, Beverly Roberts. *First and Second Thessalonians*. Interpretation. Louisville: John Knox, 1998.

1 Timothy

Deborah Krause

INTRODUCTION

First Timothy follows the form of an ancient Greco-Roman letter. It has an opening greeting that names the sender and recipient, a body, closing instructions, and a benediction. According to most scholars, however, this writing, along with 2 Timothy and Titus, are letters in outward form only. They pose as personal communication between the apostle Paul and his trusted coworkers Timothy and Titus. In this sense they are not only pseudepigraphical, but also pseudo-epistolary. Many refer collectively to 1 Timothy, 2 Timothy, and Titus as "the Pastoral Epistles" in that they all address matters of pastoral concern regarding church leadership and administration. Through the letter form, 1 Timothy, 2 Timothy, and Titus mimic Paul's practice of writing letters to instruct his churches and bear the promise of unfettered, authoritative communication of Paul's teaching for the church.

Given the rhetorical shape of 1 Timothy, 2 Timothy, and Titus, their form bears as much theological significance as their content. As writings that "stand in" for the apostle Paul, they represent part of the church's development of theological concepts regarding revelation, apostolic authority, leadership, ecclesiology, and social ethics. They portray a slice of the church's history in which different Christian communities were negotiating the absence of original revelatory leaders (e.g., Peter, Mary, James, Paul). In this period members of different Christian movements wrote within the names of their original revelatory leaders. These writings provided guides of what counted as reliable instruction and revelatory teaching. In this practice, 1 Timothy, 2 Timothy, and Titus mark an emerging consciousness within the early-second-century church of the concept of a canonical tradition and a rule of faith.

The Pastoral Epistles also represent a developing sense of the institutional church. They bear instruction about qualifications for offices of the church, appropriate compensation, and rules for expected behavior. This emphasis has led many interpreters to assess them as a less immediate expression of Christian faith than the writings of their namesake Paul. According to this assessment, interpreters often characterize the writings as a sellout of the Pauline legacy, seeing them more as glossy junk mail than vital communications of Christian witness. This perspective, however, obscures that these writings do not describe the entire second-century church, but rather prescribe their writer's understanding of what the church should be. They provide a glimpse into a particular church leader's use of the Pauline legacy to articulate his particular vision of the church in the guise of a general Pauline teaching. They may not bear Paul's same impassioned rhetoric about the experience of faith, but they give witness to a struggle to define the church (in the face of perceived opposition), right belief, and the nature of the church's leadership. Whether or not Christians today are compelled by the vision of the church offered in 1 Timothy, 2 Timothy, and Titus, the writings stand as a testimony to a period of fervent negotiation and conflict in the church's early history.

The Pastoral Epistles contain different layers of theological tradition. One layer is found in the embedded forms of liturgical texts (e.g., hymn fragments), and another layer is found in the theological perspective of the author of the writings. The theological claims in these different layers do not always cohere and this variety gives the writings an eclectic and uneven texture. Again, the theological significance of the writings is found less in their specific content, and more in their overall form as testimonies of the apostle Paul's thoughts regarding the administration of the church universal. The purpose of the Pastoral Epistles, to lay down a general and authoritative set of instructions for church leadership in the name of Paul, marks their most important theological contribution to the history of Christian literature and developing canon.

COMMENTARY

First Timothy presents Paul as the sender and Timothy as the recipient of the letter. The scenario presumed by the writing is that Paul has left Timothy, his trusted coworker, in Ephesus to manage the church in his stead. The occasion of the writing is to confer Paul's direction about maintaining a particular teaching against opponents (1:3) and promoting correct behavior within the church (3:15). As such the letter presumes in particular what was true in general for the second-century church. Paul was physically absent not because he had simply traveled away but because he had died. The promise of this instruction, then, to one who was well known as one of Paul's most trusted coworkers (1 Cor. 16:10–11; 2 Cor. 1:1, 19), is that it contains Paul's clear convictions about matters of the church and its leadership. Above all else one could trust a communication between Paul and Timothy to be an accurate reflection of Paul's thinking about the administration of the church. What better vessel within which to pour the ecclesial vision of an embattled second-century church leader?

The Acts of the Apostles presents Timothy as a disciple whom Paul first meets in Iconium in the region of Galatia (Acts 16:1ff.). According to Acts Timothy is half Jewish (by his mother) and half Greek, and Paul was compelled to circumcise him in order to meet the expectations and concerns of Jewish Christians as he traveled with Timothy throughout Asia Minor. Luke presents Timothy as one with whom Paul traveled (Acts 16:4), sent to carry out the mission (19:22), and left in his stead to continue the ministry of the church in his absence (17:14). From Acts' account it is clear that by the late first century Timothy was known as one who extended Paul's teaching and leadership in the church as it spread throughout the world. Timothy's name on the letter lends the writing the theological significance associated with the mission to the Gentiles and God's universal saving work in the church.

The most overt theological claims of 1 Timothy focus on God's universal saving purposes. Hymnic fragments throughout the letter (e.g., 1 Tim. 2:5–6a; 3:16) represent ancient claims to the saving work of God on behalf of "all people." In 2:6a Jesus Christ is celebrated as one "who gave himself as a ransom for all," and 3:16 proclaims that Jesus was "believed in throughout the world." These ancient expressions of God's saving purposes are echoed, and yet subtly altered by the letter writer. In referring to God's saving purpose, the writer nuances the theological claim with his own agenda to instruct his readers in right belief: "God is the savior of all people, *especially of those who believe*" (4:10).

The writer's primary concern is the subject of belief and its connection to the church's practice of worship, church administration, and social relationships. The writer devotes most of his time to instructing "Timothy" in the defense of that belief, and therefore does not take time to define the theological content of the belief itself. It is as if the theological content of correct belief is understood between the writer and the intended recipients of the letter. Whoever the readers are, they do not need theological instruction. Therefore, the theological content of the letter writer's belief must be reconstructed from between the lines of the writer's challenge to false teaching and defense of the "teaching that is in accord with all godliness" (6:3, my trans.).

In arguing against the authority of women within the church as teachers (2:13–14), the letter writer cites Gen. 2–3 as a creation template for the untrustworthiness of women (Eve) and the superiority of men (Adam). While contemporary readers may chafe at this interpretation of Genesis, the letter writer reveals that he holds the created order to be of God's making and purpose, and that it sets an authoritative and eternal guide for human social relationships. Furthermore, as the writer argues that his opponents forbid marriage and demand abstinence from foods, he proclaims that they misunderstand the truth of God as these things are created by God and that "everything created by God is good and nothing is to be rejected, provided it is received with thanksgiving" (1 Tim. 4:3–4). These claims regarding the goodness of God's creation alongside an affirmation of the law (1:8) may reflect the writer's challenge to early gnostic and Marcionite ideas regarding the fallen and evil nature of this world. In this context, the affirmation of God's sovereign and

creative purposes for the world is a declaration of a church leader resisting the introduction of divergent theological claims into the communities of his church.

Further theological content may be glimpsed between the lines of the writer's rhetoric about the office of widows (5:3–16), the compensation of elders (5:17–22), and the treatment of slaves (6:1–2). As the writer seeks to restrict the qualifications for membership to the order of widows to those whom he classifies as "real widows," as he advocates for the double compensation of elders who rule well, and as he commands those who are slaves to accord their masters honor, his proclaimed intention to protect the faith seems to veer toward a protection of self-interest. The widows are curtailed on the basis that God approves of those who care for the financial needs of those in their private families (5:4). Elders are afforded "double honor" (payment) on the basis of proof texts taken from the Torah ("Do not muzzle the ox when treading the grain," Deut. 25:4) and Jesus' wisdom ("the laborer deserves to be paid," Luke 10:7). Slaves are commanded to serve their masters all the more, because their masters are believers and so it is God's beloved who are benefiting.

While the theological bases of these claims are thin within the letter itself, their theological significance is remarkable when supported by the authority of Paul. The letter writer manages to draw his particular ecclesial concerns into the eternal revelatory wisdom of the apostle Paul. Importantly, the historical Paul never had this opportunity in his own ministry. His letters reveal that he regularly had to defend his apostolic authority to lead and teach in the church (e.g., 1 Cor. 15:8–11; 2 Cor. 10–12). It is only in second-century texts, drawing on what had become the legend and tradition of the apostle, that the writer's particular concerns become a general and ultimately canonical church teaching. In this sense, what may be understood historically as relatively insignificant theological claims about church order have stood in the canon of

Christian Scripture as authoritatively pronounced directives for the church universal. In the context of Paul's expanding authority, the writer's claim of women's subservient status and call for slaves to submit to their masters have been heard as divinely inspired teaching. They have guided the development of the church throughout its history and into the contemporary era. They have stood and continue to stand in many parts of the church as fences to full participation and justifications for human degradation. While not commendable, the theological and ecclesiological implications of such claims in their canonical context are enormous. Such an insight brings into clear focus the importance of social and historical as well as canonical context in the interpretation of such traditions.

Bibliography

Krause, Deborah. *1 Timothy*. New York: Continuum, 2004.

MacDonald, Dennis R. *The Legend and the Apostle: The Battle for Paul in Story and Canon*. Philadelphia: Westminster, 1983.

Quinn, Jerome D., and William C. Wacker. *The First and Second Letters to Timothy*. Eerdmans Critical Commentary. Grand Rapids: Eerdmans, 2000.

Tamez, Elsa. *Struggles for Power in Early Christianity: A Study of the First Letter to Timothy*. Translated by Gloria Kinsler. Maryknoll, NY: Orbis, 2007.

Towner, Philip H. *The Letters to Timothy and Titus*. New International Commentary on the New Testament. Grand Rapids: Eerdmans, 2006.

2 Timothy

Deborah Krause

INTRODUCTION

Contrary to what its canonical name implies, 2 Timothy is not merely a sequel to 1 Timothy. While most scholars understand that 1 Timothy, 2 Timothy, and Titus are pseudepigraphical writings of the same author (see the introduction to 1 Timothy), 2 Timothy takes on an additional form of a testament from Paul to Timothy, written while Paul was imprisoned in Rome (1:8) and awaiting death (4:6). With this added element, the writer deepens the drama of the fictive letter. More than the intimate communication between Paul and his trusted coworker, the teaching of 2 Timothy stands as Paul's final words unveiling what to him must have been his most pressing concerns and fervent hopes for the church. Given the legend of the apostle Paul as it had developed into the second century, the recipients would appreciate the writing as a trove of authoritative wisdom and essential teaching. This celebrated reception would have no doubt surprised the historical Paul greatly!

In terms of content 2 Timothy, like 1 Timothy and Titus, contains several citations of early Christian liturgical texts. These citations bear theological and confessional claims that give some indication of the author's theological perspective. In addition, the opponents of the letter writer are characterized in fairly generic derogatory terms, and in this conflicted rhetoric, one can discern some of the theological concerns of the writer and his churches. As Paul's "last will and testament," however, the primary theological significance of 2 Timothy is its reference to the example of Paul in his suffering and endurance for the faith. The writer holds up this claim as the paradigm of church leadership and the ultimate testament to God's faithfulness and trustworthiness.

While the original order of the Pastoral Epistles is not known, it is clear that its current order, like all the Pauline writings, is based upon length, going from longest to shortest. Whatever the original order, a dramatic and compelling order of the corpus would be 1 Timothy and Titus concluded by the poignant and powerful "last words of Paul" as found in 2 Timothy.

COMMENTARY

In reading 2 Timothy as a testament of Paul, one is struck by the absence of language about the cross and the crucifixion of Christ. In the undisputed letters of Paul (Romans, 1 and 2 Corinthians, Galatians, Philippians, 1 Thessalonians, and

Philemon), he frequently mentions the centrality of Jesus Christ crucified and the significance of the cross. In 1 Cor. 2:2 he says this quite plainly: "I decided to know nothing among you except Jesus Christ, and him crucified." In Gal. 6:14 Paul asserts, "may I never boast of anything except the cross of our Lord Jesus Christ, by which the world has been crucified to me, and I to the world." In Paul's theology the cross was the center of his understanding of redemption and salvation, which makes its absence from the Pastoral Epistles remarkable. More generally Christ's death is not mentioned, except as it relates to encouraging the persistence of present-day Christians: "If we have died with him, we will also live with him" (2 Tim. 2:11). In 2 Timothy it is as if the model of perseverance in suffering has shifted from Jesus to Paul. In this sense the writer of 2 Timothy commands in vivid contrast to 1 Cor. 2:2: "Remember Jesus Christ, raised from the dead, a descendant of David—that is my gospel, for which I suffer hardship even to the point of being chained like a criminal, but the word of God is not chained" (2:8–9). The legend of Paul, his suffering endurance, and his sacrifice have taken on a revelatory role of their own, and the glory of Jesus, his resurrection, and his eternal reign are what is primarily significant about God's work in Jesus Christ.

Like 1 Timothy, 2 Timothy reflects developing ideas within the early church about Scripture and its authority. In 1 Tim. 5:18 it appears as though the writer designates both Deut. 25:4 and a saying of Jesus found in Luke 10:7 as "scripture." In 2 Tim. 3:16 the writer asserts: "All scripture is inspired by God and is useful for teaching, for reproof, for correction, and for training in righteousness." If some of the writer's opponents are seen as early gnostics or Marcionites, the writer may be offering the countervailing theological claim of the divine nature of Israel's scriptural tradition. Certainly a global claim such as *"all* scripture is inspired by God" seems to suggest the intention to affirm an entire collection in the face of those who seek to narrow the definition of the contents of Scripture.

As 2 Timothy has been interpreted in the history of the church, however, this text has been cited in debates not about the content of Scripture, but about the perception of the authority of Christian Scripture texts in a literalist interpretive vein. In these debates the claim "all scripture is inspired by God" (or "God-breathed," NIV) proves that every word is inspired as it appears on the page (often of a particular translation). In this sense, what may have been the writer's struggle to define the content of Scripture has been interpreted in later contexts to authorize the divine inspiration and authority of each and every word therein.

As noted above, the vast majority of 2 Timothy is devoted to profiling the suffering and enduring witness of Paul. With the backdrop of Paul's imprisonment and his impending death, the writer enjoins Timothy to "rightly explain the word of truth." For the writer this takes place in opposition to liars, those who counterfeit the faith, and corrupt the minds of the people (e.g., 3:1–9). While these labels do not offer much particular content regarding the opponents' beliefs, they do imply that the opponents are themselves church leaders (just like the writer and Timothy). They carry out teaching, instruction, and explanation of the faith. What 2 Timothy (along with 1 Timothy and Titus) represents, therefore, is a rhetorical battle between different interpreters of early Christian belief and practice. In some senses it may seem as though the writer of 2 Timothy is completely intolerant of theological difference. He is certainly not an advocate of what today may be called ecumenical dialogue! Yet the writer does show some signs of measured response to his opponents. The writer enjoins Timothy to show patience in teaching (4:2), to avoid quarrels and controversies (3:23–23), and to be gentle with opponents (3:24–25). Using Paul's example of steadfast endurance and suffering, the writer enjoins Timothy to "be sober, endure suffering, do the work of an evangelist, carry out your ministry fully" (4:5). For the writer, the treacherous teaching of the opponents will be defeated not by violence or enmity, but by faithful and devoted adherence to teaching the message.

Bibliography

MacDonald, Dennis R. *The Legend and the Apostle: The Battle for Paul in Story and Canon.* Philadelphia: Westminster, 1983.

Quinn, Jerome D., and William C. Wacker. *The First and Second Letters to Timothy.* Eerdmans Critical Commentary. Grand Rapids: Eerdmans, 2000.

Schüssler Fiorenza, Elisabeth. *In Memory of Her: A Feminist Theological Reconstruction of Christian Origins.* New York: Crossroad, 1983.

Titus

Deborah Krause

INTRODUCTION

The rhetoric and content of Titus closely resemble that of 1 Timothy. As with 1 Timothy, the writing follows elements of the Greco-Roman letter form and contains directions for adhering to sound teaching, citations of early liturgical and creedal texts, and denouncements of opponents. With its brief serial directions about qualifications for church leadership (1:5–9), older men and women and young men (2:1–8), and slaves (2:9–10), the writing reads like an abbreviation of 1 Timothy. In many senses, the writing provides the opportunity to extend the fiction of Paul's communication to his trusted companions in ministry, and thereby to broadcast further the writer's particular interpretation of the Pauline tradition.

Paul refers to Titus in Gal. 2:1–10 as one who accompanied him to Jerusalem with Barnabas. In this reminiscence, Paul recalls that Titus, though he was Greek, was not compelled by those in Jerusalem to be circumcised (Gal. 2:3). For Paul this is an important witness to the Jerusalem church's acceptance of his mission. While that acceptance was later strained and even broken, the person of Titus stands within Paul's legacy as a symbol of the validity of Paul's mission to the Gentiles and interpretation of the gospel of Jesus Christ. While Titus is not mentioned in the Acts of the Apostles, Paul refers to him in 2 Corinthians as one who worked on the collection for the poor in Jerusalem among the Gentile churches (2 Cor. 8). This association would further commend Titus's role within the Pauline legacy as a worker of reconciliation among the Jerusalem church and the Gentile churches of Paul's mission. The use of Titus as a recipient of the letter may well reflect a theological vision of his reconciliatory role in Paul's ministry and in the broader church.

COMMENTARY

The writing presumes that Titus is working on Paul's behalf, "putting in order what remained to be done" (1:5), in the church in Crete. In the pseudepigraphical and pseudo-epistolary fiction, the letter offers guidance to Titus in his administration of the church. While neither Paul's Letters nor the Acts of the Apostles mention that Paul founded churches in Crete, the writer does not go to great lengths to establish the veracity of Paul's mission within the Cretan context. The only detail relevant to Crete in the letter comes in the writer's quote of an epithet about

Cretans: "Cretans are always liars, vicious brutes, lazy gluttons," and his affirmation that this saying is true (1:12–13). Crete likely does not appear in the letter as a genuine place name, but rather as a symbolic reference to the difficulty of administering the church in different contexts. Given that the writing was intended for church leaders, there is no doubt that they would commiserate with Titus as he worked to establish and teach the faith among a group of "Cretans."

The instructions of the writer about teaching "sound doctrine" reinforce cultural expectations of Greco-Roman household codes. Appended to the lists of expected virtues (e.g., temperance, seriousness, prudence for older men; self-control, chastity, good management of households, and submission to husbands for older and younger women) are formulaic Christian phrases (e.g., "so that the word of God may not be discredited," 2:5; "so that they may be an ornament to the doctrine of God our Savior," 2:10). These phrases reveal the writer's appropriation of Christian tradition to enforce the cultural codes. While one could argue that such a rhetorical move may or may not have merit within a given context, the canonical location of Titus imbues this amalgamation of Christian tradition and Greco-Roman values with the eternal and creative purposes of God.

Another element of accommodation within Titus (and found within the rhetoric of 1 and 2 Timothy as well) is the use of religious language associated with the cult of the Roman ruler to articulate the Christian gospel. The irony of this accommodation is striking. As the writer instructs Titus to keep the teaching pure against his opponents, he in turn engages in syncretistic references to the cult of the Roman ruler to proclaim that same teaching (e.g., Titus 3:4). As the emperor was honored as a "savior who appeared," so too, according to the writer, is God. As the emperor was celebrated for showing "goodness and loving kindness," so too is God. While some cultural interaction is endemic to all religious discourse, the writer's intolerance for others who pervert the teaching seems to beg for insight into his own double standard.

Titus and the other Pastoral Epistles stand as a powerful witness to the difficult circumstances of the church in the early second century. As the church confronted the reality of dying founders, diverse interpretations, and divergent practices, the writer of the Pastoral Epistles responded with his own quest for apostolic authority, traditional dependability, and uniform ecclesiology. In spite of his intentions for purity, however, the writer's rhetoric reveals the influence and appropriation of diverse cultural ideas and religious beliefs. Titus and the Pastoral Epistles bear witness to one eternal truth of the church, namely, that the church does not operate generally, but contextually and specifically. Even when the church asserts itself as the church universal, it is always engaged in particular contexts, navigating authority, and discerning the presence and purpose of God in the midst of human culture and history.

Bibliography

Towner, Philip H. *The Letters to Timothy and Titus*. New International Commentary on the New Testament. Grand Rapids: Eerdmans, 2006.

Philemon

James Buchanan Wallace

INTRODUCTION

Paul could have written this letter to Philemon, a Christian of Colossae, anytime between 54 and 63 CE; he wrote while a prisoner, probably in Rome or Ephesus. Virtually no one disputes the authenticity of this, the shortest of the Pauline letters. Paul composed this rhetorical masterpiece to plead for Philemon's slave Onesimus, who has fled his master and in the meantime converted to Christianity through Paul's influence. Paul has found Onesimus a useful minister to his needs in prison, and he wishes to keep him with him in the service of the gospel. He sends Onesimus back, however, to offer Philemon the opportunity, of his own free will, both to receive Onesimus as a "beloved brother" (v. 16) and to allow him to return to Paul's service. Paul may have hoped that Philemon would free Onesimus, for he expresses confidence that Philemon will do more than has been asked (v. 21). The preservation of the letter, and perhaps Col. 4:9, may indicate that Philemon fulfilled Paul's request.

COMMENTARY

Christian life requires surrendering rights and claims of special status in imitation of Christ. Instead of calling himself an apostle, Paul opens the letter by assigning himself a low social status, that of prisoner. Paul asks Philemon to sacrifice his rights as a master, while offering to make amends for any losses Philemon may have incurred, even though Philemon is already indebted to Paul, who converted him to Christianity. Although Paul could command Philemon to make this sacrifice as a duty, he refrains so Philemon can act out of love.

Life "in Christ" transforms social relationships. Slavery in the Greco-Roman world was not always as brutal as the slavery of the eighteenth-nineteenth-century American South. Slaves could hold important positions and attain wealth, and manumission was relatively common. Nonetheless, slaves were the property of their masters, and no amount of wealth could wash off the stigma of slavery. Even a person freed from slavery retained a social stigma. Paul, however, insists that Philemon and Onesimus should cease to be master and slave and become brothers (v. 16). Only then will Onesimus become "useful" (a pun on the name Onesimus, which also means "useful") to both Philemon and Paul (v. 11).

According to this radical restructuring of the household, all Christians are equal brothers and sisters, truly useful insofar as they are all servants of the one Lord, Jesus Christ (see vv. 3, 5, and 25). Christian community requires that the most deeply ingrained social stigmas and stereotypes be overcome so Christians can serve the gospel and minister to one another. Moreover, embracing those perceived as inferior cannot be an act of condescension on the part of the powerful. Rather, it must be an acknowledgment that all human beings have a vital purpose within the Christian community. This purpose can be fully realized only in communities of equality, mutual love, and fellowship.

Bibliography

Barth, Markus, and Helmut Blanke. *The Letter to Philemon: A New Translation with Notes and Commentary.* Eerdmans Critical Commentary. Grand Rapids: Eerdmans, 2000.

Fitzmyer, Joseph A. *The Letter to Philemon: A New Translation with Introduction and Commentary.* AB 34C. New York: Doubleday, 2000.

Marshall, I. Howard. "The Theology of Philemon." In Karl P. Donfried and I. Howard Marshall, *The Theology of the Shorter Pauline Letters*, 175–91. New Testament Theology. Cambridge: Cambridge University Press, 1993.

Nordling, John G. *Philemon.* Concordia Commentary. Saint Louis: Concordia Publishing House, 2004.

Hebrews

Patrick Gray

INTRODUCTION

"A riddle wrapped in a mystery inside an enigma." Winston Churchill's description of the Soviet Union on the eve of World War II provides an apt characterization of the Letter to the Hebrews. Who wrote the letter? To whom? When was it written? Under what circumstances? Agreement among scholars on these and other basic questions is hard to find. While the letter is by no means a systematic treatise articulating a comprehensive vision of God and the world, the author nevertheless deserves a place alongside Paul and John as the foremost theologian of the New Testament. Theologians and lay readers alike have mined Hebrews for the soteriological, eschatological, and especially the christological ore it yields, as well as for its views on faith, covenant, sin, and sacrifice.

Authorship and Audience

No sooner does Paul's name emerge in the second century as the author of the letter than doubts about Pauline authorship appear, especially in the Western church. Once it was formally accepted into the canon in the fourth century, however, the assumption that it belonged among Paul's Letters was rarely questioned again until the Protestant Reformation. Similarities with the Pauline correspondence are not limited to the mention of Timothy (13:23) but extend to such matters as an emphasis on faith (11:1–40; cf. Rom. 3:21–4:25; Gal. 2:15–3:29), treatment of common OT texts (Hab. 2:4 in Heb. 10:38; Rom. 1:17; Gal. 3:11), and the image of Christ as a preexistent agent in creation and the very "reflection of God's glory" (Heb. 1:1–4; cf. 2 Cor. 4:4; Phil. 2:6–7; Col. 1:15–20). Notwithstanding these and other parallels, the differences are more pronounced. Signs of tension between Jew and Gentile are notably absent from Hebrews. Whereas Paul emphasizes Jesus' resurrection (1 Cor. 15), Hebrews dwells much more on his exaltation to "the right hand of God" (1:3–4, 13; 10:12–13). If justification is Paul's signature theme (Rom. 4:25; Gal. 2:15–16), sanctification occupies a larger place in the argument of Hebrews (2:11; 10:10). Nowhere in Paul's Letters does one find the distinctive image of Jesus as a high priest (Heb. 2:17; 5:1–10; 7:1–28), nor does the motif of the new covenant (8:1–10:18) play such a pivotal role (but see 2 Cor. 3:6; Gal. 4:24).

Theories about authorship have always tantalized—Luke, Stephen, Apollos, Barnabas, Priscilla, and Mary have all been proposed—but most scholars now agree that there is relatively little hermeneutical gain in speculating about the precise identity of the unnamed author. He (see the masculine participle at 11:32) is a Christian steeped in the Jewish Scriptures and adept at employing the conventions of Greco-Roman rhetoric. Beyond this, little can be known with certainty.

The identity of the audience is likewise uncertain. A Jewish audience fits with the heavy reliance on Scripture, even though Galatians and 1–2 Corinthians stand as examples of letters addressed to Gentile audiences that draw heavily on the Hebrew Bible. According to many scholars, that the alternative to progress in faith is described as a falling away "from the living God" and a return to the performance of "dead works" (3:12; 6:1; 9:14) also militates against a Jewish readership. Most interpreters, however, believe that a Jewish or a mixed audience in Rome is more likely.

Because it is quoted in *1 Clement*, Hebrews must have been written prior to the end of the first century. Attempts to determine a more precise date often focus on the author's interest in Jewish worship and its possible connection to the destruction of the temple in 70 CE. Due to the letter's high Christology, which has affinities with the Fourth Gospel, many scholars argue for a later date. Others believe that the temple's destruction would have seemed like divine confirmation of the author's arguments about the inefficacy of the Levitical priesthood, and thus his silence on this score counts as evidence for an earlier date. Insofar as persecution of Christians took place in Rome during the earlier reign of Nero as well as during the later reign of Domitian, either date would accommodate the experience of the audience (10:32–34; 12:4; 13:3).

Purpose

This experience of persecution informs the author's purposes in writing, which are both practical and theoretical. His immediate concern is to encourage believers who may be tempted to leave the fold in the face of mistreatment by their neighbors. Whether they are Jewish Christians who contemplate a return to the synagogue and the familiarity of its ritual practices or Gentiles who have concluded that the advantages of membership in the community no longer outweigh the disadvantages, the author wants them to stand firm. At the very least, he senses a spiritual lethargy that threatens not only community solidarity but their access to "the throne of grace" (4:16) as well. Such a situation calls for more than a generic pep talk. Extended reflection on passages from the Old Testament (e.g., Gen. 14:18–20; Pss. 40:6–8; 95:7–11; 110; Jer. 31:31–34) supplies a robust theological grounding for the author's exhortations.

Why should we remain faithful rather than fall back? To this question his response is unambiguous: "Jesus has now obtained a more excellent ministry, and to that degree he is the mediator of a better covenant, which has been enacted through better promises. For if that first covenant had been faultless, there would have been no need to look for a second one" (Heb. 8:6–7). The author therefore seeks to explain the ways in which the new covenant—God's distinctive way of dealing with humanity through Jesus—demands the utmost allegiance and remains perfectly consistent with the divine plan as disclosed under the old covenant.

COMMENTARY

1:1–2:18

God speaks. With this declaration the letter begins (and not like a letter at all but like a sermon). It should come as no surprise that a writer of such eloquence has a special interest in divine speech. God speaks, but in different ways at different times—through the prophets, through the Psalms and other Scriptures so frequently quoted in the opening chapters, and, preeminently, through the Son. Although his appearance has only occurred "in these last days" (1:2), it would be a mistake to conclude that Jesus is in any way inferior to previous modes of revelation employed by God. The author does not denigrate such precursors as the angels (1:5–14) or Moses (3:1–6). Rather, he identifies them as auxiliary agents in the work of salvation accomplished by Jesus (1:14; 3:5). The logic that governs the argument that runs through the letter depends on the validity of the message of salvation as announced in the past (2:1–4). Because it promises greater rewards and portends more dire consequences, the audience must heed the good news of Jesus even more assiduously.

Jesus' significance in Hebrews derives from more than the eschatological urgency occasioned by his exaltation. To borrow the language of the Apocalypse, he is the Alpha as well as the Omega. In the opening verses, the author attributes to Jesus a role in creation and, while stopping short of explicitly Trinitarian formulations, describes him as "the exact imprint of God's very being" (1:3). Athanasius seized on this and other verses (e.g., 13:8) as proof of Jesus' divinity and immutability. Arius and his followers countered that, to the contrary, the letter implies a subordinate status for the Son (1:4; 2:8–9; 5:7–8).

Even if patristic debates about the person of Christ sometimes prove inconclusive, Hebrews offers a poignant reflection on the incarnation and suggests an answer to Anselm's famous question, *Cur Deus Homo* ("Why did God become man?"): only by assuming flesh and blood and tasting death for everyone could Jesus destroy the devil and the fear of death he inspires. In so doing he serves as "a merciful and faithful high priest" capable of making atonement for sins (2:9, 14–17).

3:1–4:13

Despite the social and cultural barriers separating them, the author presents the exodus generation in 3:7–4:11 as evidence that God's Word confronts both ancient and modern readers with equal potency. Centuries after the Israelites wandered in the wilderness, the Holy Spirit, speaking

through the psalmist (95:7–11), issued to the Israel of his day the same warning about the dangers of disobedience. Every day is the "Today" spoken in Scripture, according to Hebrews, and thus God has extended to the audience the same promise of "rest" as to those who followed Moses: "the good news came to us just as to them" (4:2). The result of disobedience was not simply the Israelites' failure to enter the land in the past but also exclusion from God's own Sabbath in the future.

4:14–5:10

After a somber reminder that every soul is laid open to the judge before whom each "must render an account" (4:12–14), the author returns to the comforting image of Jesus as high priest. Jesus is able to sympathize with human weakness because he himself has been tempted and tried, though without sinning. The picture of the Son in tears, crying out in "godly fear" (KJV) for deliverance, "[learning] obedience through what he suffered" (5:7–8), coheres with the Chalcedonian description of Jesus as "fully human." At this point there occurs a radical shift in the letter's christological trajectory not unlike what one sees in the Christ hymn of Philippians (2:6–11). Having been made perfect, Jesus is now "the source of eternal salvation for all who obey him" (Heb. 5:9). Not simply a moral exemplar, Jesus is himself a proper object of faith and obedience. Such exclusive claims about the status of Jesus and the scope of his salvific work underscore the distinctive nature of Christian identity in relationship to other religions.

5:11–6:20

Faith cannot stand still or it will fester and die. Thus the author chides his readers for their failure to make progress beyond the basic teachings (5:11–6:2). He also suggests that "it is impossible to restore again to repentance those who have once been enlightened" (6:4) and then fallen away. These comments, where the author lays out the logical implications of Jesus' death as a once-for-all sacrifice, have stirred controversy over the centuries. Disputes about penitential discipline, "perseverance of the saints," and a host of other theological and pastoral questions have frequently hinged upon a resolution of the hermeneutical difficulties posed by this hard saying. Whether the author has in view any and all postbaptismal sin or, more likely, fullfledged apostasy, Hebrews is emphatic: because "it is impossible that God would prove false" (6:18), so too should they remain true to their baptismal vow. Comprehending the full meaning of one's conversion is possible only after the fact. The warning about the perils of denying the faith makes clear that life in Christ is not a matter of what Dietrich Bonhoeffer calls "cheap grace."

7:1–28

Few aspects of the author's reasoning strike contemporary readers as more peculiar than this midrashic comparison of Jesus to the obscure figure of Melchizedek, who makes only two brief appearances in the Old Testament (Gen. 14:18–20; Ps. 110:4). How can Christ be a priest if he is a descendant of Judah instead of Levi? His priesthood is of a different order, one that is superior to the Levitical priesthood. Are Christian claims about Jesus inconsistent with the sacerdotal system laid out in Torah? No, because the necessity of repeating the sin offerings day after day on behalf of the priest as well as the people clearly illustrates that the "weak and ineffectual" Levitical priesthood was never intended to be eternally valid (Heb. 7:11, 27; cf. 8:7; 9:25–26). Only Jesus' perfect, undefiled, singular sacrifice—of himself!—could be efficacious for all time. Rather than minimizing for apologetic purposes this "scandal of particularity," the author builds his entire argument around the claim that Jesus is the unique mediator of salvation.

8:1–10:18

Jesus' priesthood is superior, the sacrifice he offers is superior, and so it follows that the covenant he thereby inaugurates is superior. This, says the author, is "the main point" (8:1–6). His exposition of Jer. 31:31–34, one of the longest OT quotations in the New Testament, demonstrates that the concept of a "new covenant" was already present under the old covenant (Heb. 8:8–13). An extended discussion of the rituals performed in the tabernacle on the Day of Atonement further reinforces their provisional character as a remedy for the problem of sin (9:1–28; cf. Exod. 25; Lev. 16). The law had "a shadow of the good things to come" but did not fully realize them (Heb. 10:1).

In such dichotomies as image/reality, earthly/heavenly, and visible/invisible (e.g., 8:1–5; 9:11, 23–24; 11:1–3), many scholars detect the influence of Platonic dualism of the sort that was common among Christian theologians, especially in Alexandria, in the second and third centuries. Hebrews, however, turns these metaphysical, vertical distinctions on their side and views them against an eschatological, temporal horizon. Various institutions in place under the old covenant anticipate and foreshadow those of the new covenant, which brings the old to completion. Here and elsewhere in the letter one finds a biblical model for typological and allegorical readings of the Old Testament. Debate about the degree to which Hebrews represents a form of supersessionism, not coincidentally, centers on these passages and influences Jewish-Christian relations in the present.

10:19–11:40

To encourage his audience, the author uses both the carrot and the stick. Those tempted to abandon their faith in times of trouble should remember that it is "a fearful thing to fall into the hands of the living God" (10:31); willingness to suffer the plundering of their possessions, on the other hand, is evidence of a trust in "something better and more lasting" (10:34). Beginning with its famous definition—"the assurance of things hoped for, the conviction of things not seen"—chap. 11 then celebrates the glorious deeds of the heroes of Jewish history accomplished "by faith." Christian writers from Benedict to John Bunyan have described the life of faith as a journey with a destination in another world, inspired in no small part by the portrait of Abraham as a wayfarer forfeiting the comforts of home and setting out for a land of promise in obedient response to God's word (11:8–16). Faith makes it possible to be in the world but not of it and to continue the journey while awaiting God's fulfillment of the promises made to the patriarchs and matriarchs, whose fate the author ties to that of his audience: God "provided something better so that they would not, *apart from us*, be made perfect" (11:40). With this remarkable move the author seeks to impress upon his readers the gravity of the situation and the crucial role they play in salvation history. Any loss of faith on their part represents a failure, the effects of which will transcend space and time. The church universal suffers and rejoices with all its members.

12:1–29

The "cloud of witnesses" cheering on the audience as they "run the race" provides a moving depiction of the communion of saints (11:39–12:1). As it was for Jesus, "the pioneer and perfecter of our faith" (12:2), however, their race will not be without serious difficulties. They are to regard these hardships not as a sign of divine displeasure but rather as the loving discipline of a father who wants them to taste "the peaceful fruit of righteous-

ness" (12:3–11). The exhortation reveals a theodicy that resembles that of the Israelite wisdom tradition as found in Proverbs, which the author quotes. Steadfast endurance will enable the audience to arrive at Mount Zion and not lose heart. "God is a consuming fire," thus appropriate worship is accompanied by "reverence and awe" (12:28–29).

13:1–25

The remarks with which the letter closes combine moral exhortation, a call for community solidarity (which includes respect for leaders: 13:7, 17, 24), and an emphasis on sacrifice, be it in the form of good works, praise for God, or a willingness to endure abuse (13:13–15). In this last respect, the audience can aspire to be like Jesus Christ, who is "the same yesterday and today and forever" (13:8).

Bibliography

Johnson, Luke Timothy. *Hebrews: A Commentary*. New Testament Library. Louisville: Westminster John Knox, 2006.

Kim, Lloyd. *Polemic in the Book of Hebrews: Anti-Semitism, Anti-Judaism, Supersessionism?* Eugene, OR: Pickwick, 2006.

Lindars, Barnabas. *The Theology of the Letter to the Hebrews*. New Testament Theology. Cambridge: Cambridge University Press, 1991.

MacLeod, David J. "The Doctrinal Center of the Book of Hebrews." *Bibliotheca sacra* 146 (1989): 291–300.

Royster, Dmitri. *The Epistle to the Hebrews: A Commentary*. Crestwood, NY: St. Vladimir's Seminary Press, 2003.

James

Luke Timothy Johnson

INTRODUCTION

This first-generation Christian composition was probably written by James the brother of Jesus, and is addressed to Jewish Christians in the Diaspora (1:1). James's main emphasis is on acting in a manner consistent with profession: faith must be expressed in deeds. The book's powerful moral exhortation draws from Greco-Roman as well as Jewish forms of wisdom. Jesus is mentioned only twice (1:1; 2:1), and no mention is made of his deeds or his death and resurrection, but the letter is suffused with the sayings of Jesus. Those who hear in James echoes of Jesus' Sermon on the Mount have a good ear. Like his brother, James is theocentric rather than christocentric, and his moral instructions are consistently grounded in convictions concerning the God who creates, sustains, reveals, saves, and judges humans.

COMMENTARY

A good example of the way James supports moral exhortation theologically is in his concern for speech. Many of his specific instructions and prohibitions find parallels in Greek and Jewish maxims. Thus James tells his readers to be slow to speak and quick to listen (1:19), to have control over their speech (1:26; 3:1–8), to speak simply without taking oaths (5:12). But these instructions find in James a specifically theological grounding. Not controlling the tongue is the opposite of "true religion" (1:27). Uncontrolled speech is not simply a human error; it is a deadly form of evil generated by the fires of hell (3:6). Cursing one's neighbor is inconsistent with blessing God (3:9). Slandering one's neighbor is judged by God (4:11–12). Angry speech does not work God's righteousness (1:20). The proper mode of human speech is shaped by the theological conviction that humans have been created by God's "word of truth," so that they should be the "first fruits" of all creation (1:18). Their speech should, therefore, not express envy or arrogance, but a deep receptivity to God's Word. They are to "receive with meekness the implanted word that can save [their] souls" (1:21). Receptivity to God's Word (in creation, in the law, and in the gospel) is the precondition to the proper use of human speech, and all human speech stands under

All quotations from Scripture in this chapter are the author's translation.

453

God's judgment: "So speak, and so act, as those who are to be judged by the law of liberty" (2:12). Forms of such positive speech are found in the community life described in 5:12–20: God is praised through prayer and song, the sick call out and are heard, sins are confessed, and mutual correction is practiced.

A similar theological basis supports James's attack on attitudes of envy and arrogance in 3:13–5:6. James offers his readers the choice of being "friends with the world" or "friends with God" (4:4). He means that humans can live by the measure of a "wisdom from above" that comes from God, is marked by meekness and gentleness, and leads to peace (3:13, 17), or by the measure of a "wisdom from below" that leads to ruthless competition, war, and murder (3:14–16; 4:1–2). Friends of the world operate by the logic of envy, which seeks to establish the self by the elimination of others. Friends of God, in contrast, share God's own giving and generous nature. In 1:5 James says that God gives to all, generously and without grudging, and in 1:17 he declares that "every good and perfect gift comes from above from the Father of lights, who is without shadow of change or alteration." To be a friend of God, therefore, is to be humble and meek, seeking the welfare of others. To such as these, James says, God gives even more gifts (4:6). In the same verse, however, James declares that God "resists" those who are arrogant. James therefore calls his readers to "lower [themselves] so that God can exalt them" (4:7, 10). In 4:11–5:6 he shows three examples of God "resisting" those who show themselves to be arrogant. Those who slander a neighbor put themselves in opposition to God's law and must deal with the one who "is able to save and to destroy" (4:12). Those who boast about their future business plans without any reference to their own contingency or God's will "boast in [their] arrogance, and do evil" (4:13–16). And those who oppress the laborers in the field by refusing to pay their wages face God's fearful judgment (5:1–6).

James's powerful essay (2:1–26) on the need for faith to express itself in deeds reveals the same theological warrant. Both examples in this essay involve the response to the poor. Will the community show discrimination in preferring the rich to the poor (2:1–6)? If they do, they break faith with the God who chose the poor to be rich in faith and heirs of the kingdom. When confronted with the naked and hungry, do they dismiss them with pious words and no deeds (2:14–16)? If so, they do not fulfill the law of the kingdom announced by Jesus, which is to love the neighbor as the self (2:8–11). Their words are without life and show them to be unlike Abraham, "the friend of God" (2:23), and unlike Rahab, who showed her faith through her hospitality (2:25–26). The community that lives by the measure of the God who exalts the lowly and brings low the rich (1:9–11) creates a place of honor for the poor and the weak and a place of forgiveness and conversion for those who have sinned (5:13–20).

James is among the most explicitly theological writings in the New Testament. Because it addresses universal issues of social ethics (speech, poverty, peace and war) from the perspective of a monotheistic faith rather than christological confession, it is an NT witness of exceptional value in an age of religious pluralism, offering the basis for theological and ethical conversations with both Jews and Muslims.

Bibliography

Johnson, Luke Timothy. *Brother of Jesus, Friend of God: Studies in the Letter of James*. Grand Rapids: Eerdmans, 2004.

Wall, Robert W. *Community of the Wise: The Letter of James*. The New Testament in Context. Valley Forge, PA: Trinity Press International, 1997.

1 Peter

Steven J. Kraftchick

INTRODUCTION

As its opening verse indicates, 1 Peter is a circular letter sent to churches located along an ancient trade route in the northeastern section of Asia (modern Turkey). The letter likely was sent from Rome during the latter part of the first century in order to encourage its recipients to remain steadfast in their beliefs in the face of social alienation and rejection (5:12). The author identifies himself as a fellow elder (5:1), who now writes under the name of the apostle Peter. This appeal to Peter's apostolic authority is amplified by the author's use of phrases and ideas typical of Paul's Epistles and the inclusion of the names of Paul's missionary companions, Silvanus and Mark (5:12–14). By claiming the authority of Peter and Paul (both traditionally thought to have been martyred in Rome), the author assures readers that they can trust the information and instructions they find in the letter.

COMMENTARY

The letter can be divided into three related sections: (1) the new identity as God's people (1:3–2:10), (2) the responsibility of the new people to live honorably as witnesses to the truth of God's plans (2:11–4:11), and (3) the sufferings that God's people will experience as they attempt to enact this witness (4:12–5:8). The circumstances in which the churches exist are a catalyst for the author's reflections on Christ's suffering, rejection, and death (1:18–21; 2:4–6, 21–24; 3:17–20; 4:13–14).

The author creates a context for understanding the churches' present circumstances by emphasizing the crucifixion-resurrection of Christ. Unlike many NT authors, however, 1 Peter focuses on Christ's suffering more than on his death. This focus allows the author to portray Christ's actions as redemptive and as an example for the Christians' current existence. Here the author is informed by a reading of Isa. 53, which depicts the rejection of the righteous sufferer as the result of a breech of justice. Rather than retaliate, the one who was unjustly treated chooses to suffer for the benefit of the rest of the community (1 Pet. 2:22–25). Thus Christ suffered at the hands of those who misunderstood his identity and purpose and did not respond in kind. With this the author grounds the current suffering of the churches in light of the founding figure's own experience. Just as Christ suffered at the hands of those who misunderstood him, so too will those who are called to serve Christ suffer. Further, just as Christ responded with patient witness, so too should the ones who claim to be followers. Such suffering is a function and result of bringing light into a dark existence, and sometimes the response to this witness will be resistance and rejection. Hence that they are suffering social alienation should not surprise the church members but confirm their allegiance to Christ and God.

The author does not rely solely on Christ's suffering as a paradigm but refers to all aspects of Christ's existence; the past, present, and future realities of Christ provide a template by which the addressees can interpret their own existence (1:3–9). Their current suffering and status on society's margins are parallel to Christ's rejection (2:4), unmerited suffering (2:21–24; 3:18; 4:1–2), and death (1:9). However, just as Christ met this suffering with obedience and so was raised in vindication (1:11, 21; 3:22) to return in glory (1:5, 7, 13; 5:4), those who remain faithful to their calling will also experience a future salvation for which they now hope (1:4–9; 4:12–13; 5:1, 4, 10).

The metaphorical references to Rome as Babylon (5:13) and to its addressees as exiles of the Diaspora (1:1) are also keys to the letter's overall message and motifs. This symbolic designation of Rome recognizes its massive influence as the center of commerce and as the seat of military and political power, but also suggests that the power is not ultimate. Rome too will be judged. The author also uses this language to indicate that the existence of Christians in the Roman Empire was analogous to that of the Israelites under Babylonian rule during their exile. The author thus identifies the audience as "aliens" and "exiles" (1:1; 2:11). In the broadest sense, Christians should consider this world not as their final home but as a sojourn toward the eschatological blessing of dwelling with God (1:4–5, 13; 5:1, 6,

10). In a narrower but equally existential sense, Christians should recognize that they are living as "foreigners" in the midst of another culture. The Christians are not simply metaphorically strangers in a spiritual sense, but are indeed aliens to the dominant social group.

Just as Israel, the initial people of God, endured the travails of living under antagonistic rule, so also the present people of God will be required to do so (1:2; 17; 2:13–17). That they are experiencing rejection is not a reflection of their own failings or those of God. Rather, it is the natural by-product of one people living in obedience to the plan of God among those who are ignorant of it. As a result, the congregants are not only to endure social opprobrium but also to use it as an opportunity to explain why they have chosen this alternative to Rome (3:13–17).

The author emphasizes the nature of this existence further by introducing the metaphor of "the household of God" (2:5; 4:17). In place of their sense of disequilibrium and social displacement, the congregations are reminded that their real social identity and place is with God. Typically God's people have lived in sojourn, persecution, and exile (e.g., Abraham, Israel under Pharaoh, and those who dwelt in the foreign land of Babylon), so the current people of God should realize that their own experiences are consonant with their status as God's elect.

The fundamental pattern for this household of God is one of order and humility, and 1 Peter provides a distinct set of guidelines for conducting oneself. First, there is a distinction drawn between suffering that results from misbehavior and suffering that is unmerited (4:14–16). Not all suffering is a matter of following Christ. Indeed, the believer must monitor his or her behavior to see if it is consonant with the character and actions of God and Christ. Second, the author suggests that the churches adopt a dual response to their neighbors. On the one hand, since the convictions of the Christian group will inevitably result in conflict with those outside its community, the congregations should not exacerbate this conflict through some moral or ethical failure. Thus, to the degree that they are able, they should follow the social patterns of their neighbors (2:18–3:8). On the other hand, when the observance of these patterns might violate the ethical behavior required by obedience to God, they should demur from their neighbors' societal norms. The two-pronged approach has two goals: to ensure that the Christians give their neighbors no reason to reject the community's witness, and to help the Christians attain their hope of future redemption.

The congregations are repeatedly exhorted to persist in their faith despite their current circumstances as societal outsiders so that they will attain the goal of redemption. These exhortations include reminders of their identity as God's "holy people" (1:15–16; 2:9) who now serve as a "holy nation," an "elect generation," and a "royal priesthood" (2:9–10). Their present status as a "holy people" is also contrasted to their former status as those in darkness and futility, unaware of the nature of life before God (1:14–15, 18; 2:25; 4:1–4). This shift in status from "no people" to "God's people" requires a new allegiance and new behaviors consonant with it (2:9–11).

While the members of the congregations had once participated in the daily routines, civic religion, and social customs of their neighbors (4:3–4), now, because of their conversion to Christianity, they should cease to do so. By not sharing in the devotion to local cults or emperor worship, but devoting themselves to another deity and deliberately absenting themselves from social and cultural events and celebrations, the Christians would have been perceived as a superstitious and potentially destructive force within the larger society. As a result they became suspect to their neighbors and, on occasion, experienced social

opprobrium, ostracism, and physical harm (3:14; 4:4, 12). The author exhorts them to steadfastness in the face of social ostracism and cultural alienation (1:6–7; 2:4–9, 19–21; 3:13–17; 4:12–14) and encourages them: "Conduct yourselves honorably among the Gentiles, so that, though they malign you as evildoers, they may see your honorable deeds and glorify God when he comes to judge" (2:11–12; see also 3:16; 4:1–2).

Ultimately, the entire letter is framed by a belief in the complete extent of God's purposes. The same God who called them into existence will also ensure that they experience eschatological redemption—provided they remain true to the desires and pattern of God's purpose. The call to patient suffering and resistance to social pressure is predicated on the belief that every element and facet of the cosmos receives God's attention and care. Christ did not restrict the gospel message to those who were alive on earth, but announces the purposes of God even to the dead. Likewise, those who are outside the bounds of the community will one day hear of the truth of God's purposes and yield to them. In the interim, the church is called to live a life of witness among those who have not yet comprehended the nature of God's purpose and reality.

By focusing on the true identity of the Christian community and presenting practical guidelines for its social and personal behavior, 1 Peter provides its readers with strategies for a peaceful, yet faithful Christian existence among their non-Christian neighbors. By pointing to motifs from the Scriptures (especially that of God calling a people into existence), by reminding them of their originating experiences (e.g., baptism and communal worship), and by pointing to their hope in God's future redemption, the author provides a means to respond to the audience's present circumstances and to maintain a steadfastness in their beliefs and behaviors that reflect their moral and religious commitments.

Bibliography

Achtemeier, Paul. *1 Peter: A Commentary on First Peter*. Hermeneia. Minneapolis: Fortress, 1996.

Boring, M. Eugene. *1 Peter*. ANTC. Nashville: Abingdon, 1999.

Goppelt, Leonhard. *A Commentary on 1 Peter*. Edited by Ferdinand Hahn. Translated by John E. Alsup. Grand Rapids: Eerdmans, 1993.

Elliott, John H. *1 Peter: A New Translation with Introduction and Commentary*. AB 37B. New York: Doubleday, 2000.

2 Peter

Steven J. Kraftchick

INTRODUCTION

Historically, 2 Peter has not enjoyed a favored status in the church, a situation that appears to have been the case almost from its inception. This letter rarely receives much attention except when someone makes references to its memorable phrases, " a dog returns to its own vomit" (2:22) and "to the Lord one day is as a thousand years and a thousand years as a day" (3:8). Nevertheless, 2 Peter provides a window onto the struggles of the nascent church to reinterpret its fundamental beliefs.

The references to its audience as "the beloved" (1:17; 3:1, 8, 14) along with their identification as converts (3:2) suggest that 2 Peter is a real letter addressed to a real congregation. Unfortunately, the specific contours of the congregation cannot be determined because the letter begins with a generic reference to "those who have received a faith as precious as ours" (1:1) and ends it with a benediction and a doxology (3:18) instead of the more typical greetings to particular members of a church.

Like the Letter of Jude, which it uses as a source (compare Jude 4–16 with 2 Pet. 2:1–18), 2 Peter combines elements of argument and refutation with ethical and moral exhortation. The letter is therefore both a response to a group of other Christian teachers who had challenged inherited understandings of God's providence and promise of a future judgment (1:16–21; 3:5–11) and an admonition to its readers to live righteously while they await the day of judgment and salvation (1:5–11; 3:11–13, 14–15).

A specific date for the letter's composition cannot be established, but a general time frame of the late first century is likely, based on its use of Jude. Internal evidence supports this, especially the letter's recognition that the apostolic generation had passed away (3:4) and its implicit suggestion that the Pauline letters have gained authoritative status (3:15–16).

Second Peter follows ancient epistolary conventions in its opening and closing, but the rest of the document's content, particularly its warnings and exhortations, is typically found in another ancient literary convention—the farewell discourse. As Peter's last testament, the letter's warnings, arguments, and admonitions would be taken as historic and prophetic warnings that the teaching of the opposition departed from God's truth (1:16–21; 2:1–4) and that following it would lead unsuspecting believers to moral and physical destruction (2:15, 18, 19, 20–21).

All quotations from Scripture in this chapter are the author's translation.

COMMENTARY

Like most documents of this sort, the letter's theological character is discerned by considering its author's portrayal of the opponents, his expression of their teachings, and his response to them. According to the author, the opposition appears to have held four basic ideas. First, the future return of Christ as cosmic judge was not an essential part of inherited Christian teaching but a fabricated myth (1:16–21). Second, to continue believing in a future appearance of Christ as eschatological judge was untenable because the "promises" on which this belief was based had not been fulfilled (3:1–6, 8–10). Third, God does not intervene in the course of human affairs; hence there would be no future judgment of humans for their conduct. Indeed, such actions would be contrary to divine will and intent (3:5–7). Finally, either because the sins of Christians had already been forgiven or because there would be no future judgment, human beings should determine their own moral codes and conduct (2:19).

Not only does the author refute the positions of the other teachers, he imputes to them immoral motives and unethical actions. His opponents are not only wrong; they are corrupt (2:12, 17–18). The author characterizes them as "pseudoprophets" who deny Christ as Master (2:1) and who, in their ignorance, slander the divine beings (2:10). With right perception, the audience will recognize that these teachers are "blemishes on the congregation" (2:13) who speak "bombastic nonsense" and who are destined for a destruction they have brought on themselves (2:1; 3:7). Exaggerated as this portrayal may be, the author's polemics show how he connected right doctrine with right behavior. This sense that beliefs have ethical consequences and that individuals are responsible for their beliefs suffuses his letter.

The author has written this letter to reestablish the boundaries of belief, underscore the ethical dimensions of belief, and expose the opponents as apos-

tates (2:20–21). He calls the community back to its initial belief and piety by stressing three fundamental positions: first, that a relationship with God must be one of deepest trust in God's sovereignty; second, that such trust in God is made manifest through a life conducted with ethical integrity (1:5–11; 3:9); and finally, at the consummation of history a time of judgment will occur as a matter of justice and God's fidelity. That judgment will reveal that those who refused God's overtures will exist in a state of alienation from God (2:12–13; 3:7), while those who lived according to God's desires will be accepted into eternal existence with God (1:9, 11; 2:9–10).

Though this letter's theology is not particularly daring, it does provide guidelines for addressing the challenges of reinterpreting beliefs that might no longer appear viable. First, its author understood that a faithful church maintains its place as God's people only if it is oriented by a consistent reinterpretation of its traditions. However, faithful reinterpretation requires critical self-inquiry and humility. Second, an appropriate understanding of God's actions in the world and human affairs arises only in relationship to the ideas of future consummation of God's justice. Finally, it is the responsibility of a community to assess its interpretations on both doctrinal and ethical grounds, because what one believes affects how one acts, and how one lives is an indication of what one believes.

Bibliography

Bauckham, Richard J. *Jude, 2 Peter.* WBC 50. Waco: Word, 1983.

Kelly, J. N. D. *A Commentary on the Epistles of Peter and Jude.* Repr. Grand Rapids: Baker Books, 1982.

Richard, E. J. *Reading 1 Peter, Jude, and 2 Peter: A Literary and Theological Commentary.* Macon, GA: Smyth and Helwys, 2000.

1 John

Allen Dwight Callahan

INTRODUCTION

First John is not a pastoral letter, for it is not a letter at all in any formal sense. The features of an ancient Greek letter—name of the author and addressees at the beginning, thanksgiving statement, proper salutation at the end—all are missing. The writers tell us nothing of their personal background or biography; they do not even tell us their names.

Chapter 1 of 1 John is, in effect, an introduction for chaps. 2–5. Disciples of the Elder have brought together the Elder's discourses in these chapters, and they now disseminate them to shore up the embattled solidarity of their circles. This scenario explains the plural "we write" of 1:4 and the singular "I write" at the opening of the tractate's various discourses and at the closing in 5:13.

COMMENTARY

The Word of Life (1 John 1)

The central theme in 1 John 1 is the word of life, or, the living word (adjectival genitive), or, the word that is life (appositive genitive). The phrase "from the beginning" (1:1) signifies that the word of life is coeval with the experience of the community, and that there was no point when the word of life was not audible, visible, tangible.

The "life" is the life of the community. Because the issue of practical assistance to brethren in need is central to the ethics of the Johannine Epistles, we must understand the fellowship referred to here as concrete, even economic. The writers of 1 John 1 represent the teachings of the Elder in an effort to shore up their community against the appeal of less economically demanding alternatives to the common life. Apparently some members have already deserted the community of goods. The counterexample of the defectors was a threat to the unwavering, concrete commitment that the common life requires.

The writers of 1 John 1 raise the matter of sin in their discussion of conduct, that is, in the language of "walking," the Israelite root metaphor for covenantal behavior. The writers remind their addressees of the divine certainty that sin confessed is sin forgiven, and sin denied is sin condemned. Through confession God breaks the influence of sin by forgiveness and removes its effects by cleansing the confessing sinner of unrighteousness. This double movement of forgiveness and cleansing, the arrest of sin's past effects and present influence, applies for every kind of injustice. God will deal with sin. Confession determines how God does so, whether with forgiveness or with judgment.

Discourse: A New Commandment (2:1–13)

The blood of Jesus signifies his life. The blood of Jesus is not a reference to the death of Jesus: nowhere in the Epistles do we find mention of the cross or the passion. Blood is the traditional Israelite synecdoche for life (Lev. 17:11, 14). Here it is a cultic metaphor for the life poured out for the sake of others, and thus a reference to the life of Jesus that constitutes the life of the community.

Only obedience to the commandments repairs the damage done by sin. This reparation is not a narrow, sectarian reality but a possibility for all humanity, "the whole world." Obedience to God's commandments is both the reparation for sins and the confirmation that one has known God.

Verses 9–11 treat the imperative to love the fellow believers. Verse 11 conjoins an ontological description of the one who hates another believer with an ethical one: one who hates is in darkness and walks in darkness. The conjunction is epexegetical: to exist in darkness is to act in darkness. One of the basic arguments of the Elder is that ontology is ethics, being is doing.

Discourse: The Human Ages (2:14–17)

This discourse addresses the three weakest links in the chain of a community: dependent children, elderly men, and young men. This division is part of the anthropology of traditional patriarchal cultures. The Elder is concerned about this vital and fragile link in the community's intergenerational chain.

The Elder next calls his audience away from appetite, desire, and pride because they are all ephemeral. Those driven toward these three features of the world are doomed to pass away like the vanity that drives them. But the will of God endures forever. So too those who do God's will.

Discourse: Christ and Antichrists (2:18–27)

Here, as in 2 John, the term "antichrist" does not signify a mythical, eschatological figure. He is one of several who have defected from the community of writer and addressees. Those who are antichrists were once in fellowship with the community, but no longer. Because they did not remain with the community they prove themselves not to have belonged to the community. Those who are truly in solidarity remain so: the one who does the will of God remains forever in solidarity with the community of sisters and brothers to which the Elder belongs and to which he writes.

For the Elder, there is only one authentic Christ, the anointed one, and that is Jesus. Any other anointed ones are necessarily making a counterclaim to Jesus' exclusive anointing, and so deny the exclusivity of that anointing, that is, that Jesus is the Christ: not an anointed one, but *the* Anointed One, Christ. The metaphor of father and son is language that signifies this exclusivity and identifies the activity of Jesus with the agency of God. God is "the holy one," a favorite epithet for God and a respectful circumlocution for the divine name in rabbinic literature. At the same time the writer insists that those who have an anointing from God recognize this very exclusivity. The emphasis of the clause is on the definite article: the writer does not use definite articles when referring to antichrists. The counterfeit anointing of the antichrists is discerned by the genuine anointing, "an anointing from *the* Holy One," that is, from God.

The writer reaffirms the truth of the common experience of the community, and insists that those who have participated in that truth but who do not affirm it necessarily deny it. There is only confession or denial. And to deny is to lie, for to deny is to say no to the truth (2:23).

Discourse: Truth as Manifestation (2:28–3:6)

Just as the Elder assured his addressees that they have received an anointing from the Holy One, he insists that they have been born of God. Even though what they will be is not yet manifest, what they are is beyond doubt. But of course the Elder writes as he does precisely to dispel doubt, doubt sown by those who have misled his children (2:27). The Elder therefore affirms his children by reminding them of what they have and what they are. Divine anointing and divine paternity belong to all the members of the community together.

Those who have the hope of seeing the Son sanctify themselves; they exercise themselves to holiness, just as he is holy. Sanctification, setting aside oneself to be holy, is the setting aside of sins, the repudiation of discrete, specific transgressions. The point here is to appear, to be made manifest in a way consistent with one's hope. This hope does not make one holy; sanctification is the evidence of one's hope.

Discourse: Love and Justice (3:7–24)

The "message" that "God is light" is an ethical statement. The original message is one of justice. All that has been said about the message is subsumed under 3:11b, "that you might love one another."

Reference here to the Bible's first fratricide in Gen. 4 says nothing of Abel. It is not the meritorious Abel but the murderous Cain who receives exclusive attention. The problem of hatred, of violence and murder, is a problem of brothers. The hatred of fratricide is death: to remain in death (v. 14b) is to remain in its power, the destructive power of taking the life of one's brother. To remain in death is not to die, for Cain the murderer was spared from becoming the victim of murder. To remain in death is to be a killer. The life of a killer is the practice of death. The only

sure deliverance from death is the practice of love (3:14).

"We know love by this, that he laid down his life for us—and we ought to lay down our lives for one another" (3:16). This appeal to the conduct of Jesus is suggested in 2:6 as the "ought" that constitutes Christian life. There is a reprise in 4:2 with the insistence that Jesus has come in the flesh. The Elder directs attention to how Jesus lived, not how he died; he nowhere mentions the cross or even the death of Jesus. The insistence on life over death—the freely offered life, not the martyr's death—leads to reflection on the life of Jesus.

Reason and language are ultimately derivative: they derive from love (3:18). The Elder asserts that compassion is the debt of love that one owes to one's brother and sister. The concrete expression of compassion, and so God's acknowledgment of it, is greater than the subjective sensibilities of the heart (3:19–20). Even our conscience is not sufficient to judge our love (3:21). The heart must not be the final judge of truth. It is truth that judges the heart. Obedience to the commandment is the basis for confidence before God. It assures that the heart's desire and the will of God are one (3:22).

Discourse: The Spirit and the Spirits (4:1–6)

The Spirit is not mentioned in 2 and 3 John. In 1 John, however, the Elder mentions the Spirit twelve times. The Elder exhorts his audience to "discern the spirits" (4:1, my trans.). Spirituality demands critical consciousness. Just as the addressees are confronted with inauthentic messiahs, so too they are confronted with inauthentic spirits—indeed, the inauthentic spirit is defined here as antichrist presently at large in the world (4:3).

Discourse: Love and Authenticity (4:7–5:21)

The Elder points back to the love that is not contingent in that it is already accomplished, already perfect, and so he writes of it in the perfect tense. God has sent his Son. This verb emphasizes the authority of the sender and the agency of the sender realized through the one sent: the act of sending is significant because of the sender. The Elder teaches that we must love because we have been loved. God's preemptive love undoes the damage of our sin.

Discourse: Authenticity and Idolatry (4:11–5:21)

The Elder assures his "children" that those who obey God's commandments are God's children, and those who are God's children are victorious over the world. Here the Elder states the relation of love and the fulfillment of the commandments: to love God is to keep God's commandments. In their obedience, the children of God overcome the world (5:4).

A confession of truth distinguishes the community's true members (5:19). Verses 20–21 close with a reminder of the addressees' intimate knowledge of "the true God." They also contain a warning against the worship of that which, according to ancient Israelite revelation, is quintessentially inauthentic: idols. The thread that binds together the pieces of this final discursive patchwork is the question of authenticity. The children of God, commended to authentic love in giving to one another, are finally commended to the authentic God. Yet even in their authenticity the children of God must ever be on guard against the inauthentic, the false, the idols.

Bibliography

Black, C. Clifton. "The First, Second, and Third Letters of John." In *NIB* 12: 363–469.

Callahan, Allen Dwight. *A Love Supreme: A History of Johanine Tradition*. Minneapolis: Fortress, 2000.

Lieu, Judith M. *Theology of the Johannine Epistles*. Cambridge: Cambridge University Press, 1991.

Painter, John. *1, 2, and 3 John*. Collegeville: Liturgical Press, 2002.

Rensberger, David K. *The Epistles of John*. Westminster Bible Companion. Louisville: Westminster John Knox, 2001.

2 John

Allen Dwight Callahan

INTRODUCTION

Second John is an appeal to "the elect lady," a chosen authority in the community of the addressees: an alternative rendering of her title is "the chosen authority." The letter is also addressed to "her children," that is, all those under her authority. In 2 John women, "elect ladies," lead these circles, and the Elder addresses 2 John to them.

COMMENTARY

The truth is "among" the addressees insofar as they practice it, even though it is "with" them forever insofar as what is now the truth shall ever and always be so. The truth is not their property; they do not possess it. They are exhorted here to have it possess them. The Elder warns against frauds in the community, whom he calls "antichrist" (7), literally, one who is contrary to Christ. (See also the discussion of "antichrist" in the entry on 1 John.)

The Elder exhorts his addressees to boycott the inauthentic witnesses wielding influence in the community (vv. 9–11). The content of the fraud is not the denial of the historical advent of Jesus the Messiah in first-century Palestine, born to Mary and crucified under Pontius Pilate. The Elder does not charge the errant members of his community with denying the incarnation. Their error is that their practices do not sufficiently affirm that "Jesus Christ has come in the flesh." Those misleading and those being misled have failed to affirm in their communal practice that the Word of God has dwelt "among us" (John 1:14 KJV). That affirmation is expressed as caring, concrete commitment: the solidarity that is love. To "confess that Jesus Christ has come in the flesh" is to bear witness to Jesus in one's own flesh, in one's own life. Confession is not what one says, but how one lives.

The Elder desires to come in the flesh himself, to speak to his addressees (literally) "mouth to mouth"—intimately, personally, tenderly. The letter closes as it began, with direct address to the elect lady. "The children" are others under the authority of an "elect sister," a community leader whose position is presumably like that of the "elect lady."

Bibliography

Black, C. Clifton. "The First, Second, and Third Letters of John." In *NIB* 12:363–469.

Callahan, Allen Dwight. *A Love Supreme: A History of Johanine Tradition*. Minneapolis: Fortress, 2000.

Lieu, Judith M. *Theology of the Johannine Epistles*. Cambridge: Cambridge University Press, 1991.

Painter, John. *1, 2, and 3 John*. Collegeville: Liturgical Press, 2002.

Rensberger, David K. *The Epistles of John*. Westminster Bible Companion. Louisville: Westminster John Knox, 2001.

3 John

Allen Dwight Callahan

INTRODUCTION

Third John is a love letter of sorts, replete with cognates of *agapā*: the verb "love" (*agapaō*) in v. 1, the noun "beloved" (*agapētos*) in vv. 1, 2, 5, 11, and the noun "love" (*agapē*) in v. 6. The Elder is the sole writer, and, as the singular vocatives throughout attest, Gaius is the sole recipient. The writer does not further identify himself, and all of the subsequent efforts to fill out his historical identity are mere fiction.

COMMENTARY

The Elder begins by celebrating Gaius's fidelity to the truth and his love, to which unnamed "friends" testify. Some of those friends are agents of the Elder, and it is on behalf of these agents that the Elder intercedes. These itinerant agents "came out taking nothing from outsiders" (v. 7, my trans.). To be "fellow workers in the truth," or, "truly fellow workers," is by definition to lend material support to those laboring in the community. To welcome them in the church means to extend hospitality and succor to them, precisely those things that Diotrophes refuses the Elder's partisans. The Elder has tried to resolve the matter from a distance: "I wrote something to the church" (v. 9, my trans.), which "Diotrephes, who craves prominence among them," has disregarded. Diotrophes is running a propaganda campaign against the Elder's allies (v. 10).

The Elder here commends one of his allies, Demetrius, to Gaius in glowing terms. Everyone attests to Demetrius's sterling reputation, "even the church itself," the very church upon which the Elder cannot rely to assist Demetrius. Demetrius's welfare is now implicitly laid to Gaius's charge.

"I had much to write to you, but I wish not to write to you with pen and ink. Rather, I hope to see you shortly, and we shall speak face to face" (vv. 13–14, my trans.). The Elder prefers presence to paper: he would speak, as the Greek here and in 2 John 12 literally translates the Hebrew idiom, "mouth to mouth" (see Num. 12:8), to speak to another intimately, personally, tenderly.

The Elder closes the letter with "peace" (*eirēnē*): "Peace to you. The friends send you their greetings. Greet the friends there, each by name" (v. 15). *Eirēnē* translates the Hebrew *shalom*, which served as a general greeting and at the beginning and end of letters in ancient Palestine. The Elder conveys his closing salutation to "the friends." Thus the salutation is selective. All in the church are sisters and brothers. But not all are friends.

This letter provides an intimate glimpse of what is required for a Christian community to live out its faith in love. Its theology is its practice. The community's confession is meaningful only insofar as it is embodied in its conduct toward others.

Bibliography

Black, C. Clifton. "The First, Second, and Third Letters of John." In *NIB* 12:363–469.

Callahan, Allen Dwight. *A Love Supreme: A History of Johanine Tradition*. Minneapolis: Fortress, 2000.

Lieu, Judith M. *Theology of the Johannine Epistles*. Cambridge: Cambridge University Press, 1991.

Painter, John. *1, 2, and 3 John*. Collegeville: Liturgical Press, 2002.

Rensberger, David K. *The Epistles of John*. Westminster Bible Companion. Louisville: Westminster John Knox, 2001.

Jude

Steven J. Kraftchick

INTRODUCTION

This short letter, purportedly from Jude the brother of James, and by extension of Jesus, was likely written toward the latter part of the first century.

COMMENTARY

The letter begins with a typical salutation and a wish for peace (vv. 1–2) but quickly shifts to a tone of warning and intervention (v. 3). The occasion for this letter is the author's belief that a group of teachers have infiltrated the congregation and pose a genuine danger to his audience's continued existence as faithful followers of God. Because the author sensed that his readers did not recognize the erroneous teaching of the intruders, he uses stark contrasts and polemical phrasing to identify them as opponents of the truth who confuse believers with an injurious message of false freedom (vv. 4, 10, 16, 19). He hopes that his hyperbole will spur his readers to recognize the threat of the intruding teachers and to reject their ideas and ultimately to expel them from the congregation.

Because Jude wished to reveal the error of the intruders, especially their arrogant disrespect for God (vv. 4, 5, 6, 7, 10, 11, 15), Jude's goal was not to write a theological essay. Rather, he wished to make clear the implications of obedience and disobedience, and so focused on an ethics of belief. Jude is convinced that the teachers misunderstand the authority of God and therefore that they are disobedient to God's will. To demonstrate this point, he offers an interpretation of Scripture and extracanonical texts that show the calamities of disobedience (vv. 5–7, 11) and the judgment that awaits those who persist in it (vv. 14–15, 17–18).

Jude's argument is predicated upon God's holy nature and its implications for human behavior. Through references to God's benevolence toward humanity—for example, the delivery of humans from bondage and peril (v. 6), the establishment of a holy community (vv. 3 and 20), and the preservation of those who are faithful (vv. 1, 21, 24, and 25)—Jude shows that God has established a world of order, justice, and mercy. Proper responses to God must reflect this. Those who are faithful obey God (and Christ the eschatological Lord) as a natural response of trust. In contrast, the disobedient, both past and present, "pervert God's grace, turning it into licentiousness" (v. 4, my trans.). As a result their very lives become acts of rebellion (v. 15) and they will face eschatological judgment (v. 15). Once the audience recognizes the cost of disobedience, Jude hopes that they will praise and glorify God (v. 25) while they await Christ's return. Jude concludes by exhorting the audience to persist in faithfulness (vv. 20–23).

Bibliography

Bauckham, R. J. *Jude, 2 Peter.* WBC 50. Waco: Word, 1983.

Kelly, J. N. D. *A Commentary on the Epistles of Peter and Jude.* Repr. Grand Rapids: Baker, 1982.

Kraftchick, Steven J. *Jude and 2 Peter.* ANTC. Nashville: Abingdon, 2002.

Revelation

Gail R. O'Day

INTRODUCTION

The book of Revelation receives its name from its opening words, "the revelation of Jesus Christ." The Greek word for "revelation" is *apokalypsis*, from which the English words "apocalyptic" and "apocalypse" derive. Although popular interpretation often labels Revelation as the prediction and depiction of the cataclysmic end of the world, such interpretations miss the theological importance and contribution of this final book in the Christian canon. The literal translation of *apokalypsis* is "unveiling," and reclaiming this meaning of apocalyptic is essential to any theological reading of Revelation. Revelation is the unveiling of the way the world looks when viewed through the eyes of God.

John communicates to others what God, through the risen Christ, has enabled him to see (1:1–2). In this regard, John is like the prophets of the OT; he is given insight into God's vision for the world and he is commissioned to declare how the faith community and the world run counter to that vision. Like the prophetic books of the OT, Revelation is not a foretelling or prediction of the future, but a "forth" telling of God's vision of and for the world. Revelation is John's public witness to God's will and hope for the world. To underscore this public dimension, the opening words of Revelation indicate that John's words were written to be read aloud in a community worship service (1:3). John's prophetic unveiling is not a private or secret communication, intended only for a select group, or to be secreted away or feared, but is a word intended to be shared as part of the community's liturgical life.

Author and Audience

John receives his vision and writes this book while in exile on Patmos (1:9), a small island in the Aegean Sea. John identifies his testimony about Jesus as the cause of his exile. Although tradition often portrays John as writing Revelation while in prison, he says nothing about that. Revelation was probably written at the end of the first century CE, during the reign of the Roman emperor Domitian.

John was a common name in NT times. While it may be tempting to equate this John with the author of the Gospel, the Epistles, or a John known elsewhere in the New Testament, there is not enough data to do so, and pursuing such questions distracts from what is central to John's identity. The John of Revelation identifies himself to his readers based solely on his own experience as a prophet and witness to the Word of God in Jesus. John's authority comes from his vocation as a prophet and his experience of the

Word and Spirit of God, not from any other reason.

Revelation is first and foremost a pastoral letter, sent to seven churches in seven cities in Asia Minor (1:4; chaps. 2–3), modern Turkey, which was then part of the Roman Empire. Although the traditional view of Revelation was that it was written to churches undergoing severe persecution, the historical data do not support a view of widespread persecution during the reign of Domitian. The imperial cult was pervasive in Asia Minor in the first century—temples and shrines to the Roman emperors dominated the landscape of the major cities— but the punishment for not participating in the emperor cult was rarely death. The penalties were actually much more subtle, for example, social ostracism or reduced economic opportunities. For the city dwellers to whom Revelation is addressed, participation in the emperor cult, alongside their participation in Christian worship, seemed harmless enough as a way of ensuring their economic livelihood. While a few of the churches named in the book (Pergamum and Philadelphia) faced some persecution, and so received encouragement from John to persevere, most did not. Instead, for most of the readers of Revelation, John is trying to encourage resistance to the appeal of the empire. There are some "prophets" in the churches who are actively trying to help the people accommodate to the empire. In the opening letters John gives them the symbolic names of Balaam and Jezebel (2:14, 20), OT figures associated with idolatry (Num. 22–24; 1 Kgs. 18–19; 2 Kgs. 9).

The problem for most Christians in first-century Asia Minor was not persecution by the empire but accommodation to the empire. John's prophetic commission in Revelation is to give the churches new eyes through which to see themselves—to unveil the Roman Empire for what it is and to show that its claim on the churches' lives is not innocuous, but violates all that is true about God. For John, the choices for the churches are clear:

resist the pull of empire, even if that resistance may result ultimately in death, or else be consumed by the empire.

Revelation's vision is not simply an unveiling of the Roman Empire to show its destructive power, however. Revelation's vision is ultimately an unveiling of the power and mystery of God. In the place of the false power and sovereignty of the empire, John advocates for the true power and sovereignty of God. John's visions proclaim that God is the only true ruler, not the Roman emperor or any of his minions. The sovereignty of God— and the ultimate triumph of life over death, good over evil—is the heart of Revelation's theological message. This theological message is found most explicitly in the hymns of praise to God that resound throughout the book, yet it also underlies all the visions of cosmic conflict. The battle is not between "good" people and "bad" people, as much popular contemporary Christian apocalyptic thinking would have us believe, but between God's good sovereignty over creation and the sovereignty of the powers and embodiments of evil.

Language and Symbolic World

The need to unveil the truth about God and empire explains much about the language and symbolic world of Revelation. Revelation is symbolic and deeply imagistic because John is trying to help his readers see their world and their God with new eyes. Revelation is like a large, bold painting that evokes all the senses—hearing, sight, taste, smell, touch. The total effect, not the deciphering of each individual detail, gives the vision its meaning.

Revelation contains many cyclical series (the seven seals, seven trumpets, seven bowls), as well as many complementary visions of the church and of the power of evil. The repetition makes a summary or outline of the book almost impossible to create. For example, trying to answer what one would think is a straightforward question, "When is Babylon destroyed in Revelation?" is actually quite complex. References to the city falling can be found at 16:17–21, as a result of the pouring out of the seventh bowl, accompanied by the acclamation, "It is done!" But at 17:1, the same angel who poured out that bowl invites John to come and see the judgment of Babylon, as if that judgment still awaits in the future. Another angel at 17:16 also refers to the destruction of Babylon in the future tense. The cyclical patterning of Revelation conveys that the visionary series are not a literal mapping of the future. Instead these visions provide a way to view human history from the perspective of the kingdom of God. John's primary concern is the present, not the future, as he uses his images to reveal the values that underlie unexamined practices of empire—injustice, violence, and oppression. Babylon is the primary symbol for Rome and for all empire, and the goal of Revelation is to invite the churches to move out of Babylon and into the grace of the city of God.

Perhaps more than any other biblical book, Revelation is a reminder that form and content are inextricably intertwined. One cannot distill *what* Revelation says apart from *how* it says it. Many popularized appropriations of Revelation (for example, the type of interpretation found in *The Late Great Planet Earth* or the *Left Behind* series of religious novels) attempt to read past Revelation's images to get to the "real" meaning. The primary interpretive strategy in these appropriations is "decoding," the hunt for the truth that is masked by the images. But such approaches completely misjudge and misunderstand the theological and literary world of Revelation. The images and symbols are not linguistic trappings that can be discarded; they are essential to John's understanding of God and God's hopes for the world. At the heart of Revelation is the mystery of God that intentionally challenges and transcends language and categorization. To separate form and content when interpreting Revelation is to miss completely the offer of God and God's good sovereignty that this book makes available in all its imagistic richness. Through the richness of his language, John summons his readers to live in a world shaped by his unveiling of God's awesome mystery and power.

COMMENTARY

Revelation is grounded in John's central theological conviction that no power on heaven or earth can negate the fulfillment of God's hopes for creation. John uses four central images and narrative patterns to dramatize his understanding of God and God's sovereignty over creation: the heavenly throne room, cosmic conflict, the church complacent and the church triumphant, and the new Jerusalem.

The Heavenly Throne Room

The heavenly throne room, first described in Rev. 4, captures the heart of John's theological vision. All the trappings normally associated with power, wealth, and majesty are present in this heavenly throne room—precious gemstones, thrones, golden crowns—and all testify to God's sovereign rule. Displays of thunder and lightning, traditional symbols of divine power and presence (Exod. 19:16–19; Ps. 18:7–15; Isa. 29:6); the sea, normally a symbol of chaos and the absence of God (Ps. 29:10) now glass-like; the full range of God's creatures—wild beast, domestic animal, human being, and bird (Ezek. 1 and Isa. 6)—that surround the throne—all of these combine to create a vivid picture of God's vast power over all creation. The elders, political and religious leaders in John's time, cast their crowns before God's throne, and so enact the subordination of all forms of earthly power to God. The throne room symbols make vivid that God has the only real power, not any earthly king, governor, or other political leader.

John also sees (and shows) that God's sovereign power is an occasion for joyous celebration. All creatures in heaven and on earth join in hymns of praise to God. The heavenly throne room models the life of faith—unceasing and joyful praise and worship of God (Rev. 4:6b–11). These hymns express John's understanding of God: God alone is holy, ever present and enduring, and worthy of all praise (see also the hymns of praise in 7:9–17; 15:2–8; 19:1–10).

As the visions of Revelation unfold, one discovers that there is a theological edge to this heavenly worship. First, to worship God—and to recognize that God alone is holy—means that one cannot also worship idols. One of the theological tasks of Revelation is to unveil where idolatry has a hold on the faithful. The most explicit unveiling of idolatry is in Revelation's depiction of the beast and its minions (13:1–18), but Revelation also makes clear that idolatry is a threat in even the ordinary activities of the church's life (2:14–15, 20–24; 3:17–18). Second, the vision celebrated in the hymns of praise shows the triumph of God's justice and righteousness (15:3–4; 19:1–5). Revelation looks to the establishment of God's kingdom; it does not celebrate vengeance or destruction. Yet the justice inherent in God's kingdom challenges the power of the empire, and so conflict is inevitable.

The challenge to conventional understandings of power and glory is on display in chap. 5. At first, John can see no one who is worthy to open the sealed scroll that is held in the right hand of the one who sits upon the throne (5:1). One of the elders points him toward a traditional messianic figure, the lion of Judah, as one who is worthy (5:5), but when John looks he sees instead an alternative incarnation of power, "a Lamb standing as if it had been slaughtered" (5:6). A willingness to witness with one's life is now the mark of power, not the conquering military or political hero. Because of the manner of his life and death, the Lamb is worthy to open the seals and so make God's vision of justice available to the world. In response to the Lamb's worthiness, all

the creatures in the heavenly throne room sing a new song that celebrates the Lamb's death as the source of his power (5:8–10). The language of the hymn echoes early Christian liturgical and theological language ("by your blood you ransomed for God saints from every tribe and language and people and nation") and confirms that the Lamb is a symbol of Christ. All political and religious power ("kingdoms and priests") is redefined by Jesus' death.

Cosmic Conflict

To many Christians, Revelation's imagery of violent cosmic upheaval is repugnant, impossible to reconcile with a gospel message of God's love for the world. To many other Christians, by contrast, Revelation's scenes of cosmic battle are reassuring, confirming that their position among the elect is secure and that the unfaithful will rightly be excluded from the kingdom of God. To still other Christians, the struggles of Revelation are uplifting, encouraging them in their own situations of powerlessness and hopelessness. To still others, these images are a prophetic wake-up call about the abuses of power in current religious and political structures. And to still more Christians, this very range of interpretations and responses to Revelation proves that the book is too ambiguous and misleading to be included in conversations about Christian life and faith.

This range of responses points to one of the most important contributions of Revelation's scenes of cosmic conflict to NT theology: John intends to discomfit the Christian community about its perceptions of God. The violent scenarios of upheaval and destruction show that God cannot be domesticated and that God's rule is not a synonym for our rule. God, God's sovereign rule, and God's hopes for creation are bigger and other than any constructs and designs with which human beings can label them. The God of Revelation constantly unsettles human arrangements. The God of Revelation belies theologies that highlight God and Jesus as personal friends, concerned with "my" salvation and "my" experience of God's love. The scope of God's concerns and hopes in Revelation make such individualistic theologies incomprehensible.

The hymns of 5:11–14, praising God and the worthiness of the Lamb, are the immediate and necessary precursor to the Lamb's opening of the sealed scroll (6:1; cf. the scenes of worship that precede the seven trumpets, 8:2–5, and the seven bowls, 15:2–8). The scenes of cosmic upheaval originate from the throne of God; their power comes not from conventional brute force or military might, but from the power of God revealed in the life and death of Jesus.

The scenes of cosmic upheaval have direct links to the exodus tradition— both the seven trumpets (8:2–11:19) and the seven bowls (15:1–16:21) mirror the plagues recounted in Exodus. The destruction of a past empire (Egypt) anticipates the fall of the current empire (Rome). The God of Revelation is the God of the exodus, who brought a nation out of the oppressive power of an empire into new life. Yet the battle against the pervasive power of empire is ongoing throughout history, as repeating series of seals, trumpets, and bowls show. The social and communal dimension of these visions is pivotal; in John's vision the fate of the cosmos, not individual souls, hangs in the balance.

Through the repeating scenes of conflict and upheaval, John also unsettles human presumptions by unveiling the scope of human complicity in the destruction of God's creation. The four horses and their riders in the first four seals, for example, do not predict God's future punishment of the earth, but describe the destruction that humanity already visits on itself. Revelation 6:1–2 depicts the destruction of war; 6:3–4, internal conflicts that rob a society of peace; 6:5–6, the injustice of economic exploitation; 6:7–8, the raw power of death and destruction already at work in the world.

The prominence of the call to repentance in Revelation attests to human complicity (or to use a more explicit theological term, "sin"). Each of the seven letters of Revelation's opening chapters contains calls to repentance (2:5, 16, 22; 3:3, 19) or to remain steadfast (2:10, 25; 3:11), showing how human action is linked to the fate of the cosmos. God's intention is to save and redeem creation (7:2–3; 11:16–19; 21:5–8) from the acts of destruction and devastation that human beings continue to inflict, yet human beings regularly and repeatedly ignore the call to repentance.

This can be seen in the cyclical nature of the visions. The opening of the seventh seal is not a conclusion (8:1), but a pause that leads to a fresh cycle of visions, the seven trumpets (8:2). In the trumpet vision (8:2–9:21) each trumpet's damage will be limited to one-third of a given area. The goal of the vision is awakening and repentance, not total devastation. Yet even in the face of vivid evidence of the cost of human complicity, there is no repentance (9:20–21). In the plague cycle (15:1–16:21), the vision of destruction expands, involving all of the cosmos, not simply a fraction of it as in the seals and trumpets, but still there is no repentance (16:8–9).

God's judgment is the meeting place for the divine sovereignty of the throne room and human complicity. In Revelation's visions, God is the only true judge, seen most clearly in the fate of Babylon (e.g., 14:6–20; 17:1–18:24). Unlike much popular use of Revelation, judgment is not a tool of God to secure the place of the faithful. Rather, the visions of judgment are first directed to members of the faith community who are tempted toward or have already succumbed to the power and pull of Babylon, the empire (14:6–7). Revelation draws on traditional biblical images of judgment—the Son of Man (14:14; Dan. 7:13), harvest and wine press (Rev. 14:14–20; Joel 3:13; Hos. 6:11; Isa. 63:1–3)—to create a vision of God's wrath that is intended not to make community members feel superior to those "outsiders" who will feel God's wrath, but to awaken disciples to the cosmic scale of their own decisions about empire.

Human complicity in Babylon, and hence accountability for its judgment, appears in the emphasis on idolatry, faithlessness, human violence, excessive wealth and economic exploitation, corrupt and arrogant power in the description of Babylon and its destruction (17:1–18:24). Revelation's visions show that the church is called either to repent of its engagement with empire completely or to share in its judgment.

The lack of repentance highlights another central theological theme of the narratives of cosmic conflict: the very real presence and power of evil in God's created cosmos (theodicy). There is nothing subtle about Revelation's engagement with the presence of evil and God's response to it, which is one reason that many Christians shy away from the book. But as Christopher Rowland has highlighted in his commentary on Revelation, the very fact that Revelation deals so explicitly with the power of evil in all its rawness is one of the book's major contributions to theological conversations. John the seer unveils the reality of evil in a way that sets Revelation apart from other books of the NT. Evil is not merely a theological concept or universal principle, but exists as an incarnate presence in the world.

John confronts the reader with an embodied evil that is powerful and dangerous; God's response to evil is also embodied—the battle imagery, violence, and warfare are narrative enactments of the conflict between good and evil. Revelation 11:3–13 provides a snapshot of this conflict. Two prophetic figures, commissioned as witnesses by God (11:3), appear to be divinely protected from harm (vv. 5–6). Nonetheless they are killed by the beast "that comes up from the bottomless pit" (v. 7) and taunted and gloated over in death by the earth's inhabitants (vv. 8–10). The beast is a figure of evil and falsehood, and in this initial encounter, the word and witness of God appears to be no match for the powers of evil. Yet as in the story of the Lamb, who was slaughtered yet somehow lives, these two witnesses are reanimated by the breath of God and ascend in glory to heaven (vv. 11–12).

Revelation 12:1–13:18 narrates the mythic battle of good and evil much more fully. Revelation 12:9 makes the stakes in this battle clear: the dragon (and later the beast) is "that ancient serpent, who is called the Devil and Satan, the deceiver of the whole world." The players on the side of good in this cosmic battle are more varied—the "woman clothed like the sun" and her son (12:1, 5, my trans.), Michael and his angels (12:7)—but the stakes are always the same. The beast's goal is to destroy all that is good and is of God. The dragon is defeated in this round of the cosmic battle, not by conventional military and political might, but by the power that comes from the life-giving death of Jesus and the churches' testimony to it (12:11–12). The narrative makes clear, however, that the battle with evil will need to be waged again and again (12:17).

Throughout Revelation evil inhabits a variety of incarnations: a dragon, a seven-headed beast with ten horns, a two-horned beast. The indictment of empire as the realm of the beast underlies much of the symbolism of chap. 13 (e.g., vv. 4–7). To worship the emperor as a divine figure was a practice of the Roman imperial cult, and that practice is both acknowledged and parodied here. The relationship between the dragon and the beasts is a pale imitation of the relationship between God and the Lamb (vv. 2, 4); all the beast's activities are a distortion of the work of the Lamb (vv. 5–8). This signals to the perceptive reader that the power of the beast is a pale imitation of the power of God and the Lamb.

In his narratives of embodied good and evil, John attempts to move his readers out of the everyday and into the realm of the mythic in order to show what is at stake in the decisions they make about human empires. John's readers, like many contemporary Christians, discount the power of evil, but John calls the community to see that evil is resilient and always the enemy of God's justice. There is an inevitable tension in the conflict between good and evil. In the last battle, for example (19:17–21), no actual fighting is narrated (cf. 6:1–7; 9:7–19), because God's victory in the life and death of the Lamb has already taken place. Satan is defeated (20:7–10), yet the threat of evil and its pull on human community and creation remains real. The disquieting violence that pervades Revelation testifies to the power of evil and the resistance that is necessary to oppose its pull.

Does Revelation focus on the "end of the world," as so much popular usage suggests? Yes and no. Revelation envisions the end of evil, not the end of the world. The dramatic battle scenes, the images of death and destruction, portray what the world is like and will be like when the power of evil is allowed to run unchecked. Human power as an agent of destruction has no place in Revelation. Human power as the power to resist the pull of empire, to offer allegiance to God and not the state, to work for justice against the injustice of political empires, to resist the lure of economic reward when the cost is participation in empire—this form of human power has a large place in Revelation. For John, power is defined by the model of the Lamb who was slaughtered and yet still lives (5:6). The only true power is the power of God unveiled in the crucifixion and resurrection of Jesus.

The Church Complacent and the Church Triumphant

Ecclesiology (the theology of the church) is another important theological theme in Revelation. For John, this theological theme is directly connected to the character of God and the cosmic battle between good and evil, because the church is to be God's witness on earth, holding fast and testifying to God's hopes for creation. Yet because churches are human institutions, they are tempted to conform to human standards rather than to God's hopes. Although they are called to be God's witness, they can act in ways that assist evil in its battle against good. One of John's

theological and pastoral goals in Revelation is to sustain the church in its true vocation.

Revelation's opening vision focuses on the very question of the identity and vocation of the Christian faithful. Chapters 2 and 3 consist of letters to seven churches in Asia Minor, but these are no ordinary pastoral letters. The "author" of these letters is the risen and triumphant Christ (1:12–20) who commands John to write to the seven churches (1:11, 19). John is the scribe for the messages, but Jesus is the author. The words of the risen Jesus enable a church to see itself through Jesus' eyes, and these letters draw the seven churches into John's vision. The activities of the church on earth are noticed and matter in heaven.

These seven cities were cultural and economic centers. The real threat to discipleship was the appeal of the wealth and power of the Roman Empire, not widespread persecution. The negative ecclesiological image for Revelation is "the church complacent," the church that reconciles its practices and beliefs with those of the Roman Empire. To protest the pervasiveness of "the church complacent," the seven letters sound a note of warning alongside a note of promise. The risen Jesus has praise and no judgment for only two of the churches, Smyrna (2:8–11) and Philadelphia (3:7–13), because they endure hardship and embrace poverty in the face of wealth. The other five churches are called to repentance by the risen Jesus for their practices of accommodation and for defining success and triumph according to the standards of the empire instead of God's vision.

The message to Ephesus (2:1–7), for example, the largest city in Asia Minor and an important Roman and Christian center, begins with praise (vv. 1–3), but moves quickly to judgment because the Ephesian church has "abandoned the love [it] had at first" (vv. 4–5). The churches that accommodate to the empire are called to repentance by the risen Jesus; they are urged to "conquer" that which leads them away from their full witness so that they can share fully in the life of God's kingdom. Smyrna and Philadelphia, by contrast, provide a glimpse of Revelation's positive ecclesiological image, "the church triumphant"—communities who find strength in weakness, whose power derives from holding fast against the empire, not aligning themselves with the power and practices of the empire. The empire embodies and enacts evil, not good, and the churches need to separate themselves from the practices of empire to enact their vocation as witnesses to God's hopes for creation.

Throughout the violence and cosmic conflict of Revelation, John intersperses visions that offer a glimpse of the church triumphant that balance the image of the church complacent. The vision of 7:1–17, for example, gives the churches hope for their future by identifying the source of their strength. Baptism is the seal of Christians' identity as servants of God (vv. 1–3). Servanthood contradicts the empire's standards of achievement and success, but it defines the churches' hope. This vision also offers a counter to ecclesial complacency with the empire in its picture of the multitudes that share the seal of baptism (vv. 4–8). The number 144,000 is the result of multiplying 12 tribes times 12 apostles and symbolically represents the totality of God's people, yet John has a vision of even more faithful than that. He sees "a great multitude that no one could count, from every nation, from all tribes and peoples and languages, standing before the throne and before the Lamb" (v. 9). The Roman Empire has no real power over the churches because there are no national distinctions before the throne of God. Yet importantly, the churches' victory is not enacted in a demonstration of power or self-vindication, but in the unceasing praise of God and the Lamb (vv. 13–17).

John's visions in 10:1–11:14, 14:1–20, and 19:6–10 also depict a community whose triumph is defined by power in weakness and its praise of God and the Lamb. The life of the churches is crucial to John's theological vision, because it is through the practices of actual communities of faith that witness to the life and death of the Lamb is made and that God's hopes for the world are enacted. When churches complacently mimic the practices of the empire and abandon the practices of the Lamb, evil gains a toehold in creation. John's visions summon the churches to live instead as a community redeemed by the life and death of the Lamb (14:3–4), grounded in the praise of God who yearns for the healing of creation, and so render null and void the power of evil to shape the world.

New Jerusalem

Revelation ends with a vivid and dramatic image of a new heaven, a new earth, and a new Jerusalem (21:1–22:7). These concluding images depict the heart of Revelation's eschatology and show the hope toward which all the cosmic conflict moves. As noted above, Revelation's ultimate concern is not with the end of the world, but with the end of evil that distorts creation. The destruction of evil in Rev. 19:11–20:15 marks the end of the first heaven and first earth, clearing the way for the establishment of God's reign of justice on earth. The end of the sea (21:1) symbolizes the end of the power of chaos and death on earth (cf. 4:6). Importantly, the new Jerusalem descends "out of heaven from God" to the earth (21:2). John's vision of the future is creation affirming, not creation denying; his vision is not of a heavenly city, but of a new city that God sends from heaven to earth. This vision of a restored and renewed creation is consistent with the eschatological hopes of the Hebrew Scriptures (Isa. 49:10; 65:17; 66:22).

The description of the new Jerusalem (Rev. 21:9–21) recalls the vision of the new temple in Ezek. 40–48, with the critical difference that unlike the vision of Ezek. 40–48, no temple is needed in the new city, because the city itself contains the unmediated presence of God and the Lamb. The gates of the new city are always open (Rev. 21:25); its gifts are available to all, including nations and kings of the earth (21:24). The only way to be excluded from the city is to choose to practice falsehood and deceit (21:27; 22:15), practices which by definition do not belong to the city of God (cf. 21:8; 22:3). In the new earth, as in the first, people still need to choose whether they will be on the side of God's covenant or not.

Most readings of the eschatology of Revelation neglect or negate this element of choice that is present even in the new Jerusalem. The references to falsehood, deceit, and evil in this final vision (21:8, 27; 22:10, 15) are not intended to vilify the "other" but to highlight the element of choice for the faithful and the persistent appeal of that which leads away from God. That such choices must be made even in the restored creation show how theologically inaccurate and misleading it is to take Revelation as a definitive map of the end time that will result in the final destruction of creation and the affirmation of the rectitude of the faithful. John's vision is not nearly that theologically simple.

Revelation ends with an imaginative vision of life with God, of a restored creation and community that embodies the fullness of God's hopes for the world and for human life grounded in the love of the Lamb. In the visions that constitute Revelation, John has been shown two cities—Babylon, the city of the beast (17:1), and the new Jerusalem, the city of the Lamb (21:9). At the heart of John's theological vision is a call to decision: the churches to which John writes must regularly and repeatedly decide in which city they want to live.

Bibliography

Blount, Brian K. *Can I Get a Witness? Reading Revelation through African American Culture.* Louisville: Westminster John Knox, 2005.

Howard-Brook, Wes, and Anthony Gwyther. *Unveiling Empire: Reading Revelation Then and Now.* Maryknoll, NY: Orbis, 1999.

Rhoads, David, ed. *From Every People and Nation: The Book of Revelation in Intercultural Perspective.* Minneapolis: Fortress, 2005.

Rowland, Christopher. "The Book of Revelation." In *NIB* 12:501–748.

Schüssler Fiorenza, Elisabeth. *The Book of Revelation—Justice and Judgment.* 2nd ed. Minneapolis: Fortress, 1998.